SALES Management

Decision Making for Improved Profitability

Dan H. Robertson/Danny N. Bellenger

BOTH OF GEORGIA STATE UNIVERSITY

Macmillan Publishing Co., Inc.

New York

Collier Macmillan Publishers

London

This book is dedicated to Sue, Laurie, and Gary Robertson,
Mr. and Mrs. Thell W. Robertson and to Judy, Brian, and Dana Bellenger

Macmillan Publishing Co., Inc.
866 Third Avenue, New York, New York 10022

Collier Macmillan Canada, Ltd.

Library of Congress Cataloging in Publication Data

Robertson, Dan H.
    Sales management: decision making for improved
profitability.

    Includes index.
    1. Sales management—Case studies. 2. Sales
management—Problems, exercises, etc. I. Bellenger,
Danny N., 1946–   joint author. II. Title.
HF5438.4.R6   658.8′1   79–11981
ISBN 0–02–402180–6

Printing: 1 2 3 4 5 6 7 8   Year: 0 1 2 3 4 5 6

Preface

This text is intended to provide an integrated set of instructional materials in sales management. The material should help to build the student's analytical abilities as well as provide an overview of the various decision areas facing the sales manager. The analytical element is provided by a series of cases, student learning exercises, and extensive discussions of decision making in the text. Learning by doing with cases and student learning exercises is a key facet of building the student's analytical skills. In addition to providing an analytical element of sales management, this text provides a more current perspective than many alternative sources.

The text consists of three major sections: Part I, Sales Management in Perspective, is designed to provide a useful introduction to selling as a component of the promotional mix as well as sales management activities and decision areas. This section consists of three chapters (see content outline). Part II, Sales Management in Action, presents an overview of today's complex decision making environment. Nine chapters covering the various decision areas in sales management are included. The text concludes with Part III, Sales Management Tomorrow, two chapters providing both a useful synthesis and an enlightened glimpse into the future world of sales management and the management of change.

Cases that integrate major concepts from the text accompany each chapter. Key readings are also provided with each section of the text. Additionally, pragmatic student learning exercises are included that encourage the student to participate actively in the sales management environment.

D.R.
D.B.

Acknowledgments

The authors gratefully acknowledge the assistance and contributions of numerous peers, acquaintances, and students. Our present and former students have made their contribution to this book by teaching us just as we have hopefully passed on knowledge to them. Although it is impossible for us to enumerate each of these students individually, we acknowledge their collective contributions and are deeply grateful for them.

We would like specifically to recognize the fine support provided this book by the efforts of Mrs. Brenda Hemperley and Mrs. Cynthia James.

We would also like to acknowledge the fine assistance of our editor, Mr. Ken MacLeod.

Finally, we would like to acknowledge the materials provided by our association with fellow academicians and practitioners in the area of sales management. The lessons learned from years of experience at both Procter & Gamble and Baxter Laboratories, Inc., are reflected in many of the comments made throughout this book. Lastly, numerous members of Sales & Marketing Executives, International, have shared with us a wealth of information and their personal experiences. Our academic colleagues and the reviewers of this book have contributed in the most meaningful way a fellow academician can help his associates—constructive criticism.

To all of the above we owe our sincere appreciation while reserving for ourselves the responsibility for any errors of commission or omission made throughout this book.

D. R.
D. B.

Contents

PART ONE
Sales Management in Perspective

PART TWO
Sales Management in Action

PART THREE
Sales Management in the Future

Readings for Part Three

Sales Management in Perspective

1

Marketing and Sales Management

Introduction

QUOTE often attributed either to Henry Ford or to Arthur Motley adorns the desk or office walls of many sales executives. This quote reads:

Nothing happens until someone sells something

Like many adages, this phrase emphasizes a point of great importance to any business or institution, but taken literally it may be misleading or untrue.

SELLING: START OR FINISH OF THE MARKETING PROCESS?

Few management personnel in business or institutions would deny the critical importance of sales. Indeed, it is not our intent to suggest that sales are unimportant. The question here is one of sequence. Are sales the *start* of a series of activities that will hopefully result in profit to the institution? Alternatively, are sales the *end result* of a series of other antecedent activities? The answer to these questions would vary from one business to another. Some would suggest virtual total agreement with the quote given. Many "made to order" types of products depend upon selling activities to provide the initiative for later activities. A sales representative calls upon a buyer who provides "specifications" for a product, which, if produced in a manner consistent with these specifications, will be purchased at an agreed upon price with actual delivery following at some mutually agreeable future time. If we chart these activities on a temporal dimension (see Figure 1.1A), sales start the process and the "finish" provides profits to the firm.

Spokespersons for other firms would probably suggest that sales are a result of other activities. Indeed, the authors of this text would agree that, with few exceptions, a great many activities should take place *before* "someone sells something." These antecedent activities might include any one or more of the following:

Marketing research
Production of inventory

Selling
Function ────────────→ Production and Shipping ────────────→ Profits Realized
                        Other Complimentary   by the Firm
                        Functions

START_____→ FINISH
                              TIME

FIGURE 1.1A Selling: The Start of the Marketing Process

Transportation to warehouse(s)
Purchasing of raw materials (including labor)
Financing of inventory and/or raw materials
Storage of finished inventory
Construction of physical plant facilities

Thus, a sequential flow of activities in this case might more closely resemble Figure 1.1B. Assuming that selling is the "start" of other activities may also be dangerous for the firm. This point will be discussed in detail later in this chapter.

SELLING—UNIQUE ACTIVITY FOR THE FIRM

Regardless of its position temporally, selling is a *unique* activity for any firm or institution. We say this because of two important and unique features that differentiate selling from other activities performed in the organization.

First, selling is unique in that it is often the *only* revenue producing activity within the firm. A quick glance back at the activities antecedent to selling listed earlier will reveal that none of them is directly revenue producing. Production, for example, is conducted at a cost to the firm that, hopefully, will result in revenue. The same statement can be made about any of the other activities. Although selling also carries a cost to the firm, it results in direct generation of revenue.

A second way that selling is unique and important is its consumer visibility. The personnel engaged in accounting, production, transportation, and other related areas are only rarely (if at all) *visible* to the consumers. Sales personnel, by the very nature of their job, are constantly visible in the eyes of different consumer audiences. Indeed, the sales representative of a firm may be the *only* person in the company who has actual face-to-face contact with a buyer. The actions, both "good" and "bad" that are taken by sales representatives are thus extremely important to the firm.

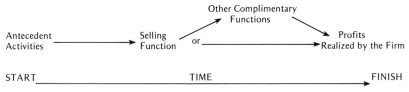

FIGURE 1.1B Selling: The End Result of the Marketing Process

SELLING DEFINED

Irving Shapiro suggests that **salesmanship** is "the art of successfully persuading prospects or customers to buy products or services from which they can derive suitable benefits, thereby increasing their total satisfactions. It is the opposite of conmanship."[1] This definition often conflicts with the experiences or expectations of students. Typically they recall their more negative experiences or interactions with a salesperson. Their experiences may be far from "deriving suitable benefits" and may, in fact, reflect an exposure to conmanship, high pressure sales tactics, or any equally distasteful episode. Despite these possible experiences, salesmanship and sales management are changing. This change is reflected in a recognition that only through the creation of *mutual satisfaction* can selling succeed in the long run. Both the buyer and the seller must benefit in the modern view of salesmanship.

A recent *Marketing News* article discusses this modern view of selling calling it "nonmanipulative selling."[2] This article stresses an approach similar to the preceding definition. Chapter 2 will present a detailed view of this new approach to selling, but it should be briefly noted that this method is based upon *mutual* satisfaction between buyer and seller. As we shall see in the following example (The Pillsbury Experience), this orientation toward mutual benefit implies an ecologically important advantage also. If the outcome of a sales transaction is mutually beneficial, society (third parties not directly involved in the transaction as buyers or sellers) should also benefit. This suggests less waste of resources in the future.

The Modern Marketing Environment

THE PILLSBURY EXPERIENCE

Many marketers would agree that the environment of marketing in this country today is far different than the environment of marketing only a few years ago. One firm whose experience has reflected these environmental changes is the Pillsbury Company. The president of this firm, Mr. Robert Keith, traced changes in environments over four distinct eras in a classic *Journal of Marketing* article.[3]

First Era—Production-Oriented Environment. For Pillsbury, this era began with the firm's formulation in 1869, continued into the 1930s, and was characterized by emphasis upon the ability to produce. Thus, develop-

---

[1] Irving J. Shapiro, *Marketing Terms*, 3rd ed. (West Long Branch, N. J., S-M-C Publishing Co., 1973), p. 147.

[2] "New Sales Technique Stresses Trust, Respect," *The Marketing News*, June 16, 1978 (Vol. XI, No. 25), p. 13.

[3] The following discussion is drawn from "The Marketing Revolution," by Robert J. Keith, *Journal of Marketing* (Vol. 26, No. 1), January 1960 pp. 35–38.

ment of sufficient productive capacity, locating and arranging purchase of raw materials (chiefly wheat), and similar activities geared toward production dominated the interests and activities of the firm during this era. Although Pillsbury is only one example, the reader should bear in mind that other firms may have experienced similar pressures to focus upon production as an outgrowth of the industrial revolution, a rapidly growing population, and so on. Thus, a production orientation would not be unusual for many firms at this point in time. In short, the emphasis was upon one question, "How can our firm produce more?"

Second Era—Sales-Oriented Environment.   By the 1930s Pillsbury had obtained reasonable facilities for production. Many other firms actually overdid their emphasis upon production facilities. This mistake proved fatal for many in the depression years that followed.

The focus in the era between 1930 and 1950 was upon selling. Considerations included not only the firm's own sales force but also development of sales support by retailers, wholesalers, distributors, and any other middlemen important in the process of selling products. The primary marketing environmental concern now shifted from a question of how to increase production capabilities to how to increase sales capabilities.

Third Era—Marketing-Oriented Environment.   The 1950s witnessed yet another change in marketing environmental considerations for Pillsbury. In this period the focus of the firm moved away from a concentration upon the sales organization per se to include related activities as well.[4] Thus, one marketing department was created that would, for example, have direct control over and sole responsibility for coordination of personal selling as well as advertising and any other forms of promotion. In addition, this marketing department would lead and broadly guide the functions of other departments within the firm—production, and so on. The focus of all Pillsbury activities was now upon Mrs. Housewife. The question was one of providing solutions to consumer needs.

Fourth Era—Marketing-Controlled Environment.   For Pillsbury the last era consisted of a change from an environment of marketing influence to one of marketing dominance. Further, marketing's sphere of influence was now extended to other areas of the firm, such as capital financing and technical research.

The reader should note that, although the changing environmental considerations of Pillsbury are not necessarily identical to those of other firms, there are many similarities noted in the marketing literature.[5] Figure 1.2 summarizes four eras of changing environmental considerations for a "typical" firm. Note that the last era mentioned in Figure 1.2— Social marketing—is somewhat different from Pillsbury's fourth era.

[4] "Related activities" as the term is used here, would overlap with many of the activities antecedent to selling mentioned earlier in this chapter.
[5] See for example, Fred J. Borch, "The Marketing Philosophy as a Way of Business Life," *The Marketing Concept: Its Meaning to Management*, Marketing Series N. 99 (New York: American Management Association, 1957), pp. 3–5.

Time Period	Orientation	Environmental Concern
1800's–1935	Production	How can our firm produce more?
Mid 1930's–1955	Sales	How can our firm sell more?
Mid 1950's–1975	Marketing	How can our firm profitably better please our consumer?
Mid 1970's–Present	Social Marketing	How can our firm utilize its resources to better benefit both society and ourselves?

FIGURE 1.2   Changes in Orientation for a Typical Firm

Social marketing would be a broader orientation than the marketing concept in that it would focus not only upon present customers of a firm but also upon society as a whole.[6] Thus, noncustomers are considered, inasmuch as they may be impacted either directly or indirectly by sales or consumption of the products involved. Consider for a moment the "societal implications" for a firm marketing birth control devices, cigarettes, or insecticides.

The Marketing Environment—An Overview

UNCONTROLLABLE VARIABLES

A more general overview of the marketing environment has been provided in the work of McCarthy.[7] Separating the major variables into "controllable" and "uncontrollable" variables, we see in Figure 1.3 that a marketer must consider the impact of five major uncontrollables. Although admittedly a sales manager can do little about changing these uncontrollables in the short run, it is nevertheless important to give consideration to them for two reasons.

First, in so doing, it may be possible to anticipate potential directions of future change. The recent bestseller by Alvin Toffler, *Future Shock*, suggests that every individual must learn to cope with changes in his/her environment. Sales managers are no exception.

Second, if they are even moderately successful in anticipating directions of future change, sales managers may avoid many of the mistakes made by other firms.[8] The classic article, "Marketing Myopia," by Theodore Levitt[9] offers a chilling testimonial to the fate that may befall the

---

[6] For a detailed discussion, see Philip Kotler and Gerald Zaltman, "Social Marketing: An Approach to Planned Social Change," *Journal of Marketing*, July 1971, pp. 3–12.

[7] E. Jerome McCarthy, *Basic Marketing*, 6th ed. (Homewood, Ill: Richard D. Irwin, Inc., 1978).

[8] Two excellent sources summarizing many such mistakes are *Mismarketing* by Thomas L. Berg (Garden City, N.Y.: Anchor Books, 1971), and Robert F. Hartley, *Marketing Mistakes* (Colombus, Ohio: Grid, Inc., 1976).

[9] Theodore Levitt, "Marketing Myopia," *Harvard Business Review*, July–August, 1960. Also reprinted September-October, 1975.

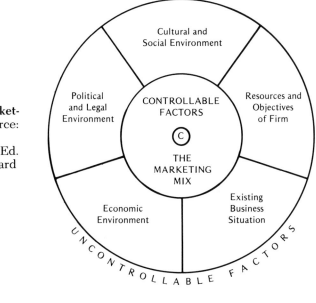

FIGURE 1.3 The Market-ing Environment [Source: E. Jerome McCarthy, *Basic Marketing*, 6th. Ed. (Homewood, Ill.: Richard D. Irwin, Inc., 1978).]

The figure shows a circular diagram. At the center: CONTROLLABLE FACTORS, ©, THE MARKETING MIX. Surrounding segments labeled: Cultural and Social Environment, Resources and Objectives of Firm, Existing Business Situation, Economic Environment, Political and Legal Environment. The outer ring reads UNCONTROLLABLE FACTORS.

firm that fails to consider the impact of change. Any sales firm, no matter how successful today, must be adequately prepared for the changes of tomorrow. Failure to be prepared for change may mean that the firm is victimized by the change and may miss specific market opportunities.

In considering these uncontrollable variables the sales manager must, of course, place anticipated changes in the context of his own product mix. Thus, although an anticipated downturn in the economic environment variable might not be critically important to a sales manager with a food product line, it might prove extremely important to a sales manager for new housing.

Let us briefly consider an example of each of the five uncontrollables.

1. *Cultural and social environment.* Women have recently become a most significant factor in the American labor force. Will such a change continue into the future? Will increasing numbers of qualified women seek to enter business generally or selling specifically. In considering this particular issue, the sales manager may see potential application to recruiting and selection of new sales representatives as well as possible "unique" management problems.[10]

2. *Economic environment.* Spiraling inflation coupled with increased taxes and social security costs have combined to reduce drastically the purchasing power of many Americans in recent years. Will this trend continue unabated in the future? If it does continue, will the rates of increase be as severe as those recently experienced? The sales manager who is considering this variable may be concerned with impact upon buyers; he might also be concerned with the variable's

---

[10] Dan H. Robertson and Donald W. Hackett, "Saleswomen: Perceptions, Problems and Prospects," *Journal of Marketing*, July 1977. Also see "Manage Sales? Yes, She Can," *Sales and Marketing Management*, June 13, 1977.

impact upon present sales personnel. If it is anticipated that this will continue, will this mean increasing pressures for salary increases to present employees?

3. *Existing business situation.* This variable concerns competition. Will a sales manager be faced with an increasing number of competitors by virtue of having new firms enter his market? Will currently existing competitors leave the business and, if so, what impact will this have upon the marketplace? These are but a few of the questions that might be asked about this variable.

4. *Political and legal environment.* This is perhaps the single most rapidly changing uncontrollable variable faced by sales managers. One example regards product liability litigation. Recently, marketers have observed a definite trend toward increasing manufacturers' legal liabilities on products. Does this mean that a sales manager should expect fewer calls from each sales representative in order to provide additional discussion time with each client concerning specific features of a liability nature? Will sales managers need to provide more technical training to the persons working for them?

5. *Resources and objectives of the firm.* Generally, this uncontrollable is the most difficult to comprehend. Perhaps this is because students often assume incorrectly that such concepts as management by objective are applied by every firm from top to bottom. In discussing this variable as it relates to sales management, keep the last word, "firm" clearly in mind. Thus, although the sales manager may have a great deal to say about resources for or objectives of the sales area, he typically would have little decision making ability for resources or objectives for the entire firm or corporation.

CONTROLLABLE VARIABLES—THE MARKETING MIX

Figure 1.4 presents the "controllable" variables. A glance back to Figure 1.3 will show that these are positioned "inside" of the uncontrollables to reflect the fact that they are affected by changes in the five uncontrollables. A change in the economic environment could thus have an impact on all, or part, of the controllables. The four controllables include price, place, promotion, and product. Whereas marketing or sales management people can do little more than be reactive to changes in the uncontrollables, they have a real chance to show their decision making ability off when it comes to the controllables. Let us examine one example for each of the four controllables.

Product. One of the major tasks or responsibilities of people in marketing or sales management is product design. That is, marketing or sales personnel are asked to act as the "eyes" of the company and constantly to suggest needed revisions in product design. This may result in additions of totally new products to a present product line, or it may simply result in slight modifications of certain existing products.

Coordination between marketing and other departments within the

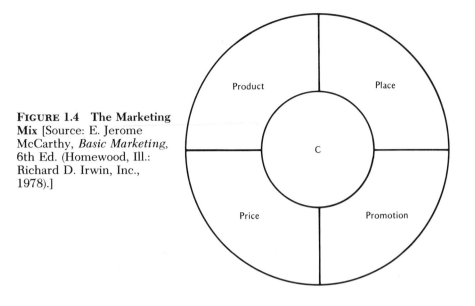

FIGURE 1.4 The Marketing Mix [Source: E. Jerome McCarthy, *Basic Marketing*, 6th Ed. (Homewood, Ill.: Richard D. Irwin, Inc., 1978).]

firm is essential in the process of product revision. Often this coordination does occur as we would hope. However, sometimes coordination is less than optimal and a situation such as the one depicted in Figure 1.5 indicates. Although a humorous example, there is a serious point to this figure. It is the needs of the customer we wish to concentrate on if the firm is to succeed. Sales management is often in the best position to obtain this information, since sales personnel are in contact with customers on a daily basis. As we shall see later, adequate sales supervision is an absolute necessity if this job is to be performed correctly.

Place. Place is a second controllable variable to which marketing or sales management can contribute. Sales personnel are often in a position to evaluate the aggressiveness of retailers by virtue of their sales call interactions. Thus, if a firm is entering a particular geographic market with a new product, it may rely upon the sales force to select from which particular retailers it is important to solicit support. Once these more aggressive or competent retailers are identified, they may then be the recipients of special information about the new product. In the automotive industry, for example, it is a fairly standard practice for certain larger volume dealers to be taken on all-expense-paid trips by the manufacturer to view new model automobiles.

One Detroit manufacturer singles out aggressive dealers and takes them on a sea cruise with new model year versions of their automobile line being previewed for this "select" group in advance of other dealers.

The point here is that sales or marketing management is attempting to elicit the best possible support for their products from the place ingredient. The reader should keep in mind that this selection process would also apply to other levels of distribution beside retailing. Indeed the entire channel of distribution may be selected on a similar basis.

As marketing requested it   As sales ordered it   As engineering designed it

As plant manufactured it   As field service installed it   What the customer wanted!!!

FIGURE 1.5

Price. Price is the third controllable variable that may benefit from marketing or sales management support. In order to thoroughly understand the essence of pricing decision making, it is important to keep in mind the fact that prices are "low" or "high" in comparison with others. Thus, "brand X" at 49¢ may be considered a "good buy" only if other similar brands do not exist at even lower prices.

The point we are making here is that marketers need constantly to monitor the selling prices of their competitors to determine whether or not their own price is "too high" or "too low." Again, sales representatives are in an excellent position to contribute pricing information, owing to their constant customer interactions. However, at least one recent study suggests that, if sales management is not vigilant, this task may not be done.[11]

Promotion. The final variable in the marketing mix is promotion. Because promotion is the very essence of sales management, it is discussed in detail in the next section.

[11] Dan H. Robertson, "Sales Force Feedback on Competitors' Activities," *Journal of Marketing* (Vol. 38, No. 2), April 1974 pp. 69–71.

The Promotional Blend

INGREDIENTS IN THE BLEND

Promotion is a broad term used to identify a variety of related, yet distinct, types of activities. To many, the term promotion may be virtually synonymous with advertising or mass media sales activities. Although promotion does include advertising, it is helpful to consider promotion as consisting of four basic elements:

1. *Advertising.* Any paid form of nonpersonal presentation and promotion of ideas, goods, or services by an identified sponsor.
2. *Personal selling.* Oral presentations in a conversation with one or more prospective purchasers for the purpose of making sales.
3. *Publicity.* Nonpersonal stimulation of demand for a product, service, or business unit by commercially significant news about it in a published[12] medium or obtaining favorable presentation of it on radio, television, or stage that is not paid for by the sponsor.
4. *Sales promotion.* Those marketing activities, other than personal selling, advertising, and publicity, that stimulate consumer purchasing and dealer effectiveness, such as displays, shows and exhibitions, demonstrations, and various nonrecurrent selling efforts not in the ordinary routine.

Thus, this text centers upon the personal selling component of promotion, but it is important to understand that it is only one of four promotional ingredients. Further, although the sales manager may not have full control over the advertising and sales promotion ingredients of the promotional blend, he is nonetheless often deeply involved in decisions regarding the degree of emphasis to be placed on each of the three components.

RELATIVE IMPORTANCE OF ADVERTISING AND SELLING

Generally firms faced with a promotional blend decision budget their total promotional funds into either advertising or personal selling budgets. Figure 1.6 depicts promotional blends selected for several different types of products. Notice that manufacturers of some products (for example, food) elect to invest all of their promotional budget in advertising, whereas others (for example, industrial equipment) might elect to invest all of their funds in personal selling. Likewise, some manufacturers (for example, lawn mowers) might elect a 1/1 ratio of funds split evenly between these two promotional ingredients. In arriving at such a decision, the decision maker must attempt to determine what promotional expendi-

[12] *Marketing Definitions: A Glossary of Marketing Terms*, compiled by the Committee on Definitions of the American Marketing Association, Ralph S. Alexander, Chairman (Chicago: American Marketing Association, 1960).

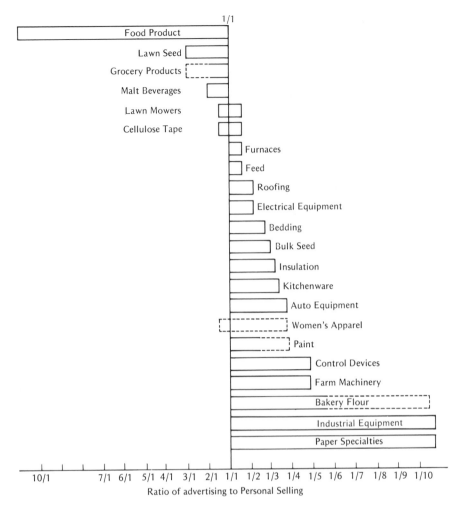

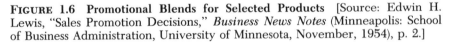

([- - - - - - - -] Indicates the Range of the Ratios)

FIGURE 1.6 Promotional Blends for Selected Products [Source: Edwin H. Lewis, "Sales Promotion Decisions," *Business News Notes* (Minneapolis: School of Business Administration, University of Minnesota, November, 1954), p. 2.]

tures will result in the most effective "blend." No one ratio will necessarily prove "right" for any one manufacturer at any one point in time. Thus, referring back to a point made earlier in this chapter, some marketing research (one possible antecedent activity) may have taken place before the decision was made to invest any funds in personal selling.

Consider for a moment a recent purchase you have made. Often our initial interest in a product or service is aroused by advertising. Perhaps you saw a television commercial or billboard ad, read a newspaper or magazine ad, or heard a radio commercial about the product or service. This, in turn, may have prompted a visit to a dealer's showroom or retail outlet to learn more about the product. Let us say for purposes of discussion that the item is a new automobile. Although advertising initially spurred your interest, personal selling will now become more important

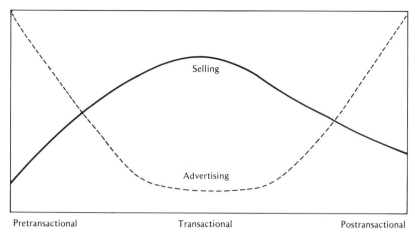

FIGURE 1.7 Advertising and Personal Selling: Effectiveness Across Time [Source: Harold C. Cash and W. J. E. Crissy, *The Salesman's Role in Marketing, The Psychology of Selling* (New York: Personal Development Associates, 1965).]

in determining whether or not you purchase the product. Thus, it can be seen that personal selling and advertising may be used to compliment each other if a coordinated "promotional blend" has been developed.

Cash and Crissy have generalized about the effectiveness of advertising and personal selling across time.[13] They contend that advertising is more important in the "pretransactional" and "posttransactional" phases of a purchase. Personal selling is more important in the "transactional" phase (that is, the time when the actual purchase is being made). Figure 1.7 depicts the relative effectiveness of these two promotional ingredients during these three stages of purchase activity. However, it must be stressed that this is a generalization and, as such, is subject to exceptions.

"PUSH" VERSUS "PULL" ALTERNATIVES

As suggested earlier, the ingredients in a promotional blend should compliment each other. However, we also noted that a manufacturer might elect to invest all promotional budget funds in one ingredient rather than blending several components. The differing blends that may be developed and their resulting efficiencies in reaching target markets are all a part of developing a promotional strategy.[14] It is useful to discuss two such strategies often used by marketers. These two alternatives focus upon a common target market—as an illustration, we will use the typical

[13] Harold C. Cash and W. J. E. Crissy, "Comparison of Advertising and Selling," in *The Salesman's Role in Marketing, The Pyschology of Selling,* (New York: Personal Development Associates, Vol. 12 (1965), pp. 56–75.

[14] The interested student will find several excellent books available which pursue this topic in detail. See for example, James F. Engel, Hugh G. Wales, and Martin R. Warshaw, *Promotional Strategy*, 3rd ed., (Homewood, Ill.: Richard D. Irwin, 1975).

American housewife. To further illustrate these two alternatives, let us assume that the marketer is a producer of detergents.

The two basic alternatives available to our detergent producer are called a "push" and a "pull" policy. Although both are aimed at the housewife, their methods of operation are very different.

A **push policy** relies heavily upon other members of the channel of distribution to assist in product promotion. In our example, let us assume the manufacturer sells detergent in carload quantities to food wholesalers. These wholesalers in turn sell in case lots (10 boxes) to supermarkets and other food retailers. In turn, the retailers sell detergent by the box to housewives. The manufacturer recognizes that the retailer and not the producer of the detergent or the wholesaler has face-to-face interaction with the consuming housewife. Thus, the manufacturer attempts to get the retailer to "push" their detergent via aggressive merchandising. Typical methods include large in-store displays, special features in retail ads, aggressive pricing, attempts to obtain disproportionately large amounts of shelf space, and so on. Although there is a wide variety of methods that may be used in pushing the brand of detergent in question, each method has one point in common—each is totally dependent upon retailer support.

A **pull policy** differs from the push policy just described in that it would attempt to reach the housewife directly. Rather than reliance upon the retailer, the manufacturer may elect to take his message directly to the target market via television, radio, magazine, billboard, or newspaper advertising. If such advertising efforts are successful, the housewife will go to the retail store and purchase the detergent, thus pulling it through the channel. The retailer would then replenish his stock by ordering from the wholesaler who, in turn, replaces his inventory by ordering from the manufacturer.

Figure 1.8 depicts the push and pull alternatives. Although exclusive reliance upon either one is possible, these two need not be thought of as mutually exclusive. In fact, many manufacturers purposely utilize both methods simultaneously for greater market impact.

Lastly, although personal selling and advertising may both be used in either a push or pull policy, typically the push policy relies more heavily upon personal selling, whereas a pull policy usually involves heavier use of advertising.

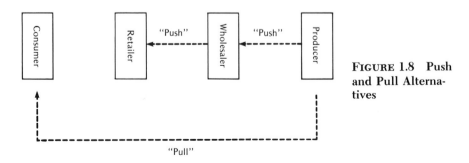

FIGURE 1.8 **Push and Pull Alternatives**

The Role of Sales Management

Earlier in this chapter we stressed the importance of sales activity to the organization. Selling is the very lifeblood of the firm since it represents the cash flow required to maintain all other activities. The person with ultimate responsibility for the sales function is the sales manager. He or she is charged with the responsibility of making prudent decisions about all areas under his/her control.

A TRADITIONAL (FUNCTIONAL) VIEW

In earlier days, sales management was narrowly viewed as consisting only of activities directly related to the selling activity itself. Typically, this traditional approach utilized a functional view of areas of responsibility. It began by giving responsibility for recruiting and selecting sales personnel to the sales manager. Additionally, sales managers were seen as being responsible for training, motivating, and finally evaluating their sales staffs. Thus, the full extent of their responsibility could be traced to one or more of these five basic activities.

A MODERN (MANAGERIAL) VIEW

Just as marketing has broadened from a strictly sales context to a social marketing context (see "Selling Defined" earlier in this chapter), so too has sales management's responsibility grown. In addition to having specific areas of responsibility such as recruiting, sales management is now seen as also having broader managerial responsibilities. A formal definition states that **sales management** means, "the planning, direction and control of personal selling, including recruiting, selecting, equipping, assigning, routing, supervising, paying and motivating as these tasks apply to the personal sales force."[15]

The preceding definition clearly suggests an overlap with the basic "functions of management" including: planning, organizing, motivating, and controlling. **Planning** in sales management revolves around two activities. First, planning relates to objectives. As we have seen earlier, the resources and general objectives of the firm typically form a starting point in the quest for specific objectives. That is, a sales manager typically reports to another marketing executive (for example, to Vice President of Sales or Vice President of Marketing). Often, this executive will provide broad objectives such as "increase sales next year by 5 per cent" or "increase gross profits on sales by 3 per cent." This does not mean that the sales manager has been given *the specific objective* he needs. He must now translate the broad objective into meaningful terms. What particular products in the entire product mix shall we emphasize to obtain

[15] Committee on Definitions, American Marketing Association, *Marketing Definitions* (Chicago: American Marketing Association, 1960), p. 20.

the sales/profit increase being sought by top management? Second, the sales manager is responsible for determining the course of action needed to achieve the specific objective(s) selected. How can these specific objectives be attained? Rue and Byars[16] suggest that planning should answer three basic questions:

1. Where are we now?
2. Where do we want to be?
3. How can we get there from here?

Chapter 5 of this text discusses planning and objectives in detail.

Organizing is a second basic management function performed by sales management. **Organizing** is the grouping of activities necessary to obtain common objectives and the assignment of each grouping to a manager who has the authority necessary to supervise the people performing the activities.[17] The sales manager thus not only supervises sales personnel but may delegate authority to them to facilitate the attainment of objectives. The concept of organizing a sales force for effective operation is the focus of Chapter 12 of this book.

Motivation suggests movement. An individual who is not "motivated" will make no movement (progress) toward the attainment of a goal. Sales management literature reflects a basic disagreement on motivation. Some sales managers believe that motivation of sales personnel cannot be accomplished by external persons or influences. That is, motivation must come from *within* the individual. Other sales managers believe that sales contests, salary or commission rate increases, and so on, will stimulate increased performance (movement) toward attainment of prescribed objectives. Chapter 8 discusses motivation and compensation of the sales force.

Controlling an operation is the final basic management function. The essence of control from a sales management viewpoint is twofold: first, a comparison must constantly be made between the expected (planned objectives) and the actual (achieved to date); second, modifications must be made as needed. Thus, a sales manager may have an annual dollar sales objective that might be reviewed on a periodic (for example, monthly) basis. Not only must the sales manager constantly evaluate the actual versus the planned objectives, he must also take necessary "corrective" steps, if needed. Often students think of such corrective steps in negative terms only. In a sales situation where the sales objective is running drastically behind schedule, it is true that personnel shifts or even termination may be called for. However, it is also true that a sales manager may engage in positive steps. The hiring of an additional sales representative, the granting of bonuses, and so on, are some of the positive steps a sales manager may engage in. Chapter 11 deals with evaluation and supervision of the sales staff.

Note that control also involves a large element of planning. Thus,

---

[16] Leslie W. Rue and Lloyd L. Byars, *Management: Theory and Application* (Homewood, Ill.: Richard D. Irwin, Inc., 1977), p. 94.
[17] Harold Koontz and Cyril O'Donnell, *Principles of Management: An Analysis of Managerial Functions,* 4th ed. (New York: McGraw-Hill Book Company, 1968), p. 231.

the prudent sales manager recognizes that these are not four separate, unrelated functions. Rather, the basic functions of planning, organizing, motivating, and controlling are *interrelated* duties.

The Environment of Sales Management

The broader areas of responsibility including planning, direction, and control suggest that a much stronger challenge faces sales management in the coming years. However, given the critical nature of sales to the firm, this is a challenge that must be met.[18] The broader environment within which sales managers of today and the future will operate will be replete with frustrations as well as challenge. Hopefully, richer rewards, both to the individual sales manager and the firm will be a partial result of successfully coping with this more complex environment. As consumer sophistication, competition, and governmental legislation increase in the future, a critical need for truly competent sales management personnel will clearly be created. It is to preparation for this challenge that the balance of this book is dedicated.

One author has examined the changing environment of sales management and concluded that specific changes in the future of the sales manager include:

1. An increase in average age due to longer training and development.
2. Increased formal education needed due to the demand for different skills.
3. Temporary assignments in other parts of the firm to decrease tunnel vision and make sales managers a more integral part of corporate management.
4. Increasing involvement in marketing planning, both as a contributor and executor.
5. The "basics" of sales management—recruiting, selecting, motivating, compensating, and evaluating will remain critically important to the firm.[19]

Summary

Although selling should not be thought of as the starting point of all other activities in the firm, it remains a critically important function. No organization can long survive if the selling function is poorly performed. The evolution of firms from emphasis upon production, selling,

---

[18] See Robert J. Holloway and Robert S. Hancock, *Marketing in a Changing Environment* (New York: John H. Wiley & Sons, Inc., 1968), pp. 357–396.

[19] R. E. Evans, "The Field Sales Manager of the Future," in *Proceedings of the American Marketing Association* Portland, 1974 Chicago, Ill.: (American Marketing Association, 1974), pp. 518–520.

marketing, and social marketing have brought about profound changes for the firm generally and sales management specifically.

Sales management takes place within a marketing environment of constant change. Certain variables in the marketing are "uncontrollable" from a sales manager's point of view whereas others are "controllable." Nevertheless, the sales manager must attempt to anticipate changes in the environment and take the required corrective action(s) within his firm.

Although selling activity is the primary focus of this text, it should be remembered that personal selling is only one of four differing but related promotional elements. Firms seek to combine these four into the proper promotional blend for their own company. Two differing types of promotional blends are characterized by a "push" and a "pull" policy.

Traditionally sales management was viewed as consisting of a narrow range of functions directly relating to personal selling. More recently a broader view of sales management has emerged that provides both for increasing challenge and responsibility.

Discussion Questions

1. Does the marketing task begin with sales activities? If not, what happens before the sale?

2. Trace the evolution of a firm from the production era through a social marketing era.

3. Discuss the "uncontrollable" elements of the marketing environment.

4. What are the elements of the marketing mix?

5. Promotion has four elements. Provide an illustration of each.

6. Differentiate between a "push" and a "pull" promotional policy.

7. Contrast a traditional (narrow) view of sales management responsibilities with a more current (broad) view. What are the differences in the responsibilities placed on sales management?

8. What specific changes are in store for sales managers of the future?

Selected References

BERG, THOMAS L., *Mismarketing* (Garden City, N.Y.: Anchor Books, 1971).
HARTLEY, ROBERT F., *Marketing Mistakes* (Columbus, Ohio: Grid, Inc., 1976).

KEITH, ROBERT S., "The Marketing Revolution," *Journal of Marketing*, January 1960, pp. 35–38.

KOTLER, PHILIP, AND GERALD ZALTMAN, "Social Marketing: An Approach to Planned Social Change," *Journal of Marketing*, July 1971, pp. 3–12.

LEVITT, THEODORE, "Marketing Myopia," *Harvard Business Review*, July–August 1960, pp. 45–56.

MCCARTHY, E. JEROME, *Basic Marketing*, 6th ed. (Homewood, Ill.: Richard D. Irwin, Inc., 1978).

TOFFLER, ALVIN, *Future Shock* (New York: Bantam Books, Inc., 1971).

CASE 1.1
The Clean Corporation

Company Background

The Clean Corporation (CC) was founded in 1848 as a partnership to manufacture and sell soaps and candles. Later in the century, the development of other lighting methods greatly reduced the demand for candles, whereas improved national cleanliness habits increased the use of soap. As a consequence, soap became considerably more important to the business than candles. Eventually, the company stopped manufacturing candles altogether.

Shortly after the turn of the century, a development occurred that was far reaching because it placed the company in the food business. CC had formed a subsidiary in 1902 to acquire and build seed crushing mills in southern cotton states to assure a constant supply of cottonseed oil for use in the manufacture of soap. The company refined some of the higher grades of the cottonseed oil and sold them to other manufacturers to be used in making salad oils. The experience gained working with this raw material prompted the company chemists to search for a way to use these vegetable oils in a shortening product that would be superior to lard. The development of an entirely new manufacturing process was the answer to this problem. The new process made it possible to convert cottonseed to a creamy form, which appears to be solid at room temperature and has almost indefinite keeping qualities. Dreamo—the first creamy, white, all-vegetable shortening, was introduced in 1912, establishing CC in the food field.

Since CC at that time was known solely as a manufacturer of soaps, the introduction of its first food product required thoughtful preparation in manufacturing, selling, and advertising. However, cooking fats were sold through the same outlets as soap, so it was important to educate

Case prepared by Dan H. Robertson, Georgia State University.

the dealer that Dreamo was a fine edible product—not a byproduct of soap. Because Dreamo represented an entirely new type of cooking fat, there would be an advantage to packing it differently from lard, which was sold at that time in cartons and bulk. The packaging problem was solved by packing Dreamo in cans, thus providing a visible form of differentiation and, also, giving the product itself added protection. Aside from helping the education of the dealer, these actions also helped educate the consumer on the existence of this new concept in food.

At the time of Dreamo's introduction, CC sold only to grocery wholesalers—not directly in food retailers. To avoid confusion, the company initially used separate salesmen to sell Dreamo to the wholesalers. After Dreamo had been introduced, however, it was added to the line of products sold by the company's Cleaning Goods Sales Department. This, of course, required careful training and indoctrination of the salesmen.

In the early 1920s, CC decided to sell directly to retailers as well as to wholesalers. The company had been concerned for some time about the cyclical buying of soap by wholesalers because of their awareness of the fluctuation in the market for tallow, then a principal ingredient in soap manufacture and an important cost factor. (Tallow, like other commodities, often ranges widely in price. For example, during the 1919–1921 period, tallow sold for as low as 5 cents a pound and as high as 21 cents a pound.) Whenever the wholesalers felt that a rise in the price of tallow was imminent, he would be inclined to order soap heavily. On the other hand, if he anticipated a price drop, he would resist ordering as long as possible. This resulted in wide swings in manufacturing schedules, with factories running day and night for certain periods and then being forced to close at other times of the year. Thus, at the manufacturing level workmen faced periods of unemployment, and at the retail level stores frequently ran out of stock and consumers were unable to buy CC products, because wholesalers sometimes waited too long to order.

A company study revealed that consumers used soap fairly constantly throughout the year. The solution, therefore, appeared to be to sell directly to retailers as well as to wholesalers and insure an even flow of CC products to the public. This meant the development of a much larger field sales organization and the reorientation of the members of the existing force. The results, however, were worth the effort. By eliminating the reasons for cyclical buying, CC was able to plan production schedules at a fairly even rate throughout the year, which provided many operating economies and stabilized employment. As a direct result, in 1928, only two years after direct retail selling was inaugurated, the company was able to initiate a plan of guaranteed annual employment under which hourly paid employees are guaranteed at least 48 weeks of work each year.

The work on synthetic detergents in Germany in the early 1920s made it possible for CC to diversify in another direction. Based on this work, CC in the early 1930s developed a synthetic detergent, Blub, which, unlike soap, did not combine with the minerals present in hard water to produce a film, or deposit, often referred to as "soap film." From this work, it became apparent to CC management that synthetic detergents should provide an excellent base for a shampoo product that would not leave a film deposit on the hair, and thus would give hair a better luster than a soap base shampoo could. CC therefore, introduced Whiz detergent shampoo in 1934 as its first entry in the beauty field.

The distribution pattern for shampoo products was different from that of soap and shortening products. At the time of the Whiz introduction, the largest percentage of shampoo sales occurred in drug and department stores rather than in grocery outlets. Soap and shortening, on the other hand, were sold almost 100 per cent in grocery stores.

CC decided, therefore, to set up a special Whiz sales force to sell only this one product. This group grew until after the war when it became the Toilet Goods Sales Department within an entirely separate Toilet Goods Division set up by CC to concentrate on health, beauty, and toiletry products. With the increased importance of the supermarkets after the war, the Toilet Goods Sales Department in many instances called on the same dealers and buyers as the Cleaning Goods Sales Department. This caused occasional confusion in dealers/buyers' minds and they sometimes resented the time required to see two separate CC salespeople.

CC adheres to a policy of promotion from within the company; consequently, practically all management personnel for the Toilet Goods Sales Department came from either the Whiz sales force or the Cleaning Goods Sales Department. After World War II, the Toilet Goods Sales Department was called upon to introduce many new brands in quick succession, including Sieria and Zing shampoos, Kurlee and Easy Time home permanents, Glisten and No D-K toothpaste, and Kool deodorant.

Current Situation

Following the war, the company also experienced substantial growth in its soap and detergent businesses, due primarily to the introduction of new synthetic detergent brands such as Zap, Happy, and others. These new brands were added to an already substantial line of cleaning products. Dreamo, however, remained the only food product sold by the Cleaning Goods Sales Department until 1975 when the company introduced golden Whippy shortening nationally. The Cleaning Goods Sales Department was selling 17 large-volume soap, detergent and food brands. The line was so large the company began to consider the desirability of establishing another sales force to handle several of these products. Further, members of the sales force were beginning to complain that they had too many brands to handle efficiently.

Recognizing the tremendous growth potential in the food business, which had resulted from a burgeoning population together with higher per capita incomes and standards of living, the company began considering the establishment of a Food Sales Department to sell Dreamo and Whippy, as well as to handle the introduction of other food products on which the company had been doing considerable research for a number of years. This food sales department, if established, would be part of a CC Food Products Division, which would operate separately from the Soap Division and the Toilet Goods Division.

Tom Williams, Vice President of Sales, must make a recommendation to CC's Board of Directors. On the one hand, Mr. Williams could see advantages to three separate sales departments. Further, he would have flexibility for adding new brands in the future. On the other hand, the cost of additional salaries, automobiles, travel expenses, administrative costs, and so on, worried him. Having been a salesman for the firm himself, he recalled the negative reaction by food buyers to two sales representatives, and he wondered if three sales representatives from his company would further aggravate the situation.

CASE 1.2
Green Film Distributors, Inc.

Company Background

Green Film Distributors, Inc. was founded in 1969 by a single owner/manager, Mr. Tom Green. Mr. Green had previously worked for 6 years as a sales representative for a large national producer of photography equipment and film. In 1969 he resigned his position to form his own company as a distributor of film produced by two large domestic firms and one foreign producer. Mr. Green thus began his business by distributing camera film for industrial applications, medical use, and as a wholesaler to discount and drug stores who sold camera film for use by ultimate consumers.

In the first 2½ years of his operation as a distributor, Mr. Green was the sole full-time employee of the firm. His previous experience in sales and his knowledge of both the technical aspects of camera film and the customers in the territory gave him distinct advantages that resulted in a rapidly increasing sales base. Sales increased by over 100 per cent in each of the first 2 full years of operation to the point where estimated sales for 1971 were over $300,000. Supplementing Mr. Green's efforts on a part-time basis was a business administration student from a local college. This student had worked for Mr. Green for over a year in two capacities. First, as bookkeeper and shipping/receiving clerk and, second, the student also took telephone messages for Mr. Green while he was in the field calling on accounts.

The typical day for Tom Green consisted of approximately 14 to 16 working hours. Typically, Mr. Green's day began around 6 A.M. when he would go by the office/warehouse combination to check on both incoming telephone messages from the preceding day and current inventory levels. Often Mr. Green left notes for the college student to indicate merchandise to be ordered from one of the film producers or other important messages to be relayed to customers via telephone. Weekends, too,

Case prepared by Dan H. Robertson, Georgia State University.

were often work time for Mr. Green, inasmuch as his larger customers frequently called him at home to order film on an emergency basis. Tom Green and his wife Nancy often joked that had he worked as many hours while he worked for the national film producers as he did since opening his own business, he would certainly have become president. The few times Tom Green had kept any records, he was able to verify that he was routinely working in the neighborhood of 100 hours each week. However, his long hours were not without their rewards. Not only was Tom his own boss and sole owner of a growing business, he also was able to pay himself a rather nice salary (approximately $30,000 for this year) and still show a modest profit for the company after all additional expenses were paid.

One recurring and somewhat disconcerting thought had occupied Tom Green's mind as of late. Although his business continued to grow in terms of dollar sales, Tom was very concerned about both the number and the nature of accounts he was able to attract and retain. Over the past 4 months, for example, Tom estimated that he had spent upwards of 60 hours in the preparatory work required to obtain the business for a large hospital in the area. The hours spent on this hospital account had paid off handsomely when Mr. Green's firm was awarded the contract to provide all x-ray film used by the various x-ray machines in the hospital for the upcoming year. However, when Tom reflected back upon the telephone messages he had received and the number of small accounts that he had lost to competition while spending time on the one large hospital account, he began to wonder if it was really worthwhile. While driving home late one evening, Tom thought to himself, "Maybe what I need to do at this point is to add another full-time salesperson to my staff. After all, it's really more than I can handle right now and it seems to me that in the future my competitors will begin to take accounts away from me faster than I am able to attract new ones." Later that same evening after dinner with his wife and while watching a late night talk show, Tom found himself scribbling down on a scratch pad the following:

Current Situation

- Is the addition of another full-time salesperson the answer to my problems?
- Should I make an offer to the college student who has been working for me on a part-time basis, inasmuch as he already knows a great deal about my business and has proven himself to be dependable?
- Am I concentrating too much on selling and forgetting about marketing more generally defined?
- Should I be trying to obtain a few very large accounts or a large number of fairly small accounts?
- Should I be putting more time into attracting new accounts or simply concentrating on keeping those accounts that I have already landed?
- Should I enlarge my product line to include not only film but cameras and related photographic equipment?

- Perhaps I shouldn't be concentrating on selling; perhaps instead I should hire someone skilled in the area of advertising and provide them an advertising budget in order to increase my sales volume.
- Could telephone selling or direct mail help me cut down on the number of contact hours spent with customers?

As Tom Green drifted off to sleep that night, he rested uneasily. Thoughts about these questions and other related questions continued to bother him. One thing was certain. If Tom was to avoid becoming an insomniac, he had to find answers to some of these questions.

Student Learning Exercise / 1
Assessing Marketing Effectiveness

Objective   To measure marketing effectiveness of an organization/institution via a standardized instrument.

Overview   This chapter has presented a variety of possible orientations for a firm including production, sales, marketing, and social marketing orientations. This exercise contains a standardized auditing outline for evaluating organizations regarding their marketing effectiveness.

Exercise   Think about a marketing organization with which you have recently dealt. Note that this organization need *not* be a profit making firm. It could be your university, church, or a campus student organization. However, it could also be a profit making organization, such as the bookstore where you purchased this text, the dealer from whom you purchased your car, a restaurant where you've recently dined, and so on.

Evaluate the organization/institution you've selected on the 15 questions provided. You may need to "dig" a bit to be able to answer some of the questions. It is also possible that you will be unable to answer some questions. At the end of the questionnaire you will find a scale for evaulating marketing effectiveness.

When you have answered all the questions and derived a total score, think about the following problems:

A. What could the organization/institution you've selected do to improve its marketing effectiveness?
B. Marketing texts often mention the "marketing concept" as a philosophy. Is the organization/institution you selected following this concept? Why, or why not? If you need to review the "marketing concept" consult any current basic marketing text.

Marketing Effectiveness Rating Scale

Customer philosophy

A. Does management recognize the importance of designing the company to serve the needs and wants of chosen markets?

Score

0 ☐ Management primarily thinks in terms of selling current and new products to whoever will buy them.

1 ☐ Management thinks in terms of serving a wide range of markets and needs with equal effectiveness.

2 ☐ Management thinks in terms of serving the needs and wants of well-defined markets chosen for their long-run growth and profit potential for the company.

B. Does management develop different offerings and marketing plans for different segments of the market?

0 ☐ No.

1 ☐ Somewhat.

2 ☐ To a good extent.

C. Does management take a whole marketing system view (suppliers, channels, competitors, customers, environment) in planning its business?

0 ☐ No. Management concentrates on selling and servicing its immediate customers.

1 ☐ Somewhat. Management takes a long view of its channels although the bulk of its effort goes to selling and servicing the immediate customers.

2 ☐ Yes. Management takes a whole marketing systems view recognizing the threats and opportunities created for the company by changes in any part of the system.

Integrated marketing organization

D. Is there high-level marketing integration and control of the major marketing functions?

0 ☐ No. Sales and other marketing functions are not integrated at the top and there is some unproductive conflict.

1 ☐ Somewhat. There is formal integration and control of the major marketing functions but less than satisfactory coordination and cooperation.

2 ☐ Yes. The major marketing functions are effectively integrated.

E. Does marketing management work well with management in research, manufacturing, purchasing, physical distribution, and finance?

0 ☐ No. There are complaints that marketing is unreasonable in the demands and costs it places on other departments.

1 ☐ Somewhat. The relations are amicable although each department pretty much acts to serve its own power interests.

2 ☐ Yes. The departments cooperate effectively and resolve issues in the best interest of the company as a whole.

F. How well-organized is the new product development process?

0 ☐ The system is ill-defined and poorly handled.

1 ☐ The system formally exists but lacks sophistication.

2 ☐ The system is well-structured and professionally staffed.

Adequate marketing information

G. When were the latest marketing research studies of customers, buying influences, channels, and competitors conducted?

0 ☐ Several years ago.

1 ☐ A few years ago.

2 ☐ Recently.

H. How well does management know the sales potential and profitability of different market segments, customers, territories, products, channels, and other sizes?

0 ☐ Not at all.

1 ☐ Somewhat.

2 ☐ Very well.

I. What effort is expended to measure the cost-effectiveness of different marketing expenditures?

0 ☐ Little or no effort.

1 ☐ Some effort.

2 ☐ Substantial effort.

[* Philip Kotler, "From Sales Obsession to Marketing Effectiveness," *Harvard Business Review*, November–December 1977, Copyright © 1977 by the President and Fellows of Harvard College; all rights reserved.]

Marketing Effectiveness Rating Scale *(continued)*

	Strategic orientation

J. What is the extent of formal marketing planning?

0 ☐ Management does little or nor formal marketing planning.

1 ☐ Management develops an annual marketing plan.

2 ☐ Management develops a detailed annual marketing plan and a careful long-range plan that is updated annually.

K. What is the quality of the current marketing strategy?

0 ☐ The current strategy is not clear.

1 ☐ The current strategy is clear and represents a continuation of traditional strategy.

2 ☐ The current strategy is clear, innovative, data-based, and well-reasoned.

L. What is the extent of contingency thinking and planning?

0 ☐ Management does little or not contingency thinking.

1 ☐ Management does some contingency thinking although little formal contingency planning.

2 ☐ Management formally identifies the most important contingencies and develops contingency plans.

	Operational efficiency

M. How well is the marketing thinking at the top communicated and implemented down the line?

0 ☐ Poorly.

1 ☐ Fairly.

2 ☐ Successfully.

N. Is management doing an effective job with the marketing resources?

0 ☐ No. The marketing resources are inadequate for the job to be done.

1 ☐ Somewhat. The marketing resources are adequate but they are not employed optimally.

2 ☐ Yes. The marketing resources are adequate and are deployed efficiently.

O. Does management show a good capacity to react quickly and effectively to on-the-spot developments?

0 ☐ No. Sales and market information is not very current and management reaction time is slow.

1 ☐ Somewhat. Management receives fairly up-to-date sales and market information; management reaction time varies.

2 ☐ Yes. Management has installed systems yielding highly current information and fast reaction time.

	Total score

Rating marketing effectiveness

The auditing outline can be used in this way. The auditor collects information as it bears on the 15 questions. The appropriate answer is checked for each question. The scores are added—the total will be somewhere between 0 and 30. The following scale shows the equivalent in marketing effectiveness:

0–5	None
6–10	Poor
11–15	Fair
16–20	Good
21–25	Very good
26–30	Superior

The audit can be kept and used again, say at the end of a year, to determine the progress that has been made in the five major areas it covers. Combined, they add up to marketing effectiveness, whether it be of the company as a whole, a division, or a product line.

The Personal Sales Component of Promotion

As indicated in Chapter 1, the focus of this book is upon the management of the personal selling function. Nevertheless, it is important to maintain a perspective of personal selling as it fits into the overall promotional program of the firm. We have also indicated that the promotional blend selected by one firm might utilize personal selling more heavily than that selected by another firm. Promotional mixes heavily dependent upon advertising and those heavily concentrated on personal selling were called "pull" and "push" strategies, respectively.

Figure 2.1 presents an overview of personal selling as it relates to the overall promotional mix selected by the marketing organization. In addition, it also shows the relationship of the basic managerial activities of planning, organizing, motivating, and controlling to the personal sales organization. Note that the sales manager has specific responsibilities in each of the four sales management decision areas.

Personal Selling: An Overview

Chapter 1 mentioned a view of personal selling that stresses the concept of a mutually beneficial exchange between buyer and seller. The salesperson may derive personal satisfaction from having helped another individual find the solution to a problem. In addition, the salesperson is ultimately

FIGURE 2.1 Personal Selling in Perspective

paid by his/her firm in the form of a salary, commission, or bonus—or in some combination of these three forms of compensation. The selling firm typically receives satisfaction through profits accruing from the sale. The buyer receives benefits from the purchase in the form of solutions to his/her problem.

The following section examines some differing approaches to interactions between buyer and seller. Note that a variety of interactions are possible. The purpose of this section is to acquaint the student with some of the more common types of views of the sales interaction situation.

THREE DIFFERING VIEWS ON SELLING

Selling is not really a single activity. There are differing types of salespeople for differing products. However, this point is easy to overlook since we have all had interaction with sales personnel. Hence, there is a tendency to equate selling with our previous personal experience. An illustration outside of the sales field might prove helpful.

A student you meet tells you he plays football for your university. The words "football player" lend themselves to stereotyping as a result of your previous experience. However, if you truly wished to understand the nature of this student's task, you would ask, "What position do you play?" This would lead to better understanding. You might determine that he is an offensive rather than defensive player, or lineman rather than back, or possibly even a kicking specialist. The point we wish to make here is that "football player" could convey a wide variety of meaning, extending from someone who merely sits on the bench to an active "star" for the team. So it is in selling.

The work of Harold Cash and W. J. E. Crissy provides one example of the possible variety of views on selling.[1] They suggest three possible categories of selling based upon the interpersonal relationships and exchanges over time between salesperson and customer.

The Stimulus-Response View of Selling. The simplest of these three theories of selling is called a stimulus-response view. Based upon the classic work of the Russian scientist Pavlov, this theory recognizes that a given stimulus (food) would produce a given response (salivation). A direct application to selling suggests that each sales representative would have a variety of stimuli in the form of things to say, examples, and so on, that would produce a response in the prospect. The ultimate response, of course, would be that the prospect becomes a customer by purchasing the product or service the sales representative is selling. Note that this view of selling assumes that a positive response (purchase) is the typical outcome of the exchange between buyer and seller.

Not all stimuli will necessarily elicit a positive response. There are things that prospects can learn about a product that may act as deterents

[1] Harold C. Cash and W. J. E. Crissy, *Psychology of Selling*, Vol. 1 (Flushing, N.Y.: Personnel Development Associates, 1958).

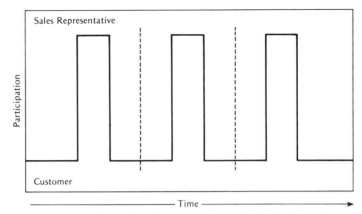

FIGURE 2.2 A Stimulus-Response View of Selling [Based on Harold C. Cash and W. J. E. Crissy, *Psychology of Selling*, Vol. 1 (Flushing 58, N.Y.: Personnel Development Associates, 1958).]

to purchase. You may see an ad for a watch in a magazine, but, when you visit a dealer or call, you find the price exceeds what you are willing to pay. Your original response to the ad was positive, but your second response (having learned the price) is negative.

Examining this approach to seller in actual use over a given time period, we would see a pattern of participation by sales representative and customer such as is shown in Figure 2.2. As can be seen, the sales representative dominates the interchange from the start. The stimuli provided by the sales representative are aimed at a desired positive response. The dotted lines represent possible ends to the sales transaction. Thus, if response one is characterized by agreement on the part of the customer, the salesman would close the interchange by again dominating to finalize details of the sale (price, delivery date, method of payment, and so on).

Obviously, a memorized or "canned" sales presentation lends itself to the stimulus-response approach. National Cash Register is often recognized as the first company to utilize a canned sales talk. Beginning in the 1920s, the firm analyzed the sales talk of some of their most successful sales personnel. This analysis led to a standard company message that NCR sales representatives were told to memorize and use. The successful results obtained by NCR prompted quick adoption by other firms. Among the advantages of the standard memorized or canned sales presentation are the following:

Arguments in favor of the use of the standard memorized sales presentation[2]

1. It insures that the salesman will tell the complete and accurate story about his company's products and policies.

---

[2] Carlton A. Pederson and Milburn D. Wright, *Salesmanship: Principles and Methods,* 5th ed. (Homewood, Ill.: Richard D. Irwin, Inc., 1971), p. 335.

2. It encompasses the best techniques and methods used by the most successful salesmen.
3. It aids the new and inexperienced salesmen.
4. It eliminates repetition and saves time for both the salesman and the buyer.
5. It guarantees the most effective presentation by having the sales points arranged in a logical and systematic sequence.
6. It provides the salesman with effective answers to all possible objections that might be raised by the prospects, and thus gives the salesman additional confidence.
7. Most salesmen tend to standardize their sales talks anyway, so why not standardize on the "one best way"?

The stimulus-response approach may also be used successively in a variety of selling situations where the dollar value of the sales transaction is relatively low and the sales effort is reasonably brief. However, this method also has drawbacks. The arguments against this process includes:

Arguments against the use of the standard memorized sales presentation[3]

1. It is too flexible and artificial and tends to make a mechanical robot out of the salesman. The salesman thus loses his enthusiasm and originality.
2. It cannot be used in certain types of selling where the salesman makes regular calls upon his customers.
3. It discourages or prevents the prospect from participating in the sales conversation. This prevents the salesman from finding the true needs and wants of each prospective buyer, and his sales story tends to become a monologue.
4. When the salesman relies on a memorized presentation, he often has difficulty getting started again after he has been interrupted by the prospect.
5. It is not practical to use the standard memorized presentation when the salesman sells many products.

It has been suggested that the major disadvantage of this method is that there is too much control or dominance of participation by the sales representative. Thompson states:

The *major disadvantage* is that the salesman who follows the stimulus-response method *controls* the sales interview and gives his "pitch" with little regard for the customer's viewpoint. He doesn't develop two-way communication. He doesn't get much feedback.[4]

This point needs further elaboration. Since the salesperson dominates the exchange (Figure 2.2), the prospective customer has very little opportunity to say anything. In Figure 2.2, the sales representative permits the customer to respond only when he is attempting to close the presenta-

    [3] Ibid. pp. 335–336.
    [4] Joseph W. Thompson, *Selling: A Managerial and Behavioral Science Analysis*, 2nd ed. (New York: McGraw-Hill Book Company, Inc., 1973), p. 149.

tion. As indicated by the dotted lines, if the closure attempt were not successful (that is, the prospect does not agree to buy), the sales representative would immediately launch stimulus two. This might consist of a summary of key points in the preceding exchange, or it may bring in new stimuli (product features, advantages of ownership, and so on). Likewise, if the prospect still resists purchasing, a third round may follow, and on it goes. The fact that truly tenacious sales personnel may continue in this process over many different sales calls is born out in the saying, "I never met a prospect I couldn't sell; of course, there are a few I still haven't closed."

One last note on the stimulus-response approach to selling. Note that the needs of any individual prospect are virtually ignored. It is *assumed* that the product or service the salesperson offers is of value to the customer. In fact, many sales personnel are specifically told in training that "everyone needs this product" or "everyone needs this service."

The Selling Formula View of Selling. A differing view of selling is provided by the selling formula approach. Also known as the *standardized learning approach*,[5] this view has application in advertising and other forms of promotion as well as personal selling. The basic concept is that the marketer must first get the prospect's attention. Thus, a commercial might begin with a loud nose, a perplexing question, or a stimulus that causes the audience to concentrate upon the commercial. As we shall see, this view concludes with an appeal to action. Typically, a commercial may suggest, "so rush right out to your local store and buy one today," and numerous other action appeals. Commenting on this philosophy as applied in personal selling, Britt states: "This theory implies that it is necessary and desirable to treat all customers alike."[6] Further, this method views prospects as moving through various steps, stages, or levels leading up to a purchase. Often a canned sales talk is used in following this method of selling as was also true with the stimulus-response approach.

Research on the subject of canned sales presentation points out a fundamental problem in discussing this approach. Typically, a canned versus uncanned type of dihotomy comes to mind that is misleading. Jolson[7] suggests that there are at least five levels of a sales presentation on the continuum that are perceivable. These include:

- *Fully Automated.* Sound movies, slides, or film strips dominate the presentation. The salesman's participation consists of setting up the projector, answering simple questions, and/or writing up the order. Many audiovisual systems are available.
- *Semiautomated.* The salesman reads the presentation from copy

---

[5] For further detail, see David L. Kurtz, H. Robert Dodge, and Jay E. Klompmaker, *Professional Selling* (Dallas, Texas: Business Publications, Inc., 1976), pp. 70–71.

[6] Steuart Henderson Britt (ed.), *Consumer Behavior and the Behavioral Sciences* New York: John Wiley & Sons, Inc., 1968), p. 484.

[7] Marvin A. Jolson, "Should the Sales Presentation Be Fresh or Canned?" *Business Horizons,* October 1973, pp. 81–88.

TABLE 2.1   Sales Presentation Methods Currently in Practice (N = 75)

	Fully Automated	Semi-automated	Memorized	Organized	Unstructured
Percentage of firms using each presentation type	9.3	33.3	24.0	85.3	76.0
Percentage of firms preferring each presentation type*	2.7	4.0	9.3	44.0	40.0

* ($x^2 = 61.7$, significant at .001 level)

printed on flip charts, read-off binders, promotional broadsides, or brochures. He adds his own comments when necessary.

- *Memorized.*   The salesman delivers a company prepared message that he has memorized. Supplementary visual aids may or may not be used.
- *Organized.*   The salesman is allowed complete flexibility of wording; however, he does follow a company pattern, check list, or outline. Visual aids are optional.
- *Unstructured.*   The salesman is on his own to describe the product any way he sees it. Generally, the presentation varies from prospect to prospect.

As this overview suggests, there are several degrees of canned presentations, not simply one extreme.

In order to determine which level of the five sales presentations were being used, a mail questionnaire was sent to 147 firms. Responses were received from top field sales executives in 75 of the original 147 firms (a 51 per cent response rate). Some of the findings[8] are shown in Table 2.1 The reader will notice that the percentages exceed 100 per cent, since some firms use or prefer more than one of the presentation methods.

This research suggests that the organized or unstructured types of presentations are more popular than the three more structured alternatives. The author of this study did note a preference for more structure as the desire for an accurate, authoritative, and ethical sales message increased. Commenting on the fully-automated method, Jolson states:

These data support the proposition that substantial presentation structure is perceived by management as being programmed against inaccurate or unethical statements by the sales force member. A highly structured approach is also effective when the seller wishes to deliver a one-way, standard message to all prospects. However, it is not conducive to customer interruptions, out-of-sequence inquiries, or requested short-cuts.[9]

As earlier stated, the selling formula approach views the sale as a result of a series of steps such as attention, interest, desire, and action.

[8] Jolson, ibid., quoted in *Contemporary Readings in Sales Management,* Marvin A. Jolson (ed.) (New York: Mason/Charter Publishing, Inc., 1977), p. 132.
[9] Jolson, op. cit., p. 135.

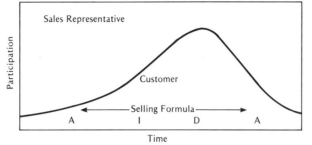

FIGURE 2.3 A Selling Formula View of Selling [Based on Cash and Crissy, *Psychology of Selling,* Vol. 1.]

The salesperson would thus first concentrate on obtaining the prospect's attention. This gives way to interest, desire by the prospect to own the product or secure the service and, thus, taking action to make the purchase.

Similar to the earlier view of the stimulus-response approach, Figure 2.3 presents a graphic view of the sales formula approach. Note that the particular formula utilized here (A-attention, I-interest, D-desire, A-action) is but one of several alternative selling formulas.

Note that there are some similarities between the stimulus-response view of selling and the selling formula. For example, early in the interchange between buyer and seller, the sales representative is clearly dominant in both views. That is, the sales representative is doing most of the talking with the prospect usually listening. Also notice that the salesperson becomes dominant again near the conclusion of both processes. As noted earlier in the stimulus-response view, dominance by the salesperson near the end of the interchange is to close the sale.

The selling formula approach also has advantages and disadvantages. Proponents of this view of selling point out that adherence to this approach insures that all important information relating to the produce or service will be transmitted to the prospect. That is, when following the formula, the sales representative is less likely to forget or leave out salient product or service information.

A major disadvantage that may arise is that the potential customer may not experience the states in the sequence suggested. Will awareness lead to interest, interest to desire, and desire to action? Research suggests that this sequence will occur when customers are interested in the generic product (versus specific brand), perceive that difference exist between alternative brands, feel that advertising concerning the product is important, and the product has recently been introduced to the market.[10]

One last comment on both the stimulus-response and selling formula views of selling should be made. Note that both methods analyze the situation from the salesperson's perspective rather than that of the customer. Both concentrate on the salesperson closing the role and merely *assume* buyer satisfaction will be an automatic outcome of a successful close. Both are characteristic of the sales oriented environment discussed earlier in Chapter 1.

[10] Michael L. Ray, "Marketing Communication and the Hierarchy-of-Effects," Working Paper (Cambridge, Mass.: Marketing Science Institute, 1973), pp. 6–7.

The Need-Satisfaction View of Selling.   A third view of selling is offered in the need-satisfaction approach to selling. A basic assumption of this theory is that purchases occur in order to satisfy needs. It follows that if one accepts this premise, the need(s) of the customer must be understood by the sales representative. In contrast to the two earlier views of selling, which examine the sales interaction from the sales representative's view, this approach focuses upon the interaction from a customer-oriented perspective. Figure 2.4 depicts a sales interaction where the need-satisfaction concept is being utilized. Note the distinctive departure from the two previous methods in terms of participation in the interaction process. In this view of selling, the customer dominates the early interaction and participates much more than the sales representative, but how will this be accomplished?

The first phase of the interchange between the sales representative and the prospective customer is called the **need-development** phase. This phase (extending up to point *X* in Figure 2.4) is characterized by the salesperson asking questions that are designed to shed light upon the prospective customer's needs. This approach requires much prethought and planning on the part of the sales representative. Consideration of this point will suggest that it is much easier to be a "talker" than it is to be a good listener. Not only are many salespeople poor listeners, they often epitomize the old Indian adage of "one who speaks much but says little."

The need-development phase may not conclude in a few minutes of exchange. In fact, many firms who use this approach in selling find that two or perhaps three sales calls may be spent determining the prospective customer's need(s).

The need-satisfaction view is not an idle theory but is, in fact, utilized in many successful sales organizations. Xerox Learning Systems trains sales personnel to recognize the interaction between customer needs, the salesperson's role, and product or service features. The salesperson

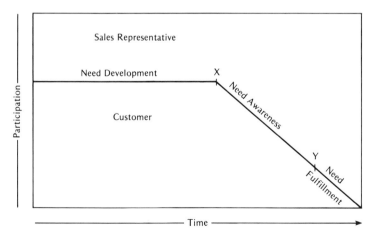

FIGURE 2.4   A Need-Satisfaction View of Selling [Based on Cash and Crissy, *Psychology of Selling*, Vol. 1.]

is trained to translate the features of their product or service into *benefits* that satisfy the customer's needs.[11]

The time and expertise needed successfully to diagnose a customer's needs should not be underestimated. Often the prospective customers cannot articulate their own needs clearly. Thus, as mentioned, the sales representative may need several calls to assess accurately the prospect's needs.

When the salesperson believes he/she has a clear picture of the prospective customer's needs, the next step involving matching these needs with the firm's product/service match in order to find a solution. We are now in the second phase of the need-satisfaction approach (between points *X* and *Y* in Figure 2.4).

The **need-awareness** phase of this approach involves the salesperson communicating to the prospective customer two items of information. First, the salesperson communicates to the prospect a complete statement of the prospect's need(s). This may serve one or two purposes. First, it provides a "check and balance" to verify that the sales representative *does* correctly and completely understand the need(s) of the prospective customer. Second, it may prove to open the prospect's eyes to a need she/he has that was not previously recognized. We have all had the experience of wrestling with a problem for a long time and then having an "outsider," who has not previously been exposed to the problem, suggest a viable solution. This often leaves us saying to ourselves, "Now why didn't I think of that?" The salesperson often serves to bring this outside perspective to the customer. At point *Y*, the customer, too, clearly sees the problem and agrees with the sales representative's view of it.

In the third and final phase, **need fulfillment,** the salesperson shows the customer the solution to the problem. The solution consists of a product/service offered by the salesperson's firm. As indicated, the sales representative does *not* stress product features, per se, but rather emphasizes the benefits of the product/service to the customer.

Notice that once point *X* is reached, participation by the salespeople increases. They now play an increasingly important role in providing information about the need(s) of the prospect and the feature(s) of the product/service solution to the need(s). If the salespeople have done a thorough job of need(s) development and need(s) awareness, then need fulfillment (point *Y*) should be both a relatively straightforward matter and one characterized by salesperson/prospective customer agreement. Namely, that the salesperson has a product/service that will meet the need(s) of the customer, thus providing a solution to the customer's problem(s).

The need-satisfaction approach is not the perfect answer to a sales strategy, however. One of the disadvantages of this method is that considerable amounts of time may be spent in defining a prospective customer's needs, only to find that the firm does not make a product or offer a service that will meet these needs. Should this occur, the salespeople have expended time and their firm has expended money on a nonproduc-

[11] *Professional Selling Skills II—Unit 1—Need Satisfaction Selling* (Greenwich, Connecticut: Xerox Learning Systems, 1976), pp. 12–19.

tive exchange. A second disadvantage of this approach is that it requires salespeople who can both ask penetrating questions and remain relatively quiet in the initial part of the exchange. It is very hard for many salespeople to let others do the talking.

The towering advantage of this method is that it does specifically attempt to determine the customer's needs. By so doing, it should also reduce the number of unsuccessful closing attempts made by a salesperson.

Together these three views of selling provide a sampling of the sales approaches and philosophies traditionally used by marketers. However, at the outset of this chapter (and earlier in Chapter 1), we noted that selling was in a transitional state. The following section offers further information on the changes taking place in selling.

THE CHANGING WORLD OF PERSONAL SELLING

Many observers believe that selling has been going through an evolutionary process. As in any evolutionary process, there must be forces or pressures bringing about this change. Four major factors are contributing to the changes currently taking place in personal selling and marketing activities in general. Mazze has suggested that these factors include:

1. *Increased competition.* This is the result of new firms entering a profitable market and also by firms in other industries looking for opportunities to diversify.
2. *Changing customer lifestyles.* The customer is better educated, more mobile, and has more income today. According to Philip Kotler in *Marketing Management,* there is a tendency for the customer to move to a life that is easy, soft, sociable, and secure.
3. *Consumerism.* This is the age of the customer. There are private groups and governmental agencies that are watching those firms which attempt to market unsafe products or engage in deceptive activities.
4. *Government.* The government has played an increasing role in regulating selling and marketing activities in recent years. Almost every sales and marketing decision needs to be approved by the firm's legal department to see if the decision will pass close government scrutiny.[12]

Certainly each of these four changes in the environment has had an impact upon marketing generally and selling specifically. The impact of each will be discussed in more detail in Chapter 13, but, for now, our purpose is to examine the evolution in personal selling brought about by these changes.

Many authors have noted a change in approaches to selling in recent years. Basically, this change is reflected in a trend away from hard-sell pressure-sales approaches to approaches similar to the need-satisfaction view. The American Management Association has offered a course enti-

---

[12] Edward M. Mazze, *Personal Selling: Choice Against Chance* (St. Paul, Minn.: West Publishing Company, 1976), pp. 29–30.

tled "Consultative Selling" to its member for the past few years. A major point in this course involves formation of a "partnership" between salesperson and customer.

One approach to selling typical of the more modern view is the **nonmanipulative** sales technique. In a recent *Marketing News* article, Professor Anthony J. Alessandra describes this approach as consisting of six steps.

It begins when the salesperson builds a trust-bond relationship with the client.

Next, the salesperson discusses the current situation with the client to determine what is being done and how well it is working. The salesperson decides whether he or she can improve the client's situation.

If he or she can help, seller and buyer together develop a plan for action, make a commitment as to when and how to put the plan into operation, and finally, the salesperson follows through to ensure that the new plan is working.[13]

One obvious contrast of this view of selling and the stimulus-response or selling formula approach is the postsales transaction consideration. Note that the AIDA (selling formula) and stimulus-response approach both terminate with an action (the purchase) by the customer. A more current view of selling recognizes that what happens *after* the sale is critical. Followup on a postsales basis by the salesperson is therfore critical.

Personal Selling Activities

As previously noted, promotion may entail four differing activities, one of which is personal selling. This is a book about sales management and as such it does not focus upon *how* to sell. Rather, it focuses upon the management of sales personnel. Naturally, a manager must have insight into the activity he or she is managing if she or he is to manage wisely. Thus, we wish to examine the sales function at least briefly at this point to determine the nature of this activity.

Numerous and differing views of selling activities abound. A close examination suggests that, although the terminology between one view of selling and another may vary considerably, the major focus of these differing views is the same. The central role of personal selling is, of course, the exchange process between the salesperson and the prospective buyer. Figure 2.5 presents an overview of the sales interview. This view centers upon six stages beginning with the approach and ending with the close. Notice that questions for the salesperson are included on the left-hand side and that the earlier stated interaction between needs of the prospective customer and benefits (rather than features) of the product/service are intrinsic to this view of selling.

[13] "New Sales Technique Stresses Trust, Respect," *The Marketing News,* June 16, 1978, p. 13.

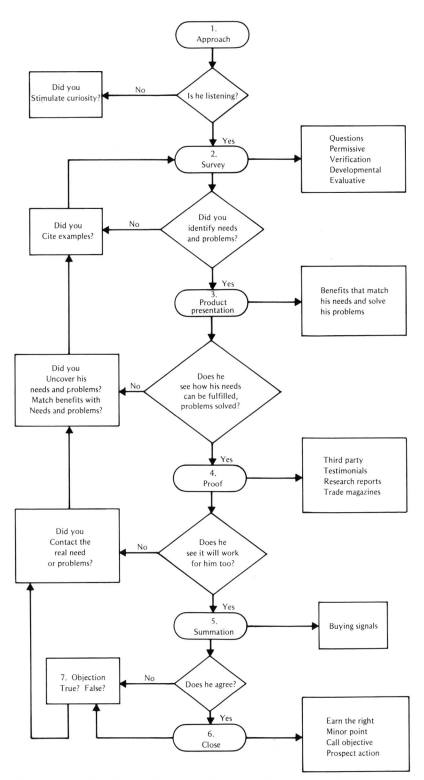

FIGURE 2.5   The Stages of the Sales Interview [Based upon H. B. Rames, *The Dynamics of Motivating Prospects to Buy* (West Nyack, N.Y.: Parker Publishing Company, Inc., 1973).]

ONE OR MANY FUNCTIONS?

Many people would suggest that there is only one function that sales personnel perform: namely, selling. However, as Figure 2.5 suggests, it may be debated that there are several sales activities to be performed instead of one. The following view of selling suggests six differing sales activites or major responsibilities.[14] Notice that these are listed in order of increasing complexity. Moreover, different sales positions require these sales activities to differing extents. Consider the following sales positions:

1. A sales position wherein the major responsibility is the *delivery* of a product. Route sales positions for vending machines, soft drinks, milk, and so on, are generally good examples. Often this position merely involves the replinishing of inventory to a previously agreed upon level. Generally little actual selling is done by these personnel.

2. A sales position where the salesperson acts as an *inside order taker*. Retail clerks often typify this type of sales position. Frequently the clerk spends time stocking shelves, and so on. The major point is that the customer comes to the clerk rather than vice versa. Often the salesperson serves as a facilitator rather than a creator of sales as such. Increasingly, this role is being filled by telephone sales personnel. In such cases, the salesperson and the customer may have little, if any, face-to-face interaction. When the position does involve face-to-face interaction, the customer has often already decided to buy. In such cases, the sales clerk merely helps the customer locate the sought item, completes the needed paperwork, and accepts payment for the item.

3. A sales position in which the salesperson is primarily an *outside order taker*. The major distinction is that in this position, the salesperson goes out and seeks out buyers. Many sales personnel calling on retail stores—for example, a person selling food goods or detergents—could be described in this manner.

4. A sales position with no direct order/sales responsibility. Contradictory as it may sound, these persons often carry the responsibility for *creating goodwill* with customers and are classified as sales personnel although they do not have direct dollar sales responsibility. These individuals also are often responsible for *conveying information* about new products or services. Missionary salespersons and detail salespersons are characteristic titles. The pharmaceutical industry is a major user of detail sales personnel. Such personnel call on physicians, pharmacists, and hospitals to convey information but often do not have dollar sales objectives.

5. A sales position like number four except that instead of product/service information being conveyed, the focus is upon *technical knowledge*. A job title often connected with this sales function is sales engineer or technical representative. Again, not having a specific dollar sales goal, these individuals nevertheless facilitate a sale made by others.

[14] This list is based upon Robert N. McMurray, "The Mystique of Super-Salesmanship," *Harvard Business Review*, March–April 1961, p. 114.

They may call upon a prospect in concert with a sales representative or alone.

6. A sales position that places primary demand upon *creative sales ability* for tangible or intangible products. Often calling "cold" (unannounced and with no previous client knowledge) upon prospects who may not recognize a need for the product/service in advance.

ORDER GETTING, ORDER TAKING, AND SUPPORTING ROLES

As the preceding descriptions indicate, it will be useful to think of selling as encompassing three different types of activities. These are order getting, order taking, and supporting activities. Although each task could be performed by a different specialist, it is also possible that any one sales representative may perform two or even all three activities in her/ his selling duties. Thus, a sales representative may have primary and secondary duties involving two or even tertiary duties involving all three.

Order getting often centers upon obtaining "new" business. This may mean that a sales representative is assigned the primary responsibility of developing new accounts (that is, gaining sales from customers who presently do not purchase from the firm). This type of sales activity is often referred to as "creative selling" or "headhunting" since it involves seeking out prospects who may have to be converted away from purchasing from a competing firm or who may presently be using a substitute product. In order to accomplish this task, an individual must have a great deal of product expertise as well as being a gifted "hunter" of prospects. Such talents are obviously not plentiful and development may require years of industry experience. Thus, this relativity rare combination of talents usually commands a handsome figure in terms of salary. Sales representatives capable of performing the order-getting duties are often compensated on a commission basis with total renumeration often reaching into six-figure ranges.

Order taking is virtually the polar opposite of order getting. Sales activity in this area is often confined to accepting payment or showing an already motivated buyer where the merchandise is located. A major distinction between order getting and order taking is that, whereas the initiative for the sale resides with the sales representative in order getting, the customer typically initiates the sale in order taking. Thus, the initiative may be the result of habit or previous promotional activities. A retail salesperson who simply states, "May I help you?" as a customer approaches a cash register with merchandise already in hand is engaging in order taking. Likewise, a route salesperson who enters a retail store and simply restocks items on a shelf to a predetermined inventory level is engaging in order taking. The same may be said of an "inside salesperson" who merely takes telephone orders. In each instance the buyer initiates the sale.

The order-taking position requires a much less competent salesperson than order getting. Consequently, the personnel performing this function tend to be young in terms of experience, paid modestly (often on a straight salary or hourly basis), and possess little sales sophistication and technical knowledge.

A supporting sales position may involve virtually no selling, per se. That is, supporting sales personnel may assist other sales personnel in obtaining an order, but they themselves may never make a single sale.

McCarthy distinguishes two types of supporting sales personnel: missionary salesmen and technical specialists.[15] Missionary salesmen typically are assigned to create goodwill or rapport between a manufacturer and other channel members. They may work at either the retail or wholesale level and often provide merchandising/promotional assistance. The set up of display materials would be a typical illustration. It should be noted, however, that another salesperson would have previously "sold" the retailer on the idea of erecting a display.

Technical specialists can assist the other sales personnel by visiting accounts either before or after a sale is made. Commonly found in industrial sales, a technical specialist might assist in the installation of a computer after it is sold and delivered. Likewise, a technical assistant might call on a *potential* customer's technical department for the purpose of advising sales personnel of the correct equipment to sell the account. In either case, just as was true of missionary salesmen, technical assistants facilitate a sale but do not personally engage in sales activities.

NEEDED: A JOB DESCRIPTION

At this point it is clear that the title of sales representative may mean many things to different people and different firms. To avoid confusion as to the specific duties of a particular salesperson, a formal written job description is both useful and desirable. Although we will have more to say concerning job descriptions in Chapter 6 (Recruiting and Selection), some basic comments are in order at this point.

First, the meaning and uses of a job description should be clarified. Second, a sample procedure for preparing a job description should be provided.

A job description is just what the term implies—that is, a written statement of both primary and secondary duties associated with a particular position in the organization. As a basic rule of thumb, if the responsibilities of a position are unclear, then management may expect a muddled performance. This written statement need not be a lengthy treatise so long as it captures the specific job-related nature of a position. The job description should be viewed as a flexible instrument changing over time. It serves both as an instrument for evaluating performance and an indication of management's expectations for the many roles a sales positition may touch upon. As we shall see in the following section, these roles do not always compliment each other.

[15] For a detailed explanation, see E. Jerome McCarthy, *Basic Marketing*, 6th ed. (Homewood, Ill.: Richard D. Irwin, Inc., 1978), p. 440.

Development of a viable job description need not be a massive or complex undertaking. A basic procedure for development of a job description has been recently provided by Lapp and Lacho.[16] This process is a nine step procedure as follows:

Step No. 1—Prepare a questionnaire to be sent to salespersons (or to employees in any positions to be analyzed), asking them to list what they feel are the major functions and sub-functions that must be performed to do their job effectively.

Step No. 2—Prior to the receipt of job descriptions from salespersons, have all executives interested in sales activities list what functions they fell *should* or *should not* be performed by salespersons.

Step No. 3—Find out from buyers what they believe should or should not be the functions of a salesperson.

Step No. 4—Tabulate the results of each of the three sources given above.

Step No. 5—Reconcile any differences between the above three viewpoints and the objectives, policies, and procedures of your company and prepare a detailed list of activities to be performed.

Step No. 6—Classify the activities either major or minor.

Step No. 7—Determine what salespersons need to know and what qualifications are necessary to perform designated activities, and specify why each activity is to be performed.

Step No. 8—Submit the results of step 7 to your salespersons for their discussion and recommendations.

Step No. 9—Revise the job descriptions following the above eight steps when you feel that changes in products, economic climate, customer demands, or custom necessitate a review of work to be performed.

Personal Selling and the Management of Conflict

In many ways the changing environmental factors mentioned earlier in this chapter—increased competition, changing customer lifestyles, consumerism, and government intervention have brought about needed and desirable changes in personal selling. Nevertheless, changes usually are accompanied by conflict. The changes in personal selling and the roles management is expected to fulfill that are accompanying the marketing environmental changes are no exception.

In many ways personal selling and sales management today reflect conflict. Not only does this conflict result from a changing marketing environment (external conflict), it may also stem from intracompany sources (internal conflict), or even intrafamily origins (miscellaneous conflict). A frank discussion of some of these types of conflict may help provide a realistic view of some problems that await sales personnel and help "set the stage" for expectations of sales management personnel.

[16] Charles L. Lapp and Kenneth J. Lacho, "Selecting the Salesperson: The Heartbeat of Sales Management," *Louisiana Business Survey*, January 1978, p. 10.

INTERNAL CONFLICT

We have seen that the role of selling has evolved over a period of time. Often this evolution has meant that formerly clear-cut lines of organizational authority and responsibility have become ambiguous. This confusion may be further aided by growth of the firm or through acquisition/merger. When this occurs, the potential for internal conflict exists.

Internal conflict means that someone or something within the organization is impeding or detracting from the efficient operation of the sales organization. Before discussing specific causes of this conflict, it should be mentioned that it is not always necessary for intent to accompany negative influences. Growth alone can impede an organization's efficiency, although the fact that growth can occur may be a healthy sign. Case 1.1 (The Clean Corporation) provides a vivid illustration of this point. Four examples of internal conflict would include the following:

- A salesperson receives a request from the accounting/credit department of his firm to collect an overdue statement from customer X during the next sales call.
- The sales representative receives a call from marketing research to "check out competitors' current prices" by acquiring copies of recent invoices to customers of his own firm who also buy from competition. This means cutting back on the time available for selling to do marketing research.
- Jim Roper, a sales representative with 5 years experience, gets a call from his boss one evening. The boss says, "Jim, I know you're busy working on our special sales promotion, but I want you to go over to a neighboring sales territory and train a new recruit for a few days." Although this is flattering to his ego, Jim wonders who gets credit for any sales made.
- The labor union producing a particular firm's products goes out on strike. Production notifies sales personnel that they may ship one-third of their normal volume. The salesperson is told it will only be possible to sell to customers in the top volume brackets for at least 60 days.

In the first instance, internal conflict exists because the salesperson is asked to play a role he/she does not normally play—that is, bill collector. If the statement is past due, there may be compelling reasons—for example, question about the sale, damaged merchandise, or a shortage in shipment, and so on. Unless this is a normal part of the salesperson's duties (and therefore a part of the job description), the accounting/credit department may be placing the salesperson in a precarious position.

In the second instance, we have an example of span of control. Does the sales representative refuse marketing research to do her/his assigned sales duties or does she/he go ahead and please marketing research while neglecting his/her sales responsibility?

The third example unfortunately occurs in many sales organizations. If sales personnel are normally paid on a commission basis, what compensation will Jim Roper receive? Given that a sales promotion is going on, should the recruit or Jim receive credit for any sales made? Is any goal or objective for the promotion to be adjusted downward in Jim's home territory?

The last illustration poses a classic dilemma that has actually happened frequently to many firms. The salesperson now faces a question of "Whom do I alienate?" and consideration as to dollar loss of immediate sales as well as future business impacts must be explored.

Internal conflicts arise across departmental boundaries, when company policies and procedures change or are unclear, and when unexpected events—for example strikes or calamities—occur. Such conflicts can be malicious and premeditated, but usually they are not the result of intentional disruption.

The point in discussing these examples of internal conflict is twofold. First, although sometimes (but not always) unintentional, internal conflicts do occur in most any organization. They are, unfortunately, a part of the job. Second, sales and management must constantly try to anticipate and seek out causes of internal conflicts. This will result in a better, more efficient organization.

EXTERNAL CONFLICTS

Much like internal conflicts, external conflict involves disruptive effects to an organization caused by someone, something, or some organization in the external environment. Prime sources of external conflict include present and former customers, competitors, and governmental agencies at local, regional, state, and/or national levels.

Four examples of external conflict follows:

- The Federal Trade Commission issues a rule removing constraints on the advertising of the price of eyeglasses, contact lenses, and eye examinations. (You are an optometrist. *Note:* whereas we often think of sales management in a company or corporation context, opthamologists, optometrists, and opticians also perform sales management functions).
- A large account with whom you as sales representative for XYZ Corporation have been doing business for years tells you, "We'll have to have a 20% discount if you want to keep us as a customer. Your competition has offered to sell us at that price. Match it or we switch our business to them."
- In a sales call on a major client, you are told that they have received another case of damaged detergent in their last shipment. You recall that this same claim has been made on your two previous calls and, although you have reimbursed the account previously, you candidly wonder if their claim is true or not.
- As a door-to-door salesperson for an encyclopedia firm, you read with interest an article in your local paper indicating that your state has just passed a "Cooling-off" law. This law allows customers to cancel commitments within 96 hours of signing a contract.

In the first instance, external conflict has occurred between an agency of the federal government and a firm. Whereas we normally think of government regulation as prohibiting an existing practice, it can also permit practices that were not permitted previously. Such is the case here. Based on a situation actually occurring at present,[17] the conflict brought about here would center upon whether or not this optometrist should start advertising. If so, what should the content of the ad be?

The second example illustrates competition's influence as a source of external conflict. A fairly common sales tactic, competition takes the offensive by setting up a "heads we win, tails you lose" type situation. Since they aren't presently selling the account, they are essentially stating we're going to make it less profitable (maybe totally *unprofitable)* for you to sell the account. If you grant the account's request, will you have to reduce your price to other accounts, too? If you do not grant the discount, will they really switch to your competitor? These are but a few of the conflicts raised. Your competition has certainly succeeded in making your job complex!

A dilemma arises in the third illustration. You can accuse the account of dishonesty. This probably means that you've lost the account. On the other hand, you can pay them for another case of damaged merchandise and ignore the problem. However, this will mean that you've now paid them three times in a row. What do you propose to do?

The last example reflects another factual change in the marketing environment. Beginning in the late 1960s many states passed such laws. By the mid 1970s over 30 states had such laws on the books.[18] As a salesperson, how will you know for sure if you've made a sale or not when you leave a consumer?

As was true with internal conflict, sales personnel and sales management must be alert for signs of external conflict. It is especially important to have vigilant sales personnel so that, if an external conflict occurs in one sales territory, management can make other sales personnel aware of it before it spreads to their territories. This is especially true of external conflicts caused by competition.

MISCELLANEOUS CONFLICT

This type of conflict is often the most insidious. It may also prove to be the most difficult to combat since it involves personal or family problems that may not be articulated.

Personal conflicts may stem from drug or alcohol addiction or related problems. If the salesperson is married, conflicts may arise between other family members. When the salesperson has to travel, conflict often arises from his/her absence from home. Conflicts with children and marital disputes often spill over into job performance.

There are so many varieties of miscellaneous conflict that illustration of examples serves no useful purpose. However, as with internal and

---

[17] For further information, see *FTC News Summary,* June 2, 1978 (No. 22, 1978), p. 1.

[18] A detailed description of cooling-off laws will be found in Orville C. Walker, Jr., and Neil M. Ford, "Can Cooling-off Laws Really Protect the Consumer?" *Journal of Marketing,* April 1970, pp. 53–58.

He came on muleback, dodging Indians as he went, with a pack full of better living and a tongue full of charms.

For he was the great American Salesman, and no man ever had a better thing to sell.

He came by rickety wagon, one jump behind the pioneers, carrying axes for the farmer, and fancy dress goods for his wife, and encyclopedias for the farmer's ambitious boy.

For he was the great practical democrat. Spreader of good things among more and more people.

He came by upper berth and dusty black coupe, selling tractors and radios, iceboxes and movies, health and leisure, ambition and fulfillment.

For he was America's emissary of abundance, Mr. High-Standard-of-Living in person.

He rang a billion doorbells and enriched a billion lives. Without him there'd be no American ships at sea, no busy factories, no sixty million jobs.

For the Great American Salesman is the great American civilizer, and everywhere he goes he leaves people better off.

FIGURE 2.6   An Idealistic View of Selling? [Source: John Hancock Mutual Life]

external conflicts, it is important to remain alert to these miscellaneous sources of conflict if their potential for damage is to be minimized.

Together, these three types of potential conflict may appear awesome. It is not our purpose to present an overly harsh view of these types of conflict. However, it is also not our purpose to paint an unrealistically romantic picture of selling either. For example, Figure 2.6 suggests a view of selling that may be both outmoded and simplistic. Although personnel in sales or sales management may wish for such an idealistic existence, they must also be realistic concerning the changes and conflicts that surround them.

The Role of Sales Management

Up to this point in this chapter, we have provided an exposure to the selling function from the point of view of sales personnel. This book as a whole is written from a differing point of view—the perspective of sales managers. The material that follows takes us back to our primary perspective, that of sales managers. Following the basic management functions of planning, organizing, motivating, and controlling discussed in Chapter 1, we begin our exposure to sales management from a decision making point of view (Chapter 3). The information provided here should be kept in mind as background for what follows.

Summary

This chapter has presented differing views of personal selling. The stimulus-response, selling formula, and need(s)-satisfaction theories were discussed in detail together with their similarities and differences. An evolving view of personal selling, nonmanipulative selling, was also explored in this chapter. Four specific causes of evolution in the personal selling function have been isolated—increased competition, changing customer lifestyles, consumer attitudes, and government intervention.

Although we may tend to think of selling in terms of a single stereotyped image, selling typically takes on differing shades of meaning from one firm to another. The multiplicity of functions that may be associated with selling from mere delivery of products to creative sales ability have been discussed. The activities associated with order getting, order taking, and supporting roles in selling were also explored. The job description was mentioned as a valued tool in clarifying the precise meaning of selling to a particular firm or individual sales applicant.

No occupation is free from drawbacks. Selling is subject to three major types of conflict—internal, external, and miscellaneous. Each of these varieties of conflict was illustrated by examples and discussed.

Last, we have suggested that, although this book focuses upon sales management, the personal sales perspective interjected by this chapter will serve as valuable and needed background for what follows in succeeding chapters.

Discussion Questions

1. Discuss the relationship of personal selling to the overall marketing mix of a firm. How would the importance of personal selling vary between a "push" and a "pull" oriented organization?

2. Given the "mutual benefit" frame of reference for personal selling, describe a recent sales transaction you have been involved in from a purchasing point of view. What satisfaction(s) did you receive? Could anything have been done to increase your satisfaction? What satisfaction(s) did the salesperson receive?

3. Think back over your past several purchases. Have you (as a buyer) ever experienced (a) stimulus-response selling, (b) selling formula selling, (c) need-satisfaction selling? If so, what are your feelings about any or all of the three?

4. Which of the three theories of selling—stimulus-response, selling formula, or need-satisfaction—most clearly reflects the "marketing concept"? Why? (If you need to review the "marketing concept" consult any current basic marketing textbook.)

5. If you were a sales manager, would you be in favor of your sales staff using a canned sales presentation? Why, or why not? Also, what alternatives are available to you other than completely canned or completely extemporaneous?

6. What forces account for the evolution occurring in personal selling? Which *single* force do you feel has been most effective in causing changes in the past? Will other forces become important in the near future? If so, discuss these briefly.

7. Discuss the role of conflict in personal selling. If you have had sales experience, have you ever been involved with any of these types of conflict? If so, discuss.

Selected References

CASH, HAROLD C., and W. J. E. CRISSY, *Psychology of Selling* (Flushing, N.Y.: Personnel Development Associates, 1958).

JOLSON, MARVIN A., "Should the Sales Presentation Be Fresh or Canned?" *Business Horizons,* October 1973, pp. 81–88.

KURTZ, DAVID L., H. ROBERT DODGE, and JAY E. KLOMPMAKER, *Professional Selling* (Dallas, Texas: Business Publications, Inc., 1976), pp. 70–71.

MAZZE, EDWARD M., *Personal Selling: Choice Against Chance* (St. Paul, Minn.: West Publishing Company, 1976), pp. 29–30.

PEDERSON, CARLTON A., and MILBURN D. WRIGHT, *Salesmanship: Principles and Methods,* 5th ed. (Homewood, Ill.: Richard D. Irwin, Inc., 1971), p. 335.

THOMPSON, JOSEPH W., *Selling: A Managerial and Behavioral Science Analysis,* 2nd ed. (New York: McGraw-Hill Book Company, Inc., 1973), p. 149.

CASE 2.1
Brown and Smith, Inc.*

Company Background

Three years ago Susan Brown and Ted Smith decided to join forces and form their own employment agency. Both had previous experience working for separate employment agencies. In addition, Ted had several years

* Case prepared by Dan. H. Robertson, Georgia State University. Original concept developed by Dr. Donald H. Hage, University of Denver.

Exhibit 1 Client Evaluation

1. George Summers teaches high school science courses during the school year. In summer, however, George works as a house-to-house salesman for the Fuller Brush Company in order to earn extra money to support his wife and four children. At first, he did not like selling products on a door-to-door basis, but lately George has adjusted quite well to his job.. "Once you learn the knack of getting your foot in the door," says George, "sales come pretty easy and the commissions add up fast. After all, people do like our products."

   a) Primary selling task: _____

   b) Secondary selling task(s): _____

   c) Comments: _____

   _____

   _____

   _____

   _____

   _____

   _____

   _____

2. Mary Andrews, a marketing major in college, went to work for Procter & Gamble as soon as she graduated. While she hopes to become a brand manager someday, Mary Presently operates as a district representative for P&G, calling on supermarkets, grocery stores, and drugstores. Mary's job is to build special displays, inform store managers of new products, provide merchandising assistance, review customer complaints, and, now and then, to suggest special orders for the stores she visits. Mary is paid a straight salary by P&G, in addition to an occasional bonus when sales in her district are good.

   a) Primary selling task: _____

   b) Secondary selling task(s): _____

   c) Comments: _____

   _____

   _____

   _____

   _____

3. Phil Brown works as a manufacturers' agent in the Boston area, representing several dozen non-competing suppliers of electrical parts and components. His customers include electrical manufacturers and distributors, building contractors, and hardware wholesalers. The electronics industry has been extremely innovative in recent years, continually introducing new products. As a result, Phil Brown has felt obliged to sell a huge variety and assortment of products to meet his customers' needs. He has found it desirable because of the complexity and variety of his lines—as part of his total effort—to spend much of his time checking his customers' parts inventories. This gives him continual customer contact and provides a useful service. He also finds time to seek new customers and is always looking for new suppliers to represent. Further, he regularly agrees to represent additional firms if their products are noncompetitive with existing suppliers' lines.

   Recently, one of his large accounts notified Brown that his services were no longer required. Apparently the supplier felt that Brown had not been aggressively promoting its products over the last few yeasr and had failed to bring in enough new business. Brown was quite bitter over losing the account. "How do they expect me to increase their sales when they don't keep their product lines up-to-date?'' he complained. ''I handle too many products to worry about just one manufacturer's offerings.''

a) Primary selling task: _____

b) Secondary selling task(s): _____

c) Comments: _____

_____

_____

_____

_____

_____

4. Joan Shaw is a cashier/clerk at the Top-Value Supermarket. According to her store manager, Joan is a ''real hustler'' with a flair for merchandising. She spends somewhat more than half her time as a ''fill-in'' cashier, but her major interest is in building displays and talking to customers. Joan is in charge of building all ''special''displays, i.e., those which require more imagination than just ''stacking cans.'' She is also responsible for stocking and displaying the high-margin non-foods merchandise, a task usually assigned to the ''best'' clerk. Sales have increased significantly since she was given these responsibilities.

Joan is very popular with customers because of the cheerful way she volunteers assistance and passes along tips about ''good buys.'' Just recently, for example, she persuaded several women to purchase Top-Value's dealer brand of liquid bleach instead of a highly advertised national brand. The two brands were chemically identical, but a gallon container of the well-known brand was priced 16¢ higher than the dealer brand.

a) Primary selling task: _____

b) Secondary selling task(s): _____

c) Comments: _____

_____

_____

_____

_____

_____

5. John Ogden holds a B.S. degree in mechanical engineering and an M.B.A. in general business. He is employed as a sales engineer by the Snyder Tool and Die Company, specializaing in made-to-order, heavy-duty automated machinery. When Synder's sales manager locates a prospect for this type of equipment, Ogden is sent out to analyze the machinery needs of the potential customer, to design a tailor-made system, and to make cost estimates. After finishing his work, Ogden reports back to Snyder's sales manager who conducts further negotiations with the customer.

a) Primary selling task: _____

b) Secondary selling task(s): _____

c) Comments: _____

_____

_____

_____

sales experience having worked for a major marketer of consumer products and an industrial marketing firm. Susan's degree was in personnel management and, other than her 4 years previous experience for the employment agency, she has had no other employment. Their organization has been formed to specialize in the area of employment for sales personnel.

Current Situation

Presently Brown and Smith, Inc. has five clients—George Summers, Mary Andrews, Phil Brown, Joan Shaw, and John Ogden. They feel that a good starting point would be to examine each of their client's present job to determine whether their primary selling tasks are those of order taker, order getter, or support salesperson. Secondly, they wish to make comments about the type of opportunity they feel would be appropriate for each client.

Act as a consultant to Brown and Smith, Inc. Indicate your thoughts as to primary and secondary sales responsibility of each of the five. Also indicate your comments about what type of future employment you feel would be most appropriate for each client (see Exhibit 1).

CASE 2.2
Busy Bee Bakers*

Company Background

Busy Bee Bakers (BBB) began as a family-owned business some 60-odd years ago in a large southeastern city. Today the sales volume of BBB is in excess of a half million dollars annually. The firm began by baking and selling to retail outlets home-baked bread. Today the firm's product line includes several different types of bread (white, whole wheat, rye, raisin, pumpernickel, and so on), cookies, pies, and assorted pastries as well as both hot dog and hamburger buns.

Reggie Thomas is the new sales manager for BBB. Mr. Thomas had been hired after completing his MBA at a prestigious eastern university, and has been with the firm for slightly over a year. The first 3 months of Mr. Thomas' experience with the firm was spent working with various field salespeople in order to obtain firsthand knowledge of their jobs and problems.

The retail salespeople for BBB had primary responsibility for delivery, sales, and display of BBB products through retail grocery outlets. This meant that they called both upon chain and independent retail food stores. Through the years BBB had taken great pride in its reputation

* Case prepared by Dan H. Robertson, Georgia State University.

for quality and had built and maintained a generally outstanding relationship with most retail food stores in their area. BBB had competition both in the form of other regional producers and national bakeries who produced similar product lines, but their reputation for quality and their good relations with the retail trade had permitted them to maintain a reasonably good market share over the years.

Current Situation

Although the reaction to Reggie Thomas as the new sales manager for BBB had been a receptive one at first, he was beginning to have some second thoughts. In a conversation with the general manager of the firm, he remarked, "I'm beginning to wonder if some of the retail salesmen don't resent me." As their conversation continued over a morning cup of coffee, Thomas went on to suggest that, whereas he could "take a joke" about his formal education and the fact that he possessed a master's degree, he was beginning to feel that some of the resentment expressed humorously might reflect hard feelings that some of the salesmen were beginning to develop. In part, he was wondering to himself if perhaps some of the positions he had taken on touchy issues were to blame for the resentment he was now beginning to feel.

One of these "touchy" issues pertained to the role of salesman. During his three months in the field, one of the things that had bothered Mr. Thomas was that he often saw salesmen spending their time in ways he felt were nonproductive.

A typical day in a salesman's life begins with the salesman driving to the bakery headquarters, loading his delivery truck with inventory needed for the day, and arriving at his first retail delivery/sales site by 7:00 A.M. The salesman would continue then upon a preestablished delivery route for that day covering approximately 15 retail accounts on a typical day. Upon arrival at a retail grocery outlet, the salesperson would enter the store and begin by checking the inventory on the shelf. Next, the individual would check with store personnel to determine whether there were any "stales" or damaged merchandise. Then the salesperson would return to the delivery truck and bring in the required inventory for filling the shelf. In addition, if there were stales or returned merchandise, replacement merchandise would be provided to the store in order to give the necessary credit. A retail clerk in the store would verify the amount of new inventory being placed on the shelf and the salesperson would leave with a signed receipt for the new merchandise.

One of the problems bothering Reggie Thomas was that he felt many of the retail salespeople spent entirely too much time on routine administrative details and too little time in actual selling activities. For example, Reggie couldn't help but notice that many of the newer products that BBB had introduced in the last few years were not really pushed aggressively by the salespeople. Instead, he observed a fairly constant replacement of inventory missing from the shelf with the same item. Rarely did Reggie observe any creativity on the part of the salesperson or any attempt either to gain additional display and retail sales space for existing items or to sell store personnel or the idea of carrying new items. As

Reggie was driving home one evening, he thought to himself, "Maybe what we really need at BBB are salespeople who are much more aggressive than the individuals we now have."

When Reggie reflected upon the actions taken by competitors, one particular development seemed to stick in his mind. This development was that a large national competitor had recently split their delivery/sales function among two different groups of employees. Salespeople for the large national competitor now engaged in no delivery or shelf stocking activities at all and, conversely, the individuals involved in delivery did no selling. However, this, of course, meant duplication both in terms of number of employees and to some extent costs for employees. Should BBB consider changing to such a system, or might there be other alternatives that Reggie has not yet thought of that BBB could consider?

Student Learning Exercise / 2
Personal Selling and You

Objective   To examine personal selling as a possible employment opportunity for yourself.

Overview   1. If you are now or have previously been employed in selling and/or sales management, provide a brief summary of this experience.
2. Obtain a copy of the Classified Ad section of a local newspaper.

This chapter has discussed personal selling in some detail. The purpose of this exercise is to stimulate further your own thoughts regarding selling as a possible occupation.

Exercise   Read through the Classified Ad section and locate an ad for sales personnel that you find attractive. Repeat this process to find an ad you find unattractive.

Discuss the features of the attractive ad that you find positive. For the unattractive ad, what features "turn you off"? In both cases, why?

Information-Based Decision Making
in Sales Management

AS indicated in Chapter 1, a basic role of the sales manager is to make decisions in those areas related to the sales function. This is, in fact, the primary task of all managers— they collectively represent the decision making core of an organization. Their decisions should be made with the intent of achieving the objectives of the total organization. Collectively the decisions made by sales management should move the organization toward greater profitability via increased sales volume and/or improved sales force productivity as expressed in the volume/cost relationship. (This concept will be discussed in detail in Chapter 4.) Specific decisions may, of course, have subobjectives that are derived from the central goals.

Sales managers, as a group within an organization, must be concerned with the several different decision areas noted earlier. The decision areas can be summarized as follows:

1. *Objectives.* Setting objectives relative to the desired level of sales and sales force productivity. This must be derived from the total corporate goals.
2. *Allocation.* The allocation of effort and resources to different products, geographic areas, and customers so as to achieve the productivity objective must be determined after the broad objective is set. This requires careful analysis of growth potential and accurate forecasting. Decisions in this area are ultimately resolved into a sales budget.
3. *Sales Plan.* The budget must then be translated into a plan of action; a sales plan. This plan includes management's decisions relative to (a) recruiting and selection of sales people, (b) sales training, (c) motivation and compensation, (d) sales territory alignment, (e) communications with and supervision of the sales force, and (f) how the sales force is to be evaluated and controlled.
4. *Organization.* Finally, a framework must be created through which the sales plan can be implemented. This requires that the sales force be organized to create an effective field unit.

The degree of success that sales managers have in making good decisions relative to these areas will materially affect the overall success of the organization. The managers must, however, make these decisions in an environment filled with risk and uncertainty. How can the decision maker cope with the complexities of the modern business environment? The best way is by approaching the decision making activity in a logical and systematic fashion. Decisions should be well thought out and based on all the relevant information available. This scientific approach to sales management can help to minimize the risk associated with making critical decisions in an ever changing world, filled with uncertainty.

The intent of this chapter is to outline and illustrate the basic approach to information based decision making in sales management. This approach can then be applied to any of the decision areas that confront the manager.

The Decision Making/Research Interaction in Sales Management

A SYSTEMATIC APPROACH TO DECISION MAKING

The first logical step in making any decision is to recognize and clearly define the managerial decision problem. This is often the most difficult step in the process. It is critical that the real problem, and not just symptoms of the problem, be isolated. A decision problem in the context used here would involve a situation within the organization requiring the sales manager to make a decision. A sales management decision problem must relate directly to one of the areas under the sales manager's control (setting objectives, allocating effort and resources, developing the sales plan, or organizing for implementation).

For example, a mediumsized chemical company, Vine Chemicals, which specializes in industrial applications in the paper industry, was experiencing a relatively low growth rate of 0–2 per cent in all of its sales territories. This symptom developed after the company had achieved a 10–15 per cent growth in sales for five consecutive years. The sales manager was concerned and started to consider possible causes of the symptom. One of his first thoughts was that perhaps the company had saturated the market, but the market share figures quickly dispelled this misconception. Next, the area of motivation and compensation was questioned. One of his assistants pointed out that the straight salary system used by the company encouraged the salespeople to concentrate on service and protecting existing business rather than trying to get new accounts. He suggested that the system be changed to provide added incentive for getting new business. The decision problem then became whether the compensation system should be changed, and, if so, whether the company should go to straight commission or to salary plus commission? After this decision was made, other decisions would need to be made to implement the change.

This particular decision problem relates to one facet of the sales plan. Other decisions must be made in each of the areas of responsibility of the sales manager. Figure 3.1 illustrates the decision making flow triggered by the definition of a decision problem.

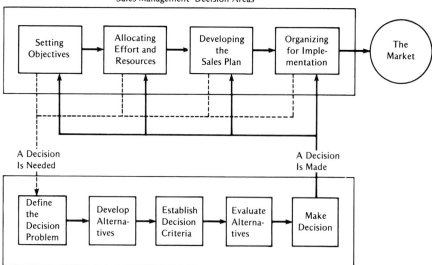

Sales Management Decision Areas

FIGURE 3.1 **The Decision Making Flow**

Note that the decision areas of sales management represent activities or tasks that must be continuously performed by the manager. The decision flow is a mental level, a sequencing of the thought process, relative to a given activity. The mental work of the sales manager is designed to provide a sound basis for his activities. If the flow of the mental decision process is logical, systematic, and well informed, the resulting activities are more likely to achieve the desired results.

After the decision problem has been clearly defined, the manager is in a position to develop alternative courses of action that may solve the problem at hand. The alternatives comprise a series of possible decisions. With Vine Chemicals the alternatives developed were (1) to stay with straight salary compensation, (2) to move to straight commission, or (3) to use a salary plus commission system. The exact nature of each plan was specified in order effectively to judge the merits of each alternative.

At this point, or in some cases earlier in the process, decision criteria must be determined. These provide a basis for evaluating the alternatives. The criteria are the objectives that need to be considered in attempting to arrive at the best decision. Should the decision lower cost, increase market share, conserve resources, enhance motivation, or accomplish some mix of objectives? The major objective or objectives to be considered in arriving at a decision comprise the decision criteria. The criteria for each decision should be derived from the overall goal for the sales function. In the case of Vine Chemical, the criteria related to the ratio between sales and cost produced by each alternative plan; that is, the direct selling cost per dollar of sales required under each of the alternative systems. The lower the cost per dollar of sales produced, the better the compensation system. Thus, if one plan was forecast to have a lower cost per sales dollar than another, it would be selected.

Now the alternatives must be evaluated by the manager. In order to do this and arrive at a logical decision, the outcome of each alternative must be projected in terms of the decision criteria. Such projections form the basis for making the decision. Decision models can be very useful in accomplishing this evaluation.

A **model** can be defined as a simplified representation of some real system or process. A decision model can be used to forecast the outcome of each alternative in terms of the decision criteria. Such a model is built by relating the important variables that exist within a particular decision environment. These variables can be divided into controllable and uncontrollable categories. In general, the controllable category for a sales manager relates to the four sets of activities mentioned earlier. The positioning of these variables may comprise alternative solutions to a given decision problem. The uncontrollable variables may involve the structure and decisions in other parts of the organization or the external environment. Corporate goals, production capacity, and other elements of the organization will influence the decisions of the sales manager but may be uncontrollable from his point of view. Likewise, the external environment comprised of the legal and political structure, the state of the economy, the social and cultural structure, the state of technology, and the basic level and determinates of demand are usually uncontrollable. When some specific uncontrollable variable can be identified as having a major effect on the outcome of a given decision and the probability of the variable being in various different positions can be subjectively estimated, the variable can be treated as what is called a **state of nature** in a decision model.

After the major controllable and uncontrollable variables have been determined for a given decision, their relationship can be outlined: Are the variables independent of each other or will manipulating one variable affect another variable? How will the outcome of positioning one variable, perhaps the compensation plan, in a specific way be affected by the state of another variable or variables, such as selling cost? This type of question can be answered only if the relationships between variables are known. One approach to developing a decision model that relates the important variables in a given decision is the decision tree. After it is constructed, such a model can be used to forecast the outcome of each alternative.

TABLE 3.1   Commission Plan

Change in Motivation	Change in Sales	Probability
Much higher motivation	20% higher	.5
Somewhat higher motivation	10% higher	.3
Same motivation	Same	.1
Lower motivation	5% lower	.1

TABLE 3.2 Salary Plus Commission Plan

Change in Motivation	Change in Sales	Probability
Much higher motivation	20% higher	.2
Somewhat higher motivation	10% higher	.5
Same motivation	Same	.2
Lower motivation	5% lower	.1

To illustrate this approach to evaluating alternatives, let us return to the Vine Chemical decision. The alternatives being considered were straight salary, a commission plan, and a salary plus commission system. The details of how each alternative would operate were specified, and the task became forecasting the direct sales cost per dollar of sales that each plan would produce. An important uncontrollable variable, state of nature, was thought to be the motivational impact of each plan on the sales force and the resulting change in sales volume. The current system would not alter the motivation; the impact of the commission plan and the salary plus commission plan were assessed based on executive judgement as shown in Tables 3.1 and 3.2.

Next, a decision tree was built by attaching the appropriate states of nature to each alternative (see Figure 3.2). The direct selling cost per dollar of sales under each combination of alternative and state of nature was then estimated. Thus, the model now complete could be used to forecast the expected cost from each alternative. Note that this particular decision tree has one set of alternatives and one set of states of nature whose probabilities vary depending upon the alternative to which they are attached. The decision tree approach, however, can be used with any manageable number of controllable and uncontrollable variables. In some cases no states of nature are involved, and the tree consists only of alternatives and their consequences.

To use the Vine Chemical decision model, the expected cost from each alternative needs to be calculated. This expected value *(EV)* is derived by multiplying the consequence of each state of nature attached to a given alternative by the probability of that state of nature occurring and summing the resulting numbers. Expected value can be defined as the average consequence from taking a given course of action an infinite number of times. For the commission plan,

$$EV = (.5 \times \$.04) + (.3 \times \$.05) + (.1 \times \$.06) + (.1 \times \$.065) = \$.04625$$

The commission system has the lowest expected direct selling cost per dollar of sales of the three alternatives.[1]

The final step in the decision flow is to resolve the decision. What course of action will be selected for implementation? The details of implementation should, of course, have been developed in the specification

[1] For a more detailed discussion of decision models, see Ben M. Enis and Charles S. Broome, *Marketing Decisions: A Bayesian Approach* (Scranton, Pa.: International Textbook Company, 1971).

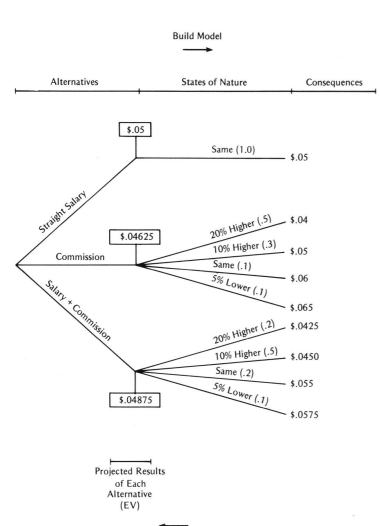

FIGURE 3.2   A Decision Model

Build Model

Alternatives   States of Nature   Consequences

$.05

Same (1.0) ———— $.05

Straight Salary

$.04625

20% Higher (.5) — $.04
10% Higher (.3) — $.05
Same (.1)
5% Lower (.1) — $.06
$.065

Commission

Salary + Commission

20% Higher (.2) — $.0425
10% Higher (.5) — $.0450
Same (.2)
5% Lower (.1) — $.055
$.0575

$.04875

Projected Results
of Each
Alternative
(EV)

Make Projections

of alternatives. Many decisions trigger a sequential decision making process, with one decision leading to another decision problem. In resolving the Vine Chemical decision, the sales manager looked at two factors: first, the lower expected cost of the commission plan and, second, the fact that this plan has a greater risk of resulting in no improvement in cost (.5 probability of no reduction) than the salary plus commission plan (.3 probability of no reduction). This was true because the commission plan allowed a higher compensation rate and needed a 10 per cent increase in sales just to get the total direct sales cost down to its current level. At this point, the extent of fixed cost was also considered because it was recognized that corporate profitability is based on more than just the direct sales cost/revenue relationship. After this additional analysis, the decision was made to go with the salary plus commission plan, which gave a good probability of lower cost per dollar of sales and higher sales volume coupled with lower risk.

The details of this illustration have been greatly simplified, but the basic flow should serve to demonstrate the concept. Some decisions need not be this highly structured, but the approach outlined here does add logic and systematic rigor to the mental decision process of the sales manager. By approaching major decisions in this fashion, the overall success of the sales management task should be enhanced.

RESEARCH SUPPORT FOR THE SALES MANAGER

Given the advantage of logical and systematic decision making by a sales manager, what is needed to make the approach work? First, the manager must understand and be committed to rigorous analytical decision making and, second, adequate information must be available. The true foundation of analytical sales management is adequate information. Information is needed in every phase of the decision flow regardless of the activity to which the decision relates. How does the manager get the needed informational inputs? Research may be the answer. Research can be broadly defined as the production of information of use to managers in making decisions. Research is, of course, not needed for all decisions. The manager may already have the information from past experience or some other source, thus removing the need for formal research.

When information gaps do exist, however, the research flow is designed to support sales management by responding to the sales manager's needs for information. Thus, the flow should start with a careful definition of the information needed for some specific decision or set of decisions. (See Figure 3.3 for the steps in the research flow.) Without this first step, research and the resulting information would have no use or value. Looking back at the Vine Chemical illustration, we can see that information was needed by the sales manager at each stage of the decision flow: (1) To identify the decision problem, the manager needed to know the sales trends and market share, along with opinions about the motivational level within the sales force. (2) In developing alternatives, information

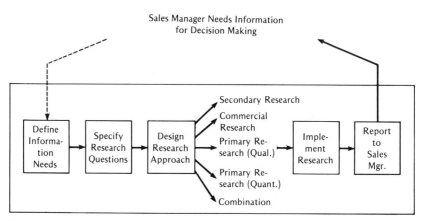

FIGURE 3.3 The Research Flow

was needed concerning various different compensation systems that might be developed. (3) Corporate goals and specific objectives for the sales function were important inputs for setting the decision criteria. These criteria were refined later in the decision flow based on other information. (4) Building the decision model for evaluation of the alternatives required a considerable body of information. The motivational impact of alternative plans had to be assessed and translated into sales volume changes. The probability of each impact needed to estimated. The cost impact of the alternatives at the various sales levels also had to be calculated. A blend of fact, impressions, and opinions were used for this purpose. (5) Finally, in resolving the decision, the decision model was used to estimate the expected cost effectiveness of each alternative and to examine risk considerations. Further information on fixed cost, sales volume, and corporate profitability were also inputs at this point. Thus, information was needed at every step of the decision flow. Some of this information was already known to the sales manager and some was produced through formal research.

When information is needed that is not already in the possession of the manager, step two of the research flow is triggered. This is the specification of research questions. These are the questions that the formal research effort will be designed to answer. They are derived from the information needs of the sales manager; by answering the question or questions, the research produces the information needed by the manager. To be useful guides to research design, the research questions should be very specific and subject to being answered via research. Many very interesting questions can be formulated that are impossible to answer through the collection and processing of data. The temptation to develop questions that are really not researchable should be avoided.

Several research questions could have been developed by the Vine Chemical sales manager. He already had much of the needed information, but two questions needed formal investigation: (1) What would be the motivational impact of the three alternative compensation plans? (2) What cost would result under each plan at various sales volumes? Research effort was then directed at these two questions.

After the research questions have been clearly stated, a research approach can be designed to produce answers. Designing the research approach should proceed in the following fashion: (1) Consider the use of *secondary research*, drawing on either internal or external sources. This type of research is usually the least expensive and should be examined first. (2) Next, consider the use of a commercial research firm. In some instances they are less expensive than doing research in-house, and quite often they have technical expertise that may not be available inside the company. (3) If the research questions cannot be answered from secondary data and using a commercial research firm is not desirable, a primary research approach should be selected. Primary research approaches can be divided into qualitative and quantitative types, with several techniques included in each category. Each of these basic types of research will be described and illustrated later in the chapter.

Vine Chemical's research approach for the motivational impact question involved the use of external secondary data and depth interviews with each salesperson. Secondary sources gave some indication as to the strengths and weaknesses of each basic type of compensation system as well as current industry practice with respect to compensation. The depth interviews with each salesperson allowed management to assess the attitudes and opinions of the sales force with respect to the present system as well as possible revisions. This provided a basis for well informed judgements concerning the motivational results of each alternative. An answer to the cost related research question was sought from internal secondary data.

After the research approaches are selected, the research is implemented by staff assistants and the results are reported to the sales manager. The information produced in the research provides inputs for the mental process of decision making. Relevant and timely information from research is the foundation on which analytical sales management is built.

RELATING RESEARCH TO DECISION MAKING

Effective decision making in sales management requires the support of sound judgements and information. Some information may come from past experience or very informal sources, whereas other information may require well-structured research support. Figure 3.4 summarizes this relationship among sales management activities or decision areas, the mental decision making flow, and the informational support provided by research. With this basic framework in mind, we will now turn to the production of information for sales management.

Producing Sales Management Information

TYPES OF SALES MANAGEMENT INFORMATION

The sales manager needs many different types of information to make decisions about the many activities under his control. A complete list of the various types of information of use to the sales manager is impossible, but a sample may help in understanding the scope of the research task. The following list indicates some of the typical types of information that can be of use in sales management on a regular basis:[2]

- The consumer
    Number of current and potential consumers
    Consumer characteristics
    Where the consumers are located
    Where the consumers buy

[2] Adapted from Danny N. Bellenger and Barnett A. Greenberg, *Marketing Research: A Management Information Approach* (Homewood, Ill.: Richard D. Irwin, Inc., 1978).

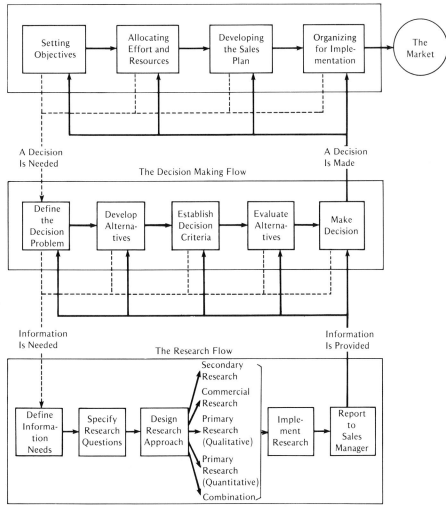

FIGURE 3.4 The Decision Making/Research Interaction

When the consumers buy

The size of purchases

How the consumers buy (relative importance of credit, brand loyalty, etc.)

Why the consumers buy (attitudes and motives)

Who influences the consumer

What changes in buying behavior are taking place

• The markets

The general business conditions

Market size

Market trends

Market potential

Geographic sales and relative profitability of different markets

Economic factors affecting sales volume
Seasonal and cyclical fluctuations
Changes in consumer group importance
- The competition
Number of competitors
Market share of each competitor
Shifts in market share
Characteristics of leading competitive products or services
Differentiation of our product or service from competitors
Policies and procedures used by the principal competitors
- The continuing products or services
Sales volume (by geographic area, type of consumer, and salesperson)
Market share
Shifts in market share
Brand repeat purchases and switching rate
Cost
Contribution to profit/unit
Consumer satisfaction with the product or service
Channel structure
Base price and alterations
Sales force effectiveness

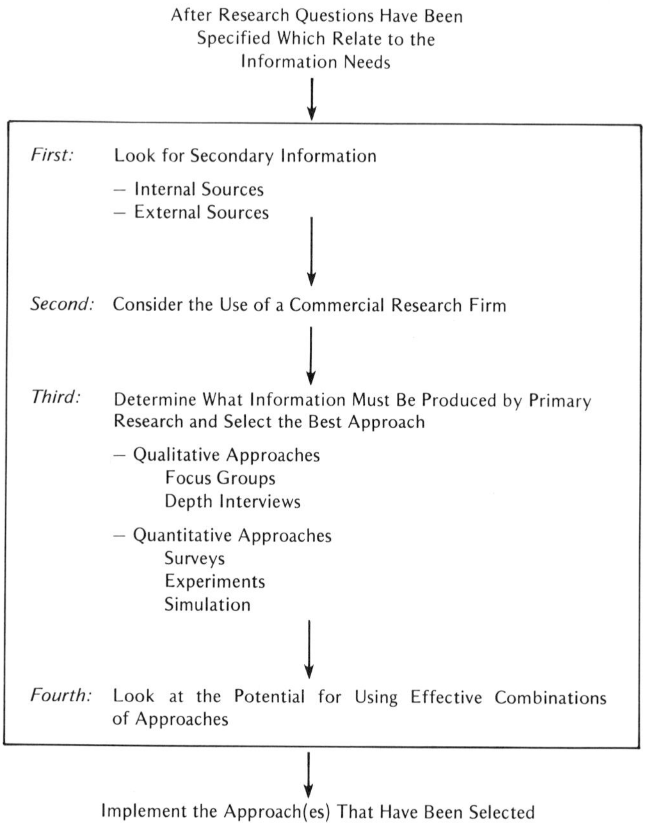

After Research Questions Have Been
Specified Which Relate to the
Information Needs

First: Look for Secondary Information

— Internal Sources
— External Sources

Second: Consider the Use of a Commercial Research Firm

Third: Determine What Information Must Be Produced by Primary Research and Select the Best Approach

— Qualitative Approaches
Focus Groups
Depth Interviews

— Quantitative Approaches
Surveys
Experiments
Simulation

Fourth: Look at the Potential for Using Effective Combinations of Approaches

Implement the Approach(es) That Have Been Selected

FIGURE 3.5 Alternative Approaches to Producing Informations for Sales Management

This type of information can create a sound base for making sales management decisions. In order to derive the maximum benefit, much of the information mentioned would be needed for each salesperson, sales district or region, as well as for the total sales force and sales territory. In addition, specific information needs arise as unique decisions confront the manager.

Many different approaches may be used to produce the needed information. These approaches and the desired sequence for considering each approach are shown in Figure 3.5. Each of these approaches can be very useful in producing sales management information. Each approach will be discussed and illustrated in the following sections.

FINDING AND EVALUATING SECONDARY INFORMATION

Secondary information is the mainstay of most sales information programs. This is true because this type of information is often less expensive than commercial or internally produced primary information. Secondary information is information that has been produced by someone else for purposes other than making the specific decisions called for in any particular organization. In contrast, primary information is produced for one organization's specific needs. Secondary information may be either internal or external. Internal secondary information is produced within a particular firm for purposes other than sales management decision making. The accounting system is usually the major source of this type of information. External secondary information is produced outside the firm. It is collected and initially processed by outside organizations either for their own or for public use. Information collected and categorized by the United States government for public use would be external secondary information for a business enterprise.

Internal Secondary Information.   To illustrate the use of internal secondary information by the sales manager, we may suppose that the manager is deciding how to allocate his sales force between alternative products carried by the company. He wants to put more effort into those products that have higher profit margins. To do this, information on the profitability of each product is needed. Suppose that the company makes and sells three different types of adding machines—full keyboard, deluxe ten-key and basic ten-key.[3] To provide the needed information, a profit and loss statement must be constructed for the marketing component being analyzed, in this case, product. "The approach consists of dividing the firm's basic costs (salaries, rent, etc.) into their functional categories (selling, advertising, etc.). The functional category amounts are then assigned within the appropriate marketing classifications."[4]

---

[3] Illustration adapted from Leland L. Beik and Stephen L. Buzby, "Profitability Analysis by Market Segments," *Journal of Marketing,* July 1, 1973, pp. 48–53.
 [4] *Ibid.*

TABLE 3.3   Product Productivity Analysis—Contribution Approach (All dollar values × 1000)

	Company Total	Full Keyboard	Deluxe Ten-Key	Basic Ten-Key
Net sales	$10,000	$5,000	$3,000	$2,000
Variable manufacturing costs	5,100	2,500	1,375	1,225
Manufacturing contribution	$ 4,900	$2,500	$1,625	$ 775
Marketing costs				
Variable:				
sales commissions	450	225	135	90
Variable contribution	$ 4,450	$2,275	$1,490	$ 685
Assignable:				
salaries—salesmen	1,600	770	630	200
salary—marketing manager	100	50	25	25
product advertising	1,000	670	200	130
Total	$ 2,700	$1,490	$ 855	$ 355
Product contribution	$ 1,750	$ 785	$ 635	$ 330
Product contribution, % of net sales	17.5	15.7	21.2	16.5
Nonassignable				
Institutional advertising	150			
Marketing contribution	$ 1,600			
Fixed-joint costs				
General administration	300			
Manufacturing	900			
Total	$ 1,200			
Net profits	$ 400			

One way to accomplish this task is the contribution approach. Table 3.3 illustrates this approach for the adding machine firm.

First, all of the variable nonmarketing costs have been assigned to products. These costs represent nonmarketing dollar expenditures which fluctuate, in total, directly in proportion to short-run changes in the sales volume of a given product. Similarly, variable marketing costs have been deducted to produce variable product contribution margins identical to those which would result from a direct costing approach.

The remaining marketing costs have been broken down into two categories— assignable and nonassignable. The assignable costs represent dollar expenditures of a fixed or discretionary nature for which reasonably valid bases exist for allocating them to specific products. For example, the assignment of salesmen's salaries in Table 3.3 might be based on Sevin's recommendation to use 'selling time devoted to each product, as shown by special sales-call reports or special studies.'[5] The marketing manager's salary could be assigned on the basis of personal records indicating the amount of time devoted to the management of each product.

[5] Charles H. Sevin, *Marketing Productivity Analysis* (New York: McGraw-Hill Book Company, 1965), p. 13.

Product advertising would be assigned by reference to the actual amount spent on advertising each product.

The use of the actual dollar level of sales was purposely avoided in choosing the allocation bases for the assignable costs in Table 3.3. Horngren, among others, has stated that when dealing with fixed or discretionary cost, 'The costs of efforts are independent of the results actually obtained, in the sense that the costs are programmed by management, not determined by sales.'[6] The nonassignable marketing costs represent dollar expenditure of a fixed or discretionary nature for which there are no valid bases for assignment to products. Consequently, institutional advertising has not been assigned to the products to avoid confounding the product profitability margins which would result from the arbitrary allocation of this cost. Since the primary purpose is calculating marketing related product contribution margins, the remaining nonmarketing costs can be taken as a deduction from the total marketing contribution margin to produce a net figure for the firm.[7]

This analysis indicates that the full keyboard machine has the highest total contribution to profit and nonassignable plus fixed cost. The deluxe ten-key model, however, has the greatest contribution per dollar of sales. This might lead the sales manager to concentrate efforts on the deluxe ten-key model in the hope of increasing its sales. At any rate, this type of internal secondary information can prove very useful in making numerous sales management decisions.

External Secondary Information.   Several types of external secondary information are available to the sales manager. To illustrate,[8] suppose that the sales manager for an industrial company manufacturing farm machinery needs to provide his sales force with a list of potential new customers in their territory. The manager wants to aim more sales effort toward getting new accounts, but the sales people need direction in identifying targets. The sales manager could use external secondary sources to provide the needed information.

First, the national input/output model published by the U.S. Commerce Department's Office of Business Economics and upgraded periodically in the Commerce Department's *Survey of Current Business* can be consulted. This model describes what industries sell to what other industries. In looking at this source, we find that there are 83 industries included; farm machinery and equipment are number 44. By looking across the row containing industry number 44, the sales volume to each of the 83 industries by the farm machinery and equipment industry can be determined. The table shows that only 30 industries buy such equipment and seven industries account for 76.9 per cent of the sales. These seven industries might be taken as the target for new potential customers.

The sales manager now knows the industry targets but he must also find detailed information on the companies such as names, addresses,

---

[6] Charles R. Horngren, *Cost Accounting: A Managerial Emphasis*, 2nd ed. (Englewood Cliffs, N.J.: Prentice-Hall, Inc., 1967), p. 381.

[7] Beik and Buzby, *op. cit.*

[8] Illustration adapted from Robert W. Haas, "Locating Industrial Customers," *Atlanta Economic Review*, September–October 1976, pp. 9–14.

sizes, and so forth? To do this, the input/output industries need to be converted to the **Standard Industrial Classification (SIC)** system. These are industrial classes established according to primary economic activity by the Technical Committee on Industrial Classification, which is a division of the Bureau of the Budget. Most detailed company information is categorized by SIC code. This conversion is not always easy, but it is possible through a combination of imagination, knowledge of the markets, and tables prepared by the Bureau of Economic Analysis.

After the SIC codes have been determined, two options are available: (1) information on potential customers in each SIC designation can be purchased from an outside source such as Dun & Bradstreet's Marketing Services Division, or (2) the information can be compiled in-house from industrial directories, *The Survey of Industrial Purchasing Power* or various United States government sources such as the *Census of Manufacturers.*

This procedure can provide the type of detailed potential customer information needed by the sales manager to direct his sales force in the attempt to attract new accounts. We have here illustrated but one of the numerous uses of external secondary information by the sales manager. Perhaps the most frequently used source is the *Survey of Buying Power,* a special issue of *Sales and Marketing Management* magazine. This source and its use will be discussed in later chapters.

The major problem in using secondary information is in finding the appropriate source. The mass of potential sources must be filtered to locate useful information. To be able effectively to find secondary sources, the sales manager should maintain an index of sources that contains previously used and potentially needed information. When needs arise, the index can be consulted. If the needed information cannot be located in the index, other sources can be searched.

In conducting such a search, the subject area should first be identified. With the subject in mind, bibliographies or indexes can be consulted. After a possible source has been identified, the manager can move on to an evaluation of the information in terms of specific needs. This evaluation should focus on such questions as:

1. Does the information meet our needs?
2. Is any bias suspected because of the sponsorship of the research?
3. Was the research design technically sound?
4. Was the research correctly implemented?
5. Are the findings properly reported?[9]

By answering these questions, the manager should be in a better position to evaluate the information for his purposes.

The well-grounded sales manager must be familiar with the basic sources of secondary information. This knowledge will better allow the manager to direct the information gathering activities of the firm and evaluate the quality of information produced.

[9] See Chapter 5 of Bellenger and Greenberg, *op. cit.,* for elaboration on this topic.

DECIDING WHEN TO USE COMMERCIAL
RESEARCH SERVICES

If the manager is not able to secure the needed information from secondary sources, another option is to use an outside research firm. Many firms produce and sell information as their business. It may be advantageous to use these organizations when a particular firm lacks the necessary expertise or when, by spreading certain technical costs over a large number of clients, an outside research firm can provide information at less expense than would be required for primary research. Commercial information may be either syndicated or custom-made. Syndicated information is produced to meet the needs of a large number of similar users. Copies of general reports are available for purchase. Custom-made information is tailored to the needs of one specific firm.

If, due to cost considerations or lack of skills, the sales manager decides to use an outside firm, an acceptable organization must be located. One good source of potential research firms is associates who have had work done in the past. The telephone directory or the American Marketing Association Directory are other potential sources. To select from among prospective research firms, several factors should be assessed:

1. What is the firm's reputation?
2. How large are they?
3. What is the background of their personnel?
4. Do they seem to understand your firm's problem?
5. Can they make a good presentation to your company personnel?
6. And, finally, how does the cost of their proposal compare with other proposals and with the cost of making a bad decision? A firm should not necessarily get the cheapest research; it should look for the least expensive research that meets its need.

The information needed by the farm machinery sales manager discussed earlier provides a good example of commercial as well as external secondary information. The manager needed details on companies in a series of SIC codes. Such information could be purchased from Dun & Bradstreet's Marketing Services Division. Dun & Bradstreet has a field force of over 2000 employees across the United States who collect information on over 300,000 manufacturing firms. The information includes, among other items: basic identification, type of activity, number of employees, and sales volume. A client of Dun & Bradstreet can get the information on each firm by paying a certain fee.

PRIMARY RESEARCH APPROACHES

If all needed information cannot be secured from secondary sources and a decision has been made not to use a commercial research firm, then primary research is required. Primary research approaches can be divided into qualitative and quantitative. Quite often both approaches may be used in a single research effort. Primary research may also be combined with secondary research and/or information from a commercial firm in any given study. For purposes of description, however, qualitative research can be thought of as involving approaches that are more subjective than quantitative research. Quantitative research approaches tend to be more objective with emphasis on producing "hard numbers" that can be subjected to statistical analysis. Numerous research approaches can be grouped into each category. The discussion here will be confined to a few of those more commonly used. In the qualitative area, focus group and depth interviews will be reviewed. Surveys, experiments, and simulation are three aspects of quantitative research that will be discussed.

Qualitative Research: Focus Group Interviews. The focus group interview is the most commonly used qualitative research procedure. It involves conducting joint discussions with small groups of usually 8 to 12 respondents. Focus group interviews typically last 1½–2 hours, which gives the moderator sufficient time to develop a good rapport with respondents and thus get candid answers. The moderator directs the group discussion but does not use a set of predetermined questions. The interview is free flowing and is designed to uncover information that might not come out in a more structured type of research.[10]

Typically two or three sessions will be conducted on a given topic. Thus, the samples are very small and the results must be treated as suggestive rather than conclusive. The information from focus groups is very useful in developing hypotheses that can be further tested in quantitative work.

To illustrate the potential usefulness of the technique to sales management, let us examine its application by one industrial products company. Owens-Corning Fiberglass is one company that has conducted research of this type.[11] The company's Transportation Marketing Division conducted a series of 15 focus group interviews with mass merchandise, oil company, and private label tire dealers. The research objective was to see what key benefits and merchandising aids would best help dealers sell radial tires with fiberglass construction. The company could then design a promotional strategy and train salespeople to assist the dealer. Previous research had shown that consumers would buy fiberglass radials provided they cost less than radials of steel construction. Owens-Corning marketing and sales personnel watched from behind a one-way mirror as a researcher got groups of 3 to 15 dealers talking about the tire business in general and fiberglass radials in particular. The managers were very surprised by what they saw, as they had been convinced that product acceptance would be smooth sailing. However, dealers talked about the problems they had had when fiberglass bias-belted tires had been introduced years previously. Even though the bias-belted tires had become big sellers, the dealers were worried that they would have similar initial problems with the fiberglass radials. As a result, the marketing and sales

---

[10] For a more complete discussion of qualitative research approaches, see Danny N. Bellenger, Kenneth L. Bernhardt, and Jac L. Goldstucker, *Qualitative Research in Marketing* (Chicago: American Marketing Association, 1976).

[11] "Owens-Corning Listens to Dealers," *Sales Management,* March 3, 1975, p. 23.

team was able to rework sales themes and promotional copy to provide a much higher probability of a successful introduction of the new product.

Depth Interviews. The depth or unstructured interview is a one-to-one interview, organized to encourage the respondent to talk freely and express ideas on the subject being investigated. As with focus groups, depth interviews are very subjective and the value of the results depends heavily on the skill of the researcher. These interviews often last for an hour or longer with the objective of getting at the respondents' underlying motives. The interviewer attempts to probe beneath surface responses. Again, as with focus groups, the sample is typically small, limiting the degree to which depth interview results can be projected to larger groups.

One company discovered that its sales force was not reporting competitive developments in their territories, even though they had been trained to do so and wanted to find out why this was happening. The company considered feedback from its sales force to be a major source of marketing intelligence about changes in the marketing strategy of its competitors. Management discovered, however, that only 5 of its 51 sales people had reported a new product of a major competitor, although all of them had been exposed to the product. A depth interview with each salesperson was conducted to discover the reasons for this lack of feedback. The major reasons uncovered were (1) "Management doesn't use it anyway." (2) "Too busy with other activities." and (3) "Not important enough to report." This information allowed the sales manager to redesign the sales feedback system in such a way as to gain greater support from the sales force.

Quantitative Research: Surveys. The most frequently used quantitative research approach is the survey. With the survey approach, a sample of some larger population is usually selected and information is collected from this sample. It is then inferred that the population has attitudes, opinions, behaviors, and so forth, similar to those of the sample. This allows the manager to gain some understanding of the group in which he is interested.

For example, suppose that a sales manager for Ford is planning the allocation of sales effort between territories for the next quarter. To do this, a forecast of sales by territory is needed. One way to produce such a forecast is an intention-to-buy survey. A sample could be drawn from each sales territory and questioned as to their intention-to-buy a Ford within the next 3 months. The survey results would provide a basis for forecasting sales in the period in question. This approach to forecasting has certain problems, which will be discussed in Chapter 4. Surveys to produce information for sales management are, however, generally very useful.

Experiments. Another quantitative approach is the experiment. The experiment allows for the production of information in a much more controlled setting than the survey. With an experiment, certain variables are manipulated and their effect on other variables is observed. A properly designed experiment can establish cause-effect relationships, whereas such relationships can only be inferred from a survey.

For example, the International Harvester Company was examining alterations in its compensation system.[12] To do this, a test group of 12 salespeople and a validation group of 11 salespeople were selected in the Philadelphia area. The salesmen sold three products and were on a salary plus commission system with all products receiving the same commission rate. The test group was changed to a system that gave a different commission rate for each product based on the product's contribution to profit. The new system also allowed the salesperson to make a higher rate of compensation on a given level of sales. The company hoped to increase overall motivation and direct more effort toward more profitable products. After the change, the effect on sales performance was monitored to assess the impact of the change.

The results of the change did not live up to management's expectations. The study also helped management to understand why the changes had failed to get the desired results. It appeared that the new plan had motivated half of the sales force but actually had had a negative reaction on the other half. This latter group was satisfied with its present income and simply sold less under the new system, preferring to keep the same income and increase leisure time. These results suggested some new directions for recruiting salespeople who would display the desired pattern of selling more to make more.

Simulation.   A final quantitative approach that holds great promise, but has yet to find wide application, is simulation. Simulation involves building an artificial environment in which information is produced. The artificial environment is usually developed in a mathematical model from survey and secondary information. The model is then used in an experimental mode. This approach allows the production of information without disrupting the actual environment. It also permits the manager to examine environments that may be projected for the future.

To illustrate,

Xerox Corporation developed a salesman allocation model employing a market grid approach.[13] A grid of intersecting horizontal and vertical lines is laid over a sales area, thus generating a set of cells which contain customers. Each cell must contain data on the expected number of customers, the expected revenue from each customer, and the expected number of calls per day per salesman. The model then allocates calls sequentially to the customer with the highest revenue per call value until all accounts in a cell are called on and all potential realized. Additional cells are combined until the salesman's maximum time limit is reached. This set of cells then constitutes the salesman's territory.[14]

---

[12] See Rene Y. Darmon, "Sales Force Response to Financial Incentive," in Marvin A. Jolson (ed.), *Contemporary Readings in Sales Management* (New York: Petrocelli/Charter, 1977), pp. 157–166.

[13] Peter J. Gray, "Computers and Models in the Marketing Decision Process," in Evelyn Konrad (ed.), *Computer Innovations in Marketing* (New York: American Management Association, 1970), pp. 158–167.

[14] James M. Comer, "The Computer, Personal Selling, and Sales Management," *Journal of Marketing*, July 1975, pp. 27–33.

THE ROLE OF THE MARKETING INFORMATION SYSTEM

After information needs have been identified by the sales manager and research approaches have been selected to produce the needed information, the research must then be implemented and the information reported to the sales manager. The employees, procedures, and equipment arranged in an institution so as to carry out research can be called an **information system.** This system in a broad sense may produce either information for one time decisions or a continual flow of information for repetitive decisions.

A system designed to implement research needs four basic components: a display unit, data collection procedures, a data bank, and an analytical bank. Part of all of these components may be housed in a computer. The elements of an information system, their relationship to each other and the system's relationship to the research flow are illustrated in Figure 3.6.

The display unit acts as an interface between the system and the research flow and, in some cases, the sales manager. It receives information requests and plans for producing the information. After the research

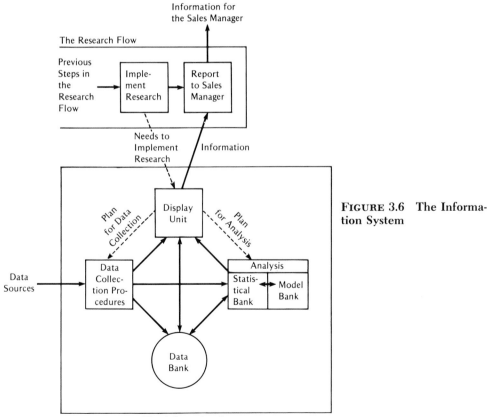

FIGURE 3.6 The Information System

is implemented, the display unit transmits the information to the researcher or the sales manager. Data collection procedures secure the needed data from internal and external sources to produce the desired information. The data bank acts as a storehouse of data and information. Finally, the analytical bank contains the statistical procedures and/or models used to transform the collected data into useful information.

Alter noted that there is a significant difference between **electronic data processing (EDP)** systems and **decision support** systems. The uses, purposes, and characteristics of each are shown in Table 3.4. Sales managers are more concerned with the decision support system as an aid in making and implementing decisions.

TABLE 3.4   Comparison of Uses, Purposes, and Characteristics of EDP Systems and Decision Support Systems

Decision Support System	
Purposes	*Uses*
Decision making	Retrieve isolated data items
Decision implementation	Use as mechanism for ad hoc analysis of data files
Characteristics	
Active line, staff, and management activities	Obtain prespecified aggregations of data in the form of standard reports
Oriented toward overall effectiveness	Estimate consequences of proposed decisions
Focus on the present and future	Propose decisions
Emphasis on flexibility and ad hoc utilization	Make decisions

Electronic Data Processing	
Purposes	*Uses*
Transaction processing	Obtain prespecified aggregations of data in the form of standard reports
Recordkeeping	
Business reporting	
Characteristics	
Passive clerical activities	
Oriented toward mechanical efficiency	
Focus on past	
Emphasis on consistency	

Source: Steven L. Alter, "How Effective Managers Use Information Systems," *Harvard Business Review* (Nov.–Dec. 1976), p. 98.

In some cases the sales manager may need to interact with the research and information system's personnel in order to direct their efforts into the most productive channels. Thus, the manager should be acquainted with the concepts and usefulness of an information system in order to take full advantage of its support potential.

Summary

Sales management can be conceptualized in terms of four sets of activities: setting objectives, allocating resources and effort, developing the sales plan, and organizing for implementation. The sales manager must make decisions related to each of these areas. This mental level of decision making should have a logical and systematic sequence. The flow starts with problem recognition and definition, and proceeds through determining alternatives, establishing decision criteria, evaluating alternatives; it concludes with making the decision. Relevant and timely information is needed to carry out this mental activity effectively. Research is designed to produce the information needed by the manager. The research flow proceeds as follows: identify needed information, specify research questions, determine research approach, implement the approach, and, finally, report the information to the sales manager.

Numerous research approaches are available to generate the desired information. These include secondary research (internal and external), use of commercial research firms, and primary research. Primary research approaches can be broken into qualitative (focus groups and depth interviews) and quantitative (surveys, experiments, and simulation). A combination of approaches is typical in most projects. The information system was presented as a structure within the institution which implements the research task.

In general this chapter provided a conceptual framework for approaching the sales management tasks. It presents a logical flow for making decisions and for informational support in this flow. This framework can be used in later chapters of the text dealing with various decision areas and in the cases provided in the text.

Discussion Questions

1. Why is it important to follow a logical and systematic approach in carrying out the sales management tasks?

2. Discuss the specific types of decisions that need to be made in each of the sales management activity sets.

3. What are the key steps in the decision flow, and what must be accomplished in each step?

4. Discuss the research flow and its relationship to decision making.

5. What are some of the problems in producing sales management information from accounting records?

6. Explain how to locate and evaluate external secondary information.

What are some of the key sources of external secondary information for the sales manager?

7. How does qualitative research differ from quantitative research?

8. Develop an example of how each of the following research approaches could be of use in sales management:
(a) focus group interviews
(b) depth interviews
(c) surveys
(d) experiments
(e) simulation

9. How are information systems related to research and sales management decision making?

10. What is the function of an information system?

Selected References

BELLENGER, DANNY, and BARNETT A. GREENBERG, *Marketing Research: A Management Information Approach* (Homewood, Ill.: Richard D. Irwin, Inc., 1978).

BESWICK, CHARLES A., and DAVID W. CRAVENS, "A Multistage Decision Model for Salesforce Management," *Journal of Marketing Research*, May 1977, pp. 135–144.

COMER, JAMES M., "The Computer, Personal Selling, and Sales Management," *Journal of Marketing*, July 1975, pp. 27–33.

DAWSON, LESLIE M., "Toward a New Concept of Sales Management," *Journal of Marketing*, April 1970, pp. 33–38.

HENRY, PORTER, "Manage Your Sales Force as a System," *Harvard Business Review*, March-April 1975, pp. 85–95.

CASE 3.1
Consolidated Food Service Supply*

Company Background Consolidated Food Service Supply was founded in 1955 as a manufacturer of restaurant equipment. During the 1960s Consolidated diversified into a product line of restaurant supplies to include tablecloths, napkins, silver-

* Case prepared by Thomas N. Ingram and Danny N. Bellenger, Georgia State University.

ware, cooking utensils, and chemicals used in the maintenance of commercial kitchens.

Consolidated had been a leader in the field since 1950 and continued to grow in the 1970s by way of acquisition. As people began eating more meals away from home, the fast food restaurant business grew dramatically. In pursuit of this market segment, Consolidated acquired a small manufacturer of disposable table and cocktail napkins in 1971 and purchased a plastic straw manufacturer in 1973 to further widen their product line. Both acquisitions proved to be excellent strategic moves as the wholesale distributors in the restaurant industry looked for suppliers, such as Consolidated, who could offer a wide line of products.

A year ago Consolidated acquired Bestware, Inc., a medium-sized manufacturer of disposable plastic beverage containers as part of their growth through acquisition strategy. Bestware was the number one supplier in the country of plastic beverage containers at the time of the acquisition. After a sales slump during the transition period when sales forces were being changed. Bestware sales volume had remained strong.

However, the market for Bestware had become extremely competitive and profit margins were unacceptably low as Consolidated began its second year with the Bestware line. The restaurant supply and paper distributors who were Consolidated's key accounts all predicted a tough, competitive market for the next year.

John Chambers had been promoted to Southeast Regional Sales Manager for Consolidated a year ago. At this time Bestware was just being added to the product line and Chambers had pushed his sales representatives hard in the past year to boost Bestware sales. In the past 90 days, sales had reached a monthly level of 9,000 cases, which meant that the first year's sales volume target for Bestware would be met.

Current Situation

Chambers was now trying to develop a strategy for the next year for all of Consolidated's products. When he started this project in July, the Bestware product line gave him considerable trouble. Strategies for the more mature products had been relatively simple to formulate compared to grappling with Bestware's problems. On July 15, Chambers requested that the marketing research department give him a current market analysis of the Bestware market in the southeastern United States and the Caribbean area.

A preliminary meeting was held with Jeff Simpson, head of the marketing research department, to spell out the specifics of the analysis. Chambers agreed to Simpson's request that Consolidated field sales representatives be used to gather some of the needed information.

It was now September 15 and Chambers had just received the Bestware market analysis from Simpson's department. The strategies for next year were to be reviewed on October 1 with George Rafferty, Regional Marketing Manager. As he sat down at his desk to read the analysis, Chambers thought, "At least our volume is strong . . . if we could only improve our profit . . ."

Objectives and Methodology

The objectives of this market analysis include:

1. A compilation of available information with regard to market size, market share by supplier, competitive characteristics, and key account performance.
2. The use of this information as a base for planning Bestware strategy for next year's plan and our three-year marketing plan.

The methods used to compile this data included:

1. Key account interviews.
2. Surveys completed in personal interview with Consolidated sales representatives.
3. Review of pertinent trade publications.
4. Review of sales and pricing history available from company sources.

Assumptions

To look at the total market size, several key assumptions were formulated based on available secondary data:

1. Of all public food and drink outlets, 16 per cent use disposable plastic beverage containers.
2. Of all institutional food and drink outlets, 12 per cent use disposable plastic beverage containers.
3. Total number of food service outlets in the United States is 460,000. Southeast Region BPI (Buying Power Index from the July issue of *Sales and Marketing Management*) is applied to estimate total number of food service outlets in the Southeast to be 69,000.
4. Average cost per meal in the public outlets is $3.00.
5. Average cost per meal in the institutional section is $2.00.

From these assumptions and other available data, the total market potential for the southeast region disposable plastic beverage container will be constructed.

Product Line Review

For the purpose of this analysis, the entire Bestware product line will be divided into the following categories:

1. Tumblers—printed and plain
2. Stemware
3. Coffee service
4. Dinnerware
5. Lids
6. Portion cups

Some competitors offer a full line similar to Bestware, whereas some compete with a limited tumbler line. More detail with regard to product line by competitor is available in a later section.

Basically, the tumbler line has 13 sizes ranging from a 4½-oz tumbler to a 16-oz tumbler. The bulk of sales within the tumbler area are in the 9- and 10-oz sizes. Approximately 70 per cent of all tumbler sales are in these two sizes. The tumbler family accounts for 92 per cent of Consolidated's total Bestware sales.

Stemware consists of specialty items for serving champagne, wine, beer, highballs, sherry, and soft drinks. Another application of certain stemware items is as a dessert container. Stemware accounts for 3.2 per cent of Bestware sales.

Coffee service, portion cups, consumer pack, and lids account for less than 4 per cent of Bestware sales. Lids have been relatively unimportant to the user of Bestware products and their competitive counterparts. However, coffee service and portion cups offer potential thus far untapped.

Dinner service is a high quality disposable sold primarily to the catering market. The dinner service items account for 2.0 per cent of sales. The sales mix June year-to-date is shown below:

Family	Case Sales	Mix, %
Tumblers	46,000	92
Printed	6,200	
Plain	39,800	
Stemware	1,500	3.0
Coffee service	300	.6
Dinner service	1,000	2.0
Lids	300	.6
Portion cups	335	.7
Consumer pack	550	1.1
Total	50,000	100.0

Market Characteristics

Total Food Service Market	
Public or commercial	
Separate eating places	$12.0 billion
Hotel/motel	2.5
Plants and factories	1.8
Separate drinking places	1.7
Retail stores	1.5
Recreation and amusement	1.2
Other	10.3
Total public	$31 billion

Market Characteristics *(continued)*

Total Food Service Market	
Institutional or noncommercial	
Schools	$ 1.9 billion
Military	3.6
Hospitals	2.3
Colleges and universities	2.0
Other	4.2
Total public	$14 billion
Total food service market	$45 billion
460,000 outlets approximately	
360,000 public and 100,000 institutional	

Food Service Market Southeast Region

Type	Number of Outlets	Annual Sales (in $ millions)	Avg. Cost Per Meal	Approx. Number Meals Per Year (in millions)
Public	54,000	4750	3.00	1600
Institutional	15,000	2000	2.00	1000
Total	69,000	6750	2.60	2600

Type	Approx. Number Meals/Yr (in millions)	Usage Plastic Bev. Containers (%)	Total Potential Number of Plastic Bev. Containers Used/Yr. (in millions)
Public	1600	12	192
Institutional	1000	16	160
Total	2600	13.5	352

With an average case pack of 500, this translates into a total annual potential market of approximately 750 thousand cases. The frequency of eating out according to these figures would be five times per month for each individual in the southeast. This rate is consistent with published studies.

Consolidated sales this year are expected to be near 100 thousand cases of Bestware products, excluding dinner service and portion cups.

Therefore, our sales are approximately 13% of the total potential for plastic beverage containers.

The total potential market is significantly larger than the market identified by sales to distributors in the southeast. Through surveys with Consolidated sales representatives and key account interviews, sales of 460 thousand cases per year have been identified in the southeast region. The difference between the identified sales of 460 thousand cases and the total market potential can be attributed to several factors:

1. Business handled on a direct basis (airlines and others).
2. Sales through southeast region distributors not identified at this time.
3. Sales from distributors outside the southeast region to end users within the region.
4. Substitute products that qualify as plastic beverage containers are being used in some parts of this market. This includes the soft-side polyethylene tumblers offered by some competitors.

The total airline tumbler usage is estimated at 100–150 million tumblers per year. By following the BPI, the airline market (usage) in the Southeast is 22.5 million tumblers per year, or approximately 45 thousand cases.

Another significant direct market is the government market, whose potential on a direct basis is unknown at this time.

Sales from outside the region are not measurable although examples are present to indicate a substantial volume. M. R. Johnson, a northeast distributor, ships regularly into Virginia. This problem is especially difficult to evaluate as, surely, there are distributors shipping from the southeast into other regions.

Probably the best explanation of the difference between the total market estimate and the identified market is that competitive sales through distributors are not completely identified. This is an area where further market contact will provide a refinement of information over time.

There is also a limitation present in the assumptions set forth at the outset. However, the per cent of public and institutional outlets using plastic beverage containers assumed is the best data available.

Market Share by Supplier

For this section, the identified distributor market is used as the base for determining market share (see table on page 86).

Characteristics of Competitive Suppliers

Airflyte. The Airflyte product line consists of nine tumbler items of a light-walled nature. The unique feature offered by Airflyte is the "crystalline" style 9- and 10-oz tumblers. This style is characterized by a crisscross design touted by Airflyte as giving the appearance of cut glass. The product line is generally regarded as being physically inferior to the Bestware tumbler line but functionally acceptable to the price

Supplier	Market Share, %	Average Case Volume/Month
Consolidated	23	9000
Gallatin	12	4500
Star	12	4500
Mystrom	8	3000
Maco	8	3000
Simpson	6	2500
Plas-Pak	6	2500
Pressly Plastics	4	1500
Thomas	4	1500
Airflyte	3	1000
Festival	3	1000
Other*	10	4500

* Other includes Bankston, Caliente, Arron, SMI, Emerald.

conscious tumbler market. Customer acceptance is based on the fact that it holds water and does so inexpensively.

Although Airflyte likes to talk about cut glass, they are at their best cutting price. The entry of Airflyte into the Southeast market late last year proved to be the beginning of drastic price reductions still occurring. Airflyte broke the price by calling on practically every possible tumbler buyer with prices up to 20 per cent below the existing market. Although not as active now in the southeast, Airflyte still poses a threat to market stability with their low priced line.

Airflyte is sold exclusively through brokers, the most active being Becker and Hayes. Their coverage is adequate, although not a particular advantage. There has been no significant promotional activity from Airflyte during the past year.

In summary, the narrow product line without print capability is a disadvantage to Airflyte when competing with Consolidated, Star, Maco, and so on. However, their low price competes most effectively on 9- and 10-oz tumblers. By doing so, Airflyte is a significant competitor in the southeast region.

Star. The Star product line offers a complete line of tumblers with a limited offering of dinnerware, stemware, and coffee service items. The stemware line does not include the 12-oz pilsner/parfait, an item whose demand exceeds Bestware's capacity to manufacture at the present time. Star offers printing, both stock and custom on 11 items in their line.

Star offers a good price/quality relationship to the industry with product generally considered to be of comparable quality to other suppliers. Pricing is competitive, with inside deals to customers considered key accounts by Bestware prior to the acquisition.

Sales coverage is provided through a strong network of brokers. Representation such as Dixie Sales in Atlanta and A. W. Archer in Nashville have done an effective job in maintaining Star's market position. In addition, key account calls are made by Star personnel who are knowledgeable in this market.

Promotional activity has been limited to a hotel/motel stock design promotion early in the year with unknown results. Since this promotion, Star has adopted a "me-too" approach with regard to Consolidated's promotional activity on the Personalized Printed Bestware program and the Christmas program. The apparent strategy is to promote only when forced to by competition.

Overall, Star's strengths include sales coverage, market knowledge, and a good price/quality relationship. With these assets, Star is a major competitor in the southeast.

Gallatin. The product line offered by Gallatin includes tumblers, medical/surgical containers, 5-oz bowls, and stemware. The tumbler line is complete and also features a lightweight 10-oz tumbler priced 17 per cent less than the regular 10-oz tumbler. Although this is not the same product as our JT-10, it does compete for the same end uses as paper and soft-side polyethylene containers.

Gallatin offers printing on only four items in the 9- and 10-oz sizes. This is largely offset by the fact that Gallatin is extremely competitive on print upcharge, adding only $2.00 per case on stock print as opposed to Consolidated's upcharge of $3.00 per case.

The medical/surgical category of Gallatin's line is one of the most complete lines offered by our competitors. The 11 items in this category include medicine cups, specimen cups, intake cups, and covers.

The stemware line is missing the pilsner/parfait and the dinnerware line is limited to 5-oz bowls in polystyrene and polypropylene.

Gallatin is sold through brokers including Atlanta Sales and Tarheel Sales. Coverage is excellent through these organizations, with Gallatin also going after airline business on a direct basis.

Price is a strong factor when competing with Gallatin, especially in the Carolinas and Virginia where their plant can offer pick-up privileges. Now that Gallatin has opened a plant in Arkansas, we can expect increased activity in Louisiana and Mississippi. During 1975, Gallatin has been more competitive on price than any supplier in the southeast with the possible exception of Airflyte. There has been no recent promotional activity from Gallatins.

Festival. Offering only a 10-oz tumbler with print capability, Festival has the narrowest product line of any of our competitors. Pricing is competitive, but the current sales volume of Festival is limited to approximately 1000 cases per month in the southeast.

Mystrom. The tumbler line of Mystrom is limited to five items: 5-oz, 7-oz, 9-oz, 10-oz, and 12-oz tumblers. Mystrom was extremely price competitive late last year and still remains competitive, although not to the degree shown last year. The Mystrom tumbler is of reasonable quality and can be combined with their dinnerware for quantity pricing.

Maco. The Maco line includes tumblers and stemware. The stemware line includes the 12-oz pilsner, a popular specialty item. Clearly Maco has clout due to their extensive food service line, which easily allows truckload and carload buying to rival Consolidated. In the Bestware area, Maco offers carload pricing to the 100-case buyer. The carload gives a 7½ per cent allowance beyond carload pricing. With a plant in Georgia, Maco has been aggressive all year in all product lines. As an example, Maco offered one case of dinnerware free with every 10 cases of drinkware purchased between February 1st and March 29th. Maco also ran a distributor prize program on wrapped tumblers during the year.

Plas-Pak. In the southeast region, Plas-Pak has not been price aggressive this year. Therefore, their volume is comparatively limited for a major supplier. The only significant activity from Plas-Pak came during their spring promotion which featured $1.00 off each case purchased of 9- and 10-oz tumblers.

The product line is excellent, with the broadest stemware line in the business. Although the product line is a plus, without competitive pricing Plas-Pak does not pose as serious a competitive problem as smaller suppliers with lower pricing.

Simpson. The lack of emphasis on tumblers by Simpson has been obvious. The great majority of their sales are by virtue of convenience to the customer buying other Simpson products rather than by sales effort by Simpson. Simpson does not regard tumblers as a major part of their business, and, therefore, sells above the price level generally available in the market. As a result, they control only small amounts of tumbler business spread throughout the southeast.

Pressly Plastics. Based in Florida, this is one competitor to keep an eye on. By being extremely price competitive, Press has begun to capture a good portion of the Miami market. Most recent reports show the same type activity in central Florida with good results.

At this point, Consolidated is the strongest supplier of Bestware type products in the southeast. The following factors are current advantages to Consolidated in the market:

1. Market share leader
2. Competitive pricing
3. Promotional activity
4. Broad product line with overall good quality

The key to volume is competitive pricing. Therefore, our major competitive threats come from Gallatin, Maco, Mystrom, and Pressly Plastics. Gallatin and Maco are especially strong as their product line is well accepted in the market. Airflyte is also a threat, but to date we have been fairly successful in limiting their volume.

Key Accounts Summary

The distribution network of Bestware-type products is characterized by a large number of distributors, with very few buying 200 cases per month or more. At times it is difficult to align distributors with suppliers on a key account relationship. Certainly the importance of price dominates the sales environment to the point of diluting loyalty of most distributors to *any* supplier.

When taking an overall view of our key accounts, the pricing strategy clearly reflects the sales volume of the first two quarters of 1975. Of the top 20 accounts, 13 are tracking behind last year's levels. This is largely a result of first quarter performance when we were not price competitive. Of the top 20, ten are ahead of first quarter sales levels during the second and third quarters. These ten are the major accounts, whereas those behind are not nearly as important from a volume standpoint. The aggressive pricing of the second quarter definitely paid volume dividends.

Summary and Outlook

Sales of Bestware products are to six key market segments. Each segment with an estimated percentage of total sales is listed:

1.	Hotel/motel	50%
2.	Recreation	15%
3.	Commercial restaurants	10%
4.	Catering	10%
5.	Bar supply	10%
6.	Health care	5%

Food service as a whole is showing only slight growth this year as compared with last year. With the economy improving, the outlook for next year is generally good. Because of the trend toward one out of two meals away from home, by 1980 growth in food service outlets should continue at least at a rate of 5 per cent per year.

The one big question mark lies within our biggest market segment, hotel/motel. The effects of anticipated increases in gasoline prices could be drastic. Next year we will most likely have to increase market share in this area to maintain our volume.

The recreation market is having a good year, with sales up 20 per cent in Florida. Major developers are bullish on the recreation/resort market for the next several years. With travel expected to increase during coming years, only fuel costs stand in the way of good growth in the recreation market.

Commercial restaurants are having a fairly good year with fast food doing better than the rest. Real growth should return to the historical level of 3–4 per cent next year. Catering and contract feeding should recover as does the economy. Health care is expected to remain relatively stable as it was last year.

The airline market is not distributor business and does not fit into our overall strategy in 1976. However, we are keeping the door open with the top airlines, should their volume warrant a direct sales approach in the future.

To look at our objectives for next year, a review of this year's accomplishments sets the stage:

1. Established base of sales at the 9,000 cases per month level.
2. Established number one position in market share.
3. Gained position as promotional leader through promotional programs and advertising.
4. Gained knowledge of market conditions and requirements.
5. Profitability unsatisfactory this year.

Next year we should strive to maintain our volume base and continue development of our combination program. We should also strive to make our activities in Bestware more profitable through the following steps:

1. Cost reduction in manufacturing and freight, if possible.
2. Improved sales mix on high margin items—stemware, dinnerware, coffee service, portion cups.
3. Price increases as market conditions allow.
4. Emphasis on printed tumblers.
5. Increased sales into the Caribbean area at favorable pricing.

CASE 3.2
Southern Equipment Manufacturing Company*

Company Background

The Product Development Committee of Southern Equipment Manufacturing Company (SEMC) recently began a review of a prospective new product. The product was basically a small version of the rotary engine. The engine would cost approximately 15 per cent more than a standard engine with the same performance characteristics. However, the new engine would provide better fuel utilization and require less maintenance, which would offset the increased initial costs of the engine within 18 months under normal operating conditions. In addition, the new engine would have an average "life span" approximately 10 per cent longer than the standard engine.

Engines in this size range are powered by gasoline, butane, or natural gas. The proposed engine would, like the standard engine, function with

* Adapted with permission from Donald S. Tull and Del I. Hawkins, *Marketing Research: Meaning, Measurement and Method* (New York: MacMillan Publishing Co., In., 1977), pp. 64–65.

any of these fuel systems. The engines are used as stationary engines; that is, they do not power moving vehicles. Instead, they operate small irrigation wells, generators, and industrial and agricultural equipment.

Current Situation

The committee in conjunction with the director of marketing research worked out sales estimates for "optimistic," "most probable," and "pessimistic" market shares. These estimates relied heavily on a series of discussions held with the firm's sales force. Both the optimistic and pessimistic forecasts were based on the assumption that there was approximately a 25 per cent chance of their being realized.

The committee developed these sales forecasts for the six-year planning period used by the firm. SEMC uses a discount rate of 12 per cent on all such projects. The profit projections for the six-year planning period are as follows.

Year	Pessimistic	Most Likely	Optimistic
1	< $ 50,000 > *	< $ 50,000 >	< $ 50,000 >
2	< 200,000 >	< 180,000 >	< 170,000 >
3	< 100,000 >	< 60,000 >	5,000
4	< 10,000 >	75,000	100,000
5	100,000	300,000	400,000
6	125,000	350,000	440,000

* <   > denotes loss.

What should SEMC do?

Student Learning Exercise / 3
Using Decision Trees

Objective

To illustrate the use of a decision tree in evaluating alternatives and selecting among them.

Overview

You will be given the necessary information to be included in your decision tree. This will be used in evaluating three proposals and selecting one of them.

The marketing manager has suggested that you—the sales manager—conduct an analysis of three states because the company is planning to expand. Your recommendation is wanted regarding the state that should be entered first, that is, in the next year.

Given the following information, construct a decision tree and make a recommendation to the marketing manager. You will be expected to justify your recommendation.

The three states are State A, State B, and State C. State B is much larger than States A or C. If the firm does extremely well in State A, expected dollar sales volume would be $780,000. The probability of this occurring is .6. If the firm does moderately well in A, sales will be $700,000. This has a probability of .3. If sales simply are average (neither good nor bad), dollar volume will be $600,000. The probability of doing average is .1.

In State B, extremely well would mean $2,500,000 in sales. The probability of this is .2. Sales of $1,800,000 would be moderately well, and this has a .3 probability. Average sales would be $1,000,000 and this probability is .5.

Doing extremely well in State C involves sales of $850,000; moderately well would be $800,000; average would be $710,000. The probabilities associated with these events are .3 (extremely well), .4 (moderately well), and .3 (average).

Total costs in State A, *excluding* travel budgets, will be 88 per cent of sales. Ten salespeople will be utilized and each will have a $3000 annual travel budget.

Total costs in B, excluding travel budgets, will be 92 per cent of sales. Since this state is larger, 15 salespeople will be needed. Each will have an annual travel budget of $4000.

Total costs in C, excluding travel budgets, will be 89.5 per cent of sales. The 10 salespeople will each have an annual $2500 travel budget.

Projected sales and costs are all assumed to be for one year.

Reading for

PART One

Manage Your Sales Force as a System

PORTER HENRY

Sales managers, according to their critics, are not sufficiently "scientific" in their decision making. They pursue volume instead of profit, make piecemeal decisions instead of comprehensive plans, rely on instinct and hunch rather than on methodical decision-making processes.

Sales managers might well reply—and often do—that they are dealing with salesmen and customers who are capricious human beings, much more difficult to predict and control than a piece of production equipment.

It is true that the sales department is a complicated communications system, influenced by many variables that are difficult to quantify and that interact in unforeseen ways. For example, a sales training program designed to help salesmen sell more of a high-profit specialty product may fail because the company's compensation plan motivates salesmen to chase the volume dollars in easy-to-sell but low-profit items. Or an increase in the size of the sales force may result in a higher proportion of calls on marginal customers, creating an increase in the sales costs ratio and a decrease in profit per sales call instead of the intended higher profitability.

Because the function they are managing is so complex, sales managers can profitably use the basic principles, if not the mathematical trappings, of the most modern of all scientific methods. Known by such terms as

From *Harvard Business Review*, March 1975, pp. 85–95. Reprinted by permission of the publisher, Harvard University Graduate School of Business Administration.

"systems engineering," "systems analysis," "the total systems concept," and "the systems approach," this method has helped Americans produce energy from atoms and place men on the moon. It can also help increase the productivity of a sales department.

Essentially, a "system" consists of various inputs that go into a process or operation of some kind and result in a measurable output. The measurement is used to adjust the inputs or the process in order to produce desired results. To describe this procedure of measurement and adjustment, systems engineers have borrowed a term from electronics: *feedback*. The methodology of systems analysis can be described in six steps:

1. Define the system to be investigated. For example, it may be an entire city, just the transportation network, or perhaps only the subway system.
2. Define what the system ought to accomplish as well as the means to measure this. For the subway system: What quality and quantity of service are desired?
3. Define the elements that make up the system and quantify their relationships. In the case of the subway system: What is the effect on passengers moved per hour of such variables as the pattern of passenger arrival frequencies at stations, length of platforms, length of trains, headway between trains, and number of doors on a car?
4. For each element, or for each major subassembly of elements, determine the measurable performance desired. To achieve the objectives of the subway system, what is required of the signals, motors, brakes and crew?
5. Consider the cost effectiveness of alternative methods to improve the performance of the system. For each dollar spent to improve the performance of one element of the system, how many dollars' worth of improvement will be obtained in the performance of the total system?
6. Implement the most desirable decisions and measure the results.

Although it may not be possible to quantify all the interacting variables that constitute the sales department of a typical company, nevertheless, "systems engineering" can be used by the sales manager to increase the overall production of his department. Let us examine the steps he takes and their potential value to him.

Defining the System

The system of concern to the sales manager is, of course, the sales department. It is a subsystem of the corporation's marketing program, which is in turn a subsystem of the corporation (see *Exhibit I*).

In the phraseology of systems engineering, the corporation's top management uses *feedback* from the marketplace and the results of previous marketing efforts to develop an *input* to the marketing system. This input includes the marketing objectives, the choice of products or services to be offered, the pricing strategy, and decisions about the resources to be committed to the attainment of marketing objectives.

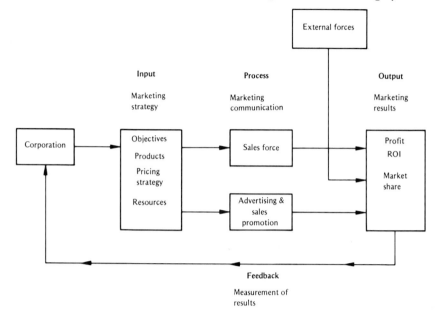

Feedback

Measurement of
results

Having developed products or services to meet identified customer needs, the corporation must then communicate their existence to potential customers. This communication is accomplished through two channels: (1) advertising and sales promotion, including every medium that reaches potential customers en masse, and (2) the sales force, which communicates to prospects primarily on a one-to-one basis.

Essential to the systems approach is the measurement of output. The output of the corporation is usually measured in terms of return on investment and/or corporate growth. Market share, profits as a percentage of sales volume, and cash flow are other measures of performance that may be stressed.

Measuring Efficiency

But the sales force is a subsystem of a larger subsystem, and return on investment, profit ratio, and market share, while good measures for the whole company, are greatly influenced by factors not completely controlled by the sales force. If these measures improve, everybody claims credit for the improvement.

Is there some way to show whether a sales force is operating at 60%, or 83.7%, or perhaps even 100% efficiency? If sales managers could agree upon two or three standard indices of sales force productivity, they could compare the effectiveness of their systems with that of other sales forces in the same industry. The following is a list of five possible yardsticks:

1. *Contribution to profit.*   The company's products can be turned over to the sales force at cost, or at cost plus some markup representing the production department's contribution to profit. The sales force

in turn sells the products at a markup. This margin, minus *all* costs of the selling operation—salesmen's salaries, sales management and supervision costs, travel and entertainment expenses, credit losses, interest on accounts receivable—represents the contribution of the sales department to corporate net profits.

2. *Return on assets managed.* The sales force requires certain capital investments—goods in warehouses, branch offices, salesmen's automobiles, money tied up in accounts receivable. If current sales expenses such as salaries, travel, and entertainment are subtracted from gross profit on sales volume, the balance represents the return on these investments.[1] If a company uses this yardstick, some costs that are now absorbed in the current budget are logically capitalized and depreciated. A sales training program useful for five years, for example, would more logically be written off over five years than in just one year.

3. *Sales cost ratio.* A frequently used index is the ratio of sales expenses divided by dollar sales volume. This ratio should be used on conjunction with other yardsticks, because a sales force selling $10 million at a 5% expense/volume ratio may not be as profitable as a sales force selling $20 million with a 7% cost ratio.

4. *Market share.* This output is influenced by variables other than sales department productivity. If, however, product quality, pricing, advertising effectiveness, and competitors' activity remain relatively constant, an increased market share could be considered an indication of increased sales force productivity.

5. *Achievement of company marketing goals.* In addition to, or instead of, indices for comparing companies in an industry, measurements of *desired* performance may be used. An example might be "to increase our market share from 15% to 25%, provided net profits as a per cent of sales do not go below 10%."

Every engineer agrees that the efficiency of an engine is its energy output divided by its energy input. Sales managers are not universally agreed upon any corresponding measurement, or even upon which activities should be considered as input and which as output. However, this state of affairs does not mean management must throw up its hands. It can and should decide what measurements best meet the needs of its company. The measurements chosen may not be perfect, but they can still be valuable, enabling management to apply the systems approach in a useful and productive way.

Improving the System

Exhibit II is a flow chart of the sales force as a system. It employs four measurements of sales force output: contribution to profit, return on assets managed, sales costs ratio, and market share. If the sales manager

---

[1] A more detailed description of this accounting method is contained in J. S. Schiff and Michael Schiff, "New Sales Management Tool: ROAM" (HBR July–August 1967), p. 59.

discovers by these measurements or any others he chooses to adopt that sales force productivity is below its desired level, he then works his way *backward* through the flow chart, from right to left, to determine which control variables at the left need adjusting. As the chart indicates, no matter what improvement the sales manager seeks in output, there are only three ways in which the salesmen can achieve the change. These ways are labeled "Salesmen's output variables" because they are the result of every input salesmen can make. The output variables are:

- An increase in total sales volume, without any change in the product mix or sales cost ratio.
- A more profitable product mix, in which the products producing a higher profit represent a larger percentage of total sales volume.
- A reduction in the sales cost ratio, which can result from increasing sales without a corresponding increase in costs, or from decreasing sales costs. (This ratio refers to *all* sales costs, including such items as price concessions, service to the account, and adjustments of complaints.)

In most cases the desired profit goal will require some improvement in all three of the output variables. However, their relative importance is likely to vary from product to product and even from salesman to salesman. In using a systems approach, therefore, it is important to determine how much and what kind of emphasis should be placed on each variable.

Analyzing Sales Activity

If we now move one step to the left in the flow chart, we arrive at the "Salesmen's input variables." These are activities salesmen can change in order to alter the output variables. The arrows emerging from each input variable indicate which of the output variables is affected. Let us now consider the nature of the input variables.

1. The Number of Sales Calls

Each salesman might be motivated to make more calls per week, or the company total could be increased by hiring more salesmen. An increased number of sales calls, *Exhibit II* indicates, will probably affect total sales volume and can affect the sales cost ratio—adversely, if additional sales calls are made on unprofitable prospects.

2. The Quality of the Sales Calls

This input is measured by such yardsticks as calls per order, dollar sales or profits per call, or percentage of calls that achieve specific objectives. In this context, a sales call refers to a salesman's conversation with one or more individuals. The "call" on a major plant might involve sales calls on many buying influences, but these calls should be considered separately in evaluating their quality and in establishing the frequency

EXHIBIT II

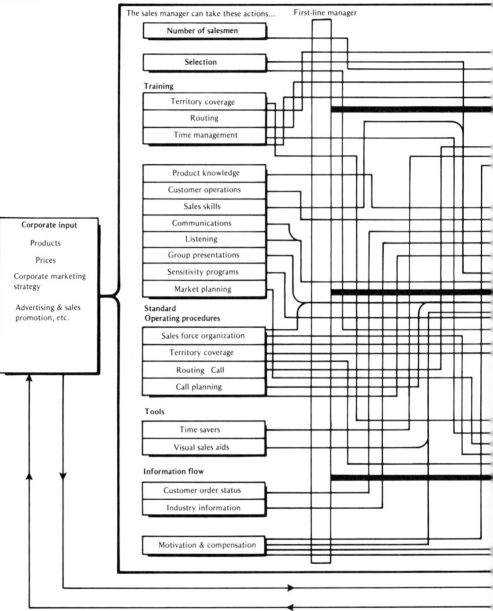

Sales manager's control variables

The sales manager can take these actions...   First-line manager

Number of salesmen

Selection

Training
 Territory coverage
 Routing
 Time management

Product knowledge
Customer operations
Sales skills
Communications
Listening
Group presentations
Sensitivity programs
Market planning

Corporate input
 Products
 Prices
 Corporate marketing strategy
 Advertising & sales promotion, etc.

Standard Operating procedures
 Sales force organization
 Territory coverage
 Routing Call
 Call planning

Tools
 Time savers
 Visual sales aids

Information flow
 Customer order status
 Industry information

Motivation & compensation

with which the buying influences should be contacted. As the flow chart indicates, call quality consists of these elements:

- The information content of the call. Is the salesman adequately informed about the customer's problems or plans, as well as about his own products and their applications?
- The effectiveness of the call as an act of communication: Does the salesman deliver the message in an understandable and convincing manner? (This is where visual sales aids may be useful.) Is the salesman

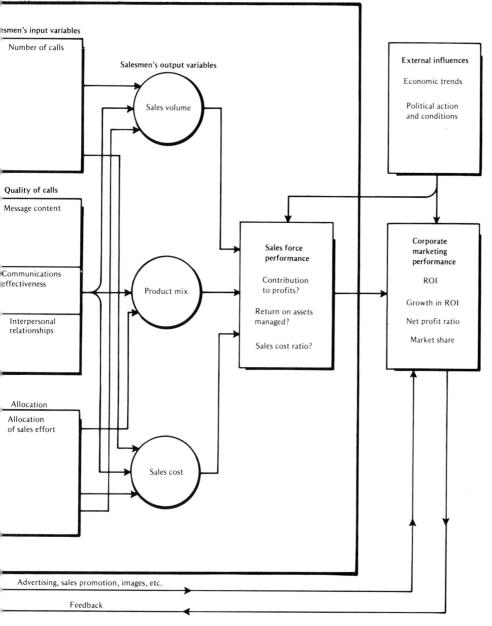

esmen's input variables

Number of calls

Salesmen's output variables

Sales volume

External influences

Economic trends

Political action
and conditions

Quality of calls

Message content

Communications
effectiveness

Product mix

**Sales force
performance**

Contribution
to profits?

Return on assets
managed?

Sales cost ratio?

**Corporate
marketing
performance**

ROI

Growth in ROI

Net profit ratio

Market share

Interpersonal
relationships

Allocation

Allocation
of sales effort

Sales cost

Advertising, sales promotion, images, etc.

Feedback

effective while on the receiving end of the conversation? That is, is
he a good questioner and listener?

- The interpersonal aspects of the call. Does the salesman rub the customer the wrong way without being aware of it? When the customer's
"inner child" speaks, does the salesman's "inner child" respond?

Most companies do a reasonably good job of giving the salesman information on customer needs and product applications, or at least make
it possible for the salesman to absorb it. Many companies try to upgrade

salesmen's skills in communication and interaction by using some kind of standardized training program. (Too often, though, the program tends to concentrate on one element while ignoring the other.) Few companies take the trouble to investigate the basic question: If our sales calls are not good enough, what is the nature of their weakness?

Improvement in call quality can increase any of the three output variables—total volume, product mix, and sales costs. The content of the training will determine which of the three is most affected. Occasionally, a sales manager may ask himself which of these outputs most needs changing, but many of us never see this happen. Instead, before launching a training program or procedural change, sales managers opt for training that is mostly motivational, without first identifying desired behavioral changes.

3. THE ALLOCATION OF SALES EFFORT

For each salesman and for the sales force as a whole, there is some optimum frequency of calls on large, medium, and small customers, and on large, medium, and small prospects, that will maximize the profit return per unit of sales effort expended. (Of course, customers may also be classified according to industry, geographical location, and other factors, but for the sake of simplicity let us assume here that volume and profit are the classifications used.)

Allocation of effort based on product profitability is related to allocation of calls by customer sizes or types: to sell more of the high-profit product, more time must be spent with customers who may buy it. If a salesman spends too much time with little customers, he will lose some of the additional potential volume from his key customers. On the other hand, if he calls too much on key customers, he will be trapped by the law of diminishing returns, for there comes a point at which additional calls could more profitably be made to smaller customers or prospective customers. If the salesman neglects prospect calls in favor of present customers, the inevitable attrition among those present customers will cost him future profits.

Except for those people following a rigid call schedule based on account classification and routing, most salesmen do not allocate their time for maximum returns. Selling is often a lonely and discouraging occupation, so it is only human to spend too much time with the friendly customers and easy buyers, while neglecting those psychologically chilling calls on hard-nosed buyers and nonbuying prospects.

Many companies attempt to solve this problem by establishing a standard procedure for classifying accounts into groups, such as A, B, and C, and assigning a call frequency to each group. The procedure itself, however, is usually based on seat-of-the-pants judgment rather than on objective methods of optimizing the allocation of sales effort.

An improvement in this salesmen's input variable usually has a marked effect on product mix, for the sales efforts are more heavily concentrated on prospective users of the more profitable products. Total sales volume and the sales cost ratio may go either up or down, but net profitability will go up.

Intermediate Measures

Many sales managers set up budgets for salesmen's output variables—sales volume by product, and sales costs—but few attempt to establish quantified goals for all of the input variables—number of calls, quality of calls, and allocation of sales effort. Since it is fairly easy to set targets for the number of calls a salesman should make, this is likely to be the only input goal established. Such a practice is extremely frustrating to the conscientious salesman, who rightfully insists that the quality of his calls is at least as important as the sheer number of calls.

Measurements of call quality can be established. They can consist of such indices as the ratio of calls to orders or to long-range purchases, the average order size, the number of different items purchased by each customer ("across-the-board" selling), the ratio of proposals to sales, and many others. And it is relatively easy to set targets for the allocation of sales effort.

Such measurements of the intermediate functions in selling can be highly important in providing prompt feedback to salesmen involved in lengthy or highly technical selling, where the sale itself usually takes place so long after the initial contact that it neither motivates the salesman nor helps him correct his weaknesses on a week-to-week basis.

Deciding on Changes

Once the sales manager can compare his salesmen's present performance with the desired level of input variables, he can determine which of the "Sales manager's control variables" should be adjusted. There are 22 of these. Listed at the left of the flow chart in Exhibit II, these control variables fall into seven categories:

1. The number of salesmen.
2. The selection of salesmen.
3. Training programs of various types.
4. Standard operating procedures.
5. Selling tools (visuals, demonstrators, films, and so on).
6. Information flow to and from salesmen.
7. Motivation, which also includes the practice of incentive compensation.

The colored arrows emerging from each control variable indicate which of the salesmen's input variables it primarily influences. For readers who do not like to trace colored arrows, Part A of *Exhibit III* lists the controls and the variables each affects; Part B works in reverse, showing for each desired behavior change the necessary control changes.

Standard operating procedures divide as follows:

Sales force organization. This category concerns such questions as: Should all salesmen sell all products, or should they be specialists in mar-

EXHIBIT III   Managerial Control and Salesmen's Action

A
Effect of manager's control variables

The manager can make the following decisions:	These actions of the salesman are most affected:	The manager can make the following decisions:	These actions of the salesman are most affected:
Number of salesmen	Number of calls	**Standard operating procedures**	
Selection of salesmen	Call quality, primarily in communications effectiveness and interpersonal relationships	Sales force organization	All three salesmen's input variables
Training		Territory coverage	Number of calls, allocation of sales effort
Territory coverage	Number of calls, allocation of sales effort	Routing	Number of calls
Routing	Number of calls	Call planning	Call quality (message content and communications effectiveness)
Time management	Number of calls, allocation of sales effort	**Sales tools**	
Product knowledge	Call quality (message content)	Time savers (dictating equipment, calculators, etc.)	Number of sales calls
Customer operations	Call quality (message content)	Visual sales aids	Call quality (communications effectiveness)
Sales skills, communications, listening, and group presentations	Call quality (communications effectiveness)	**Information flow**	
Sensitivity programs	Call quality (interpersonal relationships)	Customer order status and industry conditions	Call quality (message content)
Market planning	Allocation of sales effort	**Motivation**	
		Incentive pay, contests, recognition, opportunities for personal growth and promotion, etc.	All three salesmen's input variables

B
Salesmen's input variables affected by control variables

The salesman can take the following actions:	These actions of the manager influence the salesman:	The salesman can take the following actions:	These actions of the manager influence the salesman:
Number of sales calls	Number of salesmen	**Quality of sales calls** continued	
	Training in territory coverage, routing, and time management	b Communications effectiveness	Salesmen selection
	Standard operating procedures for sales force organization, territory coverage, and routing		Training in sales skills, communications, listening, and group presentations
	Tools for time-saving		Standard operating procedures for sales force organization and call planning
	Motivation and compensation		Visual sales aids
Quality of sales calls			
a Message content	Training in product knowledge and customer operations	c Interpersonal relationships	Salesmen selection
	Information flow on customer status, industry trends, and call planning		Sensitivity training
			Motivation and compensation
		Allocation of sales effort	Training in territory coverage, time management, and market planning
			Standard operating procedure for sales force organization and territory coverage
			Motivation and compensation

kets or products? How many salesmen should report to each first-line manager? Should the manager have account responsibilities of his own?

Development of routines. If some part of the salesman's job can be reduced to a standard operating procedure, it is easier and more effective to hand him the procedure than to train him in the skill of designing his own procedure. This approach to productivity is often overlooked.

If, for example, salesmen are required to develop an annual territory marketing plan, it is easier to provide them with a form to fill out than to give them a course in territory planning. Again, it is easier and more effective to establish a standard method of classifying accounts into sales call frequencies than to train salesmen in time allocation.

This approach does not mean that the company is trying to make robots of its salesmen or is ignoring the potential for job enrichment. It does mean that if some aspect of the salesman's function can be routinized, it makes sense to provide the routine and free more of the salesman's time for the creative aspects of his job that cannot be condensed into a procedure.

Power of the First-line Manager

The sales manager has one other control variable at his command. It is unique in that it can either weaken or amplify the effects of changes in the other control variables.

As the flow chart indicates, this multiplier variable is the first-line sales manager. In larger companies this is the district, divisional, or branch manager; in smaller companies it may be the sales manager himself, or even the owner.

Any actions taken to improve call quantity, call quality, or time allocation will not be fully effective unless the first-line manager follows through on them. There are times, in fact, when his operations are the only control variable the sales manager needs in order to fine-tune—when any desired changes in the salesmen's actions can be achieved through the training, supervision, and motivation provided by the first-line sales manager.

A sales manager can upgrade the performance of the field managers by employing any of the variables listed for salesmen; that is, he can provide more managers, he can do a better job of selecting, training, and motivating them, or he can provide them with better procedures, tools, or information.

With some notable exceptions, primarily in the pharmaceutical and packaged consumer goods industries, the importance of first-line sales management tends to be underestimated. Many companies do not give their field managers the necessary training in how to observe, evaluate, and develop the individual salesman. Yet, second only to better sales time allocation, improved field supervision is usually the simplest and fastest way to improve sales force productivity.

Approaching Major Decisions

In using the systems approach to increase sales force productivity, the sales manager works backward through the flow chart, first setting his improvement objectives and then tracing back through the salesmen's output and input variables to determine which control variables should be changed. His analysis will usually suggest the desirability of improving several of the control variables. To determine how much time or money should be invested in improving each control, the manager can ask himself these questions:

- *How important is this variable in affecting the salesmen's input variable I am trying to improve?* If its influence is small, it can be omitted from the productivity improvement plan. A good way to assess the relative importance of the control variables is to assign to each one a weight from 1 to 10. This weight will vary greatly from company to company. Information about previous orders and shipments, for example, would be highly valuable to a salesman making repeat calls to industrial purchasers, but of no value to a one-call, door-to-door sales operation.
- *How well am I handling this control variable now?* Percentage ratings are useful for this answer. For example, is our performance half of what it should be, or 90%? The industrial company mentioned in the previous paragraph might rate its flow of information to the salesman at only 50%, although its weight might be 9 or 10.

The weight is a judgment of the importance of this function in a particular company; the rating is a judgment of how well it is being performed. Although these numbers are not an accurate, objective measurement, they do make it easier to consider a complex array of variables. Whether he realizes it or not, a sales manager goes through a similar mental process in deciding how much of his available funds to spend on sales training, contests, or salary increases.

- *What would it cost to improve the performance of a function?* Here the manager needs to be mindful of the S-shaped curve, which indicates that the better a function is now being handled, the more difficult it is to produce an improvement in it. While it takes a certain amount of effort to raise the rating of a function from 50% to 55%, it might take three times as much effort to raise it from 90% to 95%.

- *How would sales force productivity be affected by the projected improvement in this variable?* This question calls for an estimate of the increase in profit contribution, minus the immediate and continuing costs of the improvement in the control variable.

By using the systems engineer's approach, the sales manager can establish more useful long-term objectives. He can identify the most important changes that must be made to increase sales force productivity. And he can establish interim progress measurements for both himself and his salesmen.

Sales Management in Action

Goals and Objectives of the Sales Function

ONE of the first decision areas with which the sales manager must deal is setting objectives for the sales function. These objectives provide decision criteria for making other decisions related to allocating resources, designing the sales plan, and organizing for implementation. All sales management decisions are, of course, very closely related and in many cases are overlapping and actually inseparable. For example, setting objectives implies that resources will be allocated in such a way as to accomplish the stated objectives. Both types of decisions are based on information about market opportunities and anticipated sales, the sales forecast. For purposes of discussion, however, these decisions along with those involved in developing the sales plan and organization will be considered separately. Setting objectives for the sales function will be discussed in this chapter along with analyzing market opportunities. Forecasting will be treated in Chapter 5 along with sales budgeting, the mechanism for allocating resources and effort.

The Nature and Function of Sales Objectives

WHAT ARE OBJECTIVES AND WHY ARE THEY NEEDED?

Objectives are essentially statements of the desired course of events. What do we want to happen in some specified future time period with regard to some variable or variables? If we want a $50,000 profit from one product in our line for the first quarter of next year, this is an objective. An objective, then, has three facets: (1) a key variable, or variables, within the environment such as profit, sales, expense, or some other important variable; (2) a desired state or level for this variable; and (3) a specified time period.

Since the sales organization is a part of a larger unit, usually a corporation, the objectives for the sales function must be derived from the corporate objectives. In terms of the decision flow presented in Chapter 3, the corporate objectives provide the decision criteria for evaluating alternative sales function objectives. The sales objectives in turn provide decision criteria for other sales management decisions. The sales objectives must be consistent with and support the corporate objectives. The sales manager, to set sales objectives successfully, must understand the corporate objectives, translate them into sales objectives, and then transmit these sales objectives to subordinates in the department.

Well defined objectives for the sales function serve many useful purposes:

1. Direction.   They provide direction for the sales effort by establishing the desired course of events. Sales objectives act as decision criteria for evaluating alternatives in the other sales management decision areas.
2. Coordination.   Clearly stated objectives also help to insure a coordinated sales program. When all decisions are made with a common set of objectives, they tend to have a uniform thrust. Thus, the multitude of diverse decisions related to the sales effort are more likely to form a coherent program if sales objectives are established early in the planning and implementation process.
3. Control.   Finally, sales objectives are an important ingredient in evaluation and control. In order to control the sales function the manager must be able to assess the performance of the sales plan and organization. This requires that actual performance be measured and compared to some standard. Performance standards for evaluating the success or failure of some facet of the operation are derived from the sales objectives.

Although clearly stated objectives have numerous benefits, they can be very frustrating to establish. Different objectives can often be at odds with one another. Rapid growth may not be consistent with short-term profits, for example. When these conflicts arise, the manager must establish priorities: which objectives are most important, and which can be sacrificed to accomplish the others.[1] The criteria for making such a decision must be the corporate objectives. Objectives may also change as the environment changes. The sales manager must be able to adapt to new conditions by altering the department's objectives, its plans, and the organization designed to achieve those objectives. Objectives tend to become obsolete as changes occur in the firm and its environment. Thus, the task of setting objectives is continuous.

CORPORATE OBJECTIVES

Since sales objectives flow from the corporate objectives, the sales manager must understand the goals of the company prior to undertaking the task of developing objectives for his department. Corporate objectives

[1] See Charles H. Goranger, "The Hierarchy of Objectives," *Harvard Business Review*, May–June, 1964, pp. 63–74.

should be based on an analysis of the company's market opportunities (this topic will be discussed in more detail later in the chapter). A careful analysis of market opportunities is also an important input into the development of the sales forecast. To determine the market opportunities for the firm, two areas should be explored: The environment should be examined with attention to market segmentation, demand, channels, the industry, and competition. When combined with an analysis of the corporate philosophy, resources, and other strengths and weaknesses, this understanding of the environment can lead to the identification of market opportunities for the firm. A clear and realistic picture of the firm's market opportunities is basic to setting corporate objectives.

Corporate objectives can be of many different types. Profit, sales volume, market share, growth, and return on investment are a few of the commonly used variables for establishing objectives. A desired sales volume of $200,000 for a given product next year may be a corporate objective. Most corporate objectives can be related to the more general goal of profit. Sales, market share, growth, and so forth, are really subobjectives which need to be accomplished to achieve the desired level of profit. Growth or sales for their own sake would have little meaning. Thus, some acceptable level of profit, given the nature of market opportunities, occupies the top position in the corporate hierarchy of objectives. For nonprofit organizations the delivery of some specific level of service at a certain cost is a typical objective.

Once the corporate objectives have been established, a marketing strategy can be designed to accomplish these objectives. As discussed in Chapter 1, the marketing strategy involves the use of all controllable variables at the disposal of the marketing manager—product, price, distribution, and promotion. The sales effort is a part of this total marketing strategy. A sales forecast can be developed based on the market opportunity analysis and the general market strategy to be used. This sales forecast along with the analysis on which it is based should be considered in formulating sales objectives. (Forecasting will be discussed in the first half of Chapter 5.)

SALES OBJECTIVES

After corporate objectives have been set, the general marketing strategy determined, and the sales forecast made, the sales manager is ready to establish objectives for the sales function. Given the profit orientation of the corporate objectives, the sales objectives must be designed so as to contribute to corporate profitability. This can lead to two basic types of sales objectives, which work together to insure that the company's sales effort contributes to profitability. These are

1. Sales volume and activity objectives
2. Sales productivity objectives

The sales volume and activity objectives can apply to either dollars (or units) or to activities such as sales calls. Productivity implies a relationship between inputs and outputs. Inputs in this context can be reduced to cost and expenses whereas outputs involve sales volume. The sales cost/sales volume ratio is a convenient statement of sales productivity. Several subobjectives can be developed under each of these basic categories. Both volume and productivity objectives will be discussed in more detail in the following sections of the chapter.

After the sales objectives have been set, the sales manager must deal

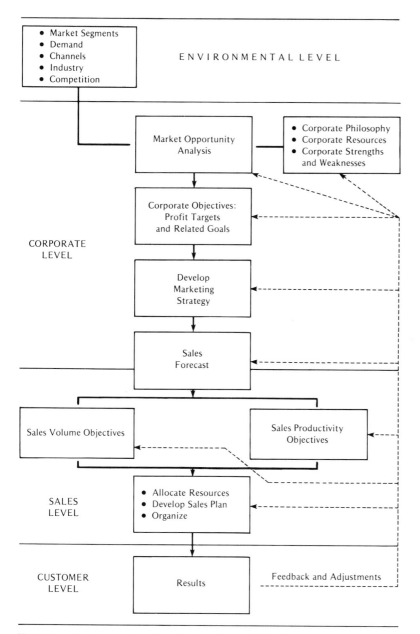

FIGURE 4.1 Inputs for Developing Sales Objectives

with other activities—allocating resources, developing the sales plan, and organizing for implementation—in such a way as to achieve the objectives. The results of the total sales effort is then assessed based on customer response. Results are feedback into the manager's decision making, and adjustments are made where needed. Goals and objectives are vital ingredients for the control of the sales function. This control aspect of sales management is discussed in greater detail in Chapter 11, Evaluating and Supervising the Sales Staff. The flow of inputs into the development of sales objectives is shown in Figure 4.1.

Sales Targets and Quotas

THE NATURE AND PURPOSE OF TARGETS AND QUOTAS

Sales volume and activity objectives are one of the two basic types of sales objectives confronting the sales manager. Targets and quotas provide a concrete statement of this type of objective.

DEFINITION

A sales target as used here is the desired level of sales for a given product or product line in a specified time period. For example, how many onyx bases do we want to sell next quarter? The target can be further subdivided by geographic area and/or customer type. Corporate profit objectives, sales forecast, and marketing strategy must all be considered in establishing these targets. In many instances the sales forecast, as it is formulated, revised, and negotiated between different levels of the company, actually becomes the sales target.

A sales quota can be defined as a "fair share" of the overall sales target allocated to a salesman, territory, or some other segment of the operation.[2] The determination of a "fair share" requires the use of managerial discretion along with a considerable amount of information on past performance, market conditions, and the like.

TYPES OF TARGETS AND QUOTAS

Many different types of targets and quotas are used in different circumstances and for different purposes. Variations between companies are considerable, but most can be classified into four basic categories: sales volume, activities, budget, and combinations. Budget and combined targets and quotas actually move the sales function objectives into the realm of productivity, which will be discussed in the next section.

Sales Volume. Here a desired or expected level of sales is established as a basic objective. This is the most common single form of target or

[2] George Risley, "A Basic Guide to Setting Quotas," *Industrial Marketing,* July, 1961.

quota and is used by a large percentage of all firms. It gives a guide for allocating resources and effort to various segments of the operations as well as evaluating performance.

Activities.   An activity target or quota can use one or a combination of many factors that are related to desired performance. "Such factors include the number of calls made (for sales, service, or missionary work), new or reactivated accounts, prospects, demonstrations, displays secured, progressive steps toward order placement, bids made—and any other units of measurement of activity."[3] This allows for the direction of some resources and effort toward service and other longer range business development. It can also be used to encourage the salesman to do a good job with day-to-day nonselling activities. Quotas of this type also overcome one of the major criticisms of most quota systems; that is, that they place too much stress on short-term sales volume often at the expense of long-term success.

One major shortcoming of activity targets and quotas when they are used alone is that they tend to stress quantity rather than quality of work. Objectives and resulting reward structures are based on inputs rather than output. Thus, activity objectives should be used in combination with others or the sales manager will need to supervise the sales force very closely to insure the quality of its work.

Budgets.   Budget targets and quotas can be used as noted earlier to interject a productivity element into the sales function objectives. Here the emphasis on sales effort is shifted to cost reduction or increasing profits. Two types of budget targets or quotas are commonly used—expenses and profit margin.

Desired levels of certain expenditures may be established as objectives. These levels are typically formalized in a sales budget (to be discussed in Chapter 5). Expense targets and quotas may be either dollar amounts or percentages of sales (a productivity concept). Sales compensation may then be tied in some way to expense reduction (achieving or bettering the budgeted amount). The problem with this approach, if used in isolation, is that it may make the sales person overly cost conscious. If expenses are cut to the point where sales drop and profits decline, the corporate objectives may not be met. Tight expense quotas are most useful and appropriate where the market is saturated and the company has little opportunity to increase its market share.

Another possibility is to set targets and quotas in terms of contributions to profits. This usually results in a compensation system that rewards the sale of high margin products more than those with lower margins. The sales force's efforts may thus be directed into the most profitable product lines.

Although this is the type of sales objective that is most directly related to corporate profitability, it does have many problems. Defining and measuring contribution to profit can be a very difficult task. The complexity

---

[3] *Ibid.*

of this process often leads to a system that is difficult for the sales force to understand. When this occurs, the value of the objectives can easily be lost. This may lead the sales manager to develop a set of targets and quotas relating to the various components of the operation that affect profit. These simpler objectives can be better understood and, when taken together, add up to the desired level of profit. Combination targets and quotas can thus be very desirable.

Combinations. With this approach, targets and quotas are established in two or more different areas. This promotes a balance between sales, activities, and sales force productivity (the cost/volume ratio). By considering both sales volume and the cost incurred to achieve that level of sales, the sales manager had indirectly addressed the corporate profitability objective.

In a combination system, the factors to be used must be determined and the relative importance of each factor weighed. To apply this concept in evaluating salespeople, each person would be evaluated on each factor. Then the attainment on each factor would be multiplied by the weight of that factor. These values would then be summed to determine the relative position of each salesperson.

This can be a reasonably precise but possibly complex system for establishing departmental and individual objectives. Where the sales force is properly oriented, however, it can be a very effective approach.

THE PURPOSE OF TARGETS AND QUOTAS

As noted earlier, sales targets and quotas have several different purposes. First, they provide a basis for planning. The sales plan is designed to accomplish certain things during some future time period. But what? Sales objectives are necessary prior to development of an intelligent sales plan. The sales objectives provide targets at which the sales plan is aimed.

Targets and particularly quotas can also provide incentive to the sales force. When coupled with the compensation system, the quota becomes a basis for rewards and, perhaps, punishment. Thus, quotas can be used to motivate salespeople to channel their efforts in specific directions.

Finally, sales targets and quotas provide a basis for evaluation. They are benchmarks against which actual performance can be compared. This is their most common use. For the sales manager to control the sales operation and make adjustments where needed, variances from the desired course of events must be detected. This requires clearly stated objectives as well as a careful monitoring of actual performance.

LIMITATIONS OF SALES TARGETS AND QUOTAS

Sales targets and quotas have many uses in sales management and can be of considerable value. They do, however, have certain limitations, or problems, which must be overcome to derive maximum benefit.

Given that motivation is one of the purposes of a target or quota, it may not match the actual sales or even the sales forecast. As managerial discretion is exercised in the decisions related to setting targets and quotas, they may be raised or lowered to achieve the desired effect. Thus the targets and quotas may not be accurate sales objectives in all cases, given the varied purposes they serve. Variances from the established objectives should be expected. The important thing is to determine the reasons for the deviations, both favorable and unfavorable, so that corrective action can be taken where needed.

The fact that targets and quotas are not always accurate, or even intended to be accurate, raises the question of fairness. This is a major reason for the controversy over the use of sales quotas in compensation systems. The notion of fairness in this context has two basic components—equity and completeness.[4]

Equity means that divisions or salespeople receive equal treatment in setting their objectives. This does not mean that all targets or quotas are set at the same level because territories, products, and customers are different. Rather, they should all have the same level of difficulty. In a smaller territory, or in one where competition is particularly intense, the quota should be set lower. Salespeople of varying ability, experience, and training may also be given different objectives. The individual circumstances of each situation should dictate the "fair" target or quota.

Completeness refers to the extent to which the stated target or quota accounts for the total range of responsibilities. If a salesperson is expected to perform planning, information gathering, and similar tasks, this must be taken into account in setting objectives. An unrealistically high sales goal may lead to neglect of other duties. Combination targets and quotas can help to overcome this difficulty.

Another potential problem with targets and quotas is lack of acceptance of the sales force or by management. Even if the objectives are accurate and fair, there may be a fear that they will show up a lack of ability or effort. Without objectives for performance standards, no real evaluation can take place. Thus, no one is found lacking. Setting targets and quotas puts added pressure on the sales force and management to perform. To help in overcoming this limitation, both the mechanics and the intent of the objectives should be completely explained to both the sales force and management. Recruiting and selecting personnel who are comfortable in this type of environment is also a key factor in the success of such a system.

DEVELOPING TARGETS AND QUOTAS

Developing targets and quotas can be viewed as a three-step decision sequence as follows: (1) select types, (2) determine the relative importance of each type, and (3) set the level of each type.[5] This flow is illustrated in Figure 4.2. The degree of sales force participation is another important

[4] Thomas R. Wotruba, "A Systematic Approach to Setting Quotas," *Atlanta Economic Review*, April 1972, p. 19.
[5] Thomas R. Wotruba, *Sales Management: Planning, Accomplishment and Evaluation* (New York: Holt, Rinehart and Winston, Inc., 1971), p. 201.

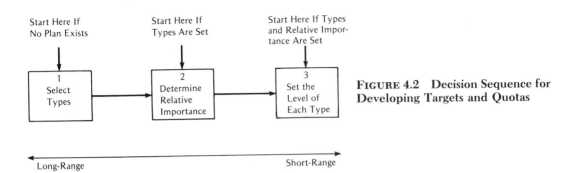

FIGURE 4.2 Decision Sequence for Developing Targets and Quotas

consideration in developing targets and quotas. This will be discussed after the three basic steps have been examined.

Select Types. As previously mentioned, there are several possible types of targets and quotas. These include sales, activities, budgets, and combinations. The first step in developing this sort of sales objective is to decide which types to use. This is a relatively long-range decision that must relate to corporate goals. The basic types of targets and quotas used for developing sales objectives are changed much less frequently than their weights and levels. In selecting the types of targets and quotas to be used the manager should analyze the nature of the sales force and the selling task in the company: How experienced is the sales force? How much detailed control is needed? Are the products all equally profitable or should some get special emphasis? How important is regular service of accounts? Are some expense categories a key to profitability? Such questions as these can help the sales manager in selecting the proper types of targets and quotas.

For example, the manager might select the following set:

Types
Sales volume
New accounts
Calls

Determining the Relative Importance of Each Type. The second step is to establish the relative importance of each type of target or quota. This involves setting a weight for each of the types of targets or quotas to be used. Sales volume might be considered three times as important as calls; thus, its weight would be three times as great. These weights may be varied from one area to another if circumstances differ. In a new territory, for example, call might be given equal weight with sales volume, whereas in an area that is more developed, sales volume could have a much higher weight. The establishment of weights allows the sales manager to direct the sales forces' efforts into the most productive sales activities.

With the types of targets or quotas noted above, we might attach the following weights:

Types	Weights
Sales volume	2
New accounts	1
Calls	1

Setting the Level of Each Type.   Finally, the desired level must be established for each type of target or quota. This tends to be a shorter range decision that is varied much more often than the others. Here the expected or desired level of sales, number of calls, and so forth must be set. Many different bases can be used for setting these levels, depending on the type of target or quota involved. Some possible bases are shown in Table 4.1.

To illustrate the application of a quota plan, suppose that two salespeople have their quota levels set as shown in Table 4.2. The performance of each salesperson can be determined by first computing the percentages of the quota attained. Second, the attained percentage on each quota type is multiplied by its weight. Third, the performance index is found by dividing the sum of the weighted attainment percentages by the sum of the weights. This allows the manager to compare the performance of the two salespeople.

The time period to be used for the target or quota must be established

TABLE 4.1   Bases for Determining Target and Quota Levels

Bases for Sales Volume

1. Previous sales
2. Sales potential
3. Sales forecast

Bases for Activities

1. Characteristics of the territory
2. Salesmen's reports
3. Marketing research

Bases for Budgets

1. Previous financial data
2. Sales budget
3. Profit and other goals

Source: Adapted from Thomas R. Wotruba, *Sales Management: Planning, Accomplishment and Evaluation* (New York: Holt, Rinehart, and Winston, Inc., 1971), p. 213.

TABLE 4.2   Operation of a Sales Quota Plan
Salesperson: Fred Adams

Types	Level	Actual	Percentage Attained	Weight	Weighted Attainment Percentage
Sales volume	$200,000	$180,000	90	2	180
New accounts	10	11	110	1	110
Calls	80	60	75	1	75
				4	365

$$\text{Performance Index} = \frac{365}{4} = 91.25$$

Salesperson: Jill Greenberg

Types	Level	Actual	Percentage Attained	Weight	Weighted Attainment Percentage
Sales volume	$150,000	$150,000	100	2	200
New accounts	8	6	75	1	75
Calls	75	75	100	1	100
				4	375

$$\text{Performance index} = \frac{375}{4} = 93.75$$

with the purposes of the system in mind. It is important to review the system regularly to adjust the levels to account for new circumstances. The basic structure of the plan may also require revisions but typically less frequently than the target and quota levels.

Sales Force Participation.   Another important consideration in the development of sales targets and quotas is the degree to which the sales force should participate. Wortruba and Thurlow investigated the level and impact of sales force participation in quota setting and forecasting in a 1974 survey of members of the Sales and Marketing Executives-International chapters in San Francisco and Los Angeles.[6] Of the responding firms 75 per cent reported the use of quotas and 56 per cent requested that their salespeople submit estimates of what they thought the quota should be. Approximately half of the companies used only sales volume in their quota plan. Others used profits, expenses, and various combinations. Firms that sought sales force participation reported more accurate quota setting than those that did not. The per cent of overestimates versus underestimates in these firms was approximately equal; 75 per cent reported a degree of error of 10 per cent or less. It thus appears that sales force participation increases the accuracy of quota setting as

[6] Thomas R. Wotruba and Michael L. Thurlow, "Sales Force Participation in Quota Setting and Sales Forecasting," *Journal of Marketing*, April 1976, pp. 11–16.

well as forecasting. This is probably true for two basic reasons: First, the salespeople are very familiar with the environment, territory, and customers, giving them a good basis on which to make inputs. Second, the fact that they are allowed to voice an opinion gives them added commitment to the stated quota. Of course, the sales force inputs are only one of the factors to consider in establishing the final quota plan.

Sales Force Productivity

THE COST/VALUE PRODUCTIVITY

Definition. In addition to sales objectives relating to absolute levels (sales volume, number of calls, and so forth) the sales manager must be concerned with sales force productivity. That is, the ratio of sales volume to sales cost. In order for the sales function to contribute to corporate profitability, it must produce the needed level of sales at an acceptable cost.

The concept of productivity has been traditionally applied to manufacturing but to develop sales objectives that truly relate to profits the sales manager must move into this area.[7] Objectives that relate to improved productivity imply some sort of standards against which actual performance can be judged. Most sales managers would never think of applying a stopwatch to the salesperson's work, but cost ratio can be very useful. If used in isolation, the cost ratio can push sales objectives away from profitability, but, when coupled with volume targets, cost ratio can aid in providing a balanced set of objectives. Some sales managers resist objectives of this type owing to a general distaste for productivity standards, lack of staff support, or a lack of information on exactly what the cost ratio for their business should be. Sales force effectiveness as expressed in a cost/volume ratio is sufficiently important, however, that the manager should attempt to deal with these roadblocks.

The major component of sales cost is associated with the compensation and support of the sales force. Thus, as a general proposition, when volume per salesperson goes up the sales cost ratio goes down. This will occur if there are any fixed elements in the sales cost, which is generally the case. Figure 4.3 illustrates this relationship. The ratio could be lowered by either getting more sales volume per salesperson or by shifting the curve down via more efficient management. The perplexing problem for the sales manager is deciding what the cost ratio should be, given the sales target, and, perhaps even more importantly, how can the cost ratio be improved?

Setting Cost/Volume Objectives. There are several different approaches for setting the expenditure on sales effort given the sales targets. These

---

[7] For an excellent discussion of sales force productivity, see William P. Hall, "Improving Sales Force Productivity," *Business Horizons*, August 1975, pp. 32–42.

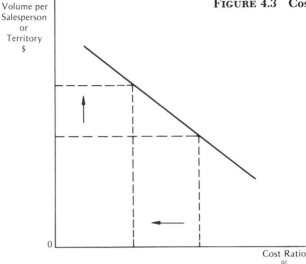

FIGURE 4.3   Cost/Volume Relationship

Volume per Salesperson or Territory $

0

Cost Ratio %

As volume per salesperson or territory goes up, the cost ratio (cost/sales) goes down.

methods can be labeled as historical, available funds, meeting competition, accomplishing objectives, return on investment and incremental.[8] In determining the expenditures for the sales function, management has in effect set the cost ratio objectives (assuming that a sales target has been established) and established the total sales budget.

With the historical approach, the sales expenditures are usually set at the same percentage of sales that occurred last year. If last year's selling cost was 5 per cent of sales and this year's sales target is $500,000, then $25,000 is set as the new selling expense target. This approach simply accepts past performance as the new cost ratio objective. Historical performance can be a useful guide if management is satisfied with the sales productivity, but the logic here is weak. In this approach sales expenditures are based on sales volume. In fact, sales effort helps to create the volume; thus, there is something of a cause-effect reversal.

With the available funds approach, all funds left after other costs are covered is devoted to sales. This residual method gives no consideration to the objectives in terms of volume and is generally a poor approach.

The sales cost/volume objective might be established by looking at competition. Sales management might assume that, if the firm's percentage selling cost and resulting budget is equal to competition, it will do equally well in the marketplace. This is not necessarily the case. Every sales cost dollar does not produce equivalent results. Financial strength also varies from company to company. The competitive parity approach does have merit, however, in that sales productivity is affected by competition. Industry practices should be considered in setting cost ratio targets. Information on such averages is another matter. It may

[8] All but the last of these approaches, as they are applied to advertising budgeting, were discussed by Joel Deal, "How Much to Spend on Advertising," *Harvard Business Review*, January-February 1951, pp. 65–74.

be possible to gain much information from trade associations, industry studies, or government studies, but this type of information is usually very difficult to find.

The three approaches mentioned so far have the common fault of failing to take into account the sales volume objectives and the level of effort needed to accomplish that volume. Given that conditions are variable from one situation to another, the level of expenditures needed to achieve the desired level of sales cannot be expected to be the same in all instances. Certain tasks must be accomplished in order to reach the sales and profit targets. Thus, one approach to arriving at a cost ratio target is to analyze the nature of the tasks that must be performed and budget the funds needed to carry out those tasks. So long as the tasks are related to the sales and profit targets, the cost ratio should be justified. This approach allows for variations in the cost target based on competitive conditions, the level of expertise in the sales force, and other important variables. It is also a pragmatic approach that can be readily applied in actual situations. As such, it is typically the most desirable approach.

Two methods that produce theoretically accurate cost ratios, but prove difficult to apply, are the return on investment and the incremental approaches. With the return on investment approach, the allocation of funds to the selling function would be based on the profit returned from that use versus the profit derived from alternative uses of the funds. This concept is a longer run approach to sales budgeting. Its major problem is the lack of information or inability to calculate the return on invested dollars in sales.

The incremental method would allocate funds to the selling effort until the marginal cost is equal to the marginal revenue. This would insure that the selling expenditures contribute to maximizing the firm's profitability. Again, however, the lack of information problem makes the approach difficult if not impossible to apply.

Several factors should be kept in mind when attempting to establish cost/volume ratio targets irrespective of the basic approach to be used.[9]

1. Inflation will shift the sales volume/cost ratio curve to the right. This means that the volume per salesperson must rise with inflation in order to maintain the same cost ratio.
2. The cost ratio will vary from industry to industry. The cost ratio in steel is much lower than in shoes, for example. Very few studies exist that give industry data on the cost ratio, but trade association data, conversations with business acquaintances, and a general knowledge of the industry should provide some insights. One study of plumbing distributors by the American Supply Association showed a 3 per cent average ratio for that industry. In other industries ratios of 10 per cent or more would not be unusual.
3. The cost ratio represents only half of the profitability picture. Volume must also be considered in assessing the sales functions contributions to the corporate objectives. Thus the sales manager must keep a bal-

[9] Hall, *op. cit.*, pp. 35–36.

anced perspective between increasing volume and reducing cost as the department's objectives are formulated.

4. Finally, the compensation plan significantly affects the cost ratio. A straight salary plan allows this fixed cost to be spread over more sales dollars as the volume rises, thus lowering the cost ratio. With a straight commission system, the sales compensation may rise in proportion to sales volume leaving the cost ratio the same as volume shifts. There are numerous considerations in selecting a compensation plan that will be discussed in Chapter 8, but significant cost ratio reductions are very difficult under a commission plan.

In attempting to improve sales force productivity the sales manager is faced with many problems: costs are rising due to inflation, market and marketing institutions are changing, the number of products carried by a firm are increasing, and competition is becoming more intense. The sales environment is becoming increasingly complex. This has led to considerable differences in sales force productivity even within the same industry. Many opportunities for improvement exist. The sales manager should attempt to set realistic cost ratio targets and then strive to find ways to achieve those objectives.

OPPORTUNITIES FOR IMPROVED PRODUCTIVITY

The Sales Audit.   After cost ratio targets have been established, the sales manager should attempt to locate opportunities for improved productivity. As these opportunities are located they may become subobjectives for the department. A careful analysis of the sales operation is needed as a basis for locating opportunities to improve. Such an analysis can be called a sales audit. Hall has outlined the major phases of a sales audit as follows:

Marketing Profile.   This phase involves identifying company objectives, strategies, market position, sales organization, territorial coverage, sales results, costs, and profit results. It establishes the basic framework within which improvement opportunities can be identified.

Definition of Selling Function.   This step identifies the major functional components of the field sales job in terms of current practices versus both management objectives and market requirements. The components of the job may include planning, travel, waiting, face-to-face selling, service, and paper work.

Evaluation of Effectiveness.   Somewhat different from how a salesman is spending his time is the question of his effectiveness, again relative to company objectives, market requirements, and competitive activists.

Analysis of Territory Configuration and Coverage.   This step is concerned with the nature and rationale for the current sales territories in terms of geographical configurations, sales potentials, sales goals, and workload (time available and calls made).

Review of Information System.   It is important to determine whether information is adequate and timely to serve sales managements and permit performance measurement.

Evaluation of Sales Management.   This phase calls for an evaluation of the field sales organization structure (including direct selling, supervisory, and support personnel), an appraisal of the effectiveness of personnel, and an indication as to whether the compensation plans at all levels of the sales force are supportive of management objectives and strategies.

Ranking of Improvement Opportunities.   As the result of the previous six analyses, a number of improvement opportunities are typically identified. Because, in our experience, a smorgasboard of ideas evolves, it becomes critical to rank the opportunities in terms of importance and pay-off potential. Without setting priorities, the effort can degenerate into an exercise in fighting brush fires.

Development of an Implementation Program.   The final step is to create a work plan calling for specific action within each top priority area, identifying program responsibilities, establishing time schedules, and setting up monitoring procedures.[10]

Ways to Improve Sales Force Productivity.   Many different types of improvement opportunities may come out of the sales audit. Some of the more typical can be grouped under the headings of better time management, sales force specialization, and improved analysis and planning.

The sales audit may reveal that the salespeople are using their time in inefficient ways. Routing and scheduling of sales calls may need to be improved. The sales force may need to put more time on larger accounts, for example. The sales manager can encourage improved time management via supervision or modifications in the compensation and quota plans.

Another common area for improving productivity is by specializing the sales force in narrower responsibility areas. The sales force might be specialized by customer type, products and so forth. Another possibility is to separate new account development from servicing existing accounts. This type of job specialization allows the salesperson to concentrate on a narrower set of duties and thus become more efficient in carrying out the assigned tasks.

One final area where most firms find room for improvement is in the analysis and planning done by the sales management itself. To develop sales plans that encourage sales productivity, the manager needs accurate and timely information and a well-conceived planning process. Information on profitability by product line may not be available, for example. By producing this information, the sales manager can better plan the use of sales resources to concentrate on more profitable lines.

Once these opportunities for improved productivity and for increased volume have been identified, they become a vital link between the sales objectives and the other decisions made to accomplish those objectives. The opportunity statements give more precise direction as to how the sales manager can work to accomplish the sales objectives. This discussion has centered on opportunities for improving sales productivity (the cost ratio). Now, let us turn to identifying opportunities for improved sales volume.

---

[10] Hall, *op. cit.,* p. 41.

Analyzing Market Opportunities

In addition to the general sales volume targets, the sales manager should establish subobjectives that, if accomplished, will move the organization toward the volume targets. These subobjectives generally relate to specific actions directed at selected parts of the market. In order to locate opportunities for increased sales, the manager needs to analyze the market. Such an analysis should be conducted with a specific product and geographic area in mind. For example, a sales manager for a rubber company may be looking for opportunities to increase tire sales in the western region. Note that a market analysis may provide a basis for setting volume targets and the interrelated sales forecasting effort in addition to isolating targets of opportunity for increasing volume.

LOCATING OPPORTUNITIES FOR INCREASED SALES

Woodruff has pointed out that market opporutnities for a given product within a given geographic area depend upon (1) the size of the market, (2) the marketing program requirements to satisfy the market wants, and (3) the extent and quality of service to the market by other firms.[11] A fourth factor might be added to the list: (4) the ability of the organization to meet the expectations of the market. By analyzing these four factors, the sales manager may be able to find groups within the market that can be induced to purchase more of the firm's products or services. To aid in this analysis and thus in locating opportunities for increased sales, the manager can follow the sequence of steps presented in Figure 4.4.

The process should start with an estimate of the size of the market for the product of interest in a particular sales territory. How many buyers are there and how much do they buy?—remembering that a buyer must be both able and willing to purchase the product. This estimate of market potential will give the manager an indication of whether the market is sufficiently large to provide significant opportunities. If the market does have adequate potential, the second step is to identify market segments that might become targets for the firm.

Segmentation is typically designed to discover the subgroups within the market that have different wants or needs in terms of the product or service in question. In estimating the market potential, the total number of computer buyers and their total needs may have been determined. But does every buyer want exactly the same computer and service? Subgroups may exist within the market that cannot be served with the same market offering. Segmentation is aimed at identifying groups or segments of customers who have similar wants and needs within the segment but whose needs are different from other segments. For example, an industrial equipment supplier might find it logical to subdivide the market by industry. The transportation industry, steel industry, and petroleum industry

[11] Robert B. Woodruff, "A Systematic Approach to Market Opportunity Analysis," *Business Horizons*, August 1976, p. 57.

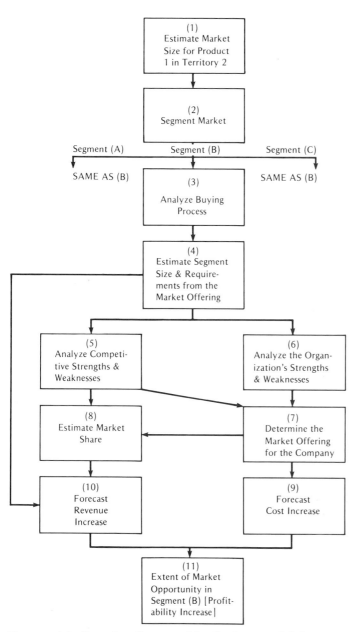

FIGURE 4.4   Locating Opportunities for Increased Sales

might be considered separate market segments because they have similar needs within each industry, but the needs and expectations are different from one industry to another. This segmentation allows the manager to tailor the market offering to selected target groups. Note that a target segment may include current customers who are not presently buying all of their needs from our firm.

In addition to identifying subgroups with similar needs, the manager should analyze the buying behavior of each segment. How do they buy, from whom, in what quantitites, and what factors influence the purchase decision? For example, how important is price relative to service in the selection of a supplier?

The next step is to estimate the size of each segment and its requirements from the market offering. That is, what does each expect in terms of product, service, price, delivery, and so forth? After the manager has determined what the buyers in a particular market segment expect, the abilities of a particular firm versus competition to satisfy the demand can be compared. This requires an analysis of the manager's firm and of competing organizations. Relative to competition, how well are they meeting the expectations of various market segments? To determine this, we may start with the industry and work down to the individual competitors: What are their strengths and weaknesses? What segments are they appealing to? How are they marketing to each segment? By answering such questions as these, the manager can begin to identify segments where the firm can attract sales from competition.

By matching the company's capabilities with the expectations of the market, the manager can begin to determine the most effective market offering for the company. This market offering (or program) in comparison to that of competition would then determine the market share the company could expect. Such considerations as the channels of distribution needed to service the market are important in this regard. Do effective channels exist for serving a given market segment and if so, who controls them? In order to have a viable market opportunity, the firm has to have access to channels needed to service the market. The type of market offering that the company establishes would also set the cost of the program.

With an estimate of the segment's size and the company's market share, the manager is now able to estimate revenue—market size multiplied by the market share. Finally, by subtracting cost from revenue, the profitability of attacking a particular segment is established. If the profit increase is sufficiently large to justify any needed investments, a market opportunity has been identified. The opportunity may relate to some new market segment or to an increase in sales in a segment currently served. In either case, the responsibility for locating opportunities for increasing sales profitability often falls on the sales manager.

USES OF THE MARKET OPPORTUNITY ANALYSIS

The market opportunity analysis has several different applications. It can provide information for setting sales objectives and for developing the marketing strategy as well as the sales plan. It also helps the sales manager in locating specific targets where sales may be increased and provides direction in accomplishing this increase. Finally, the market opportunity analysis is basic to and interrelated with sales forecasting. Understanding the market is essential for developing accurate forecasts, and market potential estimates are actually a part of the market analysis. Thus, these two analytical tasks usually overlap and are both designed to produce the information needed to make sound sales management decisions.

Summary

Setting objectives for the sales function is one of the first decision areas that faces the sales manager. In addressing this task, the manager must keep in mind the corporate objectives. Sales objectives should flow from the corporate objectives, which typically relate to profitability. In order to design a set of sales objectives that address corporate profits, two areas should be included. One area relates to volume or activity levels and the other to sales productivity.

Sales targets and quotas should be established in the three-step decision sequence: (1) select types, that is, volume, activities, budget, or combination; (2) determine the relative importance; and (3) set the level of each type. The sales forecast can be an important input into setting the sales volume target.

Sales productivity refers to the cost/volume ratio. The target cost per dollar of sales can be set in several different ways. The objective/task method is probably the best of the pragmatic approaches. The sales audit is one way to discover opportunities for improving sales force productivity.

Opportunities for increasing sales volume may be discovered via market opportunity analysis. This type of analysis investigates (1) the size of the market, (2) the marketing program requirements to satisfy the market wants, (3) the extent and quality of service to the market by other firms and (4) the ability of our firm to meet the expectations of the market. The information produced is helpful in setting subobjectives for the basic volume target, in designing the sales forecast.

Discussion Questions

1. Why does the sales manager need to be concerned with setting sales objectives?

2. Discuss the basic types of sales objectives.

3. Outline the procedure for establishing sales targets and quotas.

4. Should the sales force participate in the setting of sales quotas? Why or why not?

5. Why is it important to establish cost ratio targets?

6. Discuss the basic approaches to setting the cost ratio.

7. What is the function of a sales audit and how should such an audit be conducted?

8. What factors determine a firm's market opportunities?

9. How can the results of a market opportunity analysis be of use to the sales manager?

10. In what way is the sales forecast related to setting sales objectives?

Selected References

HALL, WILLIAM P., "Improving Sales Force Productivity," *Business Horizons*, August 1975, pp. 32–42.

JACKSON, DONALD W., JR. and RAMON J. ALDAG, "Managing the Sales Force by Objectives," *MSU Business Topics*, Spring 1974, pp. 53–59.

WINER, LEON, "The Effect of Product Sales Quotas on Sales Force Productivity," *Journal of Marketing Research*, May 1973, pp. 180–183.

WOODRUFF, ROBERT B., "A Systematic Approach to Marketing Opportunity Analyses," *Business Horizons*, August 1976, pp. 55–65.

WOTRUBA, THOMAS R., "A Systematic Approach for Setting Effective Quotas," *Atlanta Economic Review*, April 1972, pp. 18–20.

CASE 4.1
Russell Oil Company*

Company Background

Russell Oil Company was founded in 1950 in Texas as a small refiner of crude oil. Several years later, Russell began retailing their product and eventually opened their own service stations in the western United States. The marketing strategy of Russell was to franchise its operations, with selected dealers investing approximately $15,000 to become a Russell dealer.

The expansion of self-service operations had enabled Russell to grow rapidly, as consumers began preferring lower prices rather than full service. Russell had been one of the first to offer self-service in California and had become known as the market leader in offering low prices to the public. However, most Russell outlets had full-service islands as well as self-service facilities. This arrangement was well liked by the dealers,

* Case prepared by Thomas N. Ingram and Danny N. Bellenger, Georgia State University.

128 *Sales Management in Action*

who benefited from increased gasoline volume from self-service and the tire, battery, and accessory sales from full-service operations.

The Los Angeles market had been an extremely good market for Russell since the mid-1960s. In the metropolitan area, Russell operated 75 service stations, all of them offering full and self-service. There were four retail sales representatives covering the Los Angeles area, all of whom reported to Dick Fisher, the Area Sales Supervisor.

The Russell sales representatives had a wide range of job activities. They were involved in every part of the retail operation including dealer recruiting, sales promotion, training, and business counseling for their dealers (see Exhibit 1, Sales Representatives' Objectives). In addition, the Russell representatives were responsible for sales to their dealers of the following products: (1) gasoline, (2) motor oil, (3) tires, (4) batteries, and (5) automotive accessories.

In the past, Russell had easily attracted potential dealers, since the profit from a Russell operation averaged approximately $20,000 per year. However, a major oil company had increased their recruiting activities in Los Angeles in the past year, with Russell being adversely affected.

The strategy of the major oil company was to recruit experienced dealers by offering a guaranteed income of $20,000 per year—without investment. The recruited dealers then became managers for company-owned service stations. As company employees, the dealers were covered by group insurance and other free benefits they would have had to pay for if they had remained independent franchise dealers.

Within the past 6 months, Russell had lost eight of its top dealers to the major oil company. Four of the eight had been replaced, but two of these dealers were not meeting expectations.

Dick Fisher had been frustrated by the empty service stations and the unsuccessful attempts to find good dealers. He realized that the market had grown more competitive and the risk on the part of a new dealer had increased as a result.

Fisher had been discussing the subject of closed service stations with his sales representatives on a weekly basis for the past 3 months, but the results he had expected had not been forthcoming. The sales representatives were spending valuable time each day trying to recruit new dealers, but had not firm prospects. According to the sales representatives, the guaranteed income plan of the major oil company was attracting most of the potential dealers in the Los Angeles area.

It was Monday morning and the words of Ray Lunceford, Area Marketing Manager, were still ringing in Dick Fisher's ears. Ray had told Fisher, "Dick, I don't know what the problem is, but I do know that you will not meet your sales quotas if you don't get those four stations open immediately. You have got to make something happen, and soon!"

Fisher decided to try a different approach. He sent each of his sales representatives a copy of the attached letter expressing his views on the subject (see Exhibit 2). All of the letters said the same thing, since each of the sales representatives had a closed station in their territory.

EXHIBIT 1   Sales Representative's Objectives, pp. 130–136.

Name   W. Miller   BUSINESS AREA: Retail

Objective: Achieve budgeted sales quotas by product line and overall

total.

Details: Achievement measured by monthly and year-to-date computer print-

outs.

Results: Mid Year				Results: Year End
Product	Quota	Sales	%	
Gasoline	$525,000	$540,750	103%	
Motor Oil	15,000	12,000	80%	
Tires	20,000	22,000	110%	
Batteries	5,000	1,500	30%	
Accessories	5,000	6,100	122%	
Total	$570,000	$582,350	102%	

Objective: Achieve quota in all sales promotions.

Details: Spring TBA promotion planned for month of March. Fall tire

promotion planned for month of October.

Results: Mid Year	Results: Year End
Spring TBA program—finished at 92%	
of quota—4th in the area.	

Objective: Conduct a comprehensive dealer training session on TBA sales.

Details: Session to be conducted prior to spring TBA sales promotion.

Results: Mid Year	Results: Year End
Program completed February 15.	

Objective: Actively recruit dealers as needed.

Details: Keep all stations open at all times.

Results: Mid Year	Results: Year End
Has had one closed station during every month this year.	

NAME: G. Mizell   BUSINESS AREA: Retail

Objective: Achieve budgeted sales by product line and overall total.

Details: Achievement measured by monthly and year-to-date computer print-outs.

Results: Mid Year				Results: Year End
Product	Quota	Sales	%	
Gasoline	$440,000	$395,000	90%	
Motor Oil	9,000	10,000	111%	
Tires	14,000	15,000	107%	
Batteries	5,000	7,500	150%	
Accessories	5,000	6,200	124%	
Total	$473,000	$433,700	92%	

Objective: Achieve quota in all sales promotions.

Details: Spring TBA promotion planned for month of March.

Results: Mid Year	Results: Year End
Spring TBA program. 125% of quota. Number one of four representatives.	

Objective: Conduct a comprehensive dealer training session on TBA sales.

Details: Session to be conducted prior to spring TBA sales promotion.

Results: Mid Year	Results: Year End
Program completed March 1.	

Objective: Actively recruit dealers as needed.

Details: Keep all stations open at all times.

Results: Mid Year	Results: Year End
Has had one closed station this year—	
it has been closed 45 days.	

Objective: Attend Retail Business Counseling training session.

Details: Session to be held February 1–10.

Results: Mid Year	Results: Year End
Session was completed.	

Objective: _____

Details: _____
_____
_____
_____

Results: Mid Year	Results: Year End

NAME: _____R. Todd_____ BUSINESS AREA: ___Retail___

Objective: Achieve budgeted sales quotas by product line and overall total.

Details: Achievement measured by monthly and year-to-date computer

print-outs.

Results: Mid Year

Product	Quota	Sales	%
Gasoline	$500,000	$530,000	106%
Motor Oil	20,000	16,000	80%
Tires	12,000	11,000	92%
Batteries	5,000	5,100	102%
Accessories	5,000	4,400	88%
Total	$542,000	$566,500	105%

Results: Year End

Objective: Achieve quota in all sales promotions.

Details: Spring TBA promotion planned for month of March. Fall tire

promotion planned for month of October.

Results: Mid Year	Results: Year End
Spring TBA program—101% of quota—	
finished third among the four sales	
representatives.	

Objective: Conduct a comprehensive dealer training session on TBA sales.

Details: Session to be held prior to spring TBA sales Promotion.

Results: Mid Year	Results: Year End
Program completed February 25.	

Objective: Complete a market analysis with emphasis on competitive activity.

Details: Target completion date December 1.

Results: Mid Year	Results: Year End
Not applicable.	

Objective: Actively recruit dealers as needed.

Details: Keep all stations open at all times.

Results: Mid Year	Results: Year End
Now has one closed station. Also had another closed station earlier in the year that took thirty days to reopen.	

NAME: E. Stewart   BUSINESS AREA: Retail

Objective: Achieve budgeted sales by product line and overall total.

Details: Achievement measured by monthly and year-to-date computer

print-outs.

Results: Mid Year				Results: Year End		
Product	Quota	Sales	%	Quota	Sales	%
Gasoline	$600,000	$580,000	97%	$600,000		
Motor Oil	22,000	25,000	114%	22,000		
Tires	15,000	14,000	93%	15,000		
Batteries	10,000	12,000	120%	10,000		
Accessories	5,000	5,200	104%	5,000		
Total	$652,000	$636,200	98%	$652,000		

Objective: Achieve quota in all sales promotions.

Details: Spring TBA promotion planned for month of March.

               Fall tire promotion planned for month of October.

Results: Mid Year	Results: Year End
Finished TBA program at 104% of quota—	
Number two of four sales representatives.	

Objective: Conduct a comprehensive dealer training session on TBA sales.

Details: Session to be conducted prior to spring TBA promotion.

Results: Mid Year	Results: Year End
Completed February 15.	

Objective: <u>Actively recruit dealers as needed.</u>

Details: _____

_____

Results: Mid Year	Results: Year End
Has had one closed station so far this	
year. It has been closed 60 days.	

Exhibit 2   Russell Oil Company

SUBJECT: Closed Service Stations

Mr. R. Todd:

As you are aware, we are in a serious position on closed service stations. As of this date, this is how we stand:

Station	Representative	Comments	
2122	Todd	Closed 90 days. Outlook—Poor.	*No Firm Prospects.*
0342	Miller	Closed 30 days. Outlook—Poor.	*No Firm Prospects.*
7988	Stewart	Closed 60 days. Outlook—Poor.	*No Firm Prospects.*
8064	Mizell	Closed 45 days. Outlook—Poor.	*No Firm Prospects.*

Sad review, isn't it? Over seven months of lost volume and TBA sales. At 35,000 gallons per store, we missed almost 250,000 gallons of gasoline. On gasoline alone, we lost over $15,000 in profit. Serious, wouldn't you say?

Be advised that between now and August 30, each one of us will concentrate our efforts to daily recruit and secure qualified people to enter our closed stations. The August 30th date is your personal deadline to have your territory clean of these problems. Failure to accomplish this goal will result in a complete review of your daily effort and personal approach to this very serious situation.

I have heard the phrase "fails to make things happen" used in many situations—none of them good. I am dedicated to the fact that my area will not be branded with this tag. No matter what it takes, I am committed to one goal—making things happen in a positive sense.

Your ability to anticipate and handle these kinds of problems will be weighed heavily. in reviewing performance appraisals and will reap considerable benefits if handled correctly.

I suggest you continue or set up a daily recuriting effort to insure your personal compliance with the August 30th deadline. Don't wait until the last minute—it will be too late!

Richard C. Fisher
Area Sales Supervisor

As he was reading over the letter, Fisher thought to himself, "If this doesn't get some action, I don't know what will!"

CASE 4.2
Hart International*

Mr. Green, Vice President for Sales with Hart International, was disturbed. He'd tried just about everything he could think of but to no avail. James Martin's sales unit was still far below their performance goals.

    When James had first hired on, he'd been the real hotshot. His ambitions and hard work were eventually rewarded with a promotion.

    James reported directly to Mr. Green, who felt they'd always been able to talk easily about performance goals and their attainment. As a matter of fact, it had been James' idea to set specific sales goals for his group. The goals were expressed in terms of volume, new accounts, market share, and direct selling cost/dollar of sales.

    Mr. Green and James had quickly agreed on the original goals they had jointly set for the unit; they were, consequently, surprised when the unit failed to meet the goals. After reevaluating the group and the goals, they revised the sales goals downward slightly. Even though they both felt that the first target figures were completely reasonable, they were willing to try again for lower targets.

    James had just left Mr. Green's office after a discussion of the latest figures for his unit. Not only were the lower goals still not being met, but results were lower than *last* month!

Company Background

After having stared in disbelief at the figures, James obviously was more than a little upset.

    "I've done everything I can to get my people on the ball . . . I've threatened them, I've hollered at them, I've even tried giving time off to the ones who work best! It's not me to mollycoddle and pamper people . . . what counts is how well they do their jobs and how willing they are to work. The real workers I don't mind, but you know *those* people—they just basically don't want to work."

    Mr. Green mulled over for some time what James had said, then thoughtfully looked over an action request from industrial relations staff. James' unit compared quite unfavorably with the other units in number of grievances filed, rate of absenteeism, and turnover rate, as well as in sales results.

Current Situation

* Adapted from Robert M. Fulmer and Theodore T. Herbert, *Exploring the New Management* (New York: Macmillan Publishing Co., Inc., 1974), pp. 69–70. Used with permission.

Mr. Green wondered if James' slip about the minority group workers (who comprised a large majority of the unit) meant anything, or perhaps if the targets themselves had anything to do with the unit's record. He had to make some changes to get the unit back on target.

Student Learning Exercise /4
Selecting Goals for the Sales Force

Objective   To analyze the various options available for evaluating a sales force's performance as to the strengths and weaknesses inherent in each.

Overview   Presented in this exercise are several methods by which a sales force can be evaluated. The appropriateness of each is determined in large part by the organization itself and its goals.

Exercise   Assume that you are the sales manager for a company that has previously evaluated its sales force solely on their dollar sales volume compared to their quota. You suspect that better methods could be used in evaluating your individual salespeople and have developed a list of other methods. Discuss the strengths and weaknesses of each of the following evaluative criteria and suggest any other techniques that might be of value.

Possible Techniques   Dollar sales volume
Number of new accounts
Number of lost accounts
Amount over or under expense account budget
Average number of sales calls per week
Average number of hours spent in office per week
Average number of hours spent in field per week

Allocating Effort and Resources:

Forecasting and Budgeting

A S indicated in Chapter 4, setting objectives and allocating effort and resources to accomplish those objectives are very closely related tasks. The allocation of efforts and resources should flow directly from the stated objectives for the sales function. This allocation is ultimately resolved into a sales budget that in turn, aids in the development of a sales plan. Sales objectives and the resources available to achieve the objectives provide parameters and constraints within which the plan must be developed.

Accurate and timely sales forecasts are needed for both setting objectives and for devising realistic budgets. The first part of this chapter will be devoted to a discussion of forecasting techniques. The development of sales budgets will be discussed later in the chapter.

Forecasting

TYPES OF FORECASTS

Several different types of forecasts are relevant in sales management decision making. One important division is into market potential, company sales potential, and company sales forecasts.[1] **Market potential** is the total possible sales of the product or service in question by the entire industry. **Company sales potential** refers to the total possible sales for a given company, whereas the **company sales forecast** is the realistic estimate of actual sales in dollars or units that the company expects to achieve in some future time period under proposed marketing plans and in the anticipated external environment. Company potential and forecasts will be below the market potential, given any competition, and the company forecast may be below the company sales potential. Lack of resources,

---

[1] Richard R. Still, Edward W. Cundiff, and Norman A. P. Govoni, *Sales Management: Decision, Policies, and Cases,* 3rd ed. (Englewood Cliffs, N. J.: Prentice-Hall, Inc., 1976), pp. 18–19.

economic uncertainty, and so forth may keep a company from reaching its potential.

Measuring market potential requires that the market be clearly defined and that the buying behavior of the market be clearly understood. Appropriate forecasting methods can then be selected and the forecast developed. The methods selected at this level usually involve the projection of historical trends or the selection of market factors closely related with demand. For example, the *Sales and Marketing Management Buying Power Index,* which combines effective buying income, retail sales, and population into a single index, is a very useful grouping of market factors for forecasting the market potential of several consumer goods. After the market potential is established, the company sales potential and forecast may be derived by establishing probable market share relationships.

Note that the flow in developing forecasts may run from either the top down or from the bottom up. The top down approach starts with the market potential and then derives the forecasts for various subdivisions. With the bottom up approach, forecasts for various segments are made first and then combined to form a composite. Different situations may call for different approaches. The type and accuracy of information available should be a key consideration in the selection of approach.

In addition to the industry versus company specific dimension, forecasts have a number of other levels that must be considered. A forecast may be needed for some specific time period in the immediate future: a quarter or an entire year, typically. These may be called short-run forecasts. Projections that extend beyond the immediate future for 3, 5, or 10 years may be called long-run forecasts. Each type presents different problems for the manager and may require different methods. Geographic, customer type, and product considerations, as discussed in Chapter 3, also affect the nature of the forecasting task. Figure 5.1 presents

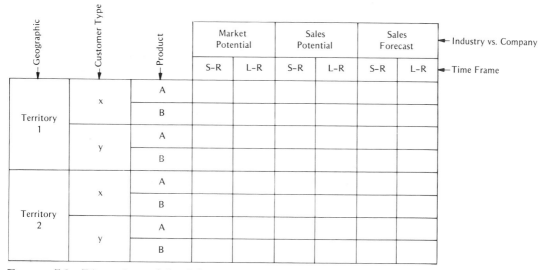

FIGURE 5.1   Dimensions of the Sales Forecast

a summary of the dimensions that must be considered in planning and developing a forecast. Any given forecast would apply to a specific time period, geographic area, customer type, product or product line, and to either the industry or a given company. Knowing the dimensions of the desired forecast is the start for forecasting.

After the dimensions of the forecast have been established, the problem of forecasting tends to center on the methods to be employed. A major task in forecasting is to determine the appropriate method given the dimensions and environment of the forecast.

FORECASTING METHODS[2]

Forecasting methods have been classified in a number of ways by various authorities. One, for example, explains that "There are two main approaches in forecasting: . . . (1) non-causal methods; and (2) causal analysis."[3] The former involves analyzing historical data in order to project its pattern of movement through time. The latter involves an analysis of the factor to be forecasted as well as factors that are causally related in an attempt to define that relationship. Using the defined relationship, the factor is forecast for future time periods.

Although it is useful to consider the causal and noncausal nature of certain methods, another important classification distinguishes between "objective" and "subjective" forecasting methods. According to Bolt, "Objective forecasts tend to be of a statistical/ mathematical nature and subjective forecasts tend to be intuitive, based on the application of experience, intelligence and judgement."[4] Since the two classifications just discussed are not mutually exclusive, a third one is particularly useful for our limited discussion. In this approach:

We have grouped the techniques into three basic categories: (1) judgemental techniques; (2) time-series analysis and projection; and (3) causal models. The first category uses qualitative data (e.g., expert opinions) and information about special events, and may or may not take the past into consideration. The second focuses entirely on patterns and pattern changes and, thus relies entirely on historical data. The third uses highly refined and specific information about relationships between system elements. It is powerful to take special events formally into account, and it also uses the past as an important input.[5]

It is not possible to discuss all of the forecasting techniques in this single section. Rather, some of the more commonly used techniques are discussed and compared.

[2] This section was adapted from Danny N. Bellenger and Barnett A. Greenberg, *Marketing Research: A Management Information Approach* (Homewood, Ill.: Richard D. Irwin, Inc., 1978), Chapters 9 and 11.

[3] Vernon G. Lippitt, *Statistical Sales Forecasting* (New York: Financial Executives Research Foundation, 1969), p. 25.

[4] Gordon J. Bolt, *Market and Sales Forecasting—A Total Approach* (New York: Halsted Press, 1972), p. 179.

[5] John C. Chambers, Satinder Mullick and Donald D. Smith, *An Executives Guide to Forecasting* (New York: John Wiley and Sons, Inc., 1974), p. 42.

Jury of Executive Opinion.   The most common judgemental or subjective technique used in forecasting is the "jury of executive opinion." As the name implies, this technique involves gathering a panel of experienced executives who work together to develop a forecast or the basis for forecasting. The disadvantages of this technique are obvious. It is not scientific and relies solely on individual opinion. Less obvious, but perhaps more important, are the advantages of the jury or panel approach.

If properly conducted, the jury of executive opinion can take advantage of the observations and experience of talented executives. It is not correct to assume that this method is devoid of historical trends or anticipations of the future. The executive's ability to assimilate past experience and a knowledge of a dynamic environment in which the market operates are vital assets in this process.

Forecasts derived from the executive panel tend to decrease in quality with the passage of time. That is, they are most accurate for the short term and least accurate for the long term. Finally, the jury approach offers the advantage of a forecast which can be developed in a relatively short period of time.

Delphi Technique.   A more structured method for utilizing executive opinion employs the Delphi technique.[6] The Delphi technique is a procedure originally developed by the RAND Corporation for obtaining a greater consensus of opinion among experts about a matter not subject to precise quantification without face-to-face discussion. Face-to-face discussion is the most common procedure for generating group opinions, but this process is known to have serious shortcomings. Among these are

1. Group opinion tends to be strongly influenced by the dominant person in the group, and this dominance may have little relationship to the person's knowledge.
2. Group discussion tends to be more concerned with individual and group interests than with problem solving, and much of this type of interchange tends to be irrelevant or biased.
3. Group pressures to conform may distort individual judgements.

The objective of the Delphi technique is to achieve a consensus of opinion without the distortions caused by face-to-face discussion; this is achieved by administering a series of questionnaires interspersed with controlled opinion feedback. This procedure allows each individual to make independent judgements and then to alter those judgements based on group opinion. The procedure also provides anonymity. In short, the technique aids in generating a consensus without stifling creative or novel ideas.

[6] For additional details, see Norman P. Uhl, *Identifying Institutional Goals* (Durham, N.C.: National Laboratory for Higher Education Research Monograph Number Two, 1971), pp. 7–9; and Richard N. Farmer and Barry M. Richman, *Comparative Management and Economic Progress* (Homewood, Ill.: Richard D. Irwin, Inc., 1965), pp. 329–339.

In practice the Delphi technique applied to the panel of executives suffers the same basic disadvantages as the jury of executive opinion. That is, executive opinions, as opposed to direct market factors, are the basis for the forecasts. The Delphi technique offers an additional advantage, however, in that it is more systematic or scientific. The executives do not communicate with each other, and their responses are systematically processed to develop a consensus.

The primary disadvantage of the Delphi technique is the length of time required to develop a forecast. Whereas a jury of executive opinion can be developed within a matter of days, the Delphi technique can easily take several weeks. Although forecasts developed in this manner are still not particularly useful for the long term, the overall quality is usually improved.

Sales Force Composite. With this method, each salesperson is asked to provide a forecast for his/her respective territory; the individual estimates are then combined and modified by management to produce a company sales forecast. This is the starting point for a bottom up approach to forecasting and is often called a "grassroots approach." Sales force composites have the advantage of drawing on the knowledge and expertise of the individuals closest to the customer—the sales force. They should be aware of trends, intentions of buyers, unique economic shifts, and so forth, that may alter the sales in a given territory. This method puts the sales force under added pressure to make the forecast happen; after all, they were the ones who developed the forecast. The sales force may also have more confidence in forecasts, quotas, and budgets developed in this fashion since they were able to participate in the process. The sales force composite has the added advantage of providing ease to breakdown on the forecasting dimensions discussed earlier—product, time period, geography, or customer type. General Electric uses this approach for forecasting the sales of its various industrial products.

Numerous problems exist in the sales force composite method that may offset its advantages. The sales force often lacks training in the forecasting and forecasting methods. Salespeople also tend to be so close to the day-to-day operations that it is often difficult for them to get an objective prospective. Immediate problems may lead to excessively low forecasts, whereas recent successes may make them overly optimistic. Another problem is that the general trends in the economy may not be sufficiently considered in the salesperson's estimates. There is a strong personal interest on the part of the salesperson if quotas and compensation are related to the forecast. This can lead to distortions by individual salespeople designed to serve their personal interests. Finally, the forecast in this method depends heavily on the salesperson's knowledge of the territory, customers, unique conditions, and so forth. As turnover takes place within the sales force, new people are often required to make forecasts. They may not have the kind of detailed knowledge needed for accurate estimates. Training of the sales force in the art of forecasting and adjustment in forecasts by the manager can help to overcome some of these problems. The difficulties with the method, however, make it undesirable for most companies to rely upon it as their only forecasting method.

TIME-SERIES ANALYSIS

Regardless of the statistical methods employed, time-series analysis involves attempts to project historical patterns into the future. Time-series generally contain one or more of four types of movements:

1. *Secular trend.* Multiyear general upward or downward movements in a time series.
2. *Periodic movements.* Movements in a time-series that recur within a given period of time, such as a year, and generally referred to as seasonal movements.
3. *Cyclical Movements.* Movements that are similar to periodic movements but are of longer duration than a year and often irregular in the period of repetition.
4. *Irregular Variations.* Movements in a time-series that are the result of either a one-time specific event or minor causes, which, although they may be repetitious, are not predictable or regularly recurring.

Moving Average. The most common technique for time-series analysis is the moving average. The purpose of the moving average is to remove seasonal variations or irregular movements. This is accomplished by calculating average points from the time-series data. The average point will tend to provide a smoother time-series plot reflecting the nature of the series without undesired variations. The length of the moving average is arbitrary. In the case illustrated in Figure 5.2, the term must be less than 1 year since we are concerned with within-season irregularities. Forecasts based on moving averages are obtained by simply extrapolating the moving average for future periods. Moving averages are actually more useful as warning indicators for short-term movements in a time-series. For example, in Figure 5.2, the slight general downward movement of the moving average would help planners anticipate the general direction of the sales curve during the first quarter of the following year.

Although time-series analysis has evolved into a fairly sophisticated area of investigation, such forecasts are based on historical data only. This leaves them vulnerable to changes in the underlying conditions of the marketplace. Also note in Figure 5.2 that the calculation of a moving average results in the loss of data at the beginning and end of the series. The month is not plotted because the December figure is not available

Exponential Smoothing. One type of moving average that has received increasing acceptance in recent years is exponential smoothing. It represents a weighted sum of all past numbers in a time-series, with the heaviest weight placed on the most recent numbers.[7] One simple but widely used form of this method—using a weighed average of this year's sales, com-

---

[7] Paul E. Green and Donald S. Tull, *Research for Marketing Decisions*, 3rd ed. (Englewood Cliffs, N.J.: Prentice-Hall, Inc., 1975), pp. 666–667.

		Sales Monthly (000)	(three-term) Moving Average
1980	January	111	
	February	126	122.3*
	March	130	132.0
	April	140	135.0
	May	135	138.3
	June	140	136.0
	July	133	132.7
	August	125	128.7
	September	128	124.3
	October	120	121.0
	November	115	

*The moving average for each month was derived by taking the average sales for the month in question, the month preceding and the month following.

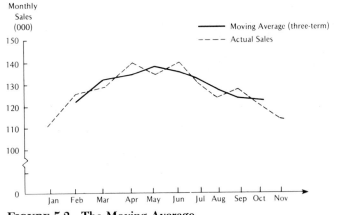

FIGURE 5.2 The Moving Average

bined with the forecast of this year's sales to get next year's forecast—will serve to illustrate. The forecast of next year's sales would be

$$y = a(x_1) + (1 - a)(x_2)$$

where y is next year's sales, x_1 is this year's sales, x_2 is this year's forecast, and a is the smoothing constant. This smoothing constant may vary between 0 and 1. Suppose that this year's sales were 400 units, the forecast was 500, and the smoothing constant has been set at .4. The forecast for next year would be:

$$y = .4(400) + (1 - .4)(500)$$
$$y = 460$$

The problem is, of course, in determining the smoothing constant. A low value of a puts more weight on the previous forecast, whereas a high value puts added weight on the actual sales. If the sales trend moves very slowly for the product, the smoothing constant should be low to retain the impact of historical data. If, however, the trend changes rapidly, the constant should be large so that the forecast will respond to recent developments. The most desirable level for a can be estimated in practice by testing several values on past forecasting data and selecting the *a* value that yields the smallest forecast error.[8]

CAUSAL METHODS OF FORECASTING

Both the judgmental and time-series analysis methods deal directly with the factor to be forecasted. That is, executive opinion or a sales trend were directly examined in order to forecast sales. When using causal methods, the researcher is seeking a better understanding of the relationships between the factor to be forecasted and other factors that cause that behavior. If a tire manufacturer wishes to forecast sales, the question might arise as to the relationship between new car sales and the demand for tires. If the sale of automobiles in an earlier period is known, and if the sale of those automobiles leads to the demand for tires in a later period, tire sales forecasts might be developed based on automobile sales as a causal factor. Although there are a number of causal methods, we will only examine three in this section. These include correlation/regression models, intention-to-buy and anticipation surveys, and leading indicators.

Correlation/Regression Methods.   One of the most commonly used, and misused, of the causal methods is the various least squares associative analyses known as correlation and regression techniques. Regression analysis in particular offers many advantages for forecasting. **Simple regression** provides an equation that can be used to determine the value of a dependent variable, the forecasted factor, given known quantities for the dependent and one independent variable; **multiple regression** involves two or more independent variables used to forecast the one dependent variable.

The first step in doing a simple regression is to develop a basic model. To do this the variables must be selected, operationally defined, and categorized into dependent and independent. The management of Arco Wire was interested in forecasting the annual market potential, by state, for a specific type of wire used for right-of-way fences on interstate highways. The sales manager knew that the market potential for wire was closely related to the number of miles of highway constructed each year. However, the waste factor, the fact that fences run in irregular patterns, and other similar considerations make the relationship less obvious. A decision was made to build a forecasting model using simple regression. The dependent variable is rolls of wire sold per year in a given state *(Y)* and the independent variable is number of miles of interstate highway constructed in the state for the year *(X)*.

To complete the decision relative to the model the form of the relationship must be decided. A linear relationship is usually assumed; however, other types of functions may also be selected. The linear function can be expressed as

$$Y = a \pm b(X)$$

where *Y* is the dependent variable, *X* is the independent variable, *a* is the *Y* intercept of the function and *b* is the slope.

[8] *Ibid.*

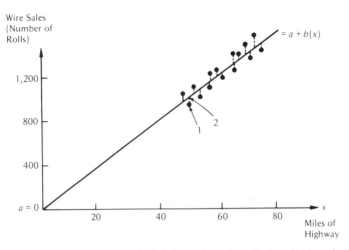

1. Each point represents an individual observation, sales and miles of highway in a given state for a given year.
2. The "least squares" method estimates the regression $[y = a \pm b(x)]$, which minimizes the sum total of the vertical distances of the data points from the line.

FIGURE 5.3   The Least Squares Method

The second step is to collect data on the variables and to fit the model to the data. From various secondary sources the number of miles of interstate highway constructed per state per year can be ascertained. The sales of wire per state per year can also be secured from trade publications. Such data were secured for the 50 states for a 3-year period. This gives 150 observations or data points in which to fit the model. The computational technique typically used in simple regression is the "least squares" method. This procedure estimates the coefficients of the equation that minimizes the sum of the squared differences between the actual values of the dependent variable for each data point and the values predicted by the equation. This can be computed by hand, but the high-speed computer makes the task relatively simple. Figure 5.3 illustrates the least squares method.

The third step is to interpret the results of the regression. Several bits of output are possible with simple regression analysis, but the most important are usually:

1. Estimates of the coefficients of the equation, a and b. These are used to build the forecasting model.
2. The coefficient of correlation (r), which is a measure of the degree of association between the variables. It can vary from -1 to $+1$, with -1 indicating a perfect fit of the model to the data in an inverse fashion, $+1$ indicates a perfect fit in a direct fashion, and 0 would mean no association.
3. The coefficient of determination (r^2), which measures the per cent of variation in the dependent variable explained by the independent variable.
4. The standard error of the estimate (SE_{est}) which can be used to translate

forecasts made using the equation for range rather than point estimates. The narrower the range, the more valuable the model is as a
forecasting tool.

The results of the simple regression might look as follows:

$$a = 0 \qquad b = +17 \qquad r = .99 \qquad r^2 = .98 \qquad SE_{est} = 12$$

The forecasting model would be $Y = 0 + 17(X)$. By inserting a value
for X the value of Y can be predicted. The r^2 indicates that 98 per cent
of the variation in sales is accounted for by variation in miles of construction. Given that this is almost all of the variation, it might be concluded
that this single variable is adequate for forecasting demand. The SE_{est}
is relatively small, which also indicates that the model is a good forecasting
tool. Suppose that the firm finds that a given state is planning 60 miles
of new interstate construction next year. To form a range estimate of
the market potential for wire, which can be said with .95 confidence
contains the true potential, the first step is to insert the 60 miles into
the predictive equation.

$$Y = 0 + 17(60) = 1020$$

Assuming a normal distribution, 1.96 SE_{est} will yield the desired level
of confidence. The confidence interval is

$$
\begin{aligned}
\text{confidence interval} &= Y \pm 1.96 \ SE_{est} \\
&= 1020 \pm 1.96 \ (12) \\
&= 996.5 \text{ to } 1043.5
\end{aligned}
$$

The Arco manager can now say that there is a .95 probability that the
true potential will fall within this range. This is, of course, assuming that
the 60 miles of construction is accurate.

Multiple regression is quite similar to simple regression with the exception that multiple regression is used with two or more independent variables. The steps in carrying out multiple regression are the same as those
for simple regression: develop a model, fit the model to collected data,
and interpret the results.

Again many different functions may be used as the basic model in
multiple regression; a linear equation is most common, however.

$$Y = a \pm b_1 \ (X_1) \pm b_2(X_2) \pm \ldots$$

Y is the dependent variable, the X's are independent variables, and a,
b_1, b_2, . . . are coefficients of the equation.

Data are fitted to the model using a computer, and the results then
interpreted. Among the more important outputs of the multiple regression analysis are

1. Estimates of the coefficients of the equation (a, b_1, b_2, . . .), which
   can be used to form a predictive model.
2. Partial coefficients of determination (r_i^2), one for each independent
   variable. These measure the per cent of variation in the dependent
   variable explained by that particular independent variable. This is
   the same as the coefficient of determination in a simple regression.

3. The coefficient of multiple determination (R^2), which indicates the per cent of variation in the dependent variable explained by all of the independent variables taken together. Note that this is not necessarily the sum of the coefficients of partial determination due to possible correlation between the independent variables.
4. The standard error of the estimate (SE_{est}), which is used in translating predictions into range estimates.

A test of significance (an F test, for example) may also be performed in the regression analysis. This allows the researcher to test for statistically significant relationships between the variables. One must be careful in interpreting statistical significance in relation to predictive value, however. Relationships may be statistically significant and still lack any real predictive ability.

A variation of multiple regression, called **stepwise regression,** performs the analysis on a variable by variable basis. The model is built by adding the most important independent variable first, the second most important next, and so forth. The results are provided after each step so that the relative importance of the variables can be evaluated. As a technical point, note that regression analysis generally requires interval data. The exception between that two-category, nominally scaled independent variables can be used. These are called "dummy" variables.

Although the technical restrictions on regression analysis are numerous, it can be a very useful analytical tool. Unfortunately, the use of the term "causal" to describe regression analysis is a misnomer. If the regression results do, in fact, describe a causal relationship, it is only because the researcher detected the relationship when defining the original model. The regression line is simply the locus of points for which the sum of squares of the vertical distances between the regression line and the actual data points is minimum. Thus, the regression line is nothing more than a statistical phenomenon. Nevertheless, a well-conceived and carried out regression analysis can provide useful forecasts for analyzing market opportunities.

Using the equation for the regression line, we can develop a confidence interval for the value of sales in a future period. Since the coefficients in the regression equation are estimates, each of which has a probability distribution, we are able to forecast a range of possible values. It remains to be seen whether the forecast is useful, given the width of the confidence interval. Since the forecast relies on systematic and logical thought in order to determine likely causal relationships, regression analysis may at times be little more than an extension of the jury of executive opinion. At least, it is always an extension of someone's opinion.

Intention-to-Buy and Anticipation Surveys. Applied to the forecasting problem as a causal method, surveys are used to determine buyers' intentions and anticipations. That is, the survey would determine estimates of future sales directly from an expression of intentions by potential buyers. This type of forecasting method is most useful as a means of monitoring market conditions. It is relatively expensive and difficult to derive actual forecasts.

The primary weakness of the survey approach is the unreliable nature of intentions as predictors of actual behavior. It is not uncommon, for example, for a survey to uncover intentions-to-purchase that vastly exceed the actual potential in a market. Frequently, this is a result of the respondent wishing to cooperate with the study or feeling intimidated if social status is attached to the purchase under study.

Leading Indicators.   Frequently, there are factors that relate to the sales or costs associated with a product, but their impact occurs after some period of time. There appears to be such a relationship, for example, between the rate of change in gross national product and the demand for air travel. When the domestic economy began to show signs of instability in the late 1960s, it was only a matter of months before the impact was felt in the airline industry. Notice that this approach to forecasting is an application, as opposed to a technique. That is, the techniques included in regression analysis and surveying are frequently used to develop leading indicators.

One of the problems associated with the use of leading indicators is complexity. Single indicators seldom prove to be adequate. A forecast of the demand for steel must take into account not only general economic conditions but specific trends in a number of industries. Some composite leading indicator indexes are published by the Census Bureau and other government and nonprofit agencies. They tend to be of greatest use to primary goods manufacturers and of less value as products approach the consumer stage.

Obviously, the type of forecasting problem, the amount of time available for forecasting, the nature of available data, and the amount of resources all affect the selection of a forecasting method. The brief discussion in this section covers only a few of the many forecasting methods that have been developed. Nevertheless, they illustrate a variety of techniques and the types of tradeoffs that the researcher faces in selecting a research approach.

USING SALES FORECASTING METHODS

Extent of Use and Accuracy.   The different forecasting methods discussed in the preceding section have found varying degrees of acceptance in the business world. They have also produced differing levels of accuracy when applied in actual forecasting. Some generalizations can be made about both the extent of use and accuracy of different forecasting methods based on past surveys of business managers.[9]

In general, the judgemental methods of jury of executive opinion and sales force composite are the most frequently used methods. These methods are less sophisticated than the others and more easily understood and applied by most sales managers. Time-series analysis involving simple

[9] See Douglas J. Dalrymple, "Sales Forecasting Methods and Accuracy," *Business Horizons*, December 1975, pp. 69–73; and *Sales Forecasting Practices* (New York: The Conference Board, Experiences in Marketing Management, 25 November 1970).

trend projections and moving averages are the next most frequently used methods. Causal methods have found the least use in actual practice.

Dalrymple reported that the average error on a 1-year forecast was 6.9 per cent.[10] Industrial firms tended to have somewhat less accurate forecasts than consumer goods firms. The most accurate methods reported were leading indicators and regression from the causal group and simple trend projections and moving averages from the time-series group. The jury of executive opinion and sales force composite were less accurate, and the intention-to-buy survey was the least accurate method. It could be implied from this that sales forecasting could be improved by a movement toward time-series and certain causal methods where these techniques can be applied.

Considerations in the Selection of Forecasting Methods. The selection of forecasting method should be based on sound logic relative to a series of basic considerations:

1. *Time.* One such consideration is the amount of time available for developing the forecast. Some methods may take longer than others if data must be collected or computer analysis performed. Lack of time may rule out the use of certain methods under given conditions.
2. *Data base.* The use of time-series analysis requires a historical data base for implementation. If adequate data does not exist, the method could not be used. This is also a consideration in the use of causal methods. If the value of the predictor variables cannot be established for the desired forecasting period, then the method cannot be employed.
3. *Costs.* Judgmental methods are generally the least expensive and causal methods the most expensive to utilize. Budget limitations may be a determining factor in the selection of forecasting method in some cases. A company would not be wise to spend a great deal of money developing a sales forecast for a product or service that accounts for a relatively small part of its total operations.
4. *Personnel.* Another key consideration is the expertise of the staff and managerial personnel of the organization. To develop meaningful forecasts, the methods and data used must be clearly understood. If a company does not have people who are well versed in the more sophisticated forecasting techniques, they will probably be well advised to stick with the simpler judgmental and trend approaches.
5. *Accuracy.* The degree of accuracy desired also affects the selection of method. If a company's planning process can function equally as well with "ballpark" estimates as with pinpoint accuracy, then the time and cost needed to implement more precise forecasting methods need not be expended. This should not, however, be used as an excuse for poor forecasting when more exact estimates would, in fact, lead to better planning and a more efficient operation.
6. *Product or service.* A final important consideration is the nature of the product or service involved in the forecast. Different products

[10] Dalrymple, *op. cit.*, p. 71.

in a company's line should typically be forecast separately, since different factors may affect their sales. The demand for some products may be relatively stable, leading to a time-series approach; whereas others may require a causal approach.

Improving Sales Forecast. Given the importance of the sales forecast in setting objectives and planning resources and effort allocation, the sales manager should continually work to improve the quality of the forecast. Donis[11] has suggested a six-step approach for improved forecast:

1. *Set general target.* Some general sales and profit targets are usually set for the sales manager by top management. They tend to assume that the trends will continue as in the past, if some internal or external forces do not act upon them. Top management is usually in a good position to evaluate the impact of external forces in particular.
2. *Make a preliminary sales forecast.* Next, the sales manager should select one or more forecasting methods and develop a preliminary sales forecast. A moving average and sales force composite might be used jointly to form the first level forecast. This is usually better done in units rather than dollars.
3. *Primary modifications.* Then, looking at each product or product line, the manager should establish a plus-minus percentage change to account for internal forces. This might include size of sales force, product life cycle movements, and so forth.
4. *Secondary modifications.* Again, a judgemental plus-minus percentage should be established to account for external forces. These tend to be even more unpredictable than the forces considered in step 3. Here the impact of technological change, legislation, business conditions, competition, and the like would be assessed.
5. *Summarize and project.* Now the modifications from steps 3 and 4 can be combined and applied to be preliminary forecasts established in step 2.
6. *Test the forecast against top management's sales and gross profit objectives.* At this point the unit's forecast is translated into dollars based on the price and gross profit margin established by top management. The forecast must ultimately be consistent with the targets of top management; if it is not consistent at this point, the sales manager should review the forecast. If differences cannot be reconciled, a conference with management to review the target and forecast is needed. It is essential that the top management's expectations and the forecast be consistent because it is from the forecast that sales objectives and budgets must be established. If top management's targets are not in line with the realities of the market as expressed in the sales forecast, the chances of the sales function fulfilling its desired corporate role are very low.

One Company's Approach to Sales Forecasting. An illustration of how one company approaches sales forecasting may be helpful at this point

[11] Jack P. Donis, "Six Steps to Forecasting for Improved Profits," *Sales and Marketing Management,* November 17, 1975, pp. 4–5.

in clarifying some of the concepts involved in the process. Dick Kahn of InterRoyal, a major supplier of commercial and institutional furniture, describes his company's approach to sales forecasting as follows:

At InterRoyal, we use two competely different forms of forecasting to give sales management the benefit of both objective and subjective predictions. The combination of the two methods produces a tool far more powerful than either one would be separately.

Our objective forecast is statistical, derived from national economic indicators and historical sales data for each product. With the aid of a computer, we can tie individual product sales to larger scale, national trends. Government and private agencies publish the indicators, from which we forecast our product sales.

The subjective forecast comes from the salesmen in the field. Their regional managers may modify the initial gut feeling of some salesmen, but there is consensus by the time the estimates of future bookings reach headquarters. This procedure works well in all three of our divisions: Office Furniture, which sells mainly through dealers; Healthcare, which sells direct to colleges, schools, hospitals, and nursing homes; and the Deluxe Div., which sells shelving and shop equipment both ways.

The two forecasts meet in the office of the national sales manager. He draws on both throughout the year to come up with the most accurate projection possible for each of our product lines.[12]

Kahn goes on to explain that the basic ingredients needed for Inter-Royal's forecasting approach are company sales records, national economic indicators, some computer capability, and a forecasting method.[13] A firm need not be large to have these basic ingredients; in fact, almost any company can develop them. Thus, the real need is for sales managers with the skills and desire to develop accurate and timely forecasts. Such forecasts provide a sound basis for making many of the more important decisions in sales management.

Budgeting

PURPOSE OF THE SALES BUDGET

Given the sales forecasts, market analysis, and sales objectives, the sales manager must decide how his department's resources and effort should be allocated. Given the planned sales in the Western territory next year and our productivity goal, how many salespeople do we need in the territory? This type of question is at the heart of the budgeting process. Answers to such questions are basic to the development of an effective sales plan.

The sales budget itself serves two basic functions. First, it is a focal point for planning how resources will be used to achieve the sales goals.

---

[12] Richard M. Kahn, "You Don't Have to be a Collosus to Forecast Accurately," *Sales and Marketing Management*, November 17, 1975, p. 7.
[13] *Ibid.*, pp. 7–8.

Priorities have been established in the form of sales and productivity objectives for various subdivisions, such as products and territories. In developing a sales budget the manager plans the allocation of the physical, financial, and human resources at his disposal to the different tasks that must be accomplished. Note that the budget acts to direct the utilization of human effort within the sales department as well as the financial resources. The relative stress desired on various territories, products, and customer types should be reflected in the budget.

The second function of the budget is control. In order effectively to evaluate and control the selling function, performance standards are needed. The sales budget provides both sales revenue and expense benchmarks against which actual performance can be compared and evaluated. When variances are found, corrective actions and supervision are needed. This topic will be explored in more detail in Chapter 11. At this point, however, let us turn to the basic principles involved in developing a budget.

BUDGETING PRINCIPLES[14]

The sales budget should provide details on both sales and expenses for all the important dimensions of the selling effort. These dimensions should be summarized into what might be called responsibility centers.

The Responsibility Center. A responsibility center is a segment of the organization to which certain responsibilities are assigned. In the sales area these centers would typically relate to specific products, customer groups, or territories. The entire sales department is, of course, a responsibility center, but in a large organization the department is generally broken into smaller units. For example, regional responsibility centers might be created to cover specific geographic areas. One manager should ultimately be responsible for planning and controlling each center. He is then accountable for that unit accomplishing its objectives. A sales budget should be developed for each center, starting from the smallest subdivision and working up the organization.

The exact nature of the budget for various centers depends upon what the manager is to be held accountable for. There are several types of centers based on this notion, with each having its uses and limitations. The various types of centers include revenue centers, cost centers, profit centers, and return-on-investment (ROI) centers.

Under the **revenue center approach,** the appropriate part of the organization is held responsible for generating its target level of sales. If the manager is simply assigned a given amount of resources and has no control over cost, then this approach may be acceptable.

With the **cost center concept,** each part of the organization is held responsible for controlling the cost incurred in carrying out its assigned

[14] For an excellent review of the basics of budgeting, see Allen Sweeny and John N. Wisner, Jr., "Budgeting Basics: A How-To Guide for Managers, Parts 1–8," *Supervisory Management,* January–August 1975.

responsibilities. The budget under this approach would involve various types of expenses. The manager is responsible for taking corrective actions when variances from the budget occur.

The limitation of both the revenue and cost center is that both cost and revenue must be considered together to account for the more basic objective of profit. As noted in Chapter 4, the objectives of the sales function should relate to both sales and sales force productivity in order to account for profit. With the **profit center approach,** the manager of a given subdivision of the organization is held responsible for both generating sales and controlling cost. Contribution to profits and nonassigned costs is a typical measure of success in the profit center approach. One problem with the profit center is that it may encourage the manager to take a narrow, short-term viewpoint. He may make "expedient" decisions that sacrifice long-term corporate objectives in favor of meeting short-term profit targets. For example, emphasis may be shifted from service to getting new accounts in order to make this year's profit look better. The company may lose in the long run from such decisions, however. This pitfall must be avoided for the profit center approach to be most effective.

A fourth approach, which has less application in sales management, is the **ROI center.** Here the manager is responsible not only for profits but also for the effective utilization of assets. Profits are divided by the total investment base for his division of the organization in order to determine the ROI for the division. The budget must, therefore, account not only for revenue and expenses but also for assets. The best organizational and budgeting approach for a given division depends on the degree of control by the manager. If the purchase and sales of significant assets are under the control of the manager, then the ROI approach may be appropriate. Sales managers generally do not have such control; thus, some version of the profit center approach is generally better. If a manager does not have control over various types of expenses, he should not be held responsible for them. Responsibility centers and the resulting budgets should be established so that the manager can control all those factors for which he is held accountable.

Cost Concepts.   The types and behavior of costs are key elements in the budgeting process, particularly with respect to what the manager should be held accountable for. Costs or expenses may be broken into variables, semivariable, and fixed. **Variable costs** vary directly with the level of activity involved. For example, sales compensation under a straight commission plan is a variable cost. **Semivariable costs** vary with the level of activity but not in direct proportion. **Fixed costs** do not vary with the level of activity, but are relatively constant over some period of time.

Costs may also be considered direct or indirect. **Direct costs** can be assigned to a specific activity or segment of the organization. Most variable and some semivariable and fixed costs are directly assignable to a particular activity. **Indirect costs** cannot be linked to a given product, territory, or customer.

In budgeting, all costs can be assigned to various subdivisions of the organization, or perhaps a better method for both planning and control purposes is direct costing. Here only direct costs are assigned to each responsibility center, and the manager is held responsible for his unit's "contribution" to profit and nonassigned costs. This contribution concept is at the heart of most sales management resources allocation decisions. The manager must budget sales and then budget funds for various activities under his control in such a way as to get the desired contribution. In budgeting the various expenses items, he is allocating a certain amount of resources, as measured in dollar terms, to the activity covered by that item—perhaps sales salaries. For managerial purposes, direct cost budgeting is typically better.

Preparing the Sales Budget.   Now that we have discussed some of the basics of budgeting, the steps in preparing the budget can be examined:

1. The first step in developing a budget for your responsibility center is a review and analysis of the situation. Note that the budgeting process for a total organization will typically start with the lowest level responsibility centers and proceed up through the organization. In the situational analysis, several things should be considered. One is the variances in last year's budget. Where was the budget off and why? By looking at this past record, similar variances may be avoided in next year's budget. Another consideration is the objectives for the upcoming budget period. Sales and productivity objectives, which should have been set prior to budgeting, give guidelines for allocating resources. The budget should reflect an allocation of resources and effort designed to meet the objectives for the sales function. Finally, changes in the business environment should be considered. The economic climate; political, regulatory, or governmental developments; changes in the distribution system; new product development; the competitive outlook; changes in promotion; and a number of other factors may affect the desired allocation of resources to achieve specific objectives.
2. Once the situation is clear, problems and opportunities should be isolated. If problems are foreseen, then corrections may be possible in the resource allocation to increase volume or profits. It may also be possible to reallocate resources in such a way as to exploit opportunities presented by either the internal or external environment.
3. The next step is to decide on the initial allocation of resources and effort to the various activities, products, customers, and territories for which the center is responsible. It is important to get the initial budget down on paper. The manager can then step back from the details of the budget and look at the total picture. Revisions may be required to make the various facets of the budget fit together in a logical fashion. Most organizations have specific formats, worksheets, procedures, and timetables for this purpose.
4. The final step is to present the budget to superiors. The manager of each responsibility center typically meets with his boss to present and explain the budget proposal. Needed modifications are worked out

before the budget is approved and made operational for the time period intended.

Monthly Budgets. After the annual budget has been approved, it must then be subdivided on a monthly basis. This requires that the manager look at the annual cycle of activity. Which months historically have higher and lower levels of sales and expeditures? Anticipated noncycle variations must also be taken into account. Such factors as planned new product introductions and advertising programs must be considered.

After the budget decisions are finally resolved, they should be monitored and adjusted as the new year progresses. Revisions may be needed as the environment changes presenting new problems and opportunities.

AN ILLUSTRATIVE SALES BUDGET

Again, as with forecasting an actual sales budgeting experience may prove helpful in understanding the basic process. Dick Grey is national sales manager for the Health Care Division of Johnson & Johnson. He is responsible for supervising the sales organization to keep goods moving to retail outlets. In describing his sales budget, he says

Basically, it's a people budget, . . . Most of our costs are directly related to the number of people I have working in the sales department—what we call a "head count."

. . . his "head count" of salesmen and saleswomen not only is reflected in salary figures but has a direct effect on other major categories, such as travel, auto expenses, and relocation costs. "These are the items that take most of the figuring," he says.[15]

Grey gives several pointers on effective sales budgeting:[16]

1. The process must be coordinated with the other marketing and financial control people. To develop an effective sales budget the sales manager needs to anticipate the number of salespeople needed to do the job effectively.

"Almost any packaged goods product introduction requires a stepped-up sales effort to go along with the ad campaign," says Greg, noting that the principal reason for that is the fight for retail shelf space. "Our salespeople have to call on each store every two or three weeks until the product has a home. In some cases, it takes several months before the product is listed in the order guide of every store manager in the chain."

Whether he decides to add to the sales force, hire part-time help, or retain an outside selling service, Grey allows for the added manpower in the tentative sales budget that he is whipping into shape. The final sales department budget will actually be a composite of 24 budget proposals submitted by his national sales manager, 20 regional and division offices, and specialists handling national accounts, trade relations, and sales administration.

[15] "At Johnson & Johnson, The Sales Budget Gets the Best of Care," *Sales Management,* May 1975, p. 9.
[16] *Ibid.,* pp. 9–10.

Classification	1974	1975	Original 1976 Budget	April Revision	July Revision	October Revision
Salaries (general)						
Travel (salesmen)						
Auto expense						
Employee moving						
Dept. supplies						

FIGURE 5.4   Sample Form for a 1976 Sales Budget

Even after the budget is complete, three departments—sales, product management, and MI & C (Marketing Information and Control)—work together throughout the year re-evaluating the figures as market conditions shift, plans change, and accounts have to be balanced. In the sales department, major alterations show up as quarterly revisions on Grey's expense sheet.[17] (See Figure 5.4.)

2. Another key issue is "what does it cost to sell our brand?" The sales force productivity targets discussed in Chapter 3 must be considered along with the sales forecast to determine the amount of expense money which is allowable.
3. Getting agreement on the budget from superiors is a key consideration. Grey notes that:

"Once all the figures are in, they are submitted to Frank H. Barker, vice president and general manager of the Health Care Div., for approval. If they fail to meet the profit objectives of the division, the departmental budgets are reworked until they are brought into line . . . The final budget must be approved by Dec. 1."[18]

4. A final point is to avoid surprises. Things must be kept flexible and constantly reviewed. If market conditions change, the budget must be revised and approval gained from superiors. To budget effectively, the sales manager must anticipate future conditions and plan effective resource utilization to take advantage of the opportunities presented.

Summary

Setting objectives and effectively allocating resources and effort to reach those objectives requires accurate sales forecasting. This forecasting task may involve several different dimensions of the organization. After the nature of the desired forecast is clear, appropriate methods must be selected and utilized. Three sets of forecasting methods were reviewed in this chapter—judgemental, time-series, and causal. Several techniques exist in each set. The jury of executive opinion and the sales force composite are the most commonly used judgemental methods and are in fact

[17] *Ibid.*
[18] *Ibid.*, p. 10.

the most widely employed of all forecasting methods. Simple trend projections, moving averages, and exponential smoothing fall in the time-series group. Regression is the most widely used causal method with intention-to-buy surveys and leading indicators also fitting in this category. Regardless of the basic methods used most initial forecasts are modified by managerial judgements concerning changes in the internal and external environment. The forecast is a vital informational input into decisions concerning the establishment of sales objectives and the allocation of resources and effort to accomplish those objectives.

Sales budgeting involves the planning of this resource allocation and is also a key standard used to evaluate and control the organization. In general, a responsibility center should only budget and be held accountable for items that it can directly influence. It is also vital that the budget be carefully monitored and adjusted as the environment changes.

Discussion Questions

1. Why are accurate forecasts important in sales management?

2. Discuss the various judgemental, time-series, and causal forecasting methods along with the advantages and disadvantages of each.

3. Develop a forecast of the market potential for new cars in your state next year.

4. How can a company derive a company potential and sales forecast from market potential estimates?

5. Discuss the procedure for developing an actual sales forecast within an ongoing business.

6. What is the function of a sales budget?

7. Discuss the concept of responsibility centers as they apply in sales budgeting.

8. What are the major advantages of the contribution concept in sales budgeting?

9. Outline the steps in developing a sales budget.

10. Why is it important for superiors to review and approve the sales budget?

Selected References

BUTLER, W. F., R. A. KAVISH, and R. B. PLATT (eds.), *Methods and Techniques of Business Forecasting* (Englewood Cliffs, N.J.: Prentice-Hall, Inc., 1974).

Chambers, John C., Satinder K. Mullick, and Donald D. Smith, *An Executive Guide to Forecasting* (New York: John Wiley and Sons, Inc., 1974).

Parker, G. C., and E. L. Segura, "How to Get a Better Forecast," *Harvard Business Review*, March–April 1975, pp. 99–109.

Sweeny, Allen, and John N. Wisner, Jr., "Budgeting Basics: A How-to Guide for Managers, Parts 1–8," *Supervisory Management*, January–August 1975.

Wotruba, Thomas R., and Michael L. Thurlow, "Sales Force Participation in Quota Setting and Sales Forecasting," *Journal of Marketing*, April 1976, pp. 11–16.

CASE 5.1
Modern Plastics*

Company Background

The Plastics Division of Modern Chemical Company was founded in 1965 when Modern Chemical purchased Cordco, a small plastics manufacturer with national sales of $15,000,000. At that time, the key products of the Plastics Division were sandwich bags, plastic tablecloths, trash cans, and plastic-coated clothesline.

Since 1965, the Plastics Division has grown to a sales level exceeding $200 million, with five regional profit centers covering the United States. Each regional center has manufacturing facilities and a regional sales force. There are three product groups in each region:

1. Food Packaging—PVC meat film, plastic bags for various food products
2. Institutional—Plastic trash bags and disposable tableware (plates, bowls, and so on)
3. Industrial—Case overwrap film, heavy duty fertilizer packaging bags, plastic film for use in pallet overwrap systems

Each product group is supervised jointly by a product manager and a district sales manager, both of whom report to the regional marketing manager. The sales representatives report directly to the district sales manager but also work closely with the product manager on matters concerning pricing and product specifications.

The five regional general managers report to Mr. J. R. Hughes, Vice-President of the Plastics Division. Mr. Hughes is located in Chicago. Although Modern Chemical is owned by a multinational paper company, the Plastics Division has been able to operate in a virtually independent manner since its establishment in 1965. The reasons for this include:

* Case prepared by Thomas N. Ingram, Danny N. Bellenger and Kenneth L. Bernhardt, Georgia State University.

1. Limited knowledge of the plastic industry on the part of the paper company management.
2. Excellent growth by the Plastics Division has been possible without management supervision from the paper company.
3. Profitability of the Plastics Division has consistently been higher than that of other divisions of the chemical company.

The institutional trash bag is a polyethyelene bag used to collect and transfer refuse to its final disposition point. There are different sizes and colors available to fit the various uses of the bag. For example, a small bag for desk wastebaskets is available as well as a heavier bag for large containers such as a 55 gallon drum. There are 25 sizes in the Modern line with 13 of those sizes being available in three colors—white, buff, and clear. Customers typically buy several different items on an order to cover all their needs.

The institutional trash bag is a separate product from the consumer grade trash bag, which is typically sold to homeowners through retail outlets. The institutional trash bag is sold primarily through paper wholesalers, hospital supply companies, and janitorial supply companies to a variety of end users. Since trash bags are used on such a wide scale, the list of end users could include almost any business or institution. The segments include hospitals, hotels, schools, office buildings, transportation facilities, and restaurants.

Based on historical data and a current survey of key wholesalers and end users in the southeast, the annual market of institutional trash bags in the region was estimated to be 55 million pounds. Translated into cases, the market potential was close to 2 million cases. During the past 5 years, the market for trash bags has grown at a rapid pace. Now a mature product, future market growth is expected to parallel overall growth in the economy. The 1978 real growth in GNP is forecast to be 4.5 per cent.

The current market is characterized by a distressing trend. The market is in a position of oversupply with approximately 20 manufacturers competing for the business in the southeast. Prices have been on the decline for several months, but are expected to level out during the last 6 months of the year.

This problem arose after a record year in 1976 for Modern Plastics. During 1976, supply was very tight due to raw material shortages. Unlike many of its competitors, Modern had only minor problems securing adequate raw material supplies. As a result, the competitors were few in 1976, and all who remained in business were prosperous. By early 1977 raw materials were plentiful, and prices began to drop as new competitors tried to buy their way into the market. During the first quarter of 1977, Modern Plastics learned the hard way that a competitive price was a necessity in the current market. Volume fell off drastically in February and March as customers shifted orders to new suppliers when Modern chose to maintain a slightly higher than market price on trash bags.

With the market becoming extremely price competitive and profits declining, the overall quality has dropped to a point of minimum standard.

Most suppliers now make a bag "barely good enough to get the job done." It is believed that this quality level is acceptable to most buyers who do not demand high quality for this type of product.

Institutional Sales Manager Jim Clayton had spent most of Monday morning planning for the rest of the month. It was early July and Jim knew that an extremely busy time was coming with the preparation of the following year's sales plan.

Current Situation

Since starting his current job less than a month ago, Jim had been involved in learning the requirements of the job and making his initial territory visits. Now that he was getting settled, Jim was trying to plan his activities according to priorities. The need for planning had been instilled in him during his college days. As a result of his 3 years field sales experience and development of time management skills, he felt prepared for the challenge of the sales manager's job.

While sitting at his desk, Jim recalled a conversation that he had a week ago with Bill Hanson, the former manager, who had been promoted to another division. Bill told him that the sales forecast (annual and monthly) for plastic trash bags in the southeast region would be due soon as an initial step toward developing the sales plan for next year. Bill had laughed as he told him, "Boy, you ought to have a ball doing the forecast being a rookie sales manager!"

When Jim had asked what Bill meant, he explained by saying that the forecast was often "winged" because the headquarters in Chicago already knew what they wanted and would change the forecast to meet their figures, particularly if the forecast was for an increase of less than 10 per cent. The experienced sales manager could throw numbers together in a short time that would pass as a serious forecast and ultimately be adjusted to fit the plans of headquarters. However, he felt an inexperienced manager would have a difficult time "winging" a credible forecast.

Bill had also told Jim that the other alternative meant gathering mountains of data and putting together a forecast that could be sold to the various levels of Modern Plastics management. This alternative would prove to be time consuming and could still be changed anywhere along the chain of command before final approval.

Clayton started reviewing pricing and sales volume history (see Exhibit 1). He also looked at the key account performance for the past 2½ years (see Exhibit 2). During the past month Clayton had visited many of the key accounts, and on the average they had indicated that their purchases from Modern would probably increase about 15–20 per cent in the coming year.

Jim had received a memo recently from Robert Baxter, the Regional Marketing Manager, detailing the plans for completing the 1978 forecast. The key dates in the memo began in only 3 weeks:

August 1   —Presentation of forecast to Regional Marketing Manager

August 10   —Joint presentation with Marketing Manager to Regional General Manager

EXHIBIT 1 Plastic Trash Bags—Sales and Pricing History, 1975–1977

	Pricing Dollars Per Case			Sales Volume in Cases			Sales Volume in Dollars		
	1975	1976	1977	1975	1976	1977	1975	1976	1977
January	$6.88	$ 7.70	$15.40	33,000	46,500	36,500	$ 227,000	$ 358,000	$ 562,000
February	6.82	7.70	14.30	32,500	52,500	23,000	221,500	404,000	329,000
March	6.90	8.39	13,48	32,000	42,000	22,000	221,000	353,000	296,500
April	6.88	10.18	12.24	45,500	42,500	46,500	313,000	432,500	569,000
May	6.85	12.38	11.58	49,000	41,500	45,500	335,500	514,000	527,000
June	6.85	12.64	10.31	47,500	47,000	42,000	325,500	594,500	433,000
July	7.42	13.48	9.90[E]	40,000	43,500	47,500*	297,000	586,500	470,000[E]
August	6.90	13.48	10.18[E]	48,500	63,500	43,500*	334,500	856,000	443,000[E]
September	7.70	14.30	10.31[E]	43,000	49,000	47,500*	331,000	700,500	489 500[E]
October	7.56	15.12	10.31[E]	52,500	50,000	51,000*	397,000	756,000	526,000[E]
November	7.15	15.68	10.72[E]	62,000	61,500	47,500*	443,500	964,500	509,000[E]
December	7.42	15.43	10.59[E]	49,000	29,000	51,000*	363,500	447,500	540.000[E]
Total	$7.13	$12.25	$11.30	534,500	568,500	503,500	$3,810,000	$6,967,000	$5,694 000

[E] July–December 1977 figures are forecast of sales Manager J. A. Clayton and other data comes from historical sales information.

EXHIBIT 2 1977 Key Account Sales History (in Cases)

Customer	1975	1976	1st 6 Months 1977	1975 Monthly Avg.	1976 Monthly Avg.	1st Half 1977 Monthly Avg.	1st Qtr. 1977 Monthly Avg.
Transco Paper Company	125774	134217	44970	10481	11185	7495	5823
Callaway Paper	44509	46049	12114	3709	3837	2019	472
Florida Janitorial Supply	34746	36609	20076	2896	3051	3346	2359
Jefferson	30698	34692	25044	2558	2891	4174	1919
Cobb Paper	13259	23343	6414	1105	1945	1069	611
Miami Paper	10779	22287	10938	900	1857	1823	745
Milne Surgical Company	23399	21930	—	1950	1828	—	—
Graham	8792	15331	1691	733	1278	281	267
Crawford Paper	7776	14132	6102	648	1178	1017	1322
John Steele	8634	13277	6663	720	1106	1110	1517
Henderson Paper	9185	8850	2574	765	738	429	275
Durant Surgical	—	7766	4356	—	647	726	953
Master Paper	4221	5634	600	352	470	100	—
D.T.A.	—	—	2895	—	—	482	—
Crane Paper	4520	5524	3400	377	460	566	565
Janitorial Service	3292	5361	2722	274	447	453	117
Georgia Paper	5466	5053	2917	456	421	486	297
Paper Supplies, Inc.	5117	5119	1509	426	427	251	97
Southern Supply	1649	3932	531	137	328	88	78
Horizon Hospital Supply	4181	4101	618	348	342	103	206
TOTAL CASES	346007	413217	156134	28835	34436	26018	17623

September 1	—Regional General Manager presents forecast to Division Vice-President
September 1–30	—Review of forecast by staff of Division Vice-President
October 1	—Review forecast with corporate staff
October 1–15	—Revision as necessary
October 15	—Final forecast forwarded to Division Vice-President from Regional General Manager

A recent study of Modern versus competition had been conducted by an outside consultant to see how well Modern measured up in several key areas. Each area was weighted according to its importance in the purchase decision and Modern was compared to its key competitors in each area and on an overall basis. The key factors and their weights are

		Weight
(1)	Pricing	.50
(2)	Quality	.15
(3)	Breadth of line	.10
(4)	Sales coverage	.10
(5)	Packaging	.05
(6)	Service	.10
	Total	1.00

As shown in Exhibit 3, Modern compared favorably with its key competitors on an overall basis. None of the other suppliers were as strong as Modern in breadth of line nor did any competitor offer as good sales coverage as that provided by Modern. Clayton knew that sales coverage would be even better next year since the Florida and North Carolina territories had grown enough to add two salespeople to the current eight in the institutional group by January 1, 1978.

EXHIBIT 3 Competitive Factors Ratings by Competitor

Weight	Factor	Modern	National Film	Bonanza	Southeastern	PBI	BAGCO	Southwest Bag	Florida Plastics	East Coast Bag Co.
.50	Price	2	3	2	2	2	2	2	2	3
.15	Quality	3	2	3	4	3	2	3	3	4
.10	Breadth	1	2	2	3	3	3	3	3	3
.10	Sales Coverage	1	3	3	3	4	3	3	4	3
.05	Packaging	3	3	2	3	3	1	3	3	3
.10	Service	4	3	3	2	2	2	3	4	3

Overall Weighted Ranking**

(1)	BAGCO	2.15	(6)	Southeastern	2.55
(2)	Modern	2.20	(7)	Florida Plastics	2.60
(3)	Bonanza	2.25	(8)	National Film	2.65
(4)	Southwest Bag (Tie)	2.50	(9)	East Coast Bag	3.15
(5)	PBI (Tie)	2.50			

*Ratings on a 1 to 5 scale with 1 being the best rating and 5 the worst.

**The weighted ranking is the sum of each rank times its weight.
  The lower the number, the better the overall rating.

Supplier	% of Market 1975	% of Market 1976
National Film	11	12
Bertram	16	0*
Bonanza	11	12
Southeastern	5	6
Bay	9	0*
Johnson Graham	8	0*
PBI	2	5
Lewis	2	0*
Bagco	—	6
Southwest Bag	—	2
Florida Plastics	—	4
East Coast Bag Co.	—	4
Miscellaneous & Unknown	8	22
Modern	28	27
	100	100

EXHIBIT 4   Market Share by Supplier, 1975 and 1976

*Out of business in 1976

National Film	Broadest product line in the industry. Quality a definite advantage. Good service. Sales coverage adequate, but not an advantage. Not as aggressive as most suppliers on price. Strong competitor.
Bonanza	Well established tough competitor. Very aggressive on pricing. Good packaging, quality okay.
Southeastern	Extremely price competitive in Southern Florida. Dominates Miami market. Limited product line. Not a threat outside of Florida.
PBI	Extremely aggressive on price. Have made inroads into Transco Paper Company during 1977. Good service but poor sales coverage.
Bagco	New competitor in 1977. Very impressive with a high quality product, excellent service, and strong sales coverage. A real threat, particularly in Florida.
Southwest Bag	A factor in Louisiana and Mississippi. Their strategy is a simple—an acceptable product at a rock bottom price.
Florida Plastics	Active when market is at a profitable level with price cutting. When market declines to a low profit range, Florida manufactures other types of plastic packaging and stays out of the trash bag market.. Poor reputation as a reliable supplier, but can still "spot-sell" at low prices.
East Coast Bag	Most of their business is from a state bid which began in January, 1976 for a two-year period. Not much of a threat to Modern's business in the Southeast, as most of their volume is north of Washington, D.C.

EXHIBIT 5   Characteristics of Competitors

Total Industry	+5.0%
Commercial	+5.4%
Restaurant	+6.8%
Hotel/Motel	+2.0%
Transportation	+1.9%
Office Users	+5.0%
Other	+4.2%
Non-Commercial	+4.1%
Hospitals	+3.9%
Nursing Homes	+4.8%
Colleges/Universities	+2.4%
Schools	+7.8%
Employee Feeding	+4.3%
Other	+3.9%

EXHIBIT 6   **1978 Real Growth Projections by Segment**

Pricing, quality, and packaging seemed to be neither an advantage nor a disadvantage. However, service was a problem area. The main cause for this, Clayton was told, was temporary out of stock situations that occurred occasionally, primarily due to the wide variety of trash bags offered by Modern.

During the past 2 years, Modern Plastics had maintained its market share at approximately 27 per cent of the market. Some new competitors had entered the market since 1975, whereas others had left the market (see Exhibit 4). The previous District Sales Manager, Bill Hanson, had left Clayton some comments regarding the major competitors. These are reproduced in Exhibit 5.

After a careful study of trade journals, government statistics, and surveys conducted by Modern marketing research personnel, projections for growth potential were formulated by segment and are shown in Exhibit 6. This data was compiled by Bill Hanson just before he had been promoted.

Jim looked back at Baxter's memo giving the time schedule for the forecast and knew he had to get started. As he left the office at 7:15 he wrote himself a large note and pinned it on his wall—"Get Started on the Sales Forecast!"

CASE 5.2
Acacia Cement Company*

The management of the Acacia Cement Company located in Los Angeles County, California, had been looking for an improved method of forecasting sales. The company's market area included Imperial, Inyo, Kern,

Company Background

* Reprinted with permission from Donald S. Tull and Del I. Hawkins, *Marketing Research: Meaning, Measurement and Method* (New York: MacMillan Publishing Co., Inc., 1977), pp. 652–656.

Los Angeles, Orange, Santa Barbara, San Bernardino, San Luis Obispo, San Diego, Riverside, and Ventura counties. Forecast errors had averaged almost 10 per cent during 1969 and 1970, and the error in the first quarter of 1971 had been almost 13 per cent.

Sales forecasts were made for two quarters ahead, with a new forecast made each quarter. The forecasting was done by the president and the marketing manager using what they referred to as their "wet finger in the wind" method. Once each quarter they met in the president's office with data on orders, construction contract awards for the market area, salesman call reports, and other information. After reviewing these data, they each wrote their forecasts for the next two quarters on a piece of paper. Differences were discussed and a final sales forecast (usually a compromise that was close to the average of their individual forecasts) was made for each quarter.

As a result of their inability to forecast accurately, the company had been forced to keep large inventories on hand to avoid losing sales when demand was unexpectedly high. Both labor and interest costs were rising in 1971, adding to the already high costs of carrying excess inventory. The president decided that some means had to be found to make better forecasts so they could reduce inventories and operating costs.

A consultant was called in to work on the problem. He found that a trade association of cement manufacturers and importers and exporters provided data on cement sales each month to contractors in each of the counties of Acacia's market area. He ran an analysis of past sales data for the industry and for Acacia and found that Acacia's market share had remained close to 9.2 per cent for some time. In discussions with the president and marketing manager, they stated that it was reasonable to expect that the company's share would continue to be at about this same level unless some major change took place in the industry.

The consultant recognized that if this were the case, the major problem was to forecast industry sales. If Acacia's share stayed relatively constant (or it changed slowly over time), finding a method of forecasting industry sales with the required degree of accuracy would permit Acacia's sales to be forecast with the accuracy needed. Acacia would only have to multiply the industry sales forecast by its estimated market share to obtain a company sales forecast.

Acacia's sales force called on contractors engaged in three different kinds of construction. Residential contractors were called on who specialized in houses and apartment buildings as were nonresidential contractors who built commercial, industrial, and military buildings. The largest contractors were those involved in construction of such projects as highways, dams, flood control, bridges, and miscellaneous other civil and military engineering projects. The consultant was aware that there was a lag time of several months between the awarding of a contract for a construction project and the use of cement in the actual construction. Although the lag was shortest for residential construction and longest for the larger engineering projects (highways and dams), the company officials believed that the average lag time was about 6 months.

Contract award data were made available each month for each of these types of construction projects from one or more governmental agencies. Data on residential construction contracts were available from the county and city agencies responsible for issuing permits and inspecting the buildings, the California Division of Highways announced awards for constructing highways and bridges, and the other state and federal agencies involved in construction activity in Southern California made similar announcements. The dollar amounts for residential and nonresidential construction contracts in each county were compiled and published each month by the research department of a bank in Los Angeles. A trade publication, the *Engineering News Record*, published information every month on awards for engineering projects. Acacia's marketing department had been collecting this information since 1966 for the salesmen to use in planning their sales calls.

The consultant decided to run some regression analysis for the period from 1966 to early 1971 to see if dollar contract awards for a given month could be used to forecast industry cement sales several months later. He planned to try lead times of 5, 6, and 7 months for the contract awards to see which one gave the regression equation that forecast cement sales most accurately. Before he could run the regressions, however, he knew that he would have to make several adjustments to the contract award data.

Current Situation

One necessary adjustment was for changes in construction costs since 1966. Costs had risen an average of 3 per cent per year since then, and so a dollar of contract award in 1971 represented substantially less actual construction (and less cement to be used in it) than a dollar in 1966.

Another adjustment was required for the different number of working days each month. After allowing for calendar variation and union holidays, the number of working days varied from as few as 18 to as many as 23 per month. Other things being equal, cement sales in an 18-workday month could be over 20 per cent less than those in a 23-workday month for this reason alone. The contract awards and industry cement sales were both converted to averages per working day in each month to allow for this factor.

An adjustment was also needed for seasonal variation in construction activity. In Southern California this was mainly the result of rain since there was no freezing weather. The months with the heaviest rain were in the winter and this was when the amount of construction was lowest.

The consultant also decided that he needed to adjust the construction award data for the effects of large engineering awards. The award for a dam, for example, was so large that it might amount to as much as one half of all other engineering awards. The effect would be to distort the relationship between contract awards and cement sales since all the cement to be used in the dam would not be used in 1 month.

After obtaining daily averages of the adjusted data for each of the three sectors of construction activity, the values were summed for each month to obtain average daily contract awards for all construction. The resulting data, along with data on industry sales of cement in Acacia's

Average Daily Construction Activity (X) and Cement Consumption (Y) In Southern California

Year	Month	X Seasonally Adjusted, 1964 Dollars (000)	Y Barrels of Cement (000)	Year	Month	X Seasonally Adjusted, 1964 Dollars (000)	Y Barrels of Cement (000)
1966	August	99.8	83.7	1969	January	108.3	89.3
	September	96.5	82.3		February	110.0	89.3
	October	99.2	80.9		March	108.3	86.9
	November	94.9	79.5		April	11.2	94.5
	December	97.6	73.5		May	109.3	94.5
					June	106.9	96.2
1967	January	93.3	75.1		July	107.5	96.3
	February	93.3	75.9		August	105.4	93.5
	March	91.7	81.3		September	106.2	88.1
	April	94.1	78.7		October	103.6	84.6
	May	91.6	77.0		November	107.0	84.9
	June	87.1	75.9		December	106.5	86.0
	July	84.7	76.3				
	August	84.8	78.2	1970	January	105.8	85.3
	September	89.2	78.2		February	102.2	86.2
	October	92.0	78.6		March	102.8	88.0
	November	90.0	75.4		April	98.3	90.2
	December	90.4	79.9		May	99.5	87.9
					June	99.8	87.9
1968	January	88.4	74.1		July	101.7	87.0
	February	93.2	70.3		August	106.2	85.4
	March	91.0	62.7		September	106.5	84.2
	April	88.9	70.3		October	108.1	80.5
	May	94.0	77.7		November	110.5	83.4
	June	103.7	83.6		December	113.4	84.6
	July	109.2	83.9				
	August	109.0	85.0	1971	January	115.0	92.1
	September	103.6	86.3		February	105.8	93.0
	October	105.0	89.4		March	102.6	93.6
	November	103.8	92.7				
	December	108.1	96.9				

market area, are given for the period from July, 1966, through March, 1971, in the following table.

The consultant planned to run simple linear regression analyses with the contract awards lagged by 5, 6, and 7 months to see which gave the best "fit." He then planned to use the regression equation for the lag period with the best fit to forecast daily average values for industry cement sales for each month for the number of months (5, 6, or 7) that the equation permitted. These forecasts could then be converted from daily averages to monthly totals by multiplying by the number of workdays in that month. He would also have to deseasonalize the forecast by multiplying each monthly total forecast by the index for that month.

He had already calculated the number of workdays in each of the next seven months and had the monthly indexes available from his earlier adjustments. These values were

	April	May	June	July	August	September	October
Number of working days in month	20.50	22.00	22.00	20.50	22.75	20.25	22.25
Monthly index of construction activity	100.3	104.3	106.0	106.0	106.3	106.3	105.0

The consultant wondered what time period was the correct one for contract awards and what a forecast for cement for cement sales would be for each such time period.

Student Learning Exercise / 5
Market Potential and Sales Forecasting

1. To develop familiarity with the types of sources of data that are available for sales forecasting.
2. To develop an understanding of how forecasting techniques are actually applied.

Objective

This exercise deals with the automobile industry. You will develop the market potential and sales forecast for a particular geographic area for a line of cars.

Overview

Assume that you are the district sales manager for a particular line of cars (for example, Oldsmobile, Chevrolet, and so on). Although you are responsible for sales in the entire district, you are particularly interested in one state. In this exercise, you will select a state and a line of cars and then determine the market potential and sales forecast within these parameters. Your boss wants this information in units, *not* dollars.

Exercise

Use the *Sales Management Survey of Buying Power* to find out the total dollar sales in the automotive industry for your entire state. Then, by investigating some trade publications such as *Automotive News* or *Automotive Industry,* approximate the sale price per car. Dividing total dollar sales by the approximate average cost will give the *unit* sales for all automobiles in your state.

Assume that your line has had the following share of the state's total automobile market over the past 5 years.

Years Ago	Share (%)
5	7.00
4	6.75
3	6.80
2	6.50
1	5.90

You already have data on the first 6 months of the current year showing your market share in the entire country and in your state.

	U.S. Share (%)	State Share (%)
January	6.00	5.93
February	5.90	5.90
March	5.60	5.90
April	5.75	5.80
May	5.80	5.95
June	5.95	6.30

Automobile sales are, of course, dependent on many things, such as the GNP, people's incomes, the price of gas, and so on. The median household cash income can be found in the *Survey of Buying Power,* listed by state. Estimates of the GNP and the general state of the economy for the next year can be found in business or economic journals or in government publications.

Prepare a market potential and sales forecast for next year along with a defense for the method and data you chose to use in developing the estimates.

Recruiting and Selection

EARLIER, in Chapter 1, a modern view of sales management was contrasted with a more traditional view. The traditional view, which is still in use by some firms today, places emphasis upon a functional approach to sales management. It originated with the sales manager's responsibility for recruiting and selecting sales personnel.

After making the types of resource allocation decisions covered in Chapter 5, sales managers turn to their personnel needs. Many firms experience severe difficulties directly or indirectly relating to recruiting and selection. It is the contention of the authors of this text that such difficulties occur for two basic reasons:

First, many firms suffer a type of myopia associated with recruiting and selection. Often sales managers view recruiting and selection of sales representatives as a *starting point*. This is a shortsighted view! If recruiting and selection is properly done, it is the *result* of a great deal of preceding time and work by sales management and others in the firm. The costs and time associated with the "homework" needed prior to the start of recruiting and selection often come at the expense of other activities. Time spent, for example, in reviewing the specific needs of a sales territory prior to actually interviewing applicants is time that must be taken away from other sales management activities.

Second, as incredible as it may sound, many firms neglect or *underestimate* the importance of recruiting and selection of sales personnel. As we shall see later in this chapter, the costs of recruiting and selection are also typically understated. Further, as discussed earlier in Chapter 3, differing objectives can often be at odds with one another. Consider the plight of a sales manager for XYZ Cosmetics. A vacancy in the firm's field sales force arose two weeks ago due to resignation. Most firms cannot afford to "drop everything" simply because of a single resignation. Should the sales manager suddenly place "top priority" on recruiting a replacement for this sales territory or should the sales manager proceed with other duties and let the territory remain vacant for a longer period of time? Our basic point of underestimating the importance of recruiting or neglecting this activity is borne out by Davis and Webster who state:

The importance of careful and continuous recruiting in developing an effective sales force should be obvious. Yet, the pressures of day-to-day operating problems often lead to neglect of this important management responsibility.[1]

These are but a few of the issues compounding the difficulties associated with the recruiting and selection of sales personnel. Together with other related issues, we will proceed to discuss methods and approaches currently used in recruiting and selection.

This chapter is structured around a sequence of three tasks that together comprise the recruiting and selection process. The first task (as we shall see below) is often neglected or totally overlooked and involves a thorough understanding of the sales task by sales management. A natural result of achieving a full understanding of the sales job is the development of a written job description. A second task concerns actual location of prospective candidates for the open sales position. As we shall see, this task involves exploration by sales management of external as well as internal sources of applicants. The third task involves the evaluation and actual selection of an individual to fill the sales position.

Understanding the Sales Task

A recent headline in a marketing periodical reads: "Sales' Execs to Waste $3 Billion."[2] The wasted dollars mentioned in this article are largely attributed to recruiting and selection. A major point of the article is that "fully half of the men and women currently selling ought not to be in sales jobs."[3] This article is one of many recent criticisms leveled at sales management for ineptness in recruiting.

Although it may at first sound like an oversimplification, a basic prob- the selling task. Despite the fact that he or she is responsible for the sales staff, a sales manager may not fully appreciate the fact that each territory may be very different from every other. How can this be if all the sales personnel in question work for the same firm and sell the same products? In order to answer this question, we must do some of the same "homework" a sales manager would do prior to the start of recruiting. In a word, we seek to *understand* the task faced by a particular sales representative assigned to a specific sales territory.

QUESTIONS PROVIDING INSIGHT

In an effort to understand better the needs in a specific sales territory, the following questions[4] may be useful for management to consider:

---

[1] Kenneth R. Davis and Frederick E. Webster, Jr., *Sales Force Management*, (New York: The Ronald Press Company, 1968), p. 385.

[2] "Sales' Execs to Waste $3 Billion," *The Marketing News*, Mid-December, 1970, p. 8.

[3] *Ibid.*

[4] Many of these questions are taken from George D. Downing, *Sales Management* (New York: John Wiley & Sons, Inc., 1969), pp. 245–246.

1. For this particular territory, what degree of sales knowledge, skill and potential is needed?
2. What does the job require in regard to "market knowledge"?
3. What type of competition is faced by the incumbent of this job?
4. How much product knowledge or technical skill with regard to product is required?
5. What is the nature of customers to be contacted? What is the range of their technology and processes? What kinds of problems do they have?
6. What kinds of individuals are there in customer organizations? Any "difficult" personalities in key positions?
7. What are the objectives of the job? What degree of managerial skill will be required of the incumbent?
8. To what extent does the job require the planning of sales strategies?
9. How important is the art of selling—that is, the communicative and personally persuasive skills needed?
10. If the sales person works through middlemen (for example, wholesalers and/or distributors), what particular problems or advantages do these middlemen have?
11. What "personal variables" (for example, extensive overnight travel) exist in this territory?
12. What is the state of the territory being filled? Is it a mature territory, characterized by heavy coverage by the sales personnel previously or is it relatively underdeveloped by the particular firm?

These are but a few of the questions management must answer if they wish to understand the vacancy they are seeking to fill.

THE GRID CONCEPT

An alternative approach to the questions developed is provided in the work of Blake and Mouton.[5] These authors developed two grids called a sales grid and a customer grid. Together these two grids may be utilized by management to understand better the type of sales person needed in a particular territory or the types of customer typically encountered in this territory.

Figure 6.1 provides an illustration of the **sales grid.** The sales grid assists management in understanding the interaction needed in a particular sales representative between "Concern for the Sale" (horizontal axis) and "Concern for the Customer" (vertical axis). Both of these factors could be estimated with a range of scores from a low of 1 to a high of 9. Thus, a salaried sales person who does not receive a commission may be expected to rate relatively low in terms of concern for the sale. Likewise, a sales representative paid on a "straight commission" basis (no sale—no pay) may be rated at 8 or 9 and viewed by potential clients as "pushy." Evaluation in terms of customer concern might also vary from

[5] Robert R. Blake and Jane S. Mouton, *The Grid for Sales Excellence: Benchmarks for Effective Salesmanship* (New York: McGraw-Hill Book Company, Inc., 1970).

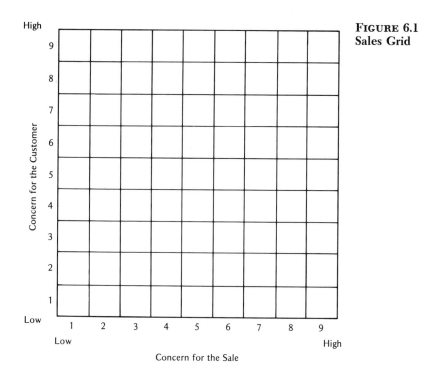

FIGURE 6.1
Sales Grid

virtually no concern (a score of 1 on the vertical scale) to great concern (a score of 9).

Sales management might find the sales grid of great use when engaging in a recruiting and selection decision. However, as noted earlier, specific

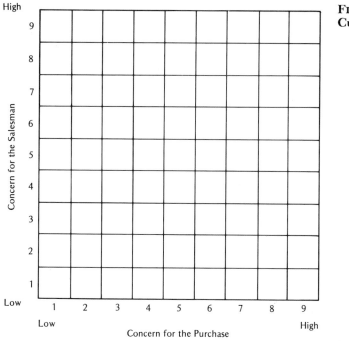

FIGURE 6.2
Customer Grid

Sales Grid Style	Customer Grid Styles				
	1, 1	1, 9	5, 5	9, 1	9, 9
9, 9	+	+	+	+	+
9, 1	0	+	+	0	0
5, 5	0	+	+	−	0
1, 9	−	+	0	−	0
1, 1	−	−	−	−	−

FIGURE 6.3 Probable Effectiveness: Sales Grid/Customer Grid Styles

Probable Effectiveness of Interaction:

+ − Likely to be effective
0 − Neutral/Cannot determine effectiveness
− − Likely to be Ineffective

knowledge of the territory in question will be needed to utilize fully this concept.

Figure 6.2 presents the **customer grid.** Similar to the sales grid, this view considers "Concern for the Purchase" (horizontal axis) and "Concern for the Salesman" (vertical axis) from the potential customer's point of view. Just as sales personnel can be judged as relatively high or low on variables in the sales grid, so too may customers be judged and plotted on the customer grid.

Used in concert, these two grids would help sales management determine in advance the probability of success (or failure) for a particular sales candidate in a particular territory. A 1,9 sales grid style would likely succeed only in a 1,9 customer grid type of territory. A 9,9 sales grid type of sales representative, on the other hand, should succeed with almost any type of customer. Likewise, a 1,1 sales grid sales representative is quite likely going to be uniformly unsuccessful with virtually any type of customer in a given territory. A table summarizing the likelihood of achieving compatibility between sales representative and customer is provided in Figure 6.3.

Prior to closing this discussion of the grid concept, a point made earlier should be stressed. Much time and cost is required in advance of recruiting and selection if this concept is to be used effectively. Further, in sales territories characterized by wide diversity between customers in the same territory, it may be necessary to carry this analysis down to the level of individual customers rather than attempting application on a territory-wide basis. In either instance, management must be willing to gather the data and spend the required time and money if the concept is to be of use.

The Job Description

Once having examined types of questions and considerations, such as those mentioned earlier in this chapter, the sales manager is now in a position to develop at least an informal job description. In preparing this description the sales manager may seek help from others in the firm. If the firm is large, personnel specialists may assist in developing the job description. In a smaller firm, the sales manager may wish to counsel with others to see if sufficient agreement exists on the job description before proceeding.

DEVELOPING A JOB DESCRIPTION

The process of reviewing the sales position is called a job analysis. The end product of a job analysis should be a written job description. Management texts see this end product as a job description that "identifies and describes the job and specifies the requirements of the job."[6] Such a job description might include the following:

1. Duties and responsibilities of the sales representative.
2. Administrative relationships indicating to whom the salesman reports.
3. Title of the specific job (for example, sales trainee versus inside salesman) together with the skills and requirements to fill the job.

Job descriptions might be developed for personnel who are involved in selling along the lines of the five basic categories of salespeople identified by *Sales & Marketing Management*. The five categories of salespeople they differentiate among include:

Account representative—A salesperson who calls on a large number of already established customers in, for example, the food, textiles, apparel, and wholesaling industries. Much of this selling is low key, and there is minimal pressure to develop new business.

Detail salesperson—A salesperson who, instead of directly soliciting an order, concentrates on performing promotional activities and introducing products. The medical detail man, for example, seeks to persuade doctors, the indirect customers, to specify the pharmaceutical company's trade name product for prescriptions. The firm's actual sale is ultimately made through a wholesaler or direct to pharmacists who fill prescriptions.

Sales engineer—A salesperson who sells products for which technical know-how and the ability to discuss technical aspects of the product are extremely important. The salesperson's expertise in identifying, analyzing, and solving customer problems is another critical factor. This type of selling is common in the chemical, machinery, and heavy equipment industries.

Industrial products salesperson, nontechnical—This salesperson sells a tangible product to industrial or commercial purchasers; no high degree of technical knowledge is required. Industries such as packaging materials or standard office equipment use this type.

Service salesperson—A salesperson who sells intangibles, such as insurance and advertising. Unlike the four preceding types, those who sell service must be able to sell the benefits of intangibles.[7]

---

[6] Leslie W. Rue and Lloyd L. Byars, *Management: Theory and Application* (Homewood, Ill.: Richard D. Irwin, Inc., 1977), p. 146.
[7] "Cost Per Call Up Sharply in 1977," *Sales & Marketing Management*, February 27, 1978, p. 21.

USES OF JOB DESCRIPTIONS

A recent study by the American Management Association reveals that aid in recruiting is only one of the functions of the job description. Other uses include use as a basis for performance appraisal, clarification of job

FIGURE 6.4 Job Description: Field Sales Representative

I. PRODUCTS SOLD:

    A. Hospital, surgical specialities, and patient-care items. All of the products sold are utilized in the diagnostic phase, in actual surgical procedures, or in the general pre- and postoperative care of the hospital patient. A portion of the product line is devoted to patient prostheses and appliances.

II. CALLS ON CUSTOMERS:

    A. Type of customers called:

        1. Recognized surgical supply distributors, who stock a wide range of hospital, physician and laity supplies. The distributor maintains an active sales force of his own and covers a representative area that includes numerous hospital and physician accounts.

        2. General and specialized hospitals that care for the ill.

        3. Physicians who specialize in the practice of urology and other specialized branches of surgery, particularly anesthesiology and cardiovascular surgery.

    B. Frequency of Calls (Minimums expected)

        1. Surgical supply distributors—as often as necessary, depending upon volume realized and cooperation received.

        2. Hospitals, under 50 beds—whenever practical (no schedule)

                50–99 beds—2 calls per year
                100–245 beds—6 calls per year
                250 and over—12 calls per year

        3. Physicians (specialized)—recognized urologists should be called on in their offices a minimum of twice per year. Urological residents should be called on each time a call is made at the hospital where they are in attendance. (It is suggested that a minimum of one physician call per day be made; more if time permits.)

    C. Personnel to be called on:

        1. Surgical supply distributors—all personnel including owners, management, purchasing, sales management, purchasing, sales management, inventory control, and all stock and order department people. In addition, the Bard representative is expected to know outside sales personnel of his distributors, and distributor sales personnel who work in his area but are associated with important customers outside his area.

        2. Hospitals.

           a. 100 beds and over—Administrator or Assistant, Purchasing Personnel, Operating Room Supervisor, Obstetrics Supervisor, Pediatric Nursing Supervisor, Cysto Supervisor, Central Supply Room Supervisor, Director of Nurses and/or Director of Nursing Services and Education, Anesthesiologicst, I.V. therapists, chest surgeons, all urologists and and urological residents, and the Cheif of Staff.

           b. Under 100 beds—Administrator, Purchasing Personnel, Operating Room Supervisor, Central Supply Room Supervisor, Cysto Supervisor, Director of Nursing, Anesthesiologist, all urologists, chest surgeon, if available.

3. Physicians (specialized)—As outlined under frequency of calls.
4. Using market potentials provided to plan work in the areas where maximum return may be expected.

D. Type of selling required:
1. Creative selling—placing sales emphasis on the needs of the buyer. Promotion of items that benefit the hospital and patient, with better patient care the end result.
2. Missionary selling—introducing new items to hospitals, distributors and physicans. Calling on prospects previously never contacted.
3. Follow up calls on accounts who have accepted new products or the general line for first time to ensure continued business. Plan and hold a sales meeting at least once a year with all dealers doing annual volume of $15,000 per year. Unless specifically directed, sales meetings with dealers having less volume is optional.
4. Promoting the established general line to all established accounts both hospital, doctor and distributor in an effort to increase the volume of items purchased.
5. Distributor calls—introduction of new items to surgical distributors. Conduct dealer sales meetings to stimulate their sales force to promote your product line. Call and procure stock orders regularly from distributors after establishing reasonable inventory levels on your merchandise.

III. OTHER PROMOTIONAL WORK REQUIRED:

A. Conduct meetings at the hospital level when necessary to indoctrinate nursing personnel on new techniques, and new products.

B. Teach dealer salesmen how to sell new items and the standard product line with emphasis on exclusive features and advantages not offered by the competition.

C. Conduct market surveys and assist in market testing new items when or if requested by marketing department.

D. Initiate and conduct Concept Procedural Studies in hospitals (outlined in Concept Selling Brochure).

IV. CLERICAL WORK REQUIRED:

A. Daily call reports. During the month of January each year, the salesmen should fill out and send to the home office and divisional managers, a Call Report on all of his hospitals listing by name and title all the people to be called on at each institution.

B. Weekly summary of calls.

C. Weekly expense report. Traveletter.

D. Filing of above forms in own file.

E. Writing up dealer stock and turnover orders on company forms.

F. Requests for samples.

G. Memos to home office and divisional managers requesting or conveying information.

H. Itinerary, advance cards, and miscellaneous records.

I. Send copies of all correspondence and reports to divisional managers.

V. RESPONSIBILITY TO IMMEDIATE SUPERVISOR:

A. Every sales representative is assigned to a division that incorporates several sales territories.

B. Each division is managed by a divisional manager who is responsible for all of the sales representatives and territories in his division.

C. All territory sales representatives are under the supervision of and accountable to the divisional manager of his division.

D. The sales representative carries out all instructions and performs all duties assigned to him by his divisional manager. He is under the supervision of his manager on all matters pertaining to the sales operation of his territory.

E. It is the responsibility of the sales representative to know and be able to advise his divisional manager what hospitals in his area are using comparable products of another manufacturer. He is expected to dispatch competitive product and price information to his manager as he learns it.

F. He should know product usage in his territory and the percentage of business by product line which he controls.

G. It is the responsibility of the sales representative to recommend to his divisional manager the addition or deletion of distributors in his territory.

VI. PERSONALITY AND PHYSICAL CHARACTERISTICS REQUIRED

A. Applicant must have the highest character evidenced by sincere, honest, and ethical behavior.

B. Well-groomed, neat appearance.

C. Good posture, sales bearing.

D. Must be in good health, able to travel by all forms of transportation.

E. Demonstrate skills of persuasion.

F. Affable, personable, and enthusiastic.

G. High degree or self-discipline and motivation.

H. Good organizer, with qualities of leadership.

I. Persistent and able to follow directions.

VII. MINIMUM REQUIREMENTS AS TO EDUCATION AND PRODUCT OR SPECIAL KNOWLEDGE:

A. College degree preferred, but not mandatory if comparable experience or knowledge is evidenced.

B. No technical education required, but strong interest in the sale of technical items used in the hospital industry is an asset.

C. Persons with successful sales records and background in any area of marketing will be extended preference.

D. Applicants with no sales background, but exhibiting strong sales desire will be interviewed and tested for sales aptitude.

E. All applicants will be personally interviewed and tested by professional testing agency examination forms.

VIII. TRAVEL REQUIRED:

A. Representative must be able and willing to routinely travel extensively within the confines of his assigned territory, remaining away from home overnight when necessary. In addition, representative will be required to travel outside of his own territory when his attendance at conventions, meetings, conferences and so on is required.

responsibilities, planning for future expansion, and so on. This study is especially useful for marketers.

Though likely more detailed than the typical firm's job description, Figure 6.4 provides an actual job description for a field sales representative of a manufacturer of health care products. Note that the detail provided in such a job description has use beyond the recruiting stage.[8]

Locating Prospective Sales Force Members

Thus far, we have proceeded through an examination of the sales job to be filled and have developed a written job description. Depending upon available time and cost considerations, we may have developed a feeling for the particular sales opening based upon customer and/or sales grids. The next step in the process of recruiting and selection is to locate prospective candidates for the sales position we wish to fill.

AN OVERVIEW

Figure 6.5 brings together many of the considerations for a sales representative that might be used in locating prospects. Notice that this view suggests that three variables are critical: (1) what the sales representative is, (2) what the sales representative knows, and (3) what the sales representative does. Some of the terminology (for example "prospecting") may require elaboration. This will be covered in the following chapter (Sales Training, Chapter 7).

Likewise, a recent *Journal of Marketing Research* article suggests that identification of successful industrial salesmen can be accomplished by starting with "major behavioral functions" of the sales job. Three such functions mentioned in this article are

- *Direct selling.* This would include activities associated with "contacting customers, making sales presentations and demonstrations, handling sales objections and closing the sale."[9]
- *Effective territory management.* This would include the salesman's "allocation of selling effort among products, customers, and prospects; planning for territory coverage and communications comprising sales plans and reports of sales activity and expenses."[10]
- *Customer service.* This includes "developing and maintaining a satisfactory business relationship between his customers and his company."[11]

[8] Jo Ann Sperling, *Job Descriptions in Marketing Management* (New York: American Management Association, 1969).
[9] Lawrence M. Lamont and William J. Lundstrom, "Identifying Successful Industrial Salesmen by Personality and Personal Characteristics," *Journal of Marketing Research* (Vol. XIV, No. 4), November 1977, pp. 517–527 at p. 518.
[10] *Ibid.*
[11] *Ibid.*

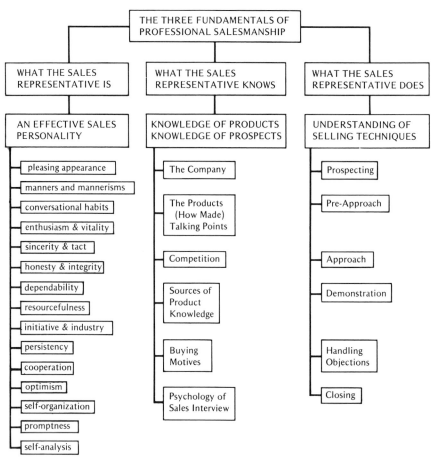

FIGURE 6.5

RECRUITING AND SELECTION: A RECIPROCAL RELATIONSHIP

As Jolson states, "Quite often, the terms recruitment and selection are used interchangeably."[12] Although this does occur, the two terms actually suggest differing activities of a reciprocal nature. Recruiting involves those activities of seeking out, interviewing, and inducing qualified applicants to apply for the open sales position. Recruiting in fact involves selling potential applicants upon the value and benefits of the job available as a sales representative. Selection, on the other hand, involves a decision making process whereby a choice is made among applicants previously recruited. If the sales manager has done a good job of recruiting, the selection process is a delightful one in that the firm may choose among several qualified recruits. In other cases where either the quality or quantity of qualified applicants is lacking, the firm may face a "lesser of evils" proposition. In such instances, a decision often must be made between

[12] Marvin A. Jolson, *Sales Management: A Tactical Approach* (New York: Petrocelli Charter Publishers, Inc., 1977), p. 170.

restarting the search and recruiting process or hiring an applicant that management views with apprehension. Clearly, this is an undesirable situation.

We have stated that the relationship between recruiting and selection is a reciprocal one. By this we mean that time well spent in recruiting, though perhaps looming large when it must be done, will pay dividends at the time of selection. Many sales managers can tell tales of woe about recruiting that was prematurely truncated when a desirable applicant was located. Then, due to a change in timing or some other uncontrollable variable, the applicant was lost to another job, leaving the original sales manager without a desirable applicant. The moral of this story is that it is generally a wise policy to *over*recruit. In fact, many firms have a formal policy of recruiting continuously, even though they may have no "open" position at the moment. Although this may be desirable from the standpoint of having a large number of qualified applicants available at any given time, many sales managers simply cannot afford the luxury of so doing. They, like the example mentioned at the start of this chapter, cannot afford to take time away from other activities unless an actual opening exists.

INTERNAL RECRUITING SOURCES

Now we turn our attention to actual sources of applicants. When a vacancy arises, many sales managers overlook a potential source of qualified applicants—internal (company) sources. Let us explore the meaning of "internal" sources.

Just as any good marketer attempts to determine how new customers learn about the firm's products and/or services, so too is it important for a firm recruiting sales candidates to determine how applicants learn about the open sales position.

We have previously indicated that a reciprocal relationship exists between recruiting and selection. Further, we indicated a need for effective recruiting in order to provide a positive selection environment. A large food marketer was interested in evaluating the effectiveness of his/her firm's recruiting. The following information in Figure 6.6 reflects three

Source	Number of Applicants	% of Total Applicants	Number of Trainees Selected	% of Total Trainees Selected	Number Completing Training	% of Placement on Source
Company Ads	104	49.1	13	32.5	12	11.5
Employment Agencies	42	19.8	6	15.0	4	9.5
Educational Institutions	36	17.0	10	25.0	10	27.8
Internal Transfers	12	5.7	6	15.0	5	41.7
Employee Recommendation	11	5.2	4	10.0	4	36.4
Unsolicited	7	3.3	1	2.5	1	14.3
Totals	212	100.1	40	100.0	36	N/A*

*Although not applicable as straight percentages, these figures are very important to management.

FIGURE 6.6   Recruiting, Selections, and Placement Data—Personal Sales Force, 1977–1978

types of useful information. First, information on sources of recruits is tabulated. Second, since many recruits are not selected for employment (review preceding discussion of selection versus recruiting if necessary), the sources of applicants selected are also identified. Last, the firm in question utilizes a standardized sales training program. Since some selected applicants are rejected or fail to complete this initial training program, we are also able to determine the sources of actual new field sales personnel. Note that Figure 6.6 represents a 2-year period and should not be used for generalization purposes since it reflects the experience of only one firm.

Notice that this firm has used six different sources for sales applicants in the 2-year period represented in Figure 6.6. Only two of these six are "internal" to the firm (internal transfers and employee recommendation). Further, an examination of the number of applicants reveals that the two "internal" sources have provided a small percentage (less than 11 per cent together) of total applicants. When one proceeds to examine the number of applicants selected (hired) by the company, these two sources have clearly provided a disproportionately large number of individuals. Further, when one examines the percentage of trainees completing the initial training program and placed in field sales assignments, the two internal sources again proved especially significant. However, these comments should not be taken to indicate that internal sources are necessarily superior to external ones. This data is for only one firm at one point in time.

Before leaving Figure 6.6 the multiple uses of such data should be stressed. The firm in Figure 6.6 might well utilize such information to make changes in recruiting procedures and policies. The company ads and employment agencies appear to be generating a very large number of initial job applicants. However, the relatively low number of trainees hired from these two "external" sources should be disturbing to sales management. Likewise, applicants obtained from these two sources seem especially vulnerable to a "drop out" effect during initial sales training. Together, these facts should "flag" these two sources for further examination. Are the firm's ads misleading? Are the employment agencies unclear as to job requirements or benefits? These are questions sales management should seek to answer.

Internal sources are certainly worthy of managerial consideration. Where available, internal sources often have advantages in terms of cost to the firm and speed. When current employees recommend a friend for a position, it generally costs the firm nothing. However, many firms make a "token" payment to the employee if the friend they recommend is selected for employment.

EXTERNAL SOURCES

External sources for sales applicants are often expensive in terms of out-of-pocket costs. Nevertheless, they frequently represent sound investments when the costs are considered in relation to the managerial time and expense. Consider a sales manager making $40,000 a year who spends 2 weeks interviewing prospective candidates for a sales position. Since 2 weeks represents roughly 4 per cent of the working time the sales manager has to invest during the year, the firm's cost of his personal interviewing time equals $1600.00. This cost alone is often sufficient to warrant use of an external source such as an employment agency. However, the point made earlier should be stressed. It is not solely the cost that the firm must consider. An employment agency that constantly provides applicants who terminate shortly after hiring represents a poor investment for the firm. In similar fashion, company ads that produce large numbers of unqualified respondents represent a poor expenditure of funds.

As a final note on internal and external sources, it should be noted that these two are not necessarily mutually exclusive. Some firms purposely elect to use both sources of applicants concurrently in order to maximize the number of sales applications received. When such a policy is followed, the sales manager is in an excellent position to compare the quality of applicants resulting.

WOMEN IN SELLING

The passage of the Civil Rights Act of 1964 resulted in drastic impacts upon all facets of company policies and operations, including recruiting and selection procedures. Guidelines for compliance with nondiscriminatory personnel policies have been developed by two government agencies, the Equal Employment Opportunity Commission (EEOC) and the Office of Federal Contract Compliance (OFCC). These guidelines are aimed at avoidance of discrimination based upon age, race, color, religion, sex, or national origin. Although significant changes have come about in selling and sales management in many of these areas, one in particular seems relatively unchanged—sex.

So ingrained is the male image in selling that we often say "sales*man*" without thinking of the implicit bias. What changes are occurring where women are concerned? What impact may these changes have upon selling and sales management?

A recent *Journal of Marketing* article provides some useful information on women and selling/sales management.[13] As background information, this article points out that women hold fewer than 18 per cent of United States managerial jobs.[14] Regarding selling specifically, results of the Research Institute of America show that 81 per cent of United States firms surveyed have not hired any saleswomen.[15] Additionally, research

[13] Dan H. Robertson and Donald W. Hackett, "Saleswomen: Perceptions, Problems and Prospects," *Journal of Marketing* (Vol. 41, No. 3), July 1977, pp. 66–71.
[14] Special Subcommittee on Education of the House Committee on Education and Labor, 1970 Hearings, *Discrimination Against Women*, Parts I and II.
[15] "RIA-SECNY Study Finds 81% of U.S. Businesses Employ No Saleswomen," *Marketing News*, July 15, 1974, p. 1. Quoted from *Women in Selling: The Problems and the Promise*, a study sponsored by Research Institute of America and Sales Executive Club of New York.

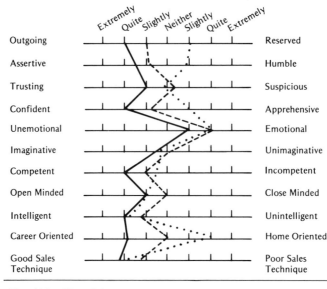

FIGURE 6.7
Profile of
Saleswomen

Mean Values Charted above are:

	Saleswomen	Salesmen	Sales Manager
Outgoing/Reserved	2.3	2.9	5.1
Assertive/Humble	2.7	2.9	5.0
Trusting/Suspicious	3.3	3.9	3.7
Confident/Apprehensive	2.2	3.4	5.0
Unemotional/Emotional	4.9	5.8	5.8
Imaginative/Unimaginative	3.7	3.9	3.5
Competent/Incompetent	1.8	3.1	3.3
Open Minded/Close Minded	2.8	3.9	3.1
Intelligent/Unintelligent	1.9	2.6	2.3
Career Oriented/Home Oriented	2.3	4.1	5.7
Good Sales Technique/Poor Sales Technique	1.8	3.1	2.4

Legend	Salesmen,	Saleswomen,	. . .	Sales Managers

Significant at .05 level.

sponsored by the 3000-member Sales Executive Club of New York revealed that women make up only 4 per cent of their members' sales forces.[16]

One of the issues explored in this research concerned the perceptions of saleswomen *vis à vis* their male sales peers. Figure 6.7 presents a comparison of perceptions of saleswomen by three groups—saleswomen

[16] John Costello, "Ms. Star in Sales," *Marketing Times,* March–April 1975, pp. 4–9.

themselves, male sales representatives, and sales managers (over 95 per cent male).

Notice that sales managers tend to view female sales representatives as significantly more reserved, humble, apprehensive, emotional, incompetent, and home oriented than their male counterparts. Taken together these factors provide some definite reasons why women have experienced only "limited" success in achieving equality in the professional sales area.

The authors of this study conclude:

Regarding perceptions by sales managers, a "show me" attitude seems to permeate attitudes toward female sales representatives. If management is to take advantage of the latent sales talent in the female work force, it would seem that the onus for change is up to both management and prospective saleswomen. To eliminate discrimination in the future, sales executives must reexamine their own attitudes toward women in sales, look at the actual data regarding women in sales, and provide them with the sales training required to perform the sales role successfully. Additionally, management must acquire a new sensitivity to women in sales and realize that perhaps personality dimensions, such as emotionality, are indeed different in men and women sales personnel and make adjustments in their interaction with women. Women must also be willing to accept some role reversal when they enter the sales arena. Commitment to the job is essential if they are to be accepted by their male peers and superiors. Additionally, travel, sales quota pressure, and such social reversals as the purchase of male clients' lunches are only a few "life style" changes saleswomen must voluntarily adopt before genuine acceptance and quality will be obtained.[17]

Additional implications concerning females in selling and sales management will be discussed in Chapter 13.

Applicant Evaluation and Selection

We have now covered the first two of three tasks associated with recruiting and selection. Specifically, we have discussed development of a thorough understanding of what is needed in the particular sales position and, secondly, we have discussed sources of applicants. We conclude this chapter with the third and final task, that of evaluation and selection.

Selection differs from evaluation in that it implies a final choice among alternatives. Evaluation makes no final choice but rather provides a ranking of alternatives on the basis of predetermined criteria.

Prior to discussing actual selection procedures, it is useful to understand some of the evaluative measures sales management may employ. One of the central concepts important for sales managers to understand is that of turnover.

TURNOVER: FRIEND OR FOE?

Turnover is the percentage of the average sales force leaving the firm's employ during a given year. The term *average* sales force is impor-

---

[17] Robertson and Hackett, *op. cit.*, p. 71.

tant since it typically fluctuates slightly from time to time in most firms. Many firms calculate average sales force size by simply taking sales force size at year's end and year's start and dividing by two.[18] Once this is accomplished, turnover is calculated:

$$\text{turnover } \% = \frac{\text{number of persons leaving the sales force}}{\text{average sales force size}}$$

Two mental biases must be guarded against in discussing turnover. First, it is typical to think of turnover as a negative. Thus, the larger the turnover percentage, the worse the effect. Second, it is also typical to think of turnover as being less that 100 per cent. Both of these mental biases can be very misleading.

Many sales organizations get into difficulties by having too low a turnover figure. This may be indicative of sales management that has become overly complacent. Likewise, it is possible, though perhaps highly undesirable, to have turnover in excess of 100 per cent. In firms where organizational structure is in a state of flux or where a large number of new sales territories have been created, turnover can run well over 100 per cent.

Sales management must continuously seek to answer two questions concerning turnover. First, why has turnover taken place? Second, what is the cost of the turnover?

Causes of turnover can include "positive" as well as "negative" factors. A sales representative promoted to management produces turnover just as does the firing of a sales representative. However, the former may be a generally healthy cause of turnover, whereas the latter may give management cause for concern.

The cost of turnover is no better understood than the costs of recruiting and selection. Two empirically based studies[19] suggest that "replacement" costs of recruiting, selecting, and training a sales representative probably exceed $10,000.00 for most firms. Clearly high turnover rates may produce an excessive drain on profits.

Another factor important in recruiting and selection is the dated, but perhaps still valid, negative image of selling. Numerous studies[20] (generally using undergraduate college students as respondents) suggest that selling produces a negative evaluation when considered as an occupation.[21] One study found that "insurance agent" and "traveling salesman for a wholesale concern" both ranked well below the average in rankings of occupational prestige for a wide variety of United States occupations.[22]

[18] See, for example, Albert H. Dunn and Eugene M. Johnson, *Managing the Sales Force* (Morristown, N.J.: General Learning Press, 1973), p. 39.

[19] See, for example, studies in *Marketing Insights*, February 12, 1968, p. 11; and "It Cost $6,685 to Fire a Man," *Sales Management*, March 15, 1955, p. 29.

[20] See, for example, John L. Mason, "The Low Prestige of Personal Selling," *Journal of Marketing* (Vol. 29, No. 4), October 1965, pp. 7–10; "Selling Is a Dirty Word," *Sales Management* (Vol. 89), October 5, 1962, pp. 44–47; and John L. Mason, "The Salesman's Prestige: A Reexamination," *Business Topics* (Vol. 10), Autumn 1962, pp. 73–77.

[21] David L. Kurtz, "Student Attitudes Toward a Sales Career: A Reexamination," *Journal of College Placement* (Vol. 30), December 1969–January 1970, pp. 85–86, 88.

[22] P. M. Hodge and P. H. Rossi, "Occupational Prestige in the United States, 1925–1963," *American Journal of Sociology* (Vol. 70), November 1964, pp. 286–302.

Thus the sales manager may face an "uphill task" in convincing qualified applicants of the merit of working as a sales representative.

EVALUATION AND SELECTION TOOLS AND TECHNIQUES

Evaluation and selection techniques vary widely from one firm to another. Some firms rely upon a subjective evaluation of potential candidates based largely upon the "chemistry" occurring in one or a few personal interviews. At the opposite end of the spectrum would be firms that assign a specific number of points to certain criteria.

The critical point for sales management is not the mechanical features of a given evaluation or selection technique but, rather, how well a group or combination of techniques work in terms of attracting desirable candidates. Commenting upon this point, other authors conclude:

No selection system is infallible; all eliminate some who would have succeeded as sales people and recommend hiring some who fail. A selection system fulfills its main mission if it improves management's ability to estimate success-and-failure probabilities of individual applicants. Every company should design its selection system to fit its own requirements.[23]

In a study published in 1970,[24] Wotruba identified selection tools and techniques used in sales recruiting in two ways. From a sample of 84 responding firms, Wotruba identified frequency of use for eight selection tools—interviews, application blanks, physical exams, references, intelligence tests, aptitude tests, personality tests, and miscellaneous. Figure 6.8 summarizes these findings. An additional finding from Wotruba's work was considered when in the recruiting process each tool was used. Figure 6.9 summarizes these findings and suggests that, although techniques such as interviews and application blanks tend to be used early in the

Selection Tool	Percent of Respondents	
	Using Tool	Not Using Tool
Interviews	100%	0%
Application Blanks	93	7
Physical Exams	83	17
References	74	26
Intelligence Tests	61	39
Aptitude Tests	50	50
Personality Tests	29	71
Others Written In	12	88

FIGURE 6.8 Incidence of Use of Salesmen Selection Tools

[23] Richard R. Still, Edward W. Cundiff, and Norman A. P. Govoni, *Sales Management: Decisions, Policies, and Cases,* 3rd ed. (Englewood Cliffs, N.J.: Prentice-Hall, Inc., 1976), p. 243.
[24] Thomas R. Wotruba, "An Analysis of the Salesmen Selection Process," *The Southern Journal of Business* (Vol. 5), January, 1970, pp. 41–51.

Selection Tool	*Percent of Respondents Checking*				
	One of First Tools Used	Used Early But Not First	Used Later But Not Last	One of Last Tools Used	Not Used Or Other Answer
Interviews	76%	16%	1%	1%	6%
Application Blanks	88	3	2	2	5
Physical Exams	7	7	23	51	12
References	17	23	24	29	7
Intelligence Tests	14	36	20	12	18
Aptitude Tests	13	33	22	11	21
Personality Tests	2	22	25	22	29

FIGURE 6.9 Ratings of Each Tool on the Basis of Its Order of Use in Selecting Salesmen

process of selection, physical exams and references tend to be used near the end of the process.

The findings in Figure 9 are hardly surprising, but they do serve to underscore an important consideration—that of cost. Since both physical and personality testing tend to be rather expensive, it seems prudent to use these only when management has previously been "sold" on the candidate.

SELECTION TOOLS AND TECHNIQUES—AN OVERVIEW

A study of the salesman selection process by Cotham[25] suggests that, in recruiting and selecting sales personnel, three basic types of information are utilized. These include cognitive factors (intelligence and sales aptitude), life history experiences (application blank items), and interpersonal measures (empathy, social intelligence, and personality). As this research suggests, although widely used by many firms, the efficacy of these as selection tools fluctuates widely. Basically, cognitive and interpersonal factors must be determined by testing, whereas life history experience can often be assessed on the basis of written information from an application blank or information conveyed orally in recruiting/selection interview sessions.

Tests have been designed to aid in the measurement of intelligence, aptitudes, personality, and other interpersonal factors. College students are often admitted or denied admission to college based upon one or more "intelligence" tests. Aptitude tests are sometimes called "ability" tests, and seek to measure existing traits. Most states include visual perceptual tests as part of their driver's license examination procedures. These perceptual tests represent aptitude tests. Lastly, personality tests seek to measure the extent to which specific personality traits exist within an individual. Personality tests vary a great deal in their length and complexity. Often these tests require clinical interpretations.

Recall the earlier comment indicating that recruiting techniques and

[25] James C. Cotham III, "Selecting Salesmen: Approaches and Problems," *MSU Business Topics,* Winter 1970, pp. 64–72.

tools are not used uniformly by all firms. Testing is no exception. Many sales executives feel that testing is "virtually worthless," whereas others feel testing can help avoid hiring individuals who do not belong in selling. An earlier reference places the "waste" brought about by hiring the wrong people as sales personnel at over $3 billion annually.[26] As these differing positions suggest, wide disagreement exists as to the value of testing in aiding sales recruiting. In order to permit students to develop their own opinion on this matter, one actual example of a test that might be used in recruiting and selection is included in the Student Learning Exercise in this chapter. If the student uses this resource, the following limitations should be noted:

1. The test included is only *one* example of many types of testing instruments.
2. Important reasons for including this test are that the test is short (typically requiring less than 15 minutes to complete); it may be self-scored (expert interpretation is *not* required), hence "privacy" of results is possible; and, lastly, "norms" for comparison are included, thus providing a *relative* dimension (your score relative to others) for score interpretation.
3. This test does not purport to measure an individual's entire or complete personality. Rather, it measures only three personality traits.
4. As with any personality test, the subjects may bias their responses if they so choose.

A last note on testing concerns legality. As of this writing, the legality of testing as a basis for applicant rejection is very unclear.[27] Some sales managers have elected to cease testing simply to avoid potential lawsuits! More will be said on this point in Chapter 13.

Just as the legality of testing is in question as a selection technique, so too is much of the information traditionally found, or expected, on employment application blanks. For example, which of the following types of application blank questions might be "hazardous" as a possible base for discrimination charges?[28]

- Age—date of birth
- Length of time at present address
- Height and/or weight
- Marital status
- Ages of children
- Occupation of spouse
- Relatives already employed by the firm
- Person to notify in case of emergency
- Type of military discharge
- References

[26] "Sales Execs to Waste $3 Billion," *The Marketing News,* Mid-December 1970, p. 8.
[27] See, for example, *Proposed Employment Testing and Other Selection Procedures* (Washington, D.C.: Office of Federal Contrast Compliance, 1971).
[28] Adapted from "Employment Application Forms: Avoiding Discrimination Problems," The Research Institute of America, Inc., in *Marketing for Sales Executives* (Vol. 4, No. 9), May 11, 1978, pp. 1–3.

The reader may be shocked to learn that *all* of these questions are potential dangers.

In summary, although the need for full background information on prospective employees is obvious, potential legal complications present a significant barrier to the acquisition of such data. Chapter 13 will discuss the implications of this point in detail.

Summary

This chapter has focused upon a time consuming and often thankless but, nevertheless, critical sales management activity—sales recruiting and selection. Three basic tasks lead to accomplishment of this activity. First, management must fully understand the particular sales position. Second, sources of potential recruits for this position must be identified. Last, recruiting techniques and selection tools were discussed.

Throughout this chapter we have stressed costs. Sales management must continuously weigh the dollar and time costs of recruiting and selection procedures against resulting benefits. One particular problem associated with this point is that costs (both time and dollar costs) impact in the short range. Benefits accruing to the firm usually appear in the long range future.

The environment of sales force recruiting and selection is currently undergoing great changes. The Civil Rights Act, current efforts to recruit women into selling, government agencies such as Equal Employment Opportunity Commission and the Office of Federal Contract Compliance are but a few of the forces producing change. Each of these has been discussed as it relates to sales recruiting and selection.

Discussion Questions

1. What difficulties do firms experience relating to sales recruiting and selection?

2. If you have recently interviewed for a sales position, do you agree with the text references (see footnote 2) of "waste" in recruiting? Why, or why not?

3. What are the three tasks that together comprise recruiting and selection from sales management's perspective? Describe each briefly.

4. In addition to the "Questions Providing Insight" part of this chapter, what additional questions might you add if you were a sales manager?

5. Explain both the sales and customer grids. How might sales management use each effectively?

6. Should a firm realistically expect a written job description for every sales position? How often, if at all, should such job descriptions be revised?

7. How are recruiting and selection interrelated?

8. Contrast internal and external sources of sales applicants.

9. What developments do you foresee for women in selling and/or sales management? Is the future a promising one? Why, or why not?

10. Discuss turnover—can it be too low?

11. What is the traditional view of selling as an occupation by students? In your own opinion, is this view changing?

12. Discuss the timing and value of some of the selection techniques mentioned in this chapter.

Selected References

BLAKE, ROBERT R., and JANE S. MOUTON, *The Grid for Sales Excellence: Benchmarks for Effective Salesmanship* (New York: McGraw-Hill Book Company, Inc., 1970).

DUNN, ALBERT H., and EUGENE M. JOHNSON, *Managing the Sales Force,* (Morristown, N.J.: General Learning Press, 1973), p. 39.

"Employment Application Forms: Avoiding Discrimination Problems," The Research Institute of America, Inc., in *Marketing for Sales Executives,* May 11, 1978, pp. 1–3.

JOLSON, MARVIN A., *Sales Management: A Tactical Approach* (New York: Petrocelli-Charter Publishers, Inc., 1977), p. 170, Chapter 8.

KURTZ, DAVID L., "Student Attitudes Toward a Sales Career: A Reexamination," *Journal of College Placement,* December 1969–January 1970, pp. 85–86, 88.

LAMONT, LAWRENCE M., and WILLIAM J. LUNDSTROM, "Identifying Successful Industrial Salesmen by Personality and Personal Characteristics," *Journal of Marketing Research,* November 1977, pp. 517–518.

LAPP, CHARLES L., and KENNETH J. LACHO, "Selecting the Salesperson: The Heartbeat of Sales Management," *Louisiana Business Survey,* January 1978, pp. 10–13, 15.

ROBERTSON, DAN H., and DONALD W. HACKETT, "Saleswomen: Perceptions, Problems, and Prospects," *Journal of Marketing,* July 1977, pp. 66–71.

"Sales Execs to Waste $3 Billion," *The Marketing News,* Mid-December, 1970, p. 8.

STILL, RICHARD R., EDWARD W. CUNDIFF, and NORMAN A. P. GOVONI, *Sales Management: Decisions, Policies, and Cases,* 3rd ed. (Englewood Cliffs, N.J.: Prentice-Hall, Inc., 1976), p. 243, Chapter 10.

Studies in *Marketing Insights,* February 12, 1968, p. 11; and "It Costs $6,685 to Fire a Man," *Sales Management,* March 15, 1955, p. 29.

WOTRUBA, THOMAS R., "An Analysis of the Salesmen Selection Process," *Southern Journal of Business,* January 1970, pp. 41–51.

CASE 6.1
Excello Oil*

Company Background   Excello Oil began in 1946 in Louisiana. At that time, a major oil company opened the Excello dealerships in an attempt to test the public reaction to discount pricing for gasoline. The Excello name was designed to insure that the general public would not associate the major oil company with the discount operation. However, existing dealers of the parent oil company discovered the operation and protested violently against the internally generated competition. After two of the Excello stations were burned to the ground by disgruntled dealers, the oil company decided to sell the remaining outlets. After the stations stood empty for 2 years, the six outlets were purchased by Crowley Oil Company, a medium-sized producer of petroleum products with a refinery located outside New Orleans.

The decision was made to retain the Excello name, advertise extensively as a low price source for gasoline, but also offer tires, batteries, and accessories supplied by local jobbers. Taking on the major oil companies in such a manner caused a lot of fireworks in the next 10 years with price wars so extreme that Crowley was often near the point of selling the Excello outlets.

However, Excello continued to expand in Louisiana and Texas with their major strength being in the larger metropolitan areas. By 1977 Excello had 200 outlets and a firmly established image, which differed considerably from their early price slashing reputation. Sales of tires, batteries, and accessories had grown to a point where Excello now offered a high quality line, most of which was manufactured for Excello according to their specifications. Crowley supplied Excello with motor oil and performance additives as well as gasoline.

Quality merchandise and a competitive but not lower than market price on gasoline were tied together with a strong sales promotion and merchandising program that gave Excello a good overall image.

Current Situation   New Orleans District Sales Manager Ray Shonner was well aware of the past history of Excello and extremely proud to be a part of a company that had fought its way into a respectable position in a tough market.

* Case prepared by Thomas N. Ingram and Danny N. Bellenger, Georgia State University.

During the past few weeks Ray had a chance to reflect on the company history as he had begun to recruit for a person to fill the Baton Rouge territory by January 1. He had told the Excello story to employment agencies, candidates who had interviewed for the job, and other people he thought might be of assistance in finding the right person for the job. Although a few candidates were referred by the Excello personnel department, Ray had the primary responsibility for recruiting sales representatives in his district.

While reviewing the company history, Ray also had a chance to think about the type of sales representation that had been primarily responsible for the excellent growth of Excello. Since he had been with the company only 4 years, Ray knew just one sales representative who had been with the company from the beginning. Stan Neville was the only original sales representative remaining with Excello, and it was his retirement at the end of the year that had promoted Ray's increased recruiting activity in the past few weeks. While a dealer sales representative in New Orleans, Ray had heard stories of how the sales representatives of the early days ran things with an iron fist. Ray had heard that on more than one occasion Stan Neville and his fellow sales representatives had threatened an uncooperative dealer with a "trip behind the station" if he did not operate as he was expected to. The bright young sales representative of today provided a strong contrast to sales representatives such as Stan Neville. Most of the current group of sales representatives came to Excello with no previous business experience and had been trained to treat the dealers as customers rather than threaten cancellation of the lease as was common in the past if dealers did not do a satisfactory job. Some competitors had even added some women sales representatives.

EXHIBIT 1

Job Description — Dealer Sales Representative

The primary responsibility of the Dealer Sales Representative is the achievement of sales quotas in the following categories:

(1) Gasoline
(2) Motor Oil
(3) Tires
(4) Batteries
(5) Accessories — includes repair parts, fuel additives, and convenience items.

These items are sold to approximately seventy-five independent dealers within a twenty-five mile radius of the sales office.

Other important activities performed by the sales representative include dealer recruiting, dealer training, sales promotion and counseling of the dealers in various business areas. To perform the counseling activities, a knowledge of salesmanship, merchandising and retail accounting is necessary. Another area of responsibility is maintaining appearance standards for the outlets and having necessary repairs made on the property by outside contractors.

Each sales representative is allocated an expense budget of ten thousand dollars per year to handle sales promotion, training and personal selling expenses. This budget is utilized by the sales representative subject to the approval of the district sales manager.

EXHIBIT 2

RESUME 1

NAME:	BETH K. ALEX	TELEPHONE:	(404) 612-3060
ADDRESS:	303 Mill Road	BIRTH DATE:	12/20/48
	Atlanta, Georgia 30303	HEALTH:	Excellent

OBJECTIVE: Leadership position in sales or product management.

EDUCATION: B.A., Economics, Gettysburg College, Pennsylvania, 1971
  GPA – 3.04 overall; 3.6 major.

BUSINESS
EXPERIENCE: March '76 to present: Hallmark Cards, Inc., Atlanta, Georgia.
  Sales and service representative for stationery departments in local department stores. Position has also included work with systems changes, installations of new departments and revisions of existing departments.

  November '75 to January '76: Atlanta Regional Commission, c/o Norrell Temporary Services, Inc., Atlanta, Georgia.
  Survey of law enforcement agencies of the seven-county Atlanta region. Information gathered, compiled and final report completed to the Director.

  July '72 to October '75: Davison's, Division of R. H. Macy, Atlanta, Georgia.
  Completed Executive Development program and progressed through a series of training assignments as Assistant Buyer in books and stationery. Promoted to Group Sales Manager in a suburban store with supervisory responsibilities for personnel, sales quotas, and merchandising in the small wares division. Brought to main store to study the feasibility of a new department in housewares and its breakdown, which included an analytical report on comparisons with other Macy stores and a synopsis of the market. Assumed position of Acting Buyer of said department; management responsibilities included planning, purchasing, advertising, merchandising, and dealing with a myriad of vendors. Consistently received outstanding reviews and salary increases.

ASSOCIATIONS: American Marketing Association – National and Atlanta Chapters.
  Junior League of Atlanta – Active member national volunteer organization. Current placement – Nearly New Thrift Shop.
  High Museum of Art Members' Guild.– Young Careers.
  Atlanta Audubon Society.

OUTSIDE
INTERESTS: Reading, appreciation of art and music, jogging, bird watching, and traveling.

REFERENCES: Available upon request.

Stan was still a crusty hard-liner, but his dealers had grown to respect him and declared their loyalty to Stan anytime Ray had visited the stations. Other indications of Stan's control were his consistent achievement of sales quota and the lowest dealer turnover rate in the district.

Exhibit 2 (cont.)

<u>RESUME 2</u>

NAME: Fred Roberts

AGE: 22

MARITAL STATUS: Married

ADDRESS: 301 Island Court, Baton Rouge, Louisiana

TELEPHONE: 602-6302

REFERENCES: Furnished upon request

<u>CAREER OBJECTIVE</u>

Seek a position in which I can use and improve my skills in acquiring and developing new sources of business for the firm; promotion of existing products and services; oral and written communication; and employee training and education. Prefer a growth oriented firm.

<u>EDUCATION</u>

Undergraduate: 9/73–6/77, Louisiana State University, B.A. in Marketing (minor in Psycyology), cum laude.

University Honors and Activities: Administrative Director and Publicity Director of Interfraternity Government; recipient of three scholarships; J-Club; Blue Key; Omicron Delta Kappa; listed in Who's Who in American Colleges and Universities; Dean's list; member of numerous university committees.

<u>WHAT FRED ROBERTS CAN DO FOR YOU</u>

WRITE

    Management summaries
    Research reports

READ A FINANCIAL STATEMENT

LEARN

    Your business
    Old axioms
    New ideas

SELL

    Your product or service

SPEAK

    Oral reports
    Company presentations
    Talks to outside groups

The dealers seemed to identify strongly with Stan who, like many of the dealers, was a high school graduate from a poor family who had worked hard to achieve success. Many of them had told Ray that they just could not get along with some of the young MBA graduates running the other territories.

EXHIBIT 2 (cont.)

RESUME 3

John J. Fields
5765 Elkridge Drive
New Orleans, Louisiana
Phone: 613-0627

Position Objective:

Position in Sales or Sales Management with a high degree of potential in
Marketing Management.

Experience:

August 1, 1974 to Present — Sales Representative, RMO Rail, New Orleans,
Louisiana. Responsible for managing sales territory in New Orleans. This
territory included several major accounts controlling business in excess of one
million dollars each.

Education:

MBA, Tulane University, 1974. Major area, Marketing. I have taken courses
in Economics, Marketing, Management and Quantitative Methods, and have
maintained a cumulative point average of 3.5 on a 4 point scale.

Bachelor of Science, Business Administration, 1972, Manhattan College,
New York. Major: Marketing. Areas of particular interest. Product Management,
Marketing Research and Advertising.

Personal Background:

Married, excellent health, six feet tall, 188 lbs., 27 years old.

Member of American Marketing Association.

Of the eight sales representatives, only one was considered a career
sales representative other than Stan. John Jarrel had been a sales representative for 10 years, enjoyed his work, and was a reasonably effective
employee. John had come to Ray the day after Stan Neville had announced his plans to retire to discuss the possibility of his taking over
the Baton Rouge territory when Stan retired. He wanted to move to
Baton Rouge primarily because that was his hometown and his wife was
anxious to return there. Ray had told John that he would be considered
for the Baton Rouge territory, but told him that it would be several
weeks before he decided anything. Of the remaining six, there were
three MBA's with less than 2 years experience and three other college
graduates filling the other slots. All six of these people were considered
to be potential management material for Excello or Crowley Oil Company.

The training program for new sales personnel lasted 6 months. After
this 6-month period, the sales representative would take over the territory. Within a year, the sales representative was expected to be performing the activities of the job with a minimum of supervision. Realizing
that the month of May was almost gone, Ray reviewed the resumes of
the top candidates he had thus far interviewed and pondered his next
step. (The sales representative job description is shown in Exhibit 1 and
the resumes of the three top candidates in Exhibit 2).

You have been retained as a consultant by XYZ Hospital Supply Corporation. Mr. Joe Smith, the sales manager of XYZ Hospital Supply, has asked you to look at his company's situation in recruiting salespeople. In particular, Mr. Smith seeks your advice regarding some of the testing procedures his company is using to select salespeople.

Company Background

In the course of your conversation with Mr. Smith, you learned his firm, XYZ Corporation, goes through a two-step process prior to selecting sales representatives. First, an ad is run in several local newspapers [ad is shown below] and promising looking respondents to the ad are then invited to attend a personal interview with Mr. Smith. At the time of the interview, Mr. Smith administers the test [that follows below] and also conducts approximately a 1-hour personal interview.

Current Situation

   One of the reasons you have been selected is that Mr. Smith feels that an outsider may bring a fresh and objective view to this process. Therefore, he has asked you to examine the ad for his corporation and to also take the test yourself in order to better advise XYZ of its merits and drawbacks. Your specific assignment is as follows:

1. Read the ad for a sales representative and offer suggestions for any changes or revisions that you feel are necessary.
2. Answer all 35 questions of the test that is included and then score your results according to the information provided. Also advise XYZ Corporation as to the merits and drawbacks of this particular test.
3. Answer the three specific questions outlined in the conclusions section at the end of this case.

SALES REPRESENTATIVE
XYZ HOSPITAL SUPPLY CORPORATION

   Dynamic marketer, a leader in the hospital supply industry, seeks candidates for the position of sales representative. College degree preferred. Previous sales experience helpful, but not required. Represent our firm to physicians and nursing/medical staff personnel located in hospitals throughout sales territory.
   Excellent compensation package including numerous company benefits. Opportunities for professional growth and advancement abound. This opening reflects growth and expansion created by our marketing management team. To learn more about this outstanding opportunity, send your resume to:

> Mr. Joe Smith, Sales Manager
> XYZ Hospital Supply Corporation
> Chicago, Illinois   12345

* Case prepared by Dan H. Robertson, Georgia State University.

In this booklet you will find a number of incomplete statements followed by six blanks. These statements describe a variety of situations. There are no "right" or "wrong" answers. In fact, people's opinions regarding each statement seem to be quite different. The purpose of this survey will be served best if you accurately report your feelings toward each statement. You may notice that many items are similar. Actually, no two items are exactly alike.

Example:	Extremely Undesirable					Extremely Desirable
Asking a friend to loan you money is:	___	X	___	___	___	___

An X has been placed in the second blank. This means that the situation described is quite undesirable to the individual concerned.

These same six blanks will be provided for each statement. Place a check mark on the blank which best expresses how desirable or undesirable the situation seems to you.

1. Being free of emotional ties with others is:

Extremely ___ ___ ___ ___ ___ ___ Extremely
Undesirable   Desirable

2. Giving comfort to those in need of friends is:

Extremely ___ ___ ___ ___ ___ ___ Extremely
Undesirable   Desirable

3. The knowledge that most people would be fond of me at all times would be:

Extremely ___ ___ ___ ___ ___ ___ Extremely
Undesirable   Desirable

4. To refuse to give in to others in an argument seems:

Extremely ___ ___ ___ ___ ___ ___ Extremely
Undesirable   Desirable

5. Enjoying a good movie by myself is:

Extremely ___ ___ ___ ___ ___ ___ Extremely
Undesirable   Desirable

6. For me to be able to own an item before most of my friends are able to buy it would be:

Extremely ___ ___ ___ ___ ___ ___ Extremely
Undesirable   Desirable

7. For me to pay little attention to what others think of me seems:

Extremely ___ ___ ___ ___ ___ ___ Extremely
Undesirable   Desirable

8. Knowing that others are somewhat envious of me is:

Extremely ___ ___ ___ ___ ___ ___ Extremely
Undesirable   Desirable

9. To feel that I like everyone I know would be:

Extremely ___ ___ ___ ___ ___ ___ Extremely
Undesirable   Desirable

10. To be able to work hard while others are elsewhere having fun is:

Extremely ___ ___ ___ ___ ___ ___ Extremely
Undesirable   Desirable

11. Using pull to get ahead would be:

Extremely ___ ___ ___ ___ ___ ___ Extremely
Undesirable   Desirable

12. For me to have enough money or power to impress self-sytle "bit shots" would be:

Extremely   _____ _____ _____ _____ _____ _____   Extremely
Undesirable   Desirable

13. Basing my life on duty to other is:

Extremely   _____ _____ _____ _____ _____ _____   Extremely
Undesirable   Desirable

14. To work under tension would be:

Extremely   _____ _____ _____ _____ _____ _____   Extremely
Undesirable   Desirable

15. If I could live alone in a cabin in the woods or mountains it would be:

Extremely   _____ _____ _____ _____ _____ _____   Extremely
Undesirable   Desirable

16. Punishing those who insult my honor is:

Extremely   _____ _____ _____ _____ _____ _____   Extremely
Undesirable   Desirable

17. To give aid to the poor and underprivileged is·

Extremely   _____ _____ _____ _____ _____ _____   Extremely
Undesirable   Desirable

18. Standing in the way of people who are too sure ot themselves is:

Extremely   _____ _____ _____ _____ _____ _____   Extremely
Undesirable   Desirable

19. Being free of social obligations is:

Extremely   _____ _____ _____ _____ _____ _____   Extremely
Undesirable   Desirable

20. To have something good to say about everybody seems:

Extremely   _____ _____ _____ _____ _____ _____   Extremely
Undesirable   Desirable

21. Telling a waiter when you have received inferior food is:

Extremely   _____ _____ _____ _____ _____ _____   Extremely
Undesirable   Desirable

22. Planning to get along with others is:

Extremely   _____ _____ _____ _____ _____ _____   Extremely
Undesirable   Desirable

23. To be able to spot and exploit weakness in others is:

Extremely   _____ _____ _____ _____ _____ _____   Extremely
Undesirable   Desirable

24. A strong desire to surpass others' achievements seems:

Extremely   _____ _____ _____ _____ _____ _____   Extremely
Undesirable   Desirable

25. Sharing my personal feelings with others would be:

Extremely   _____ _____ _____ _____ _____ _____   Extremely
Undesirable   Desirable

26. To have the ability to blame others for their mistakes is:

Extremely   _____ _____ _____ _____ _____ _____   Extremely
Undesirable   Desirable

27. For me to avoid situations where others can influence me would be:

Extremely   _____ _____ _____ _____ _____ _____   Extremely
Undesirable   Desirable

28. Wanting to repay others' thoughless actions with friendship is:

Extremely   _____ _____ _____ _____ _____ _____   Extremely
Undesirable   Desirable

29. Having to compete with others for various rewards is:

Extremely Undesirable _____ _____ _____ _____ _____ _____ Extremely Desirable

30. If I knew that others paid little attention to my affairs it would be:

Extremely Undesirable _____ _____ _____ _____ _____ _____ Extremely Desirable

31. To defend my rights by force would be:

Extremely Undesirable _____ _____ _____ _____ _____ _____ Extremely Desirable

32. Putting myself out to be considerate of others' feelings is:

Extremely Undesirable _____ _____ _____ _____ _____ _____ Extremely Desirable

33. Correcting people who express an ignorant belief is:

Extremely Undesirable _____ _____ _____ _____ _____ _____ Extremely Desirable

34. For me to work alone would be:

Extremely Undesirable _____ _____ _____ _____ _____ _____ Extremely Desirable

35. To be fair to people who do things which I consider wrong seems:

Extremely Undesirable _____ _____ _____ _____ _____ _____ Extremely Desirable

Now that you have completed the questionnaire, you may wish to know more about it. This questionnaire was developed by Joel Cohen[1] and Cohen based his questionnaire upon the earlier work of Karen Horney. Horney, along with Fromm and Sullivan, differed strongly with orthodox psychoanalysis theory. Her work at the American Institute of Psychoanalysis led to "a social orientation that greatly broadened prior instinctivist views of personality."[2] Horney did not follow the approach of merely listing a number of traits of needs. In lieu of this, Horney proposed a view of the "whole" individual. She classified individuals into three predominant orientations:

1. People who move toward other people (compliants)—These individuals desire to be included in the activities of others. They possess a marked need for affection and approval. Because of the importance of companionship and affection from others, compliant persons tend to become oversensitive to the needs of others. They also tend to be overgenerous, overgrateful, and overconsiderate. These people seek to subordinate themselves to others thereby avoiding conflict. Since many of their goals are connected with acceptance by others, they frequently go out of their way to conform to what they consider to be behavioral norms prescribed by others.

2. People who move against other people (aggressiveness)—These indi-

[1] Joel B. Cohen, "An Interpersonal Orientation to the Study of Consumer Behavior," *Journal of Marketing Research* (Vol. 4), August 1967, pp. 270–278.

[2] Joel B. Cohen, "The Role of Personality in Consumer Behavior," in Kassarjian and Robertson (eds.), *Perspectives in Consumer Behavior* (Glenview, Ill.: Scott, Foresman and Company, 1968), p. 225.

viduals desire to achieve admiration by excelling or achieving success or prestige. They view other people as rivals in their struggle. Because of this, everyone is thought to be motivated by self-interest. Expressed feelings are thought to be merely a cover to obscure real, hidden objectives. Aggressive persons admire strength, power, and unemotional realism.

3. People who move away from other people (detached)—These persons are described as desiring to put emotional distance between other persons and themselves. Detached individuals consider themselves to be unique, possessing abilities that others do not have. Intelligence and reasoning are viewed as superior to feelings because of the emotional connections with the latter. Detached individuals desire freedom from obligations and may view advances of others with distrust. Self-sufficiency is seen as highly desirable.

Thus, the three traits of personality that this questionnaire purports to measure are compliant, aggressive, and detached traits. To score yourself on this exam, use the following procedure.

Score the response to every question in the same fashion. A check in the far left (extremely undesirable column) is scored as a 1 and on across the scale in integers. Thus a check on the far right (extremely desirable) is scored as a 6.

Scoring Procedure

Extremely Undesirable					Extremely Desirable
1	2	3	4	5	6

- To find your total score on the compliant trait, add your scores on questions 2, 3, 9, 13, 17, 20, 25, 28, 32 and 35.
- To find your total score on the aggressive trait, add your scores on questions 4, 7, 8, 11, 12, 14, 16, 18, 21, 23, 24, 26, 29, 31, and 33.
- To find your total score on the Detached trait, add your scores on questions 1, 5, 6, 10, 15, 19, 22, 27, 30 and 34.

Note that the possible score on any one question is 1 through 6. Additionally, there are

- Ten questions on compliant and thus a possible range of 10 to 60 as a total score.
- Fifteen questions on aggressive and thus a possible range of 15 to 90 as a total score.
- Ten questions on detached and thus a possible range of 10 to 60 as a total score.

Now compare your results with the following "average" scores. These scores represent the average of business students like yourself and people

[3] Karen Horney, *Our Inner Conflicts* (New York, W. W. Norton & Co., Inc., 1945), pp. 48–95.

with no business affiliations (people "in general"). Note that those inclined toward business are more aggressive and less compliant, but almost identical on the detached trait.

	Compliant	Aggressive	Detached
Business	36	51	25
People in general	39	46	26

Conclusion   Now having your set of scores to use plus averages, think about testing in particular and recruiting and selection in general. Advise Mr. Smith in particular and XYZ Hospital Supply Corporation in general as to your thoughts on the following questions:

1. If you were Mr. Smith, would you hire an applicant with the scores you made? Why or why not?
2. How good a job does this test do of measuring the three traits it purports to measure? Also, are you "for" or "against" paper and pencil tests as recruiting/selection aids? Why, or why not?
3. What other information (if any) would Mr. Smith need to base his hiring/selection decision on beside your test scores?

CASE 6.3
Doncaster*

Company Background   As he was sitting in his office on the top floor of an Atlanta skyscraper late one Fall afternoon, Fritz Van Winkle picked up the phone to receive a call from Rutherfordton, North Carolina. Mr. Charles Benedict, President of Doncaster, a women's clothing manufacturing firm, was on the line. A broad smile creased Van Winkle's Robert Redfordish face as he listened, for Benedict had some good news: Doncaster was placing its business with Tucker Wayne, the national advertising agency that Van Winkle served as senior vice-president.

In addition to the normal elation over adding a new client to the agency's roster, Van Winkle was especially pleased about adding the Doncaster account. For one thing, the firm was engaged in the textile-clothing

* Case prepared by John S. Wright and Kenneth L. Bernhardt, Georgia State University. Used with permission.

manufacturing industry, and Tucker Wayne wished to expand in that product area. Furthermore, the new client was active in the specialized form of marketing known as "direct selling," which poses special challenges for the advertising agency particularly on the creative side of the business. Moreover, Doncaster appeared to be a company about to experience accelerated growth; thus, if Tucker Wayne could contribute to that growth, the agency could reasonably anticipate increased business for the firm. It all added up to an intriguing opportunity for the advertising agency.

Van Winkle immediately set up a meeting for the following Monday. Attending would be the new account team consisting of an account representative and persons from the agency's creative and media departments. At that meeting the account group would start to map out the strategy for next year's Doncaster advertising.

When contrasted to the volume of goods reaching consumers through retail outlets, direct selling to consumers is unimportant in the overall structure of American retailing. Nevertheless, for some manufacturers direct selling is the only method of distribution used to reach consumers. This is the case for Doncaster.

Direct selling organizations ordinarily use one of two selling methods: (1) door-to-door or (2) the party-plan. Manufacturers using the door-to-door plan include such familiar companies as Avon Products, Inc., Fuller Brush Company, Stanley Home Products, World Book Encyclopedia, Electrolux, and Sarah Coventry. With the door-to-door method, the sale is made to the prospect in her home by a representative of the manufacturer, usually operating as an independent contractor. This arrangement frees the manufacturer from the legal responsibilities that come with the employer-employee relationship.

Under the party-plan selling method, one customer acts as the hostess of a party to which she invites several friends. The salesperson actually stages the party and makes a sales presentation to the several guests at the party. Tupperware is a well-known user of this approach.

One practical problem for the manufacturer seeking to employ the direct selling avenue to the market is the recruitment and retention of a salesforce. For example, Avon Products, Inc., needs more than 300,000 Avon representatives to cover the United States and Canada. With an annual turnover rate exceeding 100 per cent among its salespeople, Avon must spend a great deal of effort and money in attracting new groups of women to join its salesforce.

Current Situation

Doncaster is a manufacturer of fine custom clothing for women with its factory and home office located in Rutherfordton, North Carolina. The company was founded in 1931 by the late S. B. Tanner, Jr., and originally engaged in the manufacture of men's shirts. During the following year Mrs. Tanner designed two shirtwaist-style dresses that were made of men's shirting material. This experiment met with good success and launched the company into the world of fashion.

The company has remained family-owned with the three sons of the founders now active in the management of both Doncaster and a sister firm, Tanner of North Carolina, which manufactures a line of casual dresses for sale in specialty shops and better department stores throughout the country. Doncaster's president, Charles Benedict, came to the company more than two decades ago as sales manager. His original specialization was in the field of direct selling.

The Doncaster organization manufactures two separate lines: Doncaster, which is a collection of made-to-order (custom) pants, suits, coats, skirts and similar items of women's wear; and Young Traditions (YT) which consist of ready-made sportswear items. Doncaster clothes are made to order for the customer from materials that she has selected; a pair of pants sells for about $60, a coat for $275, with the average of all items in the line coming at about $120. The YT line is lower-priced with a T-shirt selling in the $10–12 range, a coat for $130; the average price is about $40.

Doncaster clothes for women are sold directly to the consumer by approximately 1000 Doncaster saleswomen. This sales force is spread throughout the nation with some concentration in Sunbelt states. These salespeople work on commissions of 25 per cent for Doncaster items and 20 per cent for YT items. Special bonuses augment earnings for successful salespeople. As with most direct selling organizations, the sales force operates under the independent contractor form of contractual arrangement. The field force is supervised by 50 district managers, who are compensated with "overrides" (commissions) of 8 per cent of the sales generated by those saleswomen working under their supervision.

Doncaster employs an unique variation to the door-to-door method of direct selling. Instead of the Doncaster saleswoman calling at the prospect's home to make a sales presentation, the prospect is invited to a "showing," which is held in the home of the saleswoman. Showings of the Doncaster line are four times a year. Each Doncaster saleswoman sends a formal invitation to the women on her prospect list. The mailing is followed by a phone call to make a specific appointment when the prospect will come to the home of the Doncaster saleswoman to view the new offerings. Each showing lasts from ½ hour to 2 hours for each prospect who comes along. The typical showing period runs from 1 to 2 weeks, depending on the number of prospects available to the particular salesperson.

On display in the saleswoman's home are more than 100 physical samples of finished items, and there is some opportunity to try on clothing. A swatch book containing the fine materials available for use in Doncaster custom-made clothing is also on hand, as is a book of drawings featuring the current styles available for customer choice during the current season. The prospect chooses the dress, skirt, coat, and/or pants that she desires, as well as the fabric to be used in its construction. The Doncaster saleswoman assists the prospect in making the correct size choice, and the order is sent to Rutherfordton to be returned approximately 6 weeks later.

If the YT line is also featured, it is displayed in another room. Upon viewing these YT offerings, the prospect orders desired items, which are delivered several weeks later. Shipments come either directly to the customer or to the salesperson, who then calls the customer and arranges for delivery and fitting adjustments if needed.

Thus, it can be seen that the sale is a very personal event. The prospect is there because of a specific invitation from the Doncaster saleswoman, whom she probably knows from a social contact. Selections are made in a relaxed setting with very little sales pressure exerted. Many sales are made to established customers.

Doncaster management has a good idea of the type of woman who buys their expensive line of clothing. The target market profile reads:

Suburban
Affluent ($40,000 plus income)
Nonworking
Traditional lifestyle
Well-dressed, but not a fashion leader
Average age, 45 years

To reach this market, Doncaster seeks women from the same social class—social equals, as it were. Obviously special appeals need to be made to attract the right kind of women into the Doncaster sales force; money incentive is secondary as the reason for signing up. The following excerpt from the company's Information Manual illustrates the appeals used:

Bringing Doncaster service to women in your community is fun, a pleasant experience, for lots of reasons. For many women there is simply the thrill of showing beautiful clothes. For others, it is a combination of the thrill and the opportunity opened to make new friends. For all, it is a combination of these and the opportunity to earn excellent additional income. Obviously, there are innumerable reasons for desiring additional incomes, but for most women there is a specific goal. We are sure you have one, too.

The typical Doncaster saleswoman earns $1500 in commissions annually for 4–6 weeks of work. A good portion of her earnings are often used for the purchase of a personal wardrobe of Doncaster clothing.

Although direct selling organizations often encounter turnover rates in their sales forces that exceed 100 per cent annually, the Doncaster experience is a modest 30 per cent. Nevertheless, those replacements must be made. Furthermore, the company management believes that the only way for company sales to grow significantly is through an expansion in the size of the sales force. Getting increased sales volume from existing salespeople is difficult and expensive to achieve. Thus, recruitment of new Doncaster saleswomen has a very high priority in management thinking.

District managers, because of the potential implicit in sales overrides, are interested in recruiting new salespeople. Present sales force members may recommend the program to friends who live in different territories, and present customers do write in to company headquarters occasionally to ask for appointments to the sales force. Although company officials estimate that only 21 per cent of new additions to the salesforce result from media advertising at the present time, such advertising is probably

"I think how you look is important to the way you feel about yourself. That's why I wear Doncasters."

"I know when I look good in what I'm wearing.

"And when I'm dressed in a Doncaster, I look and feel my best.

"Because I know it's an exclusive design. Made up for me alone. In the color and fabric of my choice.

"Of course, custom touches like these aren't available in off-the-rack clothes. Even in the Doncaster price range—from $80 to $250.

"I also like the way Doncaster presents its collections. I go to a private showing in my Doncaster saleswoman's home.

"I can take my time looking over the dresses, suits and ensembles from Doncaster.

"And if I need sportswear, I can choose from Young Traditions, Doncaster's quality line of separates and coordinates.

"By the way, I do know something about clothes. I'm a professional model.

"So, as you can imagine, I've worn all kinds of fashions. And my personal choice is Doncaster." *doncaster*

Mike Tanner
Doncaster, Dept. NY12775
Rutherfordton, N.C. 28139

___ I'd like to be invited to the next Doncaster showing in my area.

___ I'd like information on becoming a Doncaster saleswoman.

Name _____

Address _____

City _____

State _____ Zip _____

the most important avenue—other than word-of-mouth—of recruitment available to Doncaster.

Doncaster has advertised in quality magazines for many years. For instance, in the past year advertisements were run in *New Yorker, Vogue, "W," Southern Living,* and *Smithsonian.* Media choices are made on the basis of readership demographics that correspond to the target profile described earlier.

Exhibit 1 is a reproduction of a one-column ad that appeared in the past September issue of *Vogue* and is representative of the advertising done during the past 2 years.

In evaluating the effectiveness of these magazines advertisements, Doncaster management was interested in two things: first of all, the raw number of inquiries resulting from each advertisement and, more important, the actual number of Doncaster saleswomen appointments emanating from each advertisement. Results from advertising during the previous Spring follow:

Magazine	Inquiries	Appointments
New Yorker	74	6
Vogue	76	4
"W"	59	5
Southern Living	86	2
Totals	295	17

Benedict and other members of the Doncaster management team recently concluded that the company was not getting the best possible results from its media advertising. The advertising program for the past several years had been developed by a Virginia-based agency that specialized in direct selling messages. Interpersonal relations between the advertiser and agency personnel had deteriorated, and a search for a new advertising agency was launched. Several regional advertising agencies were interviewed, and it was decided that commencing with next year's campaign Doncaster's advertising would be created by Tucker-Wayne, a large national advertising agency based in Atlanta, Georgia.

The agency was placed on a fee basis. The budget would remain the same as last year (approximately $40,000). Doncaster management's dissatisfaction with the previous agency probably springs in part from the fact that advertising objectives had not been spelled out completely enough. The former agency's approach, because of its basic orientation, was aimed at the generation of inquiries. The principal objective for the new campaign was set down as "Bringing about a significant increase in the number of new Doncaster saleswomen." Thus, Tucker Wayne was authorized to use all of the new budget for this purpose.

Van Winkle realized that the new ads would have to be created and placed in a very short period of time. He wanted to be able to present the agency's recommendation by the end of the month when a trip to Rutherfordton was scheduled.

Student Learning Exercise / 6
Sales Force Recruiting and Selection

Objective
1. To gain insight into the recruiting and selection process.
2. To isolate both effective and ineffective recruiting and selection tools.

Overview
Phone or visit your campus placement office or a placement office of a college or university nearby. Isolate a particular company that is in the process of recruiting sales personnel. Find out all you can about the recruiting and selection process this company follows. For example, does the company obtain any preliminary information before conducting campus interviews? Does it precede the campus interviews with materials of a promotional nature that might be posted or distributed elsewhere on campus? Does the company supplement its visits to campus with ads in campus newspapers or local newspapers? What happens after a successful campus interview of a candidate? And so on. Find out all you can about the process this company follows.

Prepare an audit of the recruiting and selection process followed by the organization you have selected. Constructively criticize all of the tools and methods in recruiting and selection by the organization you have selected.

Exercise
1. What are the strong points of the firm you selected regarding tools, methods, and processes used in the recruitment and selection of sales personnel?

2. What are the weak points involved in the recruiting and selection process by the firm that you selected?

3. What additional steps or processes should be followed in the recruiting and selection of salespeople that have been omitted or overlooked by this firm?

4. If the firm you selected followed all of your suggestions, including possible deletions and revisions, would their cost of recruiting sales personnel increase or decrease? Would a potential increase in the short range become a decrease in the long range or vice versa? What economic impact would your suggestions have on the recruiting and selection process?

5. Last, would the revised recruiting and selection plan you have developed result in increased or decreased turnover?

Training the Sales Force

MANY sales executives believe that sales training is the single most important activity for which they are responsible. No matter how qualified or talented the individual who has been recruited and selected (as covered in Chapter 6) for training, if the sales training received is incomplete, erroneous, outmoded, or poorly presented, the result is likely to be a discouraged or, at the very least, a highly disappointed salesperson.

By way of introduction, let us examine some "mental biases" that exist in the minds of many sales managers regarding sales training. Four points in particular need to be discussed regarding sales training before proceeding.

Sales training is for new sales personnel. One mental bias present of many sales managers when the topic of sales training is mentioned is that they automatically think of new salespeople. Although it may be true in a particular firm that the majority of training is designed for new sales personnel, other sales force members may need training, too. Ironically, it may be true that senior sales force members need retraining or additional training as much as new sales force members need initial training. Thus one of the mental biases involved in training is to avoid thinking only of new sales personnel when we refer to the concept of sales training.

Sales training is always a good investment of time and money. Although it may sound contradictory to begin a discussion of sales training by acknowledging the point, many of the resources (both time resources and dollar resources) invested in training can prove not only to be poor investments, but, in fact, may actually become counterproductive to the company's purpose. A recent article on sales training suggests that, of the estimated $12 billion spent on business training each year by American corporations, "most of it is wasted."[1] It is the contention of the authors that sales training properly received and executed can certainly help the firm, but we must be cautious not to accept sales training blindly as a "sacred cow." To the contrary, sales managements should continuously monitor the results of training via an objective and candid appraisal

[1] "Training: Critical to Marketing Success," *Marketing Times*, (Vol. XXIII, No. 1), January–February 1976, p. 3.

of both the costs of training and the benefits training provides to the firm.

A sound training program is the first step in a successful sales career with our firm. In the preceding chapter on recruiting and selecting a sales force, we suggested that, rather than a starting point, selection represents the *result* of a great deal of previous time and work invested by sales management. So, too, it is with sales training. Although it may seem obvious that much needs to be done before sales personnel are placed in a sales training program, this point is often overlooked in practice. Thus, many resources of the firm can be wasted in invalid training and such invalid training may result in higher than necessary turnover rates.

Numerous examples abound of firms who have become enchanted with training techniques or hardware. This enchantment can lead to training programs that really are not needed or are unsuitable to the particular sales force receiving the training. A recent article comments on this phenomenon by noting:

Fads and gimmicks characterize a lot of corporate training—both in-house and in outside programs. Participants may enjoy themselves and think they're learning something, but they often aren't.[2]

A sound training program does not begina with the selection of a particular speaker, technique, or training tool. Rather, a viable approach to training evolves only after management has assessed the need for training, examined training objectives as well as resources, and evaluated alternative methods of training. This chapter will begin with a model that interrelates many of the considerations management must take into account prior to the evolution of a training program per se.

Our training lasts six weeks. At the conclusion of their training program we present all trainees with an engraved certificate that acknowledges their completion of our training sequence. Then it's time for them to get to work and they are assigned to their own sales territory.

The need for training is continuous. This last "mental bias" that we need to acknowledge before proceeding, is acknowledged in the preceding quotation. Although it may sound trite to say so, it is true that the need for training is continuous. Every viable organization has a continual need for training, owing to new personnel, new products, new policies, necessary retraining of senior personnel, and changes in its marketing environment. As an example, consider the impact that the truth in lending laws had upon the financial industry. This one change in the legal and political environment, in the form of a new law, produced a dramatic need for training by many types of customer contact personnel in the financial/thrift industry. Thus, we must guard against the bias of assuming that, once sales personnel have completed a sales training course, they are "trained." As we shall see later in this chapter, the very fact that time elapses after training suggests the need for retraining. That is, the

[2] *Ibid.,* p. 4.

basic learning curve suggests that, as time elapses, the amount of information recallable from training diminishes—thus, the need for continual training.

An Overview of Sales Training: A Managerial Perspective

From a selfish point of view, sales management has much to lose by ineffective or poorly designed sales training programs. The extensive time and financial resources invested in recruiting and selection may be totally wasted if adequate training is not available to convert the newly selected sales representative into an effective performer for the firm. Effective sales training may be thought of as a bridge between the newly recruited sales representative of today and the effective sales performer of tomorrow. Figure 7.1 is a model of the training process that incorporates many of the suggestions made regarding potential "mental biases" from the preceding introductory section. Note that this model acknowledges that it is the needs of the firm rather than training per se that provide the

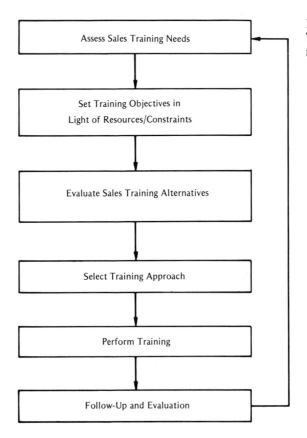

FIGURE 7.1 The Sales Training Process: A Managerial Perspective

starting point for instruction of new sales representatives. This model also suggests that the need for training is never completed, that existing personnel as well as new sales personnel may need sales training, and that there is nothing inherent in the sales training process that limits an investment in training to only positive results.

ASSESSING SALES TRAINING NEEDS

As indicated in Figure 7.1, a logical first step in the training process is to make an assessment of current sales training needs. In practice, the need for this assessment is often brought forcably to management's attention. For example, Case 7.1 (Melco Supply Company) presents just such a situation. In this case, the sales manager becomes acutely aware of the need for sales training owing to a disappointing performance of sales representatives in a role-playing exercise at a sales training meeting. In other instances management may become aware of the need for sales training through a declining market share, eroding sales profitability levels, disappointing performances by new products introduced into the market, high turnover rates, negative feedback from consumers, a large number of "lost" accounts, and so on.

Rather than wait for a negative event to occur that might suggest the need for training, it is the contention of the model presented in Figure 7.1 that sales management has a continuing responsibility for assessing sales training needs. This should not be taken to mean that sales management *personally* must perform this sales training. In fact, as we shall see, sales management may draw upon other resources, which are either internal or external to the firm, in performing the sales training function. Nevertheless, the responsibility and initiative for sales training lies with sales management.

A useful starting point in assessing sales training needs may be to conduct a mini version of a marketing audit. Kotler has defined a marketing audit as:

a periodic, comprehensive, systematic, and independent examination of the organization's marketing environment, internal marketing system and specific marketing activities with a view to determining problem areas and recommending a corrective action plan to improve the organization's overall marketing effectiveness.[3]

The objective here would be to conduct a condensed version of the marketing audit focusing solely upon the personal selling functions of the firm. Such an audit would provide an objective, current, and realistic assessment of both the strengths and weaknesses of the personal sales force of the firm.

The specific questions to be included in an audit of the sales force would naturally vary from one organization to another. Nevertheless,

[3] Philip Kotler, *Marketing Management: Analysis, Planning, and Control,* 3rd ed. (Englewood Cliffs, N.J.: Prentice-Hall, Inc., 1976), p. 448.

1. Does the sales force of our firm possess sufficient knowledge regarding our product/service mix?

2. Does the sales force of our firm possess sufficient of the policies of our company?

3. Does the sales force of our firm possess sufficient about competition?

4. Does the sales force of our firm possess sufficient knowledge about the future developments in our industry?

5. Does the sales force of our firm possess sufficient information about the inter-organizational workings of our company (are our salespeople aware of the various other departments within the firm)?

6. Does our sales staff have sufficient knowledge about the various economic, governmental, legal, and other "uncontrollable variables" influencing their day-to-day activities?

FIGURE 7.2 Potential Questions for Inclusion in a Sales Audit

in order to provide some illustrative questions, the materials in Figure 7.2 should be examined.

If sales management approaches the audit of the sales force in the correct spirit, a current and a candid appraisal of questions such as those provided in Figure 7.2 will be obtained. Answers to these questions would assist in pinpointing specific needs for additional or for new sales training programs.

An additional resource in assessing needs for the sales training is the direct approach of questioning current sales personnel. For example, current sales personnel can be asked, "Do you feel a need for additional sales training?" In addition to asking current sales personnel for their suggestions in the sales training area, sales management may also draw upon one final resource—the exit interview. What we are suggesting here is that individuals who are leaving the sales force for any reason (voluntary or involuntary) may be interviewed to determine whether faulty sales training is in part responsible. Naturally, the results obtained from individuals leaving the firm must be weighed with some degree of objective judgement by sales management.

SETTING TRAINING OBJECTIVES

As indicated in Figure 7.1, the second step in the overall model of sales training should be for management to develop objectives for the training process. The objectives developed by management should be realistic. To be sure that these objectives are not unrealistic, simultaneous consideration must be given to both the resources needed in providing training objectives and the constraints bearing upon such training.

Resources and Constraints. Let us consider an illustration of the types of resources and constraints tempering the setting of sales objectives. A national firm manufacturing computers contemplated introduction of a new model computer to the market. Because of the technical nature of this product, management felt that each sales representative would need to attend a products school lasting 6 weeks. Further, the maximum class size that would permit effective learning was felt to be classes of 20. Therefore, since the firm had roughly 200 salespeople in its sales force, it was obvious that one constraint involved in this training decision was time. It would take 60 weeks (200 salespeople ÷ 20 salespeople per class = 10 classes × 6 weeks) to train the entire sales force if the sales force were trained one class at a time. An alternative would be to run simultaneously several classes of 20 in differing locations, utilizing different training personnel. Since the management of the firm felt speed of introduction to the market was essential, it elected to run five sales training classes simultaneously in different parts of the country. The impact of resources was involved in this decision simultaneous multiple classes meant that five different training staffs had to be utilized. To accomplish this, management was forced to tie up many of their technical personnel. Although the formation of specific and measurable training objectives is critical to the process, such objectives must te tempered with realistic appraisals of both the constraints and resources bearing upon the training objectives.

Three factors seem common to all sales organizations when making decisions concerning resources and constraints in sales training. The first factor is the human factor. That is, the individuals who have been recruited become a constraint affecting the potential limits of the sales training program. If individuals of relatively low intelligence have been recruited, an organization may find it unwise to provide a highly detailed technical training program. Likewise, if individuals of relatively high intelligence have been recruited by the firm, an overly simplistic training program may leave them uninspired. A second major constraint common to most sales organizations is the cost involved in training. Although specific figures for training salespeople will be discussed in the following section, it should be noted that some firms estimate the total cost involved in changing a recruit to a productive status may be as high as $50,000.[4] This figure would include the cost for recruiting, selecting, training, and supervising the beginning salesperson. A third consideration where resources and constraints are concerned involves the length of time that will be involved in the sales training. Each of these three considerations will be discussed separately in the section that follows.

People.   The reciprocal nature of recruiting and training is apparent when the resource/constraint of people is considered. The specific group of people on whom we are focusing are the individuals who have now been hired by the firm and may carry a title such as "sales trainee." This term is used in the industry to mean "anyone who is learning about their company's products, services, and policies, as well as proven sales techniques, in preparation for a sales assignment."[5]

At this point, a valid question in the eyes of sales management may

[4] William J. Stanton and Richard H. Buskirk, *Management of the Sales Force*, 4th ed. (Homewood, Ill.: Richard D. Irwin, Inc., 1974), p. 143.
[5] "1978 Survey of Sales Costs," *Sales and Marketing Management*, (Vol. 120, No. 3), February 27, 1978, p. 62.

be "What type of people have we recruited?" and, therefore, what type of resource do we have available for sales training? A study conducted by two industrial psychologists indicated that there were two basic qualities essential to success in selling: empathy and ego drive. To elaborate:

Empathy, the important central ability to feel as the other fellow does in order to be able to sell him a product or service, must be possessed in large measure. Having empathy does not necessarily mean being sympathetic. One can know what the other fellow feels without agreeing with that feeling. But a salesman simply cannot sell without the invaluable and irreplaceable ability to get a powerful feedback from his client through empathy. . . .

The second of the basic qualities absolutely needed by a good salesman is a particular kind of ego drive which makes him want and need to make this sale in a personal or ego way, not merely for the money to be gained. His feeling must be that he *has* to make the sale; the customer is there to help him fulfill his personal need. In effect, to the top salesman, the sale—the conquest—provides a powerful means of enhancing his ego. The self-picture improves dramatically by virtue of conquest, and diminishes with failure.[6]

Hopefully the individuals recruited possess both of these basic qualities. In addition to the qualities of empathy and ego drive, it may be useful to examine some of the other characteristics and attributes sales executives seek in new applicants. A recent survey of 44 top-ranking sales executives revealed that the individual sought is "likely an enthusiastic and well organized fellow of ambition who is highly persuasive and has solid sales experience."[7] Asked to respond to a series of attributes potentially present in recruits, these sales executives indicated they would seek the following qualities in order of importance: ambition, integrity, enthusiasm, and competitiveness. If only one criterion could be used in selection, these executives indicated it would be ambition.[8]

Naturally, the sales personnel recruited by each organization will vary as to the degrees of these traits and characteristics that they possess. Hopefully, however, most of the sales personnel selected for training will possess most of these traits and characteristics to at least some moderate extent.

The Cost.   Figure 7.3 is presented in an effort to provide current and accurate information on the cost of sales training. Please note that this information is based upon an annual national survey and provides information for the year past; it is not based upon speculation about expected expenditures in a future year. Also note that the types of companies involved are classified according to whether they are involved in industrial, consumer, or service marketing. Since Figure 7.3 provides a comparison of the expenditures for 1977 with the preceding year, it should also be noted that the cost of sales training is increasing in all types of firms. Although cost information in Figure 7.3 does include salary while under-

[6] David Mayer and Herbert M. Greenberg, "What Makes a Good Salesman," *Harvard Business Review*, July-August 1964, pp. 119–125.
[7] Stan Moss, "What Sales Executives Look for in New Salespeople," *Sales and Marketing Management* (Vol. 20, No. 4), March 1978, p. 46.
[8] *Ibid.*, p. 47.

Average Cost of Sales Training per Salesman			
	Training Cost (including salary)		% Change
Type of Company	1977	1976	76–77
Industrial	$13,941	11,246	+24.0
Consumer	10,181	6,467	+57.4
Service	8,460	6,258	+35.2

*Includes Insurance, Financial, Utilities, Transportation, Retail, etc.

FIGURE 7.3 Cost: A Constraint in Setting Sales Training Objectives [Source: *1978 Survey of Selling Costs. Published by Sales and Marketing Management*, Vol. 120, No. 3 (February 27, 1978).]

going training, note that these figures specifically reflect only the cost of training and do not include, as did the earlier $50,000 estimate, any allocations for recruiting and selecting or for supervising the new sales trainee.

Time. A last constraint in setting sales training objectives common to most sales organizations is time. The same national survey used to obtain cost figures also provides some information on the length of time involved in training programs. However, it should be noted that the data presented in Figure 7.4 reflect the training period for new salespeople as opposed to the types of training programs designed for senior salespeople. Such training for senior salespeople is generally of an ongoing nature and may reflect changes in company product's service mixes, changes in company policies and procedures, or refresher training which merely recaps or summarizes training previously given to the salesperson. These programs are not included in the time increments provided and vary greatly from one firm to the other in terms of their length and time duration.

Note that while the length of training period has increased in each of the three types of companies above, the sharpest increase occurred in companies involved with industrial marketing. Industrial marketers are also much more likely to have lengthy training programs for new salespeople of over six months than are either consumer or service marketing types of firms.

Specific Goals. Having now assessed the need for sales training and also having examined the resources needed and constraints existing upon

Length of Training Period for New Salesman						
	TYPE OF COMPANY					
	Industrial		Consumer		Services*	
Time Period	'77	'76	'77	'76	'77	'76
0 to 6 wks.	23%	27%	7%	29%	50%	60%
6 wks.–3 mos.	15%	27%	33%	14%	30%	5%
3 mos.–6 mos.	8%	12%	27%	29%	10%	10%
6 mos.–12 mos.	39%	33%	13%	28%		10%
over 12 mos.	15%		20%		10%	15%
TOTAL	100%	100%	100%	100%	100%	100%
Median in weeks	26	12	20	15	7	6

*Includes Insurance, Financial, Utilities, Transportation, Retail, etc.

FIGURE 7.4 Time: A Constraint in Setting Sales Training Objectives [Source: *1978 Survey of Selling Costs. Published by Sales and Marketing Management*, Vol. 120, No. 3 (February 27, 1978).]

sales training, the sales executive is now in a position to examine specific goals for sales training. In Chapter 4, the goals and objectives for the sales function were discussed. It may be useful for the student to review quickly materials presented in Chapter 4.

The goals of training programs, of course, vary greatly from one firm to another. Nevertheless, Hughes has suggested that the following list of five goals is the most common for training programs.

1. Increased volume or profit.
2. Reducing costs, supervision, and turnover.
3. Introducing new products, markets, channels, and promotional campaigns.
4. Improving morale, motivation, and customer relations.
5. Training for management.[9]

Obviously, these five goals of sales training are not mutually exclusive. For example, if the volume sold per sales call increases, it may have the effect of reducing costs and increasing profits. Recently the Armour-Dial Division of Greyhound Corporation evaluated the effectiveness of a sales training program. The result for salespeople attending this program was a 12 per cent average increase in the number of sales calls per day, 100 per cent gain in case sales, and a 62 per cent increase in the number of displays sold.[10]

Specific goals set for sales training will revolve around increasing four areas of knowledge and expertise. These four include the company itself, the competitive environment or market the firm finds itself in, specific selling techniques and tools, and knowledge concerning the products and/or services sold by the firm.

The data presented in Figure 7.5 represents a current national breakdown of the way in which sales training time is allocated across the four areas of knowledge and expertise just mentioned. Note that the basis of this study is a current report on sales training from 156 sales executives

Subject Matter	Consumer Goods Firms	Industrial Goods Firms	Service Type Firms	All Firms
Product Knowledge	36%	47%	39%	42%
Selling Techniques	27%	21%	30%	24%
Market/Industry Orientation	20%	17%	13%	17%
Company Orientation	11%	13%	13%	13%
Other (Miscellaneous)	6%	2%	3%	4%

FIGURE 7.5 Sales Training Time for New Sales Personnel: Allocation to Knowledge Areas [Source: Adapted from information presented in *Training the Sales Force: A Progress Report* by David S. Hopkins. Published by The Conference Board, Inc., 1978.]

[9] G. David Hughes, *Marketing Management: A Planning Approach* (Reading, Mass.: Addison-Wesley Publishing Company, Inc., 1978), p. 390.
[10] This information taken from "The New Supersalesman: Wired for Success," *Business Week*, January 6, 1973, pp. 44–49.

1. Are the sales training goals explicit and measurable?

2. Are the goals selected for sales training realistic?

3. Do the resources needed to achieve sales training objectives exist?

4. Have the constraints pertaining to sales training been acknowledged realistically?

5. If multiple sales training goals exist, are the priorities on the goals clear?

6. Has a specific date for achievement of goals been isolated?

7. Has the responsibility for achieving sales training goals been clearly affixed?

8. If multiple sales training goals exist, do they complement each other or conflict?

9. Do the sales training goals established complement the overall corporate or organization goals?

10. Do the sales training goals have the support of the sales trainees?

FIGURE 7.6 Checklist of Possible Questions Pertaining to Sales Training Goals

"representing a cross-section of firms in manufacturing or service industries" having a formalized sales training program.[11]

As may be seen from the information contained in Figure 7.5, not surprisingly, industrial marketers spend more time than do consumer or service type firms on product knowledge. Likewise, service firms spend more of their training time than industrial or consumer goods firms on sales techniques. Consumer goods firms spend more time on market and industry orientation than do industrial or service types of firms. However, it should be noted that when all firms responding are considered, the amount of training time spent on product knowledge far exceeds the amount of time spent in any other area of subject matter. This is not surprising when one realizes that the training programs reflected in Figure 7.5 are only those for new sales personnel.

One last note of caution needs to be made for proceeding in our training process. Now that management has such specific training objectives with both the resources needed and constraints existing in mind, it is worthwhile to perform a check list operation to insure success of our program. Figure 6 presents several illustrative types of questions that management might ask itself about the objectives selected for sales training.

Although the types of questions presented in Figure 7.6 are, of course, appropriate, they do not represent a comprehensive or exhaustive list by any means. The purpose of such a check list is to allow management to ascertain any potentials for failure in advance of the training program itself. If any unsatisfactory answers were obtained to these or similar questions, management must, of course, proceed to remove the reason for dissatisfaction prior to beginning the sales training program.

If difficulties are encountered in the training program, it should not

[11] David S. Hopkins, *Training the Sales Force: A Progress Report.* Published by The Conference Board, Inc., 1978, p. iii.

automatically be assumed that the program itself is at fault. As Mayer and Greenberg have suggested:

Yet how often have men gone through long and expensive training programs only to fail totally when put into the field? When this happens, the trainer, and perhaps the training program itself, is blamed, and sometimes even discarded. But most often, it is neither the trainer nor the training program that is at fault; whether it is the fact that they were given the impossible task of turning a sow's ear into a silk purse. The most skilled diamond polisher, given a piece of coal, can only succeed in creating a highly polished piece of coal; but given the roughest type of uncut diamond, he can indeed turn it into the most precious stone.[12]

EVALUATION OF TRAINING ALTERNATIVES

Once the needs and training objectives are clearly in mind, the next step in the process is for the sales executive to think of all the possible training alternatives that might be utilized to achieve the training goals. For example, sales management often must wrestle with the issue of whether sales training can best be accomplished in an individual or group setting. Each approach carries its own advantages and disadvantages and neither approach is right for all occasions.

In order to be in a better position to evaluate sales training alternatives, management must understand something about learning. Basic to the learning concept is the "learning curve." The learning curve, alluded to earlier in this chapter, depicts the interaction of two forces: (1) recall of materials an individual has been exposed to and (2) intervals of time. Figure 7.7 depicts the basic learning curve.

As illustrated in Figure 7.7, the learning curve suggests that, as time intervals elapse between the initial exposure to materials, the percentage

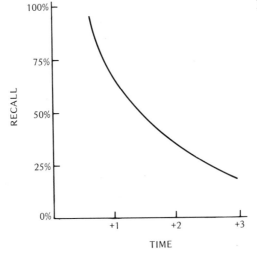

FIGURE 7.7 The Learning Curve

[12] Mayer and Greenberg, *op. cit.*, p. 125.

of the material an individual will recall declines. This has important implications for sales training. It suggests that, even though we may have senior salespeople who have been exposed to sales training information, as time elapses after their training the percentage of the information they will recall declines. Obviously, if the sales representative no longer retains information, he/she cannot pass it along to prospective buyers. A pioneering experiment in the area of retention suggested that virtually 90 per cent of the college students who were subjects in an experiment could not recall strings of three consonants given them 18 seconds earlier.[13] Thus, the obvious need for *continual* sales training.[14]

In addition to the basic learning curve depicted in Figure 7.7, sales management should also keep in mind three other rules pertaining to learning. First, experience might prove to be the most effective teaching device available for sales training. Thus, any sales training program should incorporate large doses of "active participation" on the part of sales trainees. The concept of active involvement is the heart of a quote attributed to Confucius:

"I hear and I forget. I see and I remember. I do and I understand."

Confucius

An experiment focusing upon this process of active involvement provides some interesting findings. This experiment concluded that individuals retained approximately 10 per cent of what they heard and read. If the same individuals were required to write out this material, they retained approximately 40 per cent. When the same individuals were required to discuss and talk about these materials, they retained approximately 70 per cent. When the individuals were required actively to perform and demonstrate these materials, they retained approximately 80 per cent.[15] The student may be interested to note that this same rationale is the reason for inclusion of student learning exercises in this text.

A second concept concerning learning that sales management should keep in mind is reinforcement. The concept states that rewards or praise may encourage learning and consequently discourage the kind of erosion in recall depicted in the basic learning curve in Figure 7.7. A last concept that management should keep in mind is the principle of distributed effort. Gist comments on this principle's application to learning by stating:

This rule says that learning is more effective when learning effort is evenly distributed over time rather than absorbed in the intensive bursts or cram sessions.[16]

[13] L. B. Peterson and M. J. Peterson, "Short-Term Retention of Individual Individual Verbal Items," *Journal of Experimental Psychology* (Vol. 58), 1959, pp. 192–198.
[14] For a more detailed discussion of information pertaining to retention and learning, see David Krech, Richard S. Crutchfield, and Norman Livson, *Elements of Psychology*, 2nd ed. (New York: Alfred A. Knopf, Inc., 1969) pp. 321–328.
[15] E. Jerome McCarthy, "Active (Not Passive) Learning Is the Key to Effective Education," Speech given to Conference on Experimental Learning in Marketing Education, Mid-Atlantic Marketing Association Annual Meeting, October 2, 1976, University of South Carolina, Columbia, S.C.
[16] Ronald R. Gist, *Marketing and Society*, 2nd ed. (Hinsdale, Ill.: The Dryden Press, 1974), p. 418.

The pragmatic application for sales management from the principle of distributed effort is that superior learning may take place if the effort is distributed over a longer period of time. Thus, training programs that incorporate both formal training and a return to the field for active involvement with the product may be favored over shorter, more intensive formal training sessions where an attempt is made to "cram" much information into the minds of sales trainees.

The Charles Beseler Company has found this concept to have direct application to its sales training. Searching for an innovative way to provide sales force training about a new product, the Beseler Company developed a series of color filmstrips keyed to a taped narration that could be viewed by their sales staff at home. A key aspect of this sales training approach was that the salesperson could view the filmstrips at a time convenient for her/him without cutting into the sales day. Commenting on the results, a spokesperson for the Charles Beseler Company stated:

The total cost was $10,500 or less than half what we would have spent for a sales meeting. We were right about the convenience factor, too. The salespeople spent about two days each learning the product, but they did it all on non-selling time. They learned *more* because they could run the official presentation over and over rather than seeing it 'live' just once.[17]

A wide variety of sales training techniques is used by sales organizations. Obviously, no one technique is right for all situations and circumstances. Let us briefly examine some of the more common sales training techniques. To simplify our discussion, we will divide these techniques into two basic areas. First we will explore group sales training techniques and then we will explore sales training techniques used with individuals.

Group Sales Training Techniques.   Group sales training techniques are often utilized by businesses because of the advantages provided by the group setting. A basic advantage of the group training technique is that it allows for interaction. Each member of the audience may contribute a great deal to the group training session and this contribution would, of course, be missing if the training were done on an individual basis. A second advantage of group training techniques is the advantage of time. It is obviously more efficient to train several people at one time (assuming no quality differences) than it is to train each of them in a one-on-one situation. Last, group training techniques may offer economies of scale to the firm.

The role playing method is one of the better known group sales training techniques. In this method of training, members of the audience may be selected to play certain "parts." The other members of the audience observe what is happening and may be asked to comment upon or criticize the presentation. A variation of role playing is the use of videotaping techniques, where members of the audience are assigned certain roles such as buyer or seller.

---

[17] "Look and Listen vs. Show and Tell," *Sales and Marketing Management,* (Vol. 117, No. 4), September 13, 1976, pp. 25 and 26.

Perhaps the most common group sales training technique is the speech or lecture. In this method, a speaker presents materials to the entire audience, and this speech may be followed by a question and answer session where a dialog develops between the audience and the speaker. A problem often encountered with the speech or lecture technique is that communication tends to be one way. That is, the speaker may tend to dominate the communication and direct his thoughts to the audience without permitting adequate time or opportunity for the members of the audience to respond.

A third group sales training technique currently in favor with many business is the idea of a roundtable discussion. In this approach, the members of the sales staff may have been given in advance certain cases or "real life" situations. The group then gets together to discuss various approaches and alternatives for dealing with these situations. As noted previously, one of the advantages of this technique is that the individual is exposed to solutions or suggestions brought by other members of the audience as well as his own.

Individual Sales Training Techniques. An individual training technique made popular during World War II is the on-the-job training technique. Under this method, the sales trainee learns product and selling knowledge in an actual job setting. Commenting on the use of this approach to sales training, one observer has noted:

This kind of OTJ training falls naturally into two parts: first is a period of jointly calling on accounts, to enable the trainee to absorb selling techniques and general knowledge of product features and applications; second, when the time is right, the trainee is given personal indoctrination into the specific territory for which he or she is being grouped.

There is often a progression, too, from an initial period when the neophites listen and observe the 'how and why' of the employer's approved methods of selling, on through a later period of actual sales performance under supervision, until, by degrees, there is ample opportunity to prove themselves on their own.[18]

Home study of self-instruction courses offer a second version of individual sales training techniques. Many firms choose to build a "programmed learning" approach to sales training that is sent to the sales representative for him to pursue at home. An obvious advantage of this approach is that it allows the individual to progress at his own speed and individual attention can be given to problem areas. This technique is particularly useful when the participants to be trained are widely scattered geographically or when it is difficult to bring them together for extended periods of time. Sears & Roebuck has recently experimented with a sales training program entitled "Principles of Persuasion," which includes records and related educational materials for use by the trainee in an individual setting.

A relative newcomer to the area of individual sales training techniques is the advent of computerized instruction. We are suggesting here that

[18] David S. Hopkins, *op. cit.*, p. 7.

Training Approach	Rank Order of Importance in Company						
	1st	2nd	3rd	4th	5th	6th	nr*
On-the-job	90	41	14	4	2	1	2
Classroom	46	22	27	24	7	2	26
Coaching	17	42	47	34	5	—	9
Observation	9	32	54	37	10	1	11
Home study	5	7	7	24	52	9	50
Special outside courses	1	3	5	12	21	33	79

*nr = preference not reported, or training approach listed is not used.

Base: 154 sales units reporting.

Note: The figures shown represent the number of reporting sales units that gave the indicated rank order of importance in their operations to each of the training approaches listed. (Since some gave equal ranking to two or more approaches—or failed to provide more than a few rank order votes—the figures do not add vertically to the aggregate number of sales units reporting.) The table values should be read as follows: 90 of the 154 sales units cited on-the-job training as the first (or to equal the first) in importance in their operations; 41 of them ranked this training approach as second (or equal second) in importance; and so on.

FIGURE 7.8A   Importance of Various Training Approaches for Newly Hired Sales Personnel [Source: David S. Hopkins, *op. cit.*, p. 6.]

the individual may be given access to a body of information or data via a computer terminal and may follow a previous program sequence in learning sales training materials. Recent developments have made it possible for some individuals to have access to the computer through either their work or home telephones.

In order to provide a current indication of the sales training approaches utilized by various firms, the information in Figure 7.8A and 7.8B is provided. Note that Figure 7.8A indicates training approaches used for newly hired sales personnel whereas the data in Figure 7.8B pertains to experienced sales personnel.

Training Approach	Rank Order of Importance in Company						
	1st	2nd	3rd	4th	5th	6th	nr*
On-the-job	72	26	19	16	6	1	10
Classroom	33	11	24	29	18	6	29
Coaching	25	60	28	13	3	4	17
Observation	18	32	35	21	13	2	29
Special outside courses	7	12	7	18	29	22	55
Home study	2	11	19	20	18	18	62

*nr = preference not reported, or the training approach listed is not used.

Base: 150 sales units reporting.

Note: The figures shown represent the number of reporting sales units that gave the indicated rank order of importance in their operations to each of the training approaches listed. (Since some gave equal ranking to two or more approaches—or failed to provide more than a few rank order votes—the figures do not add vertically to the aggregate number of sales units reporting.)

FIGURE 7.8B   Training Approaches for Experienced Sales Personnel [Source: David S. Hopkins, *op. cit.*, p. 16.]

SELECTING A TRAINING APPROACH

An evaluation of the various training alternatives available to sales management should result in the selection of a training approach particularly suitable to the firm involved. This approach would probably be based on one or more of the types of training techniques, or variations of these techniques, discussed previously. The specific sales approach selected for use in sales training often reflects the nature of the group to be trained. Let us consider some typical approaches that might be used for two different groups of sales personnel. First, we shall consider an approach suitable when management is training new sales personnel. Second, we will consider an approach that might be utilized if the group to be trained consists of experienced salespeople.

Jolson has suggested that a salesperson may be new in three different ways. He states, "A salesperson may be *new* to the occupation of selling, *new* to his present firm, or *new* to the product he is now selling."[19] In the example that follows, we will assume that the new salesperson is new to the occupation of selling.

Sales training is obviously essential for this new salesperson. In fact, the organization may need to provide training on the selling process. Although there are a variety of selling processes used by differing firms, the approach that follows is a reasonably standardized. The new salesperson would be taught that there are six steps involved in making a sale: prospecting, pre-approach, approach, presentation, close, and follow-up. Each of these will be discussed separately below.

Prospecting is the activity of separating qualified prospects from nonqualified. Thus, the new sales trainee must learn methods for identifying individuals who both have a need for the product or service and can afford to buy it. Good prospecting also conserves the time of the new salesperson by avoiding wastes of time on unqualified individuals.

The **pre-approach** is the second step in the sales process and consists of information that the sales representative has assembled prior to making the first call. The pre-approach would meet all of the following objectives: First, it would provide more detailed qualifying information than was available from prospecting. Prospecting only roughly separates nonqualified individuals from those who are qualified; the pre-approach should provide a much richer body of data concerning the qualifications of the prospect. A second objective is to provide information as to how best to approach the prospect. The pre-approach information, for example, might indicate that a particular industrial buyer is generally unavailable on a Monday or on a Friday. Another objective achieved by a good pre-approach is to provide information that can be utilized in making the presentation itself. Often good sales personnel learn of a problem that the prospect is currently having and center their sales presentation upon ways in which their product can provide solutions to the problem. Third, an overall objective achieved by a valid pre-approach is to build the confidence of the salesperson prior to the presentation.

[19] Marvin A. Jolson, "The Salesman's Career Cycle," *Journal of Marketing* (Vol. 38), July 1974, pp. 39–46 at p. 39.

The **approach** is the first part of the presentation and is based upon information obtained in the pre-approach. A leading salesmanship textbook suggests three objectives for the approach: first, to gain the prospect's attention; second, to stimulate his interest in learning more about the proposition; and third, to provide a smooth transition into the presentation itself.[20] The student may note similarities with the approach and the selling formula view of personal selling discussed in Chapter 2.

The next step in the selling process would be the **sales presentation.** An effective sales presentation has been defined as one having four characteristics. It should be complete, containing all of the information required by the prospect; it should eliminate competition by establishing the seller's product as the solution to the prospect's problems; it should be clear, with no ambiguities in the mind of the prospect; and it should win the prospect's confidence that the product or service has been presented in an honest light.[21]

The fifth step in the sales process is the **close.** This consists of the salesperson obtaining the order or making a sale. Obviously, in order to do this, the salesperson may not only have had to made a valid presentation, but in the process may have been required to overcome several objections.

The last step in the process is the **follow-up.** A myopic view would suggest that this step is not needed since we are assuming that the close has been made previously. Nevertheless, a good sales representative takes as a last step a follow-up after the sale has been made to insure customer satisfaction. It should be noted that salespeople who are thorough in the follow-up stage often reap the benefit of continuing customer patronage.

Now let us consider the need for training an experienced salesperson. We have previously established that even senior salespeople require continual training. This training could reflect new products or policies of the firm or it could be refresher or remedial training designed to overcome shortcomings of the particular salesperson. A common objective for training senior salespeople is to improve their time management capabilities. Symptoms indicating that this kind of training might be needed include a decline in the number of sales calls, falling sales volume or market share in a particular territory, and so on. Should this be the case, sales management must be prepared to step in and offer suggestions that may prevent the problem from compounding. Figure 7.9 presents some of the questions that might be asked to improve a salesman's thinking when planning to make a sales call.

Whether the sales training to be provided is for new or experienced sales personnel, the wise sales manager must be continuously vigilant in watching for opportunities to provide sales training. Akin to the concept of preventative maintenance is that of providing needed sales training in advance of a "breakdown." Obviously, no one sales training approach is right for every occasion and the fine tuning needed to taper sales

[20] Frederick A. Russell, Frank H. Beach, and Richard H. Buskirk, *Textbook of Salesmanship,* 10th ed. (New York: McGraw-Hill Book Company, Inc., 1978), p. 167.
[21] *Ibid.,* p. 225.

1. Is this actually a "worthwhile" account? Is it worth the time and effort? WHY?

2. Should this call have priority over other calls to be made today? WHY?

3. Should a phone call for an appointment be made? Do I want to meet with more than one individual and how can I achieve this?

4. When was my last call?

5. What happened? WHY? What am I going to do about it?

6. Whom do I plan to see? Is he the right person? What can I do about it?

7. Who can decide to change the source of supply? Who is the decision-making authority?

8. How can I reach him without antagonizing others?

9. Where does the company buy now? WHY? What percentage, if any, of its needs do we supply? Is this satisfactory? If not, what do I propose to do about it?

10. Is there really any good reason why this company should buy from us? What reason?

11. Are there any specific sales tools, samples, letters, or proposals that I should use? WHY? WHEN? WHERE? HOW?

12. Do I want to visit the plant or warehouse? How will I do this? What obstacles are likely to arise, and how can I overcome them?

13. What will I do when I do get out into the plant or warehouse?

14. Is the purpose of this call to secure an order? What order? Is this goal realistic?

15. If not to secure an order, what is the purpose of this call?

16. Is this sound?

17. If the customer is dissatisfied for any reason, how will I handle the situation?

18. Is this call an important step in the overall development of the account? HOW? If not, why not? Is this a good reason?

19. What other obstacles are likely to arise, and how will I meet them?

20. What can I do on this call, in addition to making a sale, that will lay the groundwork for another sale on my next call or in the near future? HOW? With whom? With what sales tools, aids, or samples?

FIGURE 7.9   Questions to Improve a Salesman's Thinking When Planning a Sales Call

training needs to individual requirements must be developed over a period of time.

PERFORMING SALES TRAINING

As the saying goes, there is now "nothing left but to do it." We mean by that that the next step is actually to perform the sales training that has been selected. In implementing the sales training approach selected, there are four key points to keep in mind.

First, sales management must strive to create a positive environment for the sales training. We mean by this that distractions must be minimized to the extent possible. More than one sales training session has been ruined because management in its efforts to combine "work with play" provided too great a temptation. This may be seen in classic form where the sales representative attending a group meeting and away from his home territory now kicks up his heels on the sales manager's training budget and comes into a morning training session still "hung over" from the night before. Creating a positive environment may also involve such considerations as making sure that the number of incoming phone calls or other distracting noises is minimized. Selection of a viable site for the sales training is thus no small task.

The second learning key, critically important to the success of the sales training program, is source credibility. By this we mean that the sales manager must consider the source of the training information in terms of the credibility it will have in the eyes of the individuals being trained. Thus, inclusion in a training program of individuals from top management of the firm may or may not enhance the credibility of the program. The critical variable here is the image top management has developed in the minds of the individuals to be trained. Often the revelation that an individual is from the "home office" is enough to destroy credibility in the eyes of the sales personnel. The attitude taken here is that anyone who is not directly involved in day-to-day field activities cannot possibly know what is going on. Conversely, sometimes source credibility is enhanced by including individuals who are from top management if these individuals are seen as viable members of the organization. The same argument could be made for the inclusions or exclusion of training materials or resources that are external to the firm. Consultants are often haunted by the fact that they are viewed as being from "outside our industry" and, therefore, their credibility is reduced before they have an opportunity to reveal their knowledge. In training programs dominated by sources and individuals internal to the firm, an outside speaker might well experience the reverse effect, inasmuch as that person would be viewed as bringing a "fresh and objective" viewpoint to the training program.

A third consideration involves the clarity of the information presented. Every reader can identify at least one situation in her/his life where information presented was unclear or ambiguous. To be effective, training information must be clear in the minds of the individuals receiving the training. Thus, many sales training sessions involve a summary, recap, or debriefing session aimed at making sure the information presented was really understood.

Before proceeding, we must point out that the three conditions—creating a positive environment, source credibility, and clarity of information—all have in common the fact that they can be strongly influenced by sales management. This is important inasmuch as the final key factor is somewhat immune to management control. This pertains to desire on the part of the sales trainee to learn the information being presented. It has been suggested by more than one writer in the area of sales training that ability and desire do not always complement each other in a single individual. That is, sales trainees with a great deal of ability often do not possess the desire to learn the materials being presented in sales training. Management must do all within its power to insure that it has selected from the recruiting process individuals who truly have a desire to learn how to be successful in a particular sales force.

EVALUATION OF SALES TRAINING

The evaluation of sales training may be akin to the old adage that states, "The proof of the pudding is in the eating thereof." If a similar situation does exist with regard to sales training, then sales management should be able to monitor and view the results of training in the events that follow it. Earlier it was suggested that the objectives for training should be both clear and measurable. Many firms thus conduct a pre- and posttraining evaluation to determine effectiveness of the techniques and resources used in sales training. Postevaluation was adequately illustrated earlier in the example of Armour-Dial.[22]

The key point that we wish to make with regard to the evaluation of sales training is that it is a continual process. It involves a candid appraisal and comparison of the *expected* results with the *actual* results. Rather than evolving into a situation where management attempts to affix the blame for variations between expected and actual results, the important purpose of the evaluation is to find out why such a difference exists and to determine the proper remedy. Although it rarely happens, if the actual results were even better than the expected, there is still a need to do an evaluation. If we could determine the reasons why the actual is better than the expected, we might be able to transfer the lessons learned to other divisions of the company, thus magnifying the savings and benefits.

Retraining: The Never Ending Managerial Task

We have previously stated that training should be viewed as a continuous process. Three basic motives account for the need for continuous training in a sales organization. These include

1. The firm's effort to keep salesmen up to date on changes product features, changing company policies, changing industry conditions, and changes in the competitive environment.
2. The dynamic nature of both marketing generally and personal selling specifically.
3. The need for increased productivity.[23]

[22] See footnote 10.
[23] Thomas F. Stroh, *Training and Developing the Professional Salesman* (New York: Amacon Publishing Company, 1972), p. 208.

Sales management has specific responsibility for determining when such sales force retraining is needed and the specific content of the retraining program. Jolson draws an analogy of preventative maintenance to the concept of retraining the sales force, He states:

The preventative approach looks at sales training as an ongoing, continuous process whereby management anticipates retraining needs and actually searches for symptoms and hues which will suggest the direction of retraining programs.[24]

SELECTION OF SALES PERSONNEL FOR RETRAINING

A recent study focusing upon the retraining of sales personnel has indicated four possible bases for selection of individuals to attend such retraining. These are selection on the basis of superior performance, selection on the basis of below average performance, selection on the basis of convenience to the individual, and selection on the basis of seniority.[25]

Selection on the basis of superior performance is recognition of the economics involved in retraining. If we are selecting outstanding sales performers, sales management is essentially saying that it recognizes retraining costs to be expensive and, therefore, wishes to expend dollars on individuals who are already proven performers. The Cadillac Plastic & Chemical Company of Detroit has developed an effective method for minimizing retraining costs. This method concentrates upon the use of television and allows individuals to be exposed to retraining programs without attending actual meetings through the use of television video cassettes. Carl Valduf, Director of Training for the firm, points out that the use of video cassettes "saves a bundle on staff and travel costs."[26] Yet another argument in favor of selection of outstanding sales personnel for retraining is that much may be accomplished in a small period of time inasmuch as training personnel need not be distracted by individuals who are marginal performers.

The selection of individuals who are attaining a below average performance for retraining is based upon the predication that successful retraining may be the only method for retaining the individual as a viable member of the sales force. In making such a decision, management must, of course, weigh the costs of terminating the existing poor performer and the cost of replacing this individual (through recruiting and selection of an alternative) with a candidate that *presumably* will be a better performer.

In an article entitled "The Salesman's Career Cycle," Jolson identified four stages of a salesman's career. A stage entitled "the decline" presents

[24] Marvin A. Jolson, *Sales Management: A Tactical Approach* (New York: Petrocelli/Charter, 1977), p. 212.

[25] John J. Withey, "Retraining the Experienced Salesperson," in Martin A. Jolson (ed.), *Contemporary Readings in Sales Management* (New York: Petrocelli/Charter, 1977), pp. 223–236.

[26] "Using TV for More Effective Sales Training," *Marketing for Sales Executives,* vol. 4, No. 11 (Published by the Research Institute of America, Inc., June 8, 1978), p. 3.

a similar circumstance to selection of a below average performer. Jolsen writes:

Experienced producers may begin to tire easily due to sheer physical fatigue and emotional exhaustion. Senior salesmen may begin to lose interest in their work, feelings of inadequacy may arise, and insecurity and anxiety may appear. The effects are often self-perpetuating, as tension and loss of confidence reduce the ability to solve customers' problems and the inability to solve problems increases tensions and insecurity. The salesman may begin to rationalize, denigrate himself, or withdraw psychologically or physically.[27]

Obviously, management is taking a calculated risk in selecting individuals of below average achievement for retraining.

When selection is based on the convenience of the parties involved, management may be acknowledging the cost of having territories empty. Sales management must always consider the opportunities that may be missed by an individual undergoing training. This is especially true if the individual is attending a central meeting location such as a meeting at company headquarters, for example. Although the convenience of particular sales personnel, sales management personnel, and training staff members is doubtlessly of importance, it must be weighed against the need to bring all the individuals together at the specified time and place. Some firms have solved this dilemma by selecting specific times of the year on a systematic basis for retraining. Thus, for example, the first week in January might be utilized by some firms for retraining.

Selection on the basis of seniority would appear to make a great deal of sense on the surface. However, in a recent study, Withey found that "as time on the job increases, ability and/or willingness to respond effectively in refresher type training classes decreases."[28]

Whatever basis is utilized for selection of sales personnel for retraining, sales management must be aware that this is indeed a difficult process. Retraining may carry certain positive or negative value judgments, and management must be careful to understand the political ramifications of retraining.

An overview of one individual's credo toward personal selling is depicted below. In summary, this is the type of attitude that management wishes to establish either through the initial training that the individual has received or through continual retraining.

Elbert Hubbard's Business Credo[29]

I believe in myself.

I believe in the goods I sell.

I believe in the firm for whom I work.

[27] Marvin A. Jolson, "A Salesman's Career Cycle," *Journal of Marketing*, (Vol. 38), July 1974, p. 39–46 at p. 41.

[28] *Ibid.*, p. 228.

[29] From *Sales and Marketing Management*, Oct. 9, 1978, p. 65. Excerpted from *Elbert Hubbard of East Aurora*, by Felix Shea, published by Wm. H. Wise and Co., New York. Elbert Hubbard was a classic salesman. In 1894, at the age of 35, he "retired" as a highly successful soap salesman. He later triumphed as a magazine publisher, a marketer of books, furniture, and other products, and a direct mail specialist.

I believe in my colleagues and helpers.

I believe in American Business Methods.

I believe in producers, creators, manufacturers, distributors, and in all industrial workers of the world who have a job, and hold it down.

I believe that Truth is an asset.

I believe in good cheer and in good health, and I recognize the fact that the first requisite in success is not to achieve the dollar, but to confer a benefit, and that the reward will come automatically and usually as a matter of course.

I believe in sunshine, fresh air, spinach, applesauce, laughter, buttermilk, babies, bombazine and chiffon, always remembering that the greatest word in the English language is "Sufficiency."

I believe that when I make a sale, I make a friend.

And I believe that when I part with a man, I must do it in such a way that when he sees me again, he will be glad—and so will I.

I believe in the hands that work, and the brains that think, and in the hearts that love.

Amen, and Amen.

CONTENT OF RETRAINING PROGRAM

The specific content of a retraining program will be unique to the particular business and particular salespeople who are to be retrained. However, it is possible to generalize about some potential areas for retraining. In a recent article, Withey has commented on some possible areas for inclusion. These are

- *Updating of company sales procedures and policies.* Unique or changing sales procedures and policies of the firm may be the subject for retraining. Such topics may require more than a mere explanation on the part of management and may actually involve reeducation as to new procedures and policies.
- *Usual salesmanship topics.* A particular step or a particular series of steps involved in the selling process discussed earlier in this chapter may be the focus for retraining. For example, new closing techniques or closing techniques that need to be emphasized might be the topic of a retraining session.
- *Product knowledge.* Retraining may be involved when a firm has a wide product line in which certain individual products tend to become neglected, or retraining may be involved from the standpoint of providing new applications for existing products.
- *Definition and significance of the concept of integrated marketing.* Sales management may need to point out to sales personnel the application of systems for integrated approaches to marketing. Sales personnel often view the firm from their own particular territory and do not necessarily see a more integrated and generalized systems approach to the entire firm.

- *Order processing systems.* Salesmen need to be well versed on the entire "flow" of an order from its origination to a completed delivery of merchandise. This may involve retraining sales personnel with regard to order processing information, inventory control information, credit information and how it is utilized in the firm, and so on. A useful side benefit of this is that sales personnel may develop a greater understanding for the problems associated with delivery of merchandise from the producing point.

- *The company's inventory policies.* Sales management must reeducate selling personnel occasionally as to why inventories are maintained at particular levels and why they may fluctuate throughout a particular calendar year. Sales personnel, after all, are often called upon by customers to explain why a company is out of stock or why a company is unable to fill a particular order. Such retraining information can prove invaluable in offering assistance to sales personnel in answering these types of questions.

- *Retraining of the sales force with regard to traffic and distribution questions.* Similar to the preceding point: salespeople often need to know details concerning delivery of products once they leave a particular firm's production point and are on their way to a consumer. Such a retraining session may prove an excellent opportunity to acquaint the sales force with traffic and shipping personnel, whom they do not see but who, nevertheless, may be essential to maintenance of good customer relations.

- *Expected changes in the marketing area.* Included here would be retraining of sales personnel along the lines of any expected change in the marketing environment. This would include both uncontrollable and controllable variables, as previously discussed in Chapter 1 and would suggest some of management's thinking about upcoming rather than actual events in the firm's environmental space. One illustration of these kinds of events is currently taking place in the real estate business. For example, an article in a large metropolitan newspaper indicates at least one realtor is currently providing some retraining for certain individuals in the sales force to stimulate their thinking on changes in the traditional selling environment of residential real estate. Specifically, these changes involve showing prospective buyers videotaped segments of several prospective homes that might be of interest. Heretofore, buyers have actually visited each home and/or the agent has presented "multiple listing" types of books that contain photographs of the properties.[30]

Commenting on these areas for retraining, Withey has stated:

The above eight areas of instruction tend to be universal in well-designed salesman training programs. As already specified, however, the actual curriculum will be unique to the firm and the personalities engaged in the training.[31]

[30] J. Paul Wyatt, "Realtor Shows Houses on TV," *The Atlanta Journal & Constitution* Vol. 29, No. 44, Sunday, October 22, 1978, Section H, p. 1.
[31] Withey, see pp. 230 and 231 of footnote 25.

RETRAINING TO AVOID MISTAKES

Viewing the relationship between marketing and personal selling, Peter Drucker wrote:

The aim of marketing is to make selling superfluous. The aim of marketing is to know and understand customers so well that the product or service fits them and sells itself.[32]

Drucker is implying that, if a firm is truly informed as to who their customers are and, further, if it has insight into why customers buy the products or services, selling should be relatively easy to accomplish. In order for management to fulfill this view of selling, it must continuously monitor sales force performance to correct either mistakes or bad habits. Retraining may be needed to correct these mistakes or bad habits, inasmuch as these may develop over a period of time. That is, a salesman may perform at a very acceptable level for the first 2 to 4 years of his career and then suddenly begin to develop bad habits or mistakes that management must correct.

J. Porter Henry and staff have analyzed some of the more common mistakes made by sales personnel. Any of these mistakes might be an adequate rationale for retraining. It is also possible that any individual salesman could be making a combination of the following ten mistakes.

1. Making calls instead of winning sales. One common device is for management to monitor the ratio of the number of sales calls to the number of closes. Retraining may be needed if sales management believes that the salesman is simply greeting the customer and passing the time of day without really attempting to close. This would result in an increase in the number of sales calls but a declining ratio of sales calls to closes.
2. Salesmen often need retraining because of the failure to plan. It is common for a salesperson to feel that she/he really knows a territory quite thoroughly after being assigned to it for a number of years. Thus, a failure to plan may be observed in the day-to-day operations and offer an adequate basis for a retraining program.
3. Salesmen often make the mistake of selling in the dark. We are suggesting here that, after being with the firm for a period of time, salesmen may forget to do their prospecting and pre-approach work. Thus, they may be assuming that certain motives already exist in a prospect and they are thus selling in the dark rather than determining real needs that customers have.
4. Another type of mistake that may form an adequate basis for retraining is the idea of selling bare-handed. That is, salesmen may neglect the use of visual aids, example products, and so on, and may simply attempt to walk in "bare-handed" to obtain an order from a customer.
5. A mistake that will be discussed later on, in the chapter on time

[32] Peter F. Drucker, *People and Performance: the Best of Peter Drucker on Management* (New York: Harper & Row, publishers, 1977), p. 91.

and territory management, is that of wasting time. Too often, sales-people waste time by not knowing who to see or not having planned their time sufficiently. Thus, they miss opportunities. This, too, offers fruitful grounds for retraining.

6. Yet another common mistake is the concept of selling product features rather than benefits. It has often been stated that there is a drastic difference in the point of view of manufacturers, sales personnel, and consumers. We mean by this that manufacturers often think in terms of market share or some measure of sales volume (number of cases sold, number of tons, number of units in a particular purchase, and so on). Sales personnel, on the other hand, often think in terms of commissioned dollars; that is, what they will make from a given sale or in terms of product features. Consumers, on the other hand, think in terms of benefits or in terms of finding solutions to their problems. A popular verse points this out:

So tell me quick and tell me true
Or else my friend to hell with you
Less—how this product came to be
More—what the damn thing does for me![33]

Obviously, retraining sales personnel to think in terms of consumer benefits or in terms of solutions to consumer problems is important and may produce excellent results.

7. Many salesmen make the mistake of failing to deal with emotions. We are suggesting here that the salesperson must be chameleonlike in being prepared to deal with the emotions affecting the prospect at a particular point in time of the sales call. It is possible that a salesman, who may have rehearsed a very long and detailed sales presentation, may arrive to find the prospect in a hostile state because of something totally unrelated to his call. Retraining may be able to prepare sales personnel to be flexible enough to deal with almost any emotional state of a prospect.

8. Another mistake made by many salesmen is the idea of selling in a rut. Habit provides a very "tender trap" that many sales personnel lapse into without being aware of what is occurring. Over a period of time sales representatives may develop one or two "pet" sales approaches with which they are very successful. Without realizing it, the sales personnel may neglect use of other sales approaches that might be even more effective. Retraining would have the objective of opening their eyes to sales approaches they may be overlooking by virtue of habit.

9. In the area of personal selling salesmen often make the mistake of pigeonholing customers or stereotyping customers. That is, very often sales personnel begin to think of their "average customer" and thus neglect individuals who are atypical but may provide the source of much market potential. The purpose of retraining is to recall to mind

---

[33] Source unknown. As quoted in J. Porter Henry *et al.*, "The Ten Biggest Mistakes Salesmen Make." Published by *Sales & Marketing Management*, 1975, p. 13.

that no firm has a market, rather firms have markets characterized by very different and divergent types of customers and prospects.

10. A last area for possible retraining of the sales force is the misuse of information. There are a variety of ways in which information may be misused, and each of these may offer a reason for retraining the sales force. Included are the tendency to put panic into feedback information. As an example, one particular competitor may reduce prices in a given sales territory; there might then be a tendency on the part of many sales personnel to generalize that they are therefore facing severe price competition from *all* competitors in the near future. Obviously, this may not be the case, and retraining may be needed to correct this misinterpretation of information.

All of the preceding types of mistakes are correctable by retraining. The ten areas suggested are based upon the previous work of J. Porter Henry.[34]

I. Give Him a Definite Job and a Chance to Do It

   1. Assign definite duties and responsibilities which:
      — are reasonable and practical
      — represent a challenge
      — do not conflict

   2. Make certain he clearly understands his job.

   3. Give him the tools, equipment, information, and authority necessary for his work.

   4. Give him help in learning how to handle his duties and responsibilities.

II. Stimulate and Guide His Thinking and Performance

   1. Encourage him to think for himself and to stand on his own feet.
      — let him figure out some of the answers
      — urge him to criticize your suggestions about his job
      — ask his opinion of your plans and ideas.

   2. Check his performance in terms of results and the reactions of those he contacts.

   3. By asking questions, get him to accurately appraise his plans and performance; work out ways of improving them.

   4. Back him up when he is right; give him help when he is in trouble.

III. Credit His Accomplishments, Correct His Shortcomings

   1. Praise his good work even though his overall performance is unsatisfactory.

   2. Be thorough, specific, reasonable, understanding, and constructive in discussing the shortcomings of his performance.

   3. Do the same thing about his personal shortcomings when they affect his performance or progress.

   4. Let him know where he stands and reward his progress.

IV. Insist on Results

   1. Always require his best efforts

   2. Be sure he realizes constant improvement is essential to progress.

FIGURE 7.10   How to Develop a Salesman

[34] Henry, *ibid.*

DEVELOPMENT AND RENEWAL

The purpose of retraining is twofold. First, sales management may be attempting to develop further skills already existing in the sales force. Second is the concept of renewal; sales management may hope to return an unsatisfactory level of performance by a given salesperson to a satisfactory level. Figure 7.10 summarizes many of the concepts covered in this chapter and presents an overview on development and/or renewal of sales personnel.

Summary

This chapter had focused upon the topic of sales training. We have seen that it is important for sales managers to guard against "mental biases" pertaining to training (for example, training is only for new sales personel). Likewise, we have developed a model (Figure 7.1) that provides an overview of the sales training process beginning with an assessment of sales training needs and concluding with the ongoing need for the evaluation and appraisal of training.

We have also explored the need for retraining, acknowledging that this is a continual process in a healthy sales organization. Where retraining is concerned, we have discussed the selection of personnel, the content of the retraining program, and the avoidance of mistakes. Finally, we have discussed the ultimate purposes of retraining—development and/or renewal of sales force personnel.

Discussion Questions

1. What types of training do new sales personnel need? Note "new" here means both new to selling and new to a particular firm.

2. Do you believe that a centralized location is the place for training or should it be done in an individual's own (home) territory?

3. How can a firm cut dollar expenditures on training without hurting itself in terms of long-range marketing impact?

4. Should "outsiders" be used in sales training? Why or why not? Note "outsiders" here means individuals not employed full time by the parent firm.

5. Can selling skills be taught or is the "ability to sell" something one must be born with?

6. Review Figure 7.2. What are some other questions a sales manager might ask in order to better determine training needs?

7. Review Figure 7.3. What are the implications for future training costs? Does the rapid increase, recently seen, suggest we should train all new salespeople as rapidly as possible in order to minimize costs? Should a firm attempt to hire previously trained sales personnel from competitive firms to reduce costs? Why, or why not?

8. Review the materials in this chapter on content of retraining programs. What additional topics can you suggest? Of the topics mentioned in the chapter, which should have highest priority and which lowest priority? Why?

9. Examine Elbert Hubbard's Business Credo. Does this credo typify most sales personnel today? If not, could retraining play a role in moving sales personnel in this direction? Should this be a goal of retraining? Why, or why not?

10. What time period should elapse between training and the evaluation of training? That is, how long will it take to determine whether training has "worked" or not? Be specific.

Selected References

DUNN, ALBERT H., and EUGENE M. JOHNSON, *Managing the Sales Force* (Morristown, N.J.: General Learning Corporation, 1973), Chapter 3.

HENRY, J. PORTER, *et al.*, "The Ten Biggest Mistakes Salesmen Make," *Sales & Marketing Management*, 1975.

HOPKINS, DAVID S., *Training the Sales Force: A Progress Report* (New York: The Conference Board, Inc., 1978.)

HUGHES, G. DAVID, *Marketing Management: A Planning Approach* (Reading, Mass.: Addison–Wesley Publishing Company, Inc.), p. 390.

JOLSON, MARVIN A., "The Salesman's Career Cycle," *Journal of Marketing* (Vol. 38), July 1974, pp. 39–46.

"Look and Listen vs. Show and Tell," *Sales and Marketing Management*, (Vol. 117, No. 4), September 13, 1976, pp. 25 and 26.

MAYER, DAVID, and HERBERT M. GREENBERG, "What Makes A Good Salesman," *Harvard Business Review*, July–August 1976, pp. 119–125.

STANTON, WILLIAM J., and RICHARD H. BUSKIRK, *Management of the Sales Force*, 5th ed. (Homewood, Ill.: Richard D. Irwin, Inc., 1978), Chapter 8 and 9.

STROH, THOMAS F., *Training and Developing the Professional Salesman* (New York: Amacon Publishing Company, 1972).

"Training: Critical to Marketing Success," *Marketing Times* (Vol. XXIII, No. 1), January–February 1976, p. 3.

"Using TV for More Effective Sales Training," *Marketing for Sales Executives*, (Vol. 4, No. 11), June 8, 1978, p. 3 (Published by the Research Institute of America, Inc.)

WHITHEY, JOHN J., "Retraining the Experienced Salesperson," in Martin A. Jolson (ed.), *Contemporary Readings in Sales Management* (New York: Petrocelli/Charter, 1977), p. 223–236.

CASE 7.1
Melco Supply Company*

Company Background

Melco Supply Company was founded in 1948 with the financial backing of a major soft drink manufacturer. Shortly thereafter, the soft drink manufacturer awarded Melco a substantial long-term contract to supply them with printed paper cups to be used in various promotional campaigns.

During the Korean conflict, Melco grew rapidly by securing important contracts to provide paper cups to the United States Army. Expanding into related paper and plastic food service items, Melco became the top supplier in the disposable tableware field by 1970. A national company with over $100 million in sales, Melco now sold paper and plastic plates, bowls, cutlery, tablecloths, straws, ice cream containers, and sandwich bags.

Although growth had continued to be stable in the last few years, competition was becoming more intense as new suppliers were drawn to the highly profitable field of plastic disposables. The primary threats to Melco's top position in the industry were several large oil companies who had plastic divisions with national sales coverage. Although relatively new to the food service industry, the oil companies attracted talented people and were extremely aggressive in their efforts to build market share.

Even though Melco's market share had not grown during the past two years, they still led the market with a 25 per cent market share. Future growth seemed to be a certainty, as Melco continued to lead the still-growing industry in innovative breakthroughs. In the past year, Melco had designed a disposable plastic plate that could be used with all types of food in a microwave oven with no damage to the plate. This had been a major breakthrough in the hospital, restaurant, and hotel/motel markets because previous plates melted when greasy foods such as bacon were cooked in the microwave ovens. Also, customers seemed to prefer the appearance of this new plate, which Melco planned to market under the name "Melco Microware."

* This case was prepared by Tom Ingram and Dan Robertson, both of Georgia State University.

Microware had passed the test market stage with high marks and had entered into production just a week ago. It would take approximately 60 days to reach an acceptable inventory level, at which time Melco planned a national sales promotion to introduce the product. Regional sales meetings were scheduled for May 15, when the sales representatives would be given product knowledge and training, as well as sales strategy training for Microware.

Central Region Sales Manager Craig Burns knew the importance of a well-trained sales force in the introduction of a new product. He had seen competitors' products fail completely because the sales representatives simply did not know enough about the product to sell it. Melco had experienced very few product failures in their history, particularly not those due to poor training.

However, Burns was concerned with the training job to be done prior to the introduction of Microware. Two months ago he had held a sales meeting for the Central Region sales force and had been disppointed with the performance of six of the eight sales representatives during a role-playing training exercise.

The importance of the role-playing had been minimized prior to the meeting, with the sales representatives being told to prepare a presentation on an assigned product. Each person presented a different product to another sales representative, who played the role of the prospective buyer.

The presentations were viewed by the rest of the sales force, Burns, and Bob Jamison, the Regional Marketing Manager. After each of the presentations was completed, Burns had led an oral group critique of the presentation to point out areas of strength and weakness.

Looking back on the generally weak performances, Burns reflected on the total training programs used by Melco. Most of the sales representatives coming to work for Melco had 1–3 years of sales experience in related industries. All were college graduates and four of the eight reporting to Burns had advanced degrees. All eight of the representatives wanted to advance into management with Melco, and Burns felt that each of them had the potential to become Melco managers in the future.

Burns reviewed the training each of his representatives had received in their respective careers. All had received formal training from Melco consisting of product knowledge, salesmanship, administrative procedures, and Melco manufacturing methods. As part of his regular territory visits, Burns conducted critiques after each call with regard to the effectiveness and professionalism of the call.

Up until the January meeting, Burns had felt that his sales force was highly professional—a conclusion supported by their results during the last 2 years. He thought that possibly the sales representatives had a temporary letdown after a tough year and perhaps felt they did not need the role-playing exercise since they had experienced similar training in the past.

Also Burns felt the sales representatives would have done better had he stressed "doing a better job" on the presentations prior to the meeting. However, he had taken Bob Jamison's advice who told him, "Craig, don't build up the role-playing prior to the meeting. I would like to see how your people respond on their *own* initiative."

Further, a couple of the sales representatives had told Burns that they felt "uncomfortable" doing a presentation in front of their peers. Greg Cochran had told Burns that he felt like he was "auditioning rather than selling" during his presentation.

Jamison had expressed his displeasure with the outcome of the role-playing by telling Burns, "With the excellent performance of your people in the field, I was shocked at their performance. I would like to see another role-playing exercise at the May 15 meeting, and I know that their performance will be improved."

Since the January meeting, Burns had discussed the presentations with each of the representatives. Most expressed surprise at Burns' critical evaluations and seemed defensive about their shortcomings. Burns was not trying to revise the role-playing exercise in preparation for the May 15 meeting. He had reviewed his notes of each evaluation (attached) and was now trying to plan the specific points he wanted to review with Jamison in 2 weeks. Burns felt that the exercise must be designed to reinforce the enthusiasm of the group prior to the introduction of Microware, since a successful Microware program would be crucial in attaining this year's sales targets. But Burns was still bothered by the numerous weaknesses revealed in his notes of January 10. What went wrong in the January presentations? What should I do before the May 15 meeting?

1. Greg Cochran — The best presentation of the group. Seemed a little nervous. Good use of sales literature and samples. Strong close and overcame several objectives along the way.

2. Walt Waxhall — Poorly prepared. Unable to answer several questions. No samples used in presentation. Tried to close before overcoming all objections.

3. Tom Latham — Lackadaisical. Seemed to perform more for the viewers than for the buyer. Argued with the buyer rather than presenting facts to counter objections.

4. Dave Taggart — Good presentation, although a little "low key." Nervous at the outset, but settled down. Could have handled price objection in a more positive manner.

5. Jim Lawrence — Would have never known he was our top sales representative. No supporting material used. Tried to overcome objections in a superficial manner. Very relaxed — in fact, too relaxed. Slouched in his chair as he talked with buyer.

6. Ray Maless — Very ill at ease. Appeared slow to respond to buyer's questions. Seemed relieved when the presentation ended, even though buyer failed to buy.

7. John Winder — Average presentation. No glaring weakness, but lacked John's usual creative flare in moving to close the sale.

8. Dan Wilson — Followed all the right techniques, but seemed like he was "going through the motions." Made a statement about product performance that he knew not to be true.

January 10 Sales Meeting

Maybe I should just let the January sessions become "water under the bridge" and not worry about it—after all, they're all good men.

CASE 7.2
Community Bank and Trust Company (Part A)*

Company Background

In 1957, a group of investors, made up of prominent citizens in the Mason City area, purchased a small bank from a statewide bank holding company. This bank was located in downtown Mason City, a community with approximately a 500,000 population. The newly acquired bank was named the Community National Bank and was the twenty sixth largest bank in size in the metropolitan area.

State law did not permit branch banking, thus resulting in a community of many small unit banks. Each bank was therefore a separate corporate entity. In an area with branch banking, a customer of the bank could make a deposit or withdrawal at any member bank in the system. In contrast, in a nonbranching area, a customer could only transact his business with the particular bank where he has his account.

By 1970, the Community National Bank had grown in size to the position of the fourth largest bank in the city. However, this fact tended to be somewhat misleading, as the city's three largest banking institutions were significantly larger than the Community National Bank. As an example, the deposit structure compared as follows:

	Demand Deposits Dec. 31, 1970
State National Bank	$337,130,448
County National Bank	312,187,000
City National Bank	298,898,311
Community National Bank	137,634,987

In mid-1970, the bank decided to develop a trust department. Permission from the Comptroller of the Currency to start a trust department was received in 1971. Sam Watson was hired in early 1972 as Vice President and Senior Trust Officer and was given the responsibility to develop and manage the trust department. Sam reported directly to the president of the bank.

* This case was prepared by Robert L. Berl and Dan H. Robertson, both of Georgia State University.

In late 1972, the bank's management decided to change its name to the Community National Bank and Trust Company.

The scope of activities in a bank trust department is extremely broad. Exhibit 1 outlines the various functions performed by most trust departments.

Between 1972 and 1975, considerable progress was achieved in getting the trust department on a firm foundation. By 1975, the department had grown to approximately $32,000,000 in "assets under management" and $234,000,000 in "custodial assets." Approximately 56 per cent of the "assets under management" were employee benefit plans with the majority of the remainder being personal trusts and agencies. The "assets under management" produced roughly two thirds of the departments gross fee income, and the "custodial assets" made up the remaining one third. A comparison of assets and revenues is as follows:

	Assets		Revenue	
	Dollars (000,000)	Percentage	Dollars (000)	Percentage
Assets under management				
Personal trusts	$ 12	38%	$25	41%
Employee benefit plans	18	56%	33	54%
Other	2	6	3	5%
	$ 32	12%	$61	68%
Custodial assets	234	88%	29	32%
	$266	100%	$90	100%

In addition to the manager, Sam Watson, the department had two other trust officers—Ann Leslie, Trust Operations Officer, and Harry Smith, Assistant Trust Administrative Officer, two secretaries and a part-time clerk. A functional breakdown of activities is as follows:

PRESIDENT, TRUST DEPARTMENT

Sam Watson, Manager

Trust Operations	Corporate Trust	Personal Trust	Employee Benefit Plans	Investments	New Business
Ann Leslie, T.O.	Ann Leslie, T.O.	Ann Leslie, T.O.	Harry Smith, A.T.O.	Sam Watson, V.P.	Sam Watson, V.P.
		Harry Smith, A.T.O.			

As the organizational chart depicts, there is a wide range of activities which are spread over a limited number of people. This is typical of a small trust department. It takes many years for a bank trust department to acquire a sufficient volume of business to become profitable. At this stage of development, expenses exceed revenues and, consequently, staffing is held at a minimum. Approximately 25–30 per cent of Sam's time is devoted to the active solicitation of trust business. Bank management and Sam were aware that, as the department grew, progressively more of Sam's energies would be devoted to general management and the administrative and investment functions and less time to the solicitation and acquiring of new trust customers.

Current
Situation

The bank's Board of Directors has decided to accelerate the growth of the trust department and has given Sam Watson permission to hire a Trust New Business Officer. Sam would like to hire an experienced trust salesman or an individual who has related experience such as law, investment brokerage experience, or life insurance sales. However, the entry level salary of such a person would probably far exceed the maximum amount that had been budgeted for this position. Sam is also aware that a person without experience would take a great deal more of his time and the bank's money to train before becoming productive. Sam also feels that such factors as age and education should influence his hiring and training decision.

As a basis for designing a training program for a trust officer, Sam has asked for and received a copy of a trust training program (see Appendix on page 249) from a large out-of-town correspondent bank. He wonders if such a training program is appropriate for Community Bank and Trust. If not, what additions and/or changes should be made?

APPENDIX
Trust Services

A trust department is a fiduciary. A fiduciary is an individual, or an institution, with the duty of acting for the benefit of another party. An agent and his principal, an attorney and his client, and a trustee and a beneficiary are all examples of fiduciary relationships.

(1) *Settlement of Estates*—A major service is the settlement of estates of deceased persons. The trust department's main duties are to assemble the assets; to pay the administrative expenses, taxes, and debts; and to distribute the net estate in accordance with the will or applicable state laws.

(2) *Administration of Trusts*—A second service performed for individuals is the administration of trusts. A trust is a fiduciary relationship in which one person (the trustee) is the holder of the legal title to property (trust property) subject to an equitable obligation (an obligation enforceable in a court of equity) to keep or use the property for the benefit of another (the beneficiary). Such trusts can be divided into several primary classifications: those created by a will and those created by agreement. The trust department performs those duties that are delineated in the trust agreement, holds the assets, keeps complete records, receives and disburses income, and invests the assets as it deems appropriate to achieve the objectives of the trust. Assets that the trust department is actively managing are referred to as "assets under management."

(3) *Performance of Agencies*—A main characteristic of an agency is that the title to the property does not pass to the trust institution, but remains in the name of the owner of the property, who is known as the principal. There are two major types of agency accounts. First, a custodial account in which the bank's responsibility is the safekeeping of assets, record keeping, and receiving and disbursing income. Second, an investment agency account. Here the bank performs all the functions described in the custodial agency plus the analysis and selection of investments for purchase or sale and keeping the customer's account under continuous supervision.

Services to Individuals

(1) *Administration of Employee Benefit Trusts*—Pension plans and profit sharing plans are the two principal types of employee benefit plans. A company establishes a pension plan to provide its employees with a guaranteed retirement income. In contrast, profit sharing plans are designed to share a portion of a company's profits with the employees, but no guarantees are made regarding an employee's retirement bene-

Services to Business

Week Number	Topic	Reading Schedule
1	(I) Orientation and Indoctrination (A) Personnel Department Orientation (B) Tour of trust and investment departments (C) Introduction to key personnel (D) Discussion of the trust function	(Weeks 1-6) (I) Orientation (A) Personnel Manual (B) Bank's-Annual Report (C) Amer. Bankers Asso. Glossary of Fiduciary Terms (D) State Bankers Asso. Trust Manual Chapter A (E) Trust Department Policy & Procedure Manual (F) Amer. Institute of Banking "Trust Department Services." Chapters I, II, IX, XIX, XX
2	(II) Trust Operations Division (A) Orientation (B) Securities control, income, transfers, etc. (C) Cash control, checkwriter (D) Common trust fund (E) Systems, auditing	(II) Trust Operations Division (A) State Bankers Asso. Trust Manual, Chapters B & E
3	(III) Trust Property (A) Set-up (B) Sale and maintenance (C) Review procedure (D) Property Management	(III) Trust Tax Division (A) CCH Guides on forms #1040, #1041 & #706 (B) State Bankers Asso. Trust Manual Chapter F (C) "Comparison of F Estate Taxes & State Inheritance Taxes"
4-6	(IV) Trust Tax Division (A) Orientation (B) Fiduciary returns (C) Death and gift tax returns (D) Personal returns (Examination on the first six weeks)	
7	(V) Bond Department (A) Orientation (B) Money Market (C) Bond analysis and purchase (Municipals, Corporates and Federals) (D) Common Trust Fund - philosophy & operation	(Weeks 7-10) (IV) Bond & Investment Department (A) State Bankers Asso. Trust Manual Chapter D & review of Chapter E (B) Amer. Institute of Banking-"Trust Department Services, "Chapter (C) Investments text selected by investment department
8-10	(VI) Investment Department (A) Orientation (B) Operations (Procedures & securities: sales and purchases) (C) Security analysis (D) Portfolio management (Examination on weeks eight through ten)	
11-12	(VII) New Business Division (A) Orientation (B) Marketing and advertising programs (C) Interviews and estate planning problems (D) Business planning problems	(Weeks 11-20) (V) New Business Division (A) State Bankers Asso. Trust Manual, Chapter G (B) "Agreement of State Bar Asso. and the State Bankers Asso." (C) Casey — "Estate Planning Desk Book" (D) O'Keefe — "Estate Planning Primer"
13	(VIII) Corporate Trust Division (A) Orientation (B) Functions of transfer agent & registrar	(VI) Administration: Corporate, Private and Employee Benefits (A) State Bankers Asso. Trust Manual, Chapter C (B) Redfern — "State Probate" (C) Amer. Institute of Banking "Trust Department Services" Chapters III-VIII inclusive XI-XIV, inclusive & XVI
14-18	(IX) Employee Benefit Division (A) Orientation (B) Administration (Pension plans & profit sharing plans)	
19-25	(X) Private Trust Division (A) Orientation (B) Administration (Practical experience in the private trust function)	(VII) Commercial Bank Training (A) New Accounts Manual (B) Loan & Administrative Manuals
25-29	(XI) Commercial Banking (A) New Accounts (B) Lending	
30	Review and Examination	Additional reading assignments may be added during training.

Trust Training Program

fits. The business and individual trust functions are identical; however, on a day-to-day basis they are quite different . . . different record keeping, different government forms, different investment environment, and so on.

(2) *Administration of Corporate Trusts*—The most frequent service in this category is acting as trustee under a bond indenture. Security is pledged or mortgaged by the borrower (normally a major corporation) to be held in trust by a responsible, disinterested trustee. Lenders are given notes or bonds. If the borrower meets its obligation promptly, the trustee releases the collateral to the borrower; however, if the borrower defaults on the payment of the obligation, the trustee could enforce the rights of the bondholders against the borrower and against the security.

(3) *Performance of Agencies*—Two significant services are transfer agent and registrar. As transfer agent for stocks or bonds, the trust department issues and transfers the security to the various owners. It protects the company and stockholders against improper transfer of stock or bonds, failure to effect transfer, and other errors. As registrar, the trust department's function is to prevent the over-issuance of stock. The duties include checking the original issue, checking each transfer made by the transfer agent to insure the genuiness of the certificates presented for transfer, making sure that the old certificates are canceled, and seeing that the number of shares represented by new certificates do not exceed the number of shares represented by new certificates being presented for transfer. If the security is listed on a major stock exchange, no single institution can perform both the transfer and registrar functions.

This is an overview of the major services performed by a bank trust department. Many other services can be performed, and there are occasionally exceptions to the functions as they have been explained.

Student Learning Exercise / 7
Development of a Sales Training Program

To stimulate student thinking concerning the ingredients, timing, costs, and benefits of sales training.   *Objective*

This chapter has focused upon sales training via the use of a basic model. This exercise will lend itself to use of such a model or an alternative.   *Overview*

Exercise   Visit a retail automobile agency selling new cars near your university. Try to find out as much as you can about the specific duties of sales personnel working for the car dealer. When you feel you have adequate background, answer the following questions.

1. What type of sales training program would you design for an individual who is both new to the agency and new to personal sales? Be specific as to training content, length of time, and cost.
2. Now assume you are asked by the owner to develop a retraining program for senior sales personnel who have recently started "downhill." Again, be specific as to retraining content, length of time, and cost. Also, explain how you would gain the cooperation of senior sales personnel to undergo retraining.
3. If the sales training programs in 1 and 2 were being developed for a national marketer of industrial goods and products, how would it differ in terms of length of time, location where training was conducted, and costs? Why would there be differences in these programs?

Present highlights of the answers you've developed in questions 1–3 to other class members. Defend your training program specifics against those suggested by other class members.

Motivating and Compensating

the Sales Force

THE area of sales compensation and motivation represents one of the biggest single challenges to sales management. As we have seen from the preceding chapters, management has expended a tremendous amount not only of dollar resources but of time and personnel resources in the process of locating, recruiting, selecting, and training sales staff members. If a new individual has been recruited, selected, and trained for the sales force, it is common for a firm to have invested as much as $50,000 in this recently hired individual. Motivation and compensation, therefore, are critical management decision areas, inasmuch as successes in this area will determine how well the investment has paid off.

It may be surprising, therefore, for the student to learn that many sales managers are notoriously poor motivators of sales personnel. They may themselves have been excellent salespeople, but they are often woefully lacking in their knowledge of how to approach the motivation of other personnel.

As we shall see in the sections that follow, it is quite common for sales management to make three major mistakes in the area of motivation and compensation. These three include

1. A tendency to equate motivation with compensation.
2. A tendency to focus upon motivation and compensation from a group rather than from an individual salesperson's point of view.
3. A tendency to think that once a "good" compensation and motivation system has been developed, it will remain viable and effective over a long period of time.

While these mistakes are by no means mutually exclusive, the combination of two or more of these three mistakes can often prove fatal to a sales firm. Even if these mistakes do not prove fatal, they can obviously seriously handicap and reduce the efficiency of operation of a sales force. In the sections which follow we shall talk about these problems and ways of dealing with them. In addition, we shall also explore differing approaches to motivation and compensation. We will examine some non-compensation approaches to providing motivation for the sales force and we shall examine some different types of compensation plans.

Motivation Versus Compensation

As part of the student learning exercise connected with chapter six, you were asked to examine some ads in a newspaper for sales positions. A typical ad that you might have encountered might read something like the one which follows.

The ad in Figure 8.1 is intended as a stereotype typical of the ad placed by many firms in newspapers when they seek new sales personnel. This type of ad provides some tipoffs to the philosophy of sales management concerning compensation and motivation. As noted above, it is common for many sales managers to consider compensation and motivation as being synonymous. *This is a mistake.*

FIGURE 8.1   Typical Ad for Sales Representative

> SALES REPRESENTATIVE SOUGHT
>
> Large, national marketing firm seeks sales representative for local territory. Must be self starter with strong desire to excel and succeed. Potential earnings of $40,000 in first year with base salary of $20,000–$25,000 plus bonus, depending upon qualifications. Other fringe benefits include company automobile, all expenses paid, group hospitalization, etc. For further information, respond to P.O. Box 123, Anywhere, U.S.A.   12345.

Motivation refers to a predisposition to act. It then represents a force or a pressure reflecting an individual's perceptions, needs, and environmental influences. Compensation, on the other hand, is a tool available to management that may help in providing motivation. However, it is erroneous to think that compensation is the only tool that can be used for motivating salespeople. In a study concerning the effect of compensation upon sales performance, Morse and Weiss found that over 90 per cent of the salesmen they interviewed would continue to perform their sales jobs even if their economic needs were already satisfied (via the form of a large inheritance).[1] Thus, monetary rewards alone do not appear to explain the full reasons for performing a job.

The ad that appears in Figure 8.1 does, however, provide some insight into management's thinking where motivation and compensation is concerned. Many sales managers take the view that motivation cannot be stimulated. That is, an individual who is performing a sales task will either be motivated to accomplish a good job or he or she will not. This type of thinking is displayed by the specific wording of the ad in Figure 8.1. The use of the words "self-starter" and phrases such as "strong desire to excel and succeed" are indications that management may find these

---

[1] Nancy C. Morse and Robert S. Weiss, "The Function and Meaning of Work in the Job," *American Sociological Review* (Vol. 20), April 1955, p. 197.

to be qualities they seek in individuals they would hire. This may reflect a tacit admission by management that they are either unwilling or unable to attempt to motivate sales personnel by any means other than income. On the other hand, the stress upon the income and relatively high salary reflect management's view that financial income is the single method by which salesmen may be motivated.

There is a great deal of disagreement among sales managers as to whether or not motivation may be stimulated. Some sales managers subscribe to the view that motivation is either present in an individual or it is not, and that short of financial rewards there is nothing that can be done to stimulate it. Other sales managers subscribe to the view that there are numerous nonfinancial motives that may be used to inspire sales personnel. Such motives would include

1. The desire to be needed or accepted.
2. The desire for praise or recognition.
3. The avoidance of monotony and boredom.
4. Personal pride in achievement or self-image improvement.
5. Freedom from fear and worry.[2]

The authors of this text would subscribe to the view that, although financial rewards are one very important method of achieving motivation, the use of other motivational techniques and tools is certainly appropriate; in fact, in many cases, these may prove more effective than mere financial rewards. This should not be taken to mean that financial motives for job performance are unimportant. Obviously, in an age of increasing inflation, dollar income is critically important. However, reliance upon compensation as the *sole* means of motivating the sales force is both erroneous and short sighted.

A psychologist and management theorist, Frederick Herzberg, has provided an interesting view of employee motivation. In Figure 8.2, we see a representation of some of the factors resulting in job satisfaction and job dissatisfaction. As depicted in Figure 8.2, Herzberg maintains that the external factors surrounding a job, including the financial rewards, are hygiene. If poor hygiene exists, management will face employee dissatisfaction, poor morale, and poor job performance. Good hygiene however, does not result in motivation. Hygiene needs elevate, and the zero point (the dividing point in Figure 8.2) escalates or moves to the right in the figure. For example, if the sales person receives a raise in pay of $100 per month, the sales person would quickly adjust to the new salary level and become dissatisfied again in a very short period of time. The higher base income then becomes a new level from which the individual would bargain. The adjustment on the part of the sales person would occur very quickly; thus, the increase in salary would have little effect on motivation in the long range and only a very short-lived, positive effect in the short range. To the right of the center in

---

[2] W. L. Burton, "There's More to Motivating Salesmen than Money," in T. W. Meloan and J. M. Rathmell (eds.), *Selling: Its Broader Dimensions* (New York: Macmillan Publishing Co., 1960), p. 63.

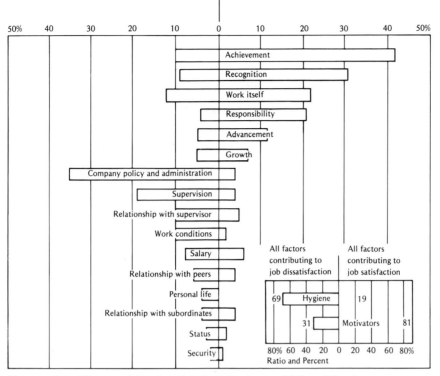

FIGURE 8.2 Factors Affecting Job Satisfaction and Dissatisfaction
[Source: Frederick Herzberg, "One More Time: How Do You Motivate
Employees?" *Harvard Business Review* (Jan.–Feb. 1968), p. 57.]

Figure 8.2, we see the factors that produced job satisfaction, and to the
left of the center we see the frequency with which these same factors
produce dissatisfaction among the individuals Herzberg surveyed.

Herzberg would suggest that the effect produced by money is short-
lived. Thus, given a high enough financial reward, an individual might
perform a task they find personally repugnant. However, the individual
would quickly adjust to the new and higher level of income and would
sequentially resist a second, third, or fourth opportunity to perform the
same distasteful task.[3]

Thus, the challenge for management in terms of motivation is to provide reasons for performing the sales task that relate to personal growth,
satisfaction, and/or achievement. This was one of the major points we
sought to make in Chapter 7 concerning training.

We shall have more to say about the specific topic of compensation
later in this chapter. For the present, however, we will simply state that
a major objective of this section was to establish that compensation is
merely *one* method of achieving motivation.

[3] Frederick Herzberg, "One More Time: How Do You Motivate Employees?" *Harvard
Business Review*, January-February 1968, p. 57.

The Sales Force: Group or Individual Orientation?

It is much easier to deal with human problems from the group perspective than from the individual perspective. Thus, for example, professors often think of group norms or group ratings when considering student satisfaction, rather than focusing upon the feelings of each individual student in a class. So it is with sales managers, who may commonly think of satisfaction within the sales force as opposed to satisfaction of an individual sales representative.

One way to avoid the mistake of overlooking individual feelings where motivation is concerned is to employ the concept of market segmentation in application to the sales force. Included in this text is a reading that stresses this point. In commenting upon use of segmentation for sales force motivation, the authors state:

> The concept of sales force segmentation should be relatively easy for the marketing manager to accept and adopt. In working with markets, the marketing manager easily accepts the fact that he is dealing with many different parts of the market and that each market must be approached (i.e., motivated to use a similar terminology) in a different manner. To accomplish this task, he uses different marketing mixes to accomplish the job. For segmenting his sales force, he needs to transfer the approach to the management of his sales force.[4]

Others have criticized this concept as being impractical or impossible to implement, and we should keep in mind that any issue involving segmentation does raise a question as to how finitely, segmentation is to be accomplished. For example, if the sales manager of a firm had a sales force consisting of over a hundred sales representatives, it quite likely would be impossible to segment down to the individual salesperson level, inasmuch as this would involve over 100 different segments. However, it might be possible to segment the sales force down to four groups of perhaps equal or differing numbers having similar compensation or motivational needs. An illustration is provided in the article by Mossien and Fram in the form of a marketer of industrial products in the scientific field. Observing this particular company, the authors commented "Ideally, each salesman should be motivated individually, but costs and a lack of trained supervisors prevent this. . . . Our observations and analyses indicated that a division into three groups was desirable and reasonable from a time standpoint."[5]

Perhaps the best single known theory dealing with individual motivation is provided in the work of A. H. Maslow. One of the most important parts of Maslow's theory is his development of a model consisting of

---

[4] Herbert Mossien and Eugene H. Fram, "Segmentation for Sales Force Motivation," *Akron Business and Economic Review,* Winter 1973, pp. 5–12. Note this reading is included in this text.

[5] *Ibid.,* p. 7.

several different levels of needs that exist in a human being and relate to each other via a "need hierarchy." Maslow has differentiated between five levels of needs. The first of these concerns itself with physiological needs, that is, hunger, thirst, and other basic drives. All living beings, regardless of their level of maturity, possess physiological needs. Note that physiological needs are omnipresent and are of a recurrent nature.

One of the misunderstandings associated with Maslow's theory is that he believes these five needs to be mutually exclusive. That, in fact, is not the intent of Maslow. To the contrary, several of these needs may occur simultaneously for any one individual and the relative importance of each need for any one individual determines the hierarchy involved. Thus, returning to physiological needs, once an individual's income is adequate to provide for his or her family's physiological needs the individual would continue in an upward direction in the hierarchy to concentrate upon additional needs.

Safety and security needs are second in Maslow's hierarchy. As Mescon, *et al.*, have commented:

The difference between the safety and security needs and the basic physiological needs is actually somewhat hazy. The theory implies that after having met one's basic physiological needs, one now starts planning to insure the continued fulfillment of these needs. Therefore, one has established a certain degree of safety and security in relation to one's physiological well being. This is a slight extension of the previously indicated basic needs.[6]

Third in Maslow's hierarchy of needs are the love needs. Sales managers sometimes become concerned with this category of needs because individual salespeople may either possess marked needs for belonging and being a member of an organization or are characterized by a strong degree of independence and prefer to act autonomously from others in the sales organization.

The fourth level of needs in Maslow's hierarchy are the esteem needs. One very important aspect of sales management and one we shall discuss in detail later in this chapter is motivation via peer group recognition.

The fifth and highest level in Maslow's needs hierarchy is the need for self-actualization or self-fulfillment. This need has been defined as "the need of a person to reach his full potential in terms of the application of his own abilities and interests in functioning in his environment. This need is concerned with the will of man to operate at his optimum and thus receive the rewards that are the result of that attainment, not only in terms of economic and social reimbursement, but also in terms of psychological reimbursement."[7]

It is important in discussing these levels of Maslow's hierarchy to point out two additional factors. First, Maslow has clearly indicated that these five levels of needs operate on an unconscious level. That is, the individual

[6] Michael H. Mescon *et al.*, *The Management of Enterprise* (New York: Macmillan Publishing Company, 1973), pp. 144–145.
[7] *Ibid.*, p. 146.

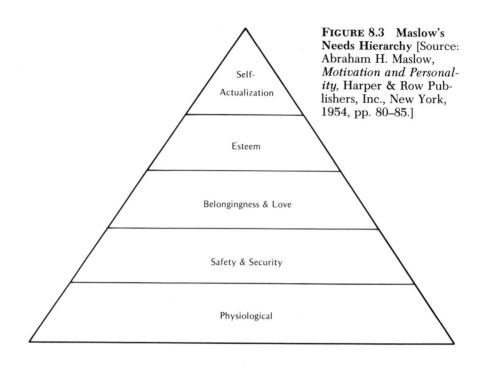

FIGURE 8.3 Maslow's Needs Hierarchy [Source: Abraham H. Maslow, *Motivation and Personality,* Harper & Row Publishers, Inc., New York, 1954, pp. 80–85.]

Self-Actualization

Esteem

Belongingness & Love

Safety & Security

Physiological

is probably not aware of concentration upon one particular need or one assortment of needs. A second factor that we should point out is that there is a strong organizational, cultural, and societal influence upon these needs. Important to sales managers would be the influence of the formal sales organization on the varying needs.[8]

The student has doubtless been exposed to Maslow's needs hierarchy previously. Figure 8.3 depicts the five levels of needs contained in Maslow's theory. Although we have cautioned the reader previously, it is worth repeating that we must avoid the temptation of a literal interpretation of Figure 8.3. Remember that needs may occur at more than one level simultaneously.

When we attempt to integrate Maslow's needs hierarchy with the concept of sales force segmentation discussed earlier, we can see that a sales manager might find certain subgroups in his sales force that fit together because of some homogeneity of needs. For example, it would not be unusual to find that many new and young sales personnel might well have a similar need with regard to income. Since they are new to the sales organization and since they are young chronologically, these individuals may well have young families or may be in the process of planning families; thus, they may have a similar concern for their financial status. Such individuals might well be motivated by financial needs or provision for physiological needs via a base salary. With regard to nonfinancial motivation techniques, we would probably find that these individ-

[8] The preceding discussion of Maslow's needs hierarchy is based upon: Abraham H. Maslow, *Motivation and Personality* (New York: Harper & Row Publishers, Inc., 1954), pp. 80–85.

uals also have relatively high needs for esteem. Since they are relatively new with the firm, they may be desirous of creating a good impression upon management by the actions they take early in their careers. Such individuals may respond very well to motivational techniques that provide peer group recognition or formal managerial recognition.

Yet another aspect of individual motivation is discussed in the work of French and Raven.[9] Their work concerns social power and focuses upon the relationship between an individual and an external influence. In the case of sales management, we would be talking about the potential applications of the various types of social power to a motivational situation whereby a sales manager is seeking to motivate a member of his sales force.

Social power reflects the potential ability of an "outside force" (external to the individual) to influence a person. Although the focus of this discussion will center on the sales manager as the "outside force," keep in mind that this force could consist of several persons—a reference group, another individual, a customer, or even an inanimate object such as a book or a movie, and so on. Additionally, remember that the influence exerted may *not* be in the desired direction. Thus, several forces external to the individual may combine to produce change in the direction opposite that intended by the sales manager.

Five types of social power exist. Traditionally, sales managers have utilized only the first two.

- *Reward power.*   This type of power is based upon person P's perception of the sales manager's (O's) ability to reward them. Keep in mind that "rewards" would include nonfinancial rewards as well as direct financial compensation. Traditionally, however, sales managers have concentrated reward power in the form of raises in salary or commission and other financial rewards.
- *Coercive power.*   This type of power stems from the expectation on the part of P that he will be punished by O if he fails to conform to the influence attempt. The punishment need not be as extreme as firing the salesman. In fact, coercive power punishment can be as trivial as a raised eyebrow or a frown by the sales manager.
- *Legitimate power.*   This type of power is based on the perception by the salesperson or sales trainee P that the sales manager O has a legitimate power or right to prescribe behavior for him. A timely issue in this regard is style of dress for the sales force. Does the firm have the right to tell me (a salesperson or sales trainee) how to dress or what length my hair should be?
- *Referent power.*   This type of power is based upon the sales person P's identification with the sales manager O. Does P see O as "one of the team" or does he view him as "the other side?" If positive identification exists, it is much easier to produce change. However, change may still occur even if P views O as an adversary.

[9] John R. P. French, Jr., and Bertram Raven, "The Bases of Social Power," in Dorwin Cartwright and Alvin Zander (eds.) *Group Dynamics*, 3rd ed. (New York: Harper & Row Publishers, 1968), pp. 259–269.

- *Expert power.* This type of power is dependent upon P's perception of O's knowledge on a given subject. Generally, P will evaluate O's knowledge in light of his own knowledge and others in the external environment. A basic consideration is, "Does O know what he's talking about?" As a general rule in sales management, the knowledge that is involved stems from one of two sources. P's evaluation of O's knowledge will typically center upon O's knowledge of the product/service mix sold by the firm or upon O's knowledge of selling and sales concepts generally.

As indicated, sales managers have generally neglected the last three types of social power. In our discussion of nonfinancial forms of motivation later in the chapter, we will refer to these in greater detail.

An interesting extension of the concept of power as a motivational device has recently been provided in the research of McClelland and Burnham. They have observed:

Good managers are not motivated by a need for personal aggrandizement, or by a need to get along with subordinates, but rather by a need to influence others' behavior for the good of the whole organization. In other words, good managers want power.[11]

Before leaving our discussion of individual factors connected with motivation, we will briefly explore some "intervening variables." Thomas Stroh has indicated that these "intervening variables" lie between an individual's needs and possible fulfillment.[12] Stroh has isolated four intervening variables. These include:

1. The individual's previous experience or degree of maturity.
2. The individual's level of aspiration.
3. The group norm or informal work standards made by other sales representatives.
4. The sales manager's own level of expectations.

An individual's previous experience or degree of maturity is usually evidenced in personal selling by either chronological age or length of employment as a salesperson. In Chapter 7 we referred to the salesman's career cycle concept developed by Jolson.[13] Figure 8.4 depicts this career cycle for sales personnel and is analogous to the product life cycle. This career cycle begins with the recruitment of a new salesperson and proceeds through his termination with the firm. Jolson cautions that rather than being considered a sequential step-by-step phased cycle, a salesman may repeat any particular stage of the entire cycle any number of times. From the standpoint of motivation, this concept suggests that sales man-

[11] David C. McClelland and David H. Burnham, "Power is the Great Motivator," *Harvard Business Review*, March-April 1976, pp. 100–110 at page 100.

[12] Thomas F. Stroh, *Managing the Sales Function*, (New York: McGraw-Hill Book Company, 1978), p. 279.

[13] Marvin A. Jolson, "The Salesman's Career Cycle," *Journal of Marketing* (Vol. 38, No. 3), July 1974, pp. 39–46.

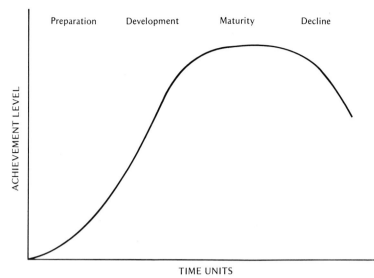

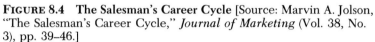

FIGURE 8.4 **The Salesman's Career Cycle** [Source: Marvin A. Jolson, "The Salesman's Career Cycle," *Journal of Marketing* (Vol. 38, No. 3), pp. 39–46.]

agement will find it relatively easy to motivate sales personnel in both the preparation and development stages. However, we should note that in the preparation stage the salesperson, although high in terms of desire, generally possesses inadequate ability due to a lack of training. On the other hand, the maturity and decline stages are stages of a salesperson's career where management will have difficulty in providing adequate motivation. Recall that in the previous chapter retraining was discussed as a possibility for a sales person at the maturity stage of the career cycle.

The second intervening variable is the individual's level of aspiration. The higher the individual's aspirations the easier it generally is for a sales manager to motivate that individual. Often the subject of a great deal of probing during the recruiting and selection process, the level of aspiration varies a greatly both across individuals and within individuals across time. The highest level of Maslow's needs hierarchy, self-actualization or self-fulfillment, is never fully attained for any one individual. As Maslow himself stated, "What a man can be, he must be."[14] During the recruiting process many sales managers ask questions such as, "What do you want to be ten years from now?" or "What position would you like to attain in our company?" Sales managers will often tell you that they are looking for answers indicating that the individual wishes to become president of the corporation or to obtain a high status in the corporation. The rationale here is that, although the individual may not become president or chairman of the board of directors, if their aspirations are truly that high, they will certainly exert great effort to succeed as sales representatives.

[14] Maslow, *op. cit.*, p. 91.

The third intervening variable is the group norm. This intervening variable is normally brought to a sales manager's attention by virtue of the negative effects it has on motivation. Chris Argyris extended Maslow's self-actualization concept in more detail. Argyris examined the needs of formal organizations together with the needs of individuals. He concludes that there may be a basic incongruity between the needs of the individual and the environment of the organization. Argyris' incongruity model, therefore, predicts that, if such incongruities occur, frustration, failure, and conflict may be the result. Argyris specifically criticizes the concepts of task specialization, chain of command, unity of direction, and span of control, suggesting that if these principles are followed individuals may become dependent, passive, and short-time oriented.[15]

One fairly common and possible side effect of the group norm or informal work rules as an intervening variable in motivation is the group pressure brought upon individual salesmen to reduce performance. Normally, this group pressure would be applied to outstanding performers in the sales force and may be exemplified by pressures to reduce dollar sales or make fewer sales calls per day. It may also be pointed out that the intervening variable of the group norm can work "for" the sales manager when it becomes a positive force. For example, in a sales force with a great deal of esprit de corps, salespersons may be positively motivated to exceed the accomplishments of particular individuals. Thus, an upward spiral develops, and the number of sales calls made or dollar sales achieved increases over time. When this occurs, it does not normally occur by accident. The sales manager must be cognizant of what is happening within the group and not only prohibit the group norm from acting as a deterrent to his goals but actually encourage group norms in a positive direction.

The last intervening variable pertains to the sales manager's expectations for members of his sales force. In a recent article pertaining to sales management, the "pygmalion effect" was discussed as it relates to motivation. The authors of this article suggest that this effect means the performance we see in others is a reflection of our own expectations. In sales management, they emphasize the need for positive rewards and reinforcements to bring about positive motivation. A brief excerpt from this article states,

The power of expectation alone can influence the behavior of others. Therefore, in many instances sales persons most often live up or down to the sales manager's expectations. Sales personnel, because of the special demands of the selling situation, need an atmosphere of positive reinforcement. Both the nature of the selling situation and the increasing emphasis on humanistic phychology suggest that sales personnel need a managerial climate and a process of motivation which underscores the importance of encouraging the achieving worker, creating the possibility for attaining self-actualizing rewards, stressing the value of a constant stream of feedback, and providing for growth and development through learning.[16]

[15] Chris Argyris, *Integrating the Individual Into the Organization*, (New York: John Wiley & Sons, Inc., 1964).

[16] Rom J. Markin and Charles M. Willis, "Sales Managers Get What They Expect," *Business Horizons*, June 1975, p. 58.

The Role of Compensation

An excellent start in the discussion of compensation is to look at the current status. A current article indicates that for 1977 experienced sales-persons earned on an average $24,500. Semiexperienced sales persons (those with 1–3 years in selling) earned on an average $18,400. And sales trainees (those with less than 1 year actual experience) earned on an average $13,500.[17]

These dollar figures actually only take on their full meaning when they are placed in a relative dimension. The Dartnell Corporation pub-lishes a biennial survey of sales force compensation. Comparing 1977 figures (those quoted above) with the 1975 data points, the dollar compen-sation figures reported represent the following increases: Experienced sales personnel have achieved a 14.9 per cent increase in compensation since 1975; semiexperienced personnel have achieved a 27.0 per cent increase since 1975; and sales trainees have experienced a 15.0 per cent increase since 1975.[18] The data utilized in this study are based upon information collected from 380 companies throughout the United States and Canada, which together employ more than 15,000 sales personnel.

It is useful to examine Figure 8.5 in order to obtain a profile of the typical salesman. This profile is based upon Dartnell's most recent survey published in 1978.

We now have a current overview of sales force compensation, and we can move on to obtain a starting point in the design of compensation programs. The sales manager must look at compensation from two points of view—that of the firm and that of the individual salesperson.

From the firm's point of view, the purpose of the compensation plan is to help provide motivation in achieving the overall goals previously determined. For example, we have seen in Chapter 4 that one of the basic tasks of sales management is to develop goals and objectives for the sales function. Likewise, we have seen in Chapter 1 that one of the "uncontrollable variables" impinging upon a sales manager's overall oper-ations would be the resources and objectives of the firm. These resources and objectives often provide basic guidelines that may dictate the limits of compensation to be provided individuals in the sales force. Obviously, the amount of compensation paid to any one individual salesperson must be sufficient to attract him/her to the firm, continually provide, together with other motivational tools, an effective level of operation, and retain this individual in the firm's sales force.

Looking more specifically at organizational goals, at least four primary objectives a compensation plan have been identified.[19]

[17] Bob Arnold, "Salescomp Outraces Inflation," *Marketing Times*, July-August 1978, pp. 3–4.
[18] *Compensation of Salesmen: Dartnell's 19th Biennial Survey*, (Chicago: Dartnell Insti-tution of Financial Research, Dartnell Corporation, 1978).
[19] Roger E. Dewhurst, John Wilding, and Waino W. Suojanen, "Managerial Goals and Individual Needs in Salesmen's Compensation Plans," *Atlanta Economic Review* (Vol. 19, No. 4), April 1969, pp. 14–16.

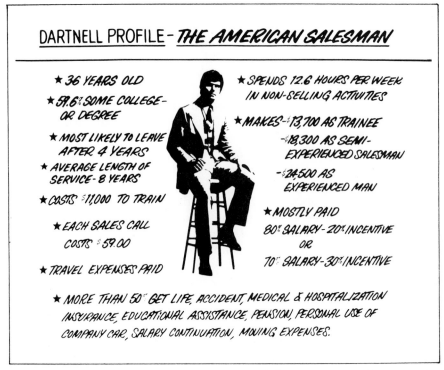

FIGURE 8.5 **A Profile of an Average American Salesman** [Source: *Compensation of Salesmen: Dartnell's 19th Biennial Survey* (Chicago: Dartnell Institution of Financial Research, Dartnell Corporation, 1978).]

1. It should encourage maximum effort on the part of the sales force toward the achievement of organizational goals.
2. It should motivate the salesmen to serve the best interests of their customers.
3. Supervision and control are basic elements in a sound compensation plan.
4. The plan should attract and retain the services of quality salesmen.

To elaborate briefly, consider the first goal. Although it may sound obvious that we wish to encourage "maximum effort," many compensation plans do not achieve this. If, for example, an individual was being paid on a hourly basis, his compensation becomes purely a function of time and does not necessarily reflect the effort he expends in that period of time. Thus, the individual may actually be encouraged to put in something less than the maximum amount of effort.

Objective two suggests that the compensation plan has a concern for customers as well as for the firm and the particular salesperson. The reader's personal experience may suggest that the customer's interest was totally disregarded. For example, many fast-talking, door-to-door sales personnel are paid on a straight commission basis. Thus, the salesperson may be encouraged to sell all of the particular product they can to any one buyer and, likewise, may be encouraged to sell the product to individ-

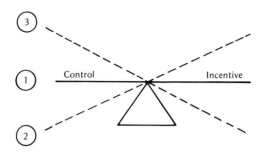

FIGURE 8.6 Control Versus Incentive: Three Possible Strategies for Sales Management

uals who may not really have a need for this product. If such a compensation system exists, it clearly may not serve or may not even consider the interests of the consumer.

The subject of control and supervision needs additional elaboration. A basic trade-off that sales management must make where a compensation system is concerned focuses upon the issue of control. Those programs that provide the greatest control may also provide the least amount of incentive and, conversely, the program providing the greatest of amount of incentive from a salesperson's point of view may provide inadequate control. We shall explore this issue later in the chapter, but for now, consider Figure 8.6. This figure attempts to point out the interrelationship between control and incentive. Position 1 in Figure 8.6 suggests that for many firms a balance between control and incentive may be the proper approach, whereas position 2 would suggest that other firms may feel that they must maintain a very strict amount of control over their sales personnel. A third position possible would have virtually no control over the sales force and, instead, would maximize the amount of incentive available.

Having now examined some of the organizational goals, let us examine the needs of the individual. One recent article has sought to integrate the basic levels of needs set forth in Maslow's hierarchy with implications for a sales compensation plan. In this article the needs of the individual were depicted in a model similar to that presented in Figure 8.7.[20] As may be seen in Figure 8.7, Maslow's hierarchy of needs is on the verticle axis and horizontally across the top are the implications for a particular compensation plan. Thus, for example, the character of monetary rewards would be in the form of a straight salary in order to provide for physiological needs and the influence of the salary would decrease as sequentially higher needs arose. Thus, at the opposite end of Maslow's needs hierarchy, where self-actualization is concerned, incentives would play the predominant role in the character of monetary rewards.

In a related article, Webster has indicated a seven-step process for developing a compensation plan for sales representatives.[21]

1. Establish clear and consistent compensation objectives.
2. Determine the level of income desired for the salesman.

[20] *Ibid.*
[21] Frederick E. Webster, "Rationalizing Salesmen's Compensation Plans," *Journal of Marketing* (Vol. 30, No. 1), January 1966, pp. 558–558.

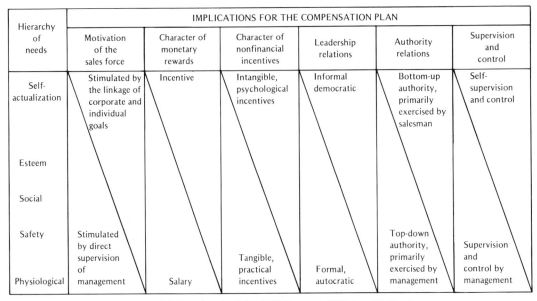

Hierarchy of needs	IMPLICATIONS FOR THE COMPENSATION PLAN					
	Motivation of the sales force	Character of monetary rewards	Character of nonfinancial incentives	Leadership relations	Authority relations	Supervision and control
Self-actualization	Stimulated by the linkage of corporate and individual goals	Incentive	Intangible, psychological incentives	Informal democratic	Bottom-up authority, primarily exercised by salesman	Self-supervision and control
Esteem						
Social						
Safety	Stimulated by direct supervision of management		Tangible, practical incentives	Formal, autocratic	Top-down authority, primarily exercised by management	Supervision and control by management
Physiological		Salary				

FIGURE 8.7   [Source: Roger E. Dewhurst, John Wilding, and Waino W. Suojanen, "Managerial Goals and Individual Needs in Salesmen's Compensation Plans," *Atlanta Economic Review*, Vol. 19, No. 4 (April 1969), pp. 14–16.]

3. Determine relative proportion of each of three elements:
   (a) Base salary.
   (b) Individual incentive.
   (c) Group incentive.
4. Establish the measurement criteria to be used to evaluate performance.
5. Relate the method of incentive payment to the measurement criteria to establish the compensation "formula."
6. Apply the "formula" to the past experience of several individuals in groups to test results on historical performance.
7. Make a field test of the new compensation plan to determine its acceptability to the sales force and to measure its influence on sales performance.

In this particular article, Webster indicated that some of the objectives to be considered would include providing maximum stimulation and motivation for sales personnel, to reward salespersons in proportion to the results that their efforts produced and to provide flexibility in compensation so that local management could adjust compensation levels fairly. To achieve step two, the field sales manager's task was to establish a "target income" based upon the individual's sales ability and experience. The results from step two became the starting point for achieving step three. In this particular study, Webster found that management agreed that base salary must be at least 65 per cent and not more than 90 per cent of the salesman's targeted income. However, we have seen in a more recent survey (see Figure 8.5) that a more common arrangement would be a 70 per cent or 80 per cent salary base with the remainder made up of incentive earnings. The guideline provided in the Webster study for 3C (group incentive) was that it should not exceed a maximum of 7 per cent of targeted income.

In the Webster study, step four was accomplished via two criteria: First, a fixed form of compensation was adopted based upon the single criterion of the sales manager's subjective estimation of how well the salesperson was doing in accomplishing both selling and nonselling responsibilities. This included provision for customer service follow-up and market investigation. The second criterion was to permit incentive income, and this was based upon the single criterion of sales volume.

The development of a formula (step 5) would of course vary from one company to another. In the particular study done by Webster, the formula called for an individual salesperson to receive an amount of commission payment that would be exactly equal the difference between the target income and base salary at 100 per cent of quota. Then, as the individual exceeded quota, he would receive additional compensation in the form of further commission payments.

The formula for the group bonus called for the entire sales group to receive a bonus equal to 5 per cent of target income if sales for the group were less than 50 per cent of quota. If sales exceeded 50 per cent but were less than 100 per cent, the bonus would be 6 per cent of target income. If the entire group achieved the quota, a bonus of 7 per cent of target income would be paid to sales personnel. Webster contends that the pretest should be checked against previous historical performance in order to determine any "fine tuning" that should be made before actual implementation.

Finally, of course, the last step consists of field testing the plan prior to implementing it for an entire sales force.

There may be hundreds of different compensation plans existing in sales management. However, it is important to understand at least some of the more basic and more common plans. In Figure 8.8 we represent a total spectrum of possible compensation arrangements along a continuum running from 100 per cent commission (straight commission) to a type of compensation plan that would consist of 100 per cent salary (straight salary). Between these two extremes are many other possible arrangements that a firm might elect to use. In order to understand better the myriad possibilities that exist, we will discuss each of the five positions illustrated on the continuum from the standpoint of some of their shortcomings and some of their advantages to sales management.

The numeral 1 at the far left of the continuum represents a compensation plan where the individual salesperson is paid on the basis of straight commission. Under this plan, the salesperson literally has license to "do

1	2	3	4	5
100% (Straight) Commission	Commission with Draw or Guaranteed Minimum	Various "Combinations"	Fixed Salary and Bonus (Incentive)	100% (Straight) Salary

FIGURE 8.8

their own thing"; that is, the sales manager really has virtually no control over what accounts the individual calls on, what sales approach is used, and so on. Also notice that the individual has no income security and receives no rewards except those directly related to the closing of a sale or obtaining a signed order. From the positive side, there are no limits set on the individual's income and from the firm's point of view a positive feature is that it can anticipate in advance the precise cost of sales in that it is a constant percentage. Likewise, the firm does not pay or incur costs for inefficient sales activity. Looking back at Figure 8.6, this particular type of compensation plan would most closely resemble position 2.

Position 2 on the continuum of Figure 8.8 is similar to position 1 except that a guaranteed minimum or a base income exists even in times when sales are poor. This is provided in the form of a draw. A **draw** is essentially a form of a cash advance or a loan made by the firm to the salesperson in anticipation of future sales. In this situation, salespersons operate in a similar fashion to position 1 with the important exception of security. That is, a sales person may anticipate the ability to draw or receive some minimum income even in times when sales are depressed. This might be very important for a firm whose sales follow seasonal trends with extreme "peaks in sales" and likewise with extreme valleys. From the firm's point of view, this option still has the advantage of providing an advance estimate of the cost of sales because they are essentially paying the salesperson a commission. The draw or the guaranteed minimum really operates only as an advance against these commissions. Likewise, the second advantage to the firm is the fact that it does provide some, although limited, control over the activities of the sales force.

Position 3 on the continuum would be represented by any of several possible "combination plans," and a typical illustration might be the type of combination we have just seen in the study by Webster. Because of the exceedingly large number of variations possible, this plan must be examined in light of the merit it has for an individual company or an individual sales force. Typically, however, combination compensation plans are somewhat expensive in terms of their administrative cost. On the other hand, proponents of combination plans contend that these combinations offer the best of all possible worlds.

Position 4 on the continuum is represented by a fixed salary plus some form of bonus or incentive and may in fact provide relatively strong security for the salesperson. From the firm's point of view, a sales manager utilizing a compensation plan similar to that depicted by position 4 has a great deal of control of the nonselling activities of the salesperson, such as obtaining their cooperation in arranging for the return of damaged merchandise, and so on. The bonuses involved in such a situation may be either of an individual nature or, as we have seen in the Webster study, of a group nature.

The final situation is Position 5, which is a straight salary position. This position, of course, encourages a great deal of company loyalty in that it maximizes security for the individual. Regardless of whether sales are good or bad in a particular quarter or month, the individuals knows that he or she can count on a given amount of income. This particular plan also maximizes the control available to a sales manager. The sales manager now has the right to tell the salespeople how to spend their time if he/she chooses to do so. On the opposite side of the coin, this particular plan may also stifle creativity, as we have noted previously. However, it may be worth considering when the effort of sales personnel and their results do not correlate well. For example, if a certain amount of service work is required with a particular group of accounts and this service work is not expected to lead to a sales order in the short range, the sales manager might well anticipate the possibility of using the straight salary method of compensation. Having this method of compensation available, the sales manager would then be in a position to strongly suggest or even "order" the sales person to call upon particular accounts in order to provide the servicing needed.

In the choice of a particular position on the continuum as the method of compensation, several facts should be kept in mind. First, in many firms, a commitment to the positions represented by numbers 1 or 2 on the continuum inadvertently may place the sales force at the mercy of other branches of the corporation. Collectively, the effects created here are known as the dependency effects; that is, the salesperson is now at the mercy of departments such as production, shipping, and so on. For example, a salesperson may obtain an order from 100 units from Account X. However, if the commission is not paid until payment has been received, the salesperson may not receive his/her commission until such time as inventories are available or until such time as it is possible to ship merchandise to the customer. Thus, even an unusual occurrence outside of the firm, such as a strike by the organization providing transportation for the product, or perhaps an inventory shortage, can prevent the salesperson from receiving his just reward for the sale.

A second point that we should make regarding the selection of any of the forms of compensation methods mentioned is that the sales manager must be careful to think whether he wishes to reward effort per se or results only. We mean by this that the sales manager might choose to reward efforts connected with nonselling activities, such as a salesperson setting up a display in a retail store, a salesperson arranging for return of damaged merchandise, a salesperson handling an erroneous, duplicate invoice issued by the firm, and so on.

Third, the choice of any particular methods of compensation is subject to cost/benefit considerations. Often sales managers neglect to determine fully the cost of a particular compensation plan. As a general rule of thumb, the more complex a particular compensation plan and the more that differing ingredients go into such a plan, the greater the cost in terms of administrative time to see that the plan operates correctly.

Last, the choice of any particular compensation plan must be tempered in light of the salesperson's ability both to understand and to agree with its fairness. If, for example, a firm elected to go with one of the many combinations illustrated by position 3 on the continuum, management must be certain that sales personnel understand the particulars of the combination form of compensation. It is important, in addition, that sales personnel feel that they are being compensated in an equitable manner and one which is fair across differing sales territories. To disregard this aspect of compensation is to invite a high degree of turnover. Sales personnel may feel, because they do not correctly understand the plan, that they may be victimized. Or, they may feel that the plan is "unfair" to them and perhaps disproportionately favors another salesperson in an adjoining territory.

Other Compensation/Motivation Approaches

In addition to the financial rewards available through a compensation program, sales management is presently considering, and in some cases has used, other motivational devices. A recent study on nonfinancial incentives for sales personnel has focused upon three kinds of motivational tools that sales management may consider.

Based upon the earlier work of Dubin, this study focused upon status pay, privilege pay, and power pay.[22] Use of the term "pay" in each of these three areas may suggest a financial type of compensation. As we shall see, this is not the case.

Status pay has to do with the public acknowledgement that management provides to an employee. In a sales force situation, status pay would have to do with peer group recognition and praise provided to an individual salesperson by a sales manager.

Privilege pay has to do with the freedom that a superior grants to subordinates to interact with him. The concept of being able to talk on "a first name basis" is an illustration of the meaning that Dubin intended for privilege pay.

Power pay has to do with the importance of a particular individual's job within the total organization. In a sales management situation, this may be accomplished by giving one sales person more responsibility and thereby acknowledging that management feels this additional responsibility is appropriate for him by virtue of his previous outstanding job performance.

In a study focusing upon these three types of "pay," Pruden, Cunningham, and English conclude, "Sales administrators should think of an incentives mix including not only base salary, commission, and bonus, but also 'privilege pay, status pay, and power pay.' "[23]

Another form of sales force motivation that lends itself to non-direct compensation or rewards is the use of sales contests. In a 1968 study it was found that the objectives for special incentive programs such as contests included a wide variety of goals related directly to sales, such as

---

[22] Robert Dubin, *Human Relations in Administration* (Englewood Cliffs, N.J.: Prentice Hall, Inc. 1968), pp. 297–299, 317–320.

[23] Henry O. Pruden, William H. Cunningham, and Wilke D. English, "Nonfinancial Incentives for Salesmen," *Journal of Marketing*, Vol. 36, No. 4 (October 1972), pp. 55–59.

	Respondents reporting use		Considered most important	
	Number	Percent	Number	Percent
Total	323	100.0%	323	100.0%
Increase overall sales	276	85.4%	217	67.2%
Find new customers	209	64.7	133	41.2
Promote special items	142	44.0	70	21.7
Obtain greater volume per call	135	41.8	89	27.6
Overcome seasonal sales slump	131	40.6	66	20.4
Introduce a new product, line or service	119	36.8	51	15.8
Get better territory coverage	103	31.9	58	18.0
Stop or slow a sales decline	92	28.5	33	10.2
Get better balance of sales	86	26.6	36	11.1
Get renewal of business with former customers	79	24.5	29	9.0
Develop new sales skills	76	23.5	23	7.1
Ease an unfavorable inventory position	66	20.4	27	8.4
Improve sales service to customers	62	19.2	24	7.4
Sell higher quality products	54	16.7	24	7.4
Build better product displays	39	12.1	17	5.3
Do self-training	38	11.8	14	4.3
Lower selling costs	33	10.2	13	4.0
Reduce selling time	14	4.3	7	2.2
Get better sales reports	12	3.7	2	0.6
Other	21	6.5	17	5.3

FIGURE 8.9 Objectives of Sales Contests [Source: Albert Haring and Malcolm L. Morris, *Contests, Prizes, Awards for Sales Motivation* (New York: Sales and Marketing Executives—International, 1968), p. 25.]

"increasing overall sales" and goals relating to non-selling activities, such as "get better sales reports" (see Figure 8.9).

There is disagreement among sales managers as to the advisability of using sales contests. Some sales managers, for example, would object to their use on the basis that salesmen are already paid for their efforts and contests involve duplication of motivational expenses. Other sales managers might agree that contests are undesirable because they may lead to disappointment by individuals who do not "win"; they may also be demotivating because the rules and regulations of contests are perceived by salesmen to be demeaning.

On the positive side, many sales managers favor the use of sales contests because they believe that they can contribute to motivation. Mr. Eli Stern, National Sales Manager of Sony Corporation, comments, "The best morale-builders are fair compensation for company sales forces, and good products and support for outside forces. So I look at the morale-building aspect of the incentives as a plus, not a primary goal."[23] Often winning the sales contest is not an end in and of itself. That is, an individual who receives a prize in the contest may also be honored or glorified in company publications or may receive peer group recognition by virtue of having his or her prize awarded at a sales meeting. In addition, plaques, certificates, and pins are also awarded, even to low-level winners in sales contests.

If the sales manager is considering the use of a sales contest, the following guidelines might prove useful. These guidelines are suggested as points that should be considered and should be characteristic of any well-run contest.

1. Any sales contest should accomplish or complement the overall goals of sales management.
2. The contest should be fair to all participants regardless of territory size or potential.
3. The contest should be clear in the eyes of the sales personnel participating. That is, the contest should be easily understood by all participants. Rules, regulations, and details should be made available in writing in advance of the contest.
4. The contest should have relatively low administrative costs versus the benefits received by the firm. That is, it should not take a great deal of management or clerical time to tabulate standings, progress, and winners in the contest unless the benefits are likewise large.
5. The contest should not encourage customer abuse. By this we mean, the contest rules should not encourage salespeople to sell customers more products than they can use nor should they encourage the "pyramiding" of the inventories in customer's warehouses or storage areas.

Lastly, in order to provide an overview of the amount of incentive spending involved, Figure 8.10 is presented. This figure represents an estimate of the amount spent nationally on merchandise and travel awards. It should be noted that this specifically excludes the cost of cash and recognition awards and thus may be an understatement of the total amount expended in sales contests.

The sales manager must always use caution in assessing whether a particular contest was beneficial or not. One of the authors of this text is currently engaged in research on the post-contest effects of a particular sales contest. Thus far, limited findings suggest that if, for example, a

| | Amount spent on merchandise and travel awards ($ millions)* | | | | |
	1978 Est.	1977 Est.	1976	1975	1974
Merchandise	$1,118.7	$1,033.9	$ 899.0	$ 787.3	$ 872.6
Travel	332.8	291.4	254.7	223.4	239.6
Total	$1,451.3	$1,325.3	$1,153.7	$1,010.7	$1,112.2

*Excludes program promotion costs and the costs of cash and recognition awards.

FIGURE 8.10 Costs on Incentive Spending [Source: *Incentive Marketing Facts*, December 1977.]

six-month sales contest is to be run, it may be to the sales manager's advantage to monitor the impact on sales not only during the six months of the contest, but in the six months following the sale. Although the data base examined thus far is quite small, it is not unusual to find a "inverted V" effect where sales contests are concerned. That is, immediately after the conclusion of the contest, sales begin to fall very rapidly in a line similar to the rapid increase experienced immediately upon announcement of the sales contest. Thus, what may be occurring in a situation like this is that salesmen are able to secure their customer's cooperation to buy larger amounts than they normally would and, therefore, enabling the sales person to place high in the contest. However, at the contest's conclusion, the customer of course has on hand more inventory than is needed and thus may postpone future purchases for an indefinite period of time or until their built-up inventory levels again diminish to normal amounts.

This section has explored the use of nonfinancial resources and, in particular, has examined both sales contests and three types of nonfinancial "pay." In addition to these nonfinancial stimuli, the reader will find other nonfinancial approaches to motivation suggested in the reading on segmentation in this book.

Summary

This chapter has focused upon motivation and compensation of the sales force. We have discussed three major mistakes made by sales management in this area, including the tendency to equate motivation and compensation, a tendency to think of motivation in group rather than individual terms, and the tendency to perceive a "good" compensation/motivation program as longer lasting than it may well prove to be.

We have suggested that there is wide disagreement among sales managers as to whether or not nonfinancial forms of motivation are viable. Nevertheless, we have explored these nonfinancial forms of motivation from the perspective of a salesperson's needs. From the rich body of management literature on employee motivation, major concepts from Herzberg, Maslow, and Argyris have been presented. In addition, and normally less well known by business students and instructors, theories from the social psychology area that apply to sales force motivation have also been presented. These theories have included works by Morse and Weiss, French and Raven, McClelland and Burnham, and others.

Regarding the specific role of compensation, a current picture of sales force financial compensation was presented depicting variations across experienced, semiexperienced, and novice sales personnel. In addition, an approach to compensation based upon objectives was presented as well as the interrelationship of both the individual's needs and those of the firm.

A specific step-by-step process for development of a compensation plan was discussed and illustrated. Following this, a discussion of five specific types of compensation plans was presented. Although these five plans are by no means exhaustive, they are illustrative of the variety of options available to sales management in selecting compensation options.

The chapter concludes with a discussion of other (nonfinancial) approaches to motivation, including status pay, privilege pay, power pay, and sales contests. The discussion of contests was enlarged to present both undesirable as well as desirable reasons for use. Finally, some suggested guidelines for compensation were presented.

A point made throughout the chapter concerns the possible approach to sales force motivation via an individual versus group approach. More detailed information is available in the reading on segmentation at the end of this part.

Discussion Questions

1. Are you surprised to learn that many sales managers make the three "major mistakes" regarding motivation and compensation discussed on page 254 of this chapter? Do you feel that one of these three is more or less important than the others? Discuss.

2. Differentiate between motivation and compensation.

3. If you were a sales manager, how might salespersons motives enter into your thinking concerning motivation and compensation? Be specific.

4. Explain Herzberg's view of factors affecting job satisfaction and disatisfaction.

5. What does "hygiene" mean according to Herzberg in relation to motivation? Also, do needs remain constant under this view?

6. Explain Maslow's needs hierarchy. Why is it important to sales managers?

7. How might sales managers utilize the concept of social power developed by French and Raven. In addition, explain the five basic types of social power they have isolated.

8. Stroh suggested that "intervening variables" are important to motivation. What are these and why are they important?

9. Explain Jolson's "salesman's career cycle" to a sales manager who is only interested in practical concepts with "real-world" implications.

10. Build the best case (that is, provide support) you can
(a) for the use of sales contests.
(b) against the use of sales contests.

Selected References

BURTON, W. L., "There's More to Motivating Salesmen than Money," in T. W. MeLoan and J. J. Rathmell (eds.) *Selling: Its Broader Dimensions* (New York: Macmillan Publishing Company, 1960).

DOWNING, GEORGE D., *Sales Management* (New York: John Wiley & Sons, Inc., 1969), Chapters 16, 17 and 18.

HERZBERG, FREDERICK, "One More Time: How Do You Motivate Employees?" *Harvard Business Review*, January-February 1968.

How to Stimulate Salesmen to Better Selling (New York: National Industrial Conference Board, Inc., 1963).

JOLSON, MARVIN A. *Sales Management: A Tactical Approach* (New York: Petrocelli/Charter, 1977), Chapter 7.

JOHNSON, H. WEBSTER, *Sales Management: Operations, Administration, Marketing,* (Colombus, Ohio: Charles E. Merrill Publishing Company, 1976), Chapter 9, 10 and 11.

MORSE, NANCY C., and ROBERT S. WEISS, "The Function and Meaning of Work in the Job," *American Sociological Review* (Vol. 20), April 1955.

MOSSIEN, HERBERT, and EUGENE H. FRAN, "Segmentation for Sales Force Motivation," *Akron Business and Economic Review,* Winter 1973. *Note:* This reading is included in this text.

STROH, THOMAS F., *Managing the Sales Function* (New York: McGraw-Hill Book Company, 1978), Chapter 12.

WORTRUBA, THOMAS R., *Sales Management Planning, Accomplishment and Evaluation,* (New York: Holt, Rinehart and Winston, Inc., 1970), Chapters 12 and 13.

CASE 8.1
F. H. Hunter Company*

During the past 10 years, the F. H. Hunter Company had grown from a small industrial chemical company with annual sales of $100,000 to a regional company with sales exceeding $10,000,000. As the company grew, the product line grew from one product (a patented chemical solution for removing rust from metal surfaces) to a line of 200 products, most of which were used by industrial customers in cleaning processes of various types.

The growth of the F. H. Hunter Company in the past decade has

Company Background

* Case prepared by Tom Ingram and Danny Bellenger, Georgia State University.

been a direct result of the efforts of the company founder and president, Frank Hunter. Mr. Hunter had started the company on a very modest scale after learning the chemical business while working with American Chemical, one of the industry leaders. Although his background was in chemical engineering, Mr. Hunter had a flair for dealing with people and had directed the sales activities of the company until recently when he decided to create the position of sales manager so that he could devote more time to raising capital for future growth.

David Ashley had been recruited from American Chemical where he had experience in sales and sales management. Mr. Hunter felt that David would bring the aggressive, full-time leadership that was required to keep the sales curve on the upswing in future years. Although Ashley would be taking over an experienced sales force, Hunter was concerned over a lack of growth during the past year. Mr. Hunter knew that the company was maturing, but he also knew that a growth rate of at least 15 per cent would be necessary to attract the desired capital for expansion and diversification in the next few years. Sales during the past year grew only 5 percent.

Current Situation

After David Ashley had gotten settled in his new job, he began to survey the situation regarding lack of sales growth. He arranged for individual meetings with each sales person in an attempt to determine what the problem was. Without exception, the sales people seemed to be satisfied with the straight salary form of compensation that the company was now using. The quality of products, service, and technical assistance were all rated highly by the sales people. Ashley also knew that the salespeople were well trained and capable, as he had competed against them during his time at American Chemical.

Ashley spent the next several evenings in the office working alone on the problem of sales growth. He reviewed his notes from territory visits and found no glaring weaknesses in sales technique or attitude. He also reviewed the salary and sales data by territory in a search for a solution to the problem (see Exhibit 1).

As Ashley spent more time on the problem, he became increasingly convinced about the company's compensation plan. He recalled a conversation with Frank Hunter a few weeks earlier when Mr. Hunter had said, "Security is important to people. The good salaries we offer result in a loyalty to the company on the part of the salespeople. Besides, look at the growth that the company has had in the past 10 years."

Sales Person	Annual Salary	Last Year's Sales	% Growth
Wilson	$17,700	$600,000	4.5%
Sheppherd	$17,580	$575,000	5.5%
Du Bois	$20,088	$658,000	4.0%
Lamont	$15,900	$530,000	6.0%
Everett	$16,900	$575,000	5.3%
Wicoff	$22,800	$740,000	4.8%
Patton	$22,000	$700,000	5.1%

EXHIBIT 1 Territory Sales, Salaries, and Growth Rate

As the third quarter staff meeting was approaching, Ashley worked hard during the next week to complete a proposal to be presented to Mr. Hunter concerning a possible new compensation plan (see Exhibit 2). Ashley had scheduled an appointment with Mr. Hunter 3 days prior to the meeting with an objective of gaining Mr. Hunter's approval of the new plan before the staff meeting. As he left the dark building, Ashley felt apprehensive about his meeting with Mr. Hunter first thing Monday morning. He was concerned about the wisdom of changing the system and about the specifics of his proposal. He had to decide soon on any modifications so that his proposal could be rewritten prior to his meeting with Mr. Hunter.

EXHIBIT 2 F. H. Hunter Company Sales Compensation Proposal

The following commission system is applicable within the sales territories assigned by F. H. Hunter Company.

1. The new system will involve salary plus commissions plus the possibility of bonuses.
2. The sales year will be January 1 through December 31 and the proposals contained herein would begin January 1.
3. The commission rate will be 3% on all products. All sales made at less than the list price shall carry a commensurate reduction in commission (e.g., a sale at 10% less than schedule shall result in a 10% reduction of normal commission rates).
4. Commissions will be paid monthly on the 15th of the following month and bonuses will be paid quarterly.
5. Quarterly Bonus: A $1,000 bonus price will be awarded to the outstanding salesman each quarter. The outstanding salesman will be defined as the person with the largest % increase in sales over the previous quarter.
6. New Product Special Commission: A special commission rate will be in effect for the first 6 months of the introduction of any new product. This rate will be determined at the time each new product is introduced and may vary across products.
7. Target Account Bonus: A $500 bonus will be paid for each target account acquired or developed by a salesman. Five target accounts shall be identified for each territory by David Ashley. Target accounts may consist of one or both of the following:

    A. A "new" account where F. H. Hunter is presently making no sales of any product.
    B. An undeveloped account which is presently buying only a few of F. H. Hunter products and can be converted to buying specified other products from us.

    The quantity of product as well as dollar volume needed to qualify as a "target" account shall be determined by David Ashley and shall be reviewed and revised as needed annually in the fourth quarter of each year. Thus, sales personnel will know the target accounts for their territory prior to the start of any calendar year.

8. All valid expenses shall be paid by the company. Last year's expenses will be used for next year's budget. This level may be exceeded, however, with management approval.
9. Regular sales meetings will be held each quarter. Other special meetings may be called as needed.
10. Compensation and Territories will be reviewed and possibly revised on an annual basis. This will be done in the fourth quarter of each year.
11. Territory Realignment Compensation: David Ashley hopes that each territory will experience significant growth over the next five years. This could necessitate the splitting of some territories in the future. In order to protect the salesman and see that he is compensated for development work in the event that his territory is split, the following system shall be used:

    When a territory is split, the salesman in the territory shall receive a sum equivalent to 1.5 times the commission earned from the accounts lost for the last full sales year preceding the split to be paid in 12 equal montly payments beginning the first month after the split is implemented.

12. In instances where products are consumed across territory boundaries, or where sales responsibility for one account extends across two or more territory boundaries, David Ashley will determine the amount of commission split on an individual case basis.

Community Bank & Trust Company (Part B)*

**Company
Background**
See the Community National Bank & Trust Company (Part A) for background on the bank and the development of the trust department.

**Current
Situation**
Sam Watson, Vice-President and Senior Trust Officer, in mid-1976 hired James Bruce to solicit new trust customers actively. During the 18 month period from June 1976, to our current time frame of late November 1977, Jim has been going through a period of extensive training in the various trust functions and their application to solving the many personal and corporate problems of the bank's customers and selected prominent and affluent persons within the metropolitan area of Mason City. For the past 6 months, Jim has been selling trust services and has been well received and accepted by his customers and the estate planning and employee benefit planning professional community (attorneys, accountants, and so on).

At the present time, Jim is receiving a straight salary of $17,000 per year. Historically, new business trust personnel are compensated on a straight salary basis. Sam is concerned because many banks have been having problems retaining qualified new business personnel who are compensated on straight salary. The normal new business trust officer receives true job satisfaction—he's helping others and exercising his knowledge and intellectual capacity to their fullest. After a short period of time, however, he may become frustrated and begin to feel that compensation limitations prevent the new business trust field from being a viable career. He may feel he is undercompensated in relation to his skills, his education, his degree of professionalism, his many contributions to the welfare of others, and, in particular, in comparison with other professionals in related fields.

Recently the literature in the field has contained several articles about various banks that are experimenting with incentive compensation plans. Sam feels the right compensation plan can be designed to retain Jim as a career employee and provide the necessary motivation to satisfy Jim's long-term compensation goals.

The compensation plan Sam is considering would pay a commission on current fee business (living trusts) and on deferred fee business (for example, executorship under will). It eliminates extraordinary services (acceptance fees, termination fees, and so on) from participating in commission payments. Jim will receive a raise of $1000 for a total annual remuneration of $18,000. One half of this base salary would be paid to

* This case was prepared by Robert L. Berl and Dan H. Robertson, both of Georgia State University.

Jim to compensate him for selling extraordinary services and performing administrative new business duties. The other half of the base salary must be validated against earned commissions.

The commission plan for current fee business is based on a series of production plateaus and a corresponding increase in the commission scale.

25 per cent of the first $15,000 of fee income
30 per cent on the next $15,000 of fee income
35 per cent on the next $15,000 of fee income
40 per cent on all fee income above $45,000

Commissions will be paid based on the actual receipt of fee income, as this eliminates the problem of the reimbursement of commissions by the salesman which were paid on the basis of accrued fees and then, for whatever reason, were not received. They are paid for 1 year. No account will be included in the fee calculation that does not at least produce a $500 annual fee. This will encourage Jim to seek out more substantial accounts. At such time as an account exceeds $1,000,000, only fees based on the first million dollars will be included in calculating fees for commission purposes. This policy should prevent Jim from taking advantage of any windfalls or falling prey to what the life insurance industry refers to as "big case-itis."

Sam feels that Jim can produce $25,000 in current fee business in the next year and $30,000 and $40,000 in the second and third years, and $50,000 or more in subsequent years.

Year	Fee Production	Gross Commissions
1	$25,000	$ 6,750
2	30,000	8,250
3	40,000	11,750
4	50,000	15,500

Sam realizes it is much more difficult to establish a commission structure on deferred fee business. Many factors (age, and so on) influence the length of time it takes from the day a will is executed to the death of the testator (creator of the will) and the bank's ability to perform its duties and earn a fee. Approximately 40 per cent of the wills that originally name the bank in an executorship role will never produce fees because the testator has moved out-of-state or has amended his/her will naming an individual or another institution as executor. Many banks use complex evaluation systems to analyze this type of business, but Sam feels that a system that is both easy to calculate and understand will best serve the bank's purposes. According to Sam's past experience, he feels Jim should be capable of producing 100 wills with an average estate value of $200,000. The number of wills produced should remain constant, but the average value per estate should increase approximately 10 per cent a year, as Jim becomes increasingly more experienced. Fee revenue projections will be discounted by 40 per cent to anticipate the loss of active wills over the years. Calculation of commissions is as follows:

Average estate	$ 200,000
Number of wills	× 100
Value of estates	$20,000,000
Executorship fees (5%)	× .05
Gross deferred income	$ 1,000,000
40% discount factor	− 400,000
Net deferred income	$ 600,000
Commission rate (½ of 1%)	× .005
Gross commission	$ 3,000

Jim's income based on Sam's projections is as follows:

Year	Number of Wills	Volume of Average Estate	Gross Deferred Income	40% Discount Factor	Net Deferred Income	Gross Commission
1	100	$200,000	$1,000,000	$400,000	$600,000	$3,000
2	100	220,000	1,100,000	440,000	660,000	3,300
3	100	242,000	1,210,000	484,000	726,000	3,630
4	100	290,400	1,452,000	580,800	871,200	4,356

Combining both current fee and deferred fee commissions, Sam projects Jim's income for the next 4 years to be as follows:

Year	Gross Current	Commission Deferred	Total Gross Commission	50% Base Salary	Net Commission	Base Salary	Total Compensation
1	$ 6,750	$3,000	$ 9,750	$9,000	$ 750	$18,000	$18,750
2	8,250	3,300	11,550	9,000	2,250	18,000	20,550
3	11,750	3,630	15,380	9,000	6,380	18,000	24,380
4	15,500	4,356	19,856	9,000	10,856	18,000	28,856

Sam feels the projections are realistic, but it would take an aggressive attitude on the part of Jim to achieve this goal. If achieved, it should satisfy Jim's long-term salary goals.

The president of the bank is currently making $60,000 per year and it was decided that at no time would Jim's total annual compensation exceed the president of the bank's annual income.

Compensation	Annual Increase	Percentage Annual Increase	Cumulative Increase	Percentage Cumulative Increase
17,000	—	—	—	—
18,750	$1,750	10%	$ 1,750	10%
20,550	1,800	10%	3,550	21%
24,380	3,830	19%	7,380	43%
28,856	4,476	18%	11,856	70%

Sam is concerned that if Jim should terminate his employment with the bank in the next couple of years he will have been overpaid for his productivity. In the event of Jim leaving the bank, Sam has established the following schedule of commission payments:

Year	Percentage of Ownership Commissions Earned but Not Paid*
1	0%
2	0%
3	10%
4	25%
5	45%
6	70%
7	100%

* Commissions earned from the last time commissions were paid.

As Sam Watson prepared to finalize the compensation plan he wondered if he had developed the "right" plan for Jim.

CASE 8.3
Outdoor Sporting Products, Inc.*

The annual sales volume of Outdoor Sporting Products, Inc., for the past six years had ranged between $1.6 million and $1.7 million. Although profits continued to be satisfactory, Mr. Hudson McDonald, president

Company Background

* Case prepared by Zarrel V. Lambert, Auburn University, and Fred W. Kniffin, University of Connecticut, Stamford. Used with permission.

and chief operating officer, was concerned because sales had not increased appreciably from year to year. Consequently, he asked a consultant in New York City and the officers of the company to submit proposals for improving the salesmen's compensation plan, which he believed was the basic weakness in the firm's marketing operations.

Outdoor's factory and warehouse were located in Albany, New York, where the company manufactured and distributed sporting equipment, clothing, and accessories. Mr. Hudson McDonald, who managed the company, organized it in 1946 when he envisioned a growing market for sporting goods resulting from the predicted increase in leisure time and the rising levels of income in the United States.

Products of the company, numbering approximately 700 items, were grouped into three lines: (1) fishing supplies, (2) hunting supplies, and (3) accessories. The fishing supplies line, which accounted for approximately 40 per cent of the company's annual sales, included nearly every item a fisherman would need such as fishing jackets, vests, caps, rods, and reels of all types, lines, flies, lures, landing nets, and creels. Thirty per cent of annual sales were in the hunting supplies line, which consisted of hunting clothing of all types including insulated and thermal underwear, safety garments, shell holders, whistles, calls, and gun cases. The accessories line, which made up the balance of the company's annual sales volume, included items such as compasses, cooking kits, lanterns, hunting and fishing knives, hand warmers, and novelty gifts.

While the sales of the hunting and fishing lines were very seasonal, they tended to complement one another. The January–April period accounted for the bulk of the company's annual volume in fishing items, and most sales of hunting supplies were made during the months of May through August. Typically, the company's sales of all products reached their lows for the year during the month of December.

Outdoor's sales volume was $1.67 million in the current year with self-manufactured products accounting for 35 per cent of this total. Fifty per cent of the company's volume consisted of imported products, which came principally from Japan. Items manufactured by other domestic producers and distributed by Outdoor accounted for the remaining 15 per cent of total sales.

Mr. McDonald reported that wholesale prices to retailers were established by adding a markup of 50 to 100 per cent to Outdoor's cost for the item. This rule was followed on self-manufactured products as well as for items purchased from other manufacturers. The resulting average markup across all products was 70 per cent on cost.

Outdoor's market area consisted of the New England states, New York, Pennsylvania, Ohio, Michigan, Wisconsin, Indiana, Illinois, Kentucky, Tennessee, West Virginia, Virginia, Maryland, Delaware, and New Jersey. The area over which Outdoor could effectively compete was limited to some extent by shipping costs, since all orders were shipped from the factory and warehouse in Albany.

Outdoor's salesmen sold to approximately 6000 retail stores in small- and medium-sized cities in its market area. Analysis of sales records showed that the firm's customer coverage was very poor in the large metropolitan areas. Typically, each account was a one- or two-store operation. Mr. McDonald stated that he knew for a fact that Outdoor's share of the market was very low, perhaps 2 to 3 per cent; and for all practical purposes, he felt the company's sales potential was unlimited.

Mr. McDonald believed that with few exceptions, Outdoor's customers had little or no brand preference and in the vast majority of cases they bought hunting and fishing supplies from several suppliers.

It was McDonald's opinion that the pattern of retail distribution for hunting and fishing products had been changing during the past 10 years as a result of the growth of discount stores. He thought that the proportion of retail sales for hunting and fishing supplies made by small- and medium-sized sporting goods outlets had been declining compared to the per cent sold by discounters and chain stores. An analysis of company records revealed Outdoor had not developed business among the discounters with the exception of a few small discount stores. Some of Outdoor's executives felt that the lack of business with discounters might have been due in part to the company's pricing policy and in part to the pressures that current customers had exerted on company salesmen to keep them from calling on the discounters.

The company's sales force played the major role in its marketing efforts since Outdoor did not use magazine, newspaper, or radio advertising to reach either the retail trade or consumers. One advertising piece that supplemented the work of the salesmen was Outdoor's merchandise catalog. It contained a complete listing of all the company's products and was mailed to all retailers who were either current accounts or prospective accounts. Typically, store buyers used the catalog for purposes of reordering.

Most accounts were contacted by a salesman two or three times a year. The salesmen planned their activities so that each store would be called upon at the beginning of the fishing season and again prior to the hunting season. Certain key accounts of some salesmen were contacted more often than two or three times a year.

Management believed that product knowledge was the major ingredient of a successful sales call. Consequently, Mr. McDonald had developed a "selling formula" that each salesman was required to learn before he took over a territory. The "formula" contained five parts: (1) the name and catalog number of each item sold by the company; (2) the sizes and colors in which each item was available; (3) the wholesale price of each item; (4) the suggested retail price of each item; and (5) the primary selling features of each item. After a new salesman had mastered the product knowledge specified by this "formula" he began working in his assigned territory and was usually accompanied by Mr. McDonald for several weeks.

Managing the sales force consumed approximately one third of Mr. McDonald's efforts. The remaining two thirds of his time was spent purchasing products for resale and in general administrative duties as the company's chief operating officer.

Mr. McDonald held semiannual sales meetings, had weekly telephone conversations with each salesman and had mimeographed bulletins con-

EXHIBIT 1 Salesmen: Age, Years of Service, Territory, and Sales

Salesmen	Age	Years of Service	Territory	Sales Previous year	Sales Current year
Allen	45	2	Illinois and Indiana	$ 82,566	$ 82,304
Campbell	62	10	Pennsylvania	298,048	345,060
Duvall	23	1	New England	—	103,664
Edwards	39	1	Michigan	—	104,854
Gatewood	63	5	West Virginia	89,632	89,638
Hammond	54	2	Virginia	103,734	103,682
Logan	37	1	Kentucky and Tennessee	—	141,930
Mason	57	2	Delaware and Maryland	161,258	206,272
O'Bryan	59	4	Ohio	135,982	143,098
Samuels	42	3	New York and New Jersey	184,256	206,118
Wates	67	5	Wisconsin	92,678	85,550
Salesmen terminated in previous year				457,204	—
House account				64,346	61,120
Total				$1,669,704	$1,673,290

taining information on products, prices, and special promotional deals mailed to all salesmen each week. Daily call reports and attendance at the semiannual sales meetings were required of all salesmen. One meeting was held the first week in January to introduce the spring line of fishing supplies. The hunting line was presented at the second meeting which was scheduled in May. Each of these sales meetings spanned four to five days so the salesmen were able to study the new products being introduced and any changes in sales and company policies. The production manager and comptroller attended these sales meetings to answer questions and to discuss problems which the salesmen might have concerning deliveries and credit.

On a predetermined schedule each salesman telephoned Mr. McDonald every Monday morning to learn of changes in prices, special promotional offers, and delivery schedules of unshipped orders. At this time the salesman's activities for the week were discussed, and sometimes the salesman was asked by Mr. McDonald to collect past due accounts in his territory. In addition, the salesmen submitted daily call reports which listed the name of each account contacted and the results of the call. Generally, the salesmen planned their own itineraries in terms of the accounts and prospects that were to be contacted and the amount of time to be spent on each call.

Outdoor's sales force during the current year totaled 11 full-time men. Their ages ranged from 23 to 67 years and their tenure with the company from one to ten years. Salesmen, territories, and sales volumes for the previous year and the current year are shown in Exhibit 1.

Current Situation

The salesmen were paid straight commissions on their dollar sales volume for the calendar year. The commission rate was 5 per cent on the first $75,000, 6 per cent on the next $25,000 in volume and 7 per cent on all sales over $100,000 for the year. Each week a salesman could draw all or a portion of his accumulated commissions. Mr. McDonald encouraged the salesmen to draw commissions as they accumulated since he felt the men were motivated to work harder when they had a very small or zero balance in their commission accounts. These accounts were closed at the end of the year so each salesman began the new year with nothing in his account.

The salesmen provided their own automobiles and paid their traveling expenses, of which all or a portion were reimbursed by per diem. Under the per diem plan, each salesman received $30 per day for Monday through Thursday and $14 for Friday, or a total of $134 for the normal workweek. No per diem was paid for Saturday, but a salesman received an additional $30 if he spent Saturday and Sunday nights in the territory.

In addition to the commission and per diem, a salesman could earn cash awards under two sales incentive plans that were installed two years ago. Under one which was called the Annual Sales Increase Awards Plan, a total of $5,200 was paid to the five salesmen having the largest percentage increase in dollar sales volume over the previous year. To be eligible for these awards, a salesman had to show a sales increase over the previous year. These awards were made at the January sales meeting, and the winners were determined by dividing the dollar amount of each salesman's increase by his volume for the previous year with the percentage increases ranked in descending order. The salesmen's earnings under this plan for the current year are shown in Exhibit 2.

Under the second incentive plan, each salesman could win a Weekly Sales Increase Award for each week in which his dollar volume in the current year exceeded his sales for the corresponding week in the previous year. Beginning with an award of $2 for the first week, the amount of the award increased by $2 for each week in which the salesman surpassed his sales for the comparable week in the previous year. If a salesman produced higher sales during each of the 50 weeks in the current year, he received $2 for the first week, $4 for the second week, and

EXHIBIT 2 Salesmen's Earnings and Incentive Awards in the Current Year

| Salesmen | Sales | | Annual sales increase awards | | Weekly sales increase awards | Earnings* |
	Previous year	Current year	Increase in sales (percent)	Award	(Total accrued)	
Allen	$ 82,566	$ 82,304	(0.3%)	—	$ 506	$10,000†
Campbell	298,048	345,060	(15.8	$1,500 (2d)	1,122	22,404
Duvall	—	103,664	—	—	—	10,000†
Edwards	—	104,854	—	—	—	10,000†
Gatewood	89,632	89,638	(0.1)	200 (5th)	552	10,000†
Hammond	103,734	103,682	—	—	—	4,628
Logan	—	141,930	—	—	—	10,000†
Mason	161,258	206,272	27.9	2,000 (1st)	1,722	12,689
O'Bryan	135,982	143,098	5.2	500 (4th)	756	8,267
Samuels	184,256	206,118	11.9	1,000 (3d)	650	12,678
Wates	92,678	85,550	(7.7)	—	306	4,383

*Exclusive of incentive awards and per diem.
†Guarantee of $200 per week or $10,000 per year.

$100 for the fiftieth week, or a total of $2550 for the year. The salesman had to be employed by the company during the previous year to be eligible for these awards. A check for the total amount of the awards accrued during the year was presented to the salesmen at the sales meeting held in January. Earnings of the salesmen under this plan for the current year are shown in Exhibit 2.

The company frequently used "spiffs" to promote the sales of special items. The salesman was paid a "spiff," which usually was $2, for each order he obtained for the designated items in the promotion.

For the past 3 years in recruiting salesmen, Mr. McDonald had guaranteed the more qualified applicants a weekly income while they learned the business and developed their respective territories. During the current year, five salesmen, Allen, Duvall, Edwards, Hammond, and Logan, had a guarantee of $200 a week, which they drew against their commissions. If the year's cumulative commissions for any of these salesmen were less than their cumulative weekly drawing accounts, they received no commissions. The commission and drawing accounts were closed on December 31 so each salesman began the new year with a zero balance in each account.

The company did not have a stated or written policy specifying the maximum length of time a salesman could receive a guarantee if his commissions continued to be less than his draw. Mr. McDonald held the opinion that the five salesmen who currently had guarantees would quit if these guarantees were withdrawn before their commissions reached $10,000 per year.

Mr. McDonald stated that he was convinced the annual earnings of Outdoor's salesmen had fallen behind earnings for comparable selling positions, particularly in the past 6 years. As a result, he felt that the company's ability to attract and hold high-caliber professional salesmen was being adversely affected. He strongly expressed the opinion that each salesman should be earning $20,000 annually.

In December of the current year, Mr. McDonald met with his comptroller and production manager, who were the only other executives of the company and solicited their ideas concerning changes in the company's compensation plan for salesmen.

The comptroller pointed out that the salesmen having guarantees were not producing the sales that had been expected from their territories. He was concerned that the annual commissions earned by four of the five salesmen on guarantees were approximately half or less than their drawing accounts.

Furthermore, according to the comptroller, several of the salesmen who did not have guarantees were producing a relatively low volume of sales year after year. For example, annual sales remained at relatively low levels for Gatewood, O'Bryan, and Wates, who had been working 4 to 5 years in their respective territories.

The comptroller proposed that guarantees be reduced to $100 per week plus commissions at the regular rate on all sales. The $100 would not be drawn against commissions as was the case under the existing plan but would be in addition to any commissions earned. In the comptrol-

EXHIBIT 3 Comparison of Earnings in Current Year Under Existing Guarantee Plan with Earnings Under the Comptroller's Plan*

Salesmen	Sales	Existing Plan			Comptroller's plan		
		Commissions	Guarantee	Earnings	Commissions	Guarantee	Earnings
Allen	$ 82,304	$4,188	$10,000	$10,000	$4,188	$5,000	$ 9,188
Duvall	103,664	5,506	10,000	10,000	5,506	5,000	10,506
Edwards	104,854	5,590	10,000	10,000	5,590	5,000	10,509
Hammond	103,682	5,508	10,000	10,000	5,508	5,000	10,508
Logan	141,930	8,185	10,000	10,000	8,185	5,000	13,185

*Exclusive of incentive awards and per diem.

ler's opinion, this plan would motivate the salesmen to increase sales rapidly since their incomes would rise directly with their sales. The comptroller presented Exhibit 3 which showed the incomes of the five salesmen having guarantees in the current year as compared with the incomes they would have received under this plan.

From a sample check of recent shipments, the production manager had concluded that the salesmen tended to overwork accounts located within a 50-mile radius of their homes. Sales coverage was extremely light in a 60- to 100-mile radius of the salesmen's homes with somewhat better coverage beyond 100 miles. He argued that this pattern of sales coverage seemed to result from a desire by the salesmen to spend most evenings during the week at home with their families.

He proposed that the per diem be increased from $30 to $36 per day for Monday through Thursday, $14 for Friday, and $36 for Sunday if the salesman spent Sunday evening away from his home. He reasoned that the per diem of $36 for Sunday would act as a strong incentive for the salesmen to drive to the perimeters of their territories on Sunday evenings rather than use Monday morning for traveling. Further, he believed that the increase in per diem would encourage the salesmen to spend more evenings away from their homes which would result in a more uniform coverage of the sales territories and an overall increase in sales volume.

The consultant from New York City recommended that the guarantees and per diem be retained on the present basis and proposed that Outdoor adopt what he called a "Ten Percent Self-Improvement Plan." Under the consultant's plan each salesman would be paid, in addition to the regular commission, a monthly bonus commission of 10 percent on all dollar volume over his sales in the comparable month of the previous year. For example, if a salesman sold $20,000 worth of merchandise in January of the current year and $18,000 in January of the previous year, he would receive a $200 bonus check in February. For salesmen on guarantees, bonuses would be in addition to earnings. The consultant reasoned that the bonus commission would motivate the salesmen, both those with and without guarantees, to increase their sales.

He further recommended the discontinuation of the two sales incentive plans currently in effect. He felt the savings from these plans would nearly cover the costs of his proposal.

Following a discussion of these proposals with the management group, Mr. McDonald was undecided on which proposal to adopt, if any. Further, he wondered if any change in the compensation of salesmen would alleviate all of the present problems.

Student Learning Exercise / 8
Designing Non-Financial Motivation

Learning Objective   To cause students to think about non-financial approaches to sales force motivation.

Overview   You are asked to give advice to a sales manager whose firm has previously used only financial motivation as a basis for paying and motivating their sales force. Remember that your suggestions must be realistic and that the firm will examine them in terms of a cost/benefit analysis.

Exercise   The Ethical Drug Company has been operating successfully for over 90 years. Mr. Ted Thomas, sales manager for the firm, has asked your assistance in "improving our sales force's motivation." Thomas explains that most of their sales representatives are paid very well. To substantiate this, he provides you with a chart (Figure 1) indicating that during the current year Ethical's three categories of sales personnel received:
"In our business, we can't do a lot of the "hot shot" types of things a soap or food type company can do," states Thomas. "After all, our business involves selling prescription drug products to physicians, wholesale druggists, and retail pharmacists. How can you motivate a sales person in this business in any way other than salary?" asks Thomas.

Category of Ethical Salesmen	Average Total Compensation	Range
Senior Sales Representatives (Over 10 years experience with the firm)	$27,500	$32,500
		$22,500
Sales Representatives (Between 2 and 10 years experience with the firm)	$26,000	$30,000
		$21,000
Sales Trainees (Less than 2 years experience with the firm)	$18,500	$23,500
		$16,000

FIGURE 1   **Average Income**

1. Is it possible that Ethical Drug Company may already be using resources to motivate sales personnel other than financial compensation?

2. Does the information on financial compensation cause you any concern? If so, why? Be specific.

3. Can you suggest alternative approaches for Ethical Drug to consider?

4. What would the effects of your suggestions mean in the long and short range for both the firm and the sales force? Elaborate.

5. Can sales contests be used in a situation such as this? If you, describe how to proceed.

Territory Decisions in Sales Management

In the past several years, American citizens have been increasingly concerned over the escalating price of oil and gasoline products. The reason for this concern is the impact of the rising prices on our personal budgets. The operational costs of an automobile are obviously affected by an increase in the price of oil. So, too, are sales managers, who must be concerned about the increasing costs of sales calls. A sales call is any face-to-face interaction between a member of the sales force and a current or potential buyer. It may be of relatively long or somewhat short duration. It may result in an order or it may not. However, the reason for management's concern about sales calls is the cost of making a sales call.

Figure 9.1 presents the average current cost figures for several varieties of sales calls. These cost figures are broken down for two different types of sales territories. One is a metropolitan area where prospects and buyers are in close proximity to each other. The other is for nonmetropolitan areas where a great deal of geographical distance may exist between prospects or customers. Note that the cost figures depicted in Figure 9.1 represent only direct costs per call and, thus, would not include such factors as hospitalization insurance, sample costs, return merchandise costs, managerial overhead allocation, and so on.

The analogy of the increasing cost of oil to the operation of an automobile and that of the increasing costs of sales calls and the operation of a sales force is a good one. As may be interpreted from Figure 1, the average cost of a sales call increased 12.0 per cent in 1977 over 1976. Thus, any inefficient operation in the sales force will indeed prove costly to a sales manager. Obviously, the need for an efficiently designed and operated sales territory exists. The major focal point of this chapter will be to discuss the basis for sales territories and concepts of better sales management for existing sales territories.

As may be seen then in Figure 1, the cost of an individual sales call (whether it results in an order or not) varies from a high of $50 for an account representative's call in a non-metropolitan area to a low of $14 for a call by either a detail salesman or a service salesman in a metropolitan area.[1] Clearly, sales management has an obligation to guide and organize

[1] *Sales and Marketing Management, 1978 Survey of Selling Costs,* Vol. 120, No. 3 (February 27, 1978), p. 25.

Type of Salesman	Costs Per Salesman's Call Metro Area	Non-Metro Area	Cost Per Call % Increase Over 1976
Account Representative	$25	$50	19.0
Detail Salesman	$14	$22	16.7
Sales Engineer	$31	$49	10.7
Industrial Products Salesman	$18	$31	5.9
Service Salesman	$14	$26	7.7

$$*\text{Direct Cost Per Call} = \frac{\text{Compensation} + \text{Auto} + \text{Travel, Food \& Lodging Cost}}{\text{Average Calls Per year}}$$

FIGURE 9.1   Direct Costs of Sales Calls, 1977 [Source: *Sales and Marketing Management, 1978 Survey of Selling Costs,* Vol. 120, No. 3 (Feb. 27, 1978), pp. 25–26.]

the calls of sales personnel and further to organize effectively sales person's territories in order that these increasing costs will still result in a profit or contribution to the firm. Wasted time caused by poorly designed sales territories will result in increasing costs and, thus, decreasing profits if the situation is not corrected. Thus, there is a need for sales management to focus attention constantly on the design of sales territories.

In the sections of this chapter that follow, we shall first look at sales territories from an overview perspective and shall examine the specific basis on which sales territories are formed. Next, we shall examine the role of sales management and shall look in particular at two techniques that sales management might utilize in making territorial decisions. These include the brand-switching matrix and the dyadic relationship. Third, we will examine situations where sales management might wish to make revisions in existing territories. Fourth, we shall examine considerations that management must bring to bear upon the establishment of new sales territories. And, finally, we shall look at the subject of more efficient routing, scheduling, and time management considerations.

Sales Territories: An Overview

Earlier in Chapters 4 and 5 we discussed the goals and objectives of the sales function, and we also discussed the allocation of effort and resources involved in sales management. At this point we wish to examine managerial decisions from a specific frame of reference. Sales managers often become frustrated when attempting to do this because they are viewing their market as a whole. As we shall see, the territorial unit offers a viable alternative for efficient planning. As stated in a recent text:

Realistic sales planning must ultimately be done on a territory-by-territory basis rather than by the total market. Characteristics of customers and prospects vary significantly from one section of the country to another, and sometimes even from one county to the next; thus, analysis of market statistics should include breakdowns for individual sales territories. For sales planning, in other words, the territory is a more homogeneous unit than the market as a whole, which frequently obscures a great deal of underlying heterogeneity.[2]

REASONS FOR THE USE OF SALES TERRITORIES

Sales managers do not always agree as to the advisability of having sales territories. For example, when the company is very small and is doing business in a local or highly restricted geographic area, it may make very little sense to establish sales territories. Likewise, when a product or service being sold is offered on the basis of personal friendships, for example, many forms of life insurance might fall into this category, it may make little sense also to establish sales territories. Clearly, what sales management wishes here is for their sales personnel to be able to call upon their friends and acquaintances regardless of the particular geographic locale in which they are located.

On the other hand, there are many reasons for the use of sales territories. First, as we have already mentioned, the existence of sales territories makes planning and resource allocation more feasible. On an overall market basis, the plight of the sales manager employed by a national firm, who faces a resource allocation decision, is dreadful. As you can well imagine, this allocation would be highly frustrating if not impossible. Thus, the existence of territories provides sales management with a more meaningful basis upon which to perform sales planning and/or resource allocation.

A second reason for the use of sales territories is to insure market coverage. If specific sales territories are not assigned, it is possible that many customers or potential customers might be overlooked. Sales personnel might tend to call only upon existing accounts and might neglect the development of potential accounts with whom the firm has not previously done business. By having specific sales territories assigned, the responsibility for calling upon such potential accounts is affixed with individual sales personnel.

A third reason for the use and existence of sales territories is additional efficiencies. If two or more sales personnel are calling upon accounts in the same geographic location, the potential certainly exists for duplication of effort. The use of sales territories should reduce the overlap in sales expenses, thus resulting in a more efficient overall operation.

WHAT IS A SALES TERRITORY?

The very word "territory" is misleading, as it is used in the connotation of a sales territory. This word, of course, suggests that we are talking about a geographic entity. In fact, as we shall see in the section that

[2] Richard R. Still, Edward W. Cundiff, and Norman A. P. Govoni, *Sales Management: Decisions, Policies and Cases,* 3rd ed. (Englewood Cliffs, N.J.: Prentice-Hall, Inc., 1970), p. 353.

follows, territories may be based upon products, customers, or geographic area.

A sales territory represents a quantifiable and identifiable group of existing and/or potential buyers. A territory thus focuses upon sales potential from the firm's point of view, and would be a slice of the total pie that the firm hopes to obtain in sales. Thus, we must guard against the tendency to think of "the Atlanta territory" or "the Denver territory" as representing geographic areas. Instead, they represent sales potential for a particular firm.

GEOGRAPHICALLY BASED TERRITORIES

As noted above, territories do not have to be based upon geography. Nevertheless, geographic considerations are probably the most common basis on which territorial decisions are made. Within the broad area of geographical bases, there is a great deal of disagreement across firms as to what specific type of geographic unit to use. Some firms, for example, will assign several states to an individual. Other firms have so many individuals on their sales force that a particular sales territory might consist of less than one county. In discussing the type of geographic base to be used, authors of a recent sales management text suggest,

It is preferable that the unit be small, for at least two reasons. First, a small unit will aid management in realizing one of the basic values of territories— the geographic pinpointing of potential. Second, the use of small control units makes it easier for management to adjust the territories.[3]

Recognizing the frequency with which geography is used as a basis in territory decisions, sales and marketing management and probably other firms publish specialized sales maps, which are aimed at assisting the sales manager in locating both retail and industrial potential as an aid in sales territory decisions.[4]

If sales management does elect to use geography as the basis for sales territory decisions, it may be doing so in recognition of at least three main factors. First, many firms select geography as their basis for dividing sales territories because it may reflect their ability to market products or services. For example, many firms market their products on a regional basis and, thus, do not view the entire country as a viable market. Under conditions such as these, geographical constraints may offer some very viable guidelines. A second reason for the selection of geography as the basis for sales territories may be the ability to provide customer service. If the product or service mix sold by a firm requires a great deal of customer contact time, then it may be physically impossible to assign

[3] William J. Stanton and Richard H. Buskirk, *Management of the Sales Force*, 5th ed. (Homewood, Ill.: Richard D. Irwin, Inc., 1978), p. 484.
[4] Sales and Marketing Management makes these "Sales Builders Maps" available either on a nationwide basis or by state or regional area. Further information may be obtained by contacting Sales and Marketing Management, 633 3rd Avenue, New York, New York, 10017.

sales territories on any basis other than geography. The support systems and support personnel needed may make adequate provision of warehouses central to particular geographic locations critical to the nature of the business. Third, geographic constraints are often used as a basis for territorial decisions when a firm is marketing through middlemen, who may have exclusive franchises or territories based upon geography. Thus, if the firm sells its product to a wholesaler, who in turn sells to retailers, it may very well wish to overlap with the wholesaler's service area by assigning a sales force to the same territory serviced by that particular wholesaler.

In basing a decision to design sales territories on geography, we might assume that all territories, therefore, would be the same geographic size. This, of course, would be a mistake since we must remember that the sales territory should reflect potential. Thus, even if we select geography as the basis for sales territories, we should expect that each territory will be very dissimilar with regard to geographic size. Thus, the sales person who covers the Rocky Mountain states might find himself faced with a territory consisting of several states, whereas an individual covering New York City might be one of two or perhaps three sales representatives covering only New York City.

CUSTOMER BASED TERRITORIES

An alternative to the use of geography in making sales territory decisions would be the use of customers as a basis. In instances where customers are utilized to design sales territories, it is common to consider both present accounts (that is, accounts who presently purchase from a particular firm) and potential accounts (that is, organizations that presently purchase from another supply).

When customers are used as the basis for a sales territory decision, we often recognize that different call frequencies are involved. By "call frequencies" we mean that some customers are called upon more frequently than others by a sales force. The Case Soap Division for Procter and Gamble, for example, has a formal policy of calling upon its largest retail accounts at least once per week, whereas smaller retail accounts may be called upon only twice in a month or perhaps only once in a month's time period. In part, therefore, the use of customers may prove a viable basis for sales territory decisions.

PRODUCT BASED TERRITORIES

Many firms elect to make their decision on organization of sales territories based upon their product lines. The Clean Corporation Case presented in Chapter 1 presents just such a possibility. The firm involved here has an existing territory structure but is contemplating revision of their sales force in light of the addition of a new food product. Inasmuch as differing products require differing amounts of service and adjustments, it is possible that a firm with a wide product line might choose to use products rather than customers or geography for selecting a basis for sales territories.

Basing sales territories on products has a distinct advantage in that it allows sales personnel to specialize. That is, sales personnel may become very knowledgeable and adept at selling particular products as opposed to using, for example, geography as a basis and having one salesperson try to span several different product lines with their sales and service knowledge. Conversely, an obvious disadvantage of this type of organization for sales territories is that several different sales personnel from the same firm may be calling upon the same account. Thus, costs associated with selling, including travel, automobiles, and so on, may be increased. Likewise, an individual responsible for buying in a given account may see several different representatives from the same firm. This, of course, lends itself to the possibility of confusion on the part of the buyer.

COMBINATIONS

Many sales organizations elect to use a combination of the geographic, customer, and product-based variables described. Burroughs Corporation, for example, today markets its computer products through a segmentation scheme that involves the use of all three variables. Their sales representatives call upon specific types of customers selling certain products produced by Burroughs within particular geographic regions fixed by the firm.

Other sales organizations might elect to use a combination of two of the three factors. For example, it is very possible that a particular firm might elect to use geographic and product bases together for the assignment of sales territories. That is, certain of their sales representatives might call upon customers in a particular geographic area selling one product of the firm, while other sales personnel might call upon either the same or differing customers selling a different type of product produced by the same firm.

Opportunity Analysis: The Role of Sales Management

In making decisions regarding sales territories, the format shown in Figure 9.2 may prove useful. Based upon the work of Vizza and Chambers, Figure 9.2 presents a model of time and territory management for salesmen. This model, of course, would be implemented by sales management, and sales management has sales responsibility for making certain that the steps listed under territorial planning are performed thoroughly and in sequence to avoid oversights.

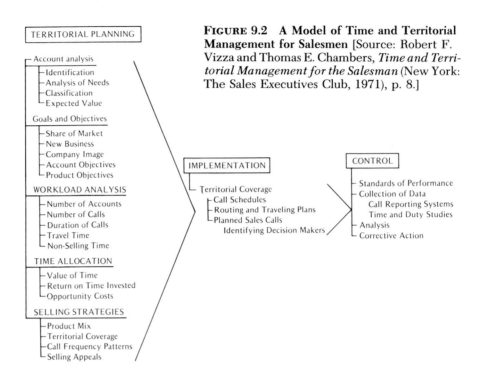

FIGURE 9.2 **A Model of Time and Territorial Management for Salesmen** [Source: Robert F. Vizza and Thomas E. Chambers, *Time and Territorial Management for the Salesman* (New York: The Sales Executives Club, 1971), p. 8.]

As suggested by the model, account analysis is the first step in establishing territories. In conducting this first step, the sales manager is required not only to identify existing accounts where we presently are doing business, but he would also have responsibility for identifying potential. Sales potential would be determined through the use of the type of analysis seen in Figure 9.3, which results in the calculation of expected values by accounts by territory.

1 Account Name and Number	2 Classification	1 Potential By Product			4 Estimated Share By Product			5 Probabilities			1 Expected Value (Col. 3x4x5)			
		X	Y	Z	X	Y	Z	X	Y	Z	X	Y	Z	Total
Totals														

Recap:

Classification	Number of Accounts
A	_____
B	_____
C	_____
D	_____
E	_____
Total	

FIGURE 9.3 **Account Analysis and Calculation of Expected Values** [Source: Same As Above, p. 12.]

A second step in the establishment of territories would pertain to goals and objectives. As we shall see in the discussion of the brand switching matrix which follows, one important aspect of this is that sales management must understand which competitors presently have a share of market and which are both vulnerable to competition and appear impregnable to competition.

The third step in the process pertains to work load analysis. At this point, the sales manager would be considering the number of accounts and calls that would be involved from the salesperson's point of view. As noted in our discussion of geographic bases for territories earlier, the sales manager must also consider travel time between accounts and the total amount of nonselling time that would be involved for a particular territory.

Time allocation will be discussed in detail later in this chapter, but for now we should note that the next step concerns calculation on the part of sales management of the value of time. Return on time invested may be calculated by dividing the average gross margin per order by the salesperson's cost per call hour. In calculating the salesperson's cost per call hour, we would take into consideration direct costs such as those mentioned at the outset of this chapter.

The last step in establishing territorial considerations would be the determination of the particular selling strategies to be employed. As we have noted previously, this would entail such considerations as establishing patterns for territorial coverage and might cause sales management to recognize that we would not necessarily expect equal call frequencies on all accounts in a particular territory. For example, those accounts identified as having high potential purchase volume might receive heavy coverage even though they are not now purchasing from the firm. In similar fashion, if sales management believes that present accounts are relatively loyal to the firm, it might elect to call on these accounts less frequently than on the high potential accounts who are not currently the firm's customers.

As may be seen, then, from Figure 9.2, these five planning steps are critical to the planning of a successful sales territory. Once the territory has been planned, the two remaining steps involve implementation by sales personnel under the supervision of sales management and control.[5]

THE BRAND SWITCHING MATRIX: SALES MANAGEMENT APPLICATIONS

A virtually unknown but nevertheless very useful tool to sales managers in arriving at territorial decisions is the brand switching matrix. Sales managers often find themselves concerned about the transient natures

---

[5] The discussion of the steps involved in territorial planning is based upon Robert F. Vizza and Thomas E. Chambers, *Time and Territorial Management for Salesmen* (New York: The Sales Executives Club, 1971), pp. 8–20.

MONTH ONE	Firm A	Firm B	Firm C	Firm D
		MONTH TWO		
Firm A (150 Purchasers)	100	15	20	15
Firm B (150 Purchasers)	10	75	15	50
Firm C (150 Purchasers)	15	25	40	70
Firm D (150 Purchasers)	0	35	35	80
TOTAL 600 Purchasers	125	150	110	215

FIGURE 9.4   A Brand-Switching Matrix

of their customers. They may be very concerned about their firm's ability to hold or retain specific customers over a given period of time. Sales managers may also be concerned about their firm's vulnerability to competition. The brand switching matrix may provide answers to these questions and, in addition, may prove very useful in making major territorial decisions.

The purpose of a brand switching matrix is to trace changes in customers' purchase behavioral patterns over a specified period of time. For purposes of illustration, a hypothetical example follows that is based on a sales territory consisting of 600 purchasers buying a nonspecified product in a monthly period. In this illustration we will assume that there are four firms that market the products in this particular area. They will be firms A, B, C, and D. To further simplify the example, let us assume that, at the beginning of this period, all four firms have an equal market share. That is, of the total 600 purchasers in this particular area, 150 have purchased from each of the four firms in month 1. During Month 2, however, these purchasers may shift their purchasing patterns to purchase from other firms. Figure 9.4 presents an illustration of a brand switching matrix designed to illustrate this data.

In the illustration provided in Figure 9.4, we are assuming that each of the purchasers has purchased only one time during a given month and further that they have purchased from only one supplier. As indicated by its purpose, the brand switching matrix thus allows us to look at the totals for Month 2 and determine which firms have actually gained purchasers and which have lost. In actual practice, since firms purchase different amounts, their purchases would be weighted to reflect volume/profit potential much as was illustrated in Figure 9.3 concerning expected value of accounts.

From the single matrix depicted in Figure 9.4, sales managers can obtain answers to the following types of questions:

1. Which firm is doing the best job of retaining its customers?
2. Which firm is making the most progress against competition?
3. How vulnerable is each firm to its competitors?
4. Against which competitor(s) is additional sales activity most likely to be effective?

Each of these four questions will be analyzed separately by comparing data from the matrix shown in Figure 9.4. It is important to understand that the 600 purchasers depicted in month 1 and month 2 are the same 600 customers (that is, no additional customers are being considered and likewise we are assuming that all 600 customers purchased both in month 1 and month 2).

Customer Retention. By examining the inner section of A with A, B with B, C with C, and D with D, we are able to ascertain that Firm A has done the best job of customer retention, inasmuch as 100 of its original 150 purchasers have stayed with this particular firm. Likewise, Firm C is doing the worst job of customer retention since it has kept only 40 out of the original 150 or roughly 27 per cent of its original market share.

The second, third, and fourth questions posed earlier can be answered by use of a net matrix. A net matrix is a device for illustrating that in every marketing situation a daily "war" is fought. This "war" is a function of both offensive and defensive effectiveness. That is, every firm both gains and loses customers in short periods of time; thus, its total effectiveness is the sum total of its gains versus the sum total of its losses. Figure 9.5 presents net matrices for each of the four firms—Firm A, Firm B, Firm C, and Firm D—involved in Figure 9.4.

An examination of each of the four net matrices will indicate how that firm is doing against each individual competitor. Looking at the net matrix for Firm A, for example, it can be seen that Firm A is losing more customers than it is gaining from all three other competitors. Given the relative magnitude of the losses, however, Firm A should be most concerned about Firm D. Firm A is losing three times as many customers

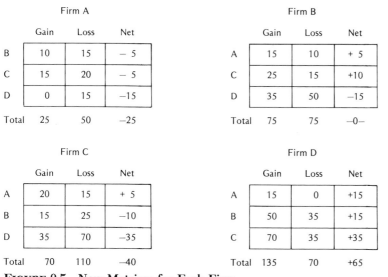

Firm A

	Gain	Loss	Net
B	10	15	− 5
C	15	20	− 5
D	0	15	−15
Total	25	50	−25

Firm B

	Gain	Loss	Net
A	15	10	+ 5
C	25	15	+10
D	35	50	−15
Total	75	75	—0—

Firm C

	Gain	Loss	Net
A	20	15	+ 5
B	15	25	−10
D	35	70	−35
Total	70	110	−40

Firm D

	Gain	Loss	Net
A	15	0	+15
B	50	35	+15
C	70	35	+35
Total	135	70	+65

FIGURE 9.5 **New Matrices for Each Firm**

to Firm D as it is to either of the other two firms with the loss to Firm D accounting for 60 per cent (15 of the 25 net customers lost) of the total net loss. The same analysis conducted for Firm B indicates that the sales manager for this firm would be pleased with the results achieved against Firm A and C, with net gains of 5 and 10 customers respectively, but concerned about the net loss of 15 customers to Firm D. Without the information available from the brand switching matrix, the sales manager for Firm B might only know that the number of customers for his firm was the same for the two periods, and mistakenly assume that there was no cause for concern. Analysis of the information in the net matrix derived from Figure 9.4 indicates that this is not the case, but that there has been considerable switching in the marketplace.

The sales manager for Firm C would recognize from the net matrix that a major problem existed and, as a result, almost half of the customers of his firm were switching to Firm D, explaining almost 90 per cent of the net loss of customers (35 of the 40 total). Analysis of the net matrix from Firm D's point of view shows that it is in an enviable position, having a net gain from each of its three competitors.[6]

Clearly, information such as that available from the brand switching matrix and the net matrices can prove useful in arriving at territory decisions. A look back at Figure 9.2 (A model of time and territorial management for salesmen) will reveal that such information would clearly be desirable from the standpoint of the goals and objectives step in territorial planning.

THE DYADIC RELATIONSHIP—TERRITORIAL CONSIDERATIONS

From sociological research, the term **dyad** has evolved to mean a situation in which two individuals interact. Applications to the area of personal selling or sales management, therefore, would lend themselves to a buyer-seller dyad. In research published in 1963, Franklin Evans investigated the buyer-seller dyad with the frame of reference being the sale of life insurance. His research concluded that the more alike sales persons and their prospects were the greater was the likelihood that their interaction would result in a sale.[7] Evans' work was based upon physical factors, such as height and age, other objectively verifiable factors, such as education and income, and personality related variables, such as whether the individual smoked or not and the individual's expressed political beliefs.[8] In some follow-up research conducted by Tosi, which focused on drug sales personnel and retail pharmacists, an addi-

---

[6] Benjamin Lipstein, "Tests for Test Marketing," *Harvard Business Review*, March–April 1961, pp. 74–77; and "The Dynamics of Brand Loyalty and Brand Switching," *Proceedings*, 5th Annual Conference, New York, Advertising Research Foundation, Incorporated, 1959, pp. 101–108.

[7] Franklin B. Evans, "Selling as a Dyadic Relationship—A New Approach," *American Behavioral Scientist* (Vol. 6, No. 9), May 1963, pp. 76–79.

[8] *Ibid.*, p. 79.

tional conclusion was drawn. The customer apparently has a preconceived perception of what a salesperson's behavior should be. How well actual behavior meshes with the prospective buyer's perception of what that behavior should be is a critical consideration in whether or not the dyadic interaction continues.[9]

Clearly, the dyadic concept is important in arriving at territorial decisions. Where possible, the sales manager should make an attempt to determine whether or not the conclusions drawn in the studies mentioned are critical to his particular business. If the sales manager feels that a similarity between buyer and seller is critical, then he should do everything in his power to obtain a good "match" between the sales person assigned to that territory and key customers in that territory. In addition to the dyadic relationship, the reader may well wish to consider the concept of the sales grid and the concept of the customer grid discussed earlier in Chapter 6.[10] A word of caution, however, should also be expressed concerning potential overlap between buyer and seller in that it may be possible to abuse the similarity of the dyad. Such abuse is one possible conclusion from a study on the life insurance business done by Gadel.[11] This study found a tendency by sales personnel to concentrate on prospects similar to themselves. This, of course, is not necessarily a negative factor, but it is one that should be considered by sales management. Obviously, the concentration by sales persons on friendly prospects who do not buy their merchandise may mean the waste of a great many sales dollars and, as we have seen earlier in this chapter, the cost of a sales call is rapidly increasing whether or not an order results. Thus, the dyad has both positive and negative implications from the territorial assignment point of view.

Specific Territory Considerations

In making decisions regarding specific territorial considerations, Still, Cundiff, and Govoni suggest that there are four main procedural steps that apply either to establishing new sales territories or making a territorial revision:[12]

1. Selecting a basic geographical control unit.
2. Determining sales potential present in each control unit.
3. Combining basic control units into tentative territories.
4. Adjusting for differences in coverage difficulty and redistricting tentative territories.

[9] Henry L. Tosi, "The Effects of Expectation Levels and World Concensus on the Buyer-Seller Dyad," *Journal of Business* (Vol. 39), October 1966, pp. 516–529.
[10] For additional information see Robert F. Blake and Jane S. Mouton, *The Managerial Grid* (Houston, Texas: Gulf Publishing Company, 1964).
[11] M. S. Gadel, "Concentration by Salesmen on Congenial Prospects," *Journal of Marketing* (Vol. 28), April 1964, pp. 64–66.
[12] Still *et al., op. cit.,* p. 358.

ESTABLISHING NEW SALES TERRITORIES

New sales territories are typically established for three reasons: First, the organization itself or the product to be sold are new. An illustration of this would be a firm that previously has not been engaged in marketing a product and suddenly decides, upon development of a new product, to market it. This, of course, means that the sales management of such an organization would have to go through the steps we have elaborated previously concerning establishment of sales territories.

Second, a new territorial arrangement may be necessitated by a change in the channel of distribution. For example, if a firm that previously operated as a manufacturer selling its output to wholesalers decides that it will market the product to retailers itself, this means that the manufacturer will have to study the retail structure and form sales territories. Essentially, in this instance the manufacturer is taking over the duty of the wholesaler by assuming it himself.

Third, new territory decisions are often necessitated by growth. For example, a firm that has continued to add products to its product mix or brands to an already large product line may find that it is necessary to reduce territory size, thus splitting the territory formerly handled by one sales representative into two or more territories; the net result would be the formation of new sales territories.

In any of the three situations listed previously, where new territories are being established, it is critical that an accurate assessment of potential be obtained by the sales manager. The reader will recall in our earlier discussion of territories that we indicated a primary consideration in establishment of territories is potential. This may sound relatively easy to do, but in practice it is often quite difficult. A further consideration concerns relative equal potential across territories. Although, as we have noted, territories may vary a great deal in terms of geographic size, the consideration of potential has important implications across sales territories. Ideally, sales territories should be of equal potential. However, in practice sales managers are often given to selecting an "easy out" and neglect to try to equate potential across territories.[13]

TERRITORY REVISIONS

There are numerous reasons why revisions are made in territories once they have become established. For one thing, sales management has a constant responsibility to review sales territories and to make changes when such changes are needed. Thus, time itself becomes one reason behind the need for revision in sales territories. With changing market conditions, changing competition, or additions in product lines, revisions in territory are often needed.

In making territory changes, sales management should keep in mind

[13] Further information on this topic may be found in J. G. Hauk, "Research in Personal Selling," in G. Schwartz (ed.), *Science and Marketing* (New York: John Wiley and Sons, Inc., 1965).

the goal of maintaining potential across differing sales territories. Thus, we are suggesting that when territory revisions are being considered the relative equality of potential across territories should be foremost in the minds of sales management. An adjustment, for example, reducing the size of the territory because the customers, both actual and potential, are not receiving the coverage management desires is really a concession on the part of management. Decisions such as these often mask a problem and treat only a symptom. For example, in this illustration, the real problem may be with motivation of the salesperson in the territory rather than coverage of the territory. A decision to reduce the territory may not, in fact, help the real problem at all and might lead to further deterioration in the attitude of the salesperson.

Territory revisions so that they result in geographic enlargements or territory shrinkages should be viewed, finally, from the point of view of the sales representative. For example, in situations where a sales territory is actually enlarged, will the salesperson be able to cover a larger geographic territory? In a situation where a sales territory is being reduced, the effect upon the ego and the morale of the salesperson must be considered in addition to the effect upon compensation and territorial coverage. Sales management must examine territorial changes from the perspective of the salesperson(s) involved. The two cases at the end of this chapter are concerned in part with the issue of territory revisions.

Effective Routing, Scheduling, and Time Management Considerations

To understand why the topics of routing, scheduling, and time management are so important for sales management, we have only to consider the amount of time that sales personnel spend in travel. Although the amount of time actually spent may vary a great deal from one firm to another, a good rule of thumb is that approximately one fourth of a salesperson's time is spent travelling. Given the cost of salespeople's time as illustrated at the outset of this chapter, sales managers need to do everything possible to insure that this unproductive time is held to a minimum and that territory coverage is possible in an efficient way.

Once a sales territory has been defined, the next step is to prepare a routing pattern analysis. Some firms choose to begin this process by having aerial photographs made of the particular territory. In other cases, mere roadmaps or city maps will suffice. In either case, the best approach is to lay out suggested coverage by actually marking locations of customers and prospective customers on a map.

In making routing decisions, there are numerous patterns that might be used. Some of the more common routing patterns include:

1. *Straight line*—Starting from the office, the salesman makes calls in one continuous direction to the end of his territory. He may make

calls on the way back along the same line, or return on another line. Thus, he alternates "lines" on each trip.

2. *Circular patterns*—These involve starting at the home office and prescribing a circle of stops, which is completed when the salesman returns to the office. There may be a series of different size circles covering the outer and inner portions of the territory, all with the home office as the common point.

3. *A clover-leaf pattern*—This is similar to the circular pattern but, instead of covering an entire territory, it circles a part of the territory. The next trip is an adjacent circle, and so on until the entire territory is covered.

5. *"Hopscotch"*—The practice of starting at the furthest point from the home office and making calls back to the office. A salesman would fly to the outer limits and drive back, for example. The next trip, he goes in the opposite direction in his territory.[14]

Scheduling considerations by and large concern call frequency. Although we have touched briefly on the concept of call frequencies before, the specific scheduling considerations that should be involved should reflect several different goals and objectives. Included here would be:

1. The expected sales volume from an existing account.
2. Potential sales volume from an account that presently does not purchase from our firm.
3. Amount of customer service needed.
4. Nonselling functions to be performed with the account, including arrangement for displays, customer participation in advertising, and so on.
5. Time needed for demonstration of new or related products.
6. Time needed with the customer for entertainment purposes.

All of the reasons cited here plus others not mentioned would affect the scheduling for a particular territory. As mentioned earlier in the chapter, it is entirely possible for different accounts to be placed on a different call frequency schedule. Thus, a large account either in terms of existing sales volume or potential sales volume will typically be seen more frequently than a smaller account.

Time management considerations are some of the most important factors that sales management should be concerned with. It is important for sales management to convey to members of the sales force the value of their time. Often sales personnel get into "ruts" and, because of their habits, they may overlook changes in time management that might prove beneficial. Since this is very difficult to talk about without direct involvement, this chapter includes a game designed by an executive who has had previous experience with sales force operations. Whether you play the game extensively or merely read over the materials included, the Time-Is-Money Game (pp. 309–315) emphasizes many major factors associated with the efficient use of sales time.[15]

---

[14] Vizza and Chambers, *op. cit.*, p. 64–65.

[15] Stewart A. Washburn, "Salesmanship: The Time-Is-Money-Game," *Sales and Marketing Management* (Vol. 116, No. 4), March 8, 1976, p. 43–49.

Salesmanship: The Time-Is-Money Game

By STEWART A. WASHBURN/
Vice President & Director of Special Projects.
Porter Henry & Co.

Ask any salesman this question: What's the difference between a good salesman—a good producer—and one who just gets by?

The chances are he'll tell you that the good producer is the one with the more persuasive communication skills. Maybe he'll tell you that the good producer is the one who knows his customers and products best. Rarely, however, will you hear that the good producer is the one who invests his time where the money is.

Yet of the three things that make for sales productivity—
☐ effective two-way communication skills
☐ knowledge of customers and products
☐ prudent investment of available sales time—the way a salesman invests his time may well be the most critical.

Salesmen can always improve their selling skills. They can always learn more about their products, their customers, and their prospects. But there is nothing they can do to expand time. There are only 250 business days per year. Most salesmen can make only five calls a day. With careful attention to routing, some salesmen can squeeze in one additional call per day. That means only 1,250 calls per year for most salesmen and 1,500 for a fortunate few. (Some consumer packaged goods salesmen are able to make 10 calls per day. With luck, they may even be able to squeeze in another call, for a total of 11. That means, for them, only 2,500 or maybe 2,750 calls per year.)

There is no way in heaven or on earth that the time budget can be increased. Yet most salesmen tend to spend about the same amount of time with all customers and prospects, invest the same amount of time with buying influences as with decision makers. And they spend sales calls as if they were limitless.

Making salesmen aware that salesmanship is a real time-is-money game is a continuing challenge for us and for anyone managing or supervising salesmen. One of the easiest ways we've found for convincing salesmen that time is indeed money is a simple paper-and-pencil game. The chips are half-hour increments of time. The game board is a territory complete with prospects, customers and less-than-ideal transportation facilities similar to those in thousands of territories. The rules and method of scoring reflect the facts of life that salesmen face every day.

Salesmanship: The Time-Is-Money Game has taught hundreds of salesmen the importance of investing available sales time wisely, as well as how to find just a little more time. We offer no money, no saving bonds, no trading stamps as an inducement to play. All we offer is an opportunity to become familiar with a device that will show your salesmen how to manage their time effectively.

Who Can Play This Game

This game is designed for any field man—manager or salesman—who may play it either alone or in competition with his peers.

This is the situation:

You represent the Great American Corp.; you are a general line salesman. Yours is the Centerville territory. You have worked the territory for several years and know it quite well.

You are about to plan your itinerary for the last four weeks of the quarter. Your quota for the quarter is $300,000. Sales for the first two months of the quarter total $280,000, leaving you only $20,000 short of your nut. It is important that you meet your quota because Great American has big plans for you if you do.

You have 14 regular customers for your products in the Centerville territory. So far during the quarter, they have bought $280,000 worth. However, you know that among them they have the potential for an additional $27,500 during the remaining month of the quarter.

You have also identified 10 nonbuying prospects in the territory. They represent an additional $39,800 in potential sales during the remaining month of the quarter. Your job is to plan the itinerary that will generate the most sales for you during the remaining four weeks of the quarter.

Details of your customers and prospects, identified by name and number, follow, as does a map of the Centerville territory showing the location of your accounts and the travel time between them.

Here Are The Rules

1. Available Selling Time

Sales time is limited to the period from 8:30 a.m. to 5:00 p.m. for five days, Monday through Friday, during the four-week period for which you are to plan the itinerary. Use the planning form on page 49. You'll need four copies, one for each week. A sample, partly filled in, is on page 48.

Sales time is reduced by the following factors:

Travel—the amount of time it takes to travel from one account to another.
Waiting time—the amount of time you must wait to see a prospect or a customer if you do not have an appointment.
Telephone time—the amount of time you spend on the phone making appointments.
Paper work—each day of selling activity generates one hour of paper work, which must be completed before the beginning of the next week.
Lunch time—unless the lunch hour is used to entertain a customer or a prospect, effective selling time is reduced by a one-hour lunch period sometimes between 11:30 and 1:30.
Don't forget holidays—your territory celebrates them all.

2. Travel Time

Travel in the Centerville territory is mostly by car. Facilities for air travel are limited. North Town Airways has an early morning turnaround flight between Centerville and North Town and a late evening turnaround flight. Service between Easton and North Town and Weston and North Town is quite frequent during the day. The current North Town Airways schedule is shown.

If you travel by air, it will take you ½ hour after your arrival to rent a car and drive to town. For example, if you fly to Easton, it will take you ½ hour to rent a car and drive to Alpha Transformer. However, if your first call after flying to Easton is to be made on the Air Conditioning Corp., it will take you ½ hour to rent a car and travel through Easton plus one hour of travel from Easton to the Air Conditioning Corp. Except in the case of air travel to North Town, travel to the first call each day may be completed by 8:30.

Hotel or motel accomodations are available within ½ hour's travel of all accounts. It is not necessary to return home each night. See travel map.

3. Making Appointments

Calls can be made cold or by appointment. Appointments can be made by phone only on the day before the call is scheduled. Three appointments can be made by phone per ½ hour. Phone calls to make appointments can be made only during normal selling/business hours; that is, from 8:20 to 5:00. Separate appointments must be made with each individual.

Calls can be made without appointments, but ½ hour of waiting time will be consumed before the person can be seen.

4. Length Of Each Sales Call

No sales call on an individual can exceed 1½ hours. However, if lunch is included, a sales call may be extended to 2½ hours.

5. Value Of Sales Time

Each half hour of sales time with a decision maker or a key buying influence increases the probability of making the sale as follows:

Calls On Present Customers

	First Call			Second Call			Third And Succeeding Calls		
	1st ½ hr.	2nd ½ hr.	3rd ½ hr.	1st ½ hr.	2nd ½ hr.	3rd ½ hr.	1st ½ hr.	2nd ½ hr.	3rd ½ hr.
Decision Maker	10	7	5	8	5	2	5	3	0
Key Buying Influence	6	4	2	5	4	3	4	3	2

Calls On Prospects

	First Call			Second Call			Third And Succeeding Calls		
	1st ½ hr.	2nd ½ hr.	3rd ½ hr.	1st ½ hr.	2nd ½ hr.	3rd ½ hr.	1st ½ hr.	2nd ½ hr.	3rd ½ Hr.
Decision Maker	5	4	3	6	7	8	10	11	12
Key Buying Influence	4	3	2	4	5	6	7	4	3

If you make an hour-and-one-half first call on the design engineer of Handwound Coil Co. and a first call on the general foreman, you will increase the probability of making the sale by 34% (10 plus 7 plus 5 plus 6 plus 4 plus 2). You will have consumed three hours of sales time. However, if you make a one-hour first call on both the design engineer and general foreman plus a half-hour second call on each, you will have consumed the same amount of time, three hours, and will have increased the probability of making the sale to 40% (1st calls: 10 plus 7 plus 6 plus 4; 2nd calls: 8 plus 5).

6. Entertainment

You can entertain only one person at a time, only at lunch, and for only one hour. Entertainment increases the probability of making the sale by a percentage equal to the value of the second half-hour of the call. You can entertain a prospect or a customer only after spending one-half hour of selling time with him in his office. With entertainment (lunch), a call may extend to 2½ hours, with extra credit for the lunch hour.

7. Scoring

For sales time to count, the probability of making the sale must be greater than 50%. To calculate the value of sales time with an account, simply multiply the total probability of making the sale (provided it is greater than 50%) by the total remaining potential of the account. Use the score sheet on page 48.

8. Winning

The winner will be the salesman who follows the rules and generates the greatest sales volume.

Customers	Sales To Date	Remaining Potential	People To See
1. Handwound Coil	$75,000	$3,000	Design Engineer* Gen. Foreman Foreman Purchasing Agent
2. General Dymo	63,000	1,500	Purchasing Agent* Design Engineer #1 Design Engineer #2
3. Superior Electric	34,000	4,000	Purchasing Agent* Design Engineer
4. Herman Transformer	28,000	1,000	Purchasing Agent*
5. Alpha Transformer	24,000	2,000	Purchasing Agent* Design Engineer
6. Circle D Centrals	9,500	3,000	Purchasing Agent* Design Engineer
7. Easton Motors	8,000	1,500	Design Engineer*
8. Fractional Motors	7,000	3,000	Design Engineer* Foreman Purchasing Agent
9. Acme Motors	7,000	2,500	Design Engineer* Purchasing Agent
10. Bartlett Transformer	6,500	1,000	Purchasing Agent*
11. Zip Electric	6,000	3,000	Purchasing Agent* Design Engineer
12. Taft Electric	6,000	500	Purchasing Agent* Design Engineer
13. Marco Electric	5,000	500	Purchasing Agent*
14. Roth Motors	1,000	1,000	Design Engineer*
Prospects			
15. ABC Transformer	—	3,000	Purchasing Agent* Design Engineer Foreman
16. Ace Motors	—	1,500	Design Engineer* Foreman Purchasing Agent
17. Air Conditioning Corp.	—	5,000	Purchasing Agent* Design Engineer
18. Amp Motors	—	3,500	Design Engineer* Foreman Purchasing AGent
19. Eastern Windings	—	1,500	Design Engineer*
20. Holmes Electric	—	3,000	Design Engineer* Purchasing Agent
21. Manual Electric	—	1,800	Purchasing Agent
22. Micro Electric	—	2,500	Design Engineer* Foreman Purchasing Agent
23. Twister Coil	—	3,000	Purchasing Agent* Design Engineer
24. U.S. Lyndon	—	15,000	Design Engineer* Foreman (1) Foreman (2) Purchasing Agent

*Decision Maker

To CENTERVILLE		
	LV.	ARR.
From North Town	6:30a —	7:30a
	8:30p —	9:30p

To EASTON		
	LV.	ARR.
From North Town	6:15a —	7:45a
	7:15a —	8:45a
	8:15a —	9:45a
	9:15a —	10:45a
	10:15a —	11:45a
	11:15a —	12:45p
	12:15p —	1:45p
	1:15p —	2:45p
	2:15p —	3:45p
	3:15p —	4:45p
	4:15p —	5:45p
	5:15p —	6:45p
	6:15p —	7:45p

To NORTH TOWN		
	LV.	ARR.
From Centerville	8:00a —	9:00a
	10:00p —	11:00p
From Easton	8:00a —	9:30a
	9:00a —	10:30a
	10:00a —	11:30a
	11:00a —	12:30p
	12:00n —	1:30p
	1:00p —	2:30p
	2:00p —	3:30p
	3:00p —	4:30p
	4:00p —	5:30p
	5:00p —	6:30p
	6:00p —	7:30p
	7:00p —	8:30p
	8:00p —	9:30p

To NORTH TOWN		
	LV.	ARR.
From Weston	7:30a —	8:30a
	8:30a —	9:30a
	9:30a —	10:30a
	10:30a —	11:30a
	11:30a —	12:30p
	12:30p —	1:30p
	1:30p —	2:30p
	2:20p —	3:30p
	3:30p —	4:30p
	4:30p —	5:30p
	5:30p —	6:30p
	6:30p —	7:30p

To WESTON		
	LV.	ARR.
From North Town	6:00a —	7:00a
	7:00a —	8:00a
	8:00a —	9:00a
	9:00a —	10:00a
	10:00a —	11:00a
	11:00a —	12:00n
	12:00n —	1:00p
	1:00p —	2:00p
	2:00p —	3:00p
	3:00p —	4:00p
	4:00p —	5:00p
	5:00p —	6:00p

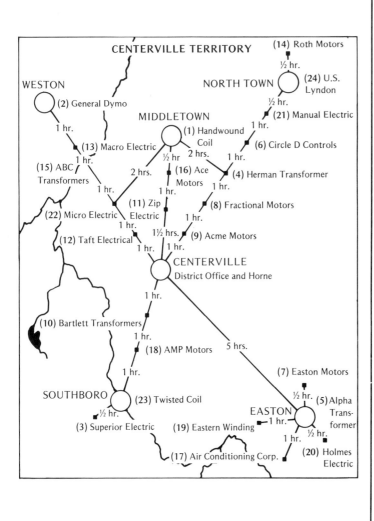

CENTERVILLE TERRITORY

Note: The information on this page completes all you will need to know to play this game. Record your solution, week by week, on the copies of the form on the opposite page. Before you do, make eight photocopies of the form—four for practice, four for record. GOOD LUCK.

Scoring Sheet

Account	(Remaining Potential)	X	(% Probability)	=	Sales Income
1. Handwound Coil	$ 3,000	X	_____ %	= $	_____
2. General Dymo	1,500	X	_____	=	_____
3. Superior Electric	4,000	X	_____	=	_____
4. Herman Transformer	1,000	X	_____	=	_____
5. Alpha Transformer	2,000	X	_____	=	_____
6. Circle D. Centrals	3,000	X	_____	=	_____
7. Easton Motors	1,500	X	_____	=	_____
8. Fractional Motors	3,000	X	_____	=	_____
9. Acme Motors	2,500	X	_____	=	_____
10. Bartlett Transformer	1,000	X	_____	=	_____
11. Zip Electric	3,000	X	_____	=	_____
12. Taft Electric	500	X	_____	=	_____
13. Marco Electric	500	X	_____	=	_____
14. Roth Motors	1,000	X	_____	=	_____
15. ABC Transformer	3,000	X	_____	=	_____
16. Ace Motors	1,500	X	_____	=	_____
17. Air Conditioning Corp.	5,000	X	_____	=	_____
18. Amp Motors	3,500	X	_____	=	_____
19. Eastern Windings	1,500	X	_____	=	_____
20. Holmes Electric	3,000	X	_____	=	_____
21. Manuel Electric	1,800	X	_____	=	_____
22. Micro Electric	2,500	X	_____	=	_____
23. Twister Coil	3,000	X	_____	=	_____
24. U.S. Lyndon	15,000	X	_____	=	_____

Total Sales Volume Generated = $ _____

DAY	MONDAY			TUESDAY			WEDNESDAY			THURSDAY			FRIDAY		
Hours	Account No.	People To See	%	Account No.	People To See	%	Account No.	People To See	%	Account No.	People To See	%	Account No.	People To See	%
8:30–9:00	24	WAIT	–												
9:00–9:30		DE	5												
10:00–10:30		DE	3												
10:30–11:00		WAIT	–												
11:30–12:00		PA	3												
12:00–12:30	LUNCH	PA	3												
12:30–1:00	//	4	–												
1:00–1:30	TEL FOR APPTS		–												
1:30–2:00		TRAVEL	–												
2:00–2:30		WAIT	–												
2:30–3:00	21	PA	5												
3:00–3:30		TRAVEL	–												
3:30–4:00		//	–												
4:00–4:30	6	PA	10												
4:30–5:00		PA	7												
Subtotals	22% FOR #14 5% FOR #21 17% FOR #6														

Summary

This chapter focuses upon the importance of territorial decisions in sales management. Initially, we discussed both the pros and the cons of using sales territories. At the outset of this chapter, we noted that, although many individuals think of territories as geographic areas, territories should be based on sales potential rather than geography. In addition to basing sales territories on geography, other possible bases include customers, products, or some combination of the three.

In examining the role of sales management where territories are concerned, we have covered two concepts that apply directly to territorial decisions. The first of these is the brand switching matrix, which offers insight into territory decisions. The second of these concerns the dyadic relationship between the buyer and the seller.

Also, covered in this chapter are specific territory considerations involved in the establishment of a new sales territory or when a territory revision is a possibility. Lastly, this chapter covered the concepts of terri-

Note: To play this game, it will be necessary for you to make *eight* copies of the Territory Planning Form below. One set of four is for practice, the other set of four for record.

TERRITORY PLANNING FORM   Week ending _____

DAY	MONDAY			TUESDAY			WEDNESDAY			THURSDAY			FRIDAY		
Hours	Account No.	People To See	%	Account No.	People To See	%	Account No.	People To See	%	Account No.	People To See	%	Account No.	People To See	%
8:30–9:00															
9:00–10:00															
10:00–10:30															
10:30–11:00															
11:00–11:30															
11:30–12:00															
12:00–1:00															
1:00–1:30															
1:30–2:00															
2:00–2:30															
2:30–3:00															
3:00–4:00															
4:00–4:30															
4:30–5:00															
Subtotals															

tory routing, scheduling, and time management considerations. Time management was covered in a unique fashion through a game developed by a sales management practitioner with a great deal of "real world" experience.

Discussion Questions

1. Present the best argument you can both for and against the use of sales territories.

2. What is a sales territory in your own words? What are the bases upon which a sales territory might be developed?

3. If you were a salesman, which of the three bases discussed in this chapter would you prefer for your own sales territory and why?

4. What is meant by a brand switching matrix?

5. How can a brand switching matrix be used to understand competitive data?

6. How is the expected value of an account computed?

7. What is the meaning of the dyadic relationship in selling and what are the implications for territorial assignments?

8. What steps should be taken in the development of a sales territory?

9. Why do new sales territories come into being in the first place?

10. What are some possible reasons affecting changes for revisions in sales territories?

11. Why place so much emphasis upon routing and scheduling where sales personnel are concerned?

Selected References

ARMSTRONG, GARY M., "The SCHEDULE Model and the Salesman's Effort Allocation, *California Management Review* (Vol. XVIII, No. 4), Summer 1976, pp. 43–50.

BLAKE, ROBERT F., and JANE S. MOUTON, *The Managerial Grid* (Houston, Texas: Gulf Publishing Company, 1964).

EVANS, FRANKLIN B., "Selling as a Dyadic Relationship—A New Approach," *American Behavioral Scientist* (Vol. 6, No. 9), May 1963, pp. 76–70.

GADEL, M. S., "Concentration by Salesmen on Congenial Prospects," *Journal of Marketing* (Vol. 28), April 1964, pp. 64–66.

LIPSTEIN, BENJAMIN, "Tests for Test Marketing," *Harvard Business Review*, March–April 1961, pp. 74–77.

LODISH, LEONARD M., "Vaguely Right Approach to Sales Force Allocations," *Harvard Business Review* (Vol. 52), January–February 1974, pp. 119–124.

STANTON, WILLIAM J., and RICHARD H. BUSKIRK, *Management of the Sales Force,* 5th ed. (Homewood, Ill.: Richard D. Irwin, 1978), Chapter 18.

STILL, RICHARD R., EDWARD W. CUNDIFF, and NORMAN A. P. GOVONI, *Sales Management: Decisions, Policies and Cases,* 3rd ed. (Englewood Cliffs, N.J.: Prenctice-Hall, Inc., 1970), Chapter 16.

Survey of Selling Costs, Sales and Marketing Management, February 27, 1978.

VIZZA, ROBERT F., and THOMAS E. CHAMBERS, *Time and Territorial Management for Salesmen* (New York: The Sales Executives Club, 1971).

CASE 9.1
Radio Station KXOV*

Radio station KXOV was first licensed by the FCC[1] in 1951 as a low-range AM station in Denver, Colorado. At this time, the station operated with a small staff during daylight hours only, featuring Western music popular at the time and hourly news. The station was owned outright by the manager, Mr. Ed White. By working as both a disc jockey and manager, to cut costs and make a small profit, Mr. White hired salesmen to "sell time" on a straight commission basis. Sales personnel were given "quarters" of the city as exclusive territories (Northeast Denver, Southwest, Southeast, and Northwest).

Company Background

By late 1967, Ed White was ready to retire. Although the station had made money in 12 of the 16 years Mr. White had operated it, he felt the station would never become a significant factor in the market owing to its low power (therefore restricted receiving range) and limited (daylight hours only) hours of operation. In 1968, White was able to "unload" the station and sold out to Ernest and Julio Weintraub. The Weintraubs were brothers who had both been disc jockeys in Los Angeles.

One of the first steps taken by the Weintraubs was to change the format of the station to "country rock." Almost immediately, the stations ARB rating[2] increased from 3 per cent of the daytime Denver listeners to over 5 per cent. The Weintraubs felt their strength was "internal" station management (employee supervision, music selection, programming direction, news editing, and so on) and delegated the "external" station affairs to Mr. Barry Johnson. Mr. Johnson had worked in Denver as a salesman for a competitive station for 2 years. Prior to that time he had become acquainted with the Weintraubs while working for another station in California. Johnson had developed quite a reputation both in California and in Denver as "one hell of a time salesman" who was energetic and hard driving.

In order to hire Johnson, the Weintraubs had to give him the title "Sales Manager" and a substantial increase in salary plus an override on the sales commissions of his staff. In addition, Johnson asked for and received "full autonomy" over sales force operations. He was also given responsibility for public relations and promotional activities.

By 1978 sales revenues had increased over 200 per cent from the original level of the station when the Weintraubs had purchased it. Although

Current Situation

* Case prepared by Dan H. Robertson, Georgia State University.
[1] Federal Communications Agency—a regulatory body of the Federal Government. Current FCC license required to broadcast.
[2] ARB is a national research firm that provides ratings (market share) of radio/television stations within specific geographic markets.

Ernest Weintraub expressed concern over the "high incomes" of the sales staff and Johnson, Julio assured him he should not worry. For the 1978 year, Johnson personally had total earnings of over $80,000.00 and the lowest paid (of six) salesman earned $32,500.00. Johnson made no bones about his high income or that of "his boys" and often reminded the Weintraubs that "if you want to make a dollar you have to spend a dime." Ernest had to admit that Johnson was a super salesman/sales manager. After all, station profits had climbed too, although not as rapidly as revenues (sales revenues increase = 212%; net profits increase = 133%).

Over coffee one day, Ernest Weintraub asked Barry what his "secret" was. Johnson replied that "brilliant internal changes in format" were largely responsible. When Ernest responded that "there must be more to it than that since sales have skyrocketed too," Barry admitted that maybe "a couple of other little old factors" had a bearing on the situation. First the "technical" factors as Barry called them. The station had been able to get approval for 24-hour operation and increased wattage (resulting in a greater listenership range). Second, the "people" factors. Barry pointed out that he had "personally hired and trained" each of the six salesmen presently on the staff (all salesmen with KXOV when the station was purchased by the Weintraub's in 1968 had left or been "encouraged to move on" by Johnson) in his 10 years as sales manager. "Why Ernest," Barry said, "my Boys would walk through fire barefooted for me."

Later that same day, Ernest found out from the treasurer that another change had been made which Barry forgot to mention. In 1969, Johnson had changed the earlier arrangement of exclusive geographic sales territories. Sales personnel now called on specified accounts. Typically, a salesman might work with two to five advertising agencies and perhaps 20 separate clients. Further, the compensation for salesmen had been changed by Barry from a straight commission basis to a base salary plus bonus. The bonus was based on the total sales of the sales staff. All salesmen received the same bonus paid at the rate of 10 per cent on every dollar over last years' total sales into a bonus pool. The pool was subsequently divided equally among the six salesmen. When Ernest confronted Johnson about these changes, Barry replied that these changes "obviously were in the best interests of KXOV." Johnson went on to point out that doing away with specific geographic territories had the advantage of leaving the sales force free to work with the accounts of advertising agencies wherever they might be located. "You see Ernest," Barry pointed out, "it's really the ad agency we need to concentrate on. My changes have resulted in a real *team* effort." Johnson went on to suggest that when geographic territories were used, "the selling got to be too cutthroat in nature."

When Ernest raised a question about the small or newly started business, Barry responded, "Hey baby—nobody wins 'em all. Besides, we're making you money aren't we? Relax and let me handle the sales staff—okay?" Ernest had to admit that Barry was right, nevertheless on more than one occasion, he had seen salesmen relaxing when he felt they should be working. They seemed to be taking the attitude that someone else would carry them in sales. Ernest wondered if a switch back to the exclusive territory arrangement or some other basis might not be more appropriate than the team approach.

Case 9.2
Meridian Manufacturing Company*

Meridian Manufacturing Company was a firm specializing in maintenance and sale of road construction and heavy-duty construction equipment. Although Meridian manufactured none of the heavy equipment itself, it operated as a wholesaler for the Centipede Manufacturing Company, which did build such heavy-duty equipment. Meridian had become a distributor for Centipede shortly after World War II, and its sales had continued to grow over the years to a present volume in excess of $3 million. Meridian was the exclusive distributor for Centipede equipment in a three-state southeastern area, including the states of Georgia, Alabama, and South Carolina. Meridian was based in Atlanta, Georgia, and had service facilities located both in other parts of Georgia and in the other two states. It also maintained small amounts of inventory in terms of parts and maintenance supplies at each of the service facilities located in the three states.

Company Background

Sales had increased fairly steadily over the years as indicated in Exhibit 1. The selling function was performed by two sales personnel, Mr. Ed

EXHIBIT 1

Year	Equipment	Parts/Supplies	Total
1974	$1,500	$ 300	1,800
1975	$1,900	$ 400	2,300
1976	$1,850	$ 550	2,400
1977	$1,900	$ 850	2,750
1978	$2,000	$1,200	3,200

Fincher and Mr. Harry Briggs, who reported to a sales manager, Mr. Bob Greenberg, in the Atlanta head office. After many long years of service to the company, Harry Briggs was preparing to retire. Previously, Harry had covered the states of Georgia and Alabama, while Ed Fincher covered the state of South Carolina.

On an early January morning, Bob Greenberg was wondering about a problem that had been troubling him greatly in the past few weeks.

Current Situation

---

* Case prepared by Dan H. Robertson, Georgia State University.

He knew that Harry Briggs was retiring as of the first of March and the problem concerning him was one of how he should reorganize the sales function in the area formally covered by Harry Briggs. Greenberg had talked with several other Centipede dealers across the country, and he knew that in many instances they assigned individual sales personnel to a state area; thus, he considered several alternatives including the following:

1. Ed Fincher was a very competent sales person and he knew he could conceivably give all three states to Ed Fincher. However, this would mean a great deal of travel on Ed's part and, because he was a loyal family man, Greenberg was somewhat concerned about the amount of travel that would be involved. Also, Greenberg knew that sales had been growing and he wondered, frankly, if any one salesperson would be able to keep up with the increasing demands of sales in a three-state area.

2. Another alternative Greenberg was considering was hiring two additional salespeople for the states of Alabama and Georgia. He realized that in the short range this would mean that two thirds of the territory covered by Meridian would be in the hands of new personnel. He also realized, however, that, if he assigned the two new salespeople to a particular state, he could avoid any possible disagreements with Fincher about the fact that Fincher had only one state. In the past, Fincher had indicated his displeasure with the fact that Briggs had two states while Fincher had only one. However, inasmuch as Briggs had been with the company longer than Fincher, Greenberg was always somehow able to justify this. He considered the point about one salesperson for one state in light of the third alternative in particular.

3. The third alternative available to Greenberg was to hire a new salesperson to cover the same territory that Briggs had been covering. Not only was this an alternative for Greenberg, it was one that had been brought forcibly to his attention now for over a year by Harry Briggs. Since Briggs had anticipated his retirement, he had mentioned on more than one occasion to Greenberg the possibility of hiring Harry's nephew. His nephew would be 23 this next spring and would be graduating from a local university as a marketing major. Greenberg's first reaction to this possibility was that, although he was glad that Briggs was concerned about his successor, in no way did he feel that the nephew was qualified for the job. Briggs had responded by reminding Greenberg that his nephew had worked for Meridian during each of the last three summers and two years ago had worked with the firm in opening up a new service and parts branch in Birmingham, Alabama.

4. Another alternative available to Greenberg was the possibility of redesigning sales territories within each of the states. He had been thinking of the possibility of dividing Alabama in half, for example, with a salesperson based in Birmingham and another based in Mobile. The logic of this argument was dictated by the fact that the firm now had service and maintenance facilities in each of these two cities and that business had been increasing rapidly not only in Alabama but in the other two states as well. Were this plan to be followed, the state of Georgia would

have an additional salesperson located in Savannah, as well as one working out of the main office in Atlanta, and the state of South Carolina would have salespeople located in Greenville and Charleston. Savannah, Georgia, Charleston, South Carolina, and Greenville, South Carolina, all were points where the firm maintained service/maintenance facilities and small inventories of parts. If Greenberg were to pursue this alternative, he anticipated being able to provide sales personnel with offices at the same physical facility stocking the inventory and parts. The fifth alternative was probably the one that concerned Greenberg the most. He was not certain that divisions along state boundaries or that the division of sales territories to reflect places where service/maintenance and parts inventories were carried was the proper basis for designing sales territories.

5. The fifth alternative was to relocate Ed Fincher, moving him to Atlanta and conceivably giving him the two states covered by Briggs. This alternative would be more acceptable to Fincher's wife who was a native of Atlanta and on numerous occasions when Bob Greenberg had worked with Fincher she had indicated a desire and willingness to return to the Atlanta area at the point in time that Briggs retired. This alternative had the additional advantage of placing the firm's only experienced salesperson in the home office; thus, giving management access to Fincher.

6. The sixth alternative was to start the process with the action indicated in alternative 5; that is, to bring Fincher to the Atlanta area. But in lieu of giving him responsibility for both the states of Georgia and Alabama, Greenberg had considered the possibility of hiring a new salesperson who would cover both Alabama and South Carolina. This would mean that Fincher could take some of his sales time for administrative activity, such as training the new salesperson, and Fincher would have only responsibility for the state of Georgia. Greenberg had also been thinking about the advantages that this might provide him in terms of getting Fincher to assist in doing some of the planning work that the president of Meridian was suggesting. In particular, he felt that Fincher might be in a better position to do the sales forecasting and development of a marketing plan that really had never been done, although the president had suggested that it be followed through on numerous occasions.

As Greenberg reflected upon the company's business, he wondered which of the preceding alternatives was the most desirable. One recurrent thought that kept bothering him, however, was that perhaps the firm was "barking up the wrong tree." By this, Greenberg meant that many of the firm's sales were now made to local government bodies or through municipalities rather than state governments. In addition, independent contractors seemed to be growing in importance, by virtue of their construction-related activities. Driving home from work late that January evening, Greenberg wondered which of the six alternatives was the most desirable. He also knew that he had a very short period of time in which to make up his mind inasmuch as it was less than 60 days before Harry Briggs retired.

Student Learning Exercise / 9
Representative Rubber Company

Objectives

1. To gain experience in time management.
2. To learn how to plan a route that meets the requirements of servicing current accounts, developing prospective accounts, and minimizing travel time.

Overview

An important ability of successful sales representatives is to know how to use their time efficiently, plan their routes, service accounts, and develop prospective accounts. Conflict often arises between the sales representative and the sales manager in developing time schedules and route plans. This exercise demonstrates how such plans should be developed, and why it is necessary to coordinate such efforts between the sales manager and the sales representative.

COMPANY BACKGROUND

**Exercise:
The Representative
Rubber Case**

Representative Rubber Company is one of several rubber producing firms in the United States. It produces a full line of tires and tubes along with other rubber products, such as hot water bottles, tennis sneakers, industrial rubber products, and so on. The firm is divisionalized, and the Tire Division sells tires and tubes to several thousand independent franchised dealers, as well as through company-owned retail tire stores. The Tire Division has sales of approximately $300,000,000 in tires, tubes, and repair materials.

Approximately 300 sales representatives are employed to cover the 48 continental states. Hawaii, Alaska, Canada, and Mexico are handled by the firm's International Division. Several years before, the firm divided the sales territories of its 300 sales representatives according to the sales volume then coming from each area. That is, sales representatives were assigned to enough counties to give each of them about $1,000,000 in sales.

The Rubber Manufacturer's Association, a trade association to which nearly all tire manufacturers belong, collects annually the tire sales data of each of its members for each county in the United States. These county data are needed for each contributor and distributed to each member. Each member, then, knows his sales and the total industry sales in each county.

SALES REPRESENTATIVE'S EFFECTIVE WORKING TIME

Sales representatives are expected to work 5 days a week. Any sales meetings are held on Saturday mornings, and *need not* be worked into the travel schedule.

Approximately 45 hours, including travel time, are available to a sales representative each week. Occasionally, a sales representative is expected to work more than the average 9 hours a day, but is not expected to work more than 45 hours in a week.

All sales representatives live within the confines of their territorial assignment and are allowed to return home each night.

PROSPECTING TIME

The Company has decided that, to ensure future business, a minimum of a sales representative's time must be spent on prospecting for new dealers. This involves making calls on competitive accounts, bankers, and others who might either be prospective representative dealers or who would know of such prospects.

DEALER CALLS

Current dealers must be called upon at the rate of *2 hours per month per $50,000 of annual current business.* This time is spent counting inventory, taking orders, training retail salespeople, helping prepare advertisements, inspecting returned tires, and so on.

Data about your territory are given in Exhibits 1–4. In Exhibit 1, you will find broad county data on auto registrations, total tire sales in dollars last year, and the firm's sales in each county. Exhibit 2 breaks the county sales down into major city and township components, and shows the total number of tire dealers in each city. Exhibit 3 is a roster of active accounts and their sales for last year. Finally, Exhibit 4 is a map of the territory and a mileage chart for the towns.

Procedure

Step 1. Before class, read the Representative Rubber Company case and answer the questions on the page entitled "Criteria for Time and Route Management for Sales Representatives."

Step 2. Also, before class, complete the "Routing Form" (prepared by sales representative). Be sure to comply with the rules prescribed by the company and to develop the routing schedule over a 4-week schedule. An example of how to fill in the form is shown below the routing schedule.

Step 3. In class, the administrator will divide the class into groups of three students per group by asking class members to count off by three. Each number 1 is the territorial sales manager, each number 2 is the sales analyst, and each number 3 is the sales representative in the territory. (5 minutes)

Step 4. Each group (comprised of a sales manager, a sales analyst, and a sales representative) will meet to develop a routing schedule for the sales representative over 4 weeks that meets the rules prescribed by the firm. (20–40 minutes)

Step 5. Fill in the "Routing Form" (prepared by sales manager). All three participants will help in developing the routing schedule; however, the sales manager is in charge and will have final authority in filling out the routing form. (5 minutes)

EXHIBIT 1 **Selected Territory Data for Representative Rubber Company, pages 324–326.**

CRITERIA FOR TIME AND ROUTE MANAGEMENT FOR SALES REPRESENTATIVES

1. Assume you are a sales representative for Representative Rubber Company. Choose a home town for yourself which takes into consideration where you would like to live and which would be centrally located insofar as covering the territory. Why did you select the town you did? (Note: you should plan to stay overnight sometime during most weeks, but certainly not every night.)

I would choose to live in _____

The reason(s) for my choice is(are): _____

_____

_____

2. What *criteria* would you use in devising a scheme for dividing your prospecting time among the counties in your territory?

Criteria: 1. _____

2. _____

3. _____

4. _____

5. _____

6. _____

7. _____

8. _____

Which, in your opinion, are the *three most important criteria?* Why these?

1._____ 2. _____ 3. _____

These criteria are the most important because: _____

_____

_____

_____

_____

ROUTING FORM
(prepared by Sales Representative)

Week	Monday		Tuesday		Wednesday		Thursday		Friday	
		Hours		Hours		Hours		Hours		Hours
1	Start		Start		Start		Start		Start	
	End	——	End	——	End	——	End	——	End	——
		Hours		Hours		Hours		Hours		Hours
2	Start		Start		Start		Start		Start	
	End	——	End	——	End	——	End	——	End	——
		Hours		Hours		Hours		Hours		Hours
3	Start		Start		Start		Start		Start	
	End	——	End	——	End	——	End	——	End	——
		Hours		Hours		Hours		Hours		Hours
4	Start		Start		Start		Start		Start	
	End	——	End	——	End	——	End	——	End	——

Example:

Monday

Start — Jefferson City	Hours
Start — Jefferson City	
Jefferson City Tire	4
Prospecting	4
Travel	0
End — Jefferson City	8

Week	Monday			Tuesday		Wednesday		Thursday		Friday
		Hours			Hours		Hours		Hours	Hours
1	Start	Start	Start		Start		Start		Start	
	End	———	End		——— End		——— End		——— End	———
		Hours			Hours		Hours		Hours	Hours
2	Start		Start		Start		Start		Start	
	End	———	End		——— End		——— End		——— End	———
		Hours			Hours		Hours		Hours	Hours
3	Start		Start		Start		Start		Start	
	End	———	End		——— End		——— End		——— End	———
		Hours			Hours		Hours		Hours	Hours
4	Start		Start		Start		Start		Start	
	End	———	End		——— End		——— End		——— End	———

Example:

Monday

	Hours
Start — Jefferson City	
Jefferson City Tire	4
Prospecting	4
Travel	0
End — Jefferson City	8

County Name	County Auto Registrations	Representative's Current Sales	Total County Tire Sales Last Year
Washington	12,000	$100,000	$ 900,000
Jefferson	11,000	450,000	750,000
Filmore	10,000	250,000	1,200,000
Arthur	4,000	200,000	260,000

EXHIBIT 2   Estimated Sales by City Last Year (and Dealer Census)

EXHIBIT 2   Estimated Sales by City Last Year (and Dealer Census)

County and City	Estimated City Sales	Est. Dealers	Our Dealers
Washington			
Adamsville	450,000	5	0
Krepson	450,000	4	1
Jefferson			
Jefferson City	450,000	6	4
Wilson	150,000	3	1
Newton	75,000	2	
Ayerville	38,000	3	1
Eaton	37,000	2	1
Fillmore			
Athens	960,000	18	4
Sparta	130,000	4	2
Rhodes	110,000	2	1
Arthur			
Lincoln	260,000	2	1

Dealer Roster	Estimated Sales
Adamsville	
Krepston	
Pioneer Tire Sales	100,000
Jefferson City	
Jefferson City Tire	150,000
Main Street Tire & Appliance	100,000
Acme Supply	50,000
Jones and Luaghter, Inc.	50,000
Wilson	
American Automotive	60,000
Ayerville	
Ace Recap Company	20,000
Eaton	
Little Accessory Corporation	20,000
Athens	
Athens Supply	50,000
Holsten and Holsten	40,000
Dearborn Tire Company	25,000
North American Auto Supply	15,000
Sparta	
Greek Gifts & Automotive	60,000
Goodbody Tires	15,000
Rhodes	
Rhodes Tire & Appliance	40,000
Lincoln	
J. W. Booth & Sons	200,000

EXHIBIT 3   Record of Dealer Sales for Last Year in This Territory

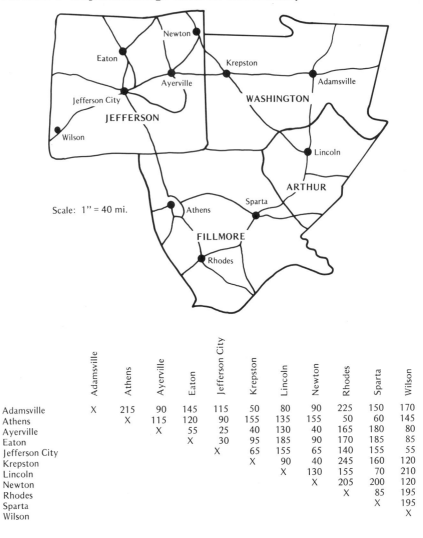

EXHIBIT 4 Map and Mileage Chart for This Territory

	Adamsville	Athens	Ayerville	Eaton	Jefferson City	Krepston	Lincoln	Newton	Rhodes	Sparta	Wilson
Adamsville	X	215	90	145	115	50	80	90	225	150	170
Athens		X	115	120	90	155	135	155	50	60	145
Ayerville			X	55	25	40	130	40	165	180	80
Eaton				X	30	95	185	90	170	185	85
Jefferson City					X	65	155	65	140	155	55
Krepston						X	90	40	245	160	120
Lincoln							X	130	155	70	210
Newton								X	205	200	120
Rhodes									X	85	195
Sparta										X	195
Wilson											X

Step 6. Complete the form "The Objectives and Criteria, Model, or Framework Used in Sales Representative Routing Procedure."

Step 7. General class discussion and instructor comments:

(a) What differences exist among groups in the decisions they reached? Why?

(b) Were differences between sales representatives' goals and company goals resolved? If so, how?

(c) From the company's point of view, what is an optimal routing solution for sales representatives? Why?

THE OBJECTIVES AND CRITERIA, MODEL, OR FRAMEWORK
USED IN SALES REPRESENTATIVE ROUTING PROCEDURE

1. The objectives we are trying to achieve for our sales representative routing schedules are:

1. _____

2. _____

3. _____

4. _____

2. The criteria, model, framework, and/or approach we are using for achieving these objectives are:

_____

_____

_____

_____

_____

_____

3. (a) The sales representative is: (circle one)
   1) very satisfied with the scheduling
   2) somewhat satisfied with the scheduling
   3) somewhat dissatisfied with the scheduling
   4) very dissatisfied with the scheduling

   (b) The reason for his or her satisfaction (or dissatisfaction) is:

   _____

   _____

   _____

4. Describe the interaction that took place in your group in developing your routing decision.

_____

_____

_____

_____

Communications to, through, and from the Sales Force

What Is Communications?

DEFINITION

EFFECTIVE communications is a key ingredient for any successful manager. This is particularly true for the sales manager. Sales managers are primarily "people" managers who must work through their salespeople to achieve the organization's goals and objectives. They must interact with both top management and with the sales force. Good communications are vital if the sales organization is to respond to a dynamic marketplace and to changing corporate directions.

In addition to the internal communications needed for effective management of the sales force, the sales organization itself is a communications arm of the firm. Thus, the sales manager must help to develop the external communications program. In this capacity the manager needs fully to understand the communications process.

Such understanding is difficult to acquire given the numerous conflicting theories of communications. Some basic points can, however, prove enlightening.[1] To communicate effectively the manager must adopt the viewpoint of the receiver of the message, for communications is perception not just information. The manager may have a full understanding of the information that is to be transmitted but still fail to communicate if the receiver perceives it differently. An old riddle illustrates the point, "Is there a sound if a tree crashes down and no one is around to hear it?" The answer is no. There are sound waves but no sound unless someone perceives it. Effective communications mean that the receiver has correctly perceived the message being transmitted.

Another important point in this regard is that to gain correct perception the message needs to be put in terms of the receiver's own experience. When talking to business people, use business metaphors. To communicate effectively the manager must use the receiver's language.

Almost all communications have both verbal and nonverbal components. The receiver experiences the total environment in which the message is being transmitted. Gestures, tone of voice, noise, and other facets of the environment may be just as important as the actual words or symbols

---

[1] For a discussion of the meaning of communication, see Peter Drucker, "What Communication Means," *Management Today*, March 1970.

used. Cultural and social relations must also be considered in the total communcations process.

One final point before moving to the development of a basic communications model. In sales management, as in most other situations, communications must produce a favorable response to be truly effective. Communications in a rational business context have a purpose and, to be effective, this purpose must be realized.

To summarize, **effective communications** can be defined as the transmission and reception of information, either verbally or nonverbally, that produces a *favorable* response. To aid in making this definition operational, a basic communications model may prove useful.

A COMMUNICATIONS MODEL

Communicating requires that the message be formulated, then translated into verbal or nonverbal symbols and these symbols be transmitted to the intended receiver of the message. The term "translation" may appear to be out of place here since we are not concerned with communicating in a different language, for example, Spanish, French, or German. The sales manager is, however, a management specialist with a jargon that may or may not be familiar to the intended receiver. Thus, the sales manager must successfully translate the message into a context that the receiver can correctly perceive.

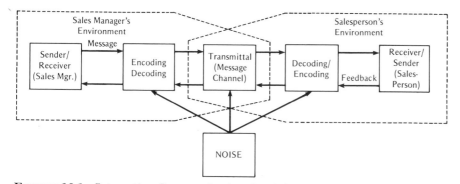

FIGURE 10.1   Interactive Communications Model

The model illustrated in Figure 10.1 represents the basic "dyadic" interactive communications model. The sales manager is the "Sender/Receiver" and the "Receiver/Sender" is the intended recipient of the message. Translation takes place in the encoding phase of the communication. The sales manager must encode a message that can be transmitted and decoded by the receiver producing a correct perception and favorable response.

A salesperson is often the intended receiver of the manager's message.

Feedback from the sales force in the communications process is a key to overcoming problems created by noise. These concepts will be discussed later in the chapter.

Encoding and Decoding. The sales manager perceives problems and solutions in the context of the surrounding sales management environment. Certain language or jargon is common to this environment but may not be understood by the salesperson. The problem in encoding is to convert the sales manager's language elements into symbols that the salesperson can decode and comprehend correctly. Thoughts formulated in the mind of one individual cannot simply be lifted and transplanted into the mind of another individual. To transmit thoughts, symbols (words, numbers, and so forth) must be selected to represent the ideas, feelings, and attitudes involved. These symbols are then presented to the receiver who must decode them and derive a meaning. To communicate effectively, symbols must be selected that will convey the desired meaning to the receiver.

To illustrate the potential problems in encoding and decoding, suppose that a sales manager is preparing an annual sales forecast. The manager plans to use a sales force composite on one approach to develop the forecast. Information is needed from the sales force, and the following memo is written:

MEMO TO: Salespeople

FROM: John Harris

SUBJECT: Annual Sales Forecast

As you know, it is time again to develop our annual sales forecast. I plan to use a sales force composite this year in addition to our standard leading indicators procedure. Would you please provide me with the needed information from your territory on an account by account basis by May 6. Thanks for your assistance.

The sales manager selected the words "sales force composite" to convey the desired meaning. If all of the salespeople are familiar with this approach, they may know what information to provide; however, if they are not, the communication will not be effective. The symbols selected may not be understood by the salespeople, thus creating a barrier to effective communications. The selection of symbols in encoding must be done with the receiver in mind. A better communication might have been:

MEMO TO: Salespeople

FROM: John Harris

SUBJECT: Annual Sales Forecast

As you know, it is time again to develop our annual sales forecast. In order to make it more accurate, I plan to use a "sales force composite" this year in addition to our standard leading indicators procedure. In order to develop the forecast, I will need your estimate of the number of units that each account in your territory will purchase from us next year. Your first hand insights about your territory will be very helpful to me in making a realistic forecast. Please contact me if you have any questions concerning this request. Thank you for your assistance.

This memo probably provides better communications because it describes the information needed in terms to which the salespeople can relate. They are more likely to decode these words and get the desired meaning from the memo. The memo also tells the salespeople that their "first hand insights" are important, thus increasing the likelihood of a "favorable response."

Feedback. Another important difference between the two memos is that the second invited feedback. If any questions occur, the salesperson will be more likely to initiate feedback to the manager. When this happens, the salesperson becomes the sender and the manager a receiver.

The role of feedback in an interactive communication system is insurance that the message has been received and correctly understood. For example, one of the salespeople upon receiving the memo may have a question: "Should I provide the estimates on a quarterly basis or for the year as a whole?" He drops by the sales manager's office to get clarification on this point. Through this feedback, the manager recognizes that the communication is not complete, so the message is further refined and is made clear. Feedback is a key element in effective communications.

Noise. Proper encoding and transmission of messages can be very difficult at times, but the additional feature of noise, or interference, makes communications an even greater challenge. Proper encoding is critical, but it cannot insure faultless communications. Noise can distort the message and can cause it to be incorrectly perceived.

Noise exerts the least impact in personal, two-party, face-to-face communications. As the number of people involved increases, and/or the medium becomes less personal, the opportunity for interference increases. When a sales manager talks to an individual salesperson, the effect of noise is minimized. The salesperson may be distracted by a telephone call, a bad cold, or other interruptions, but immediate feedback offers the opportunity for review or elaboration. The potential impact of noise is minimized by immediate feedback and the interactive nature of face-to-face communications.

The written memorandum creates additional opportunities for noise, such as misspelled words, misplaced decimal points, and time pressures on the reader. Again, if the parties involved are in close physical proximity, good feedback and interaction can remedy the problem. Noise will be discussed further in later sections of the chapter.

Transmittal: The processes of encoding and decoding occur in Figure 10.1 with the intermediate step of transmittal. Here we are concerned with the movement of an encoded message from a sender to a receiver. The subject of transmittal necessarily focuses on the various media available for communications. Although there is no such thing as a simple medium, we are usually more familiar with some than with others. Speaking, for example, is an auditory medium with which most people are quite familiar. Effective speaking, however, is not easy to achieve. The sales manager must choose media for transmitting messages that, within practical limits, enhance the total effectiveness of communications.

Media selection is a complex problem, and there is no simple solution. The discussion here is simply intended to provide a few guidelines, which, more often than not, will result in effective and efficient communications. The first principle to be followed in media selection concerns the preferences of the receiver. Second, the manager should select the simplest media available, given the communications task. Finally, media must not be called upon to do much more than carry a message. A brief discussion of each of these points follows.

The Receiver.   Each individual receiver has a particular manner, or style, in which he seeks meaning in the surrounding world. This behavioral feature is called cognitive style. Regardless of the meaning of a message, the receiver's cognitive style affects the relative effectiveness of various media. Five obvious components of cognitive style are the senses through which we receive stimuli. A written message is visual; a spoken message is auditory; the "feel of mink" is tactile, and so on. Messages can range from a presentation of a real object to a set of words and/or numbers that represent that object.

If the sales manager knows that the salespeople prefer to see and feel a real object (as opposed to reading a description), then a new product might be presented via a prototype rather than in writing, for example. A memorandum alone might prove to be relatively inefficient in this case. When the manager knows that a receiver *prefers* to hear, touch, smell, or taste, media selection can become a positive factor in his communications effort. In any event, the manager should avoid selecting media that are known to be in conflict with the receiver's cognitive style.

Keeping It Simple.   As new, more sophisticated devices for communications appear, many managers are tempted to apply the innovations in the hope of becoming more effective in reaching receivers. Examples of recent media-related innovations include multimedia presentations, highly portable film and videotape equipment, and portable computer terminals. The sales manager, as well as any other sender, should approach media selection with an eye for efficiency. The question should be, what is the simplest medium required for the desired results?

A well planned and carefully written report may be just as effective as a multimedia presentation involving audio tapes and slide projectors. Keep in mind, however, that the multimedia presentation may be the most efficient means for reaching certain people. As audio and visual components are added, costs generally increase. The more sophisticated media, such as motion picture films or videotape, incur the greatest expense and should be used only when the combination of sound, sight, and motion are all required. In light of these guidelines, it is obviously no accident that the vast majority of communications involve written or spoken words accompanied on occasion by simple visual aids.

The Limits of Media. In and of themselves, media have no magical powers over people. One of the most dramatic media tools developed in recent history is electronic data processing hardware. Laymen must be reminded constantly that computers are capable of doing only what they are made to do by their users. The same is true of other communications media. When properly used, however, a single medium can be impressively effective relative to a poor application of the same medium. If a picture is worth a thousand words to one person but fails to carry significant meaning to another, it is the receiver's cognitive style or environment, not the medium itself, that created the problem.

One must also consider the problem of noise when assessing the effectiveness of a medium. Audio channels, for example, are highly vulnerable in that receivers may be distracted and miss part of the message. In such cases, selected visual supplements, which serve as a more permanent record, may be desirable. The wise manager accepts the multitude of limitations inherent in communications and selects media that provide maximum message transmittal within desired levels of time and cost.

COMMUNICATIONS AS A SALES MANAGEMENT DECISION AREA

Effective communications in sales management involves both skill and proper decisions on the part of the manager. The discussion in this chapter deals with both the decisions that the manager must make as well as the skills necessary to carry out the decisions.

In terms of decision making, the sales manager is faced with four basic communications decisions: (1) what to communicate; (2) with whom to communicate; (3) how to encode the message; and (4) what message channel to use in transmitting the message. Certain basic communications skills (speaking, writing, good listening, and so forth) then come into play as the basic decisions are implemented. A blend of correct decisions and communications skills is needed to make the sales manager an effective and efficient communicator. In order to develop effective communications, the manager must be equipped to overcome the barriers that can block or distort the flow of messages.

Developing Effective Communications

Many factors can cause communications between human beings to break down. These problems can, however, be solved if the manager exercises proper care in making communications decisions and develops the necessary skills.

BARRIERS TO COMMUNICATIONS

What factors commonly cause communications problems? By identifying such factors, the sales manager can be alert to potential barriers and creative solutions:[2]

1. *Differences in perception.*   If the manager and the intended receiver do not share a common understanding of the symbols selected to encode the message, communications will break down. Different environments can lead to perceptual differences, which can cause the message to be lost.
2. *Lack of interest.*   If either the manager or the intended receiver are disinterested in the communication, it is likely to fail.
3. *Lack of knowledge.*   When the receiver does not have the fundamental knowledge necessary to grasp the message, a major barrier exists. For example, explaining how a chemical product works may be impossible without some basic knowledge of chemistry.
4. *Emotions.*   If the subject of the communication elicits strong emotions, the message may be overlooked. A message to a salesperson about the operation of a new rifle that is to be added to the line may not be effective if the salesperson is strongly in favor of gun control.
5. *Personality.*   Personality conflicts between the sender and receiver can make for difficult, if not impossible, communications.
6. *Appearance.*   If the intended receiver or sales manager has an appearance that distracts or annoys the other, the message may be overshadowed. For example, a salesperson may come into a sales manager's office to get information on a new prospect. If the salesperson is wearing a leisure suit but company policy calls for a coat and tie, the discussion could easily become sidetracked from its intended purpose.
7. *Prejudice.*   Preconceptions and prejudice can be very difficult barriers to effective communications. A female sales manager may have difficulty in communicating with male salespeople if they resent having a female boss.
8. *Distractions.*   This is perhaps the most common barrier to communications. In our complex and busy society, there are many things competing for a person's attention. A telephone call, a family matter, or another business problem can distract the receiver's attention and cause him/her to miss the message.
9. *Poor organization.*   If the sales manager does not organize the communication properly, the receiver may be unable to follow the intent of the message.
10. *Poor listening.*   In some cases the receiver may simply fail to listen carefully to the message, thus missing the point.

[2] See Norman B. Sigband, *Communication for Management* (Glenview, Ill.: Scott, Foresman and Company 1969); and Carl R. Rogers and F. J. Roethlisberger, "Barriers and Gateways to Communication," *Harvard Business Review,* July–August 1972, pp. 46–52.

These barriers are common problems that can interfere with almost any type of communication. Although they present a challenge to the manager, these problems can usually be solved if the communications task is approached correctly.

SOLUTIONS TO COMMUNICATIONS PROBLEMS

The key to solving communications problems is to plan the communication carefully and then to pay close attention to feedback. Feedback allows the manager to determine the reactions and level of understanding of the receiver. As difficulties arise, modifications can be made to correct any problems that arise. The manager should listen with understanding and attempt to gain insight into the receiver's perceptions by imaginative evaluation of feedback. The ability correctly to evaluate and understand feedback allows the manager to adjust and modify within the limits of the environment so the receiver ultimately receives the desired message.

The two basic solutions to most communications problems are thus:

1. To plan and execute the communication carefully.
2. Then, to pay close attention to feedback so that adjustments can be made as necessary.

Different Communications Situations Facing the Sales Manager

The sales manager is faced with many different communications situations in which the principles presented to this point can be applied. Five of the more common will be discussed in this section: person-to-person communications, sales meetings, helping salespeople with sales presentations, report writing, and feedback from the sales force.

PERSON-TO-PERSON COMMUNICATIONS

Effective person-to-person oral communications requires a certain background along with good delivery. The background for good oral communications should include knowledge, preparation, good organization, and honesty. The manager must know the subject to be effective. The message must have some significant point or points, and the manager must have the necessary facts and figures for backup. Knowing the audience can also be a key to good oral communications. In addition, the manager should be knowledgeable about opposing points of view so that responses to feedback can be direct and effective.

The manager needs to be prepared for the communications in several different ways. The major purpose of the message should be clear as well as an outline of the points to be covered. If supporting materials are to be used, these should be well thought out and integrated into the verbal presentation.

Organization is another key to effective oral communications. The discussion should be logical, concise, and clear. In a busy and complex business environment, time is at a premium. To be effective, the manager cannot afford to ramble.

A final element of background is honesty. Oral communications can be very revealing of the speaker's true nature and intent. The perceptive listener can usually tell when the speaker is being less than honest. In order to maintain goodwill, the sales manager should approach communications in an open and honest fashion.

Given the background of knowledge, preparation, organization, and honesty, the manager can then turn to the actual delivery of the message. Good delivery of oral communications focuses on the voice. Words are the symbols that carry meaning to the listener, so they should be carefully selected and properly enunciated. Eye contact is also important in securing attention of the listener and in encouraging feedback. One facet in the delivery of oral communications that is easily overlooked is gestures and posture. Body language can be a very powerful device for improving or destroying effective oral communications.[3] Certain positions and/or gestures can have significant meaning for the listener. For example, standing while talking to another person who is seated often cuts off feedback and encourages a monolog. Reading the listener's body language is also an important avenue of feedback for the careful observer.

SALES MEETINGS

Sales meetings can be very effective communications situations for the sales manager because they give an opportunity to talk to the sales force, to listen to them, and to have an open exchange of ideas. The main ingredients for effectively communicating through sales meetings are planning, site selection, staging, participation, and follow-up.[4]

Planning.   In planning the sales meeting, the manager needs to establish the purpose or purposes of the meeting and develop a detailed agenda to accomplish the goal. A sales meeting ususally has one or more of four basic purposes: informational, problem solving, training, or motivational. After the purpose of the meeting has been established, a detailed agenda or outline can then be developed to guide the meeting toward the desired result. The agenda (see Figure 10.2) when finalized should indicate the date of the meeting, location, major topic for discussion, specific items

[3] For more on this topic as it relates to sales and sales management, see SM Interviews, Julius Fast, "How Well Do You Read Body Language?" *Sales Management*, December 15, 1970, pp. 27–29.

[4] "Sales Meetings As a Communication Medium," *Sales and Marketing Management*, November 8, 1976, p. 53.

Date: November 23, 19 ___

To: Sam Adams, Art Baker, Sue Lamong, Jeff Hard, Dean Gates,
          June Still, Rick Lowe, Fred Cox

From: Joe Rowley

Subject: Sales Meeting, December 12, 19 ___
          1–4 p.m., Lounge #2

Topic for Discussion: New Product Introduction for Next Year

Specific Items for Discussion:

      1. Presentation of New Product (Uses and Technical Information)
      2. Advantages Relative to Competition
      3. Pricing
      4. Target Accounts and Sales Forecast
      5. Alternative Sales Approaches
      6. Advertising Support

FIGURE 10.2   Sample Sales Meeting Agenda

for discussion along with their sequence, and who should attend. This information should be distributed prior to the planned meeting.

Site Selection.   A site for the meeting should be selected that is consistent with the purpose. Informational meetings may be held in different locations than those intended for motivation. Cost may also become a key consideration in selecting between alternative sites.

Staging.   Proper staging helps to insure that the careful planning and site selection are not wasted. Poor staging can cause a breakdown in communications even when the meeting has been well planned. A well-run program increases the chances of getting the message through.

Some guidelines for improved staging include:

1. Get the sessions started on time; don't wait for late comers. This establishes a desirable professional tone in the meeting.
2. Keep the opening statements to a minimum. Get to the meat of the sessions as quickly as possible.
3. Keep the discussion moving, on the subject, and under control.
4. Don't let splinter groups develop. Keep the entire group together in the discussion.
5. Summarize frequently to clarify conclusions, assignments, and future actions.
6. Finally, get all the people involved in the meeting. Don't let individuals become problems and damage the meeting. Table 10.1 illustrates some of the problem people at meetings and suggests ways the manager may be able to deal with them.

Participation.   Good staging can help to insure participation, which is another key ingredient for successful meetings. In addition, the manager should attempt to accentuate the positive. Don't make negative statements unless absolutely necessary. The manager should also take care not to monopolize the meetings. Finally, avoid losing your temper; look at both sides of any disagreement that develops. Try to get disagreeing

TABLE 10.1 Problem People at Meetings

Person	How They Act	Possible Solution
Rambler	Gets off the subject.	Refocus attention by restating the relevant points.
Obstinate	Sees it one way and won't budge.	Point out that time is short and ask him to discuss it with you later.
Griper	Always has a complaint or pet peeve.	Indicate that the policy can't be changed here and offer to discuss it later in private.
Inarticulate	Can't get thoughts into words.	Say, "Let me repeat that," and then put the thoughts in better language.
Wrong	Makes comments that are incorrect.	Say, "I can see your point, but can we reconcile that with (state the true situation)."
Talkative	Well informed and anxious to show it.	Slow him down with some difficult questions or say, "That's an interesting point; let's see what the group thinks of it."
Argumentative	Combative personality.	Keep your temper in check, find a point to agree with and then shift discussion to another topic.
Helpful	Trying to help but monopolizes the discussion.	Cut across him tactfully by asking questions of others.

Source: Adapted from material by R. C. Hull, Ohio Bell Telephone Company.

Date: December 13, 19 ___

To: Sam Adams, Art Baker, Sue Lamont, Jeff Hard, Dean Gates, June Still, Rick Lowe, Fred Cox

From: Joe Rowley

Subject: Minutes of Sales Meeting Held on December 12, 19 ___ at 1 p.m., Lounge #2

Summary of Discussion:

Item 1: _____

_____

Item 2: _____

_____

Item 3: _____

_____

Assignments Made:

Sam Adams: _____

_____

FIGURE 10.3   Sample Sales Meeting Minutes

members to tell exactly where they stand on the issue, why they feel as they do, and what they recommend doing. By following these suggestions, the manager can hopefully gain the desired level of participation from the group.

Follow-Up. In order to have a progressive series of fruitful sales meetings, the sales manager needs to follow up in two ways. First, any decisions made need to be implemented so that the salespeople see immediate results from the meetings. Second, the manager needs to see that ideas communicated to the sales force at the meetings are actually being put into practice. One part of the follow-up is to prepare and distribute a summary soon after the meetings. Figure 10.3 presents a format for such a summary. This provides a record of the meetings and a basis for taking any needed action.

HELPING SALESPEOPLE WITH SALES PRESENTATIONS

The sales manager is supervising and directing a sales force that is responsible for direct communications with customers and potential customers; thus, the manager may be called upon to help salespeople with designing and making sales presentations. As discussed in Chapter 2, Cash and Crissy pointed out three different ways of looking at selling that can lead to very different types of sales presentations.[5] The three underlying theories are stimulus-response; selling formula—attention, interest, desire, action (AIDA); and need satisfaction.

The stimulus-response is the simplest and has its origin in early experiments with animal behavior. The basic concept is that various stimuli can elicit a particular response. Thus the salesperson needs a repertoire of things to say and do (stimuli) in order to get the desired response (buying). This concept typically leads to a set of points that the salesperson can use to get a desirable response. The salesperson usually dominates the interaction and becomes more effective with experience as a wider range of stimuli are learned. This approach may fit some situations, when the unit sales price is low and little time can be devoted to each interaction.

The selling formula assumes that the buying process is similar for most people and that they must be led through a series of mental states (attention, interest, desire, and action) in order to make a sale. This typically leads to a memorized or "canned" presentation. It insures that the relevant points are covered, but it also puts the emphasis on the salesperson early in the presentation. A common need is assumed among all potential customers, and the same points are made with all of them. The salesperson dominates the discussion for the majority of the interaction. This approach may work with a very universal product used by almost everyone for the same purpose, but it runs into difficulty when needs vary or the customer wants specific questions answered. Jolson

---

[5] Harold C. Cash and W. J. E. Crissy, "Ways of Looking at Selling," *Psychology of Selling* (Flushing 58, N.Y.: Personnel Development Associates, 1958).

has pointed out that the canned sales presentation does have certain advantages, particularly with new salespeople, new products, or new firms,[6] but some degree of flexibility appears to be better with most products and services where the unit price is relatively high and/or the needs and expectations are variable between customers.

Need satisfaction is based on the notion that the customer is buying to satisfy some need and that the salesperson should facilitate this need satisfaction. This approach puts the customer first and is preferable for almost all selling above the canvassing level. Here the salesperson asks questions to identify the customer's need prior to presenting the product or service. The customer dominates the early part of the interaction.

The following concepts should be recognized when attempting to put the need-satisfaction theory into effect for planning and delivering a sales presentation:

1. Establish a friendly environment. The customer should be put at ease so that he or she will feel free to talk openly with the salesperson.
2. Identify and focus attention on the customer's need. The customer is attempting to satisfy some need in the purchase process and this should be the starting point for presenting the firm's product or service. The salesperson should never launch into a discussion of products or services without first knowing what the customer wants.
3. Talk about customer benefits, not just product features. In order to make the sale the customer's need must be met by linking product/service features to customer benefits. Rather than talking about the quality of a particular fabric, the salesperson should point out how the fabric will help the customer in filling the basic need.
4. Finally, the buying decision should be made as easy as possible. Recalling the concept of closing from Chapter 2, the salesperson works toward a close that is a natural conclusion of having met the customer's need. Making it easy to say yes may also involve the presentation of positive alternatives rather than allowing the negative to come into play. A traditional example is to ask, "would you like to pay cash or charge?" rather than asking, "well, are you completely happy with the blue suit?" which might encourage the customer to think of something negative.

By keeping these concepts in mind, the manager should be more effective in helping salespeople plan and deliver sales presentations.

REPORT WRITING

In addition to the need for effective oral communications, the sales manager is faced with many situations that require written reports. Writing good reports can be a very difficult and complex task. Gallagher

[6] Marvin A. Jolson, "The Underestimated Potential of the Canned Sales Presentation," *Journal of Marketing*, January 1975, pp. 75–78.

has summarized the futility of seeking a simplistic approach to reporting by stating:

> The search for a magic formula for preparing effective reports quickly and easily has been as endless and intensive as the search for the fountain of youth, and the results have been about the same. . . . One harmful side effect, however, is that these easy remedies encourage motion without much progress, for when the writer becomes disillusioned with one, he discards it in favor of another that is easy but equally ineffective. . . . Let's be realistic then. Preparing reports is more than applying the seat of the pants to the seat of the chair. It takes time, thought, empathy, technique, and work . . .[7]

People are often shocked to hear that they cannot take written communications for granted. Most have been well prepared to read literature or express thoughts to their own satisfaction. The objective of reporting, however, is effective and efficient communications, in which success is measured by the reader's satisfaction. This focus on the needs and style of the receiver was discussed earlier in the chapter. It serves now as the starting point for an approach to producing reports that, if properly applied, will help avoid the pitfalls described by Gallagher.

Determine the Report Parameters.   A logical first step in the reporting procedure is to determine the parameters of the report. In this step the sales manager must sit back and view the message, the audience, and the resource parameters within which a successful report must be developed.

The first parameter of any report is the message it is intended to transmit. This message should be clear in the mind of the manager before the report writing starts. The intended message establishes the scope of the report. The manager should take care to insure that seemingly unimportant elements of the message, which may prove relevant later, are not overlooked.

The second parameter is the reader. Successful reporting is oriented to the needs and style of the reader. The reader's background, interest, and experience should set the tone for the style of the report. An understanding of the reader will help the manager to place meaningful limits on the scope of the report.

Last, but not least, the resources available for producing a report should be estimated. Obviously, some steps in the procedure are not necessary when a simple written memorandum is intended. In many cases, however, a rather lengthy, well-illustrated document or presentation is called for. In these cases the amount of time and money devoted to report preparation can run into weeks and many dollars. In order to plan such a task, the researcher must establish the limits of available resources.

Plan the Report.   Given the scope of the message, the reader's needs and style, and resource constraints, the manager moves on to report

[7] W. J. Gallagher, *Report Writing for Management* (Reading, Mass.: Addison-Wesley Publishing Company, 1969), p. 13.

planning. The report plan should include a content outline (including notes on the tone of the report), notes on the media for transmittal, and a production schedule.

Among the components of report planning, the outline has probably received the greatest attention. Regardless of the medium, a written outline with distinctive categories and a hierarchy of subdivisions is the preferred starting place.

Depending upon the nature of the report, content areas may be isolated based upon time periods in a historical development, geographic distribution, market segment, consumer characteristics, or some other criteria. It is important to develop content areas that are related to each other in some clear fashion. These content areas subsequently serve as the body of the report.

According to Dawe:

The finished outline will show three things: (1) the coverage, (2) the sequence, and (3) the relative importance of the parts. In the final draft, page numbers will be added so that the outline becomes the Table of Contents.[8]

The coverage and sequence are traditionally illustrated in the outline with the following major headings:

I. The Letter of Transmittal
II. The Title Page
III. Table of Contents
IV. The Synopsis
V. The Body of the Report (one or more content chapters or sections)
VI. The Addenda (bibliography, footnotes, appendices)

The relative importance of the parts of the outline are illustrated by the use of subdivisions and successive number and letter designations. Generally speaking, it is best to use descriptive terms in headings as opposed to generic headings. Furthermore, a minimum of two subdivisions are required to break down a section. Regardless of the style adopted, the report writer should maintain the same rules throughout the report.

Develop the Report.   The next task is to develop the report in accordance with the report plan. Development is more than the simple act of writing or producing. It implies a process of production, review, and revision that ultimately yields a finished product. The first step is preparation of a first draft, or script. Using the outline and the report parameters, the manager makes a first attempt to encode the message. If visual materials are involved, a storyboard or draft of visual aids is also produced at this point.

Visual aids (graphics) play a particularly important role in reporting. They include "tables, charts and graphs, and pictorial illustrations such

---

[8] Jessamon Dawe, *Writing Business and Economics Papers, Theses and Dissertations* (Totowa, N.J.: Littlefield, Adams & Company, 1965), p. 79.

as photographs, maps, and diagrams."[9] Graphics should be concise and dramatic. They act as focal points and convey large amounts of information. Shorter offers the following cautions in using graphics:[10]

1. Don't use so many charts that they overwhelm the rest of the report.
2. Use charts to explain or support the major points in the report.
3. Don't try to convey too much information on one chart.
4. Design the chart to focus on the meaning you are trying to convey.
5. Keep it simple.
6. Tie it in with your written presentation.

After the first draft is ready, the report should be reviewed and, if necessary, revised. Review is essentially an evaluation in which the report is tested against criteria developed earlier. Is the content complete? Are the needs and style of the reader accommodated? Can a finished version of the report be produced within resource parameters? Finally, is the report grammatically and otherwise technically sound? The review usually results in revisions that are subjected again to review. When no further revisions are necessary, a final version is produced and delivered to the intended reader.

A checklist can prove helpful in evaluating a report before it goes into final production. The following questions suggest areas that should be examined in any report:

1. *Summary*—Does the summary provide an overview of the entire report? The summary should cover all the major sections of the report rather than a few selected topics.
2. *Conclusions*—Are logical conclusions provided for the reader? Where appropriate, the writer should not hesitate to draw inferences from the material presented in the report.
3. *Recommendations*—Are recommendations clear and specific? All recommendations should flow from and be justified by the information in the body of the report.
4. *Introduction*—Does the introduction set the stage for the report? Adequate background and foundation information is needed before going into details of the discussion.
5. *Organization*—Is the body of the report well organized? The topics should flow logically and consistently from one to another.
6. *Headings*—Have you assisted your reader by using appropriate major and minor headings? Headings can help the reader follow the organization of the report and to find subject areas of interest more quickly.
7. *Visual aids*—Are visual aids used to the best advantage in the report? Visual aids can be very useful in presenting trends, comparing, and contrasting. They can present statistical material in a concise and dramatic fashion; however, care must be taken to select the most effective device.

[9] Leland Brown, *Effective Business Report Writing,* 3rd ed. (Englewood Cliffs, N.J.: Prentice-Hall, Inc., 1973), p. 121.
[10] R. L. Shorter, *Written Communication in Business,* 3rd ed. (New York: McGraw-Hill Book Company, 1971), p. 404.

8. *Writing style*—Does the report read easily? Business reports should be clear and concise, designed to be direct and easily understood.
9. *Documentation*—Are the sources of materials used in the report provided? Sources of basic statistics and ideas should be given so that the reader can judge the credibility of the information.
10. *Attractiveness*—Is the report inviting to the reader? An attractive report will generate more attention and interest than one that looks bad.

If you can answer yes to all the questions raised here, then you have probably written a very good report.

Production may simply involve the skills of a typist and the use of a copying machine. On the other hand, television production could involve casting, taping on location, and editing. Proper planning, particularly production scheduling, is essential for more sophisticated production efforts. Poor planning inevitably results in cost overruns as unanticipated problems arise. If the sales manager is to produce the report, simplicity is the rule. Elaborate media production (television, motion pictures, and other audiovisual formats) should be implemented by professionals, either within the firm or in the media industry. Production is the final step in the encoding process.

Deliver the Report.   Delivery is the equivalent of transmittal in the communications process (see Figure 10.1). Delivery begins when the message leaves the manager. In the case of a personal oral presentation, encoding ends with the selection of the words that form a message, and delivery begins when the words are actually spoken. The message is in transmittal as sound waves move from the speaker toward the listener. Delivery can be a frustrating experience, since the manager has relatively little control over the message while it is in transmittal. This problem, as mentioned earlier in the chapter, increases as communication becomes less personal. The manager's ability to alter a transmitted message is negligible. Most subsequent changes in the report will originate with a request from the reader.

If properly done, written reports can be very effective communications vehicles. By following the approach suggested here, the sales manager should be able to develop improved reports that effectively carry the intended message to the intended receiver.

FEEDBACK FROM THE SALES FORCE

As indicated throughout this discussion, feedback is a vital part of the communications process. This is the case both with individual communications and with the total ongoing interaction between the sales manager and the sales force. The sales manager needs feedback from the sales force in order to fulfill successfully the duties of the job.

One enlightening study of sales force feedback was concerned with the use of sales force feedback as a means of acquiring information about competitive activity.[11] Two firms with large national sales organizations agreed to cooperate in the study. The firms agreed to the following conditions:

1. Each firm would provide several units of a simulated "new" product that could be used at the discretion of the research team. These units had to be totally new to all of the firm's salesmen, and any identifying corporate seals or trademarks had to be removed. The latter requirement was necessary because the same products were to be placed in the field with actual customers of each firm, who, in turn, showed the "new" product to the salesman when he called, representing it as the new product development of a competitor.
2. Each firm agreed to cooperate with the research team and permit monitoring of all incoming communications from the salesmen to their sales managers for a period of three months after the salesman was initially exposed to the "new" product. . . . While the research team did not *personally* monitor all communications, the secretarial staffs of each firm were trained to achieve this objective.
3. Each firm selected had to have previously instituted into its sales training program a specific emphasis upon the value of feedback from the field sales force . . .
4. Lastly, it was necessary for each participating firm to suggest customer accounts that would, in turn, pass on the information to their salesmen. The research team stressed with the account the anonymity feature . . . plus the fact that since a university research team would be monitoring the feedback, no negative sanctions would be applied to nonreporting salesmen.[12]

The findings of the reporting are illustrated in Table 10.2, and the results of extensive debriefing interviews with salesmen from each firm are illustrated in Table 10.3.

In spite of the emphasis placed on sales force feedback by both of the participating firms, only 10.9 per cent of the salespeople in Corporation X and 16.7 per cent of the salespeople in Corporation Y actually

TABLE 10.2 Summary of Findings

	Corp. X	Corp. Y
Number of sales territories	46	24
Number of salesmen providing feedback	5	4
Percentage of total sales force reporting "new" product	10.9%	16.7%

Source: Dan H. Robertson, "Sales Force Feedback on Competitor's Activity," *Journal of Marketing*, April 1974, p. 71.

[11] Dan H. Robertson, "Sales Force Feedback on Competitor's Activity," *Journal of Marketing*, April 1974, pp. 69–71.
[12] *Ibid.*, p. 70.

TABLE 10.3 Salesmen's Reasons for Noncommunication

	Corp. X	Corp. Y
"Management doesn't use it anyway"	35%	29%
"Too busy with other activities"	28	42
"Not important enough to report"	20	8
All other reasons combined	17	21
	100%	100%

Source: Dan H. Robertson, "Sales Force Feedback on Competitor's Activity," *Journal of Marketing*, April 1974, p. 71.

provided feedback from the competitor's new product. Furthermore, management learned from the debriefing interviews that salespeople did not receive any particular motivation for reporting on this type of activity. Obviously, management found itself a long way from achieving the following goals:

The modern salesman, in other words, not only communicates the company's story to customers, but also feeds back customer reaction to the company. He is a vital link both in the communication and marketing processes.[13]

Psychological Factors.[14] To help minimize a situation like that found in the experiments, the following suggestions are offered:

1. *Stress the importance of sales force communications back to the company.* Be honest in acknowledging that executives can, and do, become isolated from what is happening in the field. This will not only underscore the need for the information, but it will go a long way toward convincing the salesman that management does, in fact, use the information it receives.
2. *Stress the need for information from the sales force repeatedly.* Telling a salesman to provide such information when he is undergoing his initial training won't get the job done. Repeating the importance of such information not only emphasizes its importance, but it is frequently needed, especially when there is a significant turnover rate in the sales force.
3. *When a salesman does provide such information, thank him for it but don't stop there.* Go "the second mile" by showing him how such information will be used. For example, if you learn from a salesman that a major competitor plans a price increase, show the salesman how your firm will use this advance knowledge to advantage.
4. *Recognize those salesmen who provide feedback in front of their peers.* Telling Jim that he has done a good job is fine, but doing so in front

[13] E. Jerome McCarthy, *Basic Marketing*, 4th ed. (Homewood, Ill.: Richard D. Irwin, Inc., 1971), p. 552 in Dan H. Robertson, *op. cit.*, p. 71.
[14] From Dan H. Robertson, *Sales Force Feedback and Your Firm—A Neglected Opportunity*, Monograph No. 6 (Princeton, N.J.: Center for Marketing Communications, 1976).

of other salesmen not only flatters Jim's ego but also encourages other salesmen to follow Jim's example.

5. *Lastly, recognize every salesman who reports field information.* This should hold true even if the same information has been received earlier from another salesman. Remember that it is better to receive information from several people than from none at all.

Establishing the Program. The following suggestions can prove helpful when starting or attempt to improve sales force feedback:

1. *Make the need for the program clear in the mind of every employee before you try to establish it.* Once others in your firm understand the need of such a program, they will be receptive to helping to get it operating smoothly.
2. *Stress the program's importance to secretaries, staff assistants, and other support personnel who have critical roles in assembling and transmitting information to management.* Neglecting to inform them of the importance of this program is one of the surest ways to guarantee its failure. Information can flow in from the field and reach a bottleneck if these personnel have not been properly informed of the program in advance.
3. *Provide a special form for use in this program.* This need not be an expensive undertaking. Many firms find that, once management decides what types of information are needed, personnel inside the firm can prepare the forms very inexpensively. Since marketing firms are drastically different in their operations, it is fruitless to try to develop an ideal form for all companies. Nevertheless, you should consider the following points in designing such a form:
   (a) Always provide a space for the reporting persons's name. You may need to get back in touch for additional information or clarification, and name identification will expedite this.
   (b) Make sure that the date on which this information was gathered is indicated. Knowing that Competitor X has made a significant price reduction is useless knowledge unless you know when the price cut occurred. Knowing the date will also permit a comparison across sales territories. You may find that certain competitive actions do not occur simultaneously in every geographic area.
   (c) Decide in advance who should receive copies. It is easier and safer to design a multiple carbon copy form than to try to prepare multiple photocopies of an original report later. Make certain that you leave one copy with the originating salesman. This is especially important for later follow-up purposes.
   (d) Related to the preceding point, clearly designate who is responsible in the firm for receiving and maintaining the information from such a system. This will serve two purposes. First, it will minimize confusion as to who should receive reports. Second, if you delegate an individual who is relatively high within your organization, you will be underscoring the importance of the feedback system.
4. *In training sessions with your field sales force emphasize the types*

of information that are most important. For example, your firm may be in an industry where price changes occur frequently and are of relatively little importance. On the other hand, yours might have a strong interest in learning about any new products being introduced by competition. By indicating the relative importance of various types of information, you will make the sales representative's reporting job easier.

Summary

Communication is a vital decision area and skill for any sales manager. The communications process involves formulating messages, encoding them into symbols that can be transmitted to the receiver, who then decodes the symbols to determine the sender's meaning. Many barriers can cause this process to break down and communications to be ineffective. Effective communications was defined in the chapter as the transmission and reception of information either verbally or nonverbally that produces a *favorable response.* The barriers to effective communications may be overcome by careful planning and by careful attention to feedback.

The sales manager is confronted with many different communications situations. Among these are person-to-person communications, sales meetings, helping the salespeople with sales presentations, report writing, and feedback from the sales force. Some basic requirements for success in each of these areas were discussed in the chapter.

Discussion Questions

1. What is communication?

2. Using the communications model presented in the chapter, discuss how problems may arise in the communications process.

3. Discuss some of the barriers to communications. Present an illustration of each and explain how the problem might be avoided or overcome.

4. What is feedback? How can it be encouraged? Why is it important for effective communications?

5. Discuss the requirements for good oral communications. Make a list of things that can lead to poor face-to-face communications.

6. Outline the procedure for planning and conducting effective sales meetings.

7. Discuss the three alternative theories of selling and the sales presentation that results from each.

8. Devise a checklist that could be used by a sales manager to evaluate the quality of a report.

9. What are some of the reasons for a lack of sales force feedback and how can these be overcome?

10. Discuss the ways that communications or a lack of communications can affect the success of other sales management tasks.

Selected References

CASH, HAROLD C., and W. J. E. CRISSY, "Ways of Looking at Selling," in William Lazer and Eugene Kelly (eds.), *Managerial Marketing: Perspectives and Viewpoints,* 2nd ed. (Homewood, Ill.: Richard D. Irwin, Inc., 1962), pp. 554–59.

HALL, EDWARD T., *The Silent Language* (Garden City, N.Y.: Doubleday & Company, Inc., 1959).

HOVLAND, CARL I., *et al., The Order of Presentation in Persuasion* (New Haven, Conn.: Yale University Press, 1957).

ROBERTSON, DAN H., "Sales Force Feedback on Competitor's Activity," *Journal of Marketing,* April 1974, pp. 69–71.

"Sales Meetings As a Communication Medium," *Sales and Marketing Management,* November 8, 1976.

WOLF, P. M., and R. R. AUMER, *Effective Communication in Business,* 6th ed. (Cincinnati, Ohio: Southwestern Publishing Company, 1974).

CASE 10.1
Safeco Electrical Company*

Company Background

Safeco Electrical Company was founded in the 1950s as a manufacturer of safety products for the construction industry. As a regional supplier to electrical contractors, public utilities, and municipalities, Safeco operated in ten midwestern states. Safeco had headquarters in Chicago and

---

* Case prepared by Thomas N. Ingram and Danny N. Bellenger, Georgia State University.

serviced their market through distribution centers in each of the ten states comprising their geographic market.

The primary products supplied by Safeco included insulated gloves, safety goggles, and protective plastic headgear used by electrical workers. Over the years, Safeco had built a solid reputation based on top quality products and excellent customer service.

Another strong point for Safeco was the quality of their ten field sales representatives. All were college graduates, with six having degrees in engineering.

Safeco had experienced a strong growth rate for 20 years and had established a regional market share second only to Eleco Supply Company, a large nationwide supplier. Attracted by the good reputation and growth pattern of Safeco, many larger companies had been interested in acquiring Safeco, but Safeco had not been interested in becoming part of a larger company.

In the mid-1970s, two developments occurred that had a profound impact upon the future of Safeco. First, the implementation of OSHA standards caused business to grow at an explosive pace. Manufacturing facilities had been increased to meet the demand for Safeco products. In the midst of the growth boom, Robert Hardin, the Founder and President of Safeco, died unexpectedly.

After Mr. Hardin's death, the stockholders and management began to look more favorably on the idea of being acquired by a larger company that could provide the capital needed for Safeco's future growth. A year later, Safeco was acquired by Walton Enterprises, a huge conglomerate. Walton Enterprises was highly diversified and had sales ranking them in the top 100 in the country.

At the time of the Safeco acquisition, Walton Enterprises was not involved in the electrical safety products business. The Walton plan was to have Safeco expand to other regions of the country after manufacturing and distribution facilities could be established. The overall strategy called for Safeco to be a national supplier within 3 years with an initial expansion to the northeast within 18 months.

Current Situation   Glenn Sanders was a Safeco sales representative in Missouri at the time of the acquisition by Walton Enterprises. Within 60 days, he had been promoted to Regional Sales Manager replacing Terry Flowers. Flowers had been named to a newly created position of Marketing Manager, where he would spend most of his time working on the marketing phase of Safeco's expansion program. In his new position, Sanders reported directly to Flowers.

During his first year as Regional Sales Manager, Sanders had recruited and trained a successful replacement for himself and led the sales force to a record year. Sanders had conducted four incentive programs for the sales representatives during the year, and each one produced excellent results.

Although the past year had been satisfying, Sanders was extremely concerned over the incentive portion of his sales plan for the coming year. The reason for his concern was the new incentive guidelines set forth by Walton management.

Safeco sales representatives were paid on a salary plus bonus arrangement, with the bonus tied directly to sales achieved over quota. The bonus paid was equal to 1 per cent of the annual salary for each percentage point over quota, with a maximum possible bonus of 25 per cent. The bonus plan was to remain the same this year.

Another part of Safeco's incentive program was a recognition of sales performance through the Winner's Circle Club. Basically, a sales representative was named a member of the Winner's Circle for each month that they achieved their sales quota. For being named a monthly member of the Winner's Circle, a sales representative received a merchandise certificate worth $25.00 in a Winner's Circle catalog of merchandise. Items in the catalog included clothing, athletic equipment, and home appliances. The certificates could be spent monthly or accumulated toward the purchase of more expensive merchandise.

Sanders had also used Winner's Club certificates as runner-up prizes in the four sales contests that were held last year. The first-place awards in the four contests last year were a video tape recorder, a trip to the Bahamas, a color TV, and an expenses-paid trip to the Super Bowl.

However, this year Walton guidelines stated that prizes could be awarded only in the form of Winner's Circle certificates. This meant no trips, no cash, no savings bonds—all of which had been used an incentives in the past years.

Further, the guidelines set a limit of $600 to be awarded to any one sales representative during the year. This included monthly Winner's Circle awards, as well as any incentive sales contests held during the year. If a sales representative made quota every month, Winner's Circle certificates worth $300 would be awarded, leaving the representative eligible only for $300 in additional awards throughout the year.

Sanders was faced with a dilemma—if he made the first prize on the sales contests as attractive as he had last year, a winner would be ineligible for any further prizes. On the other hand, if he made it possible for a sales representative to make quota every month, and be eligible for all contests, the contest prizes would seem trivial compared to last year.

To make matters worse, the Safeco representatives had all requested cash payments rather than certificates now that this was the exclusive form of incentive awards. They reasoned that they were being taxed as if the awards were cash; therefore, they preferred cash to merchandise certificates. Sanders had agreed with this point but had been unsuccessful in convincing Terry Flowers of his plan to pay incentive awards in cash. Flowers had told him, "Glenn, this is a new ball game. Walton feels that our sales representatives are well paid and that $600 in incentive awards for a 1-year period is enough."

Sanders was now preparing for the January sales meeting to be held in two weeks at a resort in Florida. He knew that incentive programs would be a hot topic at the meeting, and he wanted to preview the upcoming incentive programs with the sales force during the meeting.

As he reviewed last year's earnings, Sanders knew there was a good chance that some of the sales representatives could very possibly make less money this year than they had in the past year. Last year's earnings are shown below:

Sales Representative	Salary	Bonus	Monthly Awards	Program Awards	Total Compensation
F. Nelson	$16,000	$1,800	125	—	$17,925
J. Rhodes	15,500	1,700	150	75	17,350
B. Clayton	17,000	3,200	250	1,200	20,450
S. Manson	15,000	2,500	200	—	17,700
R. Miller	15,500	2,100	175	—	17,600
J. Todd	16,000	3,300	300	1,000	19,600
E. Stewart	16,750	2,900	250	900	19,900
T. Bowie	15,250	1,500	150	150	17,050
E. Stevens	15,500	1,100	150	100	16,850
P. Wright	16,000	1,900	175	175	18,075

Just as Sanders completed the review of last year's earnings, his secretary told him that Terry Flowers was on the phone. After a few minutes of conversation, Flowers said, "Glenn, the reason I called is that I want to review the incentive program plans with you prior to the sales meeting. I would like to have a written report of how you plan to communicate the situation to the sales representatives. Let's get together next week and review your report."

CASE 10.2
Ajax Company*

Company Background

The Ajax Co. is an established manufacturer of industrial products.

Current situation

"I've had it! I'm fed up to here, and I don't *have* to take it! I quit!"

With that, Sam stormed out of Mike Harrison's office, shot out of Ajax Company's headquarters building, and left for good.

Mike sat behind his desk, staring in disbelief at the still-ajar door. Sam had only been with the company for 2 years, but had already been

* Adapted from Robert M. Fulmer and Theodore T. Herbert, *Exploring the New Management* (New York: Macmillan Publishing Co., Inc., 1974), p. 149. Used with permission.

spotted as a real "comer" by the big brass. Not only was he a personable young man, but he was already one of the top industrial salesmen Ajax had, even though he still had a good bit to learn. Mike whistled softly to himself as he thought of the unbounded management potential that had just vanished.

Performance reviews always were hard on Mike, so he put them off as much as possible; still, as industrial sales manager he knew his salesmen expected the review. Sam had been such a hotshot that he'd felt it unnecessary to sit down together—all Sam needed was experience in the field, not talk.

The review—the first Sam had had—hadn't gone at all as it had been planned. Mike had reviewed Sam's sales record and his quota trends. No problem. But when he'd tried to be helpful by telling Sam that he should devote more of his attention to calling on and developing new or small accounts, and to put more emphasis on the higher profit product lines . . . well, that was a different story.

At first, Sam had just been a little uncomfortable; he must have known Mike was only trying to help, not criticize! But the more Mike talked, the surlier Sam got.

And, although he hadn't had the chance to praise Sam's initiative and efforts over the past 2 years, he *was* going to bring the matter up, as he was going to talk about the promotion in store for Sam next year. Mike wistfully thought that now he wouldn't get the chance.

He couldn't understand Sam's attitude—nor his behavior. *Why* had he been so upset? And what in the world had he meant where he said that *at last* he knew where he stood and that he was going where he knew what was expected of him and where he was appreciated!

Mike shook his head slowly, bewildered. He knew he needed to make some changes but what should he do?

CASE 10.3
Calico Candy Company*

The Calico Candy Company has manufactured salt water taffy for over 100 years and began a sideline of chocolate candy in 1970. Last year the company advertised heavily for the Christmas season, concentrating on a new salt water taffy Santa Claus. The campaign was such a success that the advertising budget for the Santa Claus taffy was tripled. Encouraged by the Christmas campaign results, the company allocated the other

Company Background

* Robert M. Fulmer and Theodore T. Herbert, *Exploring the New Management* (New York: Macmillan Publishing Company, Inc., 1974), pp. 95–96. Used with permission.

half of its advertising budget to this year's salt water taffy Easter Bunny campaign. Production was immediately put into full swing to meet the anticipated heavy demand.

Meanwhile, George King, a young sales representative calling on candy and drug stores, became increasingly dismayed by store managers' reports. These managers had ordered heavily from Calico but had been unable to sell the taffy; their inventories were therefore overstocked and the managers were pessimistic about selling the taffy, even on sale. The consensus seemed to be that taffy was no longer in demand and that chocolate candy was sweeping the tastebuds of the nation.

George reported this immediately to the advertising manager, who expressed polite interest. The advertising manager did mention George's findings to the production manager later that week over a cup of coffee. After which they had a good laugh at the thought of a decline in the popularity of their company's mainstay.

The Christmas campaign lost over $200,000; a staggering amount of candy was in stock, consisting of salt water taffy Santa Clauses and Easter Bunnies. Production was cut; but nonetheless much money had already been spent on the Easter Bunny campaign.

The Calico president was shocked about all the taffy stockpiled and the near-bankruptcy of the company. He was warned by the board of directors to correct the situation immediately. The Calico president had only to figure out how to do this.

Student Learning Exercise / 10
Report Writing and Planning Sales Meetings

Objective

1. To show the importance of encoding messages so they will produce a correct perception and favorable response.
2. To develop basic yet effective communication skills.

Overview

This exercise is twofold; you will write a memo to your sales force concerning a new product and then organize a sales meeting actually to introduce the product to them.

Exercise

Assume that you are the sales manager of a company that manufactures solar energy products. A new type of solar water heater has been developed and will be ready to go on the market in 6 weeks. Given the following information, write a memo to your sales force about the new heater. (Make assumptions concerning any additional details that are needed to write an effective memo.) Then develop an agenda for a sales meeting to explain the details of the product more fully.

Product Name: Sol-Ray Water Heater
Suggested retail price: $950.00
Dimensions: 36" diameter, 48" height
Color: Gray
Cost to install (approx.): $135.00
Life of product under normal usage: 8 years
Estimated annual savings over conventional heaters: $200–$500
Number of competitive products currently on market: 4
Advantages over competition: less expensive; smaller size; designed to harness more of the sun's rays through its unique patented components
Advertising planned for initial introduction: solar energy magazines; selected news magazines; selected home magazines

Evaluating and Supervising a Sales Staff

EVALUATION and subsequent supervision are vital components of the sales management process. The sales plan itself should provide guidelines for the evaluation of results and for corrective actions as they are needed. Both evaluation and supervision are actually part of a larger activity, which may be called **control.** The sales manager is responsible for controlling efforts to sell the firm's products and services. Control is aimed at assuring that the sales plan and its implementation are moving the organization toward the desired goals and objectives. Evaluation refers to the assessment of selected performance measured in relation to expected performance. How well is the organization doing in terms of attaining the desired levels of performance? Evaluation also involves finding the reasons for deviation from the expected performance and what should be done about these deviations. Supervision is a natural outgrowth of evaluation. When an employee is not meeting expectations, then the sales manager is responsible for taking corrective action. Not all corrective actions involve supervisory problems, but, given the "people orientation" in sales, this is frequently the case.

Evaluation

PRINCIPLES OF CONTROL

As noted, evaluation and supervision are part of the sales management control process. This process is illustrated in Figure 11.1. The sales manager is responsible for setting goals and objectives, allocating resources and effort, developing the sales plan, and organizing for implementation. The plan is then executed with the intention of accomplishing the organization's goals. A control system is needed to insure that the desired results are being achieved.

Such a system must first have performance standards on key performance criteria such as total sales volume. These standards are derived from the goals and objectives set for the organization and from the allocation of resources and effort. Next, actual performance is measured on

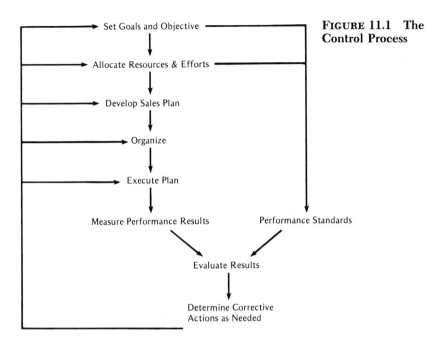

Set Goals and Objective

Allocate Resources & Efforts

Develop Sales Plan

Organize

Execute Plan

Measure Performance Results   Performance Standards

Evaluate Results

Determine Corrective
Actions as Needed

**FIGURE 11.1 The
Control Process**

each criterion and compared to the standard. If variance is discovered between the standard and the actual performance, then the performance should be evaluated to determine the cause of the discrepancy and corrective actions devised. These actions may relate to any part of the sales effort—goals, allocation of resources, the sales plan, organization, or execution of the plan.

The sales effort has certain goals and produces certain results. Various factors may intervene to prevent results from meeting the goals. When this occurs, the sales manager must recognize the fact and make needed adjustments. This is the essence of control.

One important question in establishing a control system is what variables to use for evaluation purposes? The sales effort should ultimately be geared to corporate profit objectives.[1] To produce this end, both sales volume and cost must be considered. In addition to a general analysis of sales volume and selling cost, the sales manager needs to zero in on an individual performance. By evaluating various sales volume, cost and individual performance criteria, the sales manager should be able to identify problems that may be developing and formulate corrective actions to ensure the achievement of the organization's goals.

SALES VOLUME ANALYSIS

Because almost all organizations have goals related to sales volume, various volume-related performance measures are typically evaluated for control purposes. Sales volume should be examined in terms of volume

[1] Charles W. Smith, "Gearing Salesmen's Efforts to Corporate Profit Objectives," *Harvard Business Review*, July–August 1975, pp. 8, 12, 14, 16.

by territory, product, and customers as well as total volume. There are several reasons for examining sales volume:

1. It can provide "red flags" to poor performance. If sales volume does not meet expectations, something is wrong. The difficult may be correctable. A sales territory may be too large, or a salesperson may have some personal problem. The lower than expected volume is a signal to the sales manager.

2. Sales volume analysis can also help in recognizing misdirected sales effort. A rather typical situation is that 20 per cent of the customers or perhaps products produce 80 per cent of the profits and/or sales. This is known as the **80–20 rule.** If effort and sales support have been distributed on a generally even basis, but it is discovered that most of the sales are coming from a relatively few customers, then the sales effort may be misdirected. It may be more desirable to concentrate effort on those customers, products, or territories that are producing the greatest results. This concept would apply unless the market potential is distributed in a different way than the sales results.

3. Analyzing sales volume can be helpful in identifying untapped potential for the firm. If a company has three sales territories and has its sales effort distributed equally to these territories but finds half its volume coming from one territory, then the sales effort may be misdirected. If the territories have equal potential, however, this may not be the case. By evaluating the firm's volume in relation to the market potential, an opportunity for increasing volume may be discovered. Where a larger than average gap is found between sales results and potential sales, the sales manager is alerted to a potential problem or opportunity.

Total Sales Volume. A good place to start the analysis of sales volume is with total sales. This is an indication of the aggregate performance of the organization. In doing this, the manager should look at the trend in volume compared to the sales targets. Looking at the trend is usually much more helpful than viewing any one year in isolation. It is also useful to examine the trend in sales volume as a percentage of the total industry sales. Data for such an analysis is usually relatively easy to obtain. The manager needs company sales and sales targets for the years in question along with the total industry sales in the firm's markets for those years, so that market share can be computed.

Assume that you are the sales manager for Atlantic Office Supply, a company selling office furniture and paper products to discount stores and industrial users in three sales territories. The sales trends for the last 10 years are shown in Table 11.1. The company sales trend at first looks reasonably good. The dollar increase has been around $200,000 in most years, but the percentage increase is declining from 20 per cent between 1970 and 1971 to only 8.7 per cent between 1978 and 1979. The company has typically reached its sales target or come very close, but the target has become less and less ambitious in percentage terms.

By looking at market share, it can be seen that the Atlantic Supply

TABLE 11.1 Sales Information Atlantic Office Supply

Year	Company Volume (millions)	Company Sales Target (millions)	Industry Volume (millions)	Market Share
1979	2.5	2.5	20.0	12.5
1978	2.3	2.4	18.3	12.6
1977	2.2	2.2	17.0	12.9
1976	2.0	2.1	17.5	11.4
1975	1.7	1.9	15.0	11.3
1974	1.7	1.7	13.5	13.6
1973	1.5	1.5	11.0	13.6
1972	1.3	1.3	9.0	14.4
1971	1.2	1.1	7.5	16.0
1970	1.0	.9	5.0	20.0

Company lost a big part of the increase in industry sales to competition in the early 1970s and has since stabilized in the 11–12 per cent range. This decline in market share may have resulted from internal weaknesses or from particularly aggressive competition. The sales manager should attempt to determine the cause or causes for the decline and devise ways, if possible, to shore up the company's weaknesses versus the competition. This may involve changes in any or all of the sales plans and organization.

The trend in market share, total sales, and the variance between actual and target sales can be very useful in evaluating the overall sales effort. These figures can alert the sales manager to the existence of a weakness within the sales effort. The manager must then isolate the cause of the problem and devise corrective actions.

Sales by Territory. The sales manager usually finds that an analysis of total volume is not adequate for control purposes. There is a need to isolate problems to specific territories, products, or customer groups. Doing this for sales territories involves establishing some performance standard for each territory and comparing this with actual sales. The distribution of industry sales among the various territories provides a good standard if it is available. Often it is not available, however, so the manager must turn to some index. *Sales & Marketing Management's* "Buying Power Index," is, for example, a good index for some companies. The distribution of market and sales potential among the various territories is another approach to establishing performance standards (see Chapter 5). Other companies might make use of total retail sales, automobile registrations, housing starts, or some other variable that is related to the market potential of the territory. The index is used to determine the percentage of the company's sales that might reasonably be expected to come from each territory. When the index is applied to the total sales, a volume standard is established for each territory. The percentage and dollar vari-

TABLE 11.2 Analysis of Sales by Territory Atlantic Office Supply

Territory	Index Per- centage (%)	Sales Standard ($)	Actual Sales ($)	Performance Evaluation (%)	Sales Variance ($)
1	28	700,000	900,000	129	+ 200,000
2	40	1,000,000	800,000	80	− 200,000
3	32	800,000	800,000	100	0
	100	2,500,000	2,500,000		

ance from this standard can then be evaluated to locate problem territories.

Table 11.2 illustrates this concept as applied to the three sales territories of Atlantic Office Supply. In territory 1, the company should expect 28 per cent or $700,000 of its total sales. It actually sold $900,000 in territory 1 or 129 per cent of the standard. Territory 2, on the other hand, did not live up to expectations. Sales there were $200,000 below standard. Territory 3 was on target. This evaluation identifies territory 1 as the company's strong territory with territory 2 being a "soft spot." The next step for the sales manager would be an attempt to identify the causes of variances and to devise corrective actions. Perhaps territory 2 has much stronger competition than territory 1, or perhaps the salesperson in territory 1 is for some reason not doing a satisfactory job, which could lead to supervisory actions.

Sales by Product. Another refinement of sales volume analysis that can help in pinpointing problem areas is to evaluate sales by product or product line. Again, the approach involves establishing a sales standard and comparing the acutal sales with the goal. The distribution of industry sales between the different products may be used to devise a standard or it may be necessary to turn to some index that relates to market potential.

Table 11.3 shows the standard and actual sales for Atlantic Supply's two product lines. Atlantic's performance in office furniture is shown to be much stronger than in paper products. The reason for this weakness in paper products may stem from many sources, which could be subject to corrective actions by the sales manager.

TABLE 11.3 Analysis of Sales by Product Atlantic Office Supply

Product	Index Percentage (%)	Sales Standard ($)	Actual Sales ($)	Variance ($)
Office Furniture	60	1,500,000	1,900,000	+ 400,000
Paper Products	40	1,000,000	600,000	− 400,000
		2,500,000	2,500,000	

It is often desirable to combine the product and territory analysis. The performance of various products are evaluated in each territory. This can further isolate soft spots in the company's sales that may provide opportunities for improved performance.

Sales by Customer Type. One final view of sales performance can be gained by looking at sales to key customers or customer types. The 80–20 rule often applies here more than in territories or products. Considerable misallocation of effort can result if the sales manager is not alerted to the situation.

Customers may be typed in many different ways for evaluation purposes. Classification by industry or channel of distribution are among the more common. Looking at "key" accounts as identified by size, growth potential, or some other criterion is another possibility. The sales manager should look at trends in sales for each group over a period of time both in dollar and percentage terms. Unless a careful analysis is done, the manager may simply assume that a customer group that accounts for 20 per cent of total sales accounts for 20 per cent of each product's sales. This is seldom the case. Thus, detailed evaluations of sources of sales versus the potential or expected sales from each source can prove very enlightening.

Look back to Atlantic Office Supply; if it is discovered that industrial users account for 75 per cent of the sales in the more profitable line while discount store sales are concentrated in a less profitable product group, then the sales manager may decide to shift emphasis toward industrial users. Other considerations may make another alternative more desirable, but the information on volume by customer type and product provides a basis for beginning the analysis.

Data for Sales Volume Analysis. One of the biggest problems in sales volume analysis has historically been the lack of detailed sales data. In order to do meaningful sales analysis, data is needed on sales by territory, salesperson (unless each salesperson has a separate territory), product, and customer. The data must be retained in a sufficiently disaggregated way to allow summarization in the ways most useful to the manager. Data on industry sales or market potential indexes are also needed to formulate performance standards. The use of modern computers has made the job of sales analysis much more managable.

Many companies today can provide the sales manager with up-to-the-minute sales summaries that make possible very timely evaluation and control. Pillsbury, for example, has a sales reporting system that covers over 500 salespeople selling 100 types, sizes, and flavors of products in 25 regions and 5 zones to over 40,000 retail stores plus direct accounts. The impetus for the development of this system arose out of such problems as salesperson control and the determination of which retail stores should be called on and how frequently.[2] It provides the sales manage-

---

[2] James M. Comer, "The Computer, Personal Selling, and Sales Management," *Journal of Marketing*, July 1975, p. 28.

ment at Pillsbury with the detailed performance results needed for planning and control.

The Bell System provides an interesting example of computerized sales analysis.

One of the hush-hush phases of the Bell Marketing System program is a tracking system that, for the first time, gives AT & T managers and salespeople a monthly scorecard on how performance stacks up against objectives. Called Marketing Measurement System (MMS), the program employs a massive data base with detailed profiles of business customers. Each month, operating companies transmit tapes of their customer billings to the marketing department in Morristown, N.J. Special computer techniques are used to sort the information by customer location, product line, and market segment as well as by Bell account executive (AE). AT & T, or course, has made rough stabs at measuring sales performance, but, as Sam R. Willcoxon, executive vice president of Pacific Telephone & Telegraph, points out, 'This is the first time we have been able to use Total Billed Revenue as a measure of sales performance and track it across all accounts, all markets, and by salesperson.

MMS starts with a new idea called "customer local account." Previously, operating companies identified customers by their telephone bills, but that was ineffective because a single business customer may have received several bills for different services at the same location. MMS groups all invoices by customer site. A corporate entity code covering some 3,000 corporations, ties all locations together by corporate affiliation. For example, a national account manager at AT & T's Long Lines Dept. now gets a monthly readout on all the company's revenues from Sears, Roebuck.

A special feature of MMS is that the data base includes dollar volume objectives, called 'revenue commitments,' for marketing personnel from AE up to marketing vice president. Thus, each month, as the computer matches commitment against billings, an AE and those above him in the sales hierarchy have an accurate picture of how he is doing against objectives. AEs get similar reports for individual accounts; industry managers get reports on individual AEs; and marketing managers get data broken out by industry segments.

Although MMS furnishes AT & T with its first clear picture of sales force effectiveness, James Streamo, marketing manager in charge of the data base, stresses, 'Even more importantly, it gives marketing a faster feedback on changes taking place in the market. This enables us to do a better planning job in such areas as deploying the sales force to meet emerging customer trends.'

Some operating companies are adding their own refinements. Illinois Bell, for example, has its own project, called MIDAS (Marketing Information Data Analysis System). Dave Barr, assistant vice president and director of marketing, says that MIDAS will have all accounts in it, including the smaller ones not yet a part of MMS. Also, special trend and seasonal factors have been created to make the monthly revenue commitments more consistent with the real world.[3]

Although sales volume analysis has been presented here in a rather limited fashion, there are numerous ways of recording and looking at sales data. Figure 11.2 illustrates some of the many combinations that may be used by an organization. The nature, size, and complexity of

[3] "Measuring Marketing Progress with a Computerized Monthly Scorecard," *Sales and Marketing Management,* May 1978, p. 56.

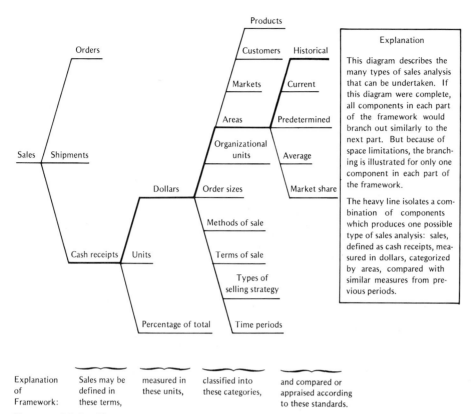

FIGURE 11.2 Alternative Views of Sales Volume Analysis [Source: Thomas R. Wotruba, *Sales Management: Planning, Accomplishment and Evaluation* (New York: Holt, Rinehart and Winston, 1971).]

the firm along with the purpose of the analysis should determine the approach used. The approach should, in turn, dictate the type of data collected for this purpose.

It should be noted at this point that the analysis of sales volume is not enough to get a complete profit picture. The manager must also analyze sales productivity and costs.

SALES PRODUCTIVITY AND COST ANALYSIS

By analyzing sales productivity and cost, the sales manager can get the other half of the total profit picture. As mentioned in Chapter 4, firms should have goals for sales productivity and cost as well as for volume. These goals can provide standards for measuring certain types of sales performance.

Most of the data for productivity and cost analysis comes from the accounting records of the firm. The accounting records are, however, typically constructed to develop financial statements (balance sheet and income statement) for external reporting purposes. The records are often too aggregated for internal planning and control use. As discussed in earlier chapters, this data must be reformulated to produce detailed cost figures for specific selling activities, territories, products, and customer groups. Cost classifications such as salaries are acceptable for the firm's income statement, but, for control purposes, the salaries need to be allocated to basic activities such as advertising, credit and collections, and selling. The costs can, in turn, be allocated to specific territories, products, and customer groups. A major decision in this process is the basis for allocating cost and which cost should be allocated. Some costs can be directly tied to one territory, product, or customer class; for example, a salesperson's salary can usually be allocated directly to a given territory. General administrative expenses are not so simple. General or nonseparable cost can be allocated equally, in accordance with volume or in proportion to the direct cost, but all of these methods are somewhat arbitrary. Another approach is to use a contribution margin, where only direct costs are allocated. This allows the manager to see the contribution to overhead and profit made by each unit of the operation.

Suppose that Atlantic Office Supply wanted to determine the contribution margin from each of three sales territories. The first step would be to compute the gross margin for each territory (sales minus cost of goods sold). Next the activity expenses would be computed and the direct cost allocated to each territory. Finally, this direct cost would be subtracted from the gross margin in each territory to determine the contribution margin. This approach is illustrated in Table 11.4. These figures show territory 2 to be somewhat weaker than the others in terms of contribution margin. This may relate in part to the product and customer mix in the territory and in part to the direct expenses. Contribution margin per dollar of sales provides a basis for comparing the relative strengths of the territories.

TABLE 11.4 Atlantic Office Supply Contribution Margin by Territory

	Territory		
	1	2	3
Net sales	$900,000	$800,000	$800,000
Less cost of goods sold	600,000	550,000	540,000
Gross margin	$300,000	$250,000	$260,000
Less direct expenses			
Direct selling	110,000	90,000	85,000
Advertising	24,000	18,000	18,000
Transportation and storage	30,000	27,000	25,000
Credit and collections	3,000	2,500	2,400
Clerical	4,000	3,000	3,000
Total direct expenses	171,000	140,500	133,400
Contribution margin	$129,000	$109,500	$126,600
Contribution margin per dollar of sales	$.1433	$.1369	$.1583

In addition to the aggregate cost and contribution margin in total, by territory, product, and customer, the sales manager should also evaluate direct selling cost. Most sales managers tend to concentrate on these costs because they have more control over selling cost than over expenses. One way to evaluate selling cost is to examine the sales budget for percentage and dollar variances. Specific types of expenses may also be compared between territories, products and/or customer groups and compared to the historical patterns. Another approach is to examine sales productivity (direct selling cost as a percentage of sales) for various subdivisions of the organization. The actual productivity should be compared to the target and to other territories, products, or customers. This can be very helpful in locating misallocated sales effort.

The analysis of selling cost and productivity should never stop with the identification of variances. The sales manager should look for the causes of the variances. If a salesperson is over budget on travel expenses owing to having worked the territory more intensively than planned and thus achieved a 20 per cent increase in sales, the expense is likely justified. The sales manager must find the cause of the variance before meaningful control is possible. By looking at cost, productivity, and volume variance in conjunction for the total operation, territories, products, and customer groups, the manager can begin to locate problem areas and identify causes. This can led to proper corrections to keep the organization on track.

Some industries are starting to take a closer look at selling cost than has been the case in the past.

Computer companies like to brag of their marketing expertise, but they turn shy when the subject of sales costs comes up. Input, a Menlo Park, Cal. research firm has taken the first small step in filling the void. Its annual survey of the $6.9 billion computer services industry reveals that in 1977 compensation of sales and marketing personnel—the biggest cost category for the industry—averaged 12.2% of revenues.

There was considerable variation among the industry's three sectors—10.1% for processing services outfits, 12.9% for professional services companies, and 18.4% for software houses (which are the most people-oriented of the three). Input president Peter Cunningham, who did the survey for the Assn. of Data Processing Service Organizations, says that after he acquires two or three years of costs data, he will build models that will match changes in marketing costs to the ups and downs of company revenues and profits.[4]

INDIVIDUAL PERFORMANCE ANALYSIS

Since the success of the sales effort of a firm depends heavily on the performance of the salespeople, individual performance needs to be evaluated along with the more general measures of corporate success. One basic performance equation for a salesperson is

[4] "In Computer Services, It's 12%," *Sales and Marketing Management,* July 1978, p. 16.

$$\text{Sales} = \text{days worked} \times \text{call rate} \times \text{batting average} \times \text{average order}$$

where

$$\text{call rate} = \frac{\text{calls}}{\text{days worked}}$$

$$\text{batting average} = \frac{\text{orders}}{\text{calls}}$$

$$\text{batting order} = \frac{\text{sales}}{\text{orders}}$$

Any weakness in the sales volume performance of a salesperson can be traced to one or more of the elements of this equation. Sales below expectations could result from too few days worked, a low call rate, a low batting average, and/or a low average order size. Any of these, however, could result from a number of different causes. Thus, an array of specific performance criteria are generally needed. These typically include both quantitative and qualitative measures. With each criterion a standard is needed to judge the actual performance. These standards are usually derived from the performance of the other salespeople or from preset quotas. The job description should also be taken into account when developing expectations relative to a salesperson's performance. An example of the application of quotas in individual performance analysis was presented in Chapter 4, thus it will not be repeated here.

An interesting view of performance analysis is provided by the "Time and Territory/Productivity Game" presented in the appendix on pages 379–382. The game is designed for self-evaluation by salespeople, but it illustrates some evaluative concepts that a sales manager may find useful.

Quantitative Evaluation. Quantitative performance criteria may include a number of objectively measurable factors related both to output or results and input or efforts. It is important to look at both input and output in evaluating a salesperson because the two do not always give the same perspective. A poor salesperson may have acceptable sales with little effort if the territory is unusually good or the competition unusually weak. On the other hand, a good salesperson who is putting forth considerable effort may have low sales owing to uncontrollable factors.

Table 11.5 provides a list of quantitative factors that may be used for evaluation purposes. To assess performance on these factors requires that they be compared to established quotas or goals, to industry averages, or to the results of other salespeople in the organization.

Qualitative Evaluation. The task of individual performance evaluation would be greatly simplified if all the evaluative factors could be easily quantified. Unfortunately, this is not the case. Qualitative factors that must be subjectively assessed by the sales manager are also important in judging the effectiveness of a salesperson. Table 11.6 shows some of the many qualitative factors that may be used for evaluative purposes.

Information for Evaluation. After a decision has been made concerning the factors to use for evaluation, the sales manager is still left with an

TABLE 11.5 Quantitative Bases for Evaluation

A. Output
   1. Sales volume
      a. In dollars and units by product, customer category, and territory as well as in total.
      b. As a percentage of quota and market potential.
   2. Gross and contribution margin by product, customer category, and territory.
   3. Orders
      a. Number
      b. Size
      c. Batting average (orders ÷ calls)
      d. Cancelled
   4. Accounts
      a. Percentage of accounts sold in the territory
      b. New accounts
      c. Accounts lost
B. Input
   1. Call rate (calls/day)
   2. Days worked
   3. Selling time versus nonselling time
   4. Direct selling expenses
      a. Total
      b. Percentage of sales volume
      c. Percentage of quota
   5. Nonselling activities such as displays set up, collections made and service calls made.

Source: Adapted from William J. Stanton and Richard H. Buskirk, *Management of the Sales Force,* 5th ed. (Homewood, Ill.: Richard D. Irwin, Inc., 1978), pp. 596–97.

often difficult problem—where to get the needed information? One source that can provide much for the information is the accounting and financial records of the firm. As mentioned earlier, with proper reformulation, various measures of sales and margin by product, territory, and customer groups can be obtained. Another important source of perform-

TABLE 11.6 Qualitative Bases for Evaluation

1. Appearance and health
2. Personality and attitude factors such as cooperativeness and aggressiveness
3. Knowledge of customers, products, competitors and the like
4. Work habits
   a. Preparation for calls
   b. Time management
   c. Quality of sales presentations

Source: Adapted from William J. Stanton and Richard H. Buskirk *Management of the Sales Force,* 5th ed. (Homewood, Ill.: Richard D. Irwin, Inc., 1978), pp. 597–98.

ance data is call reports. If the sales force is given proper incentives to provide accurate information, such reports can be very useful. Other sources include interactions with salespeople at sales meetings, travel with the salesperson in the territory, customer feedback, and the evaluation of peers by the sales staff. With careful consideration and planning, the sales manager can typically devise a procedure to produce the performance information that is essential for evaluating individuals in the sales force.

Evaluation of individual performance for salespeople provides a basis for supervision by the sales manager. When problems or opportunities are isolated in a performance review, the manager should provide the supervision needed to insure that corrective actions are taken.

Supervision

THE NEED FOR SUPERVISION

Supervision is a natural outgrowth of performance evaluation. When sales results are not up to desired levels, corrective action is needed. Since the salesperson is a major factor in this process, correction often means altering the behavior of one or more members of the sales staff.

It has been pointed out that the salesperson's performance and motivation are a function of a set of individual, interpersonal, organizational, and environmental variables.[5] The sales manager must work with the sales staff in those areas that can be controlled to insure overall success. The salesperson is constantly under pressure to succeed and is confronted with frequent rejection.[6] Coping with pressure and rejection may require supervision from the sales manager. Sales managers often find that supervision consumes a sizable portion of their time and energy. When this occurs, the problems may be traced back to poor planning, recruiting and selection, or some other part of the sales effort. Some supervision is always needed, however, even when the sales plan and organization are very carefully designed.

TECHNIQUES OF SUPERVISION

When supervision is needed, the sales manager has several different options. Since supervision is essentially a communications process, these options relate to different ways of transmitting important facts, concepts,

---

[5] Orville C. Walker, Jr., Gilbert A. Churchill, Jr., and Neil M. Forth, "Motivation and Performance in Industrial Selling: Present Knowledge and Needed Research," *Journal of Marketing Research*, May 1977, pp. 156–168.

[6] Jane Templeton, "Rejection Is Part of the Selling Job; Train Your Salesmen to Cope With It," *Sales Management*, May 1, 1972, pp. 45, 48, and 50.

ideas, or attitudes to the salesperson. One basic way of doing this is by personal contact. In a face-to-face discussion the sales manager can review performance, explore the reasons for deviations, and offer suggestions for corrective actions. A regular schedule of review periods is usually a good approach to routine supervision. The salesperson needs to know what will be evaluated and what results are accepted in each period.[7] A checklist may prove to be a good tool in these review sessions, where each performance criterion can be evaluated and shared with the salesperson. In addition to routine reviews, the sales manager may need to have special sessions when problems arise.

Other direct approaches to supervision include telephone calls, written letters or reports, and sales meetings. All of these provide for communications and, thus, the possibility of supervision. Calls and written communications often fail to give the immediate feedback and open interaction that face-to-face discussion permits. Sales meetings may provide a means for dealing with problems that the sales staff face in common, but normally not with individual situations. Calls, written communications, and sales meetings are usually supplemental in nature and cannot replace personal interaction.

Another group of supervisory techniques is the automatic devices that can cause a change in the salesperson's behavior. These are built into the system and make the salesperson aware of problems without the need for direct communication from the sales manager. Compensation, if it is geared directly to performance, can be such a device. Quotas and expense budgets can also make the salesperson aware of problems without the need for direct contact. If each salesperson is provided with detailed sales and expense reports for the territory broken down by product and customer, this can be a valuable automatic supervisory tool. The salesperson can often redirect effort into the most productive channels without the help of the sales manager if all the facts are made available.

Maryland Cup's compensation system provides an excellent example of an automatic supervisory device.

Maryland Cup's sales compensation program has the same goals as its marketing program: to sell every product possible and to increase dollar volume. Full-line salesmen, who make up over three-fourths of the 400-person sales force, earn a salary plus a bonus on their sales over quota. Moreover, the bonus paid becomes the salesmen's salary increase for the next year. The hitch is that if a salesman fails to meet his quota, his salary for the following year is cut accordingly. 'It's a funny thing,' says national sales administrator Bill Blake, 'but people will work harder to avoid a cut than to get a raise.' Naturally, the company wants its new salespeople to be the kind who work for raises, people who come from industries where, as Blake puts it, 'if you don't close, you don't eat.' Thus it takes a hard line on hiring and firing: new hires are evaluated quickly; anyone who hasn't proved himself deserving of a raise within six months is let go.[8]

[7] Robert A. Else, "Selling by Measurable Objectives," *Sales Management*, May 14, 1973, pp. 22–24.
[8] "No Paper Tigers Need Apply," *Sales and Marketing Management*, August 1978, p. 39.

One additional point on supervisory procedures should not be overlooked. People are much less likely to be productive if they are unhappy.[9] Supervision should be done in a positive rather than a negative fashion. If only the negative is emphasized, the salesperson is less likely to respond favorably to the sales manager's suggestions. Corrective actions should be put in terms of helping achieve mutual goals rather than "putting the salesperson 'right.'" By approaching potential problems in a positive way, many of them can be turned into opportunities for increased sales or increased productivity.

COMMON SUPERVISORY PROBLEMS

Some very difficult supervisory problems tend to be common in many sales staffs. One is laziness. Some people simply do not want to work hard at their job. They may make all the money they really need by working fewer hours than are desirable; they may like doing other things better; or they may have some type of psychological problem such as a depression. A salesperson who does not put in the needed effort will not get the best results for the company. In order to deal with this, the sales manager needs to locate the source of the problem. This may lead to a potential solution; however, in many cases the situation is simply beyond the power of the sales manager to correct. In these cases the salesperson may have to be replaced.

Another situation that presents similar problems is alcoholism. The sales environment often presents serious temptations for the abuse of alcohol. The salesperson is faced with the need to socialize and entertain clients and with a considerable amount of pressure to perform well in the job. Some people are physically or psychologically unable to handle this. A sales manager cannot allow the situation to persist. Customer relations are bound to suffer, and the company will be damaged. When the manager recognizes that a salesperson has this problem, firm action is needed. The salesperson should be confronted and clear guidelines of behavior set down. If this fails, the sales manager may again be faced with replacing the individual.

An additional supervisory problem that is very common is expense overruns. Again, to deal with the problem the manager must seek out its cause. It may be that the compensation system is at fault. Expense accounts are implicitly used in many organizations to provide extra compensation to the sales staff. This is generally a poor practice and can distort the planning and control value of sales budgets. A better approach is to compensate the sales force directly for performance and set expense accounts at the level needed to do a good job. Even when this is done, expense overruns may be justified if they result in better performance for the company. When overruns are found to be unjustified, the sales manager should discuss the problem with the salesperson and agree on corrective action.

[9] "A Happy Salesman Is a Productive Salesman," *Sales Management*, February 21, 1972, p. 38.

Summary

The sales manager is responsible for controlling the sales effort within the organization. This requires a mechanism for evaluating sales performance and an effort to correct situations where results are below par. In order to evaluate performance, the manager must identify the key performance criteria, set targets for the various criteria, and measure the actual results achieved. By identifying variances between desired and actual performance and the cause of the variance, the sales manager has a basis for devising corrective actions. The areas in which performance criteria should be established include sales volume, sales productivity and cost, and individual performance.

The corrective actions that result from this type of evaluation often relate to the behavior of sales personnel. This puts the sales manager into a supervisory role. Supervision, in this context, means that the manager must communicate needed adjustments to the salesperson and motivate him/her to make the required changes. This can be done in direct face-to-face discussion or at times over the phone, via letter or reports, or in sales meetings. Automatic devices such as the compensation system may also play a role in supervision. Supervision is in essence an important part of the control function of the sales manager.

Discussion Questions

1. What is control and how does it relate to sales management?

2. Discuss the various ways that sales volume can be analyzed.

3. Why is it deceptive to look only at the total volume in evaluating sales performance?

4. What are some of the alternative sources for deriving sales volume performance standards?

5. Why is it important to analyze sales productivity and cost as well as sales volume?

6. Discuss the basic performance equation for a salesperson. Will this equation give a complete picture of performance? Why or why not?

7. What are some of the key criteria for evaluating individual sales performance?

8. Why is it typically desirable to use qualitative as well as quantitative evaluative criteria?

9. What is supervision and how does it relate to evaluation?

10. Discuss some of the supervisory techniques available to the sales manager.

Selected References

CASWELL, W. CAMERON, "Marketing Effectiveness and Sales Supervision," *California Management Review,* Fall 1964, pp. 39–49.

COTHAM, JAMES C., III, and DAVID W. CRAVENS, "Improving Measurement of Salesman Performance," *Business Horizons,* June 1969, pp. 79–83.

EASTON, ALLAN, "A Forward Step in Performance Evaluation," *Journal of Marketing,* July 1966, pp. 26–32.

JACKSON, DONALD W., JR., and RAMON J. ALDAG, "Managing the Sales Force by Objectives," *MSU Business Topics,* Spring 1974, pp. 53–59.

SMITH, CHARLES W., "Gearing Salesmen's Efforts to Corporate Profit Objectives," *Harvard Business Review,* July–August 1975, pp. 8, 12, 14, 16.

APPENDIX
Time and Territory/Productivity Game

NOTE: A sales manager may find this game helpful in encouraging salespeople to evaluate
their own individual performance and in selecting evaluative criteria for assessing
sales productivity.

Work smarter, not harder. Sound familiar? Of course it does. Yet when sales management
tallies the number of calls the sales force misses, or the amount of time it loses on travel, or
the accounts it somehow ignores, management may well wonder, if anyone listening?

With every cost of selling rising, improving the productivity of salespeople has never been
so important. As a result, some old fables are being junked. One is that salespeople as a
breed "are so maverick, so much the entrepreneur" that they cannot be held to strict controls.
Another one is that too many accounts are "individualistic," that they "need customized
handling," hence they cannot be systematized. Still another legend deserving—and getting—
the scrap heap: that nobody knows the "mathematics"—such as field cost ratios—to understand, let alone build, sales force productivity. The reality is that today more companies
are mastering the techniques that ensure that their sales force win the best possible return
on their time and territories.

In this, S&MM's newest Star Salesman Game, the salesperson himself is challenged to rate
his own level of productivity. Each section of the game tests him on a different element or
technique vital to his personal productivity. (Several sections call on him to rate his management and his company's policies, and he may thereby lose points for conditions over which
he has scant control. We agree that this is unfair, but remember: the salesperson afflicted
by managerial ineptness loses in real life each day, too.)

The game is designed to be played by the salesperson himself because in any program to
build productivity, he is the star player. The questions will show him where he is succeeding in managing his time and territory for the best possible returns, and, more important,
where he is not.

How to Play the Game

1. Keep a record of your score for each category by using the total box.
2. When you have finished playing, add up your scores.
3. Then find out if you are a Star Salesman by looking up your rating in the scoring
    key which is at the back of the game.

Account Analysis
(Check only the blank that applies to you.)

I classify each of my accounts according to its present and its future potentials, using an
A, B, C or similar ranking. Yes ___   No ___

In classifying my accounts, I pay close attention to their profitabllity to my company, not
just their volume of business. Yes ___   No ___

I always keep a Call Frequency Plan—and update it regularly—to ensure that my most
important customers get my best efforts. Yes ___   No ___

I submit my Call Frequency Plan to my supervisor for his reactions. Yes ___   No ___

I know the number of calls, and their duration, each of my accounts requires for me to
get maximum results. Yes ___   No ___

I am quick to switch to telephone selling or direct mail whenever one of my accounts drops
into my least important category. Yes ___   No ___

If management decides that there are valid reasons for me to give an account to another
salesperson, I go along with the change. Yes ___   No ___

I have figured a cost ratio for doing business with each of my accounts. Yes ___   No ___

I know what it costs my company, in dollars and cents, for me to make a sales call.
Yes ___   No ___

Section Scoring: Count 1 point for each yes, 0 points for each no.

Sub totals: _____   _____

I know the number of calls I need to make in a day and how often each account should be visited for maximum productivity and profitability. Yes ___ No ___

My call frequency is at all times based on the importance of each customer—A, B, C. Thus I know each account's purchasing performance now and have estimated its future performance. Yes ___ No ___

I make every attempt to call on my accounts at the same time each week or month, especially my most important accounts. Yes ___ No ___

I never take my best accounts for granted; thus even when I intend to call on them more often, I first alert them to this development. Yes ___ No ___

I resist the temptation to boost my ego by making more calls on those customers I find to be the friendliest (even when increased business is not likely). Yes ___ No ___

I am realistic about my prospects; that is, I know when to stop trying for business I am not likely to win, no matter how tantalizing that volume of business may be. Yes ___ No ___

I avoid the urge to make as many calls as possible, regardless of results, just to appear buys. Yes ___ No ___

I recognize the folly in this statement: "The more calls I make on a customer, the more business I will do." Yes ___ No ___

Section Scoring: Count 1 point for each yes, 0 points for each no.

Sub totals: _____ _____

Your Travel Patterns
(Check only the blank that applies to you.)

Because the distribution of my accounts may change from time to time, I frequently check and revise my travel patterns. Yes ___ No ___

I alter my travel patterns, if necessary, to take advantage of changes in my product lines. Yes. ___ No ___

Each time I make an adjustment in my travel patterns, I try to avoid tampering with my A or most important accounts. Yes ___ No ___

I plan my travel at least two months in advance, using an actual map of my territory or a detailed list. Yes ___ No ___

I know almost precisely how much time I spend travelling vs. face-to-face selling. Yes ___ No ___

I do not allow my travel patterns to become a "straitjacket"; that is, I seek flexibility, so that I am prepared for the unexpected or the emergency call. Yes ___ No ___

I substitute the telephone for a personal sales call when possible. Yes ___ No ___

To save travel time and costs, when a customer has stores or outlets outside my territory, I let someone else call on those places. Yes ___ No ___

Section Scoring: Count 1 point for each yes, 0 points for each no.

Sub totals: _____ _____

The Credit Dept. Connection
(Check only the blank that applies to you.)

I encourage my company's credit manager to call on important new customers to get to know them. Yes ___ No ___

I try in every way possible to get my Credit Dept. to support sales. Yes ___ No ___

My company has flexible credit policies. Yes ___ No ___

I accept responsibility for prodding my "slow-pays". Yes ___   No ___

I avoid at all times making deliberately "foggy" statements to my customers about when they are expected to make payments. Yes ___   No ___

I tell the Credit Dept. everything I learn about my customers' payment habits—even at the risk of losing accounts. Yes ___   No ___

I tell the Credit Dept. as soon as possible about my new prospects so that it can begin its investigation early. Yes ___   No ___

Section Scoring: Count 1 Point for each yes, 0 points for each no.

Sub totals: _____ _____

Organizational Climate
(Check the Yes if you agree with the statement, the No if you don't agree.)

Productivity in this company always seems to suffer from a lack of planning and organization. Yes ___   No ___

If I make a mistake, I expect to be punished for it. Yes ___   No ___

In this company, no one trusts you to make your own decisions. Yes ___   No ___

There is a strong tendency in this company to stick to doing things "the company's way." Yes ___   No ___

Management's philosophy is that in the long run, business gets ahead faster by playing it slow and safe. Yes ___   No ___

I am convinced that management would not support me if I drastically changed my routine. Yes ___   No ___

Section Scoring: Count 1 point for each yes, 0 points for each no.

Sub totals: _____ _____

Your Top Management
(Check only the blank that applies to you.)

My top management conducts valid and periodic long-range planning. Yes ___
No ___   Seldom ___

I consider top executives at my company to be dynamic. Yes ___   No ___   So-so ___

My company's management monitors sales productivity. Yes ___   No ___   Seldom ___

Management is quick to respond to events. Yes ___   No ___   Sometimes ___

There is a strong desire by management to improve the way things are done. Yes ___
No ___   Sometimes ___

Top management carries out both territorial and customer-profitability analyses.
Yes ___   No ___   Sometimes ___

Top management knows the competition's selling costs. Yes ___   No ___   In some cases ___

Management has completed a sales audit within the past year. Yes ___   No ___   No, but one is planned ___

Management knows at all times the market demand for what it sells. Yes ___   No ___
In some cases ___

Management is careful to match incentives to company goals. Yes ___   No ___
Seldom ___

Section Scoring: Count 2 points for each yes, 0 points for each no and 1 point each for
                 seldom, sometimes, etc.

Sub totals: _____ _____

Account analysis

Call frequency

Your travel patterns

The Credit Dept. connection

Organizational climate

Your top management   _____

Your total score =   _____

Scoring Key

The maximum score is 50 points

59–50	Superior
49–45	Good, but you need to improve your performance
44–40	Average, but you must improve your performance
Below 40	You are in desperate need!

CASE 11.1
Chemco Supply, Inc.*

Company Background

Chemco Supply was founded 4 years ago in New Orleans by a group of five sales representatives and their sales manager. The six founders were unemployed at the time due to the sudden bankruptcy declaration of their employer, Gerald Ganelli and Sons. The Ganelli operation had been in existence for over 50 years, serving the institutional market as a distributor of janitorial and packaging supplies. Their primary customers had been laundries, dry cleaners, hotels, office buildings, restaurants, and athletic facilities in Louisiana.

Gerald Ganelli, Sr., had built his business from a street corner soap vendor to a company with branches in Baton Rouge, Shreveport, and Mobile, Alabama. The philosophy of the company had been to provide their customers with extraordinary service in an attempt to win customer loyalty and build market share. This had been an excellent strategy, with

* Case prepared by Thomas N. Ingram and Danny N. Bellenger, Georgia State University.

Ganelli building a dominant market share over the years. Further, the high level of service extended by Ganelli enabled the company to sell customers who were willing to pay a little more to get reliable service and therefore maximize gross margins.

Although the gross profit levels were acceptable, Ganelli & Sons did an inadequate job of controlling expenses in the mid 1970s, overextended credit to their customers, and also began to lose market share to a new competitor in the market, Asheville Chemical Company. Unable to cope with the changing conditions, Ganelli could not meet its payroll nor could the company obtain any further loans from the bank. Bankruptcy came shortly thereafter.

After the bankruptcy declaration, the elder Ganelli retired and his sons left the state to pursue careers in new fields. Of the 50 sales representatives working for Ganelli, 15 went to work with Asheville Chemical, who purchased some of the Ganelli assets. Most of the others found employment with their customers or with former suppliers to Ganelli.

The six founders of Chemco were convinced that they could be a competitive factor in the janitorial supply portion of the institutional market. John Rainey had been the sales manager of the Ganelli New Orleans branch with 16 sales representatives. At age 35, John had been building a solid career and was determined to salvage his future. It was his idea to form Chemco. With their personal savings in addition to borrowed money, the founders started Chemco with a total capital of $50,000.

By working on credit extended by suppliers and stocking only the items that would have rapid inventory turnover, Chemco experienced spectacular growth during the first 4 years, exceeding all expectations and building their market share to 40 per cent.

Current Situation

Annual sales were now at the $2.5 million level, with Chemco having branched in Baton Rouge and Jackson, Mississippi. The sales force had grown to 20. Even though John Rainey had become president of the company in the beginning, he personally directed all marketing activities until 2 years ago when he promoted two sales representatives to the positions of district sales manager. Ray Bedford supervised the 11 New Orleans area representatives and Dwight Clark supervised the nine representatives working out of Baton Rouge and Jackson.

Both Bedford and Clark had been top-notch sales representatives and had quickly produced results in the district sales management jobs. Recently Bedford and Clark had informed Mr. Rainey of problems in their respective districts that needed immediate attention. A year ago, Rainey would have probably made the decisions himself, but now he felt that his district managers must make their own decision. He had told both Bedford and Clark to keep him informed but that he expected each of them to make the final decision regarding their particular problems.

For several months, Ray Bedford had been concerned with the status of Bill Newton, his most recently hired representative. Bill was living in a small town about 90 miles from New Orleans when he was hired.

The plan was for Bill to move to New Orleans as soon as his house was sold. However, 9 months had gone by and the house was not sold and Bill was still commuting to New Orleans on Monday morning and leaving to return home on Friday evening.

When he accepted the job, Bill had said that selling his home would be "no problem." After 60 days Newton had made a request that he be allowed to remain in his hometown and commute daily to New Orleans. Newton claimed the real estate market had declined drastically and that he would have to take a loss to sell his home—a loss that he could not afford.

After a 2-month training period, Newton was assigned a New Orleans territory and had done an outstanding job. He was currently 130 per cent of quota and seemed to be getting stronger every month.

Although Newton had an excellent sales record, the fact that he had not relocated to the New Orleans area was causing significant problems. Three of the other New Orleans representatives had to move to New Orleans when hired even though all of them would have preferred to continue living where they were. Newton was not available for an emergency meeting when downtown New Orleans flooded during a weekend. As a result, other representatives were required to make emergency deliveries to his customers, causing resentment toward Newton on the part of the other representatives.

The resentment of the others was beginning to surface and one of them had told Bedford that Bill Newton had told him, "They can never make me move to New Orleans as long as I am at 130 per cent of quota." Two representatives had asked Bedford point blank why they had been required to move to New Orleans while Newton had not been required to do so.

In an attempt to clarify the situation, Bedford contacted the realtor through a friend in Newton's hometown to see if any progress had been made with regard to the sale of Newton's home. The realtor had said that she could sell the home immediately if the sale price established by Newton had been competitive with the local real estate market.

Without letting Newton know of the information he had learned indirectly from the realtor, Bedford talked with Newton and suggested that a lower price might help sell his home quickly. Newton claimed that his home had been appraised at an unacceptably low level and that his sale price represented a fair market price.

Bedford knew that Chemco would not purchase Newton's home since it was the intial move. This was a firm company policy. As he reviewed the situation, Bedford jotted down the following notes:

1. Newton has had an excellent level of performance since being assigned to the territory.
2. The morale of the other sales representatives has been hurt by the fact that Newton has not moved. They believe Newton has no intention of moving.
3. There is a question of how hard Newton is actually trying to sell his home.

4. Newton agreed to move to New Orleans as soon as his home was sold, but no specific time period was agreed on.

At this point, Bedford knew that he had to verify the true situation and remedy the problems being caused by Newton's failure to relocate to New Orleans. He considered the following alternatives:

1. If Newton has misrepresented the real estate situation, fire him.
2. Establish a deadline for moving to New Orleans. If the relocation does not take place, fire him.
3. Do nothing as long as Newton is doing an excellent sales job.

None of these alternatives particularly appealed to Bedford, but he knew that something had to be done quickly. It had been at this point that he had contacted John Rainey who had told him, "You handle it, Ray, but keep me informed."

Dwight Clark believed that competition among sales representatives was desirable and put a lot of emphasis on the "Sales Representative of the Year" competition within the Chemco organization. During the first 3 years that Chemco was in business, Carl Bridges had won the award every year. Carl was a veteran sales representative working out of the Jackson branch office. Although it was not yet publicized, Andy Hamilton of the Baton Rouge branch had won the award in the fourth year, which caused Bridges a great deal of irritation.

Bridges had loudly protested to Clark when Hamilton finished in the top spot, claiming that Hamilton had won the award unfairly. Jordeco, one of Hamilton's key accounts, had two warehouses, one in his territory and one in Bridges' territory. In the past, the Baton Rouge branch of Chemco had shipped to both Jordeco warehouses, with Hamilton receiving sales credit for shipments to the warehouse in his territory and Bridges receiving credit for products shipped to the warehouse in his territory.

Although shipments to Bridges' territory for Jordeco did continue throughout the year, the volume fell off drastically. However, total sales to Jordeco were up by 15 per cent over the previous year. Hamilton claimed that he had not influenced Jordeco's decision to bring an increased percentage of product through the warehouse in his territory. Of course, this did not satisfy Bridges, who was firmly convinced that Hamilton was giving Jordeco a "special deal" to provide them with an incentive to bring more products through the warehouse in Hamilton's territory.

To make the situation worse, Clark had heard through the grapevine that Bridges was threatening to resign on the spot if Hamilton was presented the award at the sales meeting coming up next week.

Clark wanted to preserve the integrity of the award and also wanted to get his two top sales representatives back on a friendly, cooperative basis. How to do it was the question which occupied his mind throughout the day. When he left the office late after everyone else had departed, he still had no solution to the problem.

CASE 11.2
Hanover-Bates Chemical Corporation*

***Company
Background***
James Sprague, newly appointed northeast district sales manager for the
Hanover-Bates Chemical Corporation, leaned back in his chair as the
door to his office slammed shut. "Great beginning," he thought. "Three
days in my new job and the district's most experienced sales representative is threatening to quit."

On the previous night, James Sprague, Hank Carver (the district's
most experienced sales representative), and John Follett, another senior
member of the district sales staff, had met for dinner at Jim's suggestion.
During dinner, Jim had mentioned that one of his top priorities would
be to conduct a sales and profit analysis of the district's business in order
to identify opportunities to improve the district's profit performance.
Jim had stated that he was confident that the analysis would indicate
opportunities to reallocate district sales efforts in a manner that would
increase profits. As Jim had indicated during the conversation, "My experience in analyzing district sales performance data for the national sales
manager has convinced me that any district's allocation of sales effort
to products and customer categories can be improved." Both Carver
and Follett had nodded as Jim discussed his plans.

Hank Carver was waiting when Jim arrived at the district sales office
the next morning. It soon became apparent that Carver was very upset
by what he perceived as Jim's criticism of how he and the other district
sales representatives were doing their jobs—and more particularly, how
they were allocating their time in terms of customers and products. As
he concluded his heated comments, Carver had said:

This company has made it darned clear that thirty-four years of experience don't
count for anything . . . and now someone with not much more than two years
of selling experience and two years of pushing paper for the national sales manager
at corporate headquarters tells me I'm not doing my job. . . . Maybe it's time
for me to look for a new job . . . and since Trumbull Chemical (Hanover-Bates's
major competitor) is hiring, maybe that's where I should start looking . . . and
I'm not the only one who feels this way.

As Jim reflected on the scene that had just occurred, he wondered
what he should do. It had been made clear to him when he had been
promoted to manager of the northeast sales district that one of his top
priorities should be improvement of the district's profit performance.
As the national sales manager had said, "The northeast sales district may
rank third in dollar sales, but it's our worst district in terms of profit
performance."

* Case prepared by Professor Robert E. Witt, The University of Texas, Austin. Used
with permission.

Prior to assuming his new position, Jim had assembled the data presented in Exhibits 1–6 to assist him in analyzing district sales and profits. The data had been compiled from records maintained in the national sales manager's office. Although he believed that the data would provide a sound basis for a preliminary analysis of district sales and profit perform-

Exhibit 1

HANOVER-BATES CHEMICAL CORPORATION—SUMMARY INCOME STATEMENTS: 1972-1976

	1972	1973	1974	1975	1976
Sales	$19,890,000	$21,710,000	$19,060,000	$21,980,000	$23,890,000
Production expenses	11,934,000	13,497,000	12,198,000	13,612,000	14,563,000
Gross profit	7,956,000	8,213,000	6,862,000	8,368,000	9,327,000
Administrative expenses	2,605,000	2,887,000	2,792,000	2,925,000	3,106,000
Selling expenses	2,024,000	2,241,000	2,134,000	2,274,000	2,399,000
Pretax profit	3,326,000	3,085,000	1,936,000	3,169,000	3,822,000
Taxes	1,512,000	1,388,000	790,000	1,426,000	1,718,000
Net profit	$ 1,814,000	$ 1,697,000	$ 1,146,000	$ 1,743,000	$ 2,104,000

Exhibit 2

DISTRICT SALES QUOTA AND GROSS PROFIT QUOTA PERFORMANCE–1976

District	No. of Sales Reps.	Sales Quota	Sales- Actual	Gross Profit Quota*	Gross Profit Actual
1	7	$ 3,880,000	$ 3,906,000	$1,552,000	$1,589,000
2	6	3,750,000	3,740,000	1,500,000	1,529,000
3	6	3,650,000	3,406,000	1,460,000	1,239,000
4	6	3,370,000	3,318,000	1,348,000	1,295,000
5	5	3,300,000	3,210,000	1,320,000	1,186,000
6	5	3,130,000	3,205,000	1,252,000	1,179,000
7	5	2,720,000	3,105,000	1,088,000	1,310,000
		$23,800,000	$23,890,000	$9,520,000	$9,327,000

*District gross profit quotas were developed by the National Sales Manager in consultation with the District Managers and took into account price competition in the respective districts.

Exhibit 3

DISTRICT SELLING EXPENSES–1976

District	Sales Rep. Salaries*	Sales Comm.	Sales Rep. Expenses	District Office	Dist. Mgr. Salary	Dist. Mgr. Expenses	Sales Support	Total Selling Expense
1	$177,100	$19,426	$56,280	$21,150	$33,500	$11,460	$69,500	$ 388,416
2	143,220	18,700	50.760	21,312	34,000	12,034	71,320	351,346
3	157,380	17,030	54,436	22,123	35,000**	12,382	70,010	368,529
4	150,480	16,590	49,104	22,004	32,500	11,005	66,470	348,153
5	125,950	16,050	42,720	21,115	33,000	11,123	76,600	326,558
6	124,850	16,265	41,520	20.992	33,500	11,428	67,100	315,655
7	114,850	17,530	44,700	22,485	31,500	11,643	58,750	300,258
								$2,398,915

*includes cost of fringe benefit program which was ten percent of base salary.
**salary of Jim Sprague's predecessor.

EXHIBIT 4

DISTRICT CONTRIBUTION TO CORPORATE ADMINISTRATIVE
EXPENSE AND PROFIT—1976

District	Sales	Gross Profit	Selling Expenses	Contribution to Admin. Expense & Profit
1	$ 3,906,000	$1,589,000	$ 388,416	$1,200,544
2	3,740,000	1,529,000	351,346	1,177,654
3	3,406,000	1,239,000	368,529	870,471
4	3,318,000	1,295,000	348,153	946,847
5	3,210,000	1,186,000	326,558	859,442
6	3,205,000	1,179,000	315,376	863,624
7	3,105,000	1,310,000	300,258	1,009,742
	$23,890,000	$9,327,000	$2,398,636	$6,928,324

EXHIBIT 5

NORTH EAST (3) AND NORTH CENTRAL (7)
DISTRICT SALES AND GROSS PROFIT PERFORMANCE
BY ACCOUNT CATEGORY—1976

Sales by Account Category

District	(A)	(B)	(C)	TOTAL
North East	$915,000	$1,681,000	$810,000	$3,406,000
North Central	751,000	1,702,000	652,000	3,105,000

Gross Profit by Account Category

District	(A)	(B)	(C)	TOTAL
North East	$356,000	$623,000	$260,000	$1,239,000
North Central	330,000	725,000	255,000	1,310,000

EXHIBIT 6

POTENTIAL ACCOUNTS, ACTIVE ACCOUNTS AND
ACCOUNT CALL COVERAGE: NORTH EAST AND
NORTH CENTRAL DISTRICTS—1976

District	Potential Accounts			Active Accounts			Account Coverage (Total Calls)		
	(A)	(B)	(C)	(A)	(B)	(C)	(A)	(B)	(C)
North East	90	381	635	53	210	313	1297	3051	2118
North Central	60	286	499	42	182	216	1030	2618	1299

ance, Jim had recognized that additional data would probably have to be collected when he arrived in the northeast district (District 3).

In response to the national sales manager's comment about the northeast district's poor profit performance, Jim had been particularly interested in how the district had performed on its gross profit quota. He knew that district gross profit quotas were assigned in a manner that took into account variation in price competition. Thus, he felt that poor performance in the gross profit quota area reflected misallocated sales efforts either in terms of customers or in the mix of product line items sold. To provide himself with a frame of reference, Jim had also requested data on the north-central sales district (District 7). This district was generally considered to be one of the best, if not the best, in the company. Furthermore, the north-central district sales manager, who was only three years older than Jim, was highly regarded by the national sales manager.

The Hanover-Bates Chemical Corporation was a leading producer of processing chemicals for the chemical plating industry. The company's products were produced in four plants located in Los Angeles, Houston, Chicago, and in Newark, New Jersey. The company's production process was, in essence, a mixing operation. Chemicals purchased from a broad range of suppliers were mixed according to a variety of user-based formulas. Company sales in 1976 had reached a new high of $23,890,000 up from $21,980,000 in 1975. Net pretax profit in 1976 had been $3,822,000 up from $3,169,000 in 1975. Hanover-Bates had a strong balance sheet and the company enjoyed a favorable price-earnings ratio on its stock, which was traded on the OTC market.

Although Hanover-Bates did not produce commodity-type chemicals (e.g., sulfuric acid and others), industry customers tended to perceive minimal quality differences among the products produced by Hanover-Bates and its competitors. Given the lack of variation in product quality and the industrywide practice of limited advertising expenditures, field sales efforts were of major importance in the marketing programs of all firms in the industry.

Hanover-Bates's market consisted of several thousand job-shop and captive (i.e., in-house) plating operations. Chemical platers process a wide variety of materials including industrial fasteners (e.g., screws, rivets, bolts, washers, and others), industrial components (e.g., clamps, casings, couplings, and others), and miscellaneous items (e.g., umbrella frames, eyelets, decorative items, and others). The chemical plating process involves the electrolytic application of metallic coatings such as zinc, cadmium, nickel, brass, and so forth. The degree of required plating precision varies substantially, with some work being primarily decorative, some involving relatively loose standards (e.g., .0002 zinc, which means that anything over two ten-thousandths of an inch of plate is acceptable), and some involving relatively precise standards (e.g., .0003–.0004 zinc).

Regardless of the degree of plating precision involved, quality control is of critical concern to all chemical platers. Extensive variation in the condition of materials received for plating requires a high level of service from the firms supplying chemicals to platers. This service is normally provided by the sales representatives of the firm(s) supplying the plater with processing chemicals.

Hanover-Bates and the majority of the firms in its industry produced the same line of basic processing chemicals for the chemical plating industry. The line consisted of a trisodium phosphate cleaner (SBX); anesic aldahyde brightening agents for zinc plating (ZBX), cadmium plating (CBX), and nickel plating (NBX); a protective post-plating chromate dip (CHX); and a protective burnishing compound (BUX). The company's product line is detailed in Table 1.

TABLE 1. Hanover-Bates Chemical Corporation Product-line Data

Product	Container Size	List Price	Gross Margin
SPX	400 lb. drum	$ 80	$28
ZBX	50 lb. drum	76	34
CBX	50 lb. drum	76	34
NBX	50 lb. drum	80	35
CHX	100 lb. drum	220	90
BUX	400 lb. drum	120	44

Current Situation

Hanover-Bates's sales organization consisted of forty sales representatives operating in seven sales districts. Sales representatives' salaries ranged from $14,000 to $24,000 with fringe-benefit costs amounting to an additional 10 per cent of salary. In addition to their salaries, Hanover-Bates's sales representatives received commissions of one half of 1 per cent of their dollar sales volume on all sales up to their sales quotas. The commission on sales in excess of quota was 1 per cent.

In 1974, the national sales manager of Hanover-Bates had developed a sales program based on selling the full line of Hanover-Bates products. He believed that if the sales representatives could successfully carry out his program, benefits would accrue to both Hanover-Bates and its customers: (1) sales volume per amount would be greater and selling costs as a percentage of sales would decrease; (2) a Hanover-Bates's sales representative could justify spending more time with such an account, thus becoming more knowledgeable about the account's business and becoming better able to provide technical assistance and identify selling opportunities; (3) full-line sales would strengthen Hanover-Bates's competitive position by reducing the likelihood of account loss to other plating chemical suppliers (a problem that existed in multiple-supplier situations).

The national sales manager's 1974 sales program had also included the following account call frequency guidelines: (A)-accounts (major accounts generating $12,000 or more in yearly sales)—two calls per month; (B)-accounts (medium size accounts generating $6,000–$11,999 in yearly sales)—one call per month; (C)-accounts (small accounts generating less than $6,000 yearly in sales)—one call every two months. The account call frequency guidelines were developed by the national sales manager after discussions with the district managers. The national sales manager had been concerned about the optimum allocation of sales effort to accounts and felt that the guidelines would increase the efficiency of the company's sales force, although not all of the district sales managers agreed with this conclusion.

It was common knowledge in Hanover-Bates's corporate sales office that Jim Sprague's predecessor as northeast district sales manager had not been one of the company's better district sales managers. His attitude toward the sales plans and programs of the national sales manager had been one of reluctant compliance rather than acceptance and support. When the national sales manager succeeded in persuading Jim Sprague's predecessor to take early retirement, he had been faced with the lack of an available qualified replacement.

Hank Carver, who most of the sales representatives had assumed would get the district manager job, had been passed over in part because he would be sixty-five in three years. The national sales manager had not wanted to face the same replacement problem again in three years and also had wanted someone in the position who would be more likely to be responsive to the company's sales plans and policies. The appointment of Jim Sprague as district manager had caused considerable talk, not only in the district but also at corporate headquarters. In fact, the national sales manager had warned Jim that "a lot of people are expecting you to fall on your face . . . they don't think you have the experience to handle the job, in particular, and to manage and motivate a group of sales representatives most of whom are considerably older and more experienced than you." The national sales manager had concluded by saying, "I think you can handle the job, Jim . . . I think you can manage those sales reps and improve the district's profit performance . . . and I'm depending on you to do both."

Student Learning Exercise / 11
Evaluating Salespeople

To apply the various techniques of evaluation and, based on this, to suggest any corrective supervisory action which is needed.

Objective

This exercise teaches the application of sales force evaluation techniques in a real-life situation. This is a very important situation which a sales manager must deal with quite frequently. Since the actions of the sales force play a large part in determining the amount of profits a company generates, it is vitally important for them to be evaluated and supervised on a regular basis.

Overview

In your role as sales manager, you will conduct your formal biannual evaluation of your three salespeople. After conducting your evaluation through the use of the following data, suggest any supervisory steps that you feel are necessary.

Exercise

July 1–December 31	Salesperson 1	Salesperson 2	Salesperson 3	Company Avg. from 1st 6 mos.
Territory sales potential	$1,050,000	$1,200,000	$1,800,000	$1,400,000
Sales volume ($)	192,000	189,000	180,000	187,000
Sales quota ($)	190,500	185,000	186,000	188,000
Accounts	106	112	110	108
New accounts	18	12	13	14
Lost accounts	5	2	1	2
Total expense budget	4,000	4,000	4,000	4,000
Over or (under) expense acct. budget	$ 220	$ 190	($35)	$ 68
Avg. sales calls/week	27	29	25	25
Avg. hours spent in office/week	10	11	12	10
Avg. hours spent in field/week	29	29	26	28
Total compensation	$ 19,500	$ 18,800	$ 20,500	$ 19,000

Organizing the Sales Force
for Effective Operation

PROPER organization is a vital ingredient for the effective implementation of a sales plan. Poor organization can cause potential good sales plans to fail completely. The sales manager thus needs an understanding of organizational principles in order to get the desired results for the firm. The intention of this chapter is to introduce some of the basic principles of good organization and to relate them to organizing the sales function. This should provide the prospective sales manager with a foundation for dealing with this complex decision area.

The Sales Organization and Its Purpose

The sales function occurs within the context of an organizational structure. "An organizational structure may be defined as a vertical pattern of work, people, and physical resources that contribute to the attainment of the enterprise mission."[1] "Pattern" and "structure" are key words in this definition. Regardless of its size, virtually every organization has a pattern or structure that determines which members of the group perform which specific tasks. The sales manager is responsible for developing a pattern of work, people, and resources within the enterprise that can effectively implement the sales plan to meet the goals and objectives of the enterprise.

The organizational structure brings order and structure to the enterprise, but it should never become so rigid that it actually interferes with implementing the sales plan. Both managers and employees need a degree of flexibility to function effectively. The task of organizing is, in fact, a continuous process. After a new business or division is organized, it cannot simply be left without change and expected to do the job indefinitely. The environment changes, creating a need to alter the sales organization in response to new opportunities. This decision area might actually

---

[1] J. Hodge and H. J. Johnson, *Manpower and Organizational Behavior* (New York: John Wiley & Sons, Inc., 1970), p. 158.

be better called reorganizing for effective operation since the process is continuous rather than a one-time event.

Basic Concepts of Organization

Several basic considerations in organizational structure have an impact on the effectiveness of the sales function. These considerations include: (1) delegation of responsibility, authority, and accountability; (2) fundamental organization structures; and (3) centralization and decentralization.

DELEGATION OF RESPONSIBILITY, AUTHORITY, AND ACCOUNTABILITY

An enterprise exists to accomplish one or more objectives that, ultimately, are the chief executive's responsibility. Regardless of the size or complexity of an organization, someone is ultimately responsible for performance in terms of the primary objectives. Along with this responsibility, the individual assumes a position of authority that enables her/ him to perform in the organization. The organization exists because one person is not able to perform all of the tasks required in a particular enterprise. Although the top executive retains ultimate responsibility, certain tasks must be delegated to other managers, such as sales managers, who in turn delegate tasks to various employees.

The fundamental steps in establishing a sales organization are (1) determine the tasks that must be performed to implement the sales plan (prospecting, order taking, and forecasting); (2) classify the tasks and group them into related sets (this may be done by placing tasks requiring similar skills together or by putting tasks that logically follow each other together; in a broader sense different functions, geographic areas, products, and customers must be considered in grouping sales tasks); (3) assign each set of activities to a position or positions; and finally, (4) establish the supervision and reporting relationships between positions. The completion of these steps will result in an organizational structure that can then be staffed by proper recruiting and selection.

The establishment of an organization and the subsequent delegation of tasks by the sales manager to the salesperson immediately raises the question of subordinate responsibilities. According to one popular view, three elements are derived from the delegation process: responsibility, authority, and accountability, Hodge and Johnson define these "derived ingredients" as follows:

- *Responsibility.* When personnel are assigned to work, they assume an obligation to discharge this work to the best of their ability and in accordance with the directions given them concerning it.

. . . once work is defined and assigned to an individual, an immediate result is the establishment of a unit of responsibility.

- *Authority.* Units of responsibility are the basis for the delegation of appropriate types and amounts of authority required for their discharge. Authority, then, is the right to take all actions necessary to discharge a unit of responsibility.

. . . the amount of authority a given individual holds in an organization should result from the demands of his work and his ability to accept and utilize decision making and command rights.

If organization efficiency and morale are to be optimal, responsibility and authority must be in balance; no individual should be given more authority than is necessary to discharge his responsibility, and, on the other hand, no individual should be asked to assume an obligation without receiving a commensurate amount of authority to discharge that obligation.

- *Accountability.* Accountability is the obligation of an individual to report formally to his superior on the discharge of his responsibility.

. . . authority and responsibility must be properly defined and balanced if accountability is to be a meaningfully derived ingredient in the organization structure.[2]

All three ingredients—responsibility, authority, and accountability—must exist in proper balance if a sales organization is to function effectively through the delegation process.

AT & T's recent reorganization into team marketing stresses accountability for revenue and costs (see Figure 12.1).

Team marketing under the Bell Marketing System program that went into effect at some operating companies in June 1978 had two main goals: (1) to give the

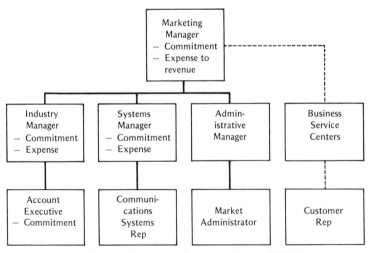

FIGURE 12.1 Team Marketing Organization at AT&T

[2] *Ibid.*, pp. 158–159.

account executive (AE) (salesperson) the technical and administrative support he needs to become a communications problem-solver and (2) to designate responsibility for attaining revenue objectives and controlling costs.

The AE develops a revenue commitment for each account, and the industry manager (sales manager) he reports to is responsible for the aggregate AEs under him, their revenue commitments, and the costs budgeted to fulfill those commitments. The systems manager, in charge of delivering technical support, has similar revenue and expense responsibilities. The AE's account plan includes the revenues that market administrators and customer reps develop for the same account through such mass market techniques as telephone selling and direct mail. (Their costs are also built into the industry manager's expense budget.)

The business service center organization, which consists of stores offering a full line of communications equipment for commercial accounts, is shown with a dotted line because it is optional. Each operating company decides whether it will open such outlets or have its marketing administrators discharge that function.[3]

FUNDAMENTAL ORGANIZATION STRUCTURES

Delegation of tasks may resolve itself into a number of different organization structures. Each of the four most commonly used has certain advantages and disadvantages. These structures are generally known as: (1) line structure, (2) line and staff structure, (3) functionalized structure, and (4) matrix structure.

Line Structure. The simplist structure is the line organization. In this structure, responsibilities are delegated from the chief executive to first level subordinates, who, in turn, delegate to second level subordinates, and so forth. The employees at the end of the organizational ladder perform some actual production, sales, or distribution function (see Figure 12.2). A pure line structure has no advisors or support specialist. The planning is centralized in the top levels of management.

The line structure has certain advantages, primarily derived from its simplicity and relatively short organizational elements. Authority and accountability channels are clearly defined and members of the organization can easily understand the structure. On the other hand, no provision is made for specialized support services, such as research and new product development. Product development is likely to occur exclusively in the production element without input from sales or marketing. Cross communications is a problem generally in line organizations. Accounting and reporting activities must be maintained in each separate subarea of the various organizational elements.

The simple line structure, to the extent that it still exists, is most commonly found in very small organizations. The need for effective internal reporting alone makes this structure undesirable for organizations of any appreciable size. The same is true for organizations in which more than one or two elements exist. The former problem is solved by a line

[3] "AT & T's team marketing stresses accountability for revenues and costs," *Sales and Marketing Management,* May 1978, p. 54.

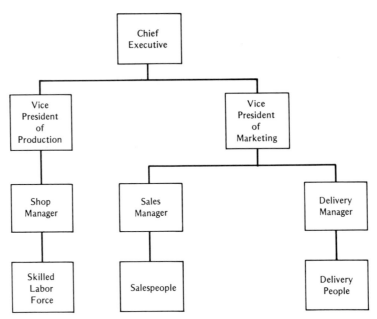

FIGURE 12.2 Line Organization Structure

and staff structure; the latter, by either a functionalized or a matrix structure.

Line and Staff Structure. The concept of staff elements appeared in organizations in the early twentieth century. Basically, the distinction between line and staff is that of decision making versus support. Marketing research, for example, is usually a staff activity, whereas sales management is a line activity.

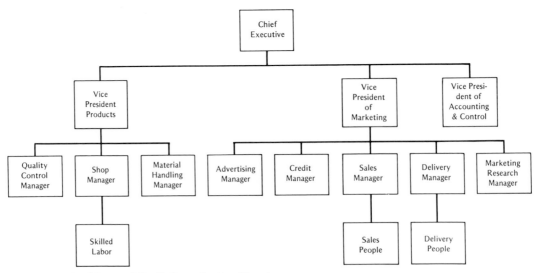

FIGURE 12.3 Line and Staff Organization Structure

In Figure 12.3 the line structure has been revised to a line and staff organization. Although the provision of staff services solves some of the problems found in line structures, it, too, suffers shortcomings. Because staff units are separate from line units, the number and complexity of communication channels can become a problem. The marketing research staff, for example, might provide information to decision makers in separate management groups for sales promotions, advertising, and sales management.

In addition, staff specialists may represent a threat to the authority of line managers. With their depth of understanding in areas of specialization, staff members of the organization are often more qualified to treat a specific problem than a line manager. It is important, however, that support staff do not assume line authority. In such cases subordinates find themselves accountable to more than one superior. Furthermore, good staff work can be so impressive as to cause line managers to accept staff findings without question. This is an equally undesirable situation in that it constitutes indirect authority outside the normal scope of staff activities. Although cited as a weakness in the line and staff structure, this violation of the "unity of command" concept becomes the basis for a functionalized structure.

Functionalized Structure. The organization chart for a highly functionalized structure resembles that of line and staff. The difference between the two is related to the decision or command authority relationships that take place in the organization. In line and staff structures, staff personnel serve in only an advisory capacity. In the functionalized structure, however, staff experts are allowed to exercise command authority over subordinates who also report to a line superior. This type of arrangement is illustrated in Figure 12.4, where the credit manager has authority over the salespeople with respect to allowing credit and setting credit terms. This concept was originally introduced by Frederick Taylor as a means

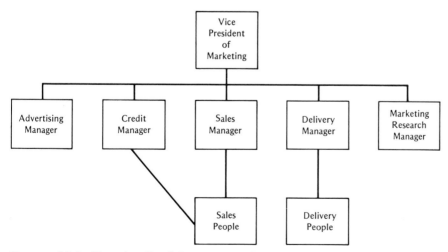

FIGURE 12.4   Functionalized Organization Structure

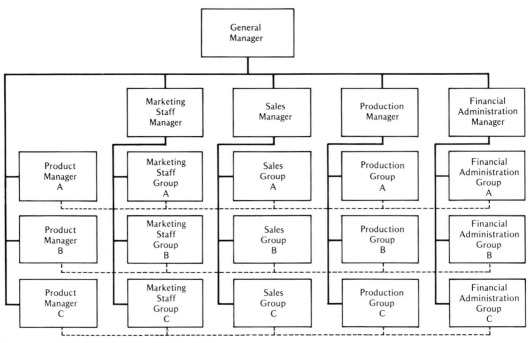

FIGURE 12.5 **Matrix Organization Structure**

of extracting maximum efficiency from specialists.[4] Thus, specialists in certain functional areas would concentrate exclusively on the application of their expertise through line authority to subordinates. A subordinate at a low level in the organization might find himself taking orders from, and accountable to, a number of specialists. Most of Taylor's work involving functionalization dealt with supervisory level management in manufacturing operations. Although functionalization is occasionally applied in special projects, its occurrence as an organizational structure is relatively rare. A more common structure for utilizing the talents of functional specialists is the matrix approach.

Matrix Structure. As illustrated in Figure 12.5 the matrix organization structure includes both functional departments (vertical lines) and a project orientation (horizontal lines). The specific project often centers on a product or brand leading to a product manager as project head. Obviously, this structure, as was the case with functionalization, violates the unity of command principle. Assigning specialists to projects, while retaining their places in functional departments, creates an environment in which confusion easily arises. The difficulties involved in coordinating personnel and resolving problems are the primary disadvantages of the matrix structure. On the other hand, the concentration of specialized talent in a project venture constitutes the primary advantage. According

[4] Fred Luthans, *Organizational Behavior: A Modern Behavioral Approach to Management* (New York: McGraw-Hill Book Company, 1973), p. 126.

to Luthans, "Many modern organizations which are facing tremendous structural and technical complexity have no choice but to move to such an arrangement."[5] The concept of product management is, however, running into difficulty, as many firms using the approach have either abandoned or significantly revised it. Some important changes in structure seem inevitable for those firms using product managers.[6]

Matrix organizations are complicated by the lack of unitary upward accountability. That is, a member of a project group is accountable to both the project manager and the manager of the department from which he is assigned. Assume for example, that a project involves the marketing of a new product. Salespeople assigned from the sales force to the new product are accountable to both the product manager and the corporate sales manager. If this relationship problem is handled well, the commitment of salespeople to the product insures the needed sales effort.

Relative Merits of Fundamental Organization Structures. Each of the fundamental organization structures has certain advantages and disadvantages as generally applied. In designing or redesigning an organization to fit a particular situation, the sales manager should keep these relative merits in mind.

A line structure is simple and usually low cost because it has few executives. It is highly centralized, allowing quick decisions and action. In larger organizations, however, it has serious drawbacks. The managers must be generalists covering a very wide range of activities. Specialized managerial skills cannot be readily directed to specific phases of the operation. Line structures can also retard the development of managerial talent within an organization. Highly centralized authority can severely restrict middle management, which is a training ground for future executives. Communications is another problem if a line organization becomes too large. Information must flow all the way to the top of the organization for decision making and directives must come back down to the lower levels. As channels become longer and the volume of information greater, barriers to efficient communication can easily develop.

A line and staff structure allows the company to have specialists on its management team. Planning and operation can be divided with staff specialists working in relatively narrow areas of expertise. This generally improves the planning process of the organization as well as its administration. On the negative side, the line and staff structure may lead to increased managerial cost as staff specialist and support personnel are hired. It can also make for slower decision making as information gathering and analysis by staff members take extra time. Such careful consideration to improve the management of the organization may be well worth the time and cost required. Another possible problem is that aggressive staff people may take line authority in some cases rather than staying in an advisory role. On the other hand, strong line executives may simply ignore

[5] *Ibid.*, p. 177.
[6] See for example, Richard M. Clewett and Stanley F. Starch, "Shifting Role of the Product Manager," *Harvard Business Review*, January–February 1975, pp. 65–73.

staff advice. Proper administration of the organization should prevent such potential conflicts.

The functionalized structure actually authorizes staff specialist to exercise direct authority over personnel who also report to line managers. This has the advantage that plans made by staff people in various functional areas cannot be ignored by line managers or salespeople. Staff specialist can directly order the implementation of their plans. This can, of course, cause serious problems if line managers, being consistently bypassed, lose influence and control. Conflicting orders can be given to subordinates when staff and line managers are not properly coordinated. This should not happen if some top manager is overseeing the total operation. The functional organization is thus an attempt to get maximum benefit from staff specialists by allowing them direct authority. The conflict and confusion that can result in such organizations, however, makes them undesirable in most situations.

Matrix structures are a more common way to bring greater staff expertise to bear in a given area. This approach allows the company to concentrate specialized talent on a specific project or product, but it also presents problems of communications and coordination. Such an organization may be necessary in industries where project or product complexities are so great that personnel must specialize to be effective, but again the difficulties are significant.

Of the four fundamental structures, line and staff remains by far the most common in moderate to larger companies. Small organizations often find the simplicity of a line structure best suited for their needs. If there is an evolutionary trend in the area of structure, it has been toward a matrix, or project, orientation. As yet, however, few organizations have been able successfully to ignore the unity of command principle.

CENTRALIZATION AND DECENTRALIZATION

Although the terms centralization and decentralization are used in varying contexts, usually the terms refer to "the degree of delegation of duties, power, and authority to lower levels of an organization."[7] Since the degree of centralization and decentralization is a function of delegation, it is not necessarily reflected in the organization chart. Furthermore, the degree of delegation in different departments and functions of an organization may vary. For example, if a large consumer goods company is organized by product lines, the sales function may also be decentralized as reflected in Figure 12.6a. On the other hand, the sales function could be centralized as illustrated in Figure 12.6b.

There is nothing intrinsically good or bad about decentralization. On the positive side one may argue that decentralization allows participation by lower levels of management in decision making. On the other hand, centralization allows top management to exercise more direct control

---

[7] H. Y. Hicks, *The Management of Organizations* (New York: McGraw-Hill Book Co., 1967), p. 349.

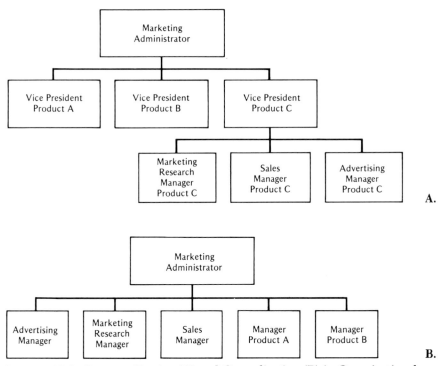

FIGURE 12.6 Decentralization (A) and Centralization (B) in Organizational Structure

over the organization and also provides uniformity and integration of inputs for planning purposes. No organization would be meaningful if centralization were carried to the extreme. Similarly, a completely decentralized organization would have no central leadership and poor coordination of efforts. Although most authorities agree that every firm operates at some point along a continuum between extreme centralization and extreme decentralization, there is considerably less agreement as to which direction is most popular.

One author states that "although decentralization has been the 'golden calf' for the past couple of decades, many scholars and practitioners are now forecasting a recentralization of organization structure. Even General Motors, the classic textbook example of decentralization, is moving toward a more centralized operating structure."[8] One group of organizational theorists explains this return to centralization by pointing out the impact of advanced information technology. They contend that the computer has enabled higher level managers to have more information in a timely fashion. Thus, fewer middle managers are required to handle the decision making chores.

Although a positive correlation between information technology and centralization is an intriguing possibility, it is only fair to point out arguments to the contrary. It can be argued, for example, that delegation is

[8] Luthans, *op. cit.*, p. 142.

more a function of the need for specialized management talent than for information. That is, getting better information to the decision maker is of no use if the manager is not capable of using it.

Obviously, factors other than information also affect organizational structure. In the case of General Motors, for example, recentralization may be a means of avoiding antitrust litigation. The company would be more difficult to split up if it were not decentralized. Again, Luthans points out:

> organizational centralization-decentralization is much broader than mere information flows. Growth, homogeneity of personnel, and . . . the environment may all play a role in the eventual organization structure. Whether the computer is of such significance that it can override these other variables is yet to be seen. But one conclusion seems certain. The computer *will* have an impact on structure as on all other areas in organization and management. The only question is *when* and *how much*.[9]

Maryland Cup's marketing committee illustrates an attempt to combine the best features of both centralization and decentralization.

Maryland Cup started out as an ice cream cone bakery in Chelsea, Mass., in 1911. Today it is a decentralized operation with divisions based in Owings Mills, Md., Wilmington, Mass., and Chicago. To make sure that everyone plays by the same rules, the company has a four-member marketing committee that meets for two days each month to discuss basic marketing and sales administration policies.

The committee members are Dick Folkoff, marketing vice president, Sweetheart Cup Div., Owings Mills, chairman; George Shumrak, vice president, Sweetheart Plastics, Wilmington; Bill Blake, national sales administrator, Sweetheart Cup Div.; and Ted Alpert, marketing vice president, Sweetheart Cup Corp., Chicago.

The agenda for a marketing committee meeting early in the summer of 1978 included the following topics:

- Proposed changes in product order units. The company follows industry practice, but it is trying to determine if a change would improve distribution.
- Development of a relocation policy for employees—a growing problem because of rising housing costs.
- A discussion of the status of containers being developed for use in convection and microwave ovens.
- The location, structure, and budgeting of the annual sales meeting.
- Compensation of salesmen and sales managers.
- Optimum territory size.
- The management-level bonus program.

The committee also holds periodic two-day meetings with regional managers, who prepare the agenda for the second day. Says Blake: "We learn because communication goes up, not down.[10]

---

[9] *Ibid.*, p. 144.
[10] "How to Market by Committee," *Sales and Marketing Management*, August 1978, p. 36.

THE HUMAN ELEMENT IN ORGANIZATION

The human element in organization cannot be overlooked in today's business environment. In the past, organization theory concentrated on doing tasks in set ways and within given time frames. Little attention was devoted to the needs of the employees or the impact that the organization had on individuals within the firm. This often led to highly structured organizations with authoritarian management. In effect, the employee was looked upon as just another piece of machinery. The sales force was frequently looked upon in this fashion along with the production workers.

In the 1930s and 1940s organization theory moved toward greater recognition of human relations. Motivation and interpersonal relationships between employees and managers were viewed as increasingly important. The authoritarian management style shifted toward greater participation. Today most managers operate somewhere between the two extremes. An element of participative management is usually present, but within a total systems framework that provides needed direction and accountability. There are significant advantages to the sales manager in recognizing that salespeople are individuals with different expectations, personalities, and abilities.

The flexibility that comes when management takes a more humanistic approach allows the organization to self-adjust as the environment changes. These shifts are often accomplished through an informal organization structure that represents the actual structure of the enterpise as opposed to the organization chart. The sales manager should realize that informal work relationships are present in most organizations. If they work to make the job more effective, they can be very useful. A sales manager may find that at times the informal organization is the best way to get a certain job done. In such case it is often better to work with it than to fight it. If the informal organization becomes destructive, some corrective action may be necessary.

Types of Sales Organizations

Discussion in the preceding section was devoted to some fundamental considerations in organizational structure. These fundamentals apply both in establishing the relationship of sales to the rest of the enterprise and in organizing the sales function itself. The following discussion will concentrate on specific organizational structures that are common in sales organizations. The subject is generally discussed in management literature under the heading of "departmentalization." Our primary concern here is specialization within the sales department. A departmentalization within the sales force is usually one of four types: (1) functional departmentalization, (2) territorial departmentalization, (3) product departmentalization, and (4) customer departmentalization. Each of these forms will be discussed briefly. Note that these organizational forms are not mutually exclusive. Most sales forces are organized with some combination of the four. They are separated here simply for ease of discussion and understanding.

SALES ORGANIZATION BASED ON FUNCTIONS

This type of organization involves specialization by tasks. Two basic types of selling tasks are sales development and sales maintenance. It is possible to organize the sales force into a sales development group that is responsible for getting new accounts and a sales maintenance group that services existing accounts.

This type of functional departmentalization is most appropriate when a firm's activities are highly centralized (geographically), the product line is relatively narrow, and the target market is not segmented. If these conditions exist, each functional group is able to service the entire market. This is not often the case, however. Thus, few sales organizations have a strictly functional basis. Another disadvantage of functionalized departments is that they tend to become very myopic. Each group sees only its own problems and concerns rather than the total scope of the enterprise. Some sales organizations have a functional element, but most use this in conjunction with some other form.

SALES ORGANIZATION BASED ON GEOGRAPHIC AREAS

Firms with widespread geographic markets are frequently faced with the necessity of organizing along the lines of geographic departmentalization. This is probably the most common form of sales organization used

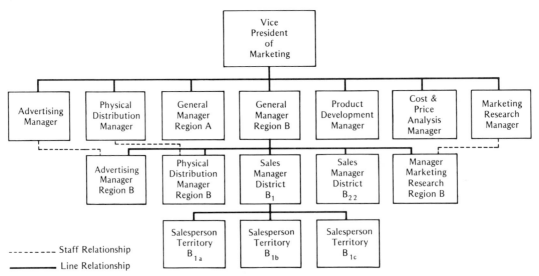

FIGURE 12.7   Organization Based on Geographic Regions

today and generally allows the most efficient utilization of the sales force in covering large geographic areas. The organization chart illustrated in Figure 12.7 represents a firm with territorial alignment of personal selling as its primary unit.

Notice that the organization is essentially a line and staff structure. The line units are organized by territory—region A, region B, and so forth. The staff functions appear at both the headquarters and region or district levels in the organization. The direct flow of line management, however, is from the region manager to the district manager and on to the salesperson in each territory.

SALES ORGANIZATION BASED ON PRODUCTS

In discussing both functional and territorial departmentalization, key assumptions were made concerning the nature of the firm's products. In each case the firm was assumed to have a single product line, or, at least, relative homogeneity among products. In many firms, however, product offerings are sufficiently diverse to require specialized treatment. A sales organization that proves to be effective for one product line might prove ineffective for a different product line. When this situation arises, the sales organization is usually built around products. This type of organization can take numerous forms, two of which are discussed in the following paragraphs.

Figure 12.8 presents an organization with two product groups, each

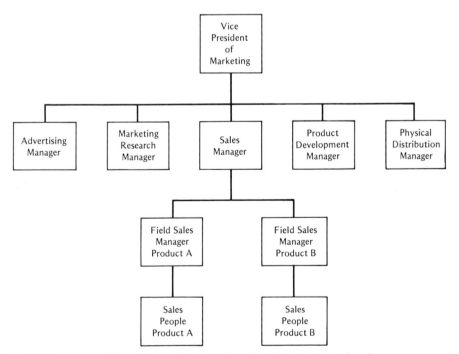

FIGURE 12.8   Sales Organization Based on Products—Centralized

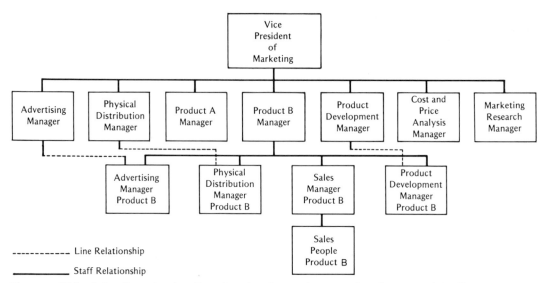

Line Relationship

Staff Relationship

FIGURE 12.9 Sales Organization Based on Products—Decentralized Line and Staff

managed by a separate assistant field sales manager. Salespeople in group A report directly to the field sales manager for product A. This type of departmentalization typically has the major drawback of overlapping territories and more than one salesperson calling on the same customer. Such duplication of effort introduces an element of inefficiency and can cause problems for the customer as well. In some cases, however, where great technical skill is needed, product specialization may be the only realistic option.

A relatively decentralized line and staff organization based on products is illustrated in Figure 12.9. In this type of organization, line authority flows from the Vice-President of Marketing through corporate level product managers and on to specialized product departments. In the case of product B, for example, the flow of line decision making is from the Vice-President of Marketing to the manager of product B to the four functional managers of product B. At the corporate level the advertising, distribution, product development, cost and price analysis, and marketing research departments are all staff functions. These departments provide the marketing administrator with information on the coordination of the various functional activities as well as basic managers. The vertical groups represent the assignment of members of functional staff departments to each project. In this manner the products receive specialized attention; the duplication of staff departments at the product and corporate levels can be avoided with a matrix structure. As noted earlier, however, matrix organizations are very difficult to implement successfully. Product managers tend to have a strong profit orientation. In a matrix structure they may lack the necessary line authority over the project team to insure attainment of profit goals.

In each of these examples, reference is made to individual products as the basis for organization. In some cases, product oriented structures are built around specific brands. The level in the organization at which product management becomes a basis for departmentalization varies from one situation to the next. Sales organizations with a product orientation are not uncommon but must also have a geographic element as well.

SALES ORGANIZATION BASED ON CUSTOMERS

A number of situations exist which could cause the firm to organize its sales effort based on customers. For example, some firms sell highly technical products that require extensive preinstallation and postinstallation service. These firms include the manufacturers of capital goods such as computers, production equipment, and major construction projects. Also included in this group are the firms that offer extensive and complex services, such as advertising and financial management. In these situations a matrix approach may be used in which the project manager is in charge of a client account. Through this organizational approach, the client-based manager is able to bring the resources of the firm directly to bear on the needs of the customer. Salespeople may be assigned directly to a specific client. As with other matrix organizations, however, the problem of motivation in the functional departments exists. It is up to the client-based manager to motivate sufficiently members of functional departments assigned to his account to take the client's interest to heart.

Another situation that leads to customer-based organization involves industry groupings. Assume, for example, that a firm sells each of its product lines to different industry groups. The sales manager assigned to a consumer-oriented market might not do a good job of simultaneously managing the sales effort in an industrial market. An illustration of marketing organization oriented to customer groups is provided in Figure 12.10.

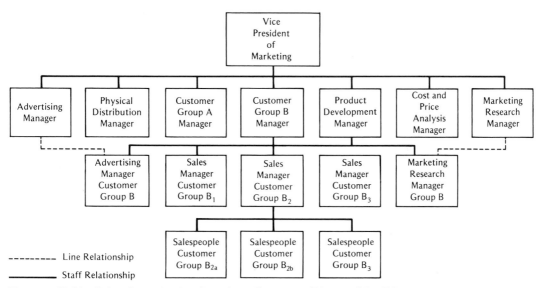

FIGURE 12.10   Sales Organization Based on Customer/Line and Staff Format

One of the obvious advantages of industry- or customer-based organization is the ability to develop and maintain close customer relations. In many cases firms that are organized along these lines become respected experts within their industry group. This type of expertise is difficult to maintain without excellent customer relations. One danger of the customer-based organization, however, is the difficulty managers have in adjusting to varying client groups. If a client group is maintained for a long period of time and subsequently declines for some reason, the manager and salespeople may find it difficult to transpose expertise to a new client group.

Reorganizing the Sales Force

As noted at the beginning of the chapter, organizing is a continual process. The organization cannot be allowed to remain static as the surrounding environment changes. It must be continually adapted to meet new challenges and opportunities. This means that the sales manager is confronted with the ongoing task of reorganizing the sales effort.

Numerous factors may create a need for reorganization. Changes in the size, number, or geographic distribution of customers or potential customers can make the old organization obsolete. New products and competitors or conflicts with distribution channel members may also cause the sales manager to think in terms of reorganization. "A sales operation ideally should be reorganized toward long-range opportunities rather than short-term problems."[11] This is often not the case, however, particularly when the goals of the sales function are all set on a short-term basis. The sequence of steps in reorganizing should be to (1) establish the new organization structure, (2) develop job description for the positions required in the new structure, and finally (3) communicate both the structure and position descriptions to the people involved.[12]

Digital Equipment Corporation's experience provides an illustration of a reorganization designed to meet a problem in dealing with national accounts.

Under Digital Equipment's former national accounts program, field salespeople were responsible for national accounts, and they called on the headquarters of those customers. But the salesmen served two masters: they reported to a local branch manager and were indirectly responsible to the corporate director of national accounts. Moreover, 10% of all sales that went outside a salesman's territory were credited to the national accounts manager. Now there are 12 national accounts managers who must see that plans are established and communications channels set up; none of them have direct sales responsibility, so there is no credit to split. One result, of course, has been a big improvement in morale. Also, says Handy, there's been an appreciable increase in total sales: "We can't

[11] Jeffrey Irving, "There's More Than Meets the Eye in Reorganizing Your Sales Force," *Sales Management*, May 1972, p. 54.
[12] *Ibid.*

honestly say it was because of this program, but we couldn't sustain it without national accounts."[13]

Ideal Toy took a somewhat different reorganizational approach to solving a similar problem.

In December (1977), a U.S. District Court judge ruled that Ideal Toy could continue selling its Star Team toys because the line did not infringe on the Star Wars Toys from General Mills' Kenner Products Div.—Kenner's toys weren't even on the market yet. With that battle decided, Ideal . . . sent out its newest star team: a reorganized sales force.

In the past, says Mort Schneider, sales vice president of the Hollis, N.Y., company, the top mass merchandisers and other retail giants were "thrown into our regional pot," sold the same way, and by the same people, as local accounts. But as Ideal's national accounts have grown—there are now 20—it became impossible for a salesperson to handle both national and local accounts, and the national accounts were extracted from the regional organization.

They, along with Ideal's five mail-order accounts, will be handled by seven people who have experience with those specific accounts. All will report to national accounts manager Jack Poovey. The remainder of the 80-person sales force, who will call on local customers in Ideal's seven regions, will work for newly named national sales manager Earl Higgins.

With the establishment of a national accounts division, Schneider says, Ideal is finally able to cater to the needs of specific types of customers; for example, drug chains. Ideal's toys, games, and dolls retail from $1.99 to $90; drug chains require a heavier concentration of $5–$10 items, Schneider says. Another target is department stores, which were "lost and forgotten" in recent years because "the margin of profit on our products wasn't to their liking." Merchandise tailored to specific market segments is now being designed and should be ready within weeks.[14]

Individuals have a natural tendency to resist change, thus unfavorable behavioral consequences often accompany a reorganization. In order to minimize such unfavorable consequences the sales manager must not only recognize that such problems are likely to arise but must also understand the basic factors underlying such behavior:

1. *Changes in the informal structure.* The informal relationship that develops within any organization may be highly complex and of importance to the individuals involved. Work and social ties develop; when reorganization alters such relationships, adverse reactions can arise.
2. *Personal characteristics.* Personal characteristics and background of the particular individuals affect their behavior toward new developments. For example, younger people with fewer years of service tend to be less opposed to change than older people with more years of service.
3. *Managerial climate.* The members of an organization are more likely to respond favorably to a proposed change if the managerial climate maintains open communications and permits all grievances to be

[13] "Sales Force Organization," *Sales and Marketing Management,* January 1977, p. 54.
[14] "Playing for Higher Stakes at Ideal Toy," *Sales and Marketing Management,* March 1978, p. 14.

heard. The method used by the sales manager to introduce a reorganization is another significant variable affecting its likelihood of success.

These and other underlying factors may generate various forms of dysfunctional behavior. Such behavior usually takes one or more of three forms, depending upon the individual's position within the organization:

1. *Aggression.* Aggressive behavior represents an attack intended to injure the object causing the problem. The most common form of aggression occurs when people attempt to "beat the system" by going around the new organizational structure.
2. *Projection.* Projection exists when people blame the changes for causing difficulties that are in fact caused by something else. Reorganization may be blamed for a poor sales showing when the real reason was the incompetence of a particular salesperson.
3. *Avoidance.* People may define themselves by simply withdrawing from the frustrating situation. They may ignore the new organization or fail to really come to terms with the new relationship created.

The sales manager should attempt to minimize dysfunctional behavior created by reorganizing. To do this, special attention should be given to the following steps:

1. *Directed toward future opportunities.* Make sure the reorganization is done with future opportunities clearly in mind. A new organizational setup should clearly improve the enterprise's ability to take fuller advantage of new opportunities. This gives the new organization a "real" advantage over the old one, which provides justification for the change.
2. *Proper atmosphere.* Critical aspects are the attitudes of both management and any affected employees toward the changes. The attitude of management should be one of full support for the reorganization. There should also be open lines of communication between different management and employees.
3. *Participation.* The salespeople should be consulted in the reorganization process. An attempt should be made to achieve harmony between individual and organizational goals.
4. *Communicate the new organization to the sales force.* The purpose and characteristics of the new organization should be as clear as possible to those who are affected by any changes. This means that the nature and details of a new organization must be fully explored and discussed with those affected before, during, and after its implementation.
5. *New challenges.* New challenges may be opened up by a reorganization. A look should be taken at what management and employees ought to be doing that is more important and satisfying than what they did before. The sales manager should discover and emphasize these positive new challenges in discussions with individuals at all levels.
6. *Reexamine performance evaluations.* Finally, as tasks change for individuals, the basis upon which their performance is judged should be reexamined. Performance standards should be updated to conform to the job requirements of the new organization.

Summary

Organizing the sales force for effective operation was presented as an ongoing task of sales management. Establishing and reformulating an effective pattern of work is a key element in attaining the goals of the enterprise.

Fundamental to any discussion of organizational structure are certain basic considerations. Management in organizations involves first the delegation of responsibility, authority, and accountability. It is particularly important that responsibility be accompanied by adequate authority to implement the delegated tasks. Four types of organizational structures were presented in the chapter, each of which involves a different concept of delegation. These include (1) line structure, (2) line and staff structure, (3) functionalized structure, and (4) matrix structure. The most common organizational structure is line and staff. Most organizations are derived from this concept. In addition to conforming to one of the fundamental organizational structures, firms tend to be relatively centralized or decentralized. In highly centralized organizations the decision making is concentrated near the top of the structure, whereas with decentralization lower levels are delegated more authority. The human element in organizational design was also presented as a vital consideration in today's business environment.

An additional consideration in building sales organizations is the nature of departmentalization. Sales organizations tend to be departmentalized along one of four dimensions: (1) functional departmentalization, (2) territorial departmentalization, (3) product departmentalization, and (4) customer departmentalization. Most sales organizations involve some combination of these basic forms.

The chapter concluded with a discussion of some of the potential problems facing the sales manager in reorganizing the sales force. Directing the reorganization toward future opportunities, proper atmosphere, participation, communicating the new organization to the sales force, pointing out new challenges and reexamining performance evaluations were suggested as steps that might help to minimize the dysfunctional behavior often resulting from reorganization.

Discussion Questions

1. What is the distinction between organization and organizing?

2. Why is an organization needed within an enterprise?

3. Discuss the types of responsibility, authority, and accountability that might be delegated to a salesperson.

4. What are some of the problems that might confront a salesperson working in an enterprise with a matrix organizational structure?

5. Why is a sales manager a line manager rather than a member of the staff?

6. Is consideration of the human element in organization more or less important to the sales manager or the production manager? Why?

7. Discuss the differences between the four types of sales organizations presented in the chapter.

8. Why is the sales organization based on geographic areas the most common?

9. Discuss the types of environmental shifts that can create a need to reorganize the sales force.

10. What are some of the dysfunctional behaviors that can result from reorganization, and what steps can a sales manager take to minimize the problems?

Selected References

BUELL, VICTOR P., "The Changing Role of the Product Manager in Consumer Goods Companies," *Journal of Marketing*, July 1975, pp. 3–11.

HANAN, MACK, "Reorganize Your Company Around Its Markets," *Harvard Business Review*, November–December 1974, pp. 63–74.

JOHNSON, H. WEBSTER, "Organizing the Sales Department," Chapter 2 in *Sales Management* (Columbus, Ohio: Charles E. Merrill Books, Inc., 1976).

KAHN, GEORGE N., and ABRAHAN SCHUCHMAN, "Specialize Your Salesmen!" *Harvard Business Review*, January–February 1961, pp. 90–98.

LUTHANS, FRED, *Organizational Behavior: A Modern Behavior Approach to Management* (New York: McGraw-Hill Book Company, 1973).

CASE 12.1
Plasti-Pak, Inc.*

Company Background Plasti-Pak was founded in the mid 1950s by a young engineering graduate who had developed an innovative method for manufacturing plastic gar-

* Case prepared by Thomas N. Ingram and Danny N. Bellenger, Georgia State University.

ment bags. The bags were used by garment manufacturers as protective covers for garments while they were in transit to retailers. The manufacturing method used by Plasti-Pak initially gave the company the lowest manufacturing cost in the industry, a position they still enjoy.

Plasti-Pak was bought in 1970 by Ames Paper Company, a large diversified multinational company. Although now a division of Ames Paper Company, Plasti-Pak retained its own name due to the excellent reputation of the company and the importance of the Plasti-Pak trademark in the plastics packaging industry.

Prior to its acquisition by Ames, Plasti-Pak had increased sales at a rapid rate to $50 million in 1970. Since becoming a division of Ames, sales had continued to increase, with current annual sales of $75 million.

The garment bag product line had been expanded to laundry and dry cleaning packaging and specialty packaging, which included a variety of plastic merchandise bags designed for retailers. All of the products in the product line were sold to distributors by a combination of company sales representatives and outside sales agents.

Bill Landis had come to work for Plasti-Pak 5 years ago after completing his MBA. Progressing rapidly through two sales positions, Bill had become a regional product manager after 3 years with the company. Just 90 days ago, Bill had been named Southwest Regional Sales Manager responsible for the activities of eight company sales representatives and six outside sales agents. His current annual sales target was $15 million.

Current Situation

After having visited all of the territories and observing the company sales representatives and agents, Landis felt he had one major problem area. Sales volume was strong in every territory and the performance of both company representatives and agents seemed to be highly professional. As a matter of fact, several customers had told Landis that the Plasti-Pak representative was the outstanding supplier representative calling on them.

The problem that concerned Landis stemmed from the fact that the company representatives geographically overlapped the outside sales agents. Although the accounts were handled by only one Plasti-Pak representative (either a company representative or an outside sales agent), the use of two representatives resulted in additional sales expense in any given territory.

After looking at all territories, Landis felt the Louisiana territory needed immediate attention with regard to this question of "double coverage." The sales agent in the Louisiana area was R. H. Baxter. Baxter combined a long association with customers, considerable skill, and a high level of knowledge to sell approximately 53 per cent of the total volume in the Louisiana territory. Baxter had been named a Plasti-Pak agent 4 years ago, after he promised Plasti-Pak the Clawson Paper Company business. Keeping his promise, Baxter secured the Clawson business and it was now the top account in Louisiana. Prior to naming Baxter as an agent, Plasti-Pak had never been able to sell Clawson.

The company representative sells the same products in Louisiana as does Baxter, but to different accounts. Accounting for 47 per cent of the total volume, the company representative also is expected to spend more time than the agent at the end-user level to build demand for Plasti-Pak products. The company representative in Louisiana was Walt Hartwell, a 10-year veteran, who often was the winner of the Top Sales Representative Award in Plasti-Pak's Southwest region.

Although Landis was extremely satisfied with the sales volume level in Louisiana, he was concerned with the expense of employing a company representative and an outside agent. However, he knew that eliminating coverage by either Baxter or Hartwell could result in volume losses for at least a year.

Since it was now October and sales forcasts and expense budgets for next year were due by November 1, Landis wanted to move as quickly as possible. He had asked Sid Johnson, his staff assistant, to complete a report on the Louisiana territory within 2 weeks so that he could make a decision prior to November 1.

TABLE 1 Sales Potential By Account

Account Name	Sales Potential (× $1000)	Account Name	Sales Potential (×) $1000)
*Adams Paper	178	*Gulfside Paper	44
*Acworth Paper	2	Haverhill Bag	15
Alesi Paper	7	*Industrial Supply	10
American Bag	43	*Institutional Supply	17
Astro Paper	53	Iverson Wholesale	2
*Azziloti Paper	30	Linild	70
Baynard Paper	19	Louverty	26
Beathard Paper	14	Malone & Harris	11
*Benson Supply	44	Miller Supply	7
*Blanks Bag Company	10	Munson Bag	3
Broussard Paper	14	*Newsom Paper	125
*Cagle Supply	4	*Parker & Sons	12
Capitol Bag	2	*Pelligreeni Paper	121
*Casio Supply	12	Pensacola Bag Company	28
Cayton's, Inc.	3	Plastic Supplies, Inc.	45
Central Bag Company	13	*Pressly Supply	19
*Church's Supply	9	Quality Bag	52
*Clawson Paper	280	Smith & Kerr	29
*Consolidated Services	42	*Snider Supply	45
Cribbin Bros.	6	*Southwest Plastics	16
*Demeter Supply	67	*Terra Wholesale	19
Durwood Company	26	*Tetley Supply	6
*G & A Supply	2	Thomas Bag Company	8
*G & M, Inc.	4	T. T. Thompson	3
Gerald Paper	30	*Warnaco Company	46
			1693

* Currently sold by R. H. Baxter.

After reading Johnson's report, Landis realized that the situation was more complicated than he had expected. Company representative or sales agent? Should there be any reorganization at all? Would cost savings offset volume loss? How would the customers react? How would Baxter and Hartwell react to a change? Those were only a few of the thoughts racing through the mind of Bill Landis as he left the office for a 3-day visit to the Louisiana territory where he planned to work with Walt Hartwell and R. H. Baxter.

MEMO TO: Bill Landis
            Regional Sales Manager

FROM: Sid Johnson

The Louisiana territory has been analyzed with regard to the current "double coverage" of our sales organization. The basic approach used to study this problem was the contribution to operating margin method.

Table 2, in the attached report, shows the expected contribution to margin if we choose to go strictly with a company representative, while Table 3 applies to the contribution expected from a sales agent organization. The average penetration rate is the percentage of total business that the respective methods could be expected to retain during the first year after a change exclusively to either one of the two methods. The penetration rates were based on information gathered from Walt Hartwell and from our own knowledge of the accounts in Louisiana. However, these rates should be regarded at best as "educated grosses."

The negative part of any organizational change in Louisiana is the possible loss of volume for at least a year at various accounts. With our overall sales target expected to increase by 15% next year, any loss of volume would be costly. However, in the long run, the savings expected would contribute significantly to Plastic-Pak's profit picture.

Another factor that should be mentioned is that the relationship between Walt Hartwell and R. H. Baxter has become less friendly as their distributors compete for end-user business. Baxter has had numerous offers to take on competitive lines and might well do so if we cut back his account responsibility. On the other hand, it seems like somewhat of a waste to have a representative of Walt Hartwell's experience and subsequent cost to the company handling less than half of the volume in Louisiana.

Regards,

Sid

Definition of Terms.

1. Selling costs—the direct costs of selling to include salaries, commissions, incentives, travel and entertainment, and other miscellaneous expenses.
2. Sales agent—an outside individual contracted by Plasti-Pak to sell their product at a set rate of commission. R. H. Baxter is the sales agent in Louisiana.
3. Company sales representative—a full-time company employee paid a straight salary plus bonus to sell the products of Plasti-Pak. Walt Hartwell is the company representative.

*Report:
Louisiana
Territory
Organiza-
tional
Considera-
tions*

TABLE 2
Calculation of Contribution to Operating Margin of a Direct Company Representative

(1)	(2)	(3)	(4)	(5)	(6)	(7)
		Sales				
Acct.		*Poten-*		*Total*	*Cost*	
Poten-	*No.*	*tial*	*Calls/*	*Calls*	*Per*	*Total*
tial	*of*	*(1) × (2)*	*Acct.*	*Needed*	*Call*	*Cost*
(× $1000)	*Accts.*	*(× $1000)*	*pr. yr.*	*(2) × (4)*	*($)*	*($)*
250–300	1	280	24	24	89	2,10
150–250	1	178	18	18	89	1,60
100–150	2	246	12	24	89	2,00
50–100	4	242	10	40	89	3,60
25–50	12	435	8	96	89	8,50
1–25	30	312	6	180	89	16,00

* C.O.M.—Contribution to Operating Margin.

4. Gross margin—equal to net sales minus manufacturing cost of goods sold.
5. Contribution to operating margin—equal to gross margin minus selling cost.

It should be pointed out that only those selling costs that are variable between the agent method and the company representative method will be considered as this question is examined. Certain costs would exist regardless of the method used by the company. These costs include training, administrative support, marketing research and promotional activity. It is assumed that these costs will be equal for the sales agent or the company representative.

Note that Table 1 shows the estimated potential sales by account for this year and which ones are sold by Baxter and which are Hartwell's accounts.

TABLE 3
Calculation of Contribution to Operating Margin for an Outside Sales Agent

(1)	(2)	(3)	(4)	(5)
Account	*Number*	*Sales*	*Average*	*Expected*
Potential	*Of*	*Potential*	*Penetration*	*Sales*
(× $1000)	*Accounts*	*(× $1000)*	*(%)*	*(× $1000)*
250–300	1	$280	100	280
150–250	1	178	90	160
100–150	2	246	90	221
50–100	4	242	50	121
25–50	12	435	60	261
1–25	30	312	50	156
			Total:	1,199

(8)	(9)	(10)	(11)	(12)	(13)
					C.O.M.
Avg.		Avg.	Avg.		Per
Penetra-	Expected	Gross	G.M.	C.O.M.*	Acct.
tion	Sales	Margin	(10 × 9)	(11) − (7)	(12) ÷ (2)
(%)	(× $1000)	(%)	(× $1000)	(× $1000)	(× $1000)
70	196	20	39.2	37.1	37.1
90	160	20	32.0	30.4	30.4
80	197	20	39.4	37.4	18.7
90	218	20	43.6	40.0	10.0
80	348	20	69.6	61.1	5.1
75	234	20	46.8	30.8	1.0
Total	1,353		270.6	236.8	

Costs of the Company Representative. In the Louisiana territory the company representative earns a salary plus bonus equal to approximately $30,000 per year. Other direct selling expenses associated with the company representative amount to $6,000 per year. Therefore, the total direct selling cost of the company representative in the territory is $36,000. When applied to the number of calls required in a year's time, the average cost per call for the company representative is $89 as shown in column 6 of Table 2.

Costs of the Outside Agent. The cost of the outside agent is computed from the commission rate paid on sales by the agent.

The agent is paid 3 per cent on sales of plastic garment bags, which make up 75 per cent of his total sales. A 5 per cent commission is paid on specialty bag sales, which make up the remaining 25 per cent of sales.

(6)	(7)	(8)	(9)	(10)
		Cost		C.O.M./
Average	Average	Comm. at		Account
Gross	Gross	Rate of	C.O.M.	
Margin	Margin	3.5%	(7) − (8)	(9) ÷ (2)
(%)	(× $1000)	(× $1000)	(× $1000)	(× $1000)
20	56.0	9.8	46.2	46.2
20	32.0	5.6	26.4	26.4
20	44.2	7.7	36.5	18.2
20	24.2	4.2	29.0	5.0
20	52.2	9.1	43.1	3.6
20	31.2	5.5	25.7	.9
	239.8	41.9	197.9	

The average commission rate is computed as follows:

Product	Sales	Commission Rate	Commission Paid
Garment bags	$ 900,000	3%	$27,000
Specialty bags	300,000	5%	15,000
Total	$1,200,000	3.5%	$42,000

This is a straight commission payable on all sales regardless of their size. There is no higher commission rate offered by Plasti-Pak as volume increases.

Gross Margin Estimates.   This estimate came directly from the year-end profit and loss statement of Plasti-Pak. The gross margin is assumed to be the same percentage for all size customers. While the cost of handling smaller orders is higher, Plasti-Pak sells the smaller accounts at a higher price, which tends to equalize gross margin among customers.

Calculation of the Contribution to Operating Margin.   The contribution to margin of the two alternatives is now calculated. The calculations are shown in Table 2 and Table 3. As defined earlier, contribution to operating margin is simply gross margin minus selling costs.

CASE 12.2
REALWAY DEPARTMENT STORE

Company Background   The sporting goods department was one of the real joys of the Realway Department Store. All six of the department's salesmen were consistently far over quota in their sales figures. And it was widely known that salesmen more knowledgeable about their wares—or more willing to help their customers—were not to be found in the greater metropolitan area, if in the entire state.

A more unlikely set of salesmen you'd be hard pressed to find anywhere, however. They ranged from a 6'6" ex-college basketball star to a 5'4" chronic overeater, from 26 to 35 years old, from bachelor to married with five kids. Only two things could you find in common among them: They loved sports and genuinely liked each other.

Adapted from Robert M. Fulmer and Theodore T. Herbert, *Exploring the New Management* (New York: Macmillan Publishing Co., Inc., 1974), pp. 85–86. Used with permission.

These six made up the department's sales staff from the beginning. On any given day off, one might easily find most of the salesmen bowling or hunting together or doing whatever the season called for. And when one was a little late getting to the store, the others would cover for him. Why, they even arranged every week for a different salesman to make sure the displays were just so and that the stock on the shelves wasn't getting low.

If, say, Rod waited on you and you wanted a rifle but were anything but an expert, Henry would help Rod out; Henry was sponsor of a boy's club rifle team and was pretty sharp on firearms. Henry would help you decide, but Rod got the commission. Naturally, Rod would return the favor when Henry was confronted with a customer interested in a motor for his fishing boat. This was a typical arrangement among all the salesmen.

As a result, each took pride in his work; customers went away satisfied, told their friends about the service, and kept coming back to Realway. Each salesman, consequently, made an extremely good living on a job he really liked.

Current Situation

Just last week the store's sales manager decided to expand the sales force and number of hours of the sporting goods department. Two new salesmen were to report to each of the experienced salesmen. To facilitate the training and to cover the new 10 A.M.–10 P.M. hours 7 days a week, the hours of each of the experienced salesmen were split up. Now, at any given time, usually just one of the "old gang" is on duty in the department.

The sales manager, in looking over the individual commission sheets for the week, is surprised that all six of the original salesmen's commissions are down substantially; he's also noticed that they don't seem as happy on the job as they used to be. The problem needed to be solved.

Student Learning Exercise / 12
Reorganizing

Objective

To gain an insight into the reorganization of a company's structure to accommodate changes in its product line or in its customers.

Overview

Based on certain changes in the product line of an expanding company, you will reorganize the company's sales area to accommodate their new needs.

Exercise

Assume that you are the sales manager for the Kelley Company. The Kelley Company has been in existence for 5 years and sells industrial screws and bolts to industrial users. They market this product in one state only and have been able to handle their volume of sales with three salespeople.

The present organization structure can be seen in the following diagram. The three salespeople are each responsible for one territory in the state and report to you (the sales manager). Working alongside you, and reporting with you to the president, are the production manager and the accounting and control manager.

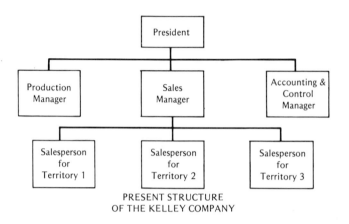

PRESENT STRUCTURE
OF THE KELLEY COMPANY

The president is in the process of negotiating a deal whereby he would acquire a new company that markets a consumer product—lawnmowers. The acquisition should become final in 4 weeks, and he has asked you to propose a reorganization that will accommodate the following changes.

In addition to acquiring a new product (and thus a new type of customer), Kelley will be taking on the three salespeople who presently work for the other firm. These salespeople cover a geographic area of three states, in one of which Kelley already does business.

Readings for

PART TWO

Sales Forecasting Methods and Accuracy

Douglas J. Dalrymple

Predictions of future revenues are important to business planning, and sales forecasts are often used to set production schedules, budget capital, and allocate resources to marketing programs. Recently, forecasting accuracy has, on the one hand, been hurt by unstable business conditions, while on the other hand, has been improved by the greater availability and use of computers. This past summer a survey was conducted to find out what methods businessmen use to predict sales, and how accurate their forecasts have been using these techniques. This article summarizes the findings of the study, and suggests ways in which businessmen can improve their own sales forecasts. From an initial mailing of 500 questionnaires (plus a follow-up letter to nonrespondents) a sample of 175 Midwestern businessmen was obtained, a 35% response rate. The composition of the sample in terms of size, age and type of firm appeared to be representative.[1]

From *Business Horizons*, Vol. 18 (December 1975), pp. 69–73. Reprinted by permission of the publisher, Graduate School of Business, Indiana University.

[1] Described in Appendix A of the author's monograph *Sales Forecasting: Methods and Accuracy*, published by the Marketing Department, School of Business, Indiana University, September 1975, p. 18.

Value of Forecasts

Sixty-four per cent of the businessmen who responded said that sales forecasting was very important to their success. Another 28% said forecasting was important, but not critical. As a group, retailers showed the most concern with forecasting. Interest was also higher than average among the larger organizations. Banks and companies with primarily local markets showed less than average interest in forecasting.

The value of sales forecasting to the firms in this study was emphasized by the large number of departments using the predictions. Table 1 shows that many different areas are involved, and that current department usage is much greater than the usage reported by a 1967 survey.[2] This suggests that sales forecasts are becoming increasingly important to business planning.

Forecasting Techniques

Respondents were asked how often they use thirteen representative forecasting techniques. Descriptions of the techniques were included in the questionnaire to reduce confusion about the methods. The techniques are listed in Table 2 according to the frequency with which they are used by the firms. The preferences shown by this study are similar to

TABLE 1 Departments Using Sales Forecasts

	Firms Responding to Current Survey (Percent)	Firms Responding to 1967 Survey (Percent)
Finance	80	32
Executive or administrative	78	10
Budgeting	63	3
Manufacturing	61	60
Inventory control	55	2
Purchasing	53	19
Planning	52	3
Accounting	44	14
Advertising	34	10
Personnel	23	8
Merchandising	22	2
Research and development	22	8
Transportation	19	6

[2] "Sales Forecasting: Is Five Percent Error Good Enough?" *Sales Management* (15 December 1967), pp. 41–48.

TABLE 2   Forecasting Techniques Used by Respondents (percentages)

Method	Used Regularly	Used Occasionally	No Longer Used	Never Tried	Short-term (one year or less)	Long-term (one to five years)
Jury of executive opinion	52	16	1	5	27	16
Sales force composite	48	15	3	9	37	6
Trend projections	28	16	1	12	13	13
Moving average	24	15	2	15	18	7
Industry survey	22	20	2	16	17	8
Regression	17	13	1	24	8	9
Intention-to-buy survey	15	17	2	23	15	3
Exponential smoothing	13	13	3	26	13	7
Leading index	12	16	1	24	12	5
Life cycle analysis	8	11	1	28	2	11
Diffusion index	8	11	—	30	9	6
Simulation models	8	8	1	35	5	5
Input/output model	6	8	1	34	6	3

those reported by a Conference Board survey published in 1970.[3] In both studies, executives reported that jury of executive opinion and sales force composite methods had significantly greater usage than other procedures.

Trend projections were used by the same number of firms for short- and long-term forecasting. This can be explained by the observation that following trends often provides good long-range predictions. Regression is used more frequently for long-range forecasts than for short-range forecasts. This is surprising, because regression is not usually a good long-range predictor. With a multiple regression equation, for example, it is difficult for executives to estimate accurately future values for independent variables that are needed to make predictions. As might be expected, the life cycle analysis method is used almost exclusively for long-range forecasts.

Space was provided on the questionnaire or businessmen to write in additional procedures used. Three firms mentioned their use of the sophisticated Box-Jenkins procedure.[4] One firm reported the use of the

[3] The 1970 study was based on responses from 161 companies and is reported in *Sales Forecasting Practices* (New York: The Conference Board, Experiences in Marketing Management, 25 November 1970), p. 10.

[4] A good description of Box-Jenkins and other techniques is contained in an article by John C. Chambers, Satinder K. Mullick and Donald D. Smith, "How to Choose the Right Forecasting Technique," *Harvard Business Review* (July–August 1971), pp. 45–74.

X-11 time series decomposition method, and another company mentioned econometric models (a set of interdependent equations). Although numerous techniques are being used, Table 2 reveals that many firms have never tried regression, exponential smoothing, leading indexes, diffusion indexes, simulation and input/output models.

Forecasting methods employed by consumer and industrial firms differ from those used by the average company. Consumer companies place greater emphasis on trend projections and exponential smoothing, and are less concerned with intention-to-buy surveys. Low usage of these surveys probably reflects their inability to predict accurately the behavior of fickle consumers. The Commerce Department recently stopped conducting consumer intention-to-buy surveys because of the high forecasting errors associated with this method. Industrial firms place more emphasis on the sales force composite and intention-to-buy methods. Success with these techniques depends on a close relationship between supplier and customer, a relationship that is traditional to industrial marketing.

Preparing Forecasts

The development of sales forecasts tended to be a group effort by the firms responding to this survey. Also, sales forecasts are most often prepared annually, with 27–30% of the firms forecasting sales on a monthly or quarterly schedule. Revisions to sales forecasts are made frequently, usually every one to three months. About half of the firms in this study said that seasonal factors are important enough to necessitate adjustments in their sales forecasts.

Respondents were also asked to evaluate the importance of a selected list of factors commonly used in preparing sales forecasts. Forty per cent of the companies indicated that past sales are very important. Among variables for which projections are frequently available, industry sales and customers' attitudes were the most popular. Surprisingly, the three factors that are used to make up the popular buying power index (retail sales, income and population) were not given high ratings in this survey. There was some interest in inventory changes, interest rates and housing starts as indicators, but businessmen have only a very limited faith in the stock market as a forecasting tool.

Two resources supposedly often used by businessmen preparing sales forecasts are consultants and computers. Table 3 shows the study indicated that consultants are used infrequently in forecasting, and computers

TABLE 3   Firms Using Forecasting Resources (percentages)

	Always Always	Frequently	Occasionally	Never	No Answer
Consultants	3	6	27	56	8
Computers	25	19	16	33	7

are employed on a regular basis by less than half of the firms in the study. The computer programs used in sales forecasting are usually developed by company personnel. The computers themselves are owned or leased by 57% of the firms, with some companies using a time sharing arrangement or obtaining access through consultants.

Forecasting Errors

Some of the most useful data collected in this study were estimates of the forecasting errors experienced by respondents. Eighty-one per cent of the firms maintain records on forecasting success and could report their past errors. The current survey showed the average error on a one-year forecast is 6.9%, considerably greater than the 5% average forecasting error reported by the 1967 survey. Reasons for increased errors mentioned in the current study were unstable business conditions, inflation, shortages of materials and unstable customer demand. Some firms indicated their errors have declined due to better data, probably from computers and improved forecasting techniques.

The survey also revealed that business firms experience a fairly wide range of forecasting error. One standard deviation of forecasting error in the current study amounted to 3.2%. This means that about 95% of the reported errors fell in the range from .5% to 13.3% error ($\pm 2\sigma$).

Forecasting errors reported by consumer-oriented companies (6.7%) were below the mean of all firms, while the average error of the industrial firms (7.6%) was above average. Apparently, demand for industrial goods is more difficult to predict because of isolation from the final consumer. Table 4 shows that errors also vary according to the type of business, with insurance companies reporting the lowest error, and manufacturers reporting the highest errors. In addition, the size of the forecasting error changes with the size of the marketing area. Firms operating in local or regional markets have smaller errors than do firms operating in national or international markets.

In contrast to previous research, forecasting errors reported in this study did not vary inversely with the size of the firm. In the 1967 study, the largest firms had the lowest errors and the smallest firms had the highest errors. In the current study, the lowest errors were reported by medium-sized firms and the highest errors by some of the largest firms.

TABLE 4   Forecasting Errors by Type of Business

Type of Business	Percent Error
Insurance	5.4
Retailing and wholesaling	6.2
Transportation	6.2
Banking	6.4
Manufacturing	7.5

TABLE 5 Forecasting Errors Reported by Firms Using Different Resources (percentages)

	Always	Frequently	Occasionally	Never
Consultants	5.4	5.8	7.7	6.9
Computers	6.9	6.3	6.3	7.6

Although size and errors did not seem to be related, the study found significant inverse relationships between errors and the age of firms, and between errors and the number of persons preparing the forecast. A negative correlation calculated between age and forecasting error ($r = -.18$) was not particularly strong, but it suggests that either firms learn more about forecasting with the passage of time, or that product lines mature with age and are easier to predict. A correlation between the number of persons and the size of the error ($r = -.17$), implies that the more people involved, the better. These results suggest that forecasts prepared by only a few persons should be avoided.[5]

Since some firms reported that consultants and computers helped reduce forecasting errors, a special tabulation was made to see if this was true for firms in the study. Responses are reported in Table 5. Although only fifteen firms said they always or frequently use consultants, these companies reported lower errors than firms who never use consultants. About one-third of the firms in the study do not use computers for forecasting, and have average errors of 7.6%. This contrasts sharply with an average error of 6.5% for companies that use computers for forecasting. Firms that always use computers had average errors (6.9%), but they are still below the forecasting errors reported by companies that never use computers.

A final tabulation of errors associated with different forecasting techniques is presented in Table 6. Note that firms reporting regular use of the two most popular techniques (jury of executive opinion and sales force composite) have errors close to the average for all firms (6.9%). However, companies who said they never tried these methods report significantly lower errors. This implies that the companies that never use the popular techniques have found better forecasting methods. Several forecasting procedures were associated with errors higher than the average.

The intention-to-buy survey, the diffusion index and exponential smoothing all performed poorly compared to the other techniques. One way to improve forecasting would be to select a technique that has been used with low error results. Methods that fall into this classification include trend projection, moving average, regression, leading index, life cycle analysis, simulation models and input/output models.

Sales forecasting is vital to business success. Forecasts are becoming

[5] Correlations are significantly different from zero with a probability of error of less than 5%.

TABLE 6   Forecasting Errors Reported by Firms Using Different
Techniques (percentages)

Method	Errors	
	Regular Use of Method	*Method Never Tried*
Life cycle analysis	4.5	7.2
Leading index	5.4	6.9
Trend projection	6.2	7.5
Moving average	6.2	7.9
Input/output models	6.2	6.6
Regression	6.4	6.8
Simulation models	6.5	6.8
Industry survey	6.7	6.0
Sales force composite	6.8	5.9
Jury of executive opinion	7.0	5.4
Exponential smoothing	7.3	7.1
Diffusion index	8.1	6.7
Intention-to-buy survey	8.5	6.2

more widely used by executives for planning purposes, but errors are increasing and forecasting personnel can expect greater pressure from management to improve accuracy. The current study indicates that errors can be reduced by adding resources to the forecasting task. When companies involve more people, hire consultants and use computers, forecasting errors decline.

Another way to reduce forecasting errors is to adopt new, more accurate methods. While no single procedure can be recommended, firms which use trend projection, moving averages, regression, leading indexes, simulation models, and input/output models have lower errors than companies employing other methods. Firms currently using intention-to-buy surveys and diffusion indexes had high forecasting error rates, indicating that these methods should be used with caution. Businessmen have traditionally relied on judgment to make sales forecasts, and the result has been an average forecasting error of 7%. Companies that want to do better should put more people and a computer to work using some of the quantitative techniques associated with lower errors.

Segmentation for
Sales Force Motivation

Herbert Mossien and Eugene H. Fram

Marketing segmentation, originally discussed by Wendell Smith in 1956, has become a significant part of our marketing lexicon and has been employed by many companies with varied success. However, better use of this concept may evolve through its extension to the management of the sales force. More dramatic results in both motivation and orders received may well be the useful product of its adoption. Modest initial experience and projections indicate interesting potential for this new application of segmentation, and suggested procedures for utilization are presented in this analysis.

Sales force segmentation involves separating the sales force into several discrete units and applying different motivation, communication, and administrative principles to each group. It calls for different motivational approaches to each group in order to achieve maximum sales potential for each. Present day sales management employs regimentation which is opposite to the suggested approach. Regimentation, observably, brings about the average, the norm, the enhancement of mediocrity. This condition is accelerated by many present day testing and selecting procedures which can eliminate the iconoclastic and creative types. In many sales forces, these types are outnumbered but produce the majority of the business. In an attempt to support individual initiative, and to appropriately encourage and reward this, we have developed the sales force segmentation concept. The current literature points to the need to consider the uniqueness of each individual and his situation as a prerequisite to better motivation.[1] It is recognized that the segmentation scheme offered does not make this provision. However, it is the conclusion of the authors (from observation and experience) that individual motivation, as recommended by many behavioral scientists, is not practical for sales management at the present time from a cost and supervision viewpoint. As the group segmentation proves itself over time from a cost/profit standpoint, further individual segmentation for motivation would be in order. The fact that job category groups show some heterogeneity is not challenged.

The need for sales force segmentation can be well illustrated by the following example from the authors' consulting experience.

Case 1.

> The scene was a familiar one to most marketing people. It was the annual sales meeting of a medium sized consumer goods firm in a plush hotel. The firm has over 400 salesmen. In the morning, the entire group attended a

From *Akron Business and Economic Review*, Winter 1973, pp. 5–12. Reprinted by permission of the publisher, the Bureau of Business and Economic Research, College of Business Administration, The University of Akron.

[1] Andrew J. DuBrin, *The Practice of Managerial Psychology* (Elmsford, New York: Pergamon Press, 1972), p. 272.

well rehearsed presentation on last year's successes and next year's opportunities in a large auditorium. At this presentation, geographical territories were mentioned for honors and various kudos given. In the afternoon session, the group was divided geographically for workshop discussions with various brand managers.

Case 1 illustrates the typical attempt to motivate the entire sales force as one monolithic group. True, the afternoon sessions were divided by product lines and by territory. But these in themselves provide no motivational inspiration for individual salesmen. The beginners were "handled" in the same ways as the veterans. Top producers were urged in the same tones and mannerisms as the middle and low producers. ("In the next three minutes, list six selling points you can relate to customers. At the end of the three minutes, we'll all compare lists.") The motivated were approached in the same manner as the unmotivated, and conformity to total group norms was encouraged.

From the case described above, the problem is clear. Yet, in consultation with a wide range of business firms by the writers, not one had even thought of segmenting its sales force beyond the common and obvious divisions of territory and product line—classifications quite unrelated to motivational variables. Anyone making the typical statement such as the following should be receptive to the sales segmentation concept: "Getting new products to market today is only half the battle. The other half is keeping them there against all the competition. To a greater extent than ever before, that now means 'segmenting' or pinpointing your products and markets."[2]

This becomes even more critical when one considers the career salesman because he has little opportunity to increase his corporate prestige and title. As will be indicated later, salary growth (his only present avenue of progressive rewards) may be quickly declining as a useful motivational tool.

Segmentation for Motivation

The need for segmenting the sales force is demonstrated by studies which indicate that the highest turnover rate is among the **most successful** and the **least successful** salesmen.[3] However, the loss of top personnel is always a concern and would indicate that improved approaches are needed to retain them. Sales force segmentation, if provided in depth, could decrease voluntary turnover among high producers. With segmentation the high producer can become distinctive, with the benefits being the same as one would achieve when one has a differentiated product. Long term improvements would be greater motivation and job enrichment. We tend, today, through constantly increased quotas, public rela-

[2] "New Products: The Push is on Marketing," *Business Week,* March 4, 1972, p. 75.
[3] Gerhard W. Ditz, "Status Problems of the Salesman," *Business Topics,* Winter 1967, p. 70.

tions, credit and repair responsibilities, to assume the salesman is motivated by this "horizontal job loading."[4] Herzberg has indicated the motivational value of job enrichment; the segmentation philosophy follows this path.[5] However, all "enrichable" jobs cannot be enriched in the same way.

The concept of sales force segmentation should be relatively easy for the marketing manager to accept and adopt. In working with markets, the marketing manager easily accepts the fact that he is dealing with many different parts of a market and that each market must be approached (i.e., motivated to use a similar terminology), in a different manner. To accomplish this task, he uses different marketing mixes to accomplish the job. For segmenting his sales force, he needs to transfer the approach to the management of his sales force. The tools are already available, as will be detailed.

To support the argument for sales force segmentation as a motivational tool, the marketing manager can look to successful applications in other fields requiring human motivation. Education is one good example. Superior grade schools, for years, have been dividing students into groups on the basis of how capable they are of learning. It is commonly accepted that the prompting for brighter students is quite different from those with average ability. These are the same people who eventually may become salesmen, and good sales force management is just as much a teaching-learning situation as any formal school situation.

Problems From "Not" Segmenting

Consulting assignments completed by the authors have provided examples of marketing problems which have or could have been solved through adoption of a segmentation approach.

Case 2

In a branch office of one of the largest industrial companies in the United States, a problem of motivating the sales force had become apparent to the district manager in November of a recent year. Business at that time was 92% of quota, and unusual circumstances would be needed to meet the quota.

The district manager had several meetings employing the usual motivating tactics and exhortations. When the authors were called to consult, it took very little examination to reveal that for purposes of motivation, the problem required segmentation of the sales force. Five of the 14 salesmen were over quota and examination revealed all in this segment were motivated to a very high degree and in every sense were professional salesmen.

[4] Frederich Herzberg, "One More Time: How do you Motivate Employees?" *Harvard Business Review*, January–February 1968, p. 59.
[5] *Ibid.*, p. 62.

Four of the men were moderately under quota, not strongly self-motivated. They were good, average salesmen who would react well to traditional motivational techniques. The remaining five were all well under quota; were having significant emotional problems at home; and were unstable under pressure. These men needed more help than it was logical to attempt in a business relationship.

With segmentation of the sales force for motivation, it was relatively easy to prescribe appropriate rewards and "punishments" for the three groups.
        Group I—Praise and attention.
                —Traditional motivation and training, i.e.,
                —product and sales technique education;
        Group II—money.
        Group III—Immediate dismissal.

After six months experience with the approach and with quotas 7% above target, the district manager offered the following reaction, ". . . we have approached many of our training (motivation) problems using the segmentation model. My judgement is that this has proved to be beneficial in many ways and affords us an opportunity to better utilize management and sales personnel time. In addition, it has improved morale."

Case 3.

A third case involved a small sales force selling a consumer product which required home sales calls based on mail leads. In this instance, the sales manager has instinctively segmented his sales force by market type—he provided carriage type salesmen with leads from the upper income sections and the "non-polished" salesmen with leads from the blue collar sections. However, in motivating the salesmen he was unable to translate this same approach; he tried to motivate the two groups in the same way, although it was quite evident to the consultants that the motivational approach needed the same segmentation as the market approach.

Case 4.

Another illustration involved an industrial product sold in the scientific field. The problem was the introduction to a new scientific instrument that had application in the education and industrial markets. The traditional approach was used with the dramatic unveiling to all the salesmen; "motivating" speeches by top executives; displays of ads and public relations releases by appropriate people. After the salesmen returned to their appropriate territory, a steady flow of communications was started to bring them new sales aids; comments on new product acceptance in other territories; user comments; etc. The program itself was not unsound, but the feedback at the end of the program was disturbing. Some salesmen liked one or more of the many promotion programs but were critical of others. Some approved of the home office presentation; others thought it "not on target."

In retrospect, and with the hindsight of segmentation, it is clear that such a shotgun approach can indeed only be "average" from the standpoint of any individual salesman. Ideally each salesman should be motivated individually, but costs and a lack of trained supervisors prevent this. In the case at hand, our observations and analyses indicated that a division into three groups was desirable and reasonable from a time standpoint (see chart for a basic model).

Changes have been partially completed in this industrial instrument company. As a first step all sales bulletins, normally sent to the sales force on a monthly basis, have been written in three ways, each appropriate to its own group. Each of the three groups comes to the home office at different times at least once a year. For example, the top producers, the master salesmen, being smaller in number have an informal dinner at the President's house where a wide variety of business problems are discussed, and "hardware" type discussions are carefully shunned. This single change alone had a marked effect on this group. Their individuality and uniqueness had been recognized. (Other variations of this will be discussed in other segments of this paper.)

It can be suggested that this form of segmentation might reduce the "team concept," but the authors' observations, re-enforced by others,[6] is that the cohesiveness of the sales force is often reduced by the presence of the superior producers.

The four cases indicate that segmentation for motivation can be a valuable tool for the marketing manager, if he is willing to transfer the knowledge he has gained from managing his markets. To accomplish this task, a number of guidelines are available.

Bases for Segmentation

The bases involve:

Segmentation for Financial Recognition
Segmentation by Job Title
Segmentation by Personal Recognition
Segmentation by Communications Differences
Segmentation by Peripheral Benefits

"Segmentation by Financial Recognition"

Financial remuneration is still a good basic approach to segmentation whether it be via salary, bonus, commission, etc. However, it is far from the ideal approach. Shown through the years is that with financial segmentation alone the "80/20 law" has remained in force; i.e., the largest share of the orders are obtained by the smallest part of the sales force. The limitations on financial recognition have been magnified in recent years with the decline in the drive for direct financial rewards.[7] As tangible evidence of the **overall business trend** involved, all one has to do is read the many stories of business executives who have resigned from high paying jobs to do "their own thing."

---

[6] Ditz, p. 74.

[7] In the May 8, 1972 issue of *The Wall Street Journal* there was a description of the importance in many companies of being able to eat in executive dining rooms.

Supporting this trend, one writer commented, "The successful sales-man . . . is typically characterized by a sense of status deprivation. For this reason, it is also relatively rare to find an outstanding salesman who feels occupationally fulfilled."[8] It appears financial segmentation while valid for the entire sales force will not cover the overall range for the high performer, who might be able to do better if segmented.

Financial segmentation, however, should not be dismissed lightly. Bo-nus segmentation is realistic and if the bonus percentage is increased for each of the segmented groups in a differentiated way, a significant additional prime motivator can be generated.

"Segmentation by Job Title"

A related problem centers around status. Under present arrangements, the salesman has little opportunity to grow in family and social status through title. This, of course, is a common route of advancement through other areas of the corporate organization.

For example, in industry one finds section heads, department heads, product managers, etc. All these will allow the recipient to report to home, society, and reference group his progress through the organization. Currently, the salesman tends to remain a salesman and must face socially the predictable comments, "Is he still a salesman?" "My gosh, he's 50 years old. Is he still selling?" Job title segmentation is applicable in those cases. For example, the following groupings could be utilized:

Trainees
Salesmen
Senior Salesmen
Master Salesmen

As time advances, it would be expected that the *average* would ad-vance to senior salesmen and the top slot would be reserved for those who consistently have outstanding records. The rate of advancement through the grades would depend upon ability. Provision should be made for outstanding personnel to advance rapidly through the grades.

"Segmentation by Peripheral Benefits"

Another method of segmenting the sales force would be by the benefits offered. For example, many salesmen have company cars, and there could be a segmented system installed based on this benefit. Other peripheral benefits would include the ability to win special trips *not* offered to sales-men in "lower categories" and special rewards given to families. What is being suggested is not the typical sales contest available to the whole group, but segmented programs aimed at rewarding those who achieve at different levels in different ways. This would provide an incentive within the segment, as well as an incentive to be upwardly mobile.

[8] Ditz, p. 75.

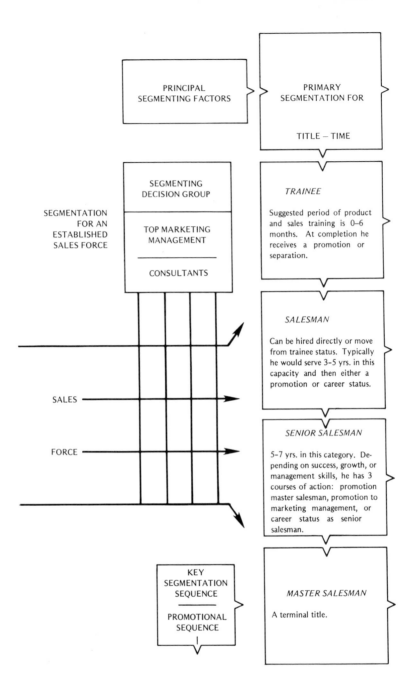

PRINCIPAL SEGMENTING FACTORS

PRIMARY SEGMENTATION FOR

TITLE — TIME

SEGMENTATION FOR AN ESTABLISHED SALES FORCE

SEGMENTING DECISION GROUP

TOP MARKETING MANAGEMENT

CONSULTANTS

TRAINEE

Suggested period of product and sales training is 0–6 months. At completion he receives a promotion or separation.

SALESMAN

Can be hired directly or move from trainee status. Typically he would serve 3–5 yrs. in this capacity and then either a promotion or career status.

SALES

SENIOR SALESMAN

5–7 yrs. in this category. Depending on success, growth, or management skills, he has 3 courses of action: promotion master salesman, promotion to marketing management, or career status as senior salesman.

FORCE

KEY SEGMENTATION SEQUENCE

PROMOTIONAL SEQUENCE

MASTER SALESMAN

A terminal title.

"Segmentation by Personal Recognition"

Since status is an acknowledged problem with the career salesman, personal recognition can be used as a basis for division. For example, the master salesmen can be expected to consult with top management several times a year or to attend annual stockholders meetings. This is

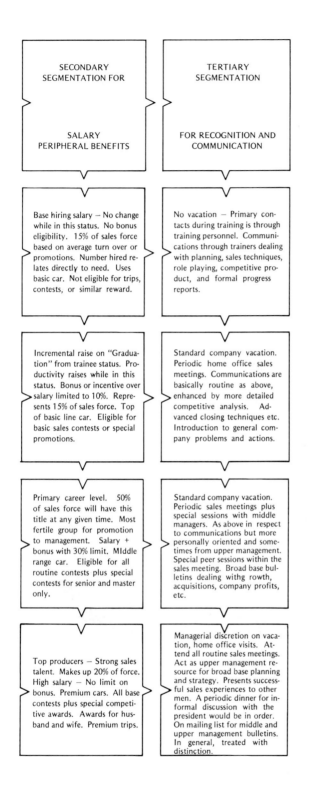

SECONDARY SEGMENTATION FOR	TERTIARY SEGMENTATION
SALARY PERIPHERAL BENEFITS	FOR RECOGNITION AND COMMUNICATION

Base hiring salary — No change while in this status. No bonus eligibility. 15% of sales force based on average turn over or promotions. Number hired relates directly to need. Uses basic car. Not eligible for trips, contests, or similar reward.

No vacation — Primary contacts during training is through training personnel. Communications through trainers dealing with planning, sales techniques, role playing, competitive product, and formal progress reports.

Incremental raise on "Graduation" from trainee status. Productivity raises while in this status. Bonus or incentive over salary limited to 10%. Represents 15% of sales force. Top of basic line car. Eligible for basic sales contests or special promotions.

Standard company vacation. Periodic home office sales meetings. Communications are basically routine as above, enhanced by more detailed competitive analysis. Advanced closing techniques etc. Introduction to general company problems and actions.

Primary career level. 50% of sales force will have this title at any given time. Most fertile group for promotion to management. Salary + bonus with 30% limit. MIddle range car. Eligible for all routine contests plus special contests for senior and master only.

Standard company vacation. Periodic sales meetings plus special sessions with middle managers. As above in respect to communications but more personally oriented and sometimes from upper management. Special peer sessions within the sales meeting. Broad base bulletins dealing withg rowth, acquisitions, company profits, etc.

Top producers — Strong sales talent. Makes up 20% of force. High salary — No limit on bonus. Premium cars. All base contests plus special competitive awards. Awards for husband and wife. Premium trips.

Managerial discretion on vacation, home office visits. Attend all routine sales meetings. Act as upper management resource for broad base planning and strategy. Presents successful sales experiences to other men. A periodic dinner for informal discussion with the president would be in order. On mailing list for middle and upper management bulletins. In general, treated with distinction.

implicit segmentation, but can provide a method of differentiating them from other salesmen. Personal recognition segmentation should bring greater motivation from those in the top group *and* those aspiring to it.

"Segmentation by Communications Differences"

Most firms communicate with their sales force in verbal and written forms in identically the same way. In segmenting for motivation, the astute sales manager would divide the approach as to the needs of the various groups under his direction. Media have been "motivating" in this manner for years with success. They acknowledge that the *New York Times* reader is different from the *Daily News* reader. Advertising copy for the *New Yorker* is obviously written to appeal to certain socio-economic groups, and people of lower social status would not be interested. *The Wall Street Journal* appeals to a specialized segment. Individual involvement in these various levels is a form of personal communication to a peer group. Why do marketing men forget this when they address sales forces and assume they all listen in the same way? A speech is not a speech, is not a speech, is not a speech! At sales meetings, it is poor judgment motivationally to address the top professional in the same manner as one addresses the neophyte.

Possible Approaches To Segmentation

Using the title segmentation developed above, Table 1 is a projected impact of the recognition system that can be extended from it.

Under this segmentation system, the salesman has a potential for job motivation through job recognition. He has an orderly progression through which he has the potential of following, and the top grade puts him in an entrepreneurial position with unlimited earnings by his own efforts. The senior salesman would have a goal for which to strive. He knows that if he exceeds his 30% maximum consistently, he has the potential of reaching the top grade.

Using better communication as an objective, this segmented sales force could be approached as illustrated in Table 2. The communication process described in Table 2 provides a growing level of sophistication as the salesman grows and responds to the motivational cues provided by a segmented approach. Good teachers have been using the same communication approach for years, and the approach would have great value in the market place.

All of the previous discussion is presented in the following model.

The Basic Segmentation And Promotion Relationships: A Model

It would be in order to indicate that a wide variety of firms use an equally wide variety of perquisites and rewards. This chart is not to be read as limiting such segmented recognitions, but merely to suggest scope

TABLE 1 Segmentation by Recognition Systems

Title	% of Force	Time*	Recognition
Trainee	15%	0–6 months	Salary (no change during period)
Salesman	15%	3–5 years	Raise at end of training period to denote a "welcome to the group." Straight salary and modest maximum 10% bonus with productivity raises for the balance of the years *or* until he is promoted to Senior Salesman.
Senior Salesman	50%	5–10 years on the average. The top of the scale for the "solid but average."	The great middle group of career men paid on a salary plus bonus, but with a 30% limit.
Master Salesman	20%	10 years to termination of career or managerial appointment.	High salary, no limitation on bonus. Extra vacation, special visits to home office with top management recognition.

* This time frame (within title sequence) is suggested for those who progress "normally." It will vary by size and type of firm and the individual involved. Some may become master salesmen in a very short time period, if they have unusual ability.

and direction. For example, airline pilots are segmented by sleeve stripes to indicate captain or co-pilot. Some firms might consider the basic units to be a small foreign car, others the regular size basic model progressing to luxury model.

The chart recognizes the possibility of hiring experienced men directly

TABLE 2 Segmentation by Communications Differences

Group	Types of Communication
Trainees	Directly supervised selling situations and critiques, role playing, basic guides to better selling, basic information on planning.
Salesmen	More product information, reports on competition analysis, less directly supervised selling situations; general sales meetings with attention getting devices.
Senior Salesmen	Special company communications from higher ranking executives. Company sales contests specially established for the group. Special sessions at sales meetings. Bulletins dealing with broader base matters.
Master Salesmen	Twice-yearly trips to confer with top management. Present successful sales experiences to other groups. Special advisory panel to sales manager. Frequent consulting requests from top management on appropriate matters.

into upper job categories, i.e., a salesman. While training, his motivating factors would be at salesman level rather than trainee. It would even be conceivable on rare occasions to hire at the master salesman level.

The authors consider the senior salesman category the most fertile source of future marketing managers. If a salesman demonstrated such ability at an early stage he would probably continue to follow sequence and be promoted to senior salesman for a reasonable time prior to promotion to management level; e.g., District Manager.

The writers have deliberately not indicated specific dollar pay ranges as these will vary among firms and industries.

Current day practice primarily deals with financial segmentation. The longer in grade the higher the salary, and the better the performance the higher the bonus. The chart clarifies such action as basic, adding title changes and goes on to demonstrate the many other possible fertile areas of segmenting.

The master salesman title has been indicated as terminal. This has been defined in the sense that such productive iconoclasts are not often promoted to management, but should be retained to retirement if possible. Segmented motivators may now make this possible.

Segmentation Is Not Easy

As with most management problems, the discussion of them is much easier than the implementation. Sales force segmentation for motivation and performance is not an exception, and it involves a number of problems.

"MAKING THE DISTINCTIONS"

At the outset of the program, distinctions in grades will have to be made, upsetting the status quo. This is a difficult process in an ongoing sales organization with an established informal or implicit hierarchy. Some of the personnel who may consider themselves to be master salesmen, may not be considered in the same light by management. However, the problem is not a unique one as it is the work of management to make decisions (in this case distinctions), and management should approach the program as just another human relations problem. A complete awareness of all portions of the program by all marketing people concerned is recommended.

"PRODUCTIVITY—HARD TO DEFINE?"

In some instances, salesmen's productivity is hard to measure. This is particularly true where service is a major facet of an operation. Related to this difficulty is the problem that the sales manager does not always have adequate opportunity to observe the particular salesman in the field. Input from district or regional managers would be helpful. It should be noted, however, that productivity must be assessed under any system to allow salary increases in the normal organization mode, and what is being suggested is just an extension of the assessment process.

"Lack of Interaction"

Segmentation of the sales force may lead to poor interaction between the various levels. Just as a child learns from observation of an adult, so should the beginning salesman learn from the superior salesman. A segmented approach, like the one being presented, would tend to widen the communications gap between the various strata of salesmen. However, as a practical matter, the authors wonder (based on their experience), how much effective interchange now takes place between the various levels. The authors' observations have reinforced the idea that the top producer tends to be a creative iconoclast and he does not think of himself as a "team player." Others have confirmed this, noting the relative absence of activities by salesmen as a cohesive group.[9]

Let's Segment For Motivation

To the action oriented manager intrigued by the potentials of this approach, a number of guidelines are available for taking the initial steps.

"Size of Sales Force"

Segmentation applies best to medium and plus sales forces i.e., 25 salesmen and up. It is always hard to divide small quantities. However, two of the four cases detailed did involve small sales forces, leaving room to modify the suggestion in particular circumstances.

"Problems of Differentiation"

The problem of assigning current personnel to various divisions is not insurmountable. Various group dynamic techniques have been used in other fields for years and can be adapted here. For example, an advisory group can be set up to include division and district managers plus a few outstanding producers who will be in the master salesman group. This panel can be helpful in setting rough criteria by which to staff the initial segments. Once established, the promotion process reverts to the normal, i.e., examination of performance related standards.

"Consultants Can be Helpful"

Since the typical marketing manager may be too close to his sales force (forest and tree problem), outside viewpoints can be helpful to aid him to put matters in perspective. For most firms, the change being proposed is a major one, and substantial decision making support may be needed, depending upon the complexity of the incumbent sales organization.

As with most changes, timing is a critical factor. For such a change, a good sales climate seems desirable. Since segmentation will disturb the current mode where everybody is a salesman, a period of declining sales may not be a desirable period. However, timing may not be a problem, if one has a good sales group which is sufficiently flexible to meet challenges and which can be even better with proper motivation.

"Experimentation"

To begin the segmentation process, it is suggested that it can be done on a small scale within a geographic area, product line or division. As an experimental division, one needs a part of the sales force which is well separated from others. The initial move likely will be quickly noted by others, and it is best to make the move with as little *outside* fanfare as possible until the inevitable bugs in the process are worked out. Supporting the move is the fact that recognition of superior performance by management has always been applauded by salesmen. Segmentation is merely an extension of the process.

Conclusion

After considerable study of available data and examination of the sales structure in local and national companies, an initial reaction is one of surprise that something so obvious as sales force segmentation has not been developed before. If the marketing community agrees, the authors think this idea may be a significant break through for the sales division.

The underlying value of this motivating method is that it provides a system by which the typical career salesman can grow in status, financial remuneration and level of communication. It gives him a career growth pattern similar to that developed for others in the corporate environment.

From the manager's viewpoint, sales force segmentation can provide a key to enabling the salesman to improve his performance and be recognized for it in a number of ways. This, in turn, should improve managements objective—increased sales and customer service productivity.

Improving Sales Force Productivity

WILLIAM P. HALL

Mention "productivity" and the typical manager thinks immediately of the manufacture of more units in less time or at less cost. Indeed, industrial engineering is a well-established profession devoted to setting work standards and constantly searching our opportunities to improve manufacturing productivity.

Less frequently does top corporate management, or marketing management, give thought to sales force productivity. Granted, most sales and marketing managers understand cost ratios and recognize the need to improve volume per salesman or territory. Yet, in attempting to achieve real breakthroughs, they typically suffer from several problems.

- Nobody is quite sure what sales cost ratios are proper for a particular business.
- Applying productivity concepts to a sales force is either unfamiliar ground, distasteful, or a "no-no" area.
  Even if the interest is there, staff support or capability is lacking.
- Solutions are applied piecemeal, or to individual territories, and are not applied as part of a total plan.

WHAT COSTS DO WE LIVE WITH?

Since most productivity improvements are geared to standards of some kind, it helps to start the exercise by giving some thought to standards. Rarely is a stopwatch applied to the activities of sales personnel. Almost never is a time study made of a salesman's day. In fact, the typical reaction of sales management may be, "Salesmen are different, so keep your stopwatch in the factory."

The closest management generally comes to worrying about a sales standard is to address the matter of cost ratios. "How do our costs compare with those of the competition? Are we above or below them?" The typical reply has been, "Well, I really don't know, but old Charlie might tell me if I spend enough time with him over a couple of martinis."

In recent years, increasingly valuable information has been developed to assist in answering the cost question. For example, the American Management Association compensation surveys provide helpful data. Surveys by The Conference Board have also advanced the cause. In recent years, *Sales Management* magazine has initiated its annual survey of selling costs. This survey provides data on levels and trends in compensation, travel, and related costs. Finally, trade associations may survey members,

From *Business Horizons* (Vol. 18), August 1975, pp. 32–42. Reprinted by permission of the publisher, Graduate School of Business, Indiana University.

as often as once a year, to develop pertinent cost and other financial ratios. Many commodity line associations in wholesaling have well organized cost surveys, and such surveys have long been common in retailing.

However, in many areas of the economy, and particularly in manufacturing, good sales cost data are either not available or are too broad in nature. That is, if available, they tend to encompass too many types of businesses and do not break down sales costs into such components as field sales force compensation, travel expenses, and supervision.

During 1974, I participated in two surveys which shed some light on how field sales costs function. Further, they provide insight into answering the perplexing question of how to know when costs are too high and, more important, what to do about it in terms of improved productivity.

Field Cost Inflation

Beginning in the early 1950s, American Supply Association (formerly Central Supply Association), which serves plumbing distributors, has been making surveys of sales compensation practices among its members. Since 1959, A. T. Kearney, Inc., has assisted ASA in preparing and interpreting a number of these surveys. Among the findings are those shown in Table 1.

Although the ratio was somewhat above 3.0 percent in 1970 and somewhat below in 1974, it is apparent that the typical ratio of sales compensation cost to sales has been very close to 3.0 percent over a long period of time. It is further apparent that, as compensation has risen with inflation, sales per territory have increased. Finally, it is clear that if sales volume lags behind salary escalation, as it did in 1970, the cost ratio increases. Or, a significant improvement in volume per territory can drive the cost ratio below the 3.0 percent average, as it did in 1974.

Looking at 1980, if the rate of inflation continues at 10 percent, then the average level of compensation will be $25,865 per salesman. The salesman, in turn, will have to generate sales per territory of $862,000, if his cost ratio is to be 3.0 percent.

TABLE 1   Trend in Salesmen's Compensation Cost Ratios, 1959–1974

Year	Average Sales Per Territory	Average Compensation	Compensation as Percent of Sales
1959	$200,000	$ 6,000	3.0%
1562	238,600	7,200	3.0
1970	322,900	11,000	3.4
1974	536,900	14,600	2.7

Source: American Supply Association

In short, average volume per territory must continue to grow with inflation, and it must be carefully monitored relative to the cost ratio it produces. Further, compensation is only part of the cost of keeping a salesman on the road. Other costs include fringe benefits, travel expenses, supervision, and miscellaneous expenses, such as telephone and office expenses. Finally, the three components of the equation (volume per salesman or territory, cost of the field effort per territory, and the resulting cost ratio) can vary widely from industry to industry.

Beating the Average

A specific survey of field sales costs which I managed in 1974 provides a revealing example of how field sales costs function. Participants were manufacturers of building materials and related products. Each participant provided, among other inputs, data as to average sales volume per sales territory and field sales cost ratios (salesmen's compensation, salesmen's expense, and overhead expense). For four companies with very similar commodity lines, average sales per salesman, and average sales cost ratios were as shown in Table 2. When graphed, the relationship between volume per territory and the cost ratio is rather dramatic, as shown in Figure 1.

Although other survey participants had results above and below the line in the graph, the conclusion is inescapable that higher volume per territory results in substantially lower field sales costs. It may be said that the results are obvious. However, I have not run into too many sales or marketing managers who have had an opportunity to view their results on such a basis. Comparative data are difficult to assemble and often show only average results (as in the ASA survey), not the dramatic differences between Company A and Company D.

Remember that these companies carry roughly similar product lines. If the difference between Company A and Company D were small, it would be easy to claim that the concept had no particular significance. However, consider the possible savings if Company D could achieve a 5.0 percent cost ratio goal (close to the average of the four companies, and yet well below the ratios of Company A and Company B).

Company D has total sales of about $57 million. One way to achieve

TABLE 2   Sales Per Territory and Sales Cost Ratios for Four Selected Companies

Company	Sales Per Salesman	Field Cost Ratio
A	$1,500,000	3.8%
B	1,250,000	4.1
C	990,000	5.3
D	760,000	6.7

FIGURE 1 Cost/Volume Relationship

better results would be to produce $75 million of sales with the same sales force. Since such an increase over current volume might be difficult, another possibility would be to maintain sales at the $57 million level and decrease the number of salesmen. As shown in Table 3, the cost savings possibilities approach $1 million.

The point to be made is that the savings potential is very large, and it is not fictional, for competitors are already enjoying such results. In fact, a 5.0 percent cost ratio is still well below the performance of companies A and B.

Further Observations on the Cost/Volume Ratio

A number of observations should be made about the functioning of the cost/volume relationship, as illustrated in Figure 1.

INFLATIONARY IMPACT

With inflation, the base line formed by the averages moves upward. That is, it functions as shown in Figure 2.

To maintain a 5.0 percent cost ratio over time and with inflation, more volume has to be sold per salesman. In other words, real improve-

TABLE 3 Savings from Inproved Sales Productivity,
Company D

	Average Cost Ratio	
	6.7%	5.0%
Total volume	$57,000,000	$57,000,000
Total field sales cost	3,819,000	2,850,000
Number of salesman	75	56
Average sales per salesman	$ 760,000	$ 1,018,000
Average cost per salesman	50,920	50,920

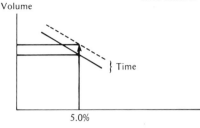

Sales Volume

FIGURE 2   Upward Movement With Time (inflation)

} Time

5.0%

ment in the ratio will only be brought about by increasing volume per territory at a rate substantially greater than the rate of inflation.

INDUSTRY DIFFERENCES

From our study of five different product groups, it is clear that the general cost/volume relationship prevailed for all five. However, the fitted curve varied as shown in Figure 3.

Clearly, cost characteristics can differ between types of products. Hence, it is important to develop the means to compare results with industry groupings which are as similar as possible. The more disparate the industries, the more invalid the comparison. For example, salesmen for steel mills generate very high volumes per individual, while salesmen of institutional furniture and equipment generate relatively low volumes per salesman. A comparison of these two industry groups might appear as in Figure 4.

Useful conclusions can be made by comparing steel companies with each other or institutional furniture companies with one another. Nothing is to be gained by comparising disparate industries, in view of the vastly different sales and product environments.

PROFITABILITY

One shortcoming of the cost/volume comparison is that it lacks any perspective on gross profit performance. It is quite valid to argue, "Sure, we have a higher field cost, but our salesmen sell a more profitable line than Company D." The argument is illustrated in Table 4.

On the one hand, the field cost ratio for Company B is lower, but so also is the profit contribution, because of the low gross profit margin.

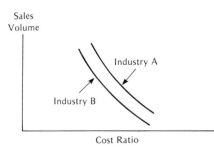

Sales Volume

Industry A

Industry B

Cost Ratio

FIGURE 3   Difference in Cost/ Volume Relationship Between Industries

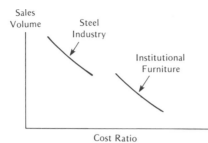

FIGURE 4   Cost/Volume Comparison of Disparate Industries

In short, the lower field cost ratio does not result in a better profit contribution.

On the other hand, the *total gross profit dollars* are higher for Company B. Unfortunately, few surveys will be able to compare both sales and gross profit results. We have been able to make some comparisons among a few wholesaler groups, but most manufacturers are reluctant to provide such data.

Accordingly, in my view, the best assumption is that, if product lines are reasonably similar, then gross profits will be sufficiently similar to allow us to return to the original premise: superior sales volume per salesman will result in a low cost ratio, and this lower ratio will favorably affect net profit.

SALES COMPENSATION PLAN

Management choice of the field sales compensation program can have an important bearing on how the cost/volume curve functions. The three forms of sales compensation are: Salary (fixed), commission (variable), and salary plus incentive (fixed plus variable). To assess the impact of each type of plan on the cost curve, let us assume three salesmen on three different plans. Their results might look as shown in Table 5 and in Figure 5.

As shown, a commission plan can be considered a "variable" expense from an accounting standpoint, in that the expense dollars rise and fall directly with sales volume. However, when looked at from the standpoint of an expense ratio, it can be considered as just the opposite—the ratio remains fixed as sales rise or fall. Conversely, the fixed cost plan (salary)

TABLE 4   Comparison of Sales Costs to Gross Profit Performance

	Company B		Company D	
	000's	*Margin*	*000's*	*Margin*
Sales per salesman	$1,250	100.0%	$760	100.0%
Gross profit	188	15.0	152	20.0
Field Sales cost	51	4.1	51	6.7
Profit contribution	$ 137	10.9%	$101	13.3%

TABLE 5 Cost Impact of Three Compensation Plans at Various Sales Levels

Type of Plan	Sales Volume (Thousands)		
	$250	$500	$750
Salary @ $25,000	$25,000	$25,000	$25,000
Commission @ 5% of sales	12,500	25,000	37,500
Salary @ $12,500 plus commission of 2.5%	18,750	25,000	31,250
Cost Ratios			
Salary plan	10.0%	5.0%	3.3%
Commission plan	5.0	5.0	5.0
Salary plus incentive plan	7.5	5.0	4.2

or fixed plus variable plan (salary plus incentive) results in significant changes in the cost ratio as sales volume rises or falls.

The importance of this analysis becomes clear. The sales/cost ratio relationship is influenced by the type of plan chosen. It is very difficult to drive the cost ratio down with a straight commission plan. However, the ratio is most responsive to a salary plan, and the ratio responds to a salary plus incentive plan. In view of the great popularity of salary plus incentive plans among businesses these days, it is probably fair to say that management has recognized them as an attractive trade-off. That is, they allow for the impact of ratio improvement and, at the same time, provide rewards to the sales force for good performance, albeit not as generous as with a straight commission plan.

In terms of total field expense (compensation, travel, supervision, etc.), almost all plans have both fixed and variable components. Some commission plans cover compensation only, and the company pays for travel expenses, which are fixed or semivariable. Others are designed so that salesmen take both income and expenses from their commission check. Even in this latter case, supervision and general sales administrative costs will result in some fixed cost portion. Nonetheless, the general conclusion prevails that it becomes much more difficult to generate field sales cost

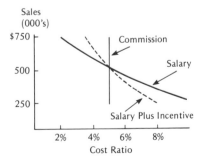

FIGURE 5 Sales/Cost Relationship Based on Various Compensation Plans

ratio improvement with a commission plan. Productivity improvement under commission plans is difficult, when considered in terms of cost ratio reduction.

FIELD MANAGEMENT PROBLEMS

Before attacking the questions of why Company A produces such demonstrably better results than Company D and what management of Company D might do about it, some comments should be made about changing conditions which have resulted in the wide variations in performance between companies. Several of these problems, when faced individually or in concert, may have confounded the management of Company D.

SALES COST ESCALATION

Ample discussion has already been given to the need to stay ahead of the inflation treadmill. Just to stay even with higher compensation costs and travel expenses, sales per territory must go up proportionately. When sales do not at least keep pace, trouble is abrewing.

MARKET CHANGES

Shifts in market size and characteristics call for different sales approaches. As one example, the growth of chain stores and decline of small food retailers has occasioned major shifts in sales approaches by both manufacturers and wholesalers.

"The sales/cost ratio relationship is influenced by the type of (compensation) plan chosen. It is very difficult to drive the cost ratio down with a straight commission plan."

PRODUCT PROLIFERATION

As product lines have grown, the sales job has become more complex and demanding. Management is faced with the question of when to drop the generalist in favor of the specialist.

CHANGING CHANNELS

The most successful channel of ten years ago may not be the best way to market today. The building material manufacturer had better have programs geared to the home improvement center chain, or he will be facing a serious loss of position.

COMPETITIVE ENVIRONMENT

Growth markets attract new competitors, and mature markets become fiercely price competitive. (At what level will the price of electronic calculators bottom out?)

The sales management equation is not a simple one; hence, achievement of better performance is bedeviled by numerous problems. Yet, these very complexities create an environment for markedly different results between companies in similar businesses. There is ample evidence that wide differences in performance exist.

OPPORTUNITIES FOR PROFIT IMPROVEMENT

In almost every company with conscientious sales management, some type of effort is being made to improve productivity. Each effort may have a modest effect, but, in combination, the results may be impressive. Some of the more productive approaches are worthy of comment. These can best be classified into three broad categories. Beginning with specific problems of territory management and moving towards broad sales/marketing management, these problem categories include territory management, job specialization/job simplification, and general sales management.

Territory Management

This facet of sales productivity improvement relates directly to the field sales effort in terms of what can be accomplished within each territory. It is directed towards the classical sales coverage, which is geographically oriented. Steps for improvement typically include (1) a time and duty analysis, (2) a customer/prospect audit and ABC analysis, and (3) changes in incentive compensation practices.

A time and duty analysis is essentially the function of the industrial engineer. It identifies the major functional components of the sales job (direct face-to-face selling, waiting, travel, and paper work) and assigns time (and costs) to these elements. It is an aspect of sales management not commonly challenged and not frequently actually studied.

One analysis of sample territories for a large greetings card manufacturer revealed that a substantial portion of the time of well-paid salesmen was being spent serving distributor inventories. This time/cost analysis led to the conclusion that significant improvement in sales force productivity could be realized if the service effort were shifted to lower cost specialists.

A fundamental approach to improved geographical coverage is through application of the ABC analysis based on the customer/prospect audit. Essentially, this technique consists of an analysis of all customers and prospects in a territory, followed by a ranking in terms of their potential into A, B, and C categories. Based on several criteria, the A category would require the most concentrated sales/marketing efforts, and the C category the least. Goals are then set in terms of sales efforts (calls), with the greatest concentration on A accounts.

For example, if a salesman can make one hundred calls per month, he might allocate them as follows: category A, seventy calls per month;

TABLE 6 Application of ABC Analysis in Seven Territories, 1970–73

Customer Ranking	Dealers		Calls		Volume (Thousands)	
	1970	1973	1970	1973	1970	1973
A	53	140	849	2,406	$ 609	$2,478
B	109	151	1,554	1,974	766	1,071
C	428	327	4,232	3,028	1,064	839
D	371	251	1,852	1,008	143	80
Total	961	869	8,487	8,416	$2,582	$4,468

category B, twenty; and category C, ten. Customers ranked below C might be covered by telephone or direct mail.

A midwestern wholesaler of farm machinery has emphasized the ABC approach since the late 1960s. Salesmen covering seven territories call on farm equipment dealers. As a result of management emphasis on building volume with A and B dealers, the customer mix shifted from 1970 to 1973 as shown in Table 6. It is interesting to note that the shift in emphasis resulted in the growth of average sales per territory from $368,000 in 1970 to $640,000 in 1973. The sales growth was substantially greater than the increase in field sales expense. Hence, the field cost ratio was reduced, and the savings went to net profit.

As pointed out earlier, profit pay-off from improved sales force productivity can be influenced by the type of sales compensation plan selected. Once the farm equipment wholesaler sold its sales management and sales personnel on the ABC approach, it changed sales compensation from a heavy commission orientation to a salary plus incentive, with the incentive heavily weighted towards products with good profitability and of interest to A and B dealers. The plan has provided improved income to salesmen, accompanied by reduced sales cost ratios. Needless to say, tying incentives to management goals is an essential ingredient of good territory management.

Job Specialization/Job Simplification

The old adage "Don't work harder, work smarter" applies quite appropriately to a growingly complex and costly sales force. As a sales force expands, cost/effectiveness benefits based on job specialization or job simplification begin to surface. This aspect of improved productivity may combine changes in territory management with some changes in supervisory or corporate roles.

Job specialization can be directed either by product or by market.

For example, AMP Incorporated may have salesmen within a territory specializing by product line. Further, they may be supported by a special task force to assist in introducing a new product or rejuvenating an old one.

Another approach is to orient salesmen by industry specialization. IBM has specialized its sales force along industry lines (banking, insurance, retailing, and wholesaling). Where market demand is shifting, the key need may be to change emphasis from one channel to another. A few years ago, swingline shifted its sales force from heavy wholesale to retail emphasis, increased the number of calls per outlet (five to seven per day) and encouraged more effective activity per call. The shift in customer emphasis and effectiveness per call resulted in substantially higher order size and output per salesman.

Impressive improvements in productivity can be generated by changing the sales job content to allow for greater specialization by function. Such approaches typically involve shifting the expensive field sales effort away from lower value and time consuming activities towards more productive pursuits. The latter activities can be taken on by a specialist who can handle them at lower cost and often with greater skill.

One example is to cover low volume accounts by telephone or by mail. U.S. Gypsum Company has initiated such a program in one of its eastern regions. A computerized analysis of accounts identified customers with consistent purchases but low volume. These accounts were taken away from salesmen and given to a telephone sales person for regular contact. In many cases, regularity of contacts has been improved, the cost of solicitation reduced, and sales increased.

In an entirely different business, a household goods moving company developed a telephone solicitation program to generate sales appointments. When implemented by the agency sales force of over 1,000 persons, the average salesman produced 1.5 times more booked business.

Another example of productivity improvement is the provision of specialty support personnel to back up the sales effort in such areas as distributor stocking and inventory control or retail shelf service. The example has already been cited of the greetings card company which identified the opportunity to shift distributor inventory servicing from salesmen to specialists. In my experience, successful food brokers have long since learned the merits of separating the sales function from the routine tasks of retail shelf service (stock checking, stock rotation, and pricing). Large brokers typically employ a small group of sales personnel who maintain sales contacts at the buyer and store manager level. These sales persons are, in turn, supported by field personnel who perform the in-store services.

A final example of the benefits to be gained from the specialist is in terms of service or technical support personnel. For example, a regional manufacturer of prefabricated and modular housing has enjoyed significant market penetration and relatively low fields sales costs because salesmen are instructed to turn all technical and service problems over to a headquarters specialist. A less effective competitor's salesmen are regularly involved in time-consuming technical and service problems.

General Sales Management

What takes place at headquarters has an important impact on sales productivity. The types of field improvement already described can best be achieved when they fit within a sound general sales management framework. Some elements include (1) a dynamic and current organization structure, (2) a good planning program, and (3) adequate analysis of territory potential and customer profitability.

A few years ago, American Seating Company made concerted effort to improve the productivity of its sales force and reduce field costs. One major initial step in the program was the reorganization of the field sales effort into three sales forces built along market lines—amusement, education, and transportation. Since the change, major shifts in demand have occurred in each market, and monitoring of sales productivity and costs has been greatly facilitated by the structural change.

Without adequate documentation of sales objectives, goals, and strategies at the headquarters, regional, and territory levels, it is almost impossible to mount a sustained improvement program. Invariably, the company with a well-thought-out plan has done its analytical homework. That is, it knows where it stands relative to competition and has ongoing plans to stay ahead or catch up. My own experience over the years (with companies making such diverse products as gloves, domestic water pumps, and compressor components) confirms that well-documented and implemented marketing plans produce beneficial profit results.

A final necessary ingredient at the headquarters level is adequate analysis, with two of the most important areas being territory potential analysis and customer profitability analysis. Although the customer/prospect audit of a territory is an invaluable sales tool, it often is subject to significant errors. When initiated at the territory level, the effort often identifies potential which is less than 50 per cent of what is actually available. To bridge the gap between what salesmen think is present as potential and what actually exists, calls for "top down," or a broad national view of potential within geographical areas (territories), wherever the exercise is practical in terms of available data. Such an analysis provides the necessary inputs for shifts in territory alignment or changes in personnel within territories. A typical type of sales performance index developed for a manufacturer of electrical parts is shown in Table 7. In this instance, some thought might be given to changing personnel in Territory A. Also, although volume in Territory C is adequate relative to potential, consideration might be given to splitting the territory.

An essential requirement in guiding field efforts is customer profitability analysis. In establishing criteria to determine what should constitute an A classification for a customer, the first ingredient should be sales potential. Often, this figure can be determined quite accurately in the field, with some assistance from headquarters market research or product management personnel who are charged with potential analysis. However, the field force is totally reliant upon its accounting department to supply customer profitability data. It is clear that such analysis provides another important criterion for ranking customers on an ABC basis. A

TABLE 7   Sales Performance Index

Territory	Potential	Sales As Percent of Total	Sales Performance Index
A	7.22%	5.77%	80
B	3.17	4.39	138
C	13.58	14.58	107
↓	↓	↓	↓
Total	100.0 %	100.0 %	100

customer with an A rating in terms of sales potential, but who provides marginal profits or losses, must clearly be rerated, perhaps to the C or D categories. Here is the means to supply the missing ingredient—profitability. The final thrust then becomes one of improving sales productivity and cost ratios, but within the constraint of a profit goal.

The Sales Audit

What have been described up to this point are a number of ingredients for improving sales force productivity. In almost all sales forces, some of the many ingredients are present, but if something is missing, a new program may provide improved results.

In many cases, dramatic opportunities for improvement can best be achieved by a broad overview of the field sales effort. Such an audit program can be undertaken by a specially appointed internal team, by a company's captive consulting group, by an outside consultant, or by any combination of the foregoing. In fact, the combination approach is often the most effective, and, in fact, is in keeping with modern practice in seeking productivity improvement. The audit should include the following:

- *Marketing Profile.* This phase involves identifying company objectives, strategies, market position, sales organization, territorial coverage, sales results, costs, and profit results. It establishes the basic framework within which improvement opportunities can be identified.
- *Definition of Selling Function.* This step identifies the major functional components of the field sales job in terms of current practices versus both management objectives and market requirements. The components of the job may include planning, travel, waiting, face-to-face selling, service, and paper work.
- *Evaluation of Effectiveness.* Somewhat different from how a salesman is spending his time is the question of his effectiveness, again relative to company objectives, market requirements, and competitive activities.

- *Analysis of Territory Configuration and Coverage.* This step is concerned with the nature and rationale for the current sales territories in terms of geographical configurations, sales potentials, sales goals, and workload (time available and calls made).
- *Review of Information System.* It is important to determine whether information is adequate and timely to serve sales management and permit performance measurement.
- *Evaluation of Sales Management.* This phase calls for an evaluation of the field sales organization structure (including direct selling, supervisory, and support personnel), an appraisal of the effectiveness of personnel, and an indication as to whether the compensation plans at all levels of the sales force are supportive of management objectives and strategies.
- *Ranking of Improvement Opportunities.* As the result of the previous six analyses, a number of improvement opportunities are typically identified. Because, in our experience, a smorgasbord of ideas evolves, it becomes critical to rank the opportunities in terms of importance and pay-off potential. Without setting priorities, the effort can degenerate into an exercise in fighting brush fires.
- *Development of an Implementation Program.* The final step is to create a work plan calling for specific action within each top priority area, identifying program responsibilities, establishing time schedules, and setting up monitoring procedures.

In some cases, top management has been worried over a "high" field sales cost, only to find that costs for the particular industry are not that far out of line, and only fine tuning or modest changes are needed. In other cases, the improvement opportunities are large and very real. I am thinking of a current study where the improvement potential in terms of cost reduction is in the magnitude of $500,000.

Where significant changes are appropriate, the time span from problem identification to implementation of improvement programs can be agonizingly slow. I remember having to wait six months to revise an incentive compensation plan, while the accounting department came up with profitability data by salesmen. Also, one change which may take a year to accomplish may necessarily precede another which, in its turn, will take a year to implement.

It is my observation, as indicating as it may sound, that such audits are seldom initiated by sales management. To begin with, there is a certain untouchable mystique about marketing costs. Often, corporate or divisional managers with backgrounds in finance, production or engineering are somewhat in awe of marketing management, and an audit is their wedge to challenge the mystique. In fairness, competent sales management will respond that the audit is not needed, because it will merely confirm superior results.

To return to the opening analysis, sales cost ratios are coming under increasing scrutiny. With inflation, sales results per salesman or per territory must be constantly improved just to maintain an even cost ratio. However, wide differences are apparent within similar industries and product groups, as to the volume that can be generated per salesman, and the results are closely correlated to cost ratios. The differences in ratio results are very large; in fact, they indicate that improvements offer substantial cost savings.

Many approaches to sales force productivity improvement are possible and have been successfully adopted by sales management. Yet, where productivity appears to be out of line, a more broad scale attack in terms of a general audit may be appropriate. While there is some risk of only a limited pay-off, the more typical outcome is a substantial change in practices and bottom line results.

Sales Management in the Future

Current and Future Challenges
in Sales Management

CHAPTER 1 discussed the evolution of the selling function within the firm. We have seen that the selling function evolved from a pure orientation to a societal focus embodying a marketing concept. This chapter turns from past evolution in sales management to concentrate on future directions.

What are some of the changes that sales management can expect in the next few years? This was the subject of a recent article in the *Marketing News,* which suggested the following changes may occur in the next few years where sales management is concerned.

Trend: The average American family is seeking a less mobile lifestyle, as revealed in Census Bureau data and in the experience of major corporations such as Delta, FMC Corp., and Polaroid.

Implication: Salespeople may resist transfer. It may become more difficult to attract new salespeople if they must move to a new area; incentives may have to be offered.

Trend: More Americans are living alone. Because of later marriages, higher divorce rates, and so on, people living alone now represent 21 per cent of all United States households—up from 17 per cent in 1970.

Implication: There is a potential for new products or for smaller portions of existing products. Marketing approaches may have to be oriented to people living alone.

Trend: The population of the country is growing older on the average. By 1990 Americans 14 to 25 will decline by 7.2 million—to 37.9 million, 16 per cent fewer than in 1975.

Implication: Look for a shift away from youth-oriented culture, tastes, and styles. In addition fewer young people may be available for the sales force.

Trend: More workers will be on the night shift because of time-of-day pricing of new electricity rates offering cheaper night-time power.

Implication: It may become necessary to develop sales staffs and methods to meet the needs of the growing night forces. Night workers may need a new range of products and services, and part-time work may increase.

Trend: Americans will be retiring later.

Implication: Older people will have more spendable income; more older people will be holding down jobs, and more will be seeking jobs. Companies will have to motivate older persons—to work or step down.

Trend: Equipment leasing is gaining popularity versus outright ownership.

Implication: Leasing may have to be incorporated into marketing efforts. It is a marketing tool that can allow a company to close sales that would have been delayed because of unavailability of capital.

Trend: Increasingly, middle managers and key employees are getting employment contracts. Employees win security and can plan career improvement. Noncompetitive stipulations aid the employer.

Implication: Great care must be exercised in selecting salespeople, since contracts tend to favor the employee.

Trend: The public sector, now about 40 per cent of the GNP, will increase to 50 per cent by the end of the century.

Implication: If you can't beat them, join them. Governments represent a vast, albeit frustrating, market.

Trend: The consumerism trend is rising, brand loyalty shrinking. The public is asking for more highly refined marketing practices in the direction of providing more information, more efficiency, and greater responsiveness.

Implication: The marketer should seek out customer opinions on product improvement and make promotional material more meaningful, incorporating consumer suggestions.

Trend: Electronic funds transfer is mushrooming in business and in government, where EFT is expected to account for 20 million transactions a month by 1981.

Implication: EFT can be developed as a customer service and as a marketing tool—and also may reduce costs.

Trend: Technology will reshape life—in communications and energy and in training and selling. By the mid-1980s, 3 million videotelephones may be in use.

Implication: Tomorrow's management will be able to use salespeople highly trained in computer technology and energy conservation and with innovative ideas on how to use new technology.

Trend: Multiearner families are on the increase, and more women will be managers. By 1990, there may be 43.7 million women in the labor force, up 22 per cent over 1974.

Implication: Management will have to become more adept in training, managing, and motivating women.

Trend: Although management has achieved some favorable results in dealing with situation stress in employees, depression is becoming the number one mental problem among salespeople and managers. Sales of tranquilizers have increased rapidly, and it is estimated that 15–20 per cent of Americans need some form of mental assistance.

Implication: Sales managers will have to learn to recognize depression symptoms; some psychological training for managers will become necessary.

Trend: Detachment will produce more "future shock" problems. More and more people are being removed from the family concept of society.

One of every three school children lives in a home headed by one parent or relative.

Implication: Management will deal less with the family as a motivating factor. Family trips and benefits and compensation programs, such as insurance, may become less attractive.

Trend: Corporate emphasis on profit on sales, rather than merely gross sales volume, is growing.

Implication: Profit performance on sales dollars may become an objective for training and rating criteria.

Trend: Foreign competition is growing and is causing major shifts in the marketplace.

Implications: Sales managers must become increasingly aware of occurrences in global, as well as domestic, markets.

Trend: Psychological testing in hiring will decrease because of right-to-work, equal opportunity, and privacy laws, plus general public antipathy.

Implication: Other evaluative criteria, such as situation testing, will move up. Attorneys will screen all tests.

Trend: Inflation and negotiated labor contracts have made it harder for sales managers to win compensation that is adequate and equitable.

Implication: Since the manager can't make much more than his force, loss of incentive may unfavorably affect companies' management selection and development plans.

Trend: Forecasting of political, social, and technological changes will decrease sole reliance on economic data.

Implication: New methods of gathering data required for sales forecasts will be developed.

Trend: Job applicants, better educated, less concerned with job-related status symbols, more concerned with "quality of life," have less respect for authority than ever.

Implication: Sales management must reevaluate its thinking about job content, sharpen personnel management techniques, and develop new reward and promotion methods.[1]

The Changing World of Sales Management

In 1970, Leslie M. Dawson published an article dealing with the future of sales management. In this article, he traces the emphasis in sales management during this century and projects into the future some changes that he foresees. Figure 13.1 summarizes the changing emphasis in sales management that Dawson provides.

Focusing upon the decade of the 70's, Dawson has suggested:

Several studies have indicated that it is lack of recognition and prestige which frustrates and demoralizes the salesman (even the successful salesman) more than

[1] Henry Lavin, "How Next Generation of Managers Sees Future," *The Marketing News* (Vol. XI, No. 20), April 7, 1978, p. 3.

	Year			
	1900 1910 1920	1930 1940	1950 1960	1970
BUSINESS RESPONSE TO PERCEIVED DOMINANT ENVIRONMENTAL CONDITIONS	Production Orientation	Sales Orientation	Marketing Orientation	Human Orientation
EMPHASIS IN MANAGEMENT'S CONCEPTION OF SALES JOB	Personality Art	"Scientific" Salesmanship	Professionalism	Personal Fulfillment
EMPHASIS IN SALES MANAGEMENT	Tight Supervision and Control	Broadened Responsibilities	Strategies and Profits	Total Human Resource Development

FIGURE 13.1   Changing Emphasis in Sales Management in This Century [Source: James M. Comer, ed., *Sales Management: Roles and Methods* (Santa Monica, Cal.: Goodyear Publishing Company, Inc., 1977), p. 361.]

any other job-related factor. Relevant also are the widely accepted estimates that one-half of all young persons who enter the sales field are unsuccessful in the career, and that 20 per cent of the nation's salesmen currently account for 80 per cent of the total sales of products and services. These indications of widespread failure and mediocrity constitute a human and economic waste of truly staggering proportions. While neither statistics nor management's concern with their impact on profits is new, what is new is the strong moral mandate for an end to this waste which a human orientation thrusts upon business management. Professional development is one part of the answer, but salesmen are whole men; thus their development within personal dimensions cannot be ignored and is likely to gain increasing attention.[2]

Clearly, the personal development of sales personnel and management's responsibility for the end of the waste of human resources has opened up a new perspective for sales management. This perspective has to do with the employment of women in both selling and sales management positions.

As Johnson has stated:

Women have held a predominant position in retail selling for many years. Now they are moving into selling jobs which previously were all staffed by men. Statistics in 1975 indicated that about 10 per cent of sales jobs were staffed by women. This trend is likely to increase as women demonstrate capacity to sell machinery, automobiles, factory supplies, and many other types of merchandise.[3]

This increasing use of women in the sales force foreseen by Johnson has in fact come to pass. Reading 1 of Part III deals with the role of women in selling and sales management.[4]

[2] Leslie M. Dawson, "Toward A New Concept of Sales Management," *Journal of Marketing* (April 1970), in James M. Comer, ed., *Sales Management: Roles and Methods* (Santa Monica, Cal.: Goodyear Publishing Company, Inc., 1977), p. 358.
[3] H. Webster Johnson, *Sales Management: Operations, Administration, and Marketing* (Columbus, Ohio: Charles E. Merrill Publishing Company, 1977), p. 89.
[4] See Dan H. Robertson and Donald W. Hackett, "Saleswomen: Perceptions, Problems, and Prospects," *Journal of Marketing*, July 1977, pp. 66–71.

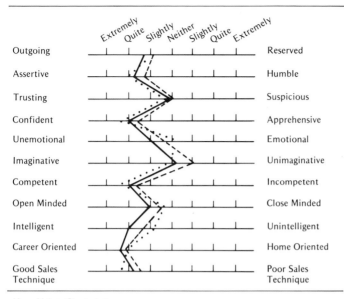

FIGURE 13.2 Profile of a Salesman [Source: Dan H. Robertson and Donald W. Hackett, "Saleswomen: Perceptions, Problems and Prospects," *Journal of Marketing* (July, 1977), p. 69.]

Mean Values Charted above are:

Characteristic	Saleswomen	Salesmen	Sales Managers
Outgoing/Reserved	2.7	3.0	2.8
Assertive/Humble	2.5	2.8	2.3
Trusting/Suspicious	3.8	3.8	3.8
Confident/Apprehensive	2.4	2.6	2.3
Unemotional/Emotional	3.4	3.7	3.8
Imaginative/Unimaginative	4.4	4.9	4.0
Competent/Incompetent	2.1	2.4	2.0
Open Minded/Close Minded	3.2	3.4	3.6
Intelligent/Unintelligent	2.2	2.6	3.2
Career Oriented/Home Oriented	1.7	2.0	2.2
Good Sales Technique/Poor Sales Technique	2.4	2.5	2.1

Legend   Salesmen,   Saleswomen,   . . .   Sales Managers

* Significant at .05 level.

Let us see how women have been perceived by both their male sales peers and by sales managers. Figure 13.2 presents a profile of salesmen as they are perceived by their fellow salesmen, saleswomen, and sales managers. In similar fashion, Figure 13.3 presents a profile of saleswomen as they are perceived by salesmen, saleswomen, and sales managers.

This article suggested that sales managers differ in their perceptions of both salesmen and saleswomen from that of the salesmen themselves and the saleswomen themselves.

In contrast to the male and female perceptions of salesmen [Figure 13.2], sales managers viewed salesmen as more assertive, imaginative and more given to utilize good sales technique. Sales managers also viewed male sales personnel as less emotional, open-minded and intelligent than did male or female sales respondents.

Sales managers also differed in their perceptions of female sales representatives. Specifically, they viewed saleswomen as more reserved, humble, apprehensive, imaginative, and home oriented than did either the male or female sales personnel

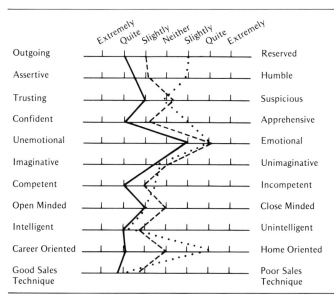

FIGURE 13.3   Profile of a Saleswoman [Source: See 13.2.]

Mean Values Charted above are:

Characteristic	Saleswomen	Salesmen	Sales Managers
Outgoing/Reserved	2.3	2.9	5.1
Assertive/Humble	2.7	2.9	5.0
Trusting/Suspicious	3.3	3.9	3.7
Confident/Apprehensive	2.2	3.4	5.0
Unemotional/Emotional	4.9	6.8	5.8
Imaginative/Unimaginative	3.7	3.9	3.5
Competent/Incompetent	1.8	3.1	3.3
Open Minded/Close Minded	2.8	3.9	3.1
Intelligent/Unintelligent	1.9	2.6	2.3
Career Oriented/Home Oriented	2.3	4.1	5.7
Good Sales Technique/Poor Sales Technique	1.8	3.1	2.4

Legend	Salesmen,	Saleswomen,	. . .	Sales Managers

Significant at .05 level.

[see Figure 13.3]. Additionally, sales managers depicted saleswomen as somewhat less competent than did either male or female sales respondents.[5]

Thus, although saleswomen are an emerging force in personal selling today, it is important to note the differing perceptions of women in selling. Likewise, as women begin to develop as sales managers, they will have to contend with such differences in perceptions.

Commenting upon the transition from females in selling to sales management, a recent article concludes:

> Some companies say, however, that fear of stubborn male chauvinism in the field has prevented them from hiring their first female sales representative, not to mention promoting women into management. At one such company, in which the average age of the salesmen is 55–60, the vice president says, "I'd be reluctant to hire a female and throw her on our salesmen's mercies. They go out of their way to find reasons not to hire women." To get the affirmative action he feels is necessary to give his company the widest possible choice of future management talent, the executive says he plans to hire a few high-potential females and direct their growth himself. "They'll work in the field, but they'll report to someone at headquarters," he says. "By the time they're ready for field management, many of our current salesmen will have retired. I feel confident that the younger people who replace them will accept women managers."[6]

Thus, if the evolution of sales management is to continue, human resources in their fullest sense must be employed.[7] One of the cases at the end of this chapter asks the student to try to resolve some of the issues concerning women in selling and sales management.

Fulfilling the Forecasts of the Past

In order to gain a fuller appreciation of the future direction of sales management, let's look at some of the forecasts that have been made for the future of sales management and examine how closely we have come to fulfilling those prophecies. In discussing the 1970s and beyond, Dawson[8] forecast three specific changes for the future. These included

1. Greater concern over personal development of sales people. We have commented upon this issue in the preceding section of this chapter;
2. A second forecast that Dawson made was the greater use of computers in sales management.
3. A third forecast was for more professionalism in the personal selling field.

---

[5] *Ibid.*, p. 70.

[6] "Manage Sales? Yes, She Can," *Sales & Marketing Management,* July 13, 1977, p. 35.

[7] The student who is interested in a role of women in selling may also wish to see Leslie Kanuk, "Women in Industrial Selling," *Journal of Marketing,* January 1978, pp. 87–91; Rena Bartos, "What Every Marketer Should Know About Women," *Harvard Business Review,* May–June 1978, pp. 78–85; and John E. Swan, Charles M. Futrell, and John T. Todd, "Same Job—Different Views: Women and Men in Industrial Selling," *Journal of Marketing,* January 1978, pp. 92–98.

[8] Leslie M. Dawson, "Toward a New Concept of Sales Management," pp. 33–39.

The second specific forecast made by Dawson, concerning the greater use of computers, has been discussed at some length by Comer.[9] In an excellent article reviewing the applications of the computer to personal selling and sales management, Comer found two general areas of application. First, he notes the application of the computer to sales reporting and analysis systems. Second, Comer noted the applications of the computer to planning-oriented systems for uses such as discussed in the last part of Chapter 9.

Regarding sales reporting and analysis systems, Comer comments:

Firms have had sales reporting and analysis systems for decades. Reporting has been as informal as casual verbal exchanges or as stringent as daily written reports. Sales managers, in most cases, conducted analysis by reading call reports and comparing them with actual sales. They were then expected to draw vital conclusions about such things as salesmen abilities and performance and customer response to programs. They were also required to make rational decisions about sales territory design, sales force size, and so on. Given these kinds of responsibilities and the expansion of sales forces over wider geographic areas, it is not surprising that published accounts in the 1960s about the innovative introduction of the computer into sales management were glowing.[10]

As Comer noted, however, further refinement needed to be made in these systems. The Pillsbury Company, for example, experimented with two such systems, one known as SOAR (Store Objectives and Accomplishments Report) and a second report known as REACH (Retail Achievement Report).[11] Both systems had as their objective to provide additional data not only on sales to particular accounts but also upon the allocation of salespeople's time. As Comer notes:

The immediate objective of such a system was to relieve sales managers of their data-matching responsibility and give them more time for certain planning activities.[12]

The REACH report put more emphasis upon salespeople's physical activities such as the building of displays, and so on. However, both SOAR and REACH are hardly the ultimate in system development. Weiss has described a differing system in which the salesperson is linked by a device that he carries to a master computer so that instantaneous changes in record and information can be transmitted electronically as they occur.[13] Suffice it to say that sales reporting has yet to reach this level of technological sophistication; nonetheless, firms have adapted the computer to suit increasingly sophisticated needs in terms of market information.

Regarding planning-oriented systems, Comer reviews developments in this field and suggests that they fall into three basic categories. These

[9] James M. Comer, "The Computer, Personal Selling, and Sales Management," *Journal of Marketing*, July 1975, pp. 27–33, in Marvin A. Jolson (ed.), *Contemporary Readings in Sales Management* (New York: Petrocelli/Charter, 1977).
[10] *Ibid.*, p. 288.
[11] *Ibid.*, p. 289.
[12] *Ibid.*, p. 288.
[13] E. P. Weiss, "The Salesman Gets Hooked into Management Systems," *Advertising Age*, June 14, 1965, pp. 84–87.

include (1) call allocation determination, (2) sales territory design, and (3) salesmen routing issues much like those discussed previously in Chapter 9 of this text. Comer concludes that a basic problem for management is to gain the internal support and cooperation of the sales force for any of these planning-oriented systems to work in a feasible manner. He suggests three particular considerations:

1. It is a tenet of human relations theory that involving people in the formulation/design of a project tends to invoke commitment. So, in the system design stage, solicit salesmen/sales manager participation wherever possible.

2. The development and installation of any new system, especially one such as this, is bound to cause anxiety about job loss or fears of inadequacy in dealing with the "monster." Although there is no perfect solution, familiarity can help reduce fears and anxieties. Therefore, introduce the system slowly and carefully, and hold frequent training sessions to educate your personnel in system use.

3. In tests, Lodish and Armstrong had salesmen use the systems on their own territories. Both reported salesmen conclusions that the program allocated calls better than they could. The implication is that the salesmen developed favorable attitudes toward the system because they could, on their own initiative, construct better call routines. The message to management is clear: to maintain salesman morale when you are instituting changes using a system, whenever possible have the salesman see for himself the beneficial effects for his territory.[14]

It is clear that a great deal of progress has been made regarding integration of the computer and computerized capabilities into the areas of personal selling and sales management. It is also clear, however, that human considerations must not be overlooked. If we are to proceed in the future to fulfill the prophecy of Comer and others regarding the capabilities of the computer, sales management must understand the inherent potential for fear and resentment on behalf of salespersons. They must also understand the need for full explanations so that sales personnel can comprehend the reasons behind the use of such systems and see for themselves firsthand the benefits that such systems can provide to the sales force.

A third change foreseen by Dawson was a change toward more professionalism in selling and sales management. Commenting on this point, Stroh has suggested:

Sales management in the next decade needs to become a profession with strict standards and entrance requirements and ongoing educational upgrading. Accountants and lawyers in business have achieved professionalism and have demonstrated how sales managers can achieve the same results.

In the insurance industry, the Certified Life Underwriter (C.L.U.) is a symbol of the professionalism of the insurance specialists. In the same way the Sales and Marketing Executives International, for example, can create the Certified Sales Manager (C.S.M.), which would distinguish the elite professional from the mass of practitioners. In a ten-year period this could become so well recognized that employers might well make it a requirement to fulfill the sales management job.[15]

[14] Jolson, *op. cit.*, pp. 295–296.
[15] Thomas F. Stroh, *Managing the Sales Function* (New York: McGraw-Hill Book Company, Inc., 1978), pp. 433–434.

Clearly, this change has not yet been fulfilled. However, strides are being made in this direction and some would contend that, viewed in retrospect, these strides represent gigantic steps forward.

Current Agents of Change

A variety of forces occurring at the present time is producing change in the area of personal selling and sales management. Included among these current forces are three prominent factors.

The Changing Legal Environment

In the past few years we have seen an increasing number of governmental agencies evolve for the purpose of regulation of business. Discussed or alluded to in earlier chapters, these agencies include the Equal Employment Opportunity Commission, the Environmental Protection

Agency	Year Enforcement Began	Complaint May Name Individual	Maximum Individual Penalty	Maximum Corporate Penalty	Private Suit Allowed Under Applicable Statute
Internal Revenue Service	1862	Yes	$5,000, three years, or both	$10,000, 50% assessment, prosecution costs	No
Antitrust Div. (Justice Dept.)	1890	Yes	$100,000, three years, or both	$1 million, injunction, divestiture	Yes
Food & Drug Administration	1907	Yes	$1,000, one year, or both for first offense, $10,000, three years, or both therafter	$1,000 for first offense, $10,000 thereafter, seizure of condemned products	No
Federal Trade Commission	1914	Yes	Restitution, injunction	Restitution, injunction, divestiture, $10,000 per day for violation of rules, orders	No
Securities & Exchange Commission·	1934	Yes	$10,000, two years, or both	$10,000, injunction	Yes
Equal Employment Opportunity Commission	1965	No		Injunction, back pay award, reinstatement	Yes
Office of Federal Contract Compliance	1965	No		Suspension, cancellation of contract	Yes
Environmental Protection Agency	1970	Yes	$25,000 per day, one year, or both for first offense, $50,000 per day, two year, or both thereafter	$25,000 per day, first offense; $50,000 per day thereafter, injunction	Yes
Occupational Safety & Health Administration	1970	No*	$10,000, six months, or both	$10,000	No
Consumer Product Safety Commission	1972	Yes	$50,000, one year, or both	$500,000	Yes
Office of Employee Benefits Security (Labor Dept.)	1975	Yes	$10,000, one year, or both, barring from future employment with plan, reimbursement	$100,000, reimbursement	Yes

*Except sole proprietorship

FIGURE 13.4   The Risks Executives Face Under Federal Law [Source: "The Law Closes in on Managers," *Business Week*, May 10, 1976, p. 113.]

Agency, the Occupational Safety and Health Administration, the Consumer Products Safety Commission, and the Federal Trade Commission. There are also, agencies created at state, municipal, and regional levels to provide business regulation. The sales manager of today and tomorrow will have increasingly to face an evolving legal environment.

Many individuals who have investigated this area feel that in the future "the manager in charge of the task will be the target for the regulators."[16] Thus, the sales manager must be aware of the changing legal environment and must be prepared to cope with such changes. A recent article in *Business Week* describes some of the risks faced by business executives under federal law alone. These risks are summarized in Figure 13.4.

Inflation: Impacts Upon Selling

In Chapters 8 and 9, we noted the increasing costs of personal selling. Compensation, for example, averaged $13,700 for sales trainees, $18,300 for semiexperienced sales personnel, and $24,500 for experienced sales personnel. These escalating salaries, of course, translate into higher selling costs for sales management to contend with. We saw, for example, in Chapter 9 that the cost of making an individual sales call can run as high as $50.00 (see Figure 9.1). Inflation has brought about increasing costs in terms of raw materials also, and together these increasing salaries, raw material costs, and costs of doing business produce a pressure which sales management must be prepared to cope with in the future.

As inflation continues to increase, management must constantly see more efficient ways of operation in order to preserve its sales in the marketplace. The impacts of inflation upon personal selling and sales management cannot be overstated. Stress is needed by management to constantly monitor the impact of inflation and its resulting impacts upon sales volume and market share.

The Changing Customer

As we have seen in the recent past, the consumer himself is changing very rapidly. By 1980, it is estimated that more than half of the United States population will be under 30 years of age. The impact of this change in age has been commented on by Stroh who suggests:

In 1980 the middle-age group, aged 35 to 54, will not grow in line with the rest of the population. This is the group that traditionally provided the managers for business and industry. By 1980, there will be only a small gain in the group from 35 to 44 and an actual drop in the group from 45 to 54. The latter is the group which has traditionally supplied the higher executives in business.[17]

[16] *Ibid.*, p. 425.
[17] *Ibid.*, p. 429.

Thus, changes in the makeup of the population have strong impacts for business, not only in terms of marketplace impacts but in terms of sources for employees. A clear implication for sales management here is that it must not only continue to monitor changes in the populus with regard to the impact such change make upon individuals as consumers but it must also consider these changes as they impact upon a firm's needs for employees. The aforementioned goal of human resource development is made clear in the efforts of at least one university (New York University) through their continuing education programs. This university conducts seminars in human resource management in a variety of locations across the United States.[18]

Summary

This chapter is focused upon both current and future changes in personal selling and sales management. The chapter began with an examination of the historical perspective of sales management and the evolutionary development of sales management up to the present. A second section of this chapter dealt with the forecasts that have been previously made for the future of sales management, and, in particular, we have examined the changes dealing with the personal development of salesmen, greater use of computers in sales management, and more professionalism in the personal selling/sales management field.

Lastly, in this chapter we have examined some of the current agents of change that are having an impact on personal selling and sales management. One current force is the changing legal environment, and we have seen some of the implications for recent legal developments where sales managers are concerned. A second current force is the impact of inflation upon selling. Lastly, we have examined some of the effects of the changing population, both as it impacts upon the populus in a marketplace fashion and as it impacts upon the populus in terms of business employees.

Discussion Questions

1. Briefly trace the development of personal selling and sales management as it has evolved during the century.

---

[18] See Brochure No. HRM-1000-1040, New York University, School of Continuing Education, Division of Career and Professional Development, 326 Shimkin Hall, New York, New York 10003.

2. Do you believe that the forecasts made for the 1970s regarding a greater human orientation, and so on, have been fulfilled? If not, why not?

3. What do you foresee regarding the use of computers in personal selling or sales management?

4. Do you believe the professionalism alluded to for personal selling and sales management personnel will evolve in the future?

5. Will the changing legal environment produce numerous lawsuits against personal salesmen and/or sales managers in the future in similar fashion to what occurred to physicians and medical personnel in the late 1970s?

6. Define the impacts of inflation upon personal selling and sales management.

7. What changes do you foresee for personal selling and sales management in the future besides those mentioned in this chapter?

Selected References

BARTOS, RENA, "What Every Marketer Should Know About Women," *Harvard Business Review,* May–June 1978, pp. 73, 85.

COMER, JAMES M. (ed.), *Sales Management: Roles and Methods* (Santa Monica, Cal.: Goodyear Publishing Company, Inc., 1977).

DAWSON, LESLIE M., "Toward A New Concept of Sales Management," *Journal of Marketing,* April 1970, pp. 33–38.

DUNN, ALBERT H., EUGENE M. JOHNSON, and DAVID L. KURTZ, *Sales Management* (Morristown, N.J.: General Learning Press, 1974), Chapter 15.

JOHNSON, H. WEBSTER, *Sales Management: Operations, Administration, and Marketing* (Columbus, Ohio: Charles E. Merrill Publishing Company, 1976), p. 89.

JOLSON, MARVIN A., *Sales Management: A Tactical Approach* (New York: Petrocelli/Charter, 1977), Chapter 13.

KANUK, LESLIE, "Women in Industrial Selling," *Journal of Marketing,* January 1978, pp. 87–91.

STANTON, WILLIAM J., and RICHARD H. BUSKIRK, *Management of the Sales Force,* 5th ed. (Homewood, Ill.: Richard D. Irwin, Inc., 1978), Chapter 24.

STROH, THOMAS F., Managing the Sales Function (New York: McGraw-Hill Book Company, Inc., 1978),

SWAN, JOHN E., CHARLES M. FUTRELL, and JOHN T. TODD, "Same Job— Different Views: Women and Men in Industrial Sales," *Journal of Marketing,* January 1978, pp. 92–98.

Disposal Systems was founded in 1960 as a distributor of commercial trash compactors, the accompanying products such as trash bags to fit the compactors, and chemicals to be used in the cleaning and maintenance of the compactors. With headquarters in central Florida, Disposal Systems originally covered the state of Florida, selling primarily to condominiums, resort facilities, and restaurants.

Company Background

The spectacular growth of the tourist business in Florida during the 1960s and early 1970s enabled Disposal Systems to expand from first year sales of $2 million to a current annual sales level of $40 million. Disposal Systems now had sales coverage in eight southeastern states with a total of 26 sales representatives.

Besides the growth in Florida, another reason for the growth of Disposal Systems was their diversification into related areas. In 1968, Disposal Systems won bids to pick up residential trash in three small Florida towns, During the next 5 years, the trash collection part of the business grew dramatically, with Disposal Systems now handling the collection of trash in 25 cities across the southeast. This business was now worth $8 million in sales per year to the company.

Another area of growth came in the compactor trash bag area. In the early days, Disposal Systems sold plastic and paper bags supplied by various manufacturers. Over the years the plastic bags had become more popular and more readily available as the manufacturers of paper bags became fewer.

In 1972, Disposal Systems hired Jim Swinson, formerly an experienced plant manager with one of the top plastic bag manufacturers. Swinson was made vice-president of manufacturing, with his first job being to design a plastic bag manufacturing plant. Within a year, Disposal Systems was manufacturing all of the trash compactor bags it needed as well as a line of institutional grade trash bags. Trash bag sales were now at an annual rate of $5 million.

Warren Kendall had been with Disposal Systems since the day the company was founded. Starting out as a truck driver, Kendall had worked his way through college and then began a sales career after graduation. Five years ago he had been named vice-president of marketing at the age of 35.

Current Situation

* This case was prepared by Tom Ingram and Danny N. Bellenger, Georgia State University.

During the past weekend Kendall had received an emergency phone call from Richard White, the Georgia/Florida District Sales Manager. Kendall had listened intently as White outlined the problem:

"As you know, Warren, we finally got the compactor bag business at Sunshine Homes, which is a large retirement community near Orlando. The residents at Sunshine Homes buy our compactor bags packed 50 to the case, break them down into packages of five and sell them to several retirement communities in the Orlando area. On our first shipment of 200 cases, 180 of the cases were anywhere from one to three bags short of the 50 count. I called Jim Swinson who assured me that he had not been aware of any shortage prior to shipment. We smoothed the situation over by sending Sunshine Homes five free cases of bags to cover the shortage. Swinson also guaranteed me that we would not have any problem like this in the future.

Competitors found out about our mistake and a couple of them started telling Sunshine Homes that Disposal Systems had a reputation for poor quality and for charging the customer the full price although shortages were common. I was able to overcome all of this until our second shipment arrived Friday. Every single case was short at least two bags, with some short as many as five bags. The people at Sunshine Homes have given me until Monday morning to show them why they should not take the following steps: (1) switch all their trash bag business to another supplier, (2) warn all other retirement communities of the deceptive practices of Disposal Systems, and (3) file a complaint with the Better Business Bureau and the state Consumer Protection Agency.

To make matters worse, one of the residents of Sunshine Homes is a retired state senator whose son is running for the state House of Representatives from the Orlando district. He hinted to me on Friday that his problem could very easily become a political issue in the election campaign."

After White had told him all the details, Kendall quickly took action. He called Martin Tyler, the president of Disposal Systems, briefed him on the situation and asked Mr. Tyler to meet him later in the day to review the situation. Next he phoned Jim Swinson. After a brief discussion, they agreed to meet at the office within an hour to work on the problem.

After giving Swinson all the details, Kendall had asked, "Jim, how could we ship the product with an incorrect count after you had been alerted to the same problem on the first shipment by Richard White?"

Swinson replied, "It is not as simple as counting the number of bags that go in the case. The mechanical counters do that. The problem is that we have been getting some variations on our manufacturing equipment which make the bags thicker than normal. As a result of increased thickness, 50 bags will not fit into the corrugated boxes we use to package our product."

Swinson went on to say that sometimes the manufacturing variation caused the customer to get more than 50 bags per case and that in the long run it "all averaged out." Swinson also said that the maximum variation to be expected should be plus or minus 3 per cent of the specified thickness of the bag. He could not explain why some of the cases shipped to Sunshine Homes were up to 10 per cent short of the specified 50 count.

As Kendall prepared for the afternoon meeting with Martin Tyler and Jim Swinson, he pondered several questions:

1. What can we do to retain the Sunshine Homes business?
2. How badly had our credibility been damaged?
3. Is Swinson trying to make his manufacturing cost look favorable at the expense of marketing?
4. How will we handle adverse publicity if the problem cannot be solved?
5. How can I insure my people in the field that this kind of problem will not persist?

As he thought over these and other questions, he called Richard White in Florida and asked him to make a Monday morning appointment for Martin Tyler and himself at Sunshine Homes. As he hung up the phone, Kendall hoped the weekend would provide enough time to answer the questions occupying his mind.

CASE 13.2
The Losmi Mine Supply Company*

The Losmi Mine Supply Company had been in existence for over 100 years. Originally begun as a firm selling supplies to gold miners in the Ricky Mountains and West Coast region, this firm's business had expanded to the point where it now was involved in the national marketing and sales of all types of mine supplies. Lawrence Losmi founded the firm in 1875 shortly after the Civil War. Beginning in San Francisco, Mr. Losmi had built a reputation for having "everything the gold miner needed" and for prompt delivery of supplies. Lawrence Losmi remained active in the management of the firm until 1930 when, upon his death, he was succeeded by his son Louis Losmi. Under Louis Losmi's direction, the firm expanded into other areas of mining to include coal mining, copper mining, and so on. Also, under Louis Losmi's direction, the firm placed a great deal more emphasis upon selling than upon merely being a source of supplies. Louis Losmi remained active in the firm until 18 months ago when he retired to be succeeded by his son Larry Losmi, who had just completed the MBA at a prestigious eastern university.

Larry Losmi felt that many changes were needed at the Losmi Mine Supply Company. One of the main things worrying Larry Losmi was the composition of the sales force. In particular, Larry was concerned

Company Background

* Case prepared by Dan H. Robertson, Georgia State University.

about two facts pertinent to the sales force. First, he noted that the average age of sales personnel was 42, although the firm did have some younger men who were in their mid to late 30s. At the opposite end of the range, however, the firm also had three individuals who were preparing for retirement and were in their early 60s. In addition to chronological age, Larry was also concerned over the fact that the sales force was 100 per cent male.

Current Situation

At a recent meeting of the Losmi Mine Supply Company management team, Larry created quite a stir when he commented, "Even a casual observer from the outside can see the need for women in our sales force. More and more we are selling to government agencies or government-supported agencies and it is clear that, with Equal Employment Opportunity pressures, our firm will soon be asked how many women we have employed. I want to be on the forefront of firms in the mine supply business who have women on their management team, and the only way I can see us accomplishing this is to get women into the sales area and let them learn our business and work their way up the ladder."

It probably would have taken an earthquake to get the same type of reaction out of the other members of management, many of whom had been with the firm for a number of years and were older. For example, later that same afternoon, when they were alone, the sales manager of the firm and the vice president of marketing were holding a private discussion on the possibility of adding women to the Losmi Mine Supply Company sales force. The sales manager remarked, "Larry must be out of his gourd. Why, there is no other firm in our industry who has female sales representatives. Furthermore, think of all the headaches this will create for me. How can women possibly go down in the mines as our male sales representatives do and become acquainted with engineers and industrial buyers? What about the problems created by overnight travel? All I need is for our firm to experience a sex scandal." The vice president of marketing was openly sympathetic to the remarks by the sales manager. Since they had known each other and worked together in their respective positions for over 10 years, they had developed a very straightforward relationship. The vice president of marketing remarked, "I see what you mean and I understand many of the problems you are getting at, but are you sure you aren't making a mountain out of a mole hill? After all, women are becoming more and more prevalent in other types of businesses as sales personnel. Why, just the other day while I was in a supermarket, I saw a female sales representative walk in carrying a detail bag and she did a very nice job in a short presentation I saw her give to a store manager." The sales manager responded, "Sure, you're right. It can happen in some industries, but this is industrial selling. It takes an entirely different 'breed of cat' to sell industrial equipment and supplies than it does to sell soap to a neighborhood grocery store."

As president of the Losmi Mine Supply Company, Larry Losmi generally was not privileged to hear of responses by other members of the management team to his ideas. However, regarding women in selling,

Larry did receive some informal feedback indicating the displeasure of the vice president of marketing and sales manager. As he sat in his paneled office gazing out the window, he wondered if he had approached this in the right manner. Perhaps, he thought, a more thoughtful and tactful approach was called for, and maybe he was a bit too brash. I was sincere in what I said, Larry thought. More and more it will be necessary for us to comply with federal regulations and rules, and, besides, even if governmental business was not important to our firm, this is a matter of principle. I believe women should be given an equal opportunity to demonstrate their capabilities, and there are a lot of bright, young women graduating from business schools these days. I should know—I had some of them as classmates in my MBA program. Isn't there any chance that women can succeed in this business? Larry wondered.

Student Learning Exercise / 13
The Future of Sales Management

Objective

To prompt student thinking about future changes in personal selling/sales management.

Overview

This chapter has focused upon changes that are occurring and may occur in the future affecting selling and/or sales management. Review these changes.

Procedure

Think about the changes impinging upon selling and sales management. Then, prepare a proposal for a sales firm in accordance with the guidelines given.

Guidelines

You have been retained as a consultant to a firm that wishes to start now in preparing for the future. In particular, advise this firm:

1. What are specific changes that you foresee for the early and middle 1980s having impacts (positive or negative) upon selling and/or sales management?
2. How may a firm prepare to meet the changes you have identified in question 1? Develop a specific plan of action.

The Management of Change

THE future is becoming the present at a seemingly increasing rate. The pace of change has accelerated over the past several years and will continue to accelerate in the future. Many of the issues discussed in Chapter 13 are relatively recent advents in sales management. When sales managers fail to focus their efforts toward the future, they may discover that they do not have much of a future. "Sales management futurism" is a state of mind and a mode of current action that addresses problems and opportunities in the future. The sales manager must first recognize the importance of changes in the environment to the success of the sales plan and then translate this realization into actions designed to take advantage of new opportunities. The future can be either a friend or an enemy, depending upon how well the manager is prepared to deal with it. If the sales manager can successfully incorporate a future perspective into today's decision making, then significant payoffs can be realized.

For those who question the need for futurism, Keane offers some interesting observations:[1]

- The United States airline industry watched a plucky and persistent Freddie Laker disrupt pricing and competitive strategy with his cut-rate service between New York and London. Sky Train Freddie claims, "a net profit of $511,634 after six weeks and a load factor that went from 71 percent the first week to 97 percent."
- The United States brewing industry whose beer may be uncharacteristically green (for envy) this year over the effervescent success of Miller's Light Beer, which stole a march on competition by boldly pioneering the light beer category.
- Or the United States auto industry. As the country's bellweather industry, Detroit saw its number one market—Los Angeles County—overtaken by foreign competition. This past year, for the first time in history, the foreign make, Toyota, became the best seller by topping Chevrolet.
- Signs are surely on the marketing wall for the food industry. My future's investigations suggest that the federal government's nutritional education emphasis alone could drastically alter the composition, consump-

---

[1] John G. Keane, "2,001 Is Approaching Fast: Are Marketers Ready to Seize Tomorrow's Opportunities?" *Advertising Age*, March 27, 1978, p. 55.

tion, and promotion of many food products in this country during the 1980s. Stubborn resistence or smug passivity to structural marketing environment shifts could devastate unwary food marketers. Conversely, selective opportunism in capitalizing on these shifts could gorge the corporate coffers of future oriented food marketers.

Some Key Dimensions of Change

In order to adopt a futuristic perspective, the sales manager must first identify some of the key dimensions of change that will affect future success. On a general level the total marketing environment is subject to change, but certain facets of this environment may impact more heavily on sales management than others. Four potentially important areas of change for the sales manager are

1. Science and new technology
2. Government regulation
3. The changing nature of growth
4. The new consumer

SCIENCE AND NEW TECHNOLOGY

The rapid advance of science and new technology is making some very important changes in the environment for sales management. This is occurring both in terms of new products and in terms of the sophistication of buyers the sales force must deal with. Toffler, in his fascinating book, *Future Shock*, pointed out the overwhelming majority of all the material things that we use in our everyday life today has been developed within this century.[2] The acceleration of new technology and new product development offers both challenges and opportunities for the innovative sales manager. Successful product introduction in a time fashion can insure corporate sales growth into the future. Frank Lynn has pointed out that the average time taken to get a major scientific discovery translated into average time taken to get a major scientific discovery translated into useful technology has been cut by 60 per cent within this century.[3] The increased educational level in the United States has brought the promise of an even more rapid development in technology. The number of scientists and engineers in this country today is vastly larger than it has ever been in the past.

Major technological changes will undoubtedly come in numerous areas. For example, transportation, communications, and computer technology are likely to undergo significant technological development within the next few years. In the case of computer technology and communica-

[2] Alvin Toffler, *Future Shock* (New York: Random House, Inc., 1970), p. 28.
[3] *Ibid.*, p. 28.

tions, the impact on sales management goes far beyond the mere introduction of new products. The entire method of decision making and control of the sales force may be materially altered by new technological innovations in these areas. For example, the computer with its advanced information storage and retrieval systems may provide the sales manager with a much greater array of data on which to base decisions than has been the case in the past.

Turning back to the area of new product development which is, at best, a risky venture for most firms, the sales manager may be confronted with new responsibilities of two types. First, the sales force may be called upon to provide an increasing flow of information from the marketplace relative to the needs and applications of new technological innovations. Secondly, the sales management will have to devise ways to accommodate the increasing complexity of the product line and the diverse requirements for selling the multitude of products that a company may decide to carry.

Science and new technology thus offer two basic challenges for sales management in the future. First, organizations that do not keep attuned to the changing consumer market may find themselves going out of business as their competitors see the opportunities revealed by technological advances. Stated positively, the future outlook for firms with the ability to match consumer needs with new technology and resulting products is very bright. Secondly, sales management is likely to become increasingly sophisticated as managerial technology moves forward in unison with new product development. This new management technology, as reflected in computer and communications developments, will increase the need for sophisticated managers to deal with the increasingly complex environment.

GOVERNMENT REGULATION

Another important dimension of the changing environment for the sales manager relates to government, and particularly to government regulation within the United States economy. Marketing and sales managers have become increasingly frustrated with the extent of regulation by government. Waste, duplication, and delay can easily be the by-products of the regulatory process. Many managers would contend that, if there are excesses on the sales and marketing side, there are surely excesses on the part of government regulatory bodies. More and more the cry for regulating the regulators is being heard in the American business community. Government regulation is, however, a part of the environment that sales managers must live with today and, almost without question, live with to an increasing degree in the future.

The sales manager of the future should attempt to approach this facet of the environment in a positive way. Too often lost in the discussions of regulation is the fact that businesses and their management have been very passive in initiating codes of conduct that go beyond the bare legal requirements. The progressive sales manager should take the initiative in incorporating social responsibility into the decision making process. Sales managers must recognize that self-interest and responsibility can be very complimentary forces to benefit the overall efforts of the firm. This is particularly true in circumstances where government regulatory bodies will impose their concepts of responsibility if the sales manager does not initiate action. As an illustration of this more positive approach, the president of the Bank America Corporation, A. W. Clawson observed:

Voluntary disclosure going beyond the minimum requirements of law seems to be the proper course. Someone had to jump into the icy water first. We thought Bank America, as the industry leader, should take the plunge first.[4]

This type of action on the part of marketing and sales management can be very beneficial to their own self-interests by providing an improved corporate image and by limiting the need for governmental regulations.

THE CHANGING NATURE OF GROWTH

The sales manager should also keep abreast of the economic dimensions of the environment. One important change that is taking place currently is in the nature of growth within the economy. Ian Wilson, along with many others, has pointed out the metabolism of growth is currently changing.[5] For example:

1. Many people are beginning to recognize that there are indeed limits to exponential growth. The concept of the S-curve as applied to physical growth of human activities has considerable validity. Much of the current thinking centers around the approach of an equilibrium in the growth of physical activities. This would be brought about because of the finite resources and space available within our planet. This equilibrium might not mean stagnation, but it would mean a slowing of the pace of growth considerably from what it has been in the past. Much of the argument today centers not on whether exponential growth has limits but on the timing of the ultimate equilibrium.
2. A second point related to growth is the increasing recognition of the need to limit population growth. If physical activity or the growth of physical activity stabilizes, then, to maintain a given standard of living, the population growth must also be stabilized. There is a distinct trend toward a stabilizing of population growth in the United States. With increased birth control technology and a movement toward quality of life choices by young married couples, the fertility rae has declined. The stabilization of the population has, in fact, become a matter of public policy that goes beyond the mere personal choices of individual families. Many communities have, for example, imposed limits on their ultimate size.

[4] "Bank America Corporation Voluntary Disclosure Code," *Bank America Corporation,* November 1976, p. 2.

[5] Ian H. Wilson, "The Changing Metabolism of Growth," remarks presented at the American Marketing Association, Atlanta Chapter, March 8, 1978.

3. There is also an increasing commitment to limit the growth of pollution within the United States. The degree of effort in this direction will undoubtedly vary from time to time, but the inevitable trend is toward environmental protection. This may force many trade-off type decisions in dealing with the development of new products and technologies along with the protection of the environment.
4. Another limit that is becoming increasingly important is the limitation on resource consumption. Both energy and raw materials are presenting short range problems in terms of availability. This has accentuated the need to plan and to develop systems for conserving and recycling raw materials.
5. Finally, evidence is accumulating that there are distinct limits to the growth of capital within our society. These limits may be more related to quality of life and environmental protection than to physical limits, but they are nonetheless real.

When taken together, these limits point to a changing growth pattern within the American economy. The likelihood is that growth will be much slower than in the past. The concept of "ecologically compatible growth" is replacing the maximum growth approach. Almost certainly the growth rate will slow from its previous high levels into the area of perhaps 3 per cent. The concepts of science and new technology mentioned earlier appear to hold the greatest promise for overcoming these apparent limits to growth. The sales manager must, however, be prepared to deal with an economic environment that is growing at a much slower rate than it has over the past several years. This situation will present new challenges for the sales manager in expanding the real sales growth of the company.

THE NEW CONSUMER

Perhaps the most important changes in the environment are taking place with the consumers themselves. The sales manager is responsible for directing a field sales effort that often has direct contact with the consumer. Thus, changes in the consumer have a very direct effect on the success of various approaches in sales and sales management. Many different forces are working to alter the buying behavior of the modern consumer. The following sections present a brief synopsis of some of the more important trends and the resulting "new consumers" that these forces are molding.[6]

New Demographics. One important force working to change the nature of the marketplace is shifts in the demography of the market. The population is growing older. As the birth rate declines, the age mix of the population will shift in favor of the older age groups. By 1985 the 25–44 age group will account for 50 per cent of the spending in the economy. The over-64 age group is also becoming very important.

[6] Adapted from a summary of trends developed by Ken Bernhardt.

The age shift is slowing the mobility of the population in a geographic sense. There is, however, a shift out of urban areas and toward the sun belt. People in their late 20s are significantly more mobile than the total population at large.

Another important demographic shift is the increasing significance of singles in the population. By 1985, 26 per cent of all households will involve people living alone. This group accounted for a total earnings of $115 billion in 1976. The singles segment has a very different spending pattern for many products, especially foods nad services.

Working women and two-earner families are also a distinct trend within the marketplace; 45 per cent of all adult women now hold jobs outside the home. In 1976, 63 per cent of all families with incomes over $25,000 had a working husband and a working wife. The traditional definition of household being defined as husband with nonworking wife and kids now account for only 25 per cent of all households. The working woman presents a family with a very different spending pattern from the traditional. Sales efforts must account for these differences in spending patterns.

Rising Levels of Education.   Consumers are becoming increasingly educated. The average number of years of formal education of those entering the work force has now risen to 12. In addition to formal education, educational television, news, and other activities have increased the general level of knowledge and awareness amongst consumers. Corporate training programs and various types of adult education courses are also moving the market in this direction. Increasing education has changed the expectations and values of the consumer. It has in general led to more innovation and to new value structures in the population.

The New Values.   Value structures amongst the population are shifting toward "people over things." Traditional values and the work ethic are on the decline. Quality of life instead of quantity of material possessions is becoming a value set held by an increasing number of consumers. Concern for ecology and the environment go hand in hand with this trend. There is also a move toward voluntary simplicity on the part of many consumers. People are learning to get pleasure from nonmaterial experiences.

The role of the woman in society is also shifting very dramatically. This is consistent with the increasing number of women in the work force. The concept of the family unit is beginning to shift away from the traditional toward singles and couples with a working wife. The importance of house cleaning and other traditional values in the home are changing.

There appears to be another trend toward fitness in the society. The "rich full life" is becoming more important. This involves the rejection of artificial elements in the diet, a decreasing consumption of alcohol, and other health-related moves. There is a general trend toward an emphasis of self and a deemphasis on self-denial. An increasing number of people are becoming more concerned about their own happiness and fitness and less concerned about denial of self to the benefit of others. This is consistent with the other trends noted concerning the quality of life and the work ethic.

It appears that even the over-60 population is having a shift in values. Many are abandoning the traditional value systems and moving toward more contemporary trends. The "gray market" is becoming an increasingly important segment within the total market structure.

The new value structures amongst the consuming public are quite consistent with the consumerism movement that we presently find in the marketplace. It is likely that consumers will become increasingly activist rather than moving in the other direction over the next few years. Many of the new values that can be seen in the marketplace are related to new economic realities that confront our society.

The New Economic Realities. Consumers are learning to live with higher inflation, higher energy costs, and a lower real growth rate in the national product. These economic trends have caused some erosion in consumer confidence in current economic conditions and the future of their own economic stability.

The entanglement of resource availability with international politics has also caused consumer concern in many areas. There appears to be a growing ethic of resource conservation and environmental protection in the public. As noted earlier, there is a changing metabolism of growth, and this new lower growth economy has had an impact on consumers and consumer values. The successful sales manager must recognize and take into account such shifts in the marketplace.

Growing Poverty of Time. Most consumers are confronted with an increasing poverty of time. Free time is more and more difficult to come by. A larger percentage of time for most people is becoming committed to various activities. Social commitments, the increase in the availability of activities, and the rising proportion of women in the labor force have all contributed to this phenomenon.

The knowledge explosion has also impacted on the amount of time necessary for various tasks. These factors influence where people shop, when they shop, how often they buy, and what they buy. Taken together these forces along with others, have worked to create new consumers.

Trends in the Marketplace. Many new types of consumers are emerging as a result of the various forces present in the market. For example, the "buy for one consumer" is becoming increasingly important. They spend their money differently, buying in smaller packages, and seeking more services, for example. There is also an increasing number of "stability-seeking consumer." These consumers seek a return to yesterday, life simplification, a return to nature, and perhaps various hobbies are of increased importance. The third new type is the "get-your-money's-worth consumer." They are more motivated by the total cost concept. Many are substituting labor for dollar cost with such things as self-service gas. The less-for-less concept is being employed by purchasing such things as powdered drinks and no name brand foods. The "time-buying consumer" is another trend to be found in the marketplace. Eating out, convenience store shopping, microwave ovens, food processors, and catalog shopping are all manifestations of the increased concern on the part of many consumers for the poverty of time. Many shoppers are willing to pay extra in order to save time that they can then use for other pursuits.

These trends toward new types of purchase behavior are manifestations of forces discussed earlier. The sales manager, in order successfully to devise and implement a sales plan, must be aware of the changing nature of the consumer.

Guidelines for the Sales Manager

Science and new technology, government regulation, the changing nature of growth, and the new consumer are but a few of the many dynamic elements in the environment of sales management. These are, however, some of the key dimensions of change that must be dealt with to insure successful operation of the enterprise. Let us now turn our attention to some guidelines that the sales manager can follow in order to manage the sales function successfully within the changing environment. These guidelines offer the prospective sales manager a framework for dealing successfully within an uncertain future. The guidelines include: plan for the future, monitor the environment, don't overreact to environmental shifts, and practice preventative management. As can be seen, planning is the central thread running through all of these guidelines; planning is in fact vital for successful sales management in a dynamic environment.

PLAN FOR THE FUTURE

In order to develop a successful sales effort, the sales manager must plan future directions carefully. Planning involves determining where the organization wishes to be at some future point and how to accomplish this objective. In order to move the sales functions toward some desired future position, the sales manager should first understand the current situation and how it came into being; even more critical, however, to the planning process is a projection of the future environment in which the sales function must operate. Thus effective planning of the sales function requires that the sales manager be in tune to shifts in the environment and be able to foresee trends that are developing that will effect the company's sales effort.

During the 1950s, planning was understood but largely ignored in many companies. They were able to succeed without careful planning because of the nature of the environment in which they were operating. By the 1970s, this environment had changed rather dramatically. The continuous and stable growth of the earlier periods was replaced by uncertainty and fear. The more volatile environment of the 1970s, which has brought increased emphasis on planning, is likely to continue into the 1980s and beyond. Ability as a planner has become a key talent for any marketing management position. This certainly holds true in the case of the sales manager. Two key factors with respect to planning are the style of the planner and the planning process or sequence itself. In order to understand better the nature of sales management planning, these two areas will be discussed in turn.

Planning Styles. To be an effective planner, the sales manager must not only appreciate the need for planning but also have a planning style that is conducive to the production of sound results. A manager's planning style can be evaluated on many different dimensions. These dimensions include gathering information, anticipating and assuming objectives, alternatives considered, implementation, and control. One way to gain a better insight into proper planning style is to consider a series of incorrect approaches. Table 14.1 illustrates five incorrect planning styles in terms of the dimensions just presented.

The "paper-shy planner" is characterized by a lack of data and a failure to commit plans to writing. This approach can create considerable confusion and generally leads to poor results. The problem with the "short-term planner" centers on the time horizon of his planning activities. This type of planner usually relies on weak data and avoids complex decision, but the key problem is planning only for the immediate future. The "do-it-yourself planner" is characterized by ignoring inputs from others. This type of planner usually shuts out feedback and selects only inputs for the planning process that fit the frame of reference already

TABLE 14.1 Incorrect Planning Styles

	PAPER-SHY PLANNER	SHORT-TERM PLANNER	DO-IT-YOURSELF PLANNER	JUST-FOR-SHOW PLANNER	SCIENCE–BLINDED PLANNER
Gathering Information	relies on instinct instead of data	acts on weak data	selects facts to fit his frame of reference	dazzles readers with biased data	screens out subjective inputs
Anticipating and Assuming	stumbles into hazards and opportunities	plans for *immediate* future: fears uncertainty	ignores inputs from others	makes unwarranted assumptions	treats assumptions like facts; future like past
Objective (Ends)	chases ad hoc objectives	wastes time and effort on *little* things	sets isolated objectives	sets politically motivated objectives	considers only quantifiable objectives
Alternatives (Means)	acts without strategy: trial-and-error	avoids multiple alternatives	ignores inputs from others	presents the *big* strategy	locks-out creative alternatives
Implementation	carries plans in his head: creates confusion	acts fast: ignores possible chain reactions	incites anti-planning	emphasizes *writing* plan—not carrying-out plan	ignores human side of planning
Control	fights fires	fights fires	shuts-out feedback	evades accountability	tracks too many variables

TABLE 14.2 Planning Profile

	A	B		C	D	
Relies on instinct	A	B	1	C	Ⓓ	Relies on data
Sets quantifiable objectives	Ⓐ	B	2	C	D	Sets ad hoc objectives
Plans short range	A	B	3	C	Ⓓ	Plans long range
Develops multiple alternatives	Ⓐ	B	4	C	D	Develops limited alternatives
Responds to priorities	Ⓐ	B	5	C	D	Responds to crisis
Locks out feedback	A	B	6	C	Ⓓ	Solicits feedback
Ignores human side of planning	A	B	7	C	Ⓓ	Involves others
Seeks plans that work	Ⓐ	B	8	C	D	Seeks plans that impress
Evades accountability	A	B	9	C	Ⓓ	Wants to be measured
Influenced by data	Ⓐ	B	10	C	D	Uses data to support opinions

established. The results of this planning style are usually very myopic and are dependent upon the accuracy of the judgements of the planner. The "just-for-show planner" uses the planning process as a shield to defend against the accountability for decisions. The objectives are often politically motivated and the planner may select data that is biased to support a particular point of view. Finally, the "science-blinded planner" tends to rule out all nonquantitative inputs into the planning process. This may inhibit creativity and cause distortions in the planning process if the future is assumed to be exactly like the past. This planning style also ignores the human side of sales management. Many human factors cannot be easily quantified and thus may be omitted from the planning process by the "science-blinded planner."

The sales manager should attempt to avoid these incorrrect planning styles. The implications for correct planning that can be drawn from Table 14.1 are that the sales manager should base plans on relevant information that can be collected about the subject in question, both quantitative and qualitative; anticipate the future environment; make assumptions where warranted that flow from the analysis of the future environment; establish a comprehensive set of objectives that the sales function is aimed at accomplishing in future time periods; carefully consider all alternatives that might be used to achieve the desired objectives before making a decision about which alternative to pursue; pay careful attention to the human side of implementing plans; and, finally, establish a system for controlling the implementation of plans that clearly sets accountability and provides for the tracking of relevant variables. Table 14.2 presents a very useful device for evaluating a planning process. By objectively positioning the sales manager's approach to planning along the ten dimensions shown, a planning profile can be developed. Although it might be reasonably asserted that a blend is needed along many of the dimensions shown, the preferred planning profile is generally indicated by the letters circled in the table.

The Planning Process. Turning now to the planning process itself, the sales manager should adopt a logical and systematic approach to the development of plans. Assume, for example, that growth is one of the objectives of the organization and that the sales manager is responsible for the development of plans to achieve this objective. Figure 14.1 illustrates a planning cycle that might be adopted by a sales manager for this purpose. The planning cycle for growth should start with an understanding of

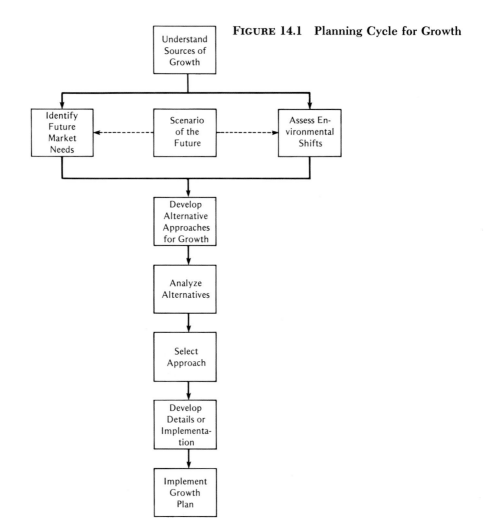

FIGURE 14.1   Planning Cycle for Growth

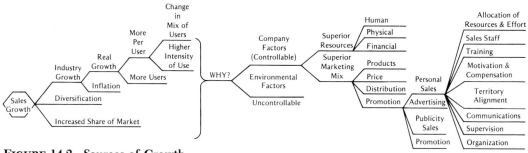

FIGURE 14.2   Sources of Growth

the alternative sources of growth. These sources are outlined in Figure 14.2. It indicates that growth may be a result of a change in the mix of users, higher intensity of use, more users, diversification, or an increase of market share. These various sources of potential growth can be triggered by internal corporate factors or by external forces.

The sales manager must zero in on the controllable company factors that can be used to promote growth within the context of environmental shifts. More specifically, the sales manager must work to develop a superior personal selling component of the total marketing effort within the organization. This might be done via better allocation of resources and effort, better sales staffing, improved training, better motivation and compensation, better territory alignment, improved communications, better supervision, or superior organization.

Given this basic understanding, the next step in the cycle is the identification of future market needs. This is perhaps the key step in the growth planning cycle. As has been pointed out many times, market factors play a more decisive role in the growth of an organization than most other environmental shifts. Thus, the planning of growth strategies should flow from an understanding of the changing nature of the marketplace. In addition, the sales manager should assess other environmental shifts that may affect growth opportunities. In order to do this, the manager must develop a scenario of the future. This future-oriented scenario should outline in detail all the key assumptions related to future-oriented events that will have a bearing on the creation of growth. Projections of the important events that are likely to occur in the future in each of the key dimensions of the evironment is a good starting point for the development of a scenario on the future. For this purpose, the manager must be able to read the present environment and to project trends into the future. Based on identification of future market needs and an assessment of environmental shifts, the manager can develop alternative approaches for growth. These approaches would relate to the alternative uses of the various controllable elements of the personal selling function within the organization.

The next step would be an analysis of the various alternative approaches in terms of resource needs, probability of success, and various related dimensions. With a careful analysis, a general approach to attaining the growth objectives can be selected. After the general approach is selected, the details of the implementation must be planned. This will include a determination of what is to be done, where, when, and by whom. Finally, the plan is put into motion to move the organization toward its growth objectives.

The use of a logical and systematic planning process is a key guideline for the sales manager in the successful management of change. When coupled with an effective planning style, the results should be very fruitful. To extend this line of thought, let us now turn to our second guideline.

MONITOR THE ENVIRONMENT

In order to develop effective plans, the sales manager should regularly assess the marketplace. This can come from word-of-mouth feedback or from some more formal system. In addition, the sales manager should have some regular direct exposure to the market. This type of direct exposure cannot be replaced by a reporting system, no matter how detailed it may be. Many companies in fact require that their management people work directly with customers at some regular interval so as to gain the hands-on familiarity with a changing market that is necessary to the development of effective plans.

In addition, the organization needs a comprehensive and coordinated marketing information system. Such a system, as discussed in Chapter 3, can provide invaluable information for the decision making process of the sales manager. This system should provide for the production of specific information required by the sales manager plus a general environmental monitoring. This will aid the manager in recognizing and appreciating shifts in the key dimensions of the organization's environment. Continuous monitoring of the environment is another important guideline for the effective management of change.

DON'T OVERREACT TO ENVIRONMENTAL SHIFTS

Although the environment should be carefully monitored, the sales manager should avoid the temptation to overreact to its changes. Many dimensions of the external environment have a cyclical behavior. A variable that starts to move in one direction may, over time, swing back. Before making long-range plans and commitments, the manager should be convinced that the trend being observed is long term. Overreaction to economic recessions is a classic example of this type of behavior. When the economy turns down, the temptation may be to cut back on staff training and other budgets. This may, however, be a very short-sighted approach to environmental change that is likely to swing back up in a relatively short period of time. The point is that careful monitoring of the environment should not be allowed to lead to short-sighted reactionary management. The sales manager should, rather, look for long-term trends in the environment and base planning on a longer term perspective.

Over correction may, in many cases, be a natural by-product of the organization's reward structure. If the organization looks only to short-term goals and success, then the planning function tends to be short-sighted. Only when the organization's goals are evaluated with a long-term perspective can the planning function gain the stability that is needed. This guideline is intended as a safeguard against potential adverse effects of careful environmental monitoring.

PRACTICE PREVENTATIVE MANAGEMENT

A final guideline that rounds out the emphasis on planning in the management of change is to practice preventative management. Rather than reacting to crises that develop, the manager should seek a regular diagnosis of developing problems and make corrective adjustments in advance. Systematic sales audits can be very useful for this purpose. By carefully analyzing the sales function on a periodic basis, early indications of trouble can be detected and plans developed to avoid situations that might prove worrisome later on. In general, it is better to try to prevent problems than to try to cure them after they have developed.

Another important concept of preventative management is contingency planning. Given that key variables in the company and the environment are to be monitored, the manager should develop contingency plans that would be put into effect if certain conditions reach predetermined boundaries. To do this, the sales manager needs to determine the critical factors that should be monitored, alternative actions that can be taken if these factors are not within acceptable bounds, and the triggering points when the contingency plans should go into action. Careful contingency planning is one way to avoid overreacting to environmental shifts. Keane has stated that:

Contingency planning is simply an attempt to minimize the impact of major negative marketing shocks and to maximize the benefit of positive marketing developments through a pre-determined monitoring system, the identification of alternative actions and likely consequences together with an implementation plan.[7]

By following the guidelines suggested here, the sales manager should become a more effective manager of change within the dynamic marketing environment of today and tomorrow.

Summary

The environment of sales management is in a constant and rapid state of change. These shifts in the environment necessitate alterations in the sales plan of an organization. The sales manager should attempt to manage

[7] John G. Keane, "Managing Marketing Change," The Ninth Annual Albert Wesley Frey Lecture: Graduate School of Business, University of Pittsburgh, April 1977, p. 8.

the changes within the sales plan so as to achieve the organization's goals in the most efficient manner. Planned change within the organization must take into account the dynamic environment and the impact of environmental shifts on the probability of success of various alternatives available to the sales manager.

In order to manage change successfully, the sales manager should be aware of certain key dimensions of change within the environment. These include science and new technology, government regulation, the changing nature of growth, and the new consumer. Changes within the consuming public are perhaps the most critical to most organizations.

In order to deal with these external forces, the sales manager needs to follow certain guidelines. Planning and futurism are the key elements of these guidelines which include: (1) plan for the future, (2) monitor the environment, (3) don't overreact to environmental shifts, and (4) practice preventative management. Effective planning involves both proper planning style and following a logical and systematic planning process. By paying careful attention to futuristic trends the sales manager should be better equipped to devise plans that will move the organization toward its goals. Careful planning is rapidly becoming an essential ingredient in successful sales management.

Discussion Questions

1. Discuss why the management of change has become more important in sales management over the last 20 years.

2. Discuss the major dimensions of change that are affecting sales managers today. What are some important changes not discussed in the text?

3. Why is the consumer the key external force in the success of most organizations?

4. Summarize the key environmental trends that should affect sales managers in the auto industry over the next 5 years.

5. Discuss the differences between effective and ineffective planning styles.

6. Using the planning profile in Table 14.2, develop a planning profile of yourself in terms of the planning of school-related work. How could this type of exercise be of use to a sales manager?

7. Discuss how scenarios of the future fit into the planning cycle.

8. In terms of planning for growth, discuss how the various elements of the sales plan relates to the basic sources of growth.

9. How does a marketing information system relate to the management of change?

10. What is meant by the concept of preventative management?

Selected References

DAVIS, KEITH, and ROBERT L. BLOMSTROM, *Business and Society: Environment and Responsibility*, 3rd ed. (New York: McGraw-Hill Book Co., 1975).

KEANE, JOHN G., "2,001 Is Approaching Fast: Are Marketers Ready to Seize Tomorrow's Opportunities?" *Advertising Age*, March 27, 1978, pp. 55–56.

LAZER, WILLIAM, "The 1980's and Beyond: A Perspective," *MSU Business Topics*, Spring 1977, pp. 21–35.

SIMMONS, W. W., "The Planning Executive of Century III—A Futuristic Profile," *Managerial Planning*, January–February 1977, pp. 19–24.

TOFFLER, ALVIN, *Future Shock* (New York: Random House, Inc., 1970).

CASE 14.1   Lone Star Life Insurance Company: Cancer Insurance Policy*

Company Background

In 1975, Don Hardy became the Georgia State Director for the National Specialty Marketing Division of Lone Star Life Insurance Company. This division is responsible for the marketing of cancer insurance. Don was responsible for building a marketing and sales organization within the state. As this effort proceeded, Don discovered in 1978 that his job was becoming more difficult due to adverse publicity. A dynamic external environment seemed to be presenting new road blocks to continuing sales growth.

This was the case even though the policy is underwritten by Lone Star Life Insurance Co., a legal reserve company of Dallas, Texas and a wholly owned subsidiary of K-Mart Corp. K-Mart is the single largest discount retailer in the United States. Lone Star is a growing company with assets in 1977 of $76,246,658, up by 21 per cent over 1976. In 1974 Lone Star had acquired Planned Marketing Associates to add cancer insurance to their line.

The company's policy, when sold direct to an individual, costs $44.00 annually for coverage of the individual or $66.00 annually for family coverage. An employer can authorize the plan for employees. The employee then pays the insurance company without payroll deduction at a rate 27 per cent below the direct sales rate. The policy is intended as supplemental coverage rather than full coverage. A schedule of benefits is shown in Exhibit 1.

* Case prepared by Danny N. Bellenger, Georgia State University.

EXHIBIT 1

SCHEDULE OF BENEFITS

BASIC BENEFITS   All Limits Shown Are Lifetime Benefits For Each Person Insured

- **HOSPITAL SCHEDULE** — $60 per day for the first 12 days of hospital confinement. $30 per day thereafter. When patient re-enters the hospital *more* than 30 days after discharge, the $60 per day again applies.

- **DRUGS AND MEDICINE** — Actual expenses to $250 for prescribed drugs and medicines or 10% of the total payable hospital confinement benefits, whichever is greater.

- **SURGICAL** — Actual fee charged to the amount shown in the policy. $50 to $750 limit. Two operations through the same incision are considered one operation. NO LIMIT ON THE NUMBER OF OPERATIONS — IN OR OUT OF HOSPITAL.

- **ATTENDING PHYSICIAN** — Actual expenses to $10 a day in hospital for physician other than surgeon; limited to $700.

- **PRIVATE NURSING** — Actual expenses to $24 daily in hospital by a registered nurse or licensed vocational nurse — limited to $1,000.

- **X-RAY, RADIUM, RADIO-ACTIVE ISOTOPES THERAPY AND CHEMOTHERAPY** — Actual expenses to $1,500 limit in or out of hospital. Hospital confinement is not required.

- **BLOOD AND PLASMA** — Actual expenses to $500 limit for charges made to insured. There is no limit for Leukemia.

- **ANESTHESIA** — Actual fee charged to $100 limit as shown in policy schedule, excpet for skin cancer operations, where the limit of $30 is applicable. No limit on number of operations.

- **AMBULANCE BENEFIT** — Actual expenses to $50 per trip, going to and from hospital where insured is admitted as patient, limited to $1,000.

- **TRANSPORATATION** — Actual charges to $600 limit for regular airplane or railroad fare to the nearest hospital providing a sepcial type of treatment for cancer.

THERE IS NO REDUCTION IN ANY COVERED BENEFIT BECAUSE OF THE AGE OF THE COVERED PERSON

EXTENDED CANCER EXPENSE BENEFITS

Hospital Confinement — Drugs & Medicine
> Beginning With The 91st Day Of Continuous Confinement Until Discharged From The Hospital, 100% Of The Actual Hospital Charges For Care and Treatment Up To $5,000 Per Month Will Be Paid.

NO DEDUCTIONS ARE MADE FOR ANY BENEFITS PAID PRIOR TO THE 91ST DAY.

THERE ARE NO LIFETIME DOLLAR MAXIMUMS NOR TIME LIMITS UNDER THIS PROVISION.

DISABILITY INCOME (LOSS-OF-TIME) OPTIONAL BENEFIT: In Lieu Of All Other Benefits*

A COVERED PERSON AT THE TIME OF CLAIM MAY CHOOSE EITHER THE BENEFITS OUT-LINED ABOVE OR THIS OPTIONAL DISABILITY INCOME AND LOSS-OF-TIME PLAN.

THIS DISABILITY COMPENSATION PROVISION, IN THAT EVENT, WILL PAY: *Thirty (30) days are considered as one.*

A. $2,000 Per Month Or $66.65 Per Day For The First Month Of Hospital Confinement;

B. $1,500 Per Month Or $50.00 Per Day For The Next Two Months Of Hospitalization; and

C. $1,000 Per Month Or $33.33 Per Day in The Hospital For Each Additional Month Thereafter When Confined To A Hospital.

A NURSING HOME OR CONVALESCENT FEATURE IS PROVIDED IN THIS BENEFIT:

After the first 90 days of hospital confinement for cancer, a covered person may, if desired, then enter a nursing home or convalescent institution. The company will then pay $200 per month or $6.65 per day for the covered person's entire lifetime while so confined.

This Option Is Not Irrevocable. The Covered Person Is Permitted To Change The Choice Of This Provision Simply By Giving Reasonable Notice To The Company.

V.A. OR GOVERNMENT HOSPITAL CONFINEMENT BENEFITS

$66.65 per day for the first month, $50 per day for the next two (2) months, and $33.33 per day thereafter, even for entire lifetime, when confined to a V.A. or Government Hospital. *Thirty (30) days are considered as one (1) month.*

**THE TOTAL MAXIMUM BENEFITS PAID UNDER THESE PROVISIONS ARE UNLIMITED
THERE ARE NO LIFETIME DOLLAR MAXIMUMS NOR TIME LIMITS**

RETROACTIVE WAIVER OF PREMIUM BENEFIT

If the named insured is continuously and totally disabled for a period of four (4) consecutive months as a result of the occurrence of cancer, to the extent that there exists the complete inability of this person to work at his or her regular profession, we will waive or refund if already paid, all premiums coming due during such disability up to (5) full years. Since this waiver of Premium Benefit is retroactive, we will also waive all premiums that had become due from the beginning of total disability during the said four (4) months.

The sales approach for the policy is generally based on statistics published by the American Cancer Society. Exhibit 2 presents a sample of statistical information used in brochures and sales presentations.

Don had entered the insurance business in 1962 after working as a reservation control agent with Southern Airways. In that year, Southern experienced its longest strike in history, so Don left the company and moved to Columbus, Georgia, to begin work with an insurance agency selling life insurance. The majority of this market was in the military field, and it proved to be very successful. After a short period of successful

EXHIBIT 2

CANCER WILL STRIKE
1 in every 4 Americans
with no partiality!

FAMILIES
20 out of every 3 families

WOMEN
Cancer is the leading killer of women between age 30 to 54 years

This year
....90,000 women will develop breast cancer.
....34,000 women will die from breast cancer.
....343,000 women will develop cancer.

CHILDREN
Cancer is the leading killing disease of CHILDREN

MEN
55% of all cancer deaths are male. 68,000 men will die from lung cancer this year. Lung cancer in men has increased 125% since 1950. Cancer death in men has increased 35% since 1950.

CANCER KILLS
5 times more Americans each year than are killed in all Automobile Accidents

CANCER KILLED
more Americans in 1975 and 1976 than died in World War I, World War II, Korea, Vietnam...combined.

The facts and figures presented above were obtained from the 1977 report published by the American Cancer Society. The information does not constitute an endorsement of the Company or the Policy described.

sales accomplishments, he moved to the home office of North American Life Insurance Company of Chicago located in Chicago for the purpose of completing a management training program. During this 18-month program, he had the opportunity to learn the company from top to bottom, beginning in the mailroom and going all the way through the entire company. The final 2 months were spent with the Chairman of the Board of the Company, Mr. C. G. Ashbrook, Sr. During this period Don attended every function that Mr. Ashbrook was involved in. After completing this 18-month training program in the home office, he was given the opportunity to move back to the South where he became an Assistant Resident Vice President for the developing of the southeastern area. The company was later acquired by the U.S. Life Corporation; at that time Don became a Regional Vice President with the North American Company for Life and Health, which is also located in Chicago. Because of numerous moves, he resigned from that company and joined the All American Life and Casualty of Chicago, serving 5 years as Regional Vice President in the southeast.

The company was then acquired also by U.S. Life Corporation. Don felt that U.S. Life would "squeeze" a short-term profit out of the company and then cast it aside. Feeling this he resigned from his company to accept his present position.

Over the past 3 years the company has provided Don with good support in terms of servicing policyholders and providing agents with accurate and timely commission statements. The relationship between the state director and the company allows the state director a great deal of freedom in building a marketing and sales program. Don has some general guidelines to follow but is given a great deal of freedom to exercise his own judgment. His success is based largely on his ability to hire and train salespeople. The state director can establish regional managers, general agents, and agents. A regional manager may in turn hire general agents and agents. Each level receives an override on commission earned by people working under them.

The state director can hire as many people as he likes, all compensated on a straight commission basis. Don attempts to show an individual how she/he can retire at the end of 5 years of marketing this product on a comfortable renewal income of $30,000 per year. This motivates some; other people it does not. They are selected based on their experience, aggressiveness, and sincerity. It is important that they understand that they are dealing in a very difficult area. Don says that "If their attitude is not right, they won't sell anything, and certainly won't be successful in our business." Due to state regulations, the individual is authorized to sell anywhere in the state of Georgia. Don does suggest, for economic reasons, that the person concentrate within a short distance around their own office or home location. Don's planning is based on how to approach economically a given area. Since the major population of the state of Georgia is in Atlanta, the planning is aimed at this market. Don sits down and works out how to arrive at his goal of producing in excess of 1000 applications per month. He has found that, in marketing this particular program, women have a very good basis for discussing cancer with other women. Don also feels that to sell the product you need salespeople in a given area who know the people and what's going on in that area.

So, the planning process really involves many variables that change constantly. The amount of time that Don may personally spend recruiting and training people is limited by his own personal income. There is no subsistence which comes from the company; what is done depends upon his own capacity to recruit and train manpower. Don has found that there are many political situations within company structures that affect the ability to sell to them. Don says that he "doesn't even like to think about competition because when you start thinking of competition, then you are not spending time actually selling your product. I thought of competition when I made the decision to go into this business, and I, in fact, eliminated competition by knowing after two months of thorough study through our insurance department and other sources that this truly is the best product on the market of its kind." This is the way he teaches his people who sell the product; he does not want them comparing the product with other companies' products; he wants them to show the benefits of their plan and sell it on its own merits.

At present Don is faced with the need for sales growth. His compensation is based on total sales so he needs to recruit and train good agents across the state. At the same time a potentially serious problem is developing

Current Situation

EXHIBIT 3 Major Points from "Cashing in on Fear: The Selling of Cancer Insurance" [Reprinted from *Consumer Reports* (June 1978), pp. 336–338.]

1. Fear is used to sell cancer insurance.
2. Cancer insurance is good for the seller but not the buyer.
3. Most pay specific amounts for a number of separate expense categories such as hospital bills, doctors' bills, etc.
4. Mutual of Omaha's approach is best. They designate all the categories as eligible expenses and after a $1,000 deductible, pay a percentage of those expenses (50% of the next $1,500 and 80% after that).
5. Benefits for stays shorter than 90 days is very limited. (The average hospital stay for cancer patients is about 15 days.) Most policies would cover less than 1/3 of the total bill for an average stay.
6. On a 40-day hospital stay which would cost $8,000, the five companies noted in the article would pay the following amounts:

Company	Annual Premium*	Payouts
Mutual of Omaha	$30	$5150
Union Fidelity Life Insurance Co.	75	3480
American Family Corporation	50	1840
Colonial Life and Accident	27	1840
Lone Star Life Insurance Co.	44	1560

*Premium given is for a 35-year-old single woman buying an individual plan. Group rates are generally somewhat lower; family-plan rates are generally somewhat higher.

7. Most policies pay all or nearly all of bills for stays lasting more than 90 days, but by government statistics this is less than 10% of all cancer patients.
8. Many policies have other limitations; for example, only Mutual of Omaha's policy covers doctors' bills when a patient is not in the hospital.
9. Three states have banned or severly restricted the sales of such policies.
10. *Consumer Reports* recommends against buying cancer insurance but if you want to buy cancer insurance, anyway, then they suggest Mutual of Omaha's policy.

due to adverse publicity concerning cancer insurance and Lone Star's cancer policy. For example, the June 1978 issue of *Consumer Reports* ran an article entitled "Cashing in on Fear: The Selling of Cancer Insurance." Key points from this article are shown in Exhibit 3. It basically advises against the purchase of cancer insurance but suggests Mutual of Omaha's policy if one is inclined to buy.

Don's reaction to the article is strongly negative.

"It is truly a shame that *Consumer Reports* does not have a person to write an article such as this who would understand the concept of cancer insurance and would write accordingly. They take the position that cancer insurance is designed to pay the total cost of cancer treatment. This is not the case at all, never has been, and never will be. If an insurance company designed a policy that would pay in total the cost of treatment of cancer, then the buying public just simply couldn't afford it. Our policies are designed to be a supplemental program to pay for costs incurred by individuals in this country who simply do not have or cannot afford adequate health insurance to cover all areas of risk.

They did a study of five companies. They gave an illustration of the annual premiums—$30, $75, $50, $27, and $44 a year for the five companies. They also indicated payouts of the benefits: $5150, $3480, $1840 and $1560. This is a totally incorrect assumption of benefits payable. Our coverage is, hospital schedules: $60 per day for the first 12 days of hospital confinement, $30 a day thereafter. The claim comparison which *Consumer Reports* makes illustrated what would be payable for a 40-day hospital stay based on a $200 per day room. Well, it is true that if you take just the hospital schedule of $60 per day for the first 12 and $30 a day thereafter, it comes out to be $1560; but when you take the *total* benefits payable, you find that the approximate payment would be $4970. Therefore, they do not give a complete statement.

In the article they go on to make a recommendation that Mutual of Omaha was the best policy if you've got to buy cancer insurance. They don't tell you in the article that Mutual of Omaha will not pay any benefits if you have an additional major medical policy. They don't bother to tell you that the true deductible on Mutual of Omaha plan is $1750 ($1000 deductible with 50 per cent of the next $1500 is truly a deductible of $1750 not $1000). So, there are so many things they leave out that the article should not have been written the way it was; and it is misleading.

They also state that the insurance company uses scare tactics to sell cancer insurance. In fact, that's the title of the article, "Cashing in on Fear—The Selling of Cancer Insurance." A number of insurance companies, the article states, are using fear of cancer to build one of the fastest growing businesses in the country. 'Cancer strikes one out of four Americans; two out of three families,' one company's brochure points out. This is not an insurance company figure—this comes from the Cancer Society and the National Cancer Institute. It is not an insurance tactic to sell insurance. It's simply stating the facts.

The article itself then is totally misleading in the way that it was written. Keep in mind that the point of this discussion is that I am unhappy that such an article would come out criticizing a program of any type, be it insurance or anything else, without giving a total presentation on the matter. If they can't give a total and fair presentation, then they should stay out of the area."

Don is now faced with two types of decisions: (1) How should the sales force be instructed to deal with the adverse publicity? (2) What plans should be made to insure the long-range growth of his Georgia operation?

CASE 14.2
Andrews Pencil Company*

*Robert M. Fulmer and Roger A. Strang, *Exploring the New Marketing* (Macmillan Publishing Company, Inc., 1976), pp. 16–17. Used with permission.

The Andrews Pencil Company was founded in 1901 and followed an aggressive cost-cutting and selling program to become the largest manufacturer in the United States by the early 1920s. The company continued to expand and by 1948 had about 45 per cent of the United States market and a substantial export business.

Company Background

In 1948, Mr. David Andrews, the grandson of the founder of the company, took over as president. Like his father who had preceded him, he had been trained as an engineer and had worked his way up through the factory. In his position as production vice-president he had played a large part in developing new machinery that substantially reduced the costs of production and allowed the Andrews Company to maintain its position as the market leader.

The Andrews Pencil Company had the largest sales force in the industry and it could usually sell all the pencils the company could manufacture. If there were any difficulty, the company would advertise or make a special cut-price offer to retailers, and any surplus production would be quickly cleared. Pencils were widely used for note taking and casual correspondence in schools, business, government, and the home and the outlook was for continued growth, especially as the postwar baby boom passed through the school system.

Current Situation

Mr. Andrews was determined to maintain his company's leadership position. He hired several able young engineers and had them working on new cost-cutting techniques. The company's research staff ensured that their full line of pencils was the best in each field, including art work and design and technical drawing. Mr. Andrews encouraged hiring an aggressive sales staff to ensure that sales levels would be maintained.

At the top he built up a "management team" of the production vice-president, sales vice-president, controller, treasurer, and research director that met frequently to formulate company strategy.

At about the same time as Mr. Andrews took over as president, the ball-point pen was introduced to the American market. Initially it was very expensive and had a number of performance faults. However, several companies were quickly into production of these pens and with competition the price rapidly dropped and performance problems were eliminated.

Mr. Andrews had noticed the introduction of the ball pen but had not seen it as a threat because he felt it would compete with fountain pens. After several years, however, the company found that pencil sales were harder to make. By 1956 the company faced its first sales decline and, although Mr. Andrews increased advertising and cut prices still further, sales continued to drop.

The profitability of the Andrews Pencil Company rapidly declined and production cutbacks and staff layoffs were ordered. By 1965 sales were half of what they had been a decade earlier and Mr. Andrews was wondering what to do to save the company.

Student Learning Exercise / 14
Finding Information for the Management of Change

Objective

To show the types and sources of information from inside and outside the firm that are needed on a continuing basis effectively to manage change.

Overview

To manage change effectively, a sales manager must first decide on the types of information that are needed. Then the sources of this information must be developed. This exercise concentrates on both internal and external information systems.

Procedure

Assume that you are the sales manager for an institutional food wholesaler. The company sells frozen, canned, and prepackaged food in bulk to various institutions such as schools, hospitals, restaurants, and fast food outlets. There are presently ten salespeople. Sales in the past have fluctuated widely, giving rise to considerable concern among the company's management.

Discuss what should be monitored inside the company and also in the external environment in order to keep track of changes and effectively respond to new developments.

Readings for

PART Three

Saleswomen: Perceptions, Problems, and Prospects

DAN H. ROBERTSON AND DONALD W. HACKETT

Confrontation on a myriad of issues represents a very real part of the dilemma facing today's marketing manager. Increasing pressure from environmentalists, government regulations, and consumerism movements are but a few of the sources of confrontation encountered. A relative newcomer to this array of confrontation issues involves participation by women in business management, generally, and marketing decision-making, in particular. Decades of frustration by females seeking to integrate heretofore closed areas of corporate operations are reflected in the following random statements generated through open ended questions collected in this study:

- On two occasions I have trained men to be my boss and have been told it was necessary since a woman could not serve at the executive level.
- My staff finds it hard to discard old biases against mingling women and decision-making.
- It's just that, especially with many old line executives, women's 'place' is in the kitchen, and the bedroom, or perhaps behind a typewriter, but not the conference room.

From *Journal of Marketing* (Vol. 41), July 1977, pp. 66–71. Reprinted by permission of the publisher, American Marketing Association.

Nevertheless, the fact is that women constitute an increasingly essential part of our nation's work force. The last three decades have witnessed extraordinary economic and social change in the status of women. The response of married women to labor market demand, changing attitudes toward careers for women outside the home, and finally, the landmark legislation prohibiting employment discrimination based on sex have all combined to produce significant gains in the participation of women in what has traditionally been male dominated positions. Aggregate statistics substantiate that gains have taken place. The census of 1970 showed a 21% increase of women in skilled and professional positions between 1960 and 1970.

Women in Business and Sales

But U.S. Department of Labor figures show females holding fewer than 18% of the U.S. managerial jobs.[1] Opportunities for women in management, while increasing, have developed gradually with spotty and uneven progress. For example, in March 1970, a survey on the employment of women, conducted jointly by the American Society for Personnel Administration and the Bureau of National Affairs, reported that, in 82% of the firms surveyed, more than 10% of the employees were women. In 31% of those firms surveyed, more than 50% of the *workers* were female; but, in the same companies, 91% reported less than 10% of their *managers* were women.[2]

The statistics pertaining to women in sales are similar. Recent survey results of the Research Institute of America,[3] showed that 81% of the U.S. companies surveyed have not hired any saleswomen; concomitantly, research sponsored by the 3,000 member Sales Executive Club of New York revealed that women make up only 4% of the member firms' sales forces.[4] Among companies that do employ women in sales, the great majority are concentrated in two or three industries. For example, the 1970 census takers found 2.1 million women "sales workers" and 3.3 million men; but, the same count showed 1.7 million of these women were salesclerks, another 93,000 sold door-to-door and 83,600 were real estate agents or brokers. Excluding these, fewer than 300,000 women are employed in industrial selling positions.

Blocks to Equal Status

The purpose of this article is not to argue whether or not discrimination exists; there is already ample evidence that it does exist in both jobs and pay.[5] However, the above figures do illustrate that discriminatory practices appear to have blocked the entry of women into selling positions to a greater degree than in other areas. What is the explanation for the slow integration of women into sales? The recent economic downturn notwithstanding, the long term demand for people to fill sales positions outstrips supply.

Traditional male attitudes and myths concerning female stereotypes which ultimately result in prejudicial action patterns seem to explain at least part of the slow integration of women into sales. Studies by Athanassiades[6] and Dipboye[7] support the notion that women in business suffer from prejudicial stereotyping. Hodges and Bernis[8] found discrimination of women to be widespread in business firms, but especially so in role supportive tasks such as sales. Epstein[9] found that women's access to the upper echelons of management is often stymied because protege systems work for males but are inoperative for females. Bass et al.[10] found male respondents' attitudes toward women in management included negative perceptions relating to dependability and career orientation.

Although there is a paucity of current information available on women in selling, three basic research questions are explored in this study. *First,* how do sales managers perceive saleswomen? This question is explored from the viewpoint of sales managers who both currently have and have not had a significant number of female sales representatives working under their supervision. *Second,* what are the perceptions of salesmen regarding saleswomen? Are women perceived as being "unfit" for sales activities? *Lastly,* how do saleswomen view themselves vis-a-vis their male counterparts? Together, these questions provide the focus of this research.

Methodology

Given the controversial nature of the subject matter, the researchers felt it was important to provide respondents in this research a guarantee of anonymity. This resulted in two separate, but related, sample populations for data collection purposes.

First, data were collected from 249 sales managers in firms who had sales staff supervisory responsibility. Although titles varied somewhat from one firm to another, this group consisted primarily of "sales managers." The data collected from this group were used to form the findings relevant to the first research question. In order to explore research questions two and three, it was necessary to gather data from personnel of both sexes who were directly involved in selling.

Exhibit 1 presents a profile of sales management respondent characteristics drawn from 249 usable returned questionnaires. In addition to questions on age and sex of the respondent, sales managers were also asked to provide an indication of the number of sales personnel in their scope of supervision unit. Finally, sales managers were classified according to whether they had a significant number (arbitrarily defined as 25% or more) of female sales personnel in their sales unit. Forty-eight (19.3%) had sales staffs with 25% or more females. Two hundred and one (80.7%) had sales staffs which were less than 25% female.

A sample of 250 sales personnel (125 male and 125 female) formed the second group. They were selected at random from the four metropolitan areas of Chicago, Atlanta, Oklahoma City and Denver. Only individuals involved in the commercial sales of real estate were considered since this is one of the few industries with heavy participation by saleswomen.

EXHIBIT 1 Sales Management Respondent Characteristics (n = 249)

	Sales Staff 25% or More Female (n = 48)	<25% of Sales Staff Female (n = 201)
Age		
Under 30	20.8%	18.4%
30–45	66.7	40.8
Over 45	12.5	40.8
Sex		
Male	95.8%	99%
Female	4.2%	1%
No. of Sales Personnel in Sales Unit[a]		
3 or less	6.3%	15.9%
4–7	31.2	48.2
8–12	22.9	19.4
13–19	20.8	12.4
20–29	12.5	2.4
Over 29	6.3	2.0
Current Annual $ Sales[b]		
$500,000 or less	20.8%	19.9%
$500,001–1,000,000	35.4	32.3
$1,000,001–5,000,000	20.8	13.9
$5,000,001–10,000,000	16.7	19.9
$10,000,001–25,000,000	4.2	9.0
Over $25,000,000	2.0	5.0

a. Total exceeds 100% due to rounding.
b. Total does not equal 100% due to rounding.

EXHIBIT 2 Sales Personnel Respondent Characteristics (n = 111)

	Salesmen (n = 59)	Saleswomen (n = 52)
Age		
Under 30	16.3%	15.0%
30–45	43.1	39.1
Over 45	40.6	45.9
Sex	53.2%	46.8%
Years of Selling Experience		
1–5 years	19.4%	25.7%
6–10 years	27.6	35.4
11–20 years	27.2	21.8
Over 20 years	25.8	17.1
Sales Performance[a]		
Top 10%	36.4%	39.2%
Top 25%	17.1	19.3
Top 50%	28.1	25.5
Other	18.4	16.0

a. Self-reported by respondents

Respondent lists were developed using the R. L. Polk City Directory for each city. Persons in the sample were mailed a questionnaire. A total of 52 women and 59 men returned usable questionnaires as a result of the first and second mailings.

The questionnaire consisted of two parts. Section I consisted of socio-economic data and personal information relating to sales experience and performance to insure the sample was normally distributed (see Exhibit 2). Section II consisted of internally scaled questions in a seven-point semantic differential format, developed so as to allow measurement of respondents' perceptions of sales personnel by sex. The bipolar adjectives and phrases were derived from previously published lists of desired personality and task competency dimensions of salespersons, as developed by Orth and Jacobs',[11] Robinson and Stidson[12] and others.[13] The personality variables related to *aggressiveness, extrovert nature, trust, imagination, emotionality,* and *open-mindedness.* The task variables were *competency, career orientation, sales technique, intelligence,* and *self-confidence.*

Data Analysis & Findings: Research Questions 2 and 3

In order to gain insight into research questions two and three, this study examined the responses of salesmen and saleswomen to determine the characteristics of salespersons that most effectively discriminate between salesmen and saleswomen. More specifically, the following two null hypotheses were tested.

H_1: *There is no significant difference in the perceptions of salesmen and saleswomen toward the male salesperson.*

H_2: *There is no significant difference in the perceptions of salesmen and saleswomen toward the female salesperson.*

Test of significance between respondent groups for each of the 11 variables applied to salesmen and saleswomen were first performed using a pooled variance T-test. This test was exploratory in nature to determine if any significant differences between groups actually existed. Examination of the direction of differences in means for the male and female respondent groups provide a basis for formulation of a descriptive profile of the perceptions of women sales personnel by saleswomen respondents, as contrasted with perceptions of women salespersons by salesmen respondents.

After the exploratory analysis by T-tests, a discriminant analysis of the data was performed. Churchill,[14] Massy,[15] Green,[16] and others have used discriminant analysis in marketing research to classify objects by a set of independent variables into one of two or more mutually exclusive and exhaustive categories. Analysis of significant grouped data in this research was performed utilizing stepwise discriminant analysis. The discriminant function—representing a linear combination of predictor variables—was computed on the assumption of known assignment of each object to one of two groups, i.e., salesmen or saleswomen. The purpose

EXHIBIT 3-A Profile of Salesmen

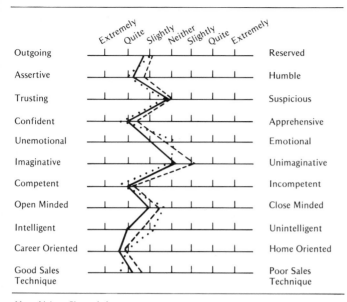

Mean Values Charted above are:

Characteristic	Saleswomen	Salesmen	Sales Managers
Outgoing/Reserved	2.7	3.0	2.8
Assertive/Humble	2.5	2.8	2.3
Trusting/Suspicious	3.8	3.8	3.8
Confident/Apprehensive	2.4	2.6	2.3
Unemotional/Emotional	3.4	3.7	3.8
Imaginative/Unimaginative	4.4	4.9	4.0
Competent/Incompetent	2.1	2.4	2.0
Open Minded/Close Minded	3.2	3.4	3.6
Intelligent/Unintelligent	2.2	2.6	3.2
Career Oriented/Home Oriented	1.7	2.0	2.2
Good Sales Technique/Poor Sales Technique	2.4	2.5	2.1

Legend——Salesmen,——Saleswomen, . . . Sales Managers

Significant at .05 level.

of using two-group discriminant analysis in this case was to find a linear combination of predictor variables that best separates the two groups and to test if the group means (centroids) have arisen from a single population versus two different populations. Predictor variables in the analysis were based on the bipolar adjective scales, and interpretation of the results was made after five steps due to the discriminatory power of predictor variables.

The first null hypothesis was supported by the survey results. There were no significant differences in the T-test of group means between male and female respondents with respect to the 11 variables when applied to salesmen. The male and female sales respondents had similar perceptions of salesmen. The results in Exhibit 3-A illustrate that both respondent groups view salesmen as *competent, highly career oriented,* and *confident.* Both groups agree that salesmen employ *good sales tech-*

EXHIBIT 3-B   Profile of Saleswomen

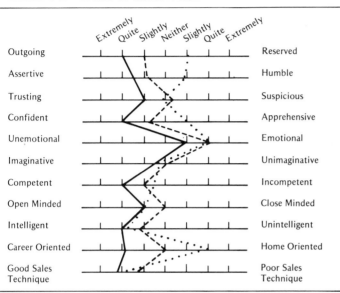

Mean Values Charted above are:

Characteristic	Saleswomen	Salesmen	Sales Managers
Outgoing/Reserved	2.3	2.9	5.1
Assertive/Humble	2.7	2.9	5.0
Trusting/Suspicious	3.3	3.9	3.7
Confident/Apprehensive	2.2	3.4	5.0
Unemotional/Emotional	4.9	5.8	5.8
Imaginative/Unimaginative	3.7	3.9	3.5
Competent/Incompetent	1.8	3.1	3.3
Open Minded/Close Minded	2.8	3.9	3.1
Intelligent/Unintelligent	1.9	2.6	2.3
Career Oriented/Home Oriented	2.3	4.1	5.7
Good Sales Technique/Poor Sales Technique	1.8	3.1	2.4

Legend	Salesmen,	Saleswomen,	. . .	Sales Managers

Significant at .05 level.

	Group Mean Scores	
Variables in Order of Appearance	Male	Female
1. Good/Poor Sales Technique	3.18	1.80
2. Career/Home Orientation	4.19	2.31
3. Open/Closed Mindedness	3.97	2.82
4. Emotional/Unemotional	5.86	5.27
5. Confident/Apprehensive	3.49	2.20

EXHIBIT 4   Summary of Stepwise Discriminant Analysis Applied to Saleswomen on Five Factors[a,b]

a. Constant Discriminatory Power index after 5 steps w
   $w^2 = .39$.
b. F Ratio after 5 steps = 13.867; significant at .05 level.

niques, are *quite intelligent* and *somewhat assertive and outgoing*. Rather neutral responses were voiced by the respondents concerning the salesman on the variables of *trustfulness, emotionality* and *open-mindedness*. At the same time, both groups viewed the salesman as *somewhat lacking in imagination*. Discriminant analysis of the respondent data pertaining to perceptions of salesmen was redundant since no significant disagreement existed between the respondent groups.

The second null hypothesis was not supported by the survey results. Pooled variance T tests applied to the two respondent groups scores of the 11 variables relating to saleswomen shows significant differences on 9 of the 11 personality and task factors, as shown in Exhibit 3-B. A linear combination of the set of variables was developed using discriminant analysis to give a more accurate account of the nature of group differences and to evaluate the relative weights and classification powers of the resulting function.

While the two respondent groups differed significantly concerning saleswomen, the discriminant analysis provided five significant predictor variables. Examination of mean differences within the five predictor variables in Exhibit 4 provides a descriptive profile of the two respondent groups. While the two groups agreed on their perceptions of salesmen, a much different perception of women in sales, based on the traditional view of the "weaker sex" seemed to be manifest among the male respondents. The male salesperson, when compared to the female salesperson respondent, pictured the saleswomen as: (1) *possessing poorer sales technique*, (2) *having less career orientation*, (3) *being less open-minded*, (4) *more emotional* and (5) *less self-confident*.

Data Analysis & Findings: Research Question 1

To obtain viable data relating to research question one it was essential to focus upon sales managers who had previous experience with *both* male and female sales personnel. Arbitrarily, the figure 25% or more female sales personnel was selected as a "cut-off point" with a follow-up question to determine if the entire sales force was female. In this way, the responses of *only* those sales managers who had a factual basis for comparison between male and female sales personnel could be isolated. All 48 sales managers who "qualified" (via the 25% figure) were males. Exhibits 3-A and 3-B also present the perceptions of sales managers for both male and female sales personnel. In contrast to the male and female perceptions of salesmen (Exhibit 3-A), sales managers viewed salesmen as *more assertive, imaginative* and *more given to utilize good sales technique.* Sales managers also viewed male sales personnel as *less emotional, open-minded* and *intelligent* than did male or female sales respondents.

Sales managers also differed in their perceptions of female sales representatives. Specifically, they viewed saleswomen as *more reserved, humble, apprehensive, imaginative,* and *home oriented* than did either the male or female sales personnel (see Exhibit 3-B). Additionally, sales managers depicted saleswomen as *somewhat less competent* than did either male or female sales respondents.

Implications & Conclusions

The findings of this study provide insights into perceptions of saleswomen by both their male peers and superiors. Additionally, it may suggest some reasons why women are having only "limited" success in achieving equality in the professional sales area.

Where peer evaluation was concerned, there were five discriminating variables that emerged from this survey. It would seem worth noting that the two highest discriminating factors occurred on the task dimension variables (good/poor sales techniques and career/home orientation), rather than the personality dimension. Of the five factors, salesmen in this sample disagreed most strongly with their female peers about women's "sales technique." Specifically, the males felt that women lacked professional expertise in the approach, set up, and closing of sales. Implied in the salesmen's reaction is that women's societal role is not best suited for sales. Analysis of the next highest discriminant variable sheds more light on this reaction since the male respondents view saleswomen as much less career oriented than necessary to be successful in sales. Within the personality dimension, a profile emerged in which salesmen viewed the saleswomen as less open-minded, more highly emotional, and less self-confident than did their female peers. Interestingly enough, both groups gave the most extreme score of all 11 variables to the emotionality of women, even though males view women as significantly more emotional than do the women themselves. On this scale one must, however, be careful with the results. Since *emotional* was placed on the negative loading of the scale one might interpret *emotional* as a negative characteristic and *unemotional* as a positive characteristic when, in fact, either argument could be made for the characteristic.

Of significance in the discriminant analysis is not only what appeared as discriminatory variables but what failed to appear. Bass,[17] it was pointed out earlier, found the factor that most highly influenced managers in their negative perception of women at work was the women's perceived *lack of dependability* and short-term *career orientation.* His findings concerning career orientation were supported by this research, but the dependability factor failed to appear among the significant variables. Additionally, two closely related variable characteristics measured in this study (i.e., *trustfulness* and *competency* of women), did not appear among the top five discriminatory variables. The fact that there is no perceived difference in the competency of saleswomen by salesmen would seem to illustrate that while women might utilize different methods and personalities in the sales environment, they still have been accepted as competent by their male peers in the profession of selling.

Regarding perceptions by sales managers, a "show me" attitude seems to permeate attitudes toward female sales representatives. If management is to take advantage of the latent sales talent in the female work force, it would seem that the onus for change is up to both management and prospective saleswomen. To eliminate discrimination in the future, sales executives must reexamine their own attitudes toward women in sales, look at the actual data regarding women in sales, and provide them with the sales training required to perform the sales role successfully. Additionally, management must acquire a new sensitivity to women in sales and realize that perhaps personality dimensions such as emotionality are indeed different in men and women sales personnel and make adjustments in their interaction with women. Women must also be willing to accept some role reversal when they enter the sales arena. Commitment to the job is essential if they are to be accepted by their male peers and superiors. Additionally, travel, sales quota pressure, and such social reversals as the purchase of male clients' lunches are only a few "life style" changes saleswomen must voluntarily adopt before genuine acceptance and quality will be obtained.

Endnotes

1. Special Subcommittee on Education of the House Committee on Education and Labor, 1970 Hearings, *Discrimination Against Women*, Parts I and II.

2. Janice Hodges and Stephen Bernis, "Sex Stereotyping: Its Decline in Skilled Trades," Bureau of the Census, *1970 Census of Population, Detailed Characteristics, U.S. Summary Report PC(1)-D*, (Washington, D.C.: U.S. Govt. Printing Office, 1973), Table 221.

3. "RIA-SECNY Study Finds 81% of U.S. Businesses Employ No Saleswomen," *Marketing News*, July 15, 1974, p. 1. Quoted from *Women in Selling: The Problems and the Promise*, a study sponsored by Research Institute of America and Sales Executive Club of New York.

4. John Costello, "Ms. Star in Sales," *Marketing Times*, March–April 1975, pp. 4–9.

5. Cynthia Epstein, "Encountering the Male Establishment: Sex Status Limits on Women's Careers in the Professions," *American Journal of Sociology*, May 1970, pp. 965–71.

6. John Athanassiades, "Myths of Women in Management," *Atlanta Economic Review*, May–June 1975, pp. 4–9.

7. Robert Dipboye, "Women as Managers—Stereotypes and Realities," *Survey of Business*, May–June 1975, pp. 22–26.

8. Hodges and Bernis, same as reference 2 above.

9. Epstein, same as reference 5 above.

10. Bernard Bass, J. Krussell, and R. N. Alexander, "Male Managers' Attitudes Toward Working Women," *American Behavioral Scientist*, Vol. 15 (1971), pp. 77–83.

11. Charles Orth and Frederick Jacobs, "Women in Management: Pattern for Change," *Harvard Business Review*, March–April 1974, pp. 45–58.

12. Patrick Robinson and Bert Stidson, *Personal Selling in a Modern Perspective* (Boston: Allyn & Bacon, 1967).

13. *Meaning in Salesmen's Performance*, Studies in Business Policy (N.Y.: National Industrial Conference Board, 1965).

14. Gilbert Churchill, Jr., N. M. Ford, and Urban Ozanne, "An Analysis of Price Aggressiveness in Gasoline Marketing," *Journal of Marketing Research* (Vol. 7), February 1970, pp. 36–42.

15. William F. Massy, "Discriminant Analysis of Audience Characteristics," *Journal of Advertising Research*, March 1965, pp. 39–48.

16. Paul Green and D. Tull, *Research for Marketing Decision*, 3rd ed. (Englewood Cliffs, N.J.: Prentice-Hall, 1975).

17. Bass, Krussell and Alexander, same as reference 10 above.

The authors acknowledge the assistance of Ms. Susan Logan, a Doctoral Candidate in Marketing at Georgia State University for her contributions.

Toward a New Concept
of Sales Management

LESLIE M. DAWSON

When efforts were being made several years ago to formulate a concept of physical distribution attuned to the modern business environment, this functional area of marketing was often referred to as *the most neglected*. Today it could be argued that the area of sales management is a prime contender for this *honor*. According to the Committee on Definitions of the American Marketing Association, sales management is:

the planning, direction, and control of the personal selling activities of a business unit, including recruiting, selecting, training, equipping, assigning, routing, supervising, paying and motivating as these tasks apply to the personal sales force.[1]

While this is no doubt a useful listing of the tasks in which the sales manager has typically become involved, it does not make clear the conceptual linkage of the sales management position to the general goals and efforts of the business organization.

This article develops the thesis that (1) top business management has always tended to operate under *some* implicit concept of the sales management function; (2) this has been evidenced by the locus of emphasis in the prescribed duties and responsibilities of managerial strata existing between the top sales executive and field selling force; and (3) having already shifted several times in this century, it would appear that the locus of emphasis is about to shift again, thereby generating a fundamental change in the nature of the sales manager's role.

A Historical Perspective

In general, the concept held by top management of the sales manager's role has always tended to be determined by the corresponding conception of the salesman's role. This role seemed to have been a function of the general tone of business' response to perceived dominant environmental forces. The process may be given a useful historical perspective by relating it to the well-known hypothesis that the dominant orientation of American business has passed through several distinct phases in this century.

From *Journal of Marketing* (Vol. 34), April 1970, pp. 33–38. Reprinted by permission of the publisher, American Marketing Association.
[1] William J. Stanton and Richard H. Buskirk, *Management of the Sales Force* (Homewood, Ill.: Richard D. Irwin, Inc., 1964), p. 7.

The Production Era

Rapid technological change dominated the business environment in the late nineteenth and early twentieth centuries. Technological progress in the fields of agriculture, transportation, and communication occurred with a swiftness as to constitute revolutions rather than evolutions. In an environment which suddenly reflected both the technical capacity for mass production and the expanded markets to absorb the increased output, the natural response of business consisted of a production orientation. Management was preoccupied with increasing volume and improving plant efficiency. While it would be an overstatement to say that market considerations were ignored during this era, there is ample foundation for Drucker's claim that "fifty years ago the typical attitude of the American businessman toward marketing was still: 'The sales department will sell whatever the plant produces.' "[2]

In the production-dominated era, the job of the salesman was not held in very high regard either by business management or the public at large. The salesman was viewed as the congenial, hail-fellow-well-met representative who built up good will for the manufacturer among the trade. This conception of the selling process as an art, not amenable to any type of scientific analysis, and of the sales job as one requiring a relatively low degree of skill and intelligence—an occupation which could naturally be expected to attract people of less than ideal character—led to a conception of sales management emphasizing *tight supervision and control*.

The Sales Era

The sales era of American business probably should be dated from the late 1920s. These years were marked by significant change in the dominant environmental forces affecting business. Unparalleled prosperity was the hallmark of the nation's economy in the post-World War I years from 1922 to 1929. Continued improvements in technology and labor efficiency propelled industrial output to a new plateau. Whereas population gained approximately 12% during these years, industrial productivity almost doubled. As assembly lines proliferated, America fast became the world's first genuine mass-production society. The demand for consumer goods could not keep up with the rapid pace of the national product, which is one reason why accumulated funds flowed into various kinds of speculation. The crash of 1929 witnessed the beginning of a depression which cast an economic pall over the nation that was never fully lifted until the start of World War II. Thus, the dominant environ-

[2] Peter F. Drucker, *The Practice of Management* (New York: Harper & Brothers, 1954), p. 38.

mental forces during this period were, first, strains of consumption saturation at an unprecedented level of industrial productivity, and ultimately, an extended period of extreme economic depression. Both of these environmental pressures tended to evoke a similar response by business. This took the form of an increased concern with the development of a mass-distribution machinery to complement the now realized mass-production system.

The stature of the sales position increased in the eyes of top management during the sales era. The fallacy of the "better mouse-trap" theorem as a workable guide to successful marketing was exposed. It became evident that something beyond congeniality was required for a salesman to sustain a consistently high volume. The term *scientific salesmanship* came into use to describe the application of sound management principles and basic behavioral science concepts to the selling process. Still, management's conception of the salesman reflected the basically company-oriented outlook of the period. His job was to generate sales, and a simple amount of product-market knowledge combined with a highly structured selling presentation was usually deemed sufficient to this end. Short-run sales volume was normally the measure of his success.

Top management's realization that the sales job required knowledge and skills beyond personality led to an emphasis on *broadened responsibilities* for sales managers. Definitions of sales management now commonly included responsibilities in such areas as recruiting, selecting, training, and compensating. The sales manager's role in overall marketing strategy and planning remained less definite. Significantly, the sales manager's performance in this era was generally measured by the *volume* produced by his selling force. Profit may not have been ignored altogether, but it was generally felt that sales volume data were easier to procure and more precise. The direct relationship between increasing sales volume and increasing profit was widely assumed.

The Marketing Era

Much has been said about the dynamic character of the business environment in the post-World War II years. The nation's economy not only recovered from the effects of the Depression, but also swiftly advanced well beyond the highest prewar levels. Postwar prosperity ushered in the age of the affluent society in the United States. The great technological surge produced by the war led to new processes and techniques which brought down traditional industry boundaries. Chemicals became the competitor of textiles; plastic of steel; and paper of glass. Rising costs and pricing constraints made the term *profit squeeze* prominent in the lexicon of business. The postwar consumer was not only better off economically, better educated, and more sophisticated, but also before long more saturated with goods. The notion of a limit to the *capacity to consume* became something more than a mere theoretical concern. As the American economy was rapidly transformed into one of abundance, the survival of the business enterprise became largely dependent upon its skill in determining, and flexibility in adjusting to, shifts in consumer tastes. An all-out commitment to market considerations became vital, and this was termed as the *marketing orientation* or the *marketing concept.*

The strategic role of the salesman as the direct link between seller and prospective buyer resulted in a virtual redefinition of the sales job in the marketing era. Numerous references have been made in the post-war literature to the death of the "old salesman" and his rebirth as the "new salesman." Several distinct attributes are supposed to differentiate the latter from his predecessor.

He is seen as a *manager of a market area* responsible for goal determination, forecasting, planning, and long-run market development. Such a managerial approach to territory cultivation is significant because "it is the difference between viewing salesmen as employees or as members of management."[3]

The new salesman is visualized as a *problem-solver.* In fact, the salesman's problem-solving abilities are recognized as often constituting the key to product differentiation, "He is a man capable of absorbing stacks of information churned out by the marketing department, and of applying it to his customer's problems. He goes forth armed with a tremendous amount of data on his customers' needs, their products, their corporate organizations, and their supply and delivery schedules."[4]

The new salesman functions as an *educator* in a technological age where effective communication across functional or disciplinary lines has become increasingly difficult. "The more effective are salesmen as educators, the more effective they will be as sales purveyors of the knowledge, concepts, and ideas contained in their sales proposals."[5]

He is an *empathizer* with a solid, often formal, grounding in the behavioral sciences which enables him to better recognize and cope with the personal need patterns of prospective buyers.

As the salesman's role has been redefined in the marketing era, a redefinition of the sales manager's role has also been necessary. For instance, the greater the degree to which firms have come to view salesmen as managers of a market area the less emphasis has been placed on field supervision and control of salesmen's activities by sales management. In general, the redefinition of the sales management job in the marketing era has tended to increase the organizational importance of the job through new emphasis in two major areas:

- The new sales manager, largely freed from day-to-day activity planning for salesmen, has become involved in creative *strategy development* at a higher marketing level. His job requires a total sales perspective wherein field sales activities are properly related to, and integrated

---

[3] Eugene J. Kelley and William Lazer, "Basic Duties of the Modern Sales Department," in *Managerial Marketing: Perspectives and Viewpoints, 3rd ed.* Eugene J. Kelley, and William Lazer (eds.) (Chicago, Ill.: Richard D. Irwin, Inc., 1967), p. 540.

[4] Carl Rieser, "The Salesman Isn't Dead—He's Different," *Fortune* (Vol. 66), November 1962, pp. 124–127, at p. 126.

[5] Joseph W. Thompson, *Selling: A Behavioral Science Approach* (New York: McGraw Hill Book Co., 1966), p. 118.

with, other elements of the total marketing mix. "Perhaps the most important change in the scope and nature of the sales manager's job . . . is that he must become a planner, a strategy developer, as well as an operator."[6]

- Due to the major influence of the computer, the sales manager of the marketing era has taken on new *profit responsibilities.* Faster and more thorough analysis of sales data facilitates the measurement of profitability of individual salesmen, products, territories, and other components of the selling operation. The profitable selling operation, instead of the high volume one, increasingly has become the criterion of successful sales management.

The 1970s and Beyond—the "Human Era"?

There has been much recent speculation as to whether business will enter a new era as it moves into the last third of the twentieth century; for example, "the age of the computer" and the "era of social responsibility." It seems clear that the environmental forces which resulted in a greater focus on the marketplace will endure and intensify in the foreseeable future. Yet, the tumultuous events ushering in the 1970s suggest that a market focus will not be sufficient in coping with a powerful new milieu of pressures emanating from the environment. The impact of computer technology on marketing management continues to grow. Not only has this often compelled the competitive firm to redesign operations and procedures, but also to deal with the human adjustments necessary in the integration of the computer in the organization system. Externally, demands mount for a deeper commitment by the business community to the solutions of the social problems which plague the United States and the world. Pressures on business leaders intensify for more action in such diverse areas at the war on poverty, pollution control, and the eradication of social injustice. Numerous recent initiatives by prominent corporations in such human need areas signify a response to such pressures and are suggestive of a possible movement beyond a *marketing orientation* to a broader *human orientation.*

A New Concept of Sales Management

It has been entirely consistent with the perspective of a marketing orientation that the sales management concept be characterized by emphasis on strategy development and profit responsibility. Both of these relate to market opportunity and the firm's search for greater profit return. But for the firm moving to a broader human orientation, the concept of the sales manager's job may be expected to reflect a very basic shift in emphasis and priorities. For such a firm the most congruous concept

---

[6] Hector Lazo and Arnold Corbin, *Management in Marketing* (New York: McGraw Hill Book Co., 1961), p. 576.

of sales management is one which revolves around the *total development of human resources*. Beyond the general thrust of a human orientation, three probable developments may be cited in support of this contention:

1. *Greater concern over personal development of salesmen.* Commensurate with the interest of progressive firms in achieving a greater measure of internal social purpose, it is clear that more attention is being paid by upper management to the capacity of all organizational roles to contribute to the self-actualization needs of organization members. Few positions require more attention in this respect than the field of personal selling. Several studies have indicated that it is lack of recognition and prestige which frustrates and demoralizes the salesman (even the *successful* salesman) more than any other job-related factor.[7] Relevant also are the widely accepted estimates that one-half of all young persons who enter the sales field are unsuccessful in the career, and that 20% of the nation's salesmen currently account for 80% of the total sales of products and services. These indications of wide-spread failure and mediocrity constitute a human and economic waste of truly staggering proportions. While neither statistics nor management's concern with their impact on profits is new, what *is* new is the strong moral mandate for an end to this waste which a human orientation thrusts upon business management. Professional development is one part of the answer, but salesmen are whole men; thus their development within personal dimensions cannot be ignored and is likely to gain increasing attention.

2. *Greater use of computers in sales management.* The impact of the computer upon the sales management function has been the topic of recent discussion. As computer applications in marketing increase in quantity and sophistication, one plausible impact upon sales management will be the greater degree to which strategic decisions in the personal selling operation will become computer-assisted, if not computer-directed. Many of the most critical kinds of strategic and tactical decisions in the personal selling area lend themselves ideally to computer analysis, particularly the simulation technique. Allocation decisions involving manpower or money, optimum sales force numbers, territorial assignments, and profitability analysis of component parts of the sales operation are all examples of key sales management decision areas which seem certain to become increasingly computer oriented. As firms move more toward the *total information system* concept, establishing procedures and routines for generating information inputs for computer analysis, the sales manager's contribution stands to be incidental or advisory. Rather than being dominated by the computer, it is far more likely that the computer's impact will be to free the sales manager from many of his present responsibilities

---

[7] See, for example, John L. Mason, "The Low Prestige of Personal Selling," *Journal of Marketing* (Vol. 29), October 1965, pp. 7–10; and F. W. Howton and Bernard Rosenberg, "The Salesman: Ideology and Self-Imagery in a Prototypic Occupation," *Social Research* (Vol. 32), Autumn 1965, pp. 277–298.

for developing strategic decisions—thus enabling him to concentrate more fully upon his responsibilities for developing people.

3. *More professionalism in the personal selling field.* Continued progress may be expected in the movement to higher professional standards for the sales career; standards pertaining to education and competence in technical, behavioral, managerial, and quantitative areas. Increased professional competence of salesmen reduces the occasions calling for direct involvement of the sales manager with customers, distributors, or other elements within the market area. The greater the degree of professionalism of salesmen, the greater the degree to which the general goal framework established by top management may be translated, adapted, and implemented directly in the field; in effect bypassing the sales management strata.

These three trends converge in such a way as to shift the logical emphasis of the sales management function. The most plausible concept of sales management for the era of the human orientation is one which has at its core a mandate for the total development of the individual members of the selling force. This development concerns not only the elevation of the salesman to the highest possible level of *professional* competence and stature, but also the creation of those conditions which will produce the highest degree of *personal* growth and fulfillment.

The New Concept and the Sales Manager's Job

The sales management concept built upon strategy development and profit responsibility focuses upon the market environment, as does the general perspective of the firm operating under a marketing orientation. The new sales management concept stresses the involvement of the sales manager in a broader environmental realm, just as the general involvement of the enterprise is so stressed under a human orientation. The impact of a sales management concept based upon the total development of human resources within the sales manager's job activities would be to require nontraditional approaches to some of the key traditional areas of sales management concern, and to involve the sales manager in some quite new areas of high priority concern. For example:

Recruitment and Selection—Sales managers have experimented with a variety of testing devices in the search for predictor variables correlated to successful sales performance. Under the new concept, the search for such variables would be broadened (or deepened) beyond *success* to include also variables predictive of an individual's potential for self-fulfillment in sales work.

Training—Sales managers have had the responsibility of equipping salesmen with the knowledge and skills necessary for effective sales performance. But, the term *training* would be inadequate to describe the design and implementation of educational experiences contemplated under the new concept. These would enable salesmen not only to develop in the various professional dimensions of their work, but also to mature in personal dimensions through better understanding of themselves and the web of their relationships to the organization, clients, and society in general.

Motivation—Sales managers have been concerned with the motivation of salesmen, as in the design of compensation plans or studies of salesmen's attitudes. Under the new concept, the search for motivating forces would probe beneath the superficial and into such areas as the complexity of self-image or basic feelings toward business values (e.g., the Protestant Ethic).

Image of Selling—Sales managers would be more concerned with improving the image of personal selling both within and without the organization's bounds. This implies a concerted and creative communication effort of major proportions among nonmarketing groups within the corporation, channel members, community groups, on college campuses, and wherever else the message can be carried.

Ethical Standards—Sales managers would be involved in establishing and promulgating a clearer picture of the ethical dimensions of the salesman's role. This implies that specific and unambiguous standards of ethical conduct need to be established pertaining to the salesman's relationship to prospects, clients, fellow employees, and other persons and groups with whom he interacts. What is envisioned here are not variations upon the *golden rule*, but instead meaningful guides to the resolution of moral conflict in personal selling which may constitute an obstacle to genuine self-fulfillment in sales work.

Social Purpose in Selling—Sales managers would become occupied with identifying and evaluating ways in which the selling force may contribute to the firm's search for greater external social purpose. This may occur, for example, when corporate sales manpower is applied in helping to solve problems of ghetto entrepreneurs. It may also occur when the problem-solving sales professional applies his ingenuity to solve an immediate customer problem in such a way as concurrently to make a positive contribution in a more significant social problem area such as pollution, safety, housing, or production cost. Certainly by virtue of size or nature of product line some organizations have a greater potential in this respect than others. But the perspective itself of the sales department as a microcosm of the larger organization, seeking ways to achieve greater social purpose concurrently with the search for profitable customer problem-solving opportunities, opens endless and fascinating possibilities. Beyond the gains to society of such a perspective, it constitutes the most fertile source of the sense of worth and accomplishment for salesmen so vital under a total development concept.

The individual circumstances of any firm will determine in large measure the requirements for the sales management position for that particular enterprise. Nonetheless, it has been the author's contention that a basic sales management concept has always tended to exist in business, evidenced by the locus of emphasis in the sales manager's responsibilities.

TABLE 1   Changing Emphasis in Sales Management in This Century

					Year			
	1900	*1910*	*1920*	*1930*	*1940*	*1950*	*1960*	*1970*
Business Response to Perceived Dominant Environmental Conditions	Production Orientation		Sales Orientation			Marketing Orientation		Human Orientation
Emphasis in Management's Conception of Sales Job	Personality Art		"Scientific Salesman-ship"			Profes-sionalism		Personal Fulfillment
Emphasis in Sales Management	Tight Supervision and Control		Broadened Responsi-bilities			Strategies and Profits		Total Human Resource Development

Table 1 illustrates the pattern of historical change relative to sales management in this century. This table indicates that the prevailing sales management concept has been a matter of changing emphasis in responsibilities rather than complete redefinition of the sales manager's role.

Conclusion

As business tends to be more responsive to the accentuation of human values occurring in society, and perhaps to move from a marketing orientation to a broader human orientation, the most congruous concept of sales management is one focused upon the total development of the individual members of the selling force. This does not necessarily imply a lesser contribution to profitability by the sales manager than has been true in the past. It does, however, imply a more subtilized view of profits, particularly as to the distinction between the short run and the long run. Aggressive sales management techniques may appear to boost short-run profit, but in the light of negative consequences on loyalty, enthusiasm, self-respect, and esprit-de-corps within the sales force, their effect on long-run profit can never be clear and may well be negative. Thus, in the long run, the total development approach may be desirable not only for humanistic reasons but also from a profit standpoint.

Index